Recreating Built Heritage for Cities

Creating Accurate HBIM 3D Buildings for Use in Unreal Engine 5

Dr. Deborah Wilson

apress®

Recreating Built Heritage for Cities: Creating Accurate HBIM 3D Buildings for Use in Unreal Engine 5

Dr. Deborah Wilson
Winchester, Hampshire, UK

ISBN-13 (pbk): 979-8-8688-1771-7   ISBN-13 (electronic): 979-8-8688-1772-4
https://doi.org/10.1007/979-8-8688-1772-4

Copyright © 2025 by Dr. Deborah Wilson

This work is subject to copyright. All rights are reserved by the Publisher, whether the whole or part of the material is concerned, specifically the rights of translation, reprinting, reuse of illustrations, recitation, broadcasting, reproduction on microfilms or in any other physical way, and transmission or information storage and retrieval, electronic adaptation, computer software, or by similar or dissimilar methodology now known or hereafter developed.

Trademarked names, logos, and images may appear in this book. Rather than use a trademark symbol with every occurrence of a trademarked name, logo, or image we use the names, logos, and images only in an editorial fashion and to the benefit of the trademark owner, with no intention of infringement of the trademark.

The use in this publication of trade names, trademarks, service marks, and similar terms, even if they are not identified as such, is not to be taken as an expression of opinion as to whether or not they are subject to proprietary rights.

While the advice and information in this book are believed to be true and accurate at the date of publication, neither the authors nor the editors nor the publisher can accept any legal responsibility for any errors or omissions that may be made. The publisher makes no warranty, express or implied, with respect to the material contained herein.

Managing Director, Apress Media LLC: Welmoed Spahr
Acquisitions Editor: Spandana Chatterjee
Development Editor: James Markham
Editorial Assistant: Gryffin Winkler

Cover designed by eStudioCalamar

Cover image designed by Unsplash

Distributed to the book trade worldwide by Springer Science+Business Media New York, 1 New York Plaza, New York, NY 10004. Phone 1-800-SPRINGER, fax (201) 348-4505, e-mail orders-ny@springer-sbm.com, or visit www.springeronline.com. Apress Media, LLC is a Delaware LLC and the sole member (owner) is Springer Science + Business Media Finance Inc (SSBM Finance Inc). SSBM Finance Inc is a **Delaware** corporation.

For information on translations, please e-mail booktranslations@springernature.com; for reprint, paperback, or audio rights, please e-mail bookpermissions@springernature.com.

Apress titles may be purchased in bulk for academic, corporate, or promotional use. eBook versions and licenses are also available for most titles. For more information, reference our Print and eBook Bulk Sales web page at http://www.apress.com/bulk-sales.

Any source code or other supplementary material referenced by the author in this book is available to readers on GitHub. For more detailed information, please visit https://www.apress.com/gp/services/source-code.

If disposing of this product, please recycle the paper

For my late husband Paul, who constantly encouraged me to write. His belief in me encouraged my approach to Apress with the outline of this book. I hope he will be proud of his little wife.

Table of Contents

About the Author xi

About the Technical Reviewer xiii

Acknowledgments xv

Introduction xvii

Chapter 1: What Is HBIM? 1

Definition and Concept of HBIM 1

Interacting with the Model 8

Case Study 1: Scan to BIM 13

    Content-Based Immersive Experience of the Basilica of Sant'Ambrogio 13

Contrasting HBIM with BIM 20

    Case Study 2: Virtual Cities 25

The Role of HBIM in Architectural Preservation 38

    Introduction 38

    Case Study 3: HBIM in Historical City Planning 47

Summary 55

References 56

Chapter 2: History and Benefits of HBIM 59

The Evolution of HBIM in the Preservation Industry 59

    Early Developments in Digital Modelling 60

    Key Milestones in HBIM Development 63

    Implementation 65

    Collaboration and Interdisciplinary Applications 68

    Advances in Visualization and Simulation 68

    Summary 69

TABLE OF CONTENTS

Advantages and Challenges of Implementing HBIM 70
- Challenges and Limitations of HBIM 70
- The Challenges of Architectural Preservation 72
- Advantages of Implementing HBIM 73
- Addressing Challenges Through Innovation 74
- Summary 76

Chapter 2 Durham Cathedral Case Study: Advantages and Challenges of Implementing HBIM 76
- The Complexities of Managing Historic Buildings with BIM 76
- Key Benefits of BIM in Historic Building Management 82

Successful Case Studies of BIM, HBIM, and VR Visualization Applications 84
- Case Study 1: HBIM Modelling of the Wang Temple in Karpacz 85
- Case Study 2: 3D Digitization of the Church in Iwięcino, Poland 89
- Case Study 3: HBIM Modelling of Big Ben 94
- Case Study 4: 3D Digitization of Hyde Abbey, Winchester, Hampshire 99
- Case Study 5: Notre-Dame Cathedral Restoration 106

Summary 113
References 114

Chapter 3: Creating an HBIM 3D Model for a City Across Different Eras 117
- Overview of the Reconstruction Process 119
  - Defining the Project Scope and Historical Context 119
  - Historical Research and Data Collection 126
  - Scoping the Reconstruction Process 130
- Selecting the Time Periods for Reconstruction 130
  - Importance of Historical Research in Era Selection 130
  - Structuring the HBIM Model by Time Period 134
- Integrating Historical Research with HBIM 148
  - Constructing the HBIM Model 148
- Summary 160
- References 161

TABLE OF CONTENTS

Chapter 4: Step One: Data Collection 163

Gathering Historical Documents, Architectural Plans, and Visuals 164
- Steventon Rectory 164
- Winchester Castle 167
- Recording the Data for Embedding into the Unreal Scenes 170
- Finding the Answers and Substantiating Data 172

Section Summary 181

Utilizing Photogrammetry and LiDAR Technology 181
- When to Model from Scratch 184
- When to Use LiDAR or Photogrammetry 185
- Example Workflow for Integrating a Scanned Historical Building into Unreal Engine 189

Section Summary 195

Collecting Geographic and Spatial Data 196
- Heightmap Data Limitations 204
- Terrain Modification and Detailing 204
- Key Considerations 205
- In Summary 206
- GIS-Based Georeferencing (Most Accurate and Scalable) 207
- Using Revit or AutoCAD for Alignment (CAD Workflow) 207
- Image Processing Automation with OpenCV (Fastest for Large Projects) 208
- Blender Projection Mapping (For 3D Surface Alignment) 208
- Which One to Choose? 208
- Creating the Landscape 209
- Cesium Step-by-Step Guide 211

Section Summary 215

References 215

Chapter 5: Step Two: Pre-processing 217

Data Preparation 218
- Phase 1: Understanding the Requirements and Defining the Data 219
- Phase 2: Creating the Data Object Parameters in Your BIM Software 221

vii

TABLE OF CONTENTS

    Phase 3: Data Management and Utilization 234

    Walls 237

Section Summary 250

How to Manage Incomplete or Missing Data 250

    A Step-by-Step Guide – Student Based 253

    Adding Data As It Becomes Available 256

    Mini Tutorial: Revit to Unreal with Update-Friendly Datasmith Workflow 264

Section Summary 269

Georeferencing and Aligning Datasets 271

    Converting 2D CAD Drawings for GIS Integration 272

    Integrating Point Clouds with GIS 273

    Step-by-Step Guide: Georeferencing Historical Maps in QGIS 274

    Step-by-Step Guide: Using CADmapper to Create a Toposolid 284

    Sculpting Imported Revit Terrain in Unreal and Using Historic Maps As Overlays 294

Section Summary 297

References 298

Chapter 6: Step Three: Building the 3D Model 299

Starting to Build with Your HBIM Software 299

    Building Steventon Rectory – Step-by-Step Exercise 301

Section Summary 355

Creating a Detailed Building Geometry 357

    Setting the Stage: The Essence of 16th/17th-Century Building for Storytelling and Recording for Future Information 357

    Adding Detail to Steventon Rectory – Step-by-Step Exercise 369

    Interior Details 399

Section Summary 422

Incorporating Historically Accurate Vernacular Materials and Textures 423

    Common Exterior Materials (16th- to 17th-century Hampshire) 429

    Common Interior Materials 429

    Creating Materials and Textures 430

    Implementation in Unreal Engine 432

    Step-by-Step Guide to Creating Master Materials in Unreal 434

Section Summary... 449

References 450

    Links to Revit Family Objects 451

    Links to Materials and Textures Assets 451

Chapter 7: Step Four: Adding Context 453

Integrating Surrounding Landscapes and Urban Features.. 454

    Copying Your Project... 455

    Initiating the Landscape for Steventon Rectory 456

    Developing Your Steventon Rectory Rural Landscape 463

Section Summary... 490

Integrating Urban Features and Infrastructure 491

    8 College Street Drawing Room Interior 495

    Creating the Portal Between 8 College Street and Steventon Rectory 512

Section Summary... 520

Capturing Historical, Social, and Cultural Context.. 521

    Beginner's Guide: HBIM Data Pop-up Panel in Unreal Engine 521

    Creating the Story for the Time Travel to Steventon Rectory........................... 540

Section Summary... 547

Documentation Glossary 548

References 548

    Images... 549

    3D Models... 550

Chapter 8: Step Five: Post-processing and Analysis 551

Refining the HBIM Model 552

    Exporting via Datasmith from Revit to Unreal... 564

    HBIM Data Feedback 570

Section Summary... 573

Assessing Historical Accuracy and Preservation Needs 574

TABLE OF CONTENTS

    Assessing Historical Accuracy 574

    The Pluses and Minuses of Virtual Reconstructed Scenes Relating to Historical Accuracy 579

    Preservation Needs 581

Section Summary 590

References 591

Chapter 9: Conclusion 593

Recapitulation of Key Findings and Insights 594

    Primary Findings 594

    Secondary Findings 597

    Strategic Implications 598

    Future Research Directions 599

    Conclusion for Primary and Secondary Findings 600

    Software Recommendations for HBIM Heritage Visualization 601

    Short-Term Development (6–18 months) 603

    Medium-Term Innovation (18 months–3 years) 604

    Conclusion 608

Reflection on the Significance of Recreating Architectural Time Periods 609

    Personal Reflection on the Evolving Role of the Practitioner 609

    Why Is It Significant to Recreate Historical Buildings, Spaces, and Places in Different Time Periods? 613

    Building a Library of Reusable Assets 615

    Conclusion: Reflecting on the Significance of Recreating Architectural Time Periods 616

Future Directions in HBIM and Architectural Preservation 617

    Backward Compatibility and Consistency Built into All Later Versions of Software 617

    Possibility of a Future Open Access HBIM Repository 618

    Other Future Areas for Focus and Consideration 621

    Future Recommendations 622

    Future of Digital Heritage Storytelling – A Personal Aim 623

References 624

Index 627

About the Author

Dr. Deborah Wilson is Owner/Designer and Creative Director of Virtual Cities Ltd and Time Tourist Ltd, building on her earlier company, The Talking Walls (est. 1996). Her work focuses on researching and designing visually rich platforms that enable users to explore cultural heritage sites through different historical time-slices – primarily guided by changes in architecture and built environments.

Before retiring from academia in early 2025, Deborah was Co-Director of the Community of Enterprise, Design & Innovation (CEDI) at the University of Winchester, where she also served as Senior Lecturer and Programme Leader for Digital Media, CAD, and 3D programs during a 15-year period.

She has led several externally funded projects and is currently developing Virtual Cities – Winchester, a prototype reconstructing sections of Winchester during the medieval and Georgian periods, in collaboration with students and external professionals. In 2023, she organized and presented at a conference on Digital Cultural Heritage Interpretation via CEDI – a research community she founded, which now continues as part of Virtual Cities Ltd.

About the Technical Reviewer

Scott Rafferty is a Lead Solutions Specialist at McLaren and an accomplished 3D visualization expert with extensive experience spanning automotive, aerospace, and emerging technology sectors. As a real-time leader in developing top-quality visuals, Scott specializes in creating cutting-edge computer-generated imagery solutions using Unreal Engine and advanced digital twin technologies.

Currently driving innovation at Mclaren, Scott leads the development of data and visualization pipelines while implementing AI strategies. His technical expertise extends across the full spectrum of digital content creation, from environment and product visualization to architectural rendering and virtual production.

Through his studio Pyre Labs, Scott delivers comprehensive B2B services including visualization, digital twins, and production across automotive, aerospace, defense, advertising, and fashion industries. His proven track record includes successful implementations at prestigious organizations like Bentley Motors and JLR, where he developed sophisticated digital twin systems and led technical visualization initiatives.

Scott combines deep technical knowledge with strategic leadership, consistently achieving measurable impacts on revenue and operational efficiency through innovative solution implementations.

Acknowledgments

I would like to express my gratitude to Spandana Chatterjee, Acquisitions Editor at Apress, for the opportunity to publish this book. I would also like to thank Deepa Shirley Tryphosa Chellappa for her guidance and feedback and Scott Rafferty, Technical Reviewer, for his thorough and in-depth feedback and encouraging words for several of the chapters.

I would like to thank my student Thomas Dulkys for agreeing to allow his project work with Winchester Castle to be included as an example of the work we have been doing on the Virtual Cities – Winchester 1400 and 1800 project.

I would also like to thank the experts who provided such excellent feedback and encouragement for the Steventon Rectory and HBIM work: Jane Austen House, Chawton, Deborah Charlton of Archaeo Briton, and Geoff Browell of XRchiving and Project Lead: Heritage Collections at King's College London.

Finally, I would like to thank my mother, daughter, and close friends for their endless support and encouragement, and of course my animals for occasionally missing their walks while I have been writing this book.

Introduction

Historic buildings are physical manifestations of cultural heritage, representing the traditions, values, and histories of the communities that built and inhabited them. They provide tangible connections to the past, allowing people to experience the architectural styles, craftsmanship, and urban planning of previous periods. This direct connection to history plays a critical role in shaping collective identity, inculcating a sense of belonging, and guaranteeing the continuity of cultural narratives.

I have always been intrigued by the stories these buildings hold, hence my early company name "The Talking Walls" in 2004, which was initially focused on Dunster Castle, Somerset (National Trust, 1999). A retired schoolteacher who became a volunteer guide at Dunster Castle informed me that the school children he took around Dunster Castle as it is today could not imagine its early history as a hill fort that gradually evolved into a stone-built castle and then the manor house it is today (Woodger, 1996). Artistic impressions of the different stages had been created, yet these beautiful drawings were not sufficiently "real" for the children to understand they really existed or that they were lived in. There were only two families that lived at the Castle: the first was the De Mohuns, who sold it to the Luttrells at the end of the 14th century. The Luttrells lived there until the 20th century when it was finally given to the National Trust (National Trust, 1999). The stories of the families and the changes they made to the castle and why, were created into digital stories of the people that lived there, with 3D reconstructions using the sketches and available floor plans. I also worked with the volunteer guide and the National Trust team to know more regarding the De Mohuns and the Luttrells in 1996 for one of my final major projects to complete my degree in Computer Animation and Illustration. From there, I didn't look back. I have been creating 3D visualizations and reconstructions of historic buildings, developing the stories of the people that lived there since then. My PhD also focuses on this area and the design of cultural heritage interpretation design. The different heritage organizations owning/caretaking these historic buildings are very aware that their buildings serve as storybooks, encapsulating the lives of those who shaped the society we live in today (Wilson, 2021). The buildings inspire curiosity and provide a sense of continuity, as younger generations experience the physical spaces that shaped their ancestors' lives.

INTRODUCTION

These buildings often embody a mix of influences, showcasing the interactions of different cultures during the course of time. From medieval abbeys to the latest architectural styles, they tell nuanced stories of cultural exchange and shared heritage. Recognizing and preserving these elements encourages inclusivity and understanding. They also anchor communities by providing a sense of place (Uzzell, 1996). Whether it is a centuries-old market square or a local church, these structures are often focal points for community identity and activity. Preserving these buildings strengthens local pride and encourages communal efforts to maintain cultural landmarks. By involving communities in preservation and interpretation efforts, these structures also encourage active participation and intergenerational learning. In an increasingly globalized society, historic buildings offer a sense of belonging and cultural specificity. They remind people of their unique cultural identities while also connecting them to shared human experiences, providing continuity (Historic England, 2019).

Historic buildings are key assets for cultural tourism, attracting visitors interested in history, architecture, and storytelling. They boost local economies by supporting businesses such as tours, museums, and hospitality services, or serve as living museums, providing valuable educational experiences for people of all ages. Revitalized historic buildings can also become thriving commercial spaces, supporting local businesses.

Programs that highlight the cultural significance of historic sites, such as guided storytelling tours, contribute to a deeper understanding of heritage while generating revenue. Historic buildings can also act as classrooms, teaching of art, technology, and culture in ways that textbooks cannot.

Historical buildings are facing rapid deterioration due to ageing and environmental factors, and the need to preserve them is becoming increasingly important (Historic England, 2020). Cities have grown and changed, in use and importance, with time, with current communities unaware of why certain buildings have changed, been erased, or why they are now in ruins. Street names highlight what once was part of the city but perhaps now does not form part of current-day culture. By recreating in different architectural time periods, it will become easier to understand why and how the city has evolved.

By preserving and celebrating historic buildings, we not only honor our past but also create opportunities to strengthen community identity, inculcate belonging, and inspire future generations. These structures are more than relics; they are active participants in the ongoing story of humanity.

This book covers the process of creating Heritage Building Information Modelling (HBIM) 3D models across different periods, using industry standard 3D modelling software (primarily Autodesk Revit/Autodesk 3DS Max) and Unreal Game Engine 5.

INTRODUCTION

The reconstruction of buildings from different time periods that no longer exist in their original form is becoming a growth area especially for heritage tourism and virtual tourism. The book will cross different architectural periods and include how to embed heritage data such as materials/interior styles/building skills used. Each building can then be explored for conservation/heritage/cultural purposes and visually explored to gain an understanding of its cultural heritage evolution.

There is considerable interest in the use of HBIM for preserving buildings; this book takes it one step further in demonstrating how a building has changed with time, the interior styling and stories of people that lived there. The book then details how to present those buildings within their city using Unreal Game Engine 5 and how to create portals for users to step through time and view the different architectural changes made by the "owners" of the time and why. Explanation of the importance of BIM software and implementation of HBIM for historical models is provided with reference for further research into both models for those interested in learning more throughout the book. Research on the standards and implementation of those standards is a growing area within academia where universities are helping in the recreation of past heritage.

This book aims to help professionals and students work through the process of recreating past times of a city and bring them to life for visitors to engage with the culture and heritage of a city across different time periods. The practical elements, exercises, and tutorials work alongside the development of a live project "Virtual Cities – Winchester 1400 and 1800" and will highlight the challenges of historical research and inputting of heritage information to guarantee accurate representation.

Explanations of why certain software should be used and the research required to reconstruct heritage buildings/spaces of significance are provided. In addition, how to represent buildings for which data cannot be found will be discussed.

Case studies including real-life applications will be a part of the book and help to illustrate the practical applications of methods and processes discussed. Visual aids and illustrations/renders will be included to enhance the understanding of the processes and further engage the readers. Future expectations will be discussed as part of the conclusion.

In summary, this book has been planned as a resource for architects, historians, urban planners, heritage enthusiasts, virtual technologists, and film/game professionals using Unreal Engine to recreate 3D environments. It would also be valuable for students on degree programs studying/creating 3D environments, architecture, level design, and 3D modelling.

INTRODUCTION

Chapter Outlines

Chapter 1: What Is HBIM? – This chapter delves deeper into the concept of HBIM, explaining what it is and how it differs from conventional BIM. It explores the fundamental principles and technologies involved in HBIM. The chapter takes a technical approach, focusing on the specific characteristics and functionalities that distinguish HBIM as a specialized tool for historical building preservation. The purpose is to educate readers on the concept and significance of HBIM as the foundation for the subsequent chapters. It makes sure that readers have a solid understanding of the main subject before moving on to practical implementation.

Chapter 2: History and Benefits of HBIM – This chapter is a historical overview of HBIM, tracing its development and adoption in the preservation industry. It highlights successful case studies that demonstrate the benefits of using HBIM for architectural heritage conservation. The chapter adopts a historical and analytical angle, presenting the evolution of HBIM as a practical solution to historical building preservation challenges. The purpose is to showcase the impact of HBIM, demonstrating its advantages and potential in addressing historical preservation needs. It motivates readers by illustrating the effectiveness of HBIM through past accomplishments.

Chapter 3: Creating an HBIM 3D Model for a City Across Different Eras – This chapter outlines the step-by-step process of creating an HBIM 3D model that spans various architectural time periods. It discusses the importance of historical research and context in selecting the periods for reconstruction. The chapter takes a practical approach, guiding readers through the methodology of creating an HBIM model that captures the essence of different historical epochs. The purpose is to introduce readers to the main focus of the book, recreating architectural time periods. It prepares readers for the technical aspects of the subsequent chapters and emphasizes the integration of historical research.

Chapter 4: Step One: Data Collection – This chapter explores the crucial phase of data collection for historical building reconstruction. It covers various data sources, such as historical documents, archives, photogrammetry, and LiDAR technology. The chapter emphasizes the importance of accurate and comprehensive data collection in the HBIM process. The purpose is to equip readers with the necessary knowledge to gather historical data effectively, as accurate data is the foundation for successful HBIM reconstruction.

Chapter 5: Step Two: Pre-processing – This chapter discusses the pre-processing stage, where data is cleaned, aligned, and prepared for integration into the HBIM model. The chapter takes a technical angle, addressing data management and preparation for use in the subsequent stages of reconstruction. The purpose is to make sure that readers understand the critical role of pre-processing in creating an accurate and cohesive HBIM model, thus avoiding potential problems in the later stages.

Chapter 6: Step Three: Building the 3D Model – This chapter focuses on the actual construction of the HBIM 3D model. It covers the selection of appropriate HBIM software, creation of building geometry, and incorporation of textures and materials. The chapter combines technical details with a creative angle, as building the 3D model requires both technical skills and an artistic understanding of architecture. The purpose is to guide readers through the process of building the HBIM model and developing a visually appealing representation of historical architecture.

Chapter 7: Step Four: Adding Context – This chapter explores the importance of context in HBIM reconstruction. It covers the integration of surrounding landscapes, urban features, transportation networks, and historical, social, and cultural contexts. The chapter takes a comprehensive view, demonstrating that historical buildings are part of a larger urban fabric that requires consideration in the reconstruction process. The purpose is to highlight the significance of context in creating accurate historical reconstructions, providing readers with a more comprehensive understanding of the past.

Chapter 8: Step Five: Post-processing and Analysis – This chapter focuses on post-processing and analytical studies. It covers refining the HBIM model and assessing structural integrity and preservation needs. The chapter adopts a problem-solving angle, addressing the challenges and considerations involved in the final stages of the HBIM process. The purpose is to emphasize the importance of quality control, accuracy, and research validation in the HBIM model. It prepares readers to critically analyze the outcomes of the reconstruction.

Chapter 9: Conclusion – The final chapter provides a comprehensive summary of the key findings and insights from the book. It reflects on the significance of recreating architectural time periods and their impact on preserving historical heritage. The chapter takes a reflective and future-oriented angle, summarizing the book's achievements and looking ahead to potential advancements in HBIM and architectural preservation. The purpose is to reinforce the main takeaways from the book and leave readers with a sense of fulfillment, understanding, and inspiration to continue exploring the field of HBIM and historical preservation.

INTRODUCTION

References

Historic England (2019) There's No Place Like Old Homes – Re-Use and Recycle to Reduce Carbon. Heritage Counts Historic England on behalf of the Historic Environment Forum. February 2020 – Project Code: HE0031 https://historicengland.org.uk/content/heritage-counts/pub/2019/hc2019-re-use-recycle-to-reduce-carbon/

Historic England (2020) Heritage at Risk in England Revealed in 2020. Available at: https://historicengland.org.uk/whats-new/news/heritage-at-risk-2020/

National Trust, (1999) Guidebook: Dunster Castle, Somerset. National Trust, London

Uzzell, David (1996) Creating place identity through heritage interpretation. International Journal of Heritage Studies 1, 4, pp. 219-228. January 1996 DOI: 10.1080/13527259608722151

Wilson, Deborah (2021) Curator, Designer and Visitor Interaction in Cultural Heritage Interpretation Design Practice. PhD Thesis, Design, University of Winchester, Hampshire

Woodger, B. (1996) Dunster Castle Volunteer Guide, Private communication

CHAPTER 1

What Is HBIM?

Historical Building Information Modelling (HBIM) is an approach that combines innovative technology with historical preservation to recreate and document historical buildings. This chapter reviews the definition and concept of HBIM, highlighting its significance in architectural preservation. We will also compare HBIM with conventional Building Information Modelling (BIM) to understand the key differences. Moreover, this chapter will explore the crucial role that HBIM plays in preserving the architectural heritage of buildings and cities and its potential applications through illustrative examples.

Definition and Concept of HBIM

Murphy, McGovern, and Pavia (2009) proposed Historical Building Information Modelling (HBIM) as a "library of parametric objects based on historic architectural data." Their paper details the use of laser scanning to create point cloud 3D surface meshes, then adding BIM objects to the 3D surface mesh to detail construction methods and material used. Arayici et al. (2017) refer to Heritage Building Information Modelling rather than Historical Building Information Modelling, stating a reference to the earliest mention of Heritage Information Modelling principles and purpose from Getty Conservation Institute's Recording, Documentation, and Information Management (RecorDIM) Initiative (2003–2007). The difference between the two, Heritage and Historical, is generally distinguished by their scope:

- Heritage BIM is a broader and more contemporary term referring to the use of Building Information Modelling for buildings or sites of cultural, historical, or architectural significance. It serves as a practical tool for preservation, restoration, facility management, and as a digital visual asset to aid communication, research, and public engagement.

- Historical BIM by contrast tends to refer more specifically to the modelling of a building's past states, chronological development, former functions, and historical contexts. Its primary goal is to document and interpret the building's evolution over time.

In summary, Heritage BIM is perceived as future-facing and management-oriented, supporting conservation and sustainable use, while Historical BIM is past-facing and research-oriented, supporting interpretation and understanding of a building's history. For this book, we are working with Heritage BIM rather than Historical BIM. HBIM is discussed widely as a specialized methodology that employs advanced digital technologies to create detailed 3D models of historical buildings and urban landscapes. Unlike BIM and traditional 3D modelling, HBIM integrates physical attributes, historical data, context, and metadata into the virtual reconstruction. At its core, HBIM captures the intrinsic characteristics of historical buildings, such as construction materials, architectural elements, and historical alterations. These attributes are digitally mapped into the virtual model, providing a comprehensive representation of the building's past and present states, making it a powerful tool for preserving architectural heritage.

The concept of HBIM emerged from the need to preserve and manage historic buildings effectively. Historically, conservation professionals used traditional methods such as hand-drawing and documentation to record historic buildings. However, these methods were time-consuming, expensive, and often failed to capture the full complexity of a building. HBIM is a significant advancement in this regard because it provides a way to create accurate digital representations of historic buildings that can be easily updated, shared, and analyzed. Adding HBIM data can also be time-consuming in researching, collating, and verifying the data that needs to be considered in the development and costing of HBIM projects. Delays to modelling can be lengthy when relying on finding data such as heights of buildings that no longer exist as we will discover later when the work involved in creating Virtual Cities – Winchester is explained.

Height in remodeling existing buildings is generally not an issue, especially with using the Scan to BIM method to capture the existing building/object. Scan to BIM is a process used to create accurate 3D models using 3D laser scanning technology to capture detailed measurements and data of the building's physical elements and converts that data into a digital BIM model. This process is particularly useful for existing heritage buildings, as it helps preserve their historical significance, document their current condition, and facilitate renovations or restoration projects. There are many examples of how useful and valuable this is in the UK and Internationally, a few of which can be seen in the case studies further in this chapter.

CHAPTER 1   WHAT IS HBIM?

Figure 1-1 details a Scan to BIM process.

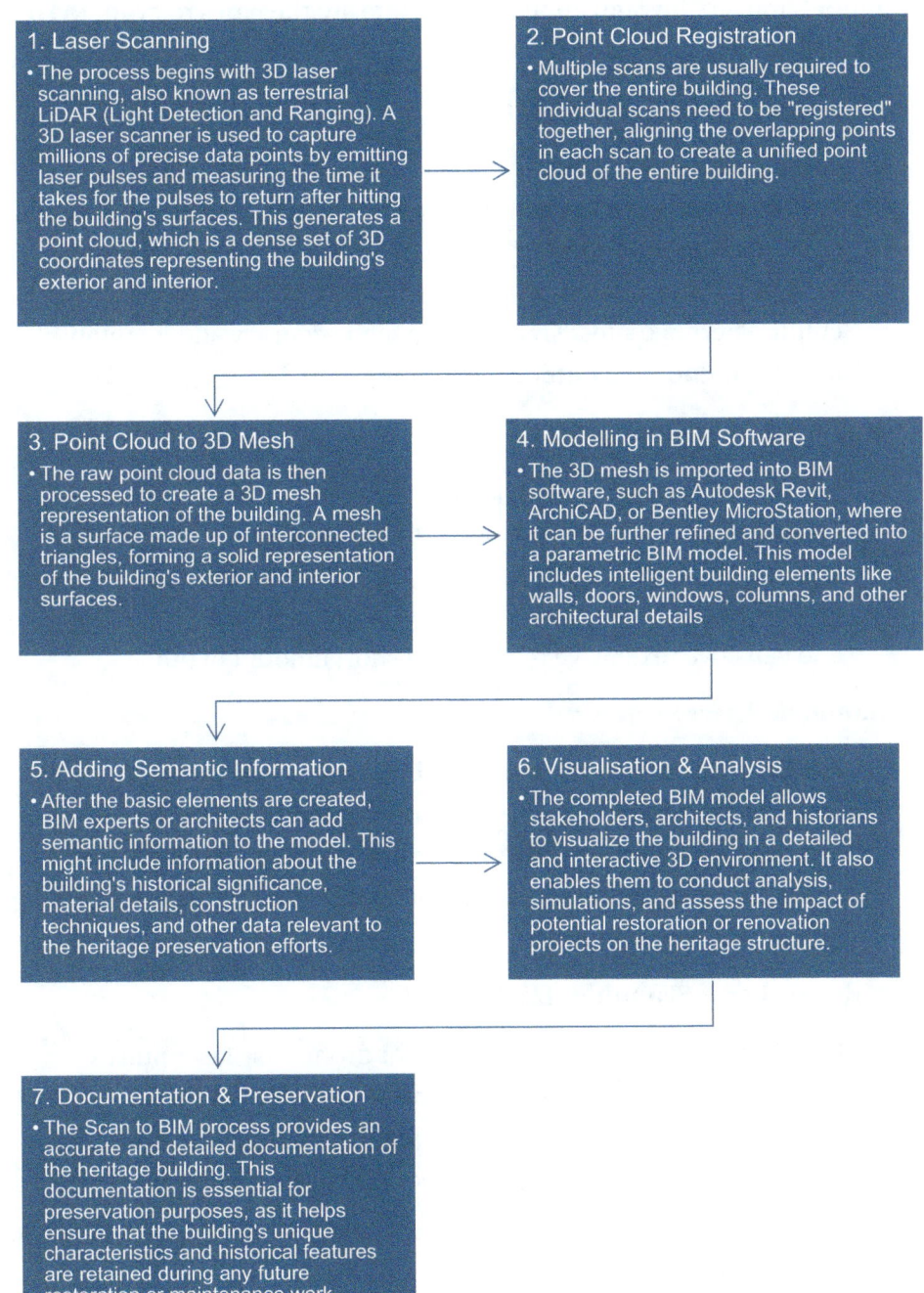

Figure 1-1. *Scan to BIM process expanding on Dore and Murphy's (2012) HBIM process workflow (Figure 1, p. 369)*

There are several different technologies available for laser scanning, each with its own unique characteristics and applications. Here are the types relevant to HBIM currently available and its primary use:

- **Terrestrial Laser Scanning (TLS)**
    - Terrestrial laser scanners are ground-based devices that use a rotating laser beam to capture 3D data points of the surrounding environment. They are commonly used for capturing detailed measurements of buildings, infrastructure, landscapes, and cultural heritage sites. TLS provides high accuracy and is suitable for both indoor and outdoor scanning.

- **Mobile Laser Scanning (MLS)**
    - Mobile laser scanners are typically mounted on vehicles, such as cars or drones, and are used to scan large areas quickly. MLS is commonly used for surveying roads, railways, highways, and other transportation networks. It allows for rapid data collection and can cover extensive regions in a short amount of time.

- **Handheld Laser Scanners**
    - Handheld laser scanners are portable devices that can be operated by hand to capture 3D data of objects or small areas. They are often used for capturing intricate details and are suitable for applications like reverse engineering, quality control, and industrial measurements.

- **Airborne Laser Scanning (LiDAR)**
    - LiDAR systems mounted on aircraft or drones use laser pulses to measure the distance between the sensor and the Earth's surface. It is widely used for topographic mapping, forestry, environmental monitoring, and floodplain modelling.

There are also several platforms available for converting the scan data to 3D mesh surfaces. The platforms mostly used are

- Reality Capture (https://www.realityscan.com/en-US, Epic Games)
- Mesh2Surface (https://www.mesh2surface.com/)

- VRMesh (https://www.vrmesh.com/)

- Geomagic (https://www.3dsystems.com/software)

- QuickSurface (https://www.quicksurface3d.com/)

- SolidWorks (https://www.solidworks.com/)

Once the data has been created as a 3D surface mesh, the model can be refined and added to as described in step 4 in Figure 1-1. By creating highly accurate 3D models of sites using BIM industry architectural software such as Autodesk Revit or ArchiCAD, researchers can gain an understanding of the structure, form, and function of the site that would not be possible without digital modelling. This is particularly important for sites that have been damaged or destroyed, as they allow for the reconstruction of these sites in a digital environment. The use of free form modelling software such as Autodesk 3DS Max or Maya, or Blender does not natively provide the same level of architectural construction nor the ability to provide data without programming additional functions.

For organizations, companies, or individuals who would like to have a 3D model of an existing building, there are companies that will capture and produce the finished 3D model for you such as Matterport who has completed several 3D projects for heritage sites, which can be seen on https://discover.matterport.com/tag/heritage. Other companies that can provide heritage 3D scanning to BIM/HBIM are growing in amount and include Multivista, Surface Scan, Point Scan, and ARTEC 3D. For existing heritage sites, this may be the route to use due to the expertise, equipment, and time required which can be costly before then being able to use and create.

The one issue I had when initially looking at 3D scanning and the 3D meshes result was the ability to walk up to the building and then into the building seamlessly, i.e., not cutting from an exterior scene to an interior scene. Admittedly this was several years ago, and since then, this has now become possible but still does require thinking about. Having a model that can only be viewed outside might be absolutely all that you need for a city/town/village scene with your users being able to explore the environment. Or perhaps you only want users to interact with the interior, for example, a museum, or a historic building such as The Dome, Edinburgh. The following images demonstrate the 3D scanned interior of The Dome Edinburgh and how the 3D data is portrayed in "doll's house" format. When you zoom in, you can see the polygons formed by the point cloud data (see Figure 1-2). When you click on the blue circles, you are taken to 360 view captures (see Figure 1-3) and can move around using a sequence of 360 views replacing the point cloud data "doll's house" model.

CHAPTER 1 WHAT IS HBIM?

Figure 1-2. *Matterport 3D scanning example of the exterior entrance – The Dome Edinburgh, Space shared by* `www.360virtualtour.co`

Figure 1-3. *Matterport 3D scanning example of an interior space – The Dome Edinburgh, Space shared by* `www.360virtualtour.co (https://matterport.com/ discover/space/CMatvVatCjc)`

Figure 1-4. *Matterport example of one of the 360 views allowing you to explore the interior spaces using the blue circles (or white floor circles) to move about the spaces*

A point cloud is a set of millions (or even billions) of individual points in 3D space, each defined by X, Y, and Z coordinates, often also with color or reflectance data. The point cloud represents the surface of objects or scenes without lines connecting them and can be detected by 3D laser scanners or photogrammetry as can be seen in Figure 1-5.

Figure 1-5. *Point cloud example by ACCA Software, 2025*

Meshing connects these dots into triangles (or polygons) to form a continuous surface. This makes the model easier to visualize, process, and use in various applications. The mesh structure may result in being a "closed mesh," i.e., completely enclosed, in which case you would need to create openings in the mesh to allow your users to walk through; makes sense, doesn't it? If the mesh is a "hollow mesh" and already has an interior space as part of the scanned data, then this should become straightforward to then walk through and explore the interior. You would need to make sure the interior geometry is detailed and not just an outer shell. Figure 1-6 shows a basic example of a mesh that is open, i.e., has holes in the mesh, and a closed mesh.

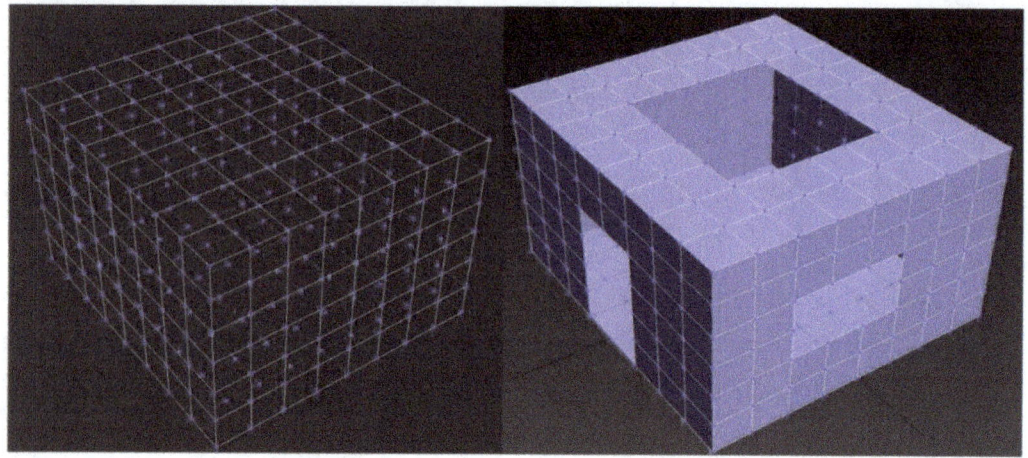

Figure 1-6. Basic Example of an Open and Closed Mesh

Interacting with the Model

For interacting with the scanned model, tools such as Unreal Game Engine allow the creation or setting up of teleportation points for transitioning between the outside and inside, which could be an engaging way of moving between the two spaces if no opening is modelled. We are using this tool in Virtual Cities – Winchester 1400 and 1800 for stepping between the two time periods to a great effect. For The Dome Edinburgh, you can zoom up to and in through the front entrance, although the method using a 360 view and clicking on the circles to move into the building is also available for a much more finished/polished view.

CHAPTER 1   WHAT IS HBIM?

The Dome Edinburgh model in Matterport includes links (the circles) that link out to information, such as the history of the Georgian building, reservations, menus, and typical web content. It appears to have been modelled to allow exploration of the building online; see the restaurant spaces and the beautiful internal detail. There isn't much other than the history page on The Dome Edinburgh's website (https://www.thedomeedinburgh.com/history) that provides detail of the building fabric or stories of the building, which for this example is perhaps all that is needed, i.e., an engaging addition/virtual tour to the website. It would, although, have been interesting to find out much more about the building, what was therefore before, and the changes to the building. The circle indicators could also have been attached to certain aspects of the building to provide detailed information, for example, the beautiful marble columns in the foyer. What happened to the previous building's material when it was demolished, was it used for another building, or at least parts of it? The following case study demonstrates how this is possible and provides the process used and how users/visitors would engage with the model.

In the Virtual Cities – Winchester case study, the project has been developed to include two different eras: 1400 and 1800. Many of the medieval buildings did not survive through to the 1800s; therefore, the use of Scan to BIM technology was not possible. The medieval and Georgian buildings have subsequently been built using Autodesk Revit. Several of our students have also used Blender, albeit in a non-BIM format. We created each building from researched floor plans, elevations, archaeological evidence, typical building styles of each period (interior and exterior), and artistic impressions/sketches and other image forms. By using Autodesk Revit, information regarding wall types/materials, window styles, and other architectural elements were included from a library of 3D components suitable for the era and specified by the research undertaken. Although Blender was not a BIM modelling software when first used, students were later able to embed HBIM data to the buildings they created by using the "BlenderBIM" add-on, recently renamed as Bonsai (Blender, 2024).

Before working at the university, I used to train Autodesk Revit to architectural practices with most of the projects worked on being new buildings and often commercial, which, in many ways, can be seen as generally much easier to model, whereas historic buildings, depending on their age, may have unique and complex features, requiring adaptation of standard BIM tools to suit the different complexities. For example, going from 500- to 1000-mm-thick medieval stone and rubble walls to added lathe and plaster and then newer additions of brick and cavity walls, therefore different levels of quite different materials and thicknesses. The use of 3D scanning therefore would perhaps be the easiest method for picking up the differences in textures and shaping of internal and external walls. The next section discusses the advantages between the two methods of creating BIM and HBIM models and the difference in BIM and HBIM.

If you are thinking about investing in being able to create 3D Scan to BIM models and be able to walk from the outside of the model to inside and vice versa, Table 1-1 is a good general guideline for process and software.

Table 1-1. *Guide to software and process*

Software	Use	Open Source	Inexpensive	Expensive
General 3D Modelling and Editing – These tools are great for preparing scanned meshes, fixing issues, and creating detailed models				
Blender	Open source software for editing, cleaning, and optimizing 3D meshes. Add openings, smooth surfaces, and enhance interior details. Offers a walkthrough mode for navigating models.	✓		
Autodesk MeshMixer	Ideal for fixing holes, smoothing meshes, and basic editing. Useful for cleaning up scanned data for walkthrough readiness.	✓		
Z-Brush	For high-quality sculpting and refining scanned models. Great if your scanned data needs artistic enhancements or detail restoration.			✓
Game Engines for Real-Time Walkthroughs – These engines provide interactivity, making it possible to walk through meshes virtually				

(continued)

Table 1-1. (continued)

Software	Use	Open Source	Inexpensive	Expensive
Unreal Engine	Industry standard for VR and interactive experiences. Supports real-time rendering, realistic lighting, and smooth transitions (e.g., portals). Easily handles large 3D scanned environments for detailed walkthroughs.	✓		
Unity	User-friendly and versatile for real-time 3D visualization. Plug-ins like Pixyz or RealityCapture streamline importing scanned meshes.	✓		
Photogrammetry and 3D Scanning Integration – These are useful for refining and importing scanned data into walkthrough-ready formats				
Reality Scan	Excellent for creating clean, navigable 3D meshes from scans or photos. Outputs optimized models compatible with game engines like Unreal or Unity.	✓		
Agisoft Metashape Standard	Produces high-resolution models from 3D scans.		✓	
Agisoft Metashape Professional	Includes tools for texture baking and mesh simplification			✓
Virtual Reality and Walkthrough Platforms – These platforms focus on immersive navigation				

(*continued*)

CHAPTER 1   WHAT IS HBIM?

Table 1-1. (continued)

Software	Use	Open Source	Inexpensive	Expensive
Twinmotion – Education	Simplified version of Unreal Engine tailored for architectural visualization. Great for nondevelopers who need to create walkthroughs quickly.	✓		
Matterport – 2 users	Focuses on real estate and building walkthroughs. Automatically converts 3D scans into navigable virtual tours.	✓		
Matterport – 10 users Professional			✓	
Matterport – 100–300 users Business				✓
Sketchfab – Free	For sharing and interacting with 3D models online. Allows basic navigation within the mesh through a browser.	✓		
Sketchfab – Paid			✓	
CAD-Specific Tools – These tools are helpful if you are working with architectural or historical reconstructions				
Autodesk Revit Student	For combining 3D scans with BIM workflows, particularly for historical buildings.	✓		
Autodesk Revit				✓
Autodesk Revit Lt			✓	
Rhino + Grasshopper Student	Supports scanned data refinement and integration with HBIM tools.		✓	
Rhino + Grasshopper Commercial			✓	

Case Study 1: Scan to BIM
Content-Based Immersive Experience of the Basilica of Sant'Ambrogio

Authors: Fabrizio Banfi, Raffaella Brumana, Chiara Stanga (2019)
University of Milan, Italy

Introduction

The Basilica of Sant'Ambrogio, located in Milan, Italy, is one of the most historically significant examples of Romanesque architecture. Its architectural complexity and cultural value make it a prime candidate for digital preservation and public education. In their 2019 study, the authors explored how immersive technologies, combined with robust data-driven models, could transform the way people interact with and understand such heritage sites. The study focuses on the integration of Historic Building Information Modelling (HBIM), virtual reality (VR), and historical narratives to create an engaging and educational experience for both experts and the general public.

Figure 1-7. *The Basilica of Sant'Ambrogio, Milan, Italy (Figure 1, p. 159)*

Objectives of the Study

Banfi, Brumana, and Stanga sought to achieve the following objectives:

1. **Cultural Preservation:** To digitally document the Basilica of Sant'Ambrogio, ensuring its preservation for future generations

2. **Public Accessibility:** To make the Basilica's rich history, art, and architecture accessible to a wider audience

3. **Educational Engagement:** To provide an immersive and content-rich experience that educates users about the Basilica's historical significance

4. **Framework Development:** To establish a replicable methodology for integrating HBIM and immersive technologies for other heritage sites

Methodology

The methodology combined advanced digital documentation techniques with interactive storytelling, ensuring a comprehensive and user-friendly experience.

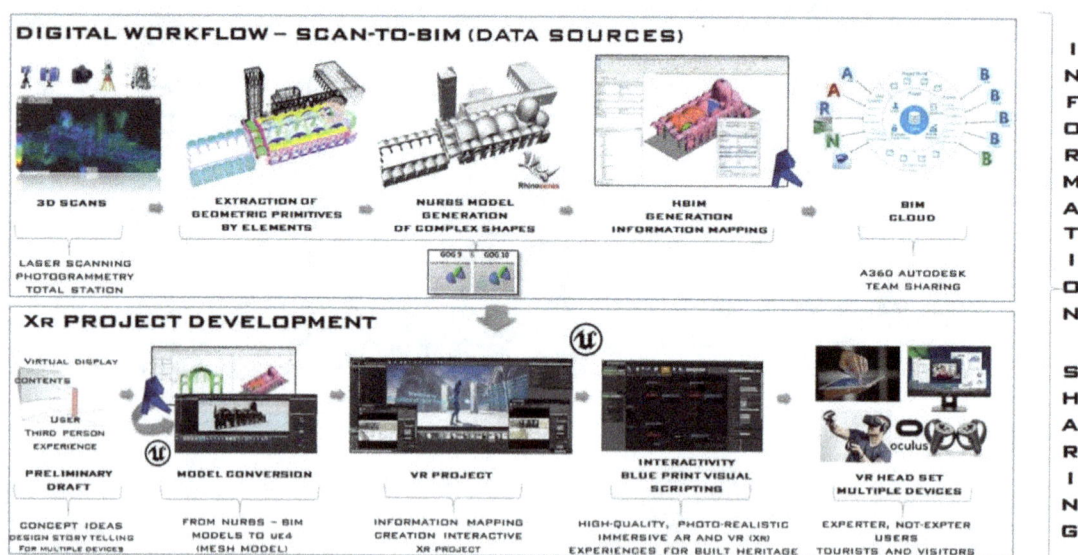

Figure 1-8. *Banfi, Brumana, and Stanga's (2019) XR Digital process workflow (Figure 2, p. 160)*

CHAPTER 1 WHAT IS HBIM?

Digital Data Collection

The authors employed state-of-the-art tools to accurately capture the Basilica's physical and historical features.

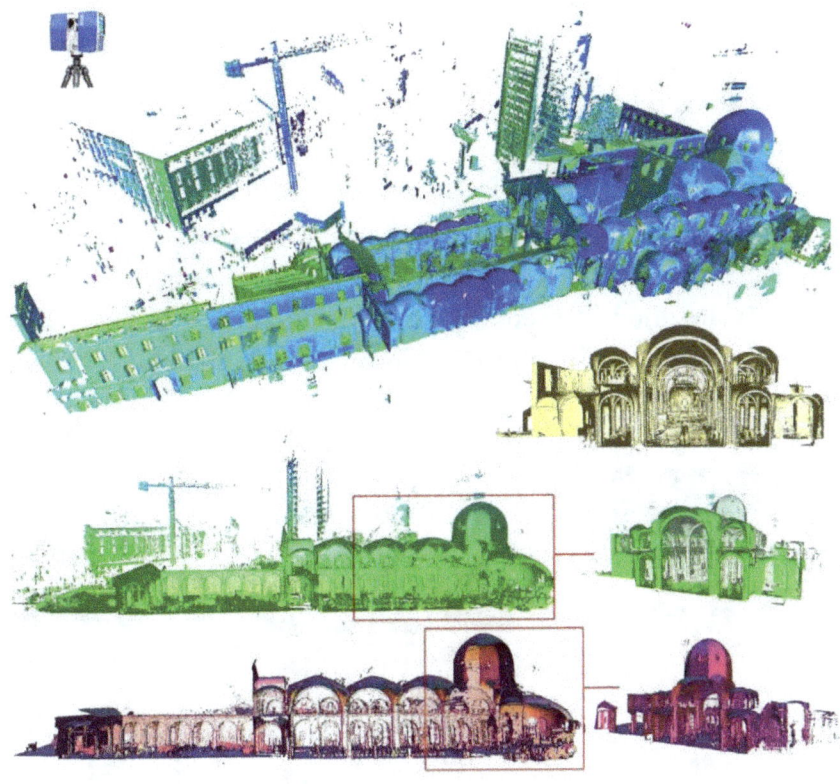

Figure 1-9. Banfi, Brumana, and Stanga's (2019) post-processing phase, orientation, cleaning, and creation of different layers of point cloud data for the generative process of Scan to BIM elements (Figure 3, p. 161)

Photogrammetry and 3D Laser Scanning
These techniques were used to produce high-resolution, accurate 3D models of the Basilica. The data provided intricate details of architectural elements, such as facades, columns, and frescoes, while ensuring spatial accuracy.

Archival Research
Historical documents, including manuscripts, drawings, and photographs, were analyzed to contextualize the Basilica's architectural evolution and cultural role.

15

Art and Iconography Documentation

Detailed information about the Basilica's artwork, such as mosaics and sculptures, was gathered to provide layers of interpretative content.

Building Information Modelling (HBIM)

HBIM served as the foundation for creating an interactive digital replica of the Basilica. This technology enabled the integration of geometrical, historical, and material data into a single platform.

The team structured the HBIM models to include metadata that could be accessed by users during the immersive experience. This data encompassed information about building materials, construction techniques, and the historical context of specific elements.

By leveraging HBIM, they ensured that the digital model was not only a visual representation but also an information-rich repository for researchers and visitors.

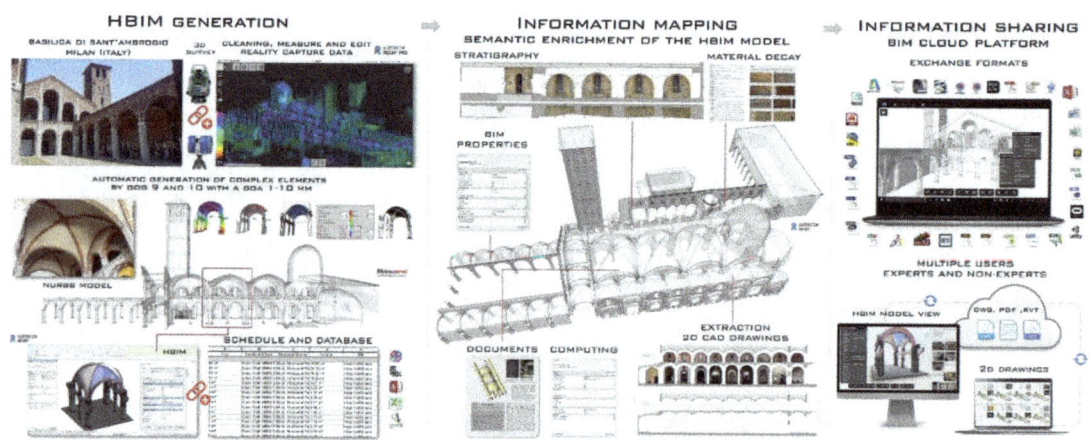

Figure 1-10. Banfi, Brumana, and Stanga's (2019) three steps applied to the HBIM model (Figure 6, p. 163)

Interactive Platforms

The immersive experience was designed to be intuitive and engaging.

> **Virtual Reality (VR):** VR allowed users to navigate the Basilica in a fully immersive environment. This approach enabled exploration of areas that might be physically inaccessible, such as elevated galleries or fragile sections of the building.

Content Integration: Interactive hotspots were embedded throughout the virtual environment, offering detailed information on architectural features, historical anecdotes, and artistic details. For example, a user could click on a mosaic to learn about its iconography and cultural significance.

User-Centered Design: The interface was developed to cater to nonspecialist audiences, ensuring that the experience was both educational and enjoyable for a diverse demographic.

Key Features of the Immersive Experience

Immersive Navigation

The VR platform provided users with the ability to "walk through" the Basilica virtually, offering a sense of presence and scale that traditional media cannot replicate. This feature allowed for exploration of lesser-known or restricted areas, enhancing the user's understanding of the Basilica's spatial organization and design.

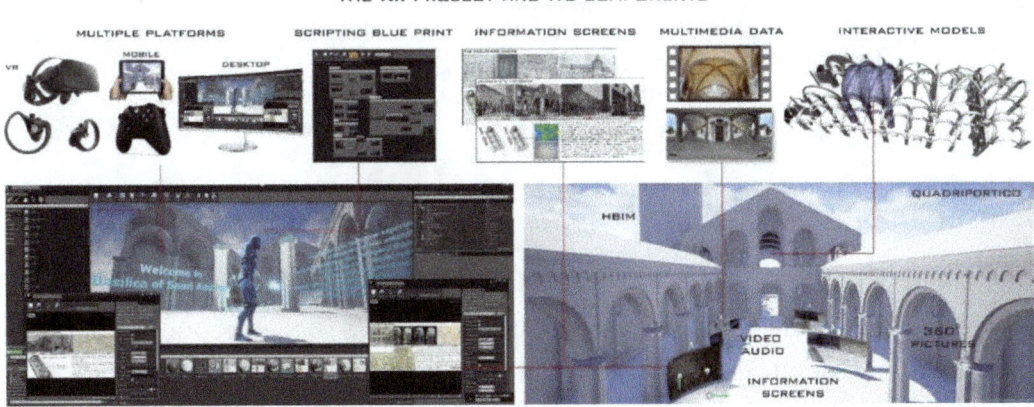

Figure 1-11. Banfi, Brumana, and Stanga's (2019) XR project has provided for the different data sources such as information screens, multimedia data, and an interactive model (Figure 8, p. 164)

Content-Rich Interaction

The experience combined high-quality visuals with detailed narratives. For example, users could examine intricate architectural elements, such as the Basilica's ribbed vaults, while accessing explanations about their engineering and aesthetic significance.

Historical layers of the Basilica, from its early Christian origins to Romanesque additions, were presented through time-lapse visualizations and accompanying text.

Multidisciplinary Integration

The authors' approach combined disciplines such as architecture, history, art conservation, and digital technologies. This holistic approach ensured that the experience was not only visually compelling but also intellectually enriching.

Outcomes

Cultural Preservation

The digital documentation of the Basilica of Sant'Ambrogio created a long-lasting resource that can be used for restoration efforts, academic research, and public engagement. By preserving both the physical and intangible aspects of the site, the project contributes to safeguarding cultural heritage in the face of threats like environmental degradation or urbanization.

Enhanced Public Accessibility

The immersive platform democratized access to the Basilica's rich heritage. People unable to visit in person, whether due to geographical, physical, or economic barriers, could still explore the site and learn about its significance.

Educational Benefits

The project provided a novel way to educate the public about architectural and historical topics. Teachers, students, and tourists could use the platform as an interactive learning tool, bridging the gap between academia and public engagement.

Framework for Future Projects

Their methodology offers a replicable framework for other cultural heritage sites. By demonstrating the feasibility of combining HBIM and immersive technologies, the study paves the way for similar initiatives worldwide.

Impact and Insights

Banfi's work highlights the transformative potential of digital tools in the field of heritage conservation and public engagement. Key insights include

> **The Power of Interdisciplinarity:** The integration of advanced digital technologies with historical research and architectural documentation enriched the user's experience and ensured academic rigor.
>
> **The Importance of Accessibility:** Immersive technologies break down traditional barriers to heritage appreciation, making historical sites accessible to a global audience.
>
> **Sustainability in Heritage Management:** Digital models can serve as tools for monitoring the condition of heritage sites and planning conservation efforts, reducing the need for invasive interventions.
>
> **Engagement Through Immersion:** By creating a sense of presence, VR fosters a deeper emotional connection with heritage sites, encouraging users to value and preserve cultural history.

Conclusion

Banfi, Brumana, and Stanga's study on the Basilica of Sant'Ambrogio demonstrates the innovative ways in which technology can enhance heritage conservation and education. The project's success underscores the potential of HBIM and immersive platforms to create meaningful, content-driven experiences that resonate with diverse audiences. Banfi's approach serves as a model for future initiatives, bridging the gap between cultural heritage and modern technology while ensuring the preservation and appreciation of our shared history.

CHAPTER 1   WHAT IS HBIM?

Contrasting HBIM with BIM

While HBIM shares similarities with conventional Building Information Modelling (BIM), there are critical distinctions that set them apart. BIM focuses primarily on the design, construction, and management of contemporary buildings, while HBIM emphasizes the preservation and analysis of historical structures.

One of the significant differences lies in the data collection and analysis processes. In BIM, data is often collected from architects, engineers, and contractors during the building's construction and life cycle. Conversely, HBIM requires the integration of historical records, documents, and archival materials into the modelling process. This integration necessitates a distinct set of skills and methodologies tailored to historical research and analysis (Historic England, 2017).

To illustrate the concept of HBIM, we will demonstrate how HBIM was instrumental in documenting and understanding the alterations made to a selection of Winchester City buildings over two centuries. Through HBIM, research, and collaboration with architectural historians, archaeologists, historians, and conservationists, we have gained valuable insights into the buildings' historical development, interior and exterior. The historical data has enabled us to connect aspects of the two periods, the changes made, why, and who by. We are then able to share this information through the 3D reconstructions, allowing others to engage with this information as they explore the city. In Virtual Cities – Winchester 1400 and 1800, once completed, there will be approximately 74 buildings that users will be able to access internally and engage with the embedded HBIM data. One such building is 8 College Street, the house in which Jane Austen spent the last six weeks of her life (see Figure 1-12).

CHAPTER 1 WHAT IS HBIM?

Figure 1-12. A render of Jane Austen's Drawing Room as it may have looked in 1817, at 8 College Street, Winchester (Wilson, 2021)

For visualization purposes, there is an element of artistic license for the layout and design of the interiors. We can use books and papers such as Crook's (1987) study of Winchester Cathedral Deanery and his (1982) study of "the Pilgrim's Hall, Winchester" that provide interior description and building materials in good detail. For the interior of Jane's room in Winchester, there were a couple of sketches that gave a glimpse of what the room may have looked like. Using these and personal photos of the style of furniture used by Jane at Chawton House helped in providing an "assumed" interior layout. This type of research is rewarding although time-consuming and requires expertise in understanding/knowing where to resource the information and how to knit it together. There is a definite need for researchers, historians, designers, archaeological professionals, and local history groups to glean the data required for HBIM models, unlike BIM that, as mentioned above, rely on architects, engineers, building contractors, and interior designers.

If the purpose of the 3D building models was purely for visualization such as The Dome Edinburgh (Matterport, 2025), i.e., did not contain additional information, then life is a little more straightforward, as the scenes can be put together so they "look right." Yet, to provide realistic representations of a building, street, or city for exploring or as part of a film set, or game environment, the materials/textures and structures still require research, such as period style, vernacular architecture, and use of the buildings. Interactive engagement with the model puts an additional layer to the data required and the level of realism. The user is able to choose how long they stay within the scene and how close they are to the model, which means they are able to "inspect" the objects/model more closely; for example, see Case Study 1 and the work that has been done for the Basilica of Sant'Ambrogio (Banfi et al., 2019). When providing animated walkthroughs or guided

21

tours of the 3D scene or building, the user can be steered from being too close or guided away from areas that are not as detailed. The movement detracts from being able to "stare" and take on board aspects that may not be as realistic, or as accurate. A decision is needed, therefore, about the level of detail (LOD) and whether the user is going to be allowed to roam and explore and whether there is a need for them to engage with any data embedded in the model. The visualization-only model was what I initially created in 1995-1996 for Dunster Castle, Somerset; Beaulieu Abbey (2009-2010) and Hyde Abbey (2015-2016) in Hampshire; and in the models our students made for Malmesbury (2020). These models were much more about animated tours and being able to "walk through" the spaces, mostly because of the availability of technology at the time. The research was about the materials and construction of each building to be able to create the 3D model, due to most of the buildings being in ruins or no longer resembled what they once were.

Having undertaken this research, it might have been worthwhile going the extra mile to add that data to the models. The issue here, though, was the additional time required, and most commercial-based projects may not have the funds, or time, to do this, as in the case of the projects mentioned above.

BIM is built into new buildings, which will ensure the future of these buildings is recorded. What seemed to be the concern, according to a plethora of academic papers, is what information and how it should be recorded. This concern resulted in the British BIM Standard BS1192, which has been recently superseded in 2019 by BS EN ISO 19650, generally shortened to ISO 19650 (UK BIM Framework, 2019) and clearly sets out what should be recorded and how to do so. BIM Level 2 compliance is now mandatory in the UK for centrally procured government projects.

HBIM builds on BIM by incorporating historical and analytical information into the model and can help with conservation, performance insights, and communicating information to a variety of audiences including researchers, visitors, and owners/stakeholders. From further research, there appears to be several suggestions of what should also be included for an HBIM set of standards. The issues being discussed are whether to include intangible data such as photographs, oral histories, video clips, and community stories (Heesom et al., 2020), and if so, how.

The tables below present a side-by-side comparison of the key characteristics of HBIM and BIM. The charts highlight their respective focuses, data sources, applications, and advantages. By juxtaposing the two methodologies, it will hopefully be easier to gain a clear understanding of the unique aspects of HBIM that cater specifically to historical preservation.

Table 1-2. There is considerable data that needs resourcing for BIM and HBIM; resourcing the information can be time-consuming and costly (Wilson, 2025)

Types of Data	BIM	HBIM	Sources of Data
Exterior measurements	X	X	Archives
Interior measurements	X	X	Community research
Construction materials	X	X	Archaeological evidence
Architectural periods	X	X	History books
Architectural changes	X	X	Historical societies
Floor plans – layouts	X	X	Planning depts
Sections and callouts	X	X	Site visits/surveys
Schedules	X	X	Artwork/paintings
Site maps	X	X	3D scans
Artistic impressions/sketches	X	X	3D surveys
Photos	X	X	Thermal imaging
Point cloud data/3D mesh	X	X	LiDAR
Thermal analysis	X	X	Photogrammetry
Video and audio/music		X	Architects
Film clips		X	Historians
Walkthroughs/animations		X	Films
Stories		X	Video and audio/music

In Table 1-3, I have highlighted the possibility that BIM could also include intangible data for new and recent significant buildings. These could be interviews with the architects and stakeholders, the reason for the building and choice of materials for example, what was on the site before the new building, and were there any archaeological finds, historical events, or similar. Even the press relating to the building may become of interest in years to come. Should it therefore be included? If captured while the building work was happening, it would not be as time-consuming if being revisited in 50 years' time.

CHAPTER 1   WHAT IS HBIM?

Table 1-3. *Why HBIM needs to be more considered regarding the type of data resourced and included in record keeping*

	Examples	Stories Culture	Significant Owners	Phases of construction	Restoration/ Repairs	Memories/Past Culture
BIM	Modern buildings Commercial, residential, industrial structures	The Shard 22 Bishopsgate Newfoundland SEGRO V-Park Grand Union Millennium Bridge	None unless a high-profile building OR interviews/ oral histories with architects and stakeholders for the future	Possibly	Generally no	Generally no	Possibly depending on why the building was built, i.e., purpose or any historical events associated
HBIM	Ruins, existing No longer existing Recent significant cultural buildings	Corfe Castle Winchester Great Hall Steventon Rectory The Shard	Yes, oral histories with community and/or descendants	In most cases	Yes	Yes	Yes

24

Table 1-4. *In terms of the outputs a BIM or HBIM model supplies, they are more or less identical. The only difference is that the Interactive HBIM model would provide more engagement to a wider demographic of users (see Table 1-3)*

	2D Plans	Elevations and Sections	Services	Schedule	3D Model	Walkthrough	Interior Layouts	Interactive Model
BIM	Yes	Yes	Yes	Yes	Yes	Yes	Yes	Yes?
HBIM	Yes	Yes	Yes	Yes	Yes	Yes	Yes	Yes

Case Study 2: Virtual Cities

Virtual Cities is currently in development as a prototype heritage interpretation project reconstructing a segment of Winchester in the Medieval period (1400) and Regency period (1800). The premise is to reconstruct cities using architectural time-slices demonstrating the architectural and cultural changes of a city across time. Buildings of the initial two periods will be pulled together in the Unreal Game Engine, enabling visitors/users to step between the two eras on screen and in VR. There are several specific buildings we are recreating, which will include historical information such as the people who lived in/used the building, its built fabric, when it was built/destroyed/changed and why, where possible, and other aspects relating to HBIM.

Figure 1-13. *Cheyney House, Winchester (Pye, H. (Student), 2022)*

Figure 1-14. *College Street, Winchester (Wilson, D and Sineiko, N. (Student), 2022)*

Background

Virtual Cities stems from an earlier concept, "The Talking Walls," in which we developed Beaulieu Abbey in three eras, rebuilding the abbey and the life of the monks and its community as a kiosk and web application (launched 2010).

Working with Beaulieu formed the basis of my PhD "Curator, Designer, and Visitor Interaction in Cultural Heritage Interpretation Design Practice."

In 2016, we worked on reconstructing Hyde Abbey, Winchester, which included the abbey precinct and surrounding landscape. This was our first time working within Unreal Game Engine.

In 2019–2020, we worked with Malmesbury Market Town in the Medieval and Anglo-Saxon periods for "Explore Malmesbury." We worked on this as a live client project with our students, using a mix of Blender, Autodesk Revit, 3DS Max, and the Unreal Game Engine.

The models created did not include HBIM or BIM information; additional data was not required for this project.

Figure 1-15. Hyde Abbey and Precinct (Wilson, 2016)

Figure 1-16. Malmesbury Medieval Reconstruction (Wilson, 2019)

How

Step 1 – Visual, historical, architectural, and archaeological research discovering specific eras of significant architectural and cultural change in the city was undertaken.

Step 2 – A buildings' list was collated of all the buildings we would create in full and those that would be generic used for visualization purposes only.

Step 3 – Started reconstruction via architectural and 3D modelling software for specific buildings/streets and constant research .

Step 4 – Collaboration with the university, external history and archaeological experts, and organizations for advice and validation was necessary for the additional skillsets.

We worked with students from different design disciplines to recreate the landscapes and buildings and source the relevant heritage building information. As the city develops, we will also work with students from history and creative writing to provide history tours, ghost trails, and similar for use with the virtual city.

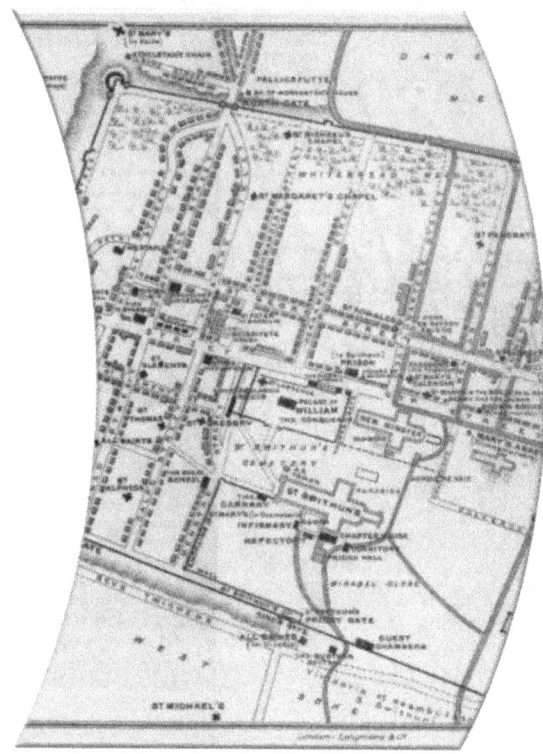

Figure 1-17. *Extracted from Chapter 2 Winchester: A City of Two Planned Towns in "The Land of the English Kin" (Biddle, 2020)*

CHAPTER 1   WHAT IS HBIM?

Winchester 1400

1400 was chosen as an initial era due to the medieval importance of Winchester, and before many of the churches were lost to decay. Also, the availability of maps for the period with sufficient detail was a deciding factor.

Figure 1-18. *A Historical Map of Winchester (Town & City Historical Maps) (Biddle, 2016) published by The Historic Towns Trust*

CHAPTER 1   WHAT IS HBIM?

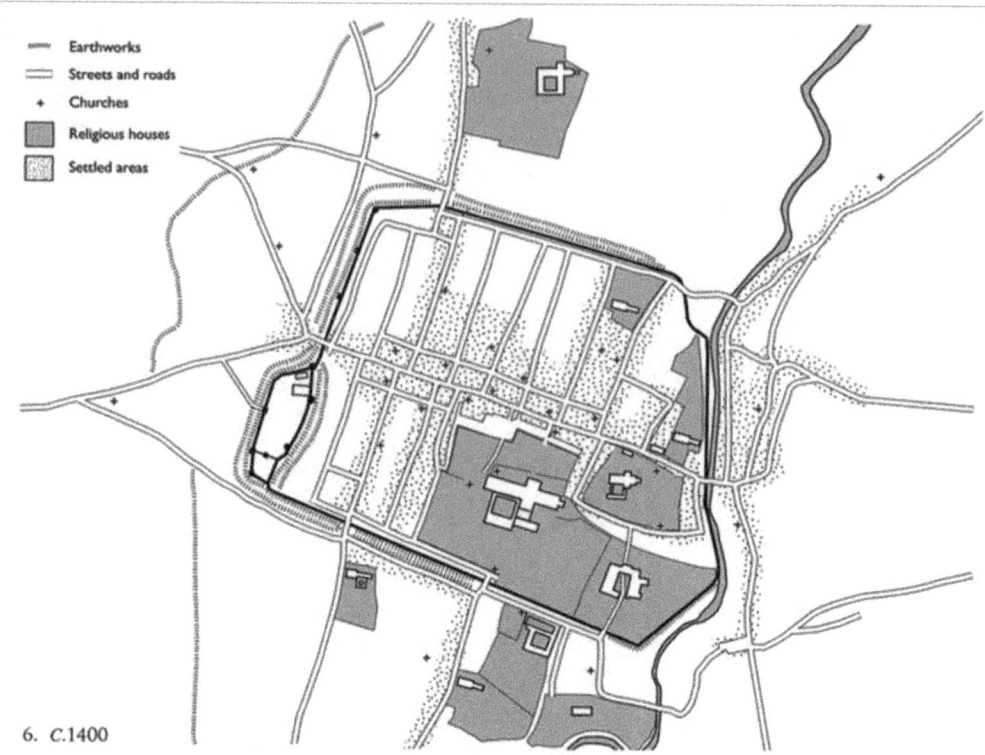

Figure 1-19. Extracted from Chapter 2 Winchester: A City of Two Planned Towns in "The Land of the English Kin" (Biddle, 2020): Figure 2.4 Winchester, the development of the city from the mid to late 2nd century B.C. to 1870, from WS 11 (Winchester Atlas) (Oxford, 2017), Figure 1. Drawn by Giles Darkes (`https://brill.com/display/book/edcoll/9789004421899/BP000004.xml`)

Winchester 1800

1800 was chosen as one of the initial eras to reconstruct mostly to be able to include Jane Austen's time in Winchester and model the building she stayed in, internally as well as externally.

It is also a good period to choose to highlight the change in buildings and urban growth from the medieval period. In addition, there would also be significant changes to notice from the current city.

Figure 1-20. *An Historical Map of Winchester (Town & City Historical Maps) (Biddle, 2016) published by The Historic Towns Trust*

Prototype

We have chosen the area from the Cathedral south to College Street and east to Wolvesey Castle for building the prototype for testing process, time, and research available.

The map we initially used was one from the 1750s. The map was one of a series of four framed prints given to me as a present. The blue line here indicates the area for the prototype originally provided to our 2nd year BSc 3D Environments (Game & Heritage) and BSc CAD students (see Figure 1-21).

The area covered provides a range of historic buildings in both the 1400 and 1800 but is also an area that changed significantly from being quite open and cultivated in 1400 to many more houses and smaller plots of land, highlighting the urban growth of the city.

CHAPTER 1   WHAT IS HBIM?

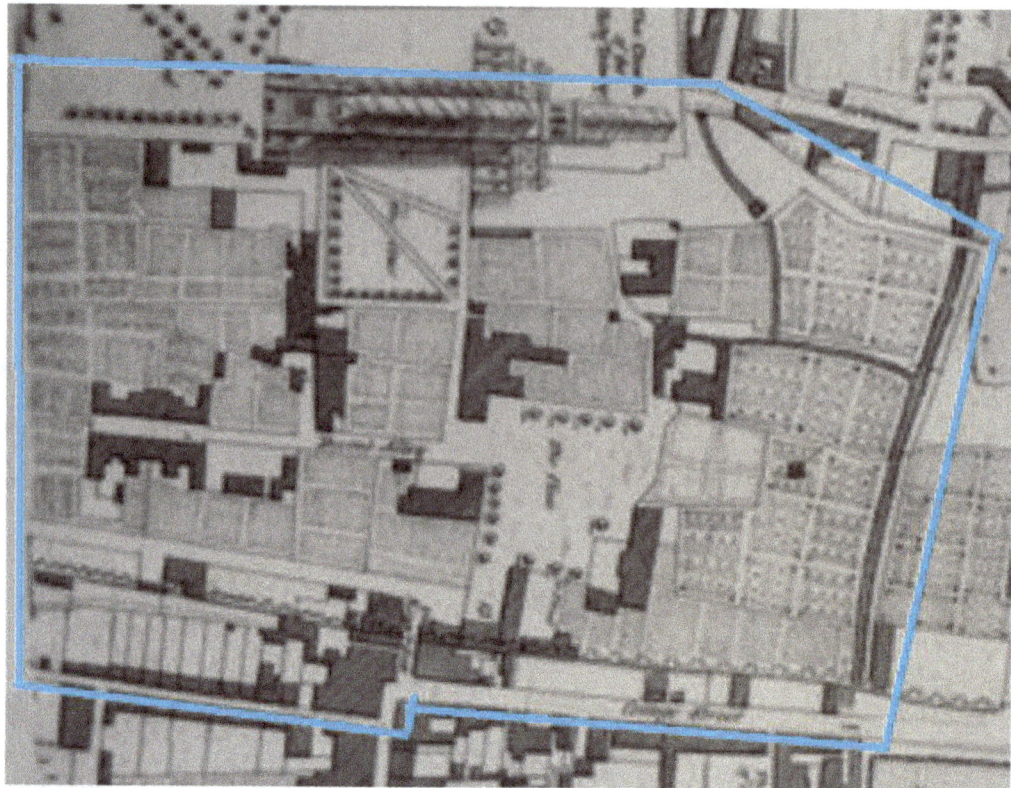

Figure 1-21. *Extract of a set of four maps created by Will Godfon in 1750. The four prints created a centerpiece of the City of Winchester with elevations and perspectives of some of the significant buildings set in each corner, with various excerpts providing the history of those buildings.*

Design Process

Action research, practice-led design, and design thinking approaches will be used for developing a prototype of an area of Winchester to the full city across the two eras. In use is a user-centered design and participatory design process with a consistent team of designers, visitor representatives, students, and local Winchester experts for the design and development of heritage site interpretation, also testing the model coming from my PhD. We may need to extend the team occasionally to include experts in areas such as medieval gardens/plants and geology.

CHAPTER 1   WHAT IS HBIM?

Our process will be recorded for educational purposes in being able to replicate processes, test, and reflect changes for implementing in future work. The main focus is on preserving and celebrating the rich cultural history of 1400 and 1800 Winchester through virtual reconstruction.

The reconstruction serves to ensure the sustainability of Winchester's cultural heritage and preservation of historical landmarks providing access to essential HBIM data.

Figure 1-22.   *External render of 15-16 Kingsgate St. (Hau, C. (student), 2022)*

The Possibles

- The Unreal scenes and individual buildings may form backdrops for multiple purposes. Jane Austen's house in College Street, remodeled with the interior designed based on research from sketches and Regency/Georgian interiors.

- Cultural Heritage Sketchfab – students' work on international display with a growing library of 3D assets.

- The Virtual City spaces/buildings could be enhanced for holding exhibitions and lectures in a choice of historical buildings.

- Linking cities with museum assets and their context via our work with The Earth Museum.

33

CHAPTER 1   WHAT IS HBIM?

- We can also place relevant Winchester objects within the virtual city and use them as a resource for local heritage museums, organizations, and The Earth Museum. More importantly, a record of historic buildings will be created, each embedded with HBIM data, forming a valuable preservation resource.

Figure 1-23. *Initial render of Jane Austen's room at 8 College Street (Wilson, 2023)*

Commercialization

Commercialization could include aspects similar to Second Life and future Metaverse creations. For example, we could gain sponsorship/fees from Winchester organizations/retail/tourism who may be interested in putting on events within the virtual city periods.

Education and craft-based scenarios could be developed to understand the culture and skills of the past. For example, skills that are disappearing could be delivered in either 2D or 3D animated scenes as a learning resource for schools, history groups, and research via the web application.

The individual architectural models could also be available to purchase along with interior fittings for each of the two time periods.

We are currently applying for funding to create the whole city in the two periods, and then for further periods, and different cities.

Figure 1-24. *Internal render of Jane Austen's room at 8 College Street (Wilson, 2023)*

Figure 1-25. *External render of 15-16 Kingsgate Street (Hau, C. (student), 2022)*

Why Now?

Software and hardware have made it much easier to create realistic scenes for walking around in VR; the headsets (Quest 3) are now wire-free; gaming laptops are more powerful, and students (and the public) are more willing to "explore" virtually.

With the recent pandemic and the focus on less travel for eco reasons, creating a virtual city in different periods allows visitors to still visit and learn about the city online and using VR.

How we now interact, visit, and engage with the world around us has changed quite quickly, especially in also thinking about Eco Footprints and travel where tourism is concerned. The Metaverse, we are told, is the next technological phase; content for the different virtual worlds is needed.

CHAPTER 1　WHAT IS HBIM?

Figure 1-26. *iStock purchase – used for Digital Media, University of Winchester*

Figure 1-27. *Hyde Abbey, Winchester (Wilson, 2016)*

CHAPTER 1   WHAT IS HBIM?

The Role of HBIM in Architectural Preservation

Introduction

Architectural preservation is a critical discipline dedicated to safeguarding our built heritage. Historical buildings embody cultural, historical, and artistic values that connect us to the past and offer insights into earlier architectural practices, societal norms, and technological advancements. However, preserving these structures presents unique challenges, such as structural deterioration, incomplete documentation, and, in some cases, the need to adapt historic buildings to contemporary requirements. HBIM plays a pivotal role in the field of architectural preservation by bridging the gap between technology and heritage conservation. Its applications extend beyond visual representations, as HBIM also facilitates analysis, documentation, and collaboration among professionals and stakeholders in the preservation process.

HBIM enables architects, historians, and conservators to collaborate effectively, combining their expertise to restore and preserve historical buildings accurately. By facilitating an immersive and interactive experience, HBIM engages the public in understanding the significance of architectural heritage, fostering a sense of cultural identity and pride.

I have shown how HBIM extends the principles of BIM to heritage contexts integrating advanced technologies, such as laser scanning, photogrammetry, and historical data integration, into a coherent digital environment. This section explores the multifaceted role of HBIM in architectural preservation, reviewing its contributions to documentation, conservation, and adaptive reuse of heritage buildings.

Virtual Reconstruction of Lost Elements

Many heritage buildings have suffered partial or total loss of certain features due to decay or past interventions. HBIM's parametric capabilities allow for the virtual reconstruction of missing elements, guided by historical documentation and expert interpretation. These reconstructions provide valuable insights for restoration efforts or virtual heritage initiatives.

Facilitating Adaptive Reuse

HBIM supports the integration of modern systems, such as HVAC, electrical, and accessibility features, into historic buildings without compromising their heritage value. BIM clash detection tools ensure that interventions are compatible with the existing structure, minimizing physical and aesthetic disruptions. By simulating different usage scenarios, HBIM aids in designing adaptive reuse solutions that respect the building's historical significance.

Enhanced Collaboration and Decision-Making

As with BIM, HBIM acts as a centralized repository of information, fostering collaboration among multidisciplinary teams. The ability to test multiple scenarios within the HBIM environment facilitates informed decision-making for buildings that require restoration or modernizing aesthetically. The visualization and different simulations help to improve stakeholder understanding of project goals and constraints.

Heritage Interpretation and Visualization Projects

The purpose of this book is primarily to aid 3D visualizers and 3D modellers and therefore more about immersive interpretational experiences, visualizations, and educational value that HBIM can provide. This includes the possibility of virtual reality (VR) and augmented reality (AR) applications based on the HBIM models to bring historical architecture to life for researchers, students, and the public. When The Talking Walls started in 1996, this was the premise for modelling different phases of Dunster Castle and telling the story of the inhabitants and their life within the Castle. Children visiting the site found it hard to visualize the building as a castle where it had changed over the years to become a grand Manor house (Woodger, 1995), a far different looking building to that of the previous castle variants. These variants had been documented by a set of wonderful sketches (see Figure 1-28) and a floor plan which formed the basis of the initial digital Talking Walls application.

CHAPTER 1   WHAT IS HBIM?

Figure 1-28. *Dunster Castle through the ages (National Trust, images by Stephen Biesty)*

Figure 1-29. *1995 Degree Project for Dunster Castle; right image is 1150 and left image is 1600, based on Stephen Biesty's images (above) drawn for the National Trust (Wilson, 1995)*

Unfortunately, technology at the time was limited to CD-ROMs and Autodesk 3DS Max. Even the later application for Beaulieu Abbey using Autodesk 3DS Max and Autodesk Revit, and launched in 2010, was for use via a kiosk (see Figure 1-30). We had hoped that the early smartphones/PDAs might be sufficiently powerful as an additional platform so tourists would be able to "roam" the Abbey and explore the application in situ; unfortunately this wasn't the case.

CHAPTER 1 WHAT IS HBIM?

Figure 1-30. *Beaulieu Abbey Kiosk Application, Beaulieu Abbey Dome Museum (Wilson, 2010)*

Figure 1-31. *Beaulieu Abbey Cloister and inside the Chapter House (Wilson, 2009)*

The Abbey was built for three phases of its life: its construction in the 13th century, its completion and heyday in the 14th century, and its dissolution in the 15th century. Reference for the Abbey involved working with Beaulieu's Archivist Susan Tomkins and Lady Mary Montagu-Scott. It also involved the use of floor plans and sketches from Fowler's (1911) book *A History of Beaulieu Abbey, A.D. 1209–1539* (see one of the sketches below and the digital interpretation in Figure 1-32).

Figure 1-32. *Beaulieu Abbey Cloister and inside the Chapter House (Wilson, 2009)*

For this project, Autodesk Revit was used to create the basic model, which was then taken into 3DS Max, the aim purely to be visual and not retain BIM data, mostly because this was not required as part of the project but also because the FBX transition to 3DS Max, at the time, did not allow the retention of the BIM data. To do so would have meant a considerable amount of programming within 3DS Max which was beyond the skillset available, and as mentioned, the scope of the project. An aspect that was a nice surprise for the client was the realization of the physical scale of the Abbey by those that saw the internal views with the monks sitting at prayer. What was interesting was the speed with which the basic model could be produced in Autodesk Revit compared to Autodesk 3DS Max during the earlier project. The elevations and a walkthrough of the basic Revit model were completed within a few days for a presentation demo to the Beaulieu team. The internal elements were later added in 3DS Max.

CHAPTER 1   WHAT IS HBIM?

Figure 1-33. *Beaulieu Abbey East Elevation Basic model in Autodesk Revit (Wilson, 2006)*

Figure 1-34. *Beaulieu Abbey South Elevation Basic model in Autodesk Revit (Wilson, 2006)*

A similar "quick" demo was created in 2009 for a concept furthering The Talking Walls' applications in which a significant person and the homes they lived in were the main premise. For the early example, we chose Jane Austen and Steventon Rectory where Jane Austen lived with her family as a child. The model of Steventon Rectory, the church, and path to the church was constructed in just a couple of days in Autodesk Revit (see Figures 1-35 and 1-36).

An animated visualization was then created with a voice-over and background music to attract interest within the Jane Austen Societies. The application would have been available via different platforms, envisioning tourists being able to visit different sites with their mobiles or tablets and seeing the digital reconstructions while at the real location. We are currently recreating this concept in full, i.e., for eight of the places Jane Austen lived, which can then be viewed in VR and AR, and on mobile devices. The buildings will be HBIM models and incorporate stories as well as construction and phase data.

CHAPTER 1   WHAT IS HBIM?

Figure 1-35. *The Talking Walls' Jane Austen Demo showing the basic Autodesk Revit model of Steventon Rectory based on Anna Lefroy's Sketch in Walker's article in "Persuasions On-Line" (2005) (Wilson, 2006)*

Figure 1-36. *The basic Autodesk Revit model of Steventon Rectory and path leading to Steventon Church based on different historical maps and Google Maps (Wilson, 2009)*

The new Jane Austen map is possible now because of the development of technology such as smartphones, tablets, VR headsets, and software over the last 15 years. Technology now allows not just mobile users to explore as they roam (or at home/school) but also using virtual reality headsets and make use of augmented or mixed reality, blending the physical building with the virtual digital model. The use of 3DS Max, Revit, Blender, and Unreal Game Engine allows modellers to create reconstructed models, add customized elements, and import to a game engine where the landscape could also be recreated authentically using historic maps. This later technology provides an exciting time for those that love history, architecture, and storytelling, to bring the past to life. In addition, the past life recreation has proven to be an area that 3D Environment and Visualization students unexpectedly enjoy, i.e., being able to undertake historical research and create environments that were "real" unlike fantasy environments that could take the form of their imagination without in-depth research.

Each of the examples above was a project designed to be interactive visually rich applications including storytelling of the inhabitants and their life and culture within the buildings. There was not a call or need for including BIM data from the clients; the brief was to engage tourists/visitors with the history and culture. This is generally the case with such heritage projects; it is only more recently that the embedding of HBIM data within the model has been considered important.

For new buildings, BIM is a requirement; for historic buildings undergoing renovation/repair, the data is being added to the digital BIM model in the process of the renovation work. As of December 2024, there is no universal mandate requiring the incorporation of HBIM data into all 3D historical reconstruction architectural models in heritage interpretation projects. However, HBIM is becoming increasingly prominent in the field of heritage conservation and interpretation due to its ability to digitally document, analyze, and manage historical structures. The additional work involved such as integrating extensive documentation, analysis, and interpretation may be too expensive to factor into a heritage project. The value with regard to preservation, building management, and resulting inclusion of the models to a digital heritage repository of information should be considered when justifying whether the cost should be included in the overall project costs.

While the adoption of HBIM is growing, its implementation varies by region and project. Some countries and organizations have embraced HBIM as standard practice for heritage projects, recognizing its benefits in conservation and restoration efforts. For example, research in Poland by Janisio-Pawłowska (2021) has demonstrated the potential of HBIM technology in cultural heritage protection, highlighting its role in creating detailed 3D models based on existing structures and historical materials.

In France, there is a strong emphasis on preserving cultural heritage, and digital technologies such as HBIM are increasingly utilized. However, specific requirements can vary depending on local regulations, project scope, and the institutions involved. In summary, while HBIM is not universally mandated for all heritage interpretation projects, its growing adoption reflects its value in the field. For specific projects, it is advisable to consult local guidelines and stakeholders to determine the necessity and extent of HBIM integration.

Future Directions and Innovations

Automation and AI in HBIM: Machine learning algorithms are being developed to automate point cloud processing and feature recognition, reducing manual effort. AI-driven analysis can assist in identifying patterns of deterioration and suggesting conservation strategies (Alshawabkeh et al., 2024; Senturk, 2024).

Integration with IoT and Smart Technologies: Sensors embedded in heritage buildings can feed real-time data into HBIM models, enabling dynamic monitoring and management (Chiabrando et al., 2016; Rolim et al., 2024).

Open Data and Collaborative Platforms: The development of open HBIM libraries and collaborative platforms will promote wider adoption and knowledge sharing (Heesom et al., 2019; Penjor et al., 2024).

Enhanced Visualization Tools: Advances in VR and AR technologies will enable more immersive and interactive applications of HBIM in education, tourism, and stakeholder engagement (Banfi, 2021; Lui et al., 2024).

For this section's case study example overleaf, I chose a 2001 heritage interpretation project that highlights the work being done with HBIM for a city. A further reason for choosing this project was because it states the limitations in the use of available technology.

The comparison of what was and what is current was also interesting and how the authors managed that process, which reminded me of the work I undertook for Dunster Castle in 1996, especially in being able to only view as a CD-ROM and Desktop/PC screen.

Case Study 3: HBIM in Historical City Planning

Exciting Understanding in Pompeii Through On-Site Parallel Interaction with Dual-Time Virtual Models

Authors: Daniela Scagliarini, Antonella Coralini, and others from the University of Bologna and collaborating institutions (2001)

In this Case Study showcase, we will explore how HBIM was instrumental in the reconstruction of a historical city, such as Pompeii in Italy. Through HBIM, researchers rebuilt sections of the city that were lost to volcanic eruptions, providing an invaluable tool for studying urban planning and architectural evolution over time.

Overview and Core Objectives

The project aimed to enhance the understanding of Pompeii's archaeological heritage by integrating advanced digital technologies into both research and public engagement practices. Central to the study is MUSE (Mobile and User-centric System for Enjoyment), a multimedia system designed to enable on-site interaction with dual-time virtual models of archaeological sites. Specifically, the study focuses on the "Casa del Centenario" in Pompeii, offering visitors a unique experience that combines physical reality with digital reconstructions.

The primary objectives included

1. Supporting archaeologists in validating reconstruction hypotheses through interactive tools

2. Providing visitors with an engaging and educational experience that bridges the past and present through synchronized models

3. Utilizing a mobile, user-centric interface to democratize access to cultural heritage sites

CHAPTER 1   WHAT IS HBIM?

Figure 1-37. *The western arm of the peristyle in an archive photo (a), in the virtual model of the current situation (b), in the virtual reconstruction (c) (graphic elaboration: E. Vecchietti, 2001)*

Figure 1-38. *The northern wall of the atrium in an archive photo (a), in the virtual model of the current situation (b) (graphic elaboration: E. Vecchietti, 2001)*

Technological Innovations

The MUSE system employed cutting-edge technology to achieve its goals, combining hardware, software, and design innovations to enhance both usability and content delivery.

1. **Dual-Time Models**
    - Two synchronized 3D reconstructions were created: the first showing the Casa del Centenario in its current state (2000–2002), and the second hypothesizing its appearance in 79 AD before the eruption of Mount Vesuvius.

- Users could switch seamlessly between these models, enabling direct comparisons of the site's transformation over centuries.
- The models integrated data from historical drawings, photographs, modern surveys, and chemical analyses.

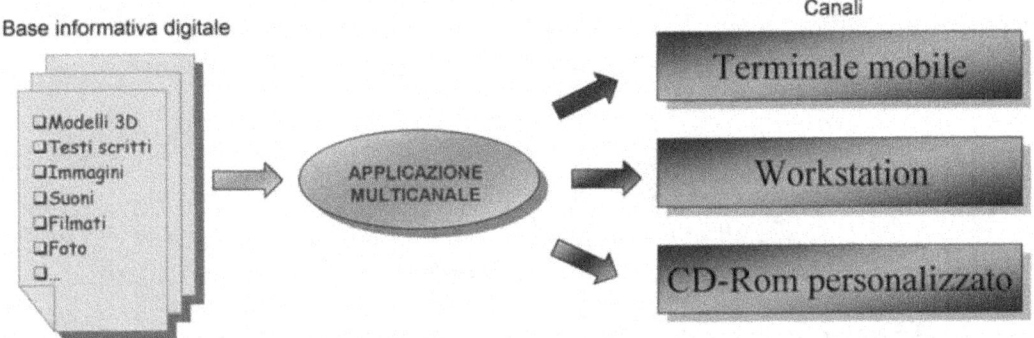

Figure 1-39. *Abstract representation of the MUSE multichannel system (graphic elaboration: A. Coralini, 2001)*

2. **Interactive Navigation**

    - Visitors interacted with the system via portable multimedia tablets featuring an intuitive navigation metaphor called "Virtual Steering by Waving." This allowed users to explore 3D spaces simply by tilting the device.
    - The tablets also served as controllers for high-performance fixed graphic stations located on-site, offering enhanced visuals on larger displays.

CHAPTER 1   WHAT IS HBIM?

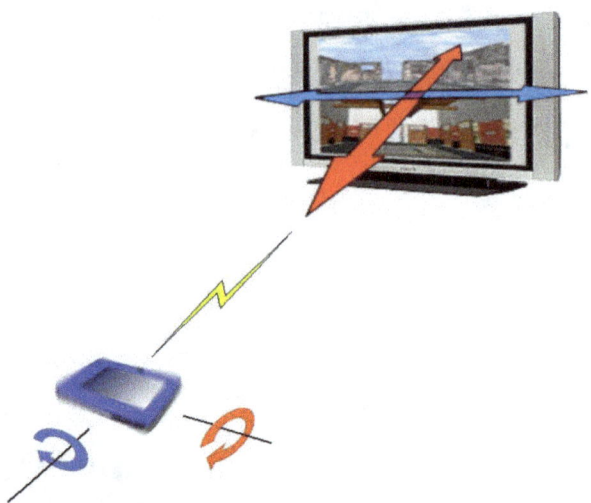

Figure 1-40. *Remote navigation metaphor (Scagliarini et al., 2001)*

3. **Wireless Connectivity**

   - A wireless local area network (WLAN) allowed tablets and graphic stations to communicate seamlessly, ensuring mobility and real-time updates.

   - The system's infrastructure adhered to IEEE 802.11 standards, balancing portability with high-performance requirements.

4. **Augmented Reality Integration**

   - The interactive system enhanced traditional museum experiences by overlaying virtual reconstructions onto physical realities, allowing users to visualize the Casa del Centenario's past while standing within its present ruins.

Case Study: Casa del Centenario

The Casa del Centenario, a Roman domus in the Insula del Centenario (Region IX, Insula 8), served as the focal point of the project. Rediscovered in 1879 during the eighteenth centennial of the eruption, the domus is renowned for its architectural complexity and decorative richness, including frescoes, mosaics, and one of Pompeii's few private baths.

Key features highlighted in the study include

- **Architectural Elements**

    The atrium tuscanicum, impluvium, and peristyle with two-floor arcades were digitally reconstructed to showcase their original forms and functions.

- **Decorative Analysis**

    Raman spectroscopy and chemical analyses were employed to identify pigments, leading to accurate color reconstructions. For instance, the dominant red shade initially hypothesized was revised based on spectroscopic findings.

- **Interactive Engagement**

    Visitors could explore reconstructed spaces like the atrium and its surrounding rooms, gaining insights into Roman architectural practices and the daily lives of Pompeii's inhabitants.

Data Collection and Methodologies

The creation of scientifically reliable 3D models required extensive and diverse data sources. The project relied on the following:

Modern Surveys: Topographical and architectural data from excavation campaigns (1999–2001) provided precise measurements for digital mapping and modelling.

Historical Archives: Drawings, watercolors, and photographs from the 19th and early 20th centuries captured details of the site's earlier states, particularly decorative elements now lost.

Chemical and Physical Analyses: Advanced techniques such as Raman spectroscopy identified the mineral composition of pigments and construction materials.

Comparative Studies: Analogous structures within the Vesuvian region informed missing architectural and decorative elements.

The integration of these sources into a centralized database ensured accuracy and transparency in the reconstruction process. The models were designed to be "works in progress," allowing updates as new findings emerged.

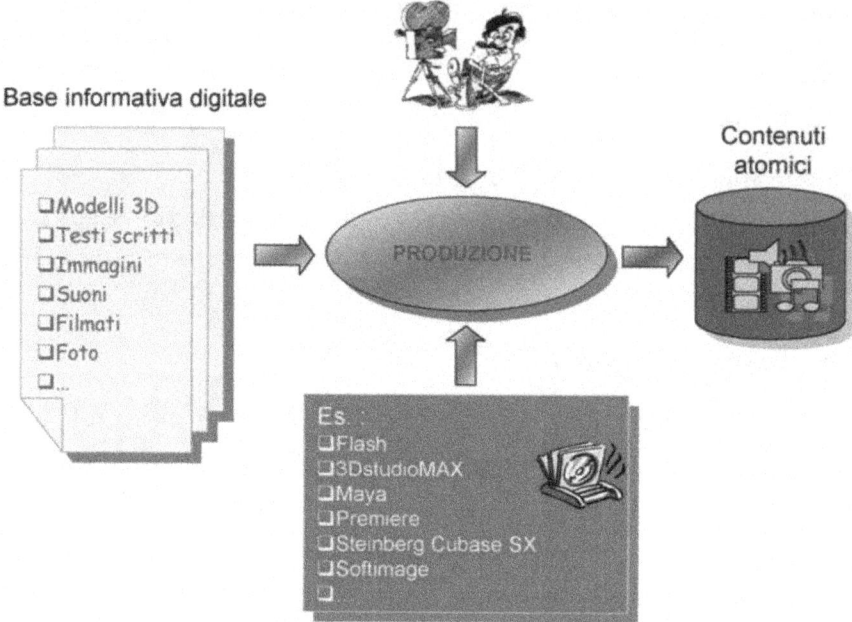

Figure 1-41. *The production and editing of multimedia content (Scagliarini et al., 2001)*

Visitor Experience and Impact

The project's dual-time interaction model aimed to enrich visitor engagement by offering both educational and emotional experiences.

> **Educational Benefits:** Visitors could actively compare the site's current ruins with its hypothesized past, gaining a comprehensive understanding of Roman architecture and urbanism. The system also emphasized critical thinking, inviting users to evaluate the archaeological interpretation process through hierarchical data structures.

CHAPTER 1   WHAT IS HBIM?

Emotional Engagement: The ability to "step back in time" fostered a deeper connection to Pompeii's history and its tragic destruction. The interactive nature of the system created a sense of personal discovery, enhancing visitor satisfaction.

Research Applications: For archaeologists, the system provided a platform for testing reconstruction hypotheses and visualizing alternative scenarios without physically altering the site. The collaborative process highlighted the importance of interdisciplinary approaches, combining archaeology, architecture, and computer science.

Challenges and Limitations

While the project achieved significant milestones, several challenges were noted:

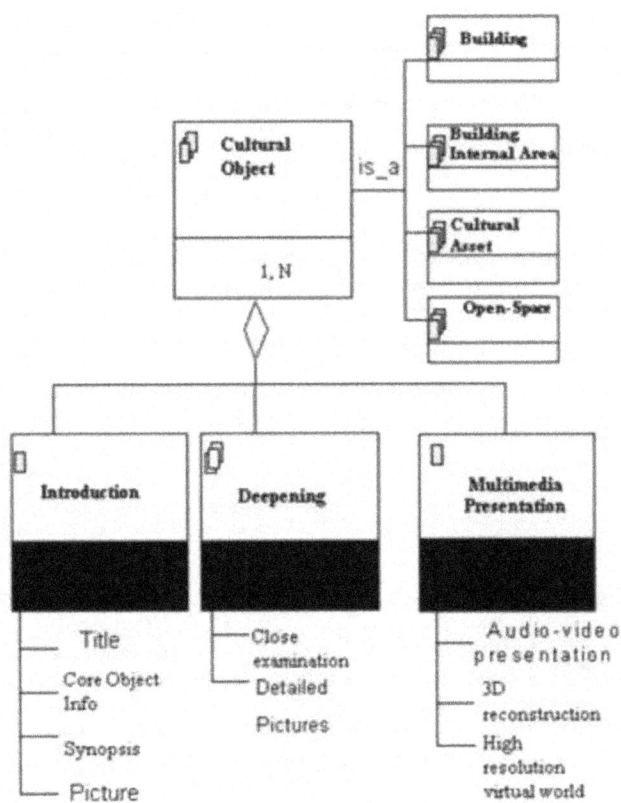

Figure 1-42. *The organization of the primary information base and the relationships between the contents (Scagliarini et al., 2001)*

1. **Hardware Limitations**
   - Portable tablets lacked the processing power for real-time interaction with large virtual environments, necessitating the use of fixed graphic stations for high-definition visuals.

2. **Incomplete Data**
   - Gaps in historical documentation required reliance on comparative studies, which introduced some degree of uncertainty into the reconstructions.

3. **User Experience**
   - Balancing technological complexity with user accessibility was an ongoing challenge, particularly for non-specialist audiences.

Future Directions

The study proposed several avenues for further development:

Enhanced Mobility: Improving tablet performance and battery life to enable seamless interaction without reliance on fixed stations.

Streaming Capabilities: Implementing on-demand streaming of multimedia content to enrich user experiences.

Expanded Applications: Adapting the MUSE system for other archaeological sites, potentially integrating it with emerging technologies such as AI and immersive VR.

Conclusion

The integration of digital technologies at the Casa del Centenario demonstrates the transformative potential of virtual archaeology. By bridging the gap between physical ruins and reconstructed hypotheses, the MUSE system not only enhanced visitor experiences but also advanced the field of archaeological research. The project underscores the importance of interdisciplinary collaboration in preserving and interpreting cultural heritage, paving the way for future innovations in the field.

Summary

HBIM enables the creation of highly detailed and accurate digital records of heritage buildings. With advanced surveying techniques, such as laser scanning, the production of point clouds can now serve as the foundation for 3D modelling. Photogrammetry complements this by providing texture and color information, enhancing the visual fidelity of models.

Historical data, including archival drawings and records, are then able to be incorporated into HBIM models to ensure historical authenticity and provide a rich data resource, especially if cultural stories of the building's life span are included.

HBIM also facilitates precise analysis of structural conditions by integrating data on material properties, structural performance, and deterioration patterns. If required, time-based data can be added to track changes over time, perhaps through the use of "Phases" within Autodesk Revit (Autodesk, 2025b), enabling continuous visual monitoring of building conditions.

Simulation tools within HBIM allow for the testing of various conservation strategies and prediction of potential outcomes.

This chapter has provided a comprehensive overview of Historical Building Information Modelling (HBIM), defining its concept, comparing it with conventional BIM, and emphasizing its role in architectural preservation. Through real-world examples and pedagogical features, readers have gained insights into the unique attributes of HBIM and its significance in preserving our architectural heritage. The subsequent chapters will delve deeper into the methodologies and processes involved in implementing HBIM for historical building reconstruction and understanding urban development across different eras.

HBIM represents a paradigm shift in architectural preservation, bridging the gap between traditional conservation practices and modern technological advancements. Its ability to integrate detailed documentation, condition assessment, and simulation within a single digital environment makes it an invaluable tool for preserving our architectural heritage. While challenges remain in terms of cost, expertise, and data integration, ongoing innovations are poised to expand HBIM's accessibility and effectiveness.

As heritage buildings continue to face threats from environmental change, urban development, and neglect, HBIM offers a proactive and informed approach to their preservation. By fostering collaboration, enhancing decision-making, and opening new avenues for education and interpretation, HBIM ensures that our built heritage is not only preserved but also celebrated and understood by future generations.

References

Alshawabkeh, Y.; Baik, A.; Miky, Y. (2024) HBIM for Conservation of Built Heritage. ISPRS Int. J. Geo-Inf. 2024, 13, 231. https://doi.org/10.3390/ijgi13070231

Arayici, Y.; Counsell, John; Mahdjoubi, Lamine; Nagy, Gehan A.; Hawas, Soheir; Dewidar, Khaled (2017) *Heritage Building Information Modelling*; Routledge: Taylor Francis Group, New York, NY, USA

Banfi, Fabrizio (2021) The Evolution of Interactivity, Immersion and Interoperability in HBIM: Digital Model Uses, VR and AR for Built Cultural Heritage. *ISPRS Int. J. Geo-Inf.* 2021, *10*(10), 685; https://doi.org/10.3390/ijgi10100685

Biddle, Martin (2020) Winchester: A City of Two Planned Towns. In book: The Land of the English Kin. DOI: 10.1163/9789004421899_004

Biddle, Martin (2016) An Historical Map of Winchester (Town & City Historical Maps). Publisher: The Historic Towns Trust. https://www.historictownstrust.uk/maps/an-historical-map-of-winchester

Blender (2024) Bonsai: A native Building Information Model authoring platform using IFC. Add-on by IfcOpenShell. https://extensions.blender.org/add-ons/bonsai/

Chiabrando, F.; Sammartano, G.; Spano, A. (2016) Historical Buildings Models and Their Handling via 3D Survey: From Points Clouds to User-Oriented HBIM. The International Archives of the Photogrammetry, Remote Sensing and Spatial Information Sciences, Volume XLI-B5, 2016 XXIII ISPRS Congress, July 12–19, 2016, Prague, Czech Republic

Crook, John (1987) Winchester Cathedral Deanery. Hampshire Field Club & Archaeological Society. Proc. Hampsh. Field Club Archaeol. Soc. 43, 1987, pp. 125–173. https://www.hantsfieldclub.org.uk/publications/hampshirestudies/digital/1980s/vol43/Crook.pdf

Crook, John (1982) Pilgrim's Hall, Winchester. Hampshire Field Club & Archaeological Society. Proc. Hampsh. Field Club Archaeol. Soc. 38, 1982, pp. 85–101. https://www.hantsfieldclub.org.uk/publications/hampshirestudies/digital/1980s/vol38/Crook.pdf

Dore, C.; Murphy, M. (2012, September). Integration of Historic Building Information Modeling (HBIM) and 3D GIS for recording and managing cultural heritage sites. In 18th International Conference on Virtual Systems and Multimedia (VSMM), pp. 369–376, Milan, Italy. https://doi.org/10.1109/VSMM.2012.6365947

Fowler, Sir James Kingston (1911) "A History of Beaulieu Abbey, A.D. 1204–1539." Published by Car Illustrated

Heesom, David; Boden, Paul; Hatfield, Anthony; Rooble, Sagal; Andrews, Kate; Berwari, Hadar (2019) Developing a collaborative HBIM to integrate tangible and intangible cultural heritage. International Journal of Building Pathology and Adaptation DOI: 10.1108/IJBPA-04-2019-0036

Historic England (2017). BIM for heritage developing a historic building information model. https://historicengland.org.uk/images-books/publications/bim-for-heritage/heag-154-bim-for-heritage/

Janisio-Pawłowska, D. (2012) Analysis of the Possibilities of Using HBIM Technology in the Protection of Cultural Heritage, Based on a Review of the Latest Research Carried Out in Poland. ISPRS Int. J. Geo-Inf. 2021, 10, 633. https://doi.org/10.3390/ijgi10100633

Liu, Junshan; Azhar, Salman; Willkens, Danielle; Li, Botao (2023) "Static Terrestrial Laser Scanning (TLS) for Heritage Building Information Modeling (HBIM): A Systematic Review." Virtual Worlds 2, no. 2, pp. 90–114. https://doi.org/10.3390/virtualworlds2020006

Lui, Zhen; He, Yunrui; Demian, Peter; Osmani, M. (2024) Immersive Technology and Building Information Modeling (BIM) for Sustainable Smart Cities. Buildings 14(6):1765 DOI: 10.3390/buildings14061765

Matterport (2025) The Dome, Edinburgh, Space shared by www.360virtualtour.co. https://matterport.com/discover/space/CMatvVatCjc

Murphy, M.; McGovern, E.; Pavia, S. (2009) "Historic building information modelling (HBIM)," Structural Survey, Vol. 27. No. 4, pp. 311–327. https://doi.org/10.1108/02630800910985108

National Trust (1999) Guidebook: Dunster Castle, Somerset. National Trust, London

Penjor, Tshering; Banihashemi, Saeed; Hajirasouli, Aso; Golzad, Hamed (2024) Heritage building information modeling (HBIM) for heritage conservation: Framework of challenges, gaps, and existing limitations of HBIM. Published in Digital Applications in Archaeology and Cultural Heritage, Vol 35, Dec 2024 e00366, ISSN 2212-0548, https://doi.org/10.1016/j.daach.2024.e00366. (https://www.sciencedirect.com/science/article/pii/S2212054824000511)

Rolim, Renan; Lopez-Gonzalez, Concepcion; Vinals, Maria J. (2024) Analysis of the Current Status of Sensors and HBIM Integration: A Review Based on Bibliometric Analysis. Heritage 2024, 7(4), pp. 2071–2087; https://doi.org/10.3390/heritage7040098

Scagliarini, Daniella; Coralini, Antonella; Vecchietti, Erika; Cinotti, Tullio Salmon; Roffia, Luca (2001) Exciting Understanding in Pompeii Through On-Site Parallel Interaction with Dual-Time Virtual Models. University of Bologna, Association for Computing Machinery, Inc., 2002. DOI: 10.1145/584993.585007

Senturk, Hilal S.; Simsek, Cemile F. (2024) HBIM Modelling Process from 3D Point Clouds by Applying Artificial Intelligence Algorithms in Cultural Heritage. Journal of Polytechnic. DOI: 10.2339/politeknik.1503631

UK BIM Framework (2019) The overarching approach to implementing BIM in the UK. https://ukbimframework.org/standards/

Walker (2005) Persuasions On-Line,

Woodger, B. (1995) Dunster Castle Volunteer Guide, Private communication

CHAPTER 2

History and Benefits of HBIM

The evolution of Historic (or Heritage) Building Information Modelling (HBIM) has revolutionized the architectural preservation industry, offering precision, collaboration, and storytelling capabilities. Emerging in the early 2000s as a specialized application of BIM, HBIM is tailored to the unique challenges of documenting, preserving, and managing historical buildings. As technology continues to advance, HBIM will play an even more critical role in safeguarding our architectural heritage for future generations, providing new methodologies to reconstruct and visualize lost structures and embed these reconstructions with rich layers of historical, cultural, and material data (Arsalan et al., 2025).

This chapter provides an overview of the historical development and transformative benefits of HBIM, including its role in fostering interdisciplinary collaboration, enhancing restoration accuracy, and engaging modern audiences through digital visualization. Its potential applications extend from cultural heritage management to urban planning, education, and immersive virtual environments. In addition, this chapter provides an overview of the advantages and challenges involved in implementing HBIM in architectural preservation projects and in this case, for visualizing heritage buildings and cities for different time periods. The last part of the chapter provides five case studies of successful applications using BIM, HBIM, and VR visualization.

The Evolution of HBIM in the Preservation Industry

The origins of HBIM lie in the technological advancements and methodologies developed for contemporary architecture. BIM, the foundation of HBIM, emerged from the fusion of CAD systems and parametric design principles (Murphy et al., 2009).

CHAPTER 2   HISTORY AND BENEFITS OF HBIM

These innovations transformed design and construction workflows by integrating 3D modelling with rich datasets, allowing for more efficient and accurate project management.

Historic Building Information Modelling (HBIM) emerged as a transformative tool for heritage preservation, allowing practitioners to digitally reconstruct, analyze, and manage historic buildings with precision. Its development stems from advancements in BIM, tailored specifically to meet the unique demands of documenting and conserving heritage structures.

HBIM required adaptations to suit the complexities of historical architecture. Unlike modern buildings, heritage structures often feature irregular geometries, unique materials, and intricate details shaped by cultural and historical contexts. The evolution of HBIM as a distinct discipline reflects the increasing recognition of these challenges and the growing demand for tools that bridge the gap between preservation and technology.

Early Developments in Digital Modelling

The foundation for HBIM can be traced to advancements in CAD and solid modelling technologies during the 1960s and 1970s. Douglas Engelbart (1925–2013) was an American inventor in the field of computing. His vision, outlined in his paper "Augmenting Human Intellect" (1962), focused on the ability to dynamically change and update information, which formed the core of parametric modelling in BIM, where changes in one part of the model automatically update related elements. The paper also outlined how computers could augment human intelligence, which is basically the driving force behind the use of BIM to improve design, construction, and facility management processes. This was before the days of the graphical interfaces that we use today, and therefore, being able to view a realistic 3D output was not possible.

During the 1970s, solid modelling became possible, and through the use of Boolean operations, users could create more complex design shapes such as doors and windows within wall representations.

In the 1980s, AutoCAD (1982) designed by John Walker, the founder of Autodesk, grew to become one of the leading 2D CAD systems. CATIA, a surface modelling program, and Pro/Engineer (1987), the first parametric modelling program, were also available.

The early CAD programs, such as AutoCAD (1982), were revolutionary for their time but lacked the parametric capabilities necessary for complex architectural modelling.

The 1990s saw the introduction of SolidWorks by Jon Hirschtick, the founder, whose aim was to create a user-friendly, low-cost 3D modelling software for Windows Desktop (Hirschtick, 2015).

The CAD programs to date were engineering-based programs, not architectural/AEC based. Architects were continuing to use drawing boards except for a few who were using AutoCAD. When I was in my first year of a degree (Computer Animation and Illustration) in 1993–1994, a local architect practice had sent a request for a student who knew how to use AutoCAD. Being the only student that did, I worked for them alongside my studies. The reason for mentioning this is that both architects had been avoiding learning/using AutoCAD as they thought it would crush creativity. They had won their bid for a tower block hotel project in the Middle East, and the work required needed to be in AutoCAD, primarily blocks of furniture items for replicating across multiple floors. It was interesting to see their views change slightly with regard to the ability and speed in replicating items and floor levels, compared to drawing them individually each time.

Architecture was quite slow in moving from the drawing board to digital drawings. The resistance for some may have been due to the steep learning curve, high cost of investing in the software, and a preference for hand-drawing, which many architects considered more intuitive and expressive. The adoption of CAD accelerated significantly once construction firms and other stakeholders in the building industry embraced digital technologies. These organizations recognized the efficiencies CAD provided in terms of precision, collaboration, and integration with other systems. As construction companies began to expect or require digital drawings, architects and design firms had to adapt to stay competitive and meet client and industry expectations.

These early versions of CAD software, except for Pro/Engineer, lacked the parametric and data-enriched capabilities of modern BIM. CAD systems were static and were not able to accommodate the complexity of nonstandard geometries often found in historical buildings.

Graphisoft ArchiCAD was being developed in the early 1980s by programmers Leonid Raiz and Gabor Bojar in Hungary (Quirk, 2012). It was initially launched for Apple Macintosh in 1984 and became the first BIM software.

Meanwhile Autodesk had developed Architectural Desktop from their AutoCAD platform. In 1997, they launched their first version "AutoCAD Architectural Desktop 1" (later known as ADT). Having been a user, teacher, and trainer of this software, it was certainly better than using just AutoCAD for creating buildings.

In 1997, Charles River Software developed another BIM software which they renamed Revit Technology Corporation in 2000. Leonid Raiz (previously with PTC's Pro/Engineer and Graphisoft) and Irwin Jungreis (previously with PTC's Pro/Engineer), aided by funding to employ software programmers and architects, developed the parametric architecturally based software for the Windows platform (Krygiel, 2014). I was introduced to Revit just before it was purchased by Autodesk, and absolutely loved the program – and still do, although I now only use it for mostly visualization purposes of historical buildings.

In 2002, Autodesk purchased Revit, adding it to their suite of modelling software. With two architecturally based programs, you might think why? Well, Revit is a parametric modelling solution, designed for collaboration. ADT had objects such as walls, doors, and windows that knew they were those things, although if you deleted a door or window, the "hole" cut into the wall for the door or window remained as a hole. Parametric modelling was not available in ADT until 2010. In addition, with ADT, it was not as easy where collaboration was required.

Autodesk Revit, Bentley Microstation, Graphisoft ArchiCAD, and Vectorworks are the four main BIM software programs. Autodesk Revit and Bentley Microstation do not have a native Macintosh version (although from 2024, Bentley Microstation is now available on Mac). Autodesk Revit still does not have a Mac version but can be used by using Bootcamp or similar on a Mac system. Autodesk Revit has become the BIM market leader with 37.8% (6Sense, 2024; Offield, 2023)

BIM has obviously become a game-changer in architectural design and construction by integrating 3D models with metadata. However, its initial focus was on contemporary buildings with standardized components. Early attempts to use BIM for historical buildings highlighted limitations, particularly the lack of libraries and tools to represent the irregular and unique features of heritage structures.

CHAPTER 2   HISTORY AND BENEFITS OF HBIM

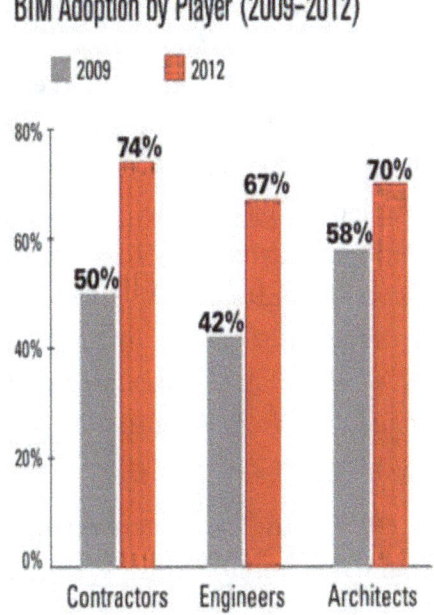

The percentage of companies using BIM jumped from 28% in 2007, to 49% in 2009, and to 71% in 2012.

For the first time ever, more contractors are using BIM than architects.

Source: The Business Value of BIM in North America: Multi-Year Trend Analysis and User Ratings SmartMarket Report, McGraw-Hill Construction, 2012.

Figure 2-1. The Business Value of BIM in North America (McGraw-Hill Construction, 2012)

Key Milestones in HBIM Development

The roots of HBIM can be traced back to the early 2000s when architects and researchers recognized the limitations of conventional BIM in handling irregular geometries and historical details. Early efforts focused on adapting BIM tools to include bespoke libraries of historic architectural elements, enabling more accurate modelling of heritage structures. Standard BIM software was designed for new construction projects, relying on libraries of predefined components like walls, doors, and windows. These components often failed to capture the unique features of historical architecture, such as Gothic arches, Baroque moldings, and irregular masonry. Over time, HBIM expanded to incorporate data from photogrammetry, LiDAR scanning, and archival research, providing a multidimensional perspective on historic buildings.

HBIM introduced parametric objects for classical architecture elements such as columns, vaults, and decorative motifs. These libraries allowed for the reconstruction of heritage buildings with greater authenticity. The use of LiDAR (Light Detection and Ranging) and photogrammetry enabled precise documentation of irregular geometries, seamlessly integrating this data into HBIM platforms. HBIM models began to incorporate layers of historical data, documenting the evolution of buildings over time, which became essential for restoration planning. Tools for assessing material degradation, structural integrity, and environmental impacts became embedded in HBIM workflows (Historic England, 2017).

Modern HBIM workflows integrate historical records, such as old photographs, architectural drawings, and maps, to reconstruct lost details (Lovell et al., 2023). HBIM platforms facilitated collaboration among architects, historians, engineers, and conservators by centralizing the relevant data.

With immersive technologies such as virtual reality (VR) and augmented reality (AR), HBIM now allows stakeholders to visualize historical sites in their original context or simulated proposed restorations. HBIM's evolution has been driven by the following three areas:

- **Technological Advancements:** Improved photogrammetry and LiDAR technologies have enhanced the accuracy and efficiency of data collection.

- **Interdisciplinary Collaboration:** Architects, historians, archaeologists, and technologists now work together to integrate diverse datasets into cohesive HBIM models.

- **Global Initiatives:** Projects like UNESCO's World Heritage Cities program have spotlighted HBIM as a critical tool for preserving culturally significant sites under threat from urbanization, climate change, or conflict.

More recently, HBIM has advanced to include 4D simulations (time-based modelling), tracking the chronological evolution of a structure. Machine learning algorithms assist in identifying architectural features from scanned data, reducing manual modelling time. In addition, artificial intelligence (AI) models are able to predict potential risks to heritage structures, aiding proactive conservation efforts (Lui et al., 2024).

The evolution of BIM to HBIM has become invaluable in its application within preservation for the following reasons:

- **Reconstruction of Lost Heritage:** HBIM recreates buildings destroyed by natural disasters or war, combining physical data with archival research.

- **Public Engagement:** Virtual tours and interactive models based on HBIM promote heritage awareness and education.

- **Policy and Regulation:** HBIM provides accurate data to support preservation policies, ensuring compliance with international heritage standards (e.g., UNESCO guidelines).

- **Sustainability:** Energy simulations and material analysis within HBIM models enable environmentally conscious preservation strategies.

HBIM has shifted from being primarily a documentation tool to a dynamic resource for restoration, education, and public engagement. Its applications now include simulating historical contexts, allowing users to visualize architectural changes across time. It has evolved to disaster recovery, for example, supporting rapid assessment and restoration efforts after events such as fires, floods, or earthquakes (please see Case Study 5 in this chapter). HBIM has also become an educational tool, enabling interactive exploration of historical sites for academics, history groups, and the public. By integrating advanced technologies and fostering collaborative workflows, HBIM continues to redefine how we approach architectural heritage.

Implementation

HBIM implementation relies on input of historical data to ensure accuracy and future value. The data may incorporate any or all of those shown in Table 2-1.

Table 2-1. *Table of possible HBIM data categories and their type and use*

Data Category	Data Type and Use
Architectural drawings and blueprints	Historical plans, sketches, and blueprints provide critical references for reconstructing heritage buildings. These documents are often digitized and imported into HBIM software as base layers
Historical photograph	Early photographs, especially stereoscopic images, offer visual details of facades, interiors, and contextual surroundings
Written records	Descriptions in historical texts, inventories, and diaries are used to interpret lost or undocumented features
Cadastral maps	These maps, often linked to property boundaries and taxation records, help identify the original footprints of historical structures

(*continued*)

CHAPTER 2   HISTORY AND BENEFITS OF HBIM

Table 2-1. (*continued*)

Data Category	Data Type and Use
Historical urban plans	Detailed plans of cities and towns from various periods contribute to understanding the evolution of urban fabric and building contexts
Artifacts and materials	Physical remnants, such as surviving decorative elements or construction materials, are analyzed and incorporated into HBIM models to ensure authenticity
Survey data from historical records	Pre-existing survey measurements and records (sometimes centuries old) offer valuable dimensional data, especially for structures no longer standing
Historical photogrammetry	Early 20th-century photogrammetry techniques and their results, including analogue aerial or terrestrial imagery, are digitized and integrated into HBIM workflows for spatial accuracy
Chronological changes	HBIM models document changes over time, creating "temporal layers" that visualize modifications, additions, or damages during various historical periods
Restoration histories	Previous restoration efforts, often recorded in detail, inform decisions about materials and techniques used in HBIM reconstructions
Access to archival repositories	Partnerships with libraries, museums, and local archives provide access to rare documents, imagery, and construction records that are otherwise unavailable
Digitization projects	Collaborative efforts have led to the digitization of large volumes of historical data, making it accessible for HBIM applications

This book is primarily about using HBIM as a visualization tool in historic recreations with the additional ability to engage with the building information as well as the people who lived there. Historically, visualizations and reconstructions of historic buildings in 3D modelling software often relied on polygonal face modelling, where 2D surfaces were used to form the building's geometry. This approach resulted in structures made up of singular, flat faces, lacking the depth until extruded, and therefore the architectural data of a typical structural design. Such a model would lack the ability to be treated as a realistic architecturally constructed model with information about different construction materials. But then, building the model was just for visualization rather than any form of formal recordkeeping or preservation as an intelligent 3D representation.

The ease with which BIM software users can create buildings using structurally correct walls, doors, windows, etc., creating a 3D model that provides data schedules, dimensions, and architectural details, has made architectural visualization so much easier to do. The addition of different rendering styles with materials already built in and the ability to create location-based land masses with planting and quickly create walkthroughs has helped to create impressive visualizations quickly.

Explaining how quickly a building can be created within the Autodesk Revit software to our students, who had only used Blender previously, was a little bit of a hard sell; they only wanted to use what they knew for creating their architectural models. Demonstrating the software and getting them to create a simple two-story building within two days, with landscape, planting, camera views, and a walkthrough, helped them to understand the speed and flexibility of the software. Several of these students have gone on to learn more about Revit and have produced some excellent models, but as yet, still without the added HBIM data, they are purely for visualization purposes. This is the case with most architectural visualizations, particularly for recreating historic environments for games such as in Assassin's Creed (Ubisoft, 2025).

The buildings forming the environment would be brought in generally via FBX exported from the majority of 3D modelling software such as 3DS Max, Blender, or Revit. Much of the BIM data would be lost if just imported. For most projects, this would be fine, i.e., using Unreal Engine for visuals, not data. With today's technology, and use of VR headsets for being able to walk within the environments and building, it would be good to explore and perhaps discover more about the buildings. For architectural projects, this seems to be becoming popular and enable architects' clients to walk around their virtual home before it is built. But is there a need beyond architectural projects? From just a few papers, mostly from international universities, there is one or two that are exploring the visualization of heritage buildings containing HBIM data which the user may be able to interact with as they explore the virtual scene. For this to happen, the FBX import needs to retain the BIM data. The best method for doing this is through importing to Unreal via Datasmith, a plug-in for Revit and other software such as Blender. Additional data can also be added in Unreal via Data Assets and Blueprints. The data can then be programmed to appear when coming up to an object, room, or building detail. This is what we are doing with Virtual Cities "Winchester City – 1400 and

1800," i.e., creating a total of 75 buildings in the 1400 and again in the 1800, to reconstruct in BIM software, embed with HBIM data, and import to Unreal Engine so that users can explore how those buildings changed and the development of the city, their fabric, and stories of people that lived there. The two scenes and the individual buildings can then also be used for heritage conservation/preservation.

The materials embedded in the BIM software may not always bring about the best result in Unreal. Unreal uses Quixel Megascans to produce realistic materials that work efficiently with Unreal's lighting system; therefore, it might be good to not bring in the materials as part of the FBX process. In our initial prototype, the models produced by the students each have a range of materials built in, some of them not translating well as textures within Unreal or their mapping is incorrect. The various materials have also "bloated" the size of the project, so we are now in the process of changing the materials and forming a library of typical Hampshire/Winchester brick and stonework to use instead.

Collaboration and Interdisciplinary Applications

One of HBIM's greatest strengths is its ability to foster collaboration among a diverse range of stakeholders. Architects, conservators, historians, engineers, and technologists work together using a shared HBIM platform to ensure the accuracy and authenticity of preservation projects. This interdisciplinary approach ensures that restoration decisions are informed by both technical precision and historical context.

For example, in the restoration of Winchester City's historical buildings, collaboration between historians and architects enables integration of lesser-known historical details, such as local folklore and construction techniques, into the HBIM model. Engineers contribute structural analysis, ensuring that proposed interventions respected both the original design and modern safety standards. This holistic process not only enriches the models but also fosters a deeper understanding of the city's evolution.

Advances in Visualization and Simulation

Modern HBIM workflows leverage immersive technologies like virtual reality (VR) and augmented reality (AR) to enhance engagement with heritage sites. These tools allow users to explore reconstructed environments, gaining insights into historical contexts that might otherwise remain inaccessible. Additionally, the development of 4D modelling, which incorporates the dimension of time enables the visualization of changes to structures over centuries.

The integration of machine learning and artificial intelligence further streamlines HBIM processes. Algorithms capable of identifying architectural features from scan data reduce the need for manual modelling, while predictive tools help assess risks to heritage structures. These advancements are transforming HBIM from a documentation tool into a dynamic platform for analysis, education, and storytelling.

Summary

The conceptual foundations of HBIM trace back to the principles underlying BIM: integrating 3D modelling with data-rich systems to support design, construction, and management. However, applying these principles to heritage buildings requires addressing a host of complexities not present in modern construction projects. Early CAD systems laid the groundwork by introducing object-based design, but their limitations, especially in representing irregular geometries, highlighted the need for more advanced, heritage-specific tools. The development of parametric modelling in software such as Revit and Graphisoft ArchiCAD provided the flexibility necessary to accurately depict historical architecture, accommodating the asymmetrical and often organic forms that characterize heritage structures.

The emergence of HBIM was driven by the integration of advanced scanning technologies, such as LiDAR (Light Detection and Ranging) and photogrammetry, which allowed for the precise capture of existing structures. These technologies complemented traditional archival research by offering new methods for documenting and analyzing historical sites. By combining these data inputs, HBIM emerged as an indispensable tool for conservators, enabling the creation of models that are both visually accurate and data rich.

By connecting historical records to 3D models, HBIM democratizes access to heritage. Its ability to visualize temporal changes fosters greater public awareness and appreciation for architectural history. Moreover, the use of HBIM to analyze materials, simulate structural integrity, and explore energy performance aligns with contemporary concerns for sustainability, bridging the past and future in innovative ways.

The introduction of HBIM marks a transformative moment in the preservation of architectural heritage. By merging cutting-edge technology with traditional conservation practices, HBIM not only enhances our ability to document and restore historical buildings but also expands the ways in which these structures can be experienced and understood. As technology continues to evolve, so too will the possibilities for HBIM, ensuring that the stories embedded in our built heritage endure for generations to come.

Advantages and Challenges of Implementing HBIM

Unlike contemporary BIM, which primarily addresses parametric design for modern construction, HBIM needs to account for the unique complexities of historical structures. These include irregular geometries, nonstandard materials, and often limited or inconsistent documentation. Such challenges arise from the diverse architectural styles and cultural influences that shaped heritage buildings, as well as the impact of time, which may have resulted in partial destruction, total destruction such as abbeys in the dissolution, replacement, or modernization of the original structures.

HBIM excels in addressing these challenges through the development of specialized parametric objects that replicate historical architectural details – Gothic arches, Baroque moldings, medieval vaulting, and classical columns. Through developing a library of objects tailored to heritage needs, HBIM extends the capabilities of traditional BIM, enabling the accurate and comprehensive documentation of historical sites.

Challenges and Limitations of HBIM

While the benefits of HBIM are transformative, its implementation poses significant challenges, which can be broadly categorized as follows:

- **Data Acquisition and Processing Such as**

    High-Resolution Data Capture: The use of advanced technologies such as laser scanning and photogrammetry demands specialized expertise and equipment. Acquiring this data can be resource intensive, particularly for large-scale sites.

    Point Cloud Processing: Cleaning and converting point cloud data into usable 3D models is a labor-intensive process, often requiring skilled professionals to interpret and validate the results.

- **Modelling Complexity, e.g.:**

  Irregular Geometries: Historical structures often feature intricate and nonstandard shapes that require custom modelling approaches. Parametric modelling of such features demands advanced skills and can be time-consuming.

  Limited Libraries: Standard BIM libraries typically lack the components needed for heritage applications, necessitating the creation of custom objects to represent unique architectural elements.

- **Integration of Historical Data which Includes:**

  Incomplete Records: Historical documents, photographs, and blueprints may be inconsistent, ambiguous, or fragmented, complicating their integration into HBIM models.

  Reconciliation with Physical Evidence: Aligning archival data with current physical conditions requires careful interpretation and expert judgment to ensure accuracy and authenticity.

- **Technical Complexity; Project Teams Need to Consider:**

  Implementing HBIM requires expertise across multiple disciplines, from digital modelling to historical research.

- **Cost and Accessibility Include:**

  High Costs: The financial burden of acquiring specialized equipment, technology such as LiDAR and photogrammetry, software licenses, and skilled personnel can be prohibitive, especially for smaller organizations.

  Uneven Accessibility: The adoption of HBIM is often limited by regional disparities in technological infrastructure and expertise.

- **Ethical Considerations; Project Teams Need to Consider:**

  Decisions about reconstruction often involve balancing historical accuracy with modern interpretations.

  Despite these challenges, the potential of HBIM to revolutionize heritage preservation outweighs its limitations, particularly as technology and methodologies continue to advance.

CHAPTER 2   HISTORY AND BENEFITS OF HBIM

The Challenges of Architectural Preservation

Preservation of historical architecture is a complex undertaking influenced by several challenges:

Documentation and Accuracy: Historic structures frequently lack detailed documentation due to their age, alterations, or the destruction of records. Traditional survey methods, though valuable, are time intensive and may fail to capture the intricacies of ornate architectural details. HBIM offers a solution, but its effectiveness depends on the availability and quality of supplementary historical data.

Deterioration and Structural Complexity: Natural ageing, environmental conditions, and human activity contribute to the deterioration of heritage buildings. Older structures often feature obsolete construction techniques and materials, posing challenges for analysis and restoration. HBIM's ability to model these complexities is vital, but it demands significant effort and expertise.

Balancing Preservation and Modernization: Adapting heritage buildings to contemporary standards for safety, accessibility, and functionality without compromising their historical integrity is a delicate task. HBIM helps stakeholders visualize potential interventions and their impact, aiding decision-making processes.

Stakeholder Collaboration: Preservation projects typically involve architects, engineers, historians, conservators, policymakers, and community members. Effective communication and coordination among these diverse groups are crucial but challenging, particularly when integrating modern technologies into traditional practices.

Advantages of Implementing HBIM

Despite these challenges, HBIM offers numerous advantages that make it an indispensable tool in heritage preservation:

Enhanced Documentation: HBIM creates comprehensive digital archives that combine geometrical accuracy with metadata. These archives are invaluable for conservation planning, restoration efforts, and long-term management.

Comprehensive Data Integration: HBIM combines architectural data with historical context, creating models that are both visually detailed and richly informative.

Enhanced Preservation Planning: Digital simulations allow stakeholders to test restoration scenarios, predict outcomes, and prioritize interventions.

Simulation and Analysis: By embedding material properties, structural information, and environmental data, HBIM enables advanced simulations. These can include structural integrity assessments, energy performance analyses, and climate resilience studies, which are critical for sustainable preservation.

Interdisciplinary Collaboration: HBIM platforms centralize diverse datasets, fostering collaboration among professionals from multiple disciplines. This holistic approach ensures that all aspects of a project, from historical accuracy to structural stability, are considered.

Public Engagement: Interactive HBIM models can be used to create virtual tours, educational content, and immersive experiences. These tools make heritage sites accessible to wider audiences, promoting awareness and appreciation of cultural history and support for heritage preservation.

Restoration of Lost Features: Through the integration of archival research and advanced modelling, HBIM allows for the accurate reconstruction of lost or damaged architectural elements. This capability is particularly valuable for structures affected by war, natural disasters, or neglect.

> **Sustainability:** HBIM supports adaptive reuse by identifying ways to preserve existing materials, reducing waste and embodied carbon.
>
> **Policy and Regulation Compliance:** HBIM provides detailed records that align with international heritage preservation standards, such as UNESCO guidelines. This ensures that restoration projects meet regulatory requirements and best practices.

Addressing Challenges Through Innovation

To overcome the limitations of HBIM, ongoing innovation and collaboration are essential. Key strategies include the following.

Advancing Technology

Machine learning – Algorithms that identify and classify architectural features from scan data can streamline modelling workflows, reducing manual effort.
Automation – Tools that automate repetitive tasks, such as point cloud cleaning or parametric object creation, can enhance efficiency.

Expanding Libraries

Developing extensive libraries of parametric objects for heritage features can reduce the need for custom modelling, accelerating project timelines.

Training and Education

Equipping professionals with the skills needed to use HBIM tools is crucial. Academic programs, workshops, and certifications can help bridge the knowledge gap.

Collaborative Frameworks

Establishing platforms for real-time collaboration can improve communication among stakeholders, ensuring that projects are informed by diverse expertise.

Funding and Support

Government grants, partnerships with cultural institutions, and private sector investments can offset the high costs associated with HBIM projects, making the technology accessible to smaller organizations.

Education and Training in HBIM

The successful adoption of HBIM relies heavily on education and training. Academic programs and workshops are critical for equipping the next generation of professionals with the skills necessary to manage heritage projects. As someone involved in teaching, I have seen the impact of introducing students to HBIM through hands-on projects. Demonstrating the practical applications of HBIM, such as creating detailed 3D models of historical buildings for visualization purposes, helps students to appreciate its potential and motivate them to explore its broader use.

Training initiatives also play a vital role in professional development. Organizations involved in heritage conservation often conduct workshops to familiarize their teams with the latest HBIM tools and techniques. These programs emphasize the integration of technology with traditional preservation practices, ensuring that professionals are equipped to handle the unique challenges of heritage projects.

Global Developments and Applications

HBIM's applications are not confined to specific regions; its impact is evident in heritage conservation projects worldwide. In Europe, HBIM has been used extensively for the restoration of UNESCO World Heritage Sites, such as the Basilica of San Francesco in Assisi, Italy (UNESCO, 2000). Advanced modelling techniques were employed to assess structural damage from earthquakes and guide restoration efforts (Croci, 2002). Similarly, in Asia, HBIM has been pivotal in preserving ancient temple complexes, where intricate carvings and fragile materials pose significant challenges (ICCROM ed. Wijesuriya and Lee, 2017).

In North America, HBIM has facilitated the adaptive reuse of historical buildings, integrating modern amenities while preserving architectural authenticity (Peek, 2024). For instance, the rehabilitation of 19th-century industrial sites into cultural centers has benefitted from HBIM's ability to document and analyze historical features. In the Middle East, HBIM is being applied to preserve archaeological sites, enabling virtual reconstructions that offer insights into ancient civilizations (Baik, 2020).

CHAPTER 2   HISTORY AND BENEFITS OF HBIM

Summary

The implementation of HBIM represents a transformative approach to heritage preservation, offering unparalleled accuracy, collaboration, and engagement opportunities. While challenges remain, the continued evolution of technology, combined with strategic investments in education and infrastructure, promises to unlock HBIM's full potential. By addressing the complexities of historical architecture and fostering interdisciplinary collaboration, HBIM ensures that the rich narratives of our built heritage endure for generations to come.

The following case study, "The Complexities of Managing Historic Buildings with BIM," highlights the advantages and challenges of implementing HBIM for work undertaken for Durham Cathedral using 3D scanning by Charlton, Kelley, Greenwood, and Moreton in 2020.

In the next section, we present five successful case studies that demonstrate the use of HBIM for heritage asset management and visualization in VR.

Chapter 2 Durham Cathedral Case Study: Advantages and Challenges of Implementing HBIM
The Complexities of Managing Historic Buildings with BIM

Authors: James Charlton, Kenneth Kelley, David Greenwood, Leo Moreton (2020)

Introduction

Historic buildings are vital cultural assets that require careful management to preserve their architectural integrity and historical value. Managing these structures presents unique challenges, particularly when modern technologies like Building Information Modelling (BIM) are introduced. In their 2020 study, Charlton et al. explored the complexities of using BIM for the management of historic buildings. The research focused on identifying key challenges, proposing strategies for overcoming these obstacles, and demonstrating the potential benefits of BIM in the heritage sector.

Objectives of the Study

The primary objectives outlined by Charlton et al. were as follows:

1. **Identify Challenges:** To analyze the specific difficulties encountered when applying BIM to historic buildings

2. **Optimize BIM for Heritage Use:** To adapt BIM methodologies for the idiosyncrasies of historic structures, including irregular geometries and incomplete records

3. **Support Conservation Efforts:** To explore how BIM can facilitate better conservation, maintenance, and management of heritage sites

4. **Bridge Knowledge Gaps:** To align modern technological tools with traditional conservation practices, promoting collaboration among stakeholders

Methodology

The study adopted a multifaceted approach to evaluate the complexities of integrating BIM into the management of historic buildings.

Literature Review

The authors conducted a comprehensive review of existing studies to establish a theoretical foundation. They identified gaps in knowledge concerning the application of BIM to historic structures and highlighted recurring challenges, such as

- The lack of standardized approaches for historic building modelling
- Difficulties in integrating BIM with existing heritage documentation systems
- Resistance to adopting BIM due to cost and technical expertise barriers

CHAPTER 2   HISTORY AND BENEFITS OF HBIM

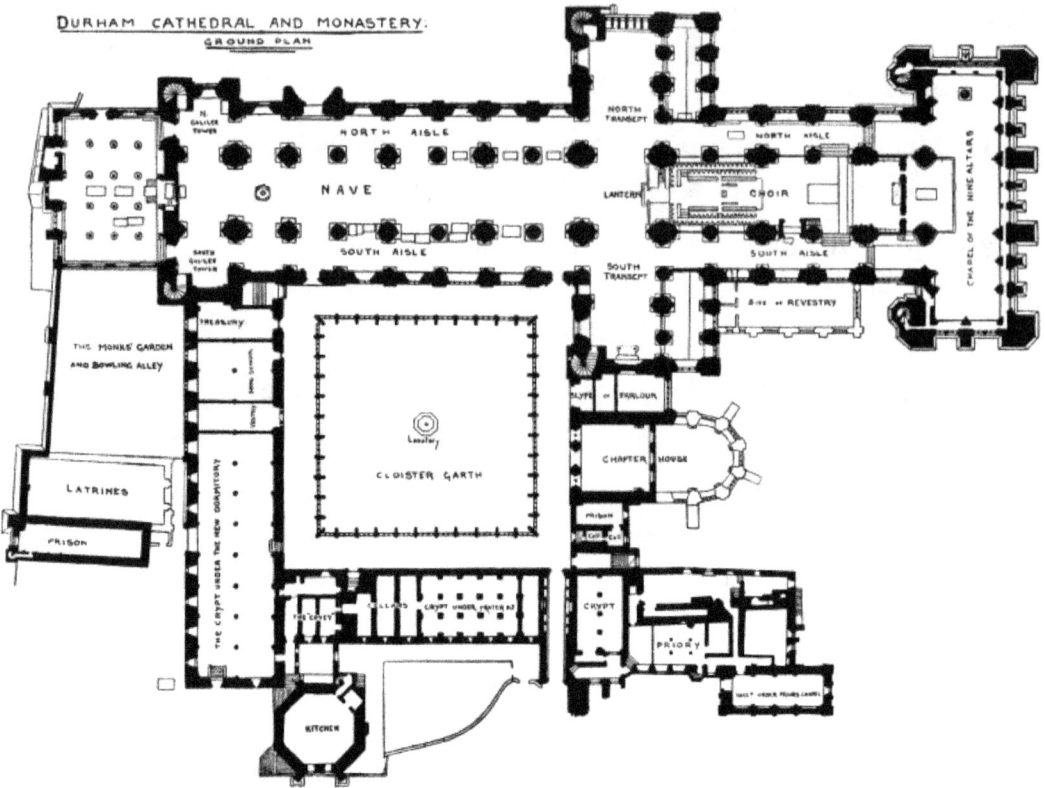

Figure 2-2. *Durham Cathedral Plan (Bygate, 1900) (Figure 1, p. 6)*

Case Studies and Interviews

The research included case studies of historic buildings where BIM had been implemented. These examples provided practical insights into the challenges and successes of using BIM in real-world scenarios. In-depth interviews with industry professionals, including architects, conservators, and BIM specialists, were conducted to capture diverse perspectives.

Analysis of BIM Methodologies

The team analyzed BIM workflows and tools, focusing on how they could be adapted to address the unique needs of heritage buildings. Particular attention was given to

- Capturing irregular geometries using advanced digital surveying techniques, such as laser scanning and photogrammetry
- Integrating historical data and conservation records into BIM models
- Balancing the technical precision of BIM with the interpretative nature of heritage work

Figure 2-3. *Charlton, Kelley, Greenwood, and Moreton's (2020) example of captured laser scan data of Durham Cathedral (Figure 3, p. 8)*

Key Challenges Identified

Data Capture and Accuracy

Historic buildings often feature irregular geometries, nonstandard materials, and layers of modifications over time. Capturing these details accurately requires advanced tools and techniques, such as

- High-resolution 3D scanning to document complex architectural features
- Combining new data with incomplete or fragmented historical records

Data Integration

Integrating diverse datasets into a single BIM model is a significant challenge. For example:

- Conservation data, such as repair history and material analysis, often exist in disparate formats.
- Aligning these datasets within a BIM framework requires custom solutions to ensure interoperability and usability.

Stakeholder Collaboration

The use of BIM in heritage projects involves multiple stakeholders, including architects, engineers, conservators, and regulatory bodies. The study highlighted challenges in fostering collaboration due to

- Differing levels of technical expertise and familiarity with BIM tools
- Varying priorities and objectives among stakeholders

Cost and Resource Constraints

Implementing BIM in heritage projects can be resource intensive. Costs associated with equipment, software, and training often deter adoption, particularly for smaller projects or organizations with limited budgets.

Adapting BIM for Heritage Contexts

Standard BIM tools and workflows are designed for new construction projects. Applying these tools to historic buildings requires significant adaptation to account for

- The interpretative nature of heritage work, where incomplete data often require assumptions and hypotheses.
- The need to preserve the historical authenticity of a site while introducing modern interventions

Strategies for Overcoming Challenges

Leveraging Advanced Technologies

The study emphasized the importance of using advanced digital tools to address the complexities of data capture and modelling. These include

- **Laser Scanning and Photogrammetry:** To create detailed and accurate 3D models of historic structures
- **Point Cloud Data Integration:** To represent the irregular geometries of historic buildings within BIM software

Developing Tailored Workflows

Adapting BIM workflows to heritage contexts involves

- Incorporating historical data as metadata within BIM models
- Using HBIM (Heritage BIM) frameworks that are specifically designed for historic buildings
- Developing templates and guidelines to standardize the documentation of heritage features

Enhancing Stakeholder Collaboration

To bridge knowledge gaps and promote effective collaboration, the authors recommended

- Training programs to familiarize stakeholders with BIM tools and methodologies
- Collaborative platforms that enable real-time data sharing and communication among project teams

Cost Management and Scaling

To address resource constraints, the study suggested

- Prioritizing key aspects of a project for BIM implementation, rather than attempting comprehensive modelling
- Exploring partnerships and funding opportunities to offset costs

Key Benefits of BIM in Historic Building Management

Improved Documentation and Analysis

BIM facilitates the creation of comprehensive digital records that combine geometrical data, historical information, and conservation details. These records serve as valuable resources for ongoing maintenance and restoration efforts.

Enhanced Decision-Making

By integrating diverse datasets into a single model, BIM provides a holistic view of a building's condition and history. This enables more informed decision-making regarding conservation and adaptation strategies.

Greater Public Engagement

Digital models created through BIM can be repurposed for public outreach and education. For example:

- Virtual tours and interactive exhibits can enhance public appreciation of heritage sites.
- BIM models can be used to simulate the impact of proposed interventions, fostering transparency and community support.

Future-Proofing Heritage Management

BIM provides a scalable and adaptable framework for managing historic buildings in the long term. Digital models can be updated as new data become available, ensuring that conservation efforts remain dynamic and responsive.

CHAPTER 2   HISTORY AND BENEFITS OF HBIM

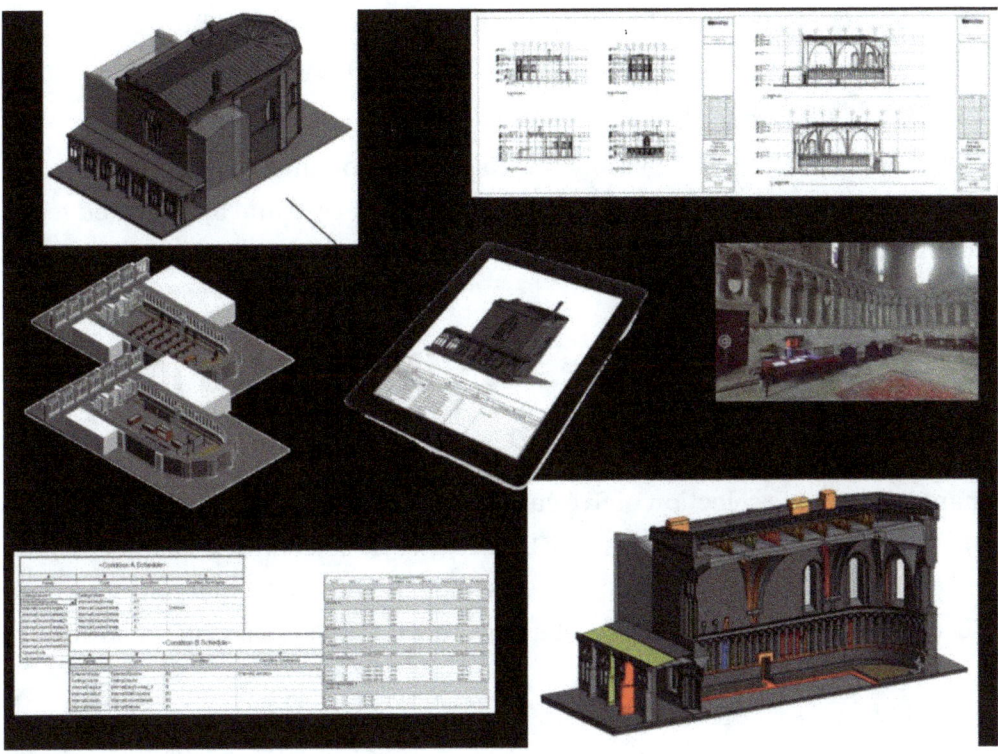

Figure 2-4. Charlton, Kelley, Greenwood, and Moreton's (2020) resulting Asset Information Model (AIM) and its features, running on a mobile device (Figure 4, p. 9)

Conclusion and Insights

The study by Charlton et al. sheds light on the unique challenges and opportunities associated with managing historic buildings using BIM. Key insights include

1. **Adapting Technology for Heritage Contexts:** Standard BIM workflows must be tailored to account for the complexities of historic structures.

2. **Collaboration Is Crucial:** Effective collaboration among stakeholders is essential for the successful implementation of BIM in heritage projects.

CHAPTER 2　HISTORY AND BENEFITS OF HBIM

3. **Balancing Costs and Benefits:** While resource intensive, BIM offers significant long-term benefits for documentation, analysis, and public engagement.

By addressing these challenges and leveraging the potential of BIM, heritage professionals can ensure that historic buildings are preserved and appreciated for generations to come.

Successful Case Studies of BIM, HBIM, and VR Visualization Applications

This chapter presents a selection of five case studies demonstrating the use of BIM software to create digital twins of historic buildings. The selection has been deliberate in highlighting that BIM projects can be focused on analysis for repair and structural modifications or for VR visualization, an aspect that has been raised in the previous sections.

The first two case studies are based in Poland and highlight the advantages and disadvantages of the projects undertaken, shown in Table 2-2 (Janisio-Pawłowska, 2021).

Table 2-2. Advantages and disadvantages of the two Polish case studies

Name of the Object of the Study	Advantages of the Study	Disadvantages
Church in Iwięcino	Advanced 3D model with moving models and conservation data, the ability to export the published resource to CAD software, access to an interactive model database, models available in VR	No BIM model, no access to a 3D model saved in an open format
Wang Temple in Karpacz	BIM model, data available solely in the application, own library database	Lack of access to the 3D model and interactive conservation data about the object, no access to the 3D model saved in an open format

What is obvious is that the two projects either incorporate accessible BIM/HBIM or 3D models that can be explored via VR. The purpose/project brief will perhaps have stated what is required, i.e., data or visualization. As an HBIM project, the route expected would be focused on data, for ensuring preservation, and knowledge about the structure, materials, and development of the building. A project focused on being able to virtually walk around the building, interact with movable objects and via 3D scanning, and capture the state of the building's structure can still be described as an HBIM project, but it is less about technical data and more about the visual state and the ability for a community (in the case of the Church in Iwięcino) to understand their building and see what repairs might be necessary in areas they may not physically be able to access.

Of course, the latter is possible because the building still exists, unlike Case Study 4, which was chosen because the building no longer exists, or any part of it. The 3D reconstruction was, at the time, to see what it would have looked like, how large, and as the "backdrop" to the life and culture of the monks, Abbots, and the resting place of King Alfred. Although Revit was used for the initial model, the internal detail was created in 3DS Max, the whole building then exported via FBX to Unreal.

Case Study 3 was chosen for the thorough use of BIM and HBIM, and because of the time taken (five years) and detail added, this iconic building has a complete digital twin for future use in preservation and for future VR visualizations.

Case Study 5 was selected for the thoroughness of the restoration using HBIM and a digital twin that had already been scanned prior to Notre-Dame's fire. This case highlights the importance of modelling a digital replica for preservation, conservation, and reconstruction purposes.

Case Study 1: HBIM Modelling of the Wang Temple in Karpacz

Information from "Analysis of the Possibilities of Using HBIM Technology in the Protection of Cultural Heritage, Based on a Review of the Latest Research Carried Out in Poland" by Dorota Janisio-Pawłowska (2021)

CHAPTER 2   HISTORY AND BENEFITS OF HBIM

1. Introduction

The Wang Temple, a Protestant church located in Karpacz, Poland, exemplifies the successful application of HBIM for heritage preservation. This 12th–13th century Norwegian stave church, built entirely of wood without nails, boasts a unique design and rich history.

Figure 2-5. *3D model of Wang Temple in Karpacz (Janisio-Pawłowska, 2021)*

2. Historical Significance and Challenges

- Originally built in Norway, the temple reflects early Christianity's entanglement with pagan beliefs in the region.

- Dismantled in the 19th century due to deterioration, it was transported to Szczecin, then Berlin, before being rebuilt in Karpacz in 1842.

- The complex history and unique wooden structure with interlocking components posed challenges for traditional documentation methods.

3. HBIM Implementation

- In 2016, researchers employed a Z+F IMAGER 5010c scanner to capture the temple's intricate details through 36 scans (12 interior, 24 exterior).

- Point cloud data was processed and refined using ZF-LaserControl software to eliminate errors.

- ArchiCAD software facilitated the creation of a 3D model, which was then enriched with textures using PointCab software.

4. HBIM Model Benefits

Detailed Architectural Representation: The HBIM model captures every aspect of the temple, including wall finishes, ridge ends, and wooden cladding, enabling faithful comparison with the actual structure (Figure 2-6).

Comprehensive Information: Each element within the model possesses definable properties like material, dimensions, function, color, and repair history, facilitating cross-sectional analysis (Figure 2-7).

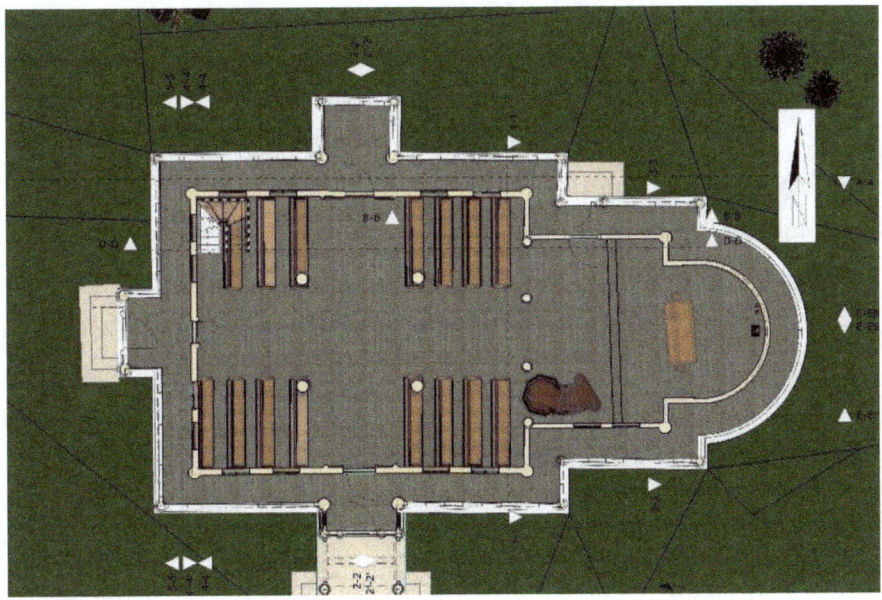

Figure 2-6. *Ground floor of Wang Temple in Karpacz (Janisio-Pawłowska, 2021)*

CHAPTER 2   HISTORY AND BENEFITS OF HBIM

Figure 2-7. Model of Wang Temple in Karpacz, cross-section (Janisio-Pawłowska, 2021)

The image presents a cross-section at arbitrarily selected location of the model, thanks to the documentation developed in HBIM technology, and fully modelled elements, e.g., beams, columns, stairs, windows, are visible at each cross-section level; furthermore, it is also possible to filter the information assigned to them.

Structural Analysis: The model incorporates structural elements like beams, columns, and stairs, allowing for transparent analysis of the building's integrity.

- **Digital Accessibility:** The freely available BIM application enables users to explore the complete HBIM model on their phones or tablets.

5. Innovation and Future Applications

Nonstandard windows were meticulously modelled as separate library objects, allowing for future editing and parameter adjustments (Table 2-3).

Table 2-3. *Example of windows modelled for the documentation of the object (Janisio-Pawłowska, 2021)*

	List of windows					
Sill height	110	306	314	419	422	513
Nominal size W x H x T	28× 3×17	48×114×17	48×114×17	22×64×17	22×64×17	80×80×17
3D Axonometry						
Quantity	5	1	1	1	4	2

The windows have been saved as library objects with the possibility of editing their parameters.

- The model's LOD 300 level of detail encompasses historical, functional, geometric, and construction information, valuable for planning future conservation efforts.
- The HBIM model serves as a foundation for ongoing monitoring of the temple's condition and further analytical work.

6. Conclusion

The Wang Temple project demonstrates the power of HBIM in documenting, analyzing, and preserving historical structures. The detailed model not only provides a permanent record of this unique building but also facilitates informed decision-making for its future conservation. This case study paves the way for wider adoption of HBIM in safeguarding cultural heritage sites around the world.

Case Study 2: 3D Digitization of the Church in Iwięcino, Poland

Information from "Analysis of the Possibilities of Using HBIM Technology in the Protection of Cultural Heritage, Based on a Review of the Latest Research Carried Out in Poland" by Dorota Janisio-Pawłowska (2021)

CHAPTER 2   HISTORY AND BENEFITS OF HBIM

1. Introduction

This case study explores the digitization project undertaken in 2019 to preserve the cultural heritage of the 14th-century church in Iwięcino, Poland. The project employed advanced digital tools to create a comprehensive 3D record of the church and its movable elements.

Figure 2-8. *The church in Iwięcino, the scanned object presented in 3D form (Janisio-Pawłowska, 2021)*

2. Historical Significance

- Located in Western Pomerania, the church is part of a unique group of 75 gothic buildings in the region.

CHAPTER 2   HISTORY AND BENEFITS OF HBIM

- The presence of Cistercian artifacts inside the church testifies to their historical presence in the area.
- The richly decorated beam ceiling with a depiction of the Judgment Day dates back to 1697.

3. Digitization Process

- A variety of tools were used to capture detailed data, including scanners (ground based and handheld), drones with high-resolution cameras, and traditional photography.
- The FARO Focus 150 terrestrial scanner and drones equipped with 6K cameras were used for large-scale data acquisition.
- White and blue structural light scanners with high resolutions were employed for capturing the intricate details of movable monuments.
- RealityCapture software facilitated the processing and integration of point clouds from laser scanning and photogrammetry.

4. Digital Deliverables

- A 3D model of the entire church with a textured surface (Figures 2-8 and 2-9)
- 3D models of individual movable objects, such as the baptismal font (Figure 2-12).
- 2D technical drawings and cross-sections generated from the 3D model (Figures 2-10 and 2-11).
- An interactive website allowing users to virtually explore the church and its artifacts in 3D or virtual reality
- Detailed information about each object, including material, style, location, and description

CHAPTER 2   HISTORY AND BENEFITS OF HBIM

Figure 2-9. *Church in Iwięcino, 3D model based on combined scans with superimposed texture (Janisio-Pawłowska, 2021)*

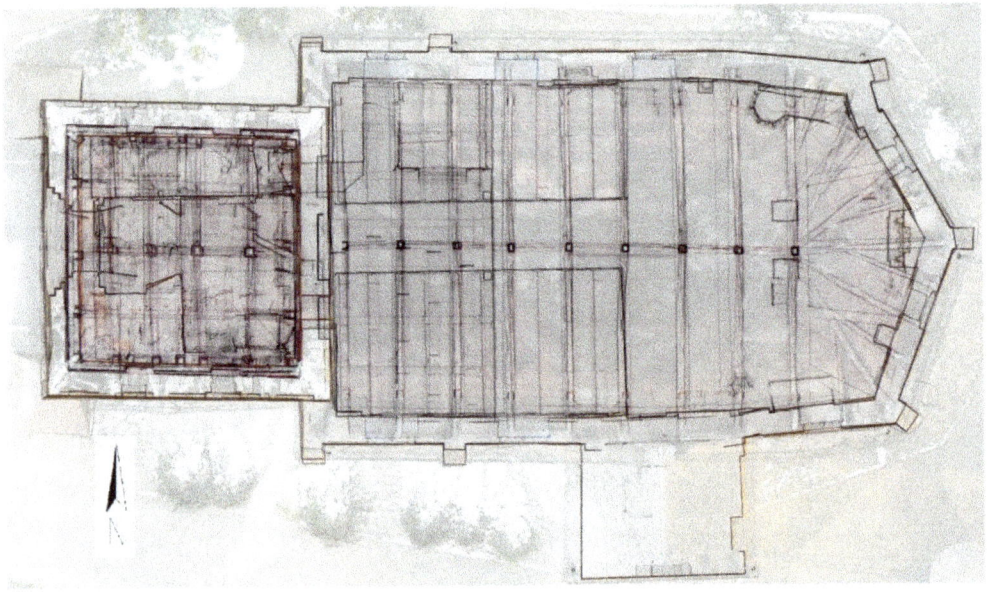

Figure 2-10. *Object projection, horizontal section, based on the model obtained from complex scans (Janisio-Pawłowska, 2021)*

Figure 2-11. *Vertical section based on the model obtained from complex scans (Janisio-Pawłowska, 2021)*

Figure 2-12. *Model of a movable object, a six-sided baptismal font from the 17th century, located in the presbytery, designed as a separate element (Janisio-Pawłowska, 2021)*

Using the interactive website, users can view all digital models of the entire study with a breakdown into objects, sculptures, arts and crafts, painting, and blacksmithing (source: Fundacja Wirtualizacji Narodowego Dziedzictwa Kulturowego).

5. Benefits and Future Potential

- The project provides a permanent digital record of the church's current state, facilitating future conservation efforts.
- The 3D models enable detailed analysis of both the church structure and individual movable objects.
- The publicly accessible website promotes the church and cultural heritage to a wider audience.
- The collected data can serve as a foundation for developing a Building Information Model (BIM) for future conservation management planning.

6. Conclusion

The Iwięcino church digitization project demonstrates the effectiveness of digital tools in preserving cultural heritage. The comprehensive 3D documentation not only provides valuable insights for conservators but also fosters public engagement with this historic landmark. This project paves the way for the integration of such data into BIM workflows for more informed decision-making regarding the church's future.

Case Study 3: HBIM Modelling of Big Ben

Information from "HBIM for Historic Buildings: Refurbishment of Big Ben for UK Parliament" by Andrew Dobson, Partner and Architect at Purcell and Autodesk University (2022), "Inside Big Ben's Makeover" by The B1M company (2020), the "Conservation of the Elizabeth Tower and Big Ben" article by UK Parliament (2022), and "The Importance of Numbering in Refurbishing Big Ben Clock Tower" by Graitec (2023)

1. Introduction

Big Ben, officially known as the Elizabeth Tower, is an iconic landmark in London and a symbol of the UK. This 96-meter-tall clock tower, part of the Palace of Westminster, underwent a major restoration project from 2017 to 2022 (UK Parliament, 2022). This case study explores the successful application of HBIM in this complex undertaking.

Figure 2-13. The Elizabeth Tower restoration project (UK Parliament, 2022)

2. Project Scope and Challenges

The restoration of Big Ben presented numerous challenges:

- **Preservation of Heritage:** Maintaining the integrity of this Grade I listed building while addressing critical safety and maintenance issues was paramount (Historic England, 2018).
- **Complexity of Structure:** The intricate Victorian Gothic architecture, with its intricate stonework, delicate clock mechanisms, and

numerous layers of construction and repair over centuries, demanded meticulous attention to detail (Parliament UK, 2022).

- **Public Scrutiny:** As a globally recognized symbol, the project faced intense public and media scrutiny, requiring transparent communication and careful consideration of public opinion.

- **Logistical Constraints:** Working on a live site within a busy parliamentary complex presented significant logistical challenges, including restricted access, noise and vibration limitations, and the need to minimize disruption to parliamentary business.

3. The Role of HBIM

HBIM played a crucial role in overcoming these challenges:

- **Comprehensive Digital Twin:** A highly detailed 3D model of the entire tower, including its internal structure, clock mechanisms, and external fabric, was created. This digital twin served as a central repository of information, accessible to all stakeholders.

- **Improved Understanding:** The model provided a deeper understanding of the building's complex construction and the impact of past interventions. It helped identify hidden defects, assess structural stability, and plan for future maintenance.

- **Enhanced Collaboration:** The digital model facilitated seamless communication and collaboration among architects, engineers, conservators, historians, and other stakeholders.

- **Risk Mitigation:** By simulating various scenarios and analyzing potential risks, HBIM helped to identify and mitigate potential problems before they occurred, minimizing delays and cost overruns.

- **Informed Decision-Making:** The model provided a powerful tool for decision-making, allowing stakeholders to visualize proposed interventions, assess their impact on the building's heritage, and select the most appropriate solutions.

- **Public Engagement:** The digital model was used to engage the public and explain the complex restoration works in an accessible and engaging

4. Key HBIM Applications

- **Laser Scanning and 3D Modelling:** High-resolution laser scanning technology was used to capture the existing condition of the tower in minute detail, creating a highly accurate 3D point cloud. This data was then used to generate a detailed 3D model of the entire structure.

- **Structural Analysis:** Finite element analysis (FEA) was performed on the 3D model to assess the structural integrity of the tower and identify areas of weakness. This informed the design of strengthening works and ensured the long-term stability of the structure.

- **Clock Mechanism Restoration:** The complex clock mechanisms were meticulously modelled and analyzed, allowing engineers to understand their operation and plan for their restoration and future maintenance.

- **Heritage Recording:** The HBIM model served as a valuable record of the building's existing condition, capturing its intricate details and historical fabric before any restoration work commenced (Graitec, 2023).

5. Benefits of HBIM

The use of HBIM in the restoration of Big Ben delivered significant benefits:

- **Improved Project Delivery:** HBIM streamlined the project delivery process, reducing delays and improving efficiency.

- **Cost Savings:** By identifying and mitigating potential problems early on, HBIM helped to avoid costly rework and minimize project overruns.

- **Enhanced Quality:** The use of HBIM ensured that the restoration work was carried out to the highest possible standards, preserving the heritage value of the building (Graitec, 2023).

CHAPTER 2   HISTORY AND BENEFITS OF HBIM

- **Improved Safety:** By identifying potential hazards and implementing appropriate safety measures, HBIM helped to ensure the safety of all workers on site.

- **Legacy for the Future:** The HBIM model will serve as a valuable resource for future generations, providing a comprehensive record of the building's history and facilitating future maintenance and repair work.

Figure 2-14. Inside Big Ben's Makeover YouTube video screenshot, presented and narrated by Fred Mills (The B1M, 2020) (*www.youtube.com/watch?v=UCwZ1iI3pdw*)

6. Lessons Learned

The restoration of Big Ben provides valuable lessons for the application of HBIM in other heritage projects:

- **Early Adoption:** Early adoption of HBIM is crucial to maximize its benefits.

- **Data Quality:** The quality of the data captured during the laser scanning and modelling process is critical to the accuracy and usefulness of the HBIM model.

- **Multidisciplinary Collaboration:** Effective collaboration among all stakeholders is essential for the successful implementation of HBIM.

- **Training and Skills Development:** Investing in the training and development of staff in HBIM technologies is essential to ensure their effective use.

- **Communication and Engagement:** Clear communication and engagement with the public are crucial to ensure their understanding and support for the use of HBIM in heritage projects.

7. Conclusion

The restoration of Big Ben demonstrates the power of HBIM as a transformative tool for heritage conservation (Dobson, 2022). By providing a comprehensive digital representation of the building, HBIM enabled a deeper understanding, improved collaboration, and informed decision-making, ultimately contributing to the successful restoration of this iconic landmark (Graitec, 2023). The lessons learned from this project can be applied to other heritage projects around the world, helping to preserve our built heritage for future generations.

Case Study 4: 3D Digitization of Hyde Abbey, Winchester, Hampshire

Information from the Hyde Abbey project by Dr. Debs Wilson and Digital Media students in 2016–2017 for Hyde900

1. Introduction

This case study explores the digitization project undertaken in 2017 and was our first project using the Unreal Game Engine. The project was funded by HLF and Hyde900 to reconstruct the abbey for which only the gatehouse and the local church survive. We worked from archaeological research and a set of sketches of the abbey dated 1500, just before the dissolution and therefore the demolition of the abbey. The reconstruction project was to produce images and backgrounds for two video tours: one for current day looking back at the past and the other as though it was in the past with the then "Abbot Aston" narrating stories of the life and Benedictine culture.

CHAPTER 2   HISTORY AND BENEFITS OF HBIM

Figure 2-15. *Hyde Abbey and curtilage, Unreal Engine scene (Wilson, 2017)*

2. Historical Significance

- Located at Hyde Mead on the northern edge of Winchester, Hyde Abbey was a large Benedictine monastery.

- The abbey was founded by Henry I and became a popular pilgrimage destination.

- The monastery was one of the wealthiest in the UK and the final resting place of King Alfred the Great, his wife Ealswitha, and Edward the Elder, their son.

3. Digitization Process

- Due to the loss of the building, the reconstruction was through the use of Revit and 3DS Max from artwork, maps, and archaeological drawings.

- The land mass was built using historical maps and visuals in the Unreal Game Engine.

- Details such as the columns and pillars were from evidence in the form of stones, i.e., parts of the columns and pillars found in walls and buildings in the local area, plus reference from historians.

- The monasterial buildings within the curtilage were also recreated using artistic sketches by Nick McPherson and research by local history group Hyde900.

4. Digital Deliverables

- Create the Abbey exterior and interior in 3D to include
  - **Interior:** Nave, Apse, Chapter House
  - **Exterior:** Hyde Abbey Church, St Bartholomew's church, Gatehouse, Almoners Hall, Precinct Boundary, The Cloister Area, Guest House
  - **Curtilage:** Various buildings in accordance with Nick McPherson's drawings, St Gall's cutaway sketch, and Hyde900's research

- Creation of an interactive abbey site in Unreal Game Engine to show historical views of the site and its buildings, with overlays of information when hovering for visitor use via the website

- An interactive website allowing users to virtually explore the abbey and its artifacts in 3D or virtual reality

- Rendered scenes from the interactive 3D abbey and site for use in the AR tour, elements in the "Series of Anecdotes" Tour and rendered stills and animations for the other three tours

CHAPTER 2   HISTORY AND BENEFITS OF HBIM

Figure 2-16. *Camera view of the Cloisters in Autodesk 3DS Max (Wilson, 2017)*

Figure 2-17. *Camera view of the Nave in Autodesk 3DS Max (Wilson, 2017)*

CHAPTER 2   HISTORY AND BENEFITS OF HBIM

Figure 2-18. *Camera view of the Choir Space and columns in Autodesk 3DS Max (Wilson, 2017)*

Using Unreal, users could walk around the site and engage with the objects. The interactive website is no longer available, although the video tours are still available on YouTube.

5. Benefits and Future Potential

- The project provided a permanent digital record of the size and importance of Hyde Abbey and the curtilage, its additional buildings and their use, facilitating visitors to see and explore the size of the building which no longer exists.

- The 3D models enabled detailed research of the church structure, individual components such as door arches, columns, pillars, and movable objects such as the crucifix given by King Canute to the Abbey at Easter.

CHAPTER 2   HISTORY AND BENEFITS OF HBIM

Figure 2-19. *King Cnut's Cross image used to recreate in the 3D model of Hyde Abbey, Winchester (Wilson, 2017)*

- Rendered stills and animations specific to the scripts for the different video tours containing a range of Points of Interest (POIs) for walking tours.

- Stories of the monks narrated by Abbot Aston (actor Nigel Bradshaw) with backgrounds of the 3D model and medieval music created originally for The Talking Walls' Beaulieu Abbey kiosk application in 2008–2009.

- The collected data can serve as a foundation for developing a Building Information Model (BIM) for future engagement with the data.

- The video stories and stills mentioned in the points above can be viewed on YouTube at `https://www.youtube.com/@hydeabbeywinchester9600/videos`.

The visuals enabled visitors to understand the scale of Hyde Abbey, which was difficult to imagine from the very little remaining evidence of such an important abbey in its time. Figure 2-20 shows the footprint of the abbey and how it has now been covered by streets of houses and their gardens.

Figure 2-20. *Site Plan of Hyde Abbey, Winchester, showing the size of the Abbey and its grounds contained by the Abbey curtilage walls (Wilson, 2017)*

6. Conclusion

The Hyde Abbey digitization project demonstrates the effectiveness of digital tools in reconstructing and preserving cultural heritage of a site that no longer exists. The comprehensive 3D library allows the ability to update the Unreal site and the 3D buildings to include HBIM data in the future. This would provide valuable insights to the life and culture of Benedictine monks and enable public engagement with a historic landmark. Hyde Abbey Garden has been designed to highlight aspects of the original abbey by markers in the form of holly trees and yew hedges. The Hyde Abbey project was created seven to eight years ago and needs updating and embedding with HBIM data, the stories of the monks told by the monks as avatars with Unreal. This is planned as part of Virtual Cities Winchester 1400–1800 as the project progresses.

Case Study 5: Notre-Dame Cathedral Restoration

Information from BIM and the Notre-Dame resurrection by Martyn Day, 2021 (AEC Magazine) (https://aecmag.com/bim/bim-and-the-notre-dame-resurrection-revit/) and "Faceting the post-disaster built heritage reconstruction process within the digital twin framework for Notre-Dame de Paris" by Antoine Gros, Anais Guillem, Livio De Luca, Elise Baillieul, Benoit Duvocelle, Olivier Malavergne, Lise Leroux, and Thierry Zimmer (2023)

Role of HBIM in the Restoration Process

The 2019 fire at Notre-Dame Cathedral in Paris was a devastating event that underscored the fragility of cultural heritage. However, it also demonstrated the transformative power of HBIM in disaster recovery and restoration.

Emergency Assessment

Within days of the fire, digital scans and archival data were mobilized to assess the damage. A pre-existing HBIM model created by art and architectural historian Andrew Tallon in 2010 provided invaluable baseline data for comparing the cathedral's condition before and after the fire. Tallon had carried out a top-to-bottom laser scan, starting at the west-side entrance. Tallon used a Leica Geosystems laser scanner (Day, 2021, Gros et al., 2023).

CHAPTER 2 HISTORY AND BENEFITS OF HBIM

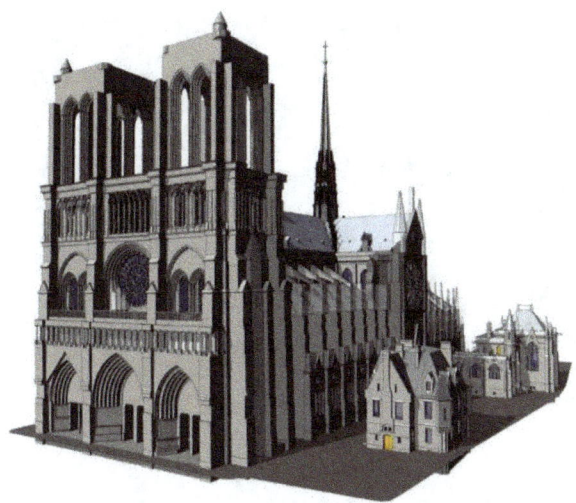

Figure 2-21. *Pre-fire model in Autodesk Revit by Andrew Tallon, 2010*

1. Collaboration and Coordination

- The restoration effort brought together architects, engineers, historians, and conservation specialists from around the world.
- HBIM served as a central platform for integrating diverse inputs, from structural analyses to historical research.

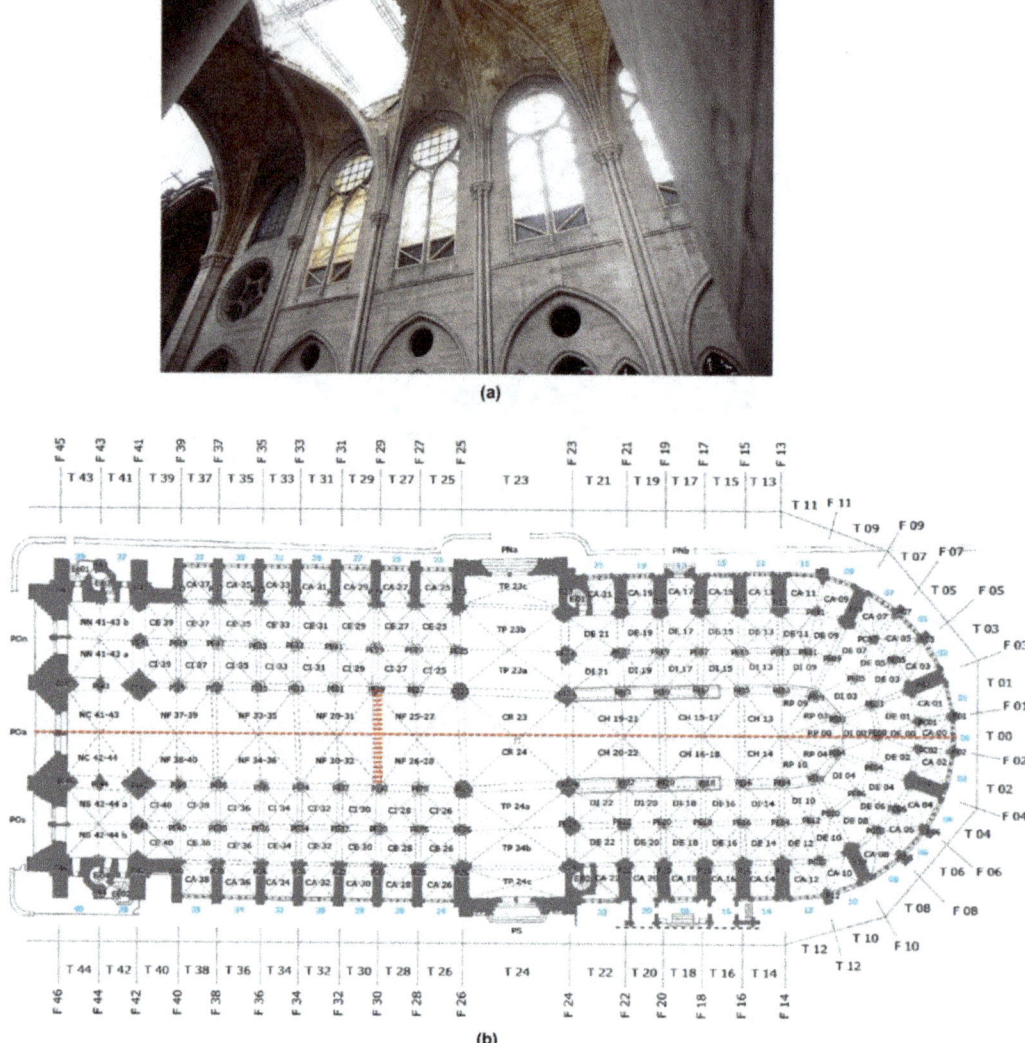

Figure 2-22. *(a) Collapsed vaults in the nave and the transept of Notre-Dame (@Bestrema); (b) situation of the collapsed nave vault on the floor plan (Gros et al., 2023)*

2. Restoration Planning

- HBIM models were used to simulate restoration scenarios, ensuring structural stability while preserving the cathedral's historical integrity. These included

    - **Data Collection:** Drones and laser scanners were used to collect billions of measurements of the cathedral.

    - **3D Modelling:** The data was used to create a 3D model of the cathedral using Autodesk software.

    - **Documentation:** The data was used to extract information about the materials used, quantities, and technical documents.

    - **Digital Representation:** The model provided architects, engineers, and other construction professional with precise measurements for their work.

    - The digital twin facilitated virtual walkthroughs, enabling stakeholders to visualize proposed interventions and anticipate challenges.

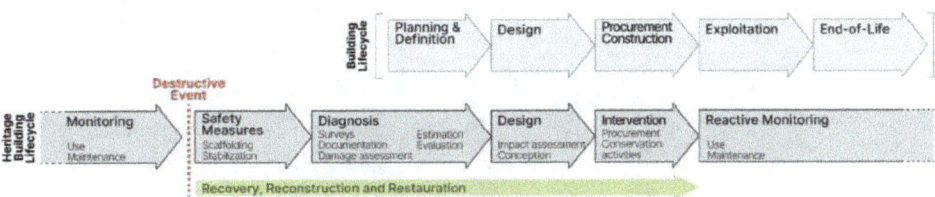

Figure 2-23. *Building life cycle and Notre-Dame restoration project as continuous cultural heritage building life cycle (Gros et al., 2023)*

CHAPTER 2   HISTORY AND BENEFITS OF HBIM

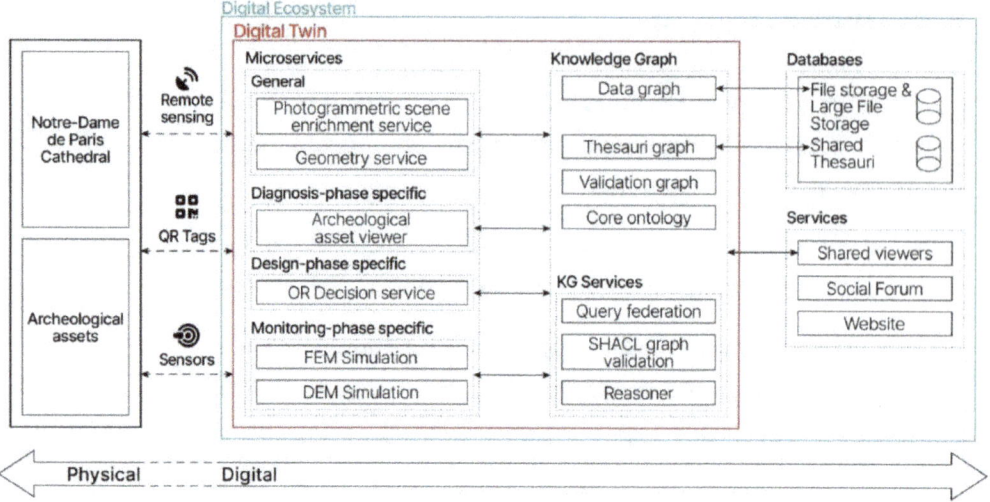

Figure 2-24. High level overview of the digital twin model composition and its links to the existing digital context (Gros et al., 2023)

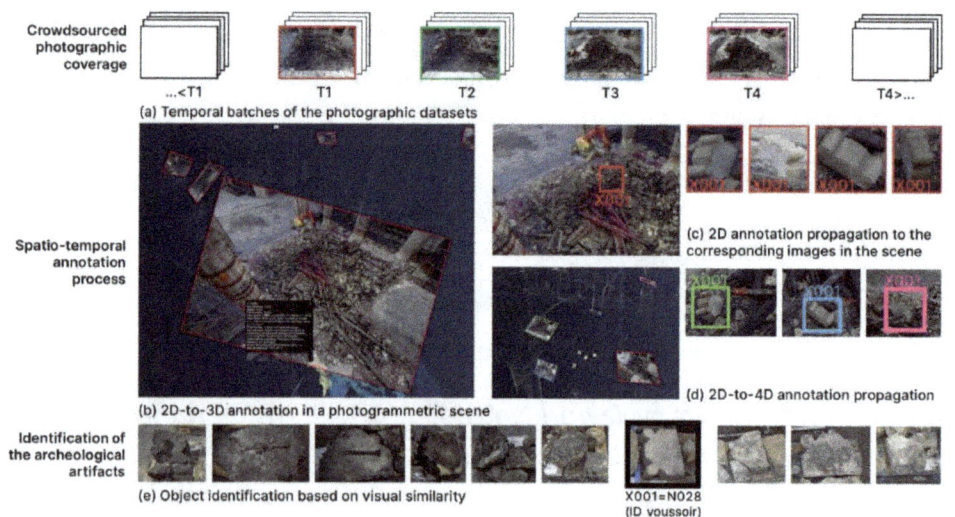

Figure 2-25. Spatio-temporal tracking in photogrammetric scenes, identification, and annotation of voussoirs in the remains during the recovery operations (Gros et al., 2023)

3. Broader Implications

The Notre-Dame restoration highlights several key benefits of HBIM:

- **Disaster Preparedness:** The existence of detailed HBIM models prior to the fire expedited recovery efforts, underscoring the importance of proactive digital documentation.

- **Accurate Reconstruction:** The model provided precise measurements and structural information, helping to ensure the cathedral was rebuilt to its original design.

- **Accelerated Process:** The model helped to accelerate the reconstruction process.

- **Insight to the Building's History:** The model can be used to reconstruct how the building looked into the past and to provide visitors with insight into its history.

- **Public Engagement:** Virtual tours and visualizations of the restoration process have kept the global community informed and invested in Notre-Dame's recovery.

- **Sustainability and Innovation:** The project has spurred innovations in materials science and digital modelling, setting new standards for heritage preservation.

By leveraging HBIM, the Notre-Dame restoration exemplifies how technology can bridge the past and future, safeguarding cultural treasures for generations to come.

CHAPTER 2 HISTORY AND BENEFITS OF HBIM

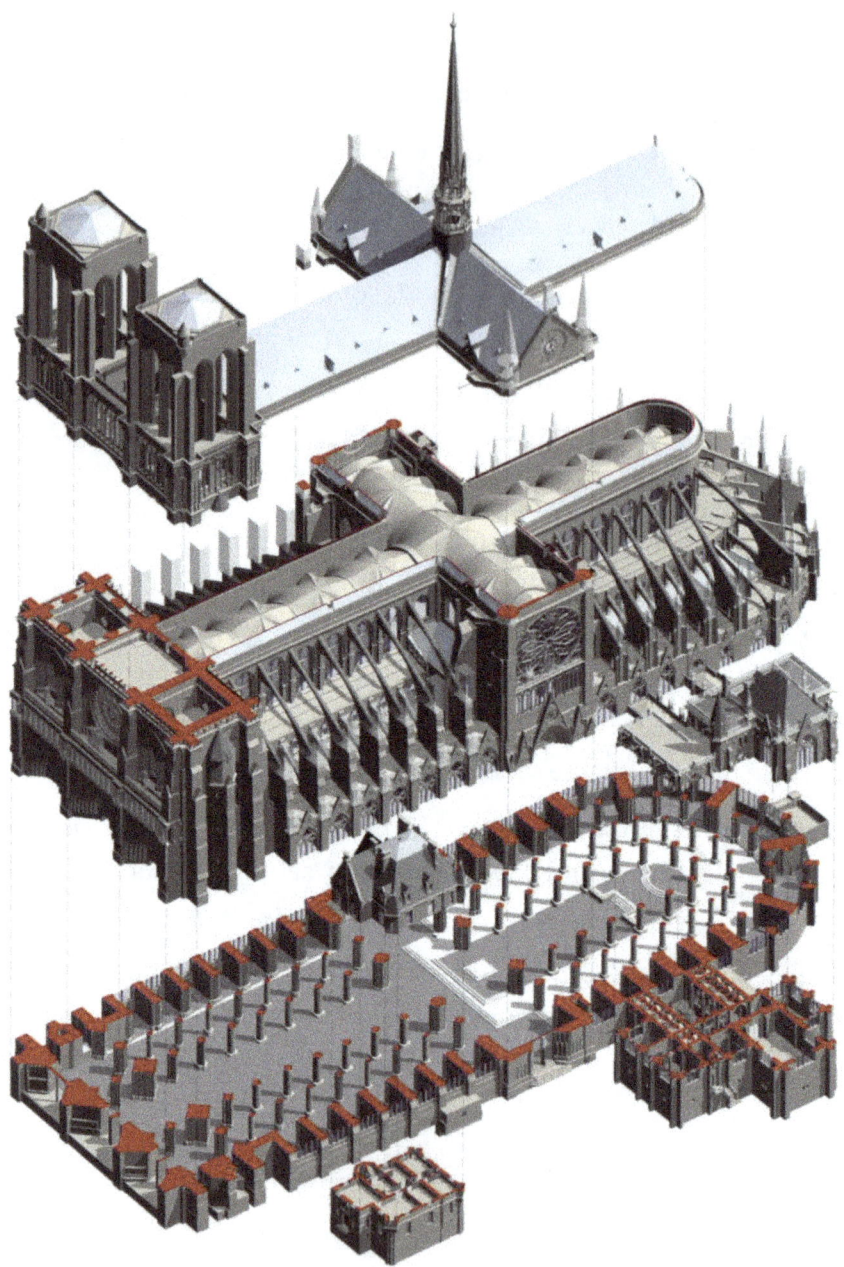

Figure 2-26. *Autodesk Revit exploded view of Notre-Dame (Day, 2021) (BIM and the Notre-Dame resurrection,* https://aecmag.com/bim/bim-and-the-notre-dame-resurrection-revit/*)*

CHAPTER 2   HISTORY AND BENEFITS OF HBIM

Summary

In the research undertaken now and in previous years, I have found that the majority of HBIM visualizations are internationally based; very few are in the UK. It certainly seems to appear that BIM and HBIM are much more about construction, repair, and analysis than visualization, which seems to be more of a by-product in these cases. The visualizations are also much more technical in appearance, perhaps straight from the BIM software rather than from taking into realistic lighting and material software for achieving more realistic results, or keeping with the scanned image, if an existing building.

The two Polish case studies highlight this quite well; one is much more about data and forming a library of that data, while the other is about being able to explore the 3D in VR.

The Elizabeth Tower (Big Ben) is about repair and therefore structural analysis, construction data, and understanding the history of the building. The images provided of the Revit model are thorough and highly detailed, which will also serve for not just the repairs undertaken between 2017 and 2022 but will be extremely valuable for future repair and possibly used as a heritage asset for tourism, i.e., exploring the buildings in VR.

The Hyde Abbey model was purely that, a model. Although built in Revit and then refined in 3DS Max, the HBIM data was not embedded for the final output. Dimensioned elevations, sections, 3D views, and plans were available from the Revit model, with doors, wall, and window schedules available if required. But they were the byproduct. What was required were the visualizations of the abbey in full, where it was no longer possible to see the Abbey church in all its glory as one of the largest Benedictine abbeys in the UK. The Malmesbury Abbey model created by one of our students was the same; it was for visualization purposes only, as was Beaulieu Abbey at Beaulieu in Hampshire.

Virtual Cities – Winchester 1400 and 1800 is different. It wasn't planned to be initially; it was going to be visualizations of the city in those two time periods to highlight the changes and growth of the city, the culture, and people that lived there. The 3D buildings were brought together in Unreal as visual assets for people to explore via VR, their devices, or on desktops. Later versions of software and technology have now made it much more feasible to include BIM/HBIM data within Unreal Engine, so it makes perfect sense to include it. The query currently is whether it is necessary. Maybe the individual buildings created should remain as individual buildings with embedded data to serve as preservation/conservation assets. The buildings taken into Unreal may, therefore, be copies of those buildings without the embedded BIM/HBIM data. A decision needs to be made whether to have two versions, one for heritage conservation, one for visualization within game like environments, aiding storytelling, with characters and interactive objects. Different users require different experiences and seek different types of knowledge. When you cannot find many examples where the buildings combine the data and the visualization aspects, it does make you wonder why. Maybe, and I think this is the case, the ability to do both is too new, too time-consuming maybe, and without many other examples, I have been unable to ascertain whether the value is there, i.e., will people want to explore the more technical data?

With the growing interest in heritage and HBIM, the discussions in the advantages and challenges of HBIM, and many more examples of HBIM in use than a few years ago, it makes sense to add the data and continue to add the data as further research is undertaken. It might be, though, that the projects that combine HBIM data and visual storytelling would mostly be undertaken by academic organizations who are able to access funding, rather than small companies, or perhaps a mix of academia and commercial organizations, as in the case of the Virtual Cities Winchester project.

References

6Sense (2024) Autodesk Revit (Market Share). Available at https://6sense.com/tech/bim-and-architectural-design-software/autodesk-revit-market-share

Arsalan, Hord; Heesom, David; Moore, Nigel. (2025). From Heritage Building Information Modelling Towards an 'Echo-Based' Heritage Digital Twin. Heritage. 8. 33. 10.3390/heritage8010033

Autodesk (1982) Autodesk AutoCAD. Available at https://www.autodesk.com/uk/solutions#architecture-engineering-and-construction

Baik, Ahmad (2020) Heritage building information modelling for implementing UNESCO procedures: challenges, potentialities, and issues. Abingdon, Oxon; New York, NY: Routledge. ISBN 9781003036548. https://lccn.loc.gov/2020006639

Charlton, James; Kelley, Kenneth; Greenwood, David; Moreton, Leo (2020) The Complexities of Managing Historic Buildings with BIM. Engineering, Construction and Architectural Management, 28 (2). pp. 570–583. ISSN 0969-9988. Available at https://doi.org/10.1108/ECAM-11-2019-0621

Croci, Giorgio (2002) The restoration of the Basilica of St Francis of Assisi. In: Estrategias relativas al patrimonio cultural mundial. La salvaguarda en un mundo globalizado. Principios, practicas y perspectivas. 13th ICOMOS General Assembly and Scientific Symposium. Actas. Comit Nacional Espaol del ICOMOS, Madrid, pp. 134–136 [Book Section]

Day, Martyn (2021) BIM and the Notre-Dame resurrection. AEC Magazine BIM/Features/Reality Modelling [https://aecmag.com/bim/bim-and-the-notre-dame-resurrection-revit/]

Dobson, Andrew (2022) HBIM for Historic Buildings: Refurbishment of Big Ben for UK Parliament. Autodesk University Class Presentation

Graitec (2023) The Importance of Numbering in Refurbishing Big Ben Clock Tower. Available at https://graitec.com/uk/customerstories/the-importance-of-numbering-in-refurbishing-big-ben-clock-tower/

Gros, Antoine; Guillem, Anaïs; De Luca, Livio; Baillieul, Élise; Duvocelle, Benoit; Malavergne, Olivier; Leroux, Lise; Zimmer, Thierry. Faceting the post-disaster built heritage reconstruction process within the digital twin framework for Notre-Dame de Paris. Sci Rep **13**, 5981 (2023). Available at https://doi.org/10.1038/s41598-023-32504-9 https://www.nature.com/articles/s41598-023-32504-9

Hirschtick, Jon (2015) Why We Started From Scratch (Again) in the CAD Business. Medium, originally published in Onshape News. Available at https://medium.com/onshape-news/why-we-started-from-scratch-again-in-the-cad-business-39ff2575c5fc

Historic England (2017) BIM for heritage developing a historic building information model. Available at https://historicengland.org.uk/images-books/publications/bim-for-heritage/heag-154-bim-for-heritage/

ICCROM ed. Wijesuriya and Lee (2017) Asian Buddhist Heritage – Conserving the Sacred. ICCROM-CHA Conservation Forum Series. International Centre for the Study of the Preservation and Restoration of Cultural Property

Janisio-Pawłowska, D. (2021) Analysis of the Possibilities of Using HBIM Technology in the Protection of Cultural Heritage, Based on a Review of the Latest Research Carried Out in Poland. ISPRS Int. J. Geo-Inf. 2021, 10, 633. Available at https://doi.org/10.3390/ijgi10100633

Krygiel, Eddy (2014) Autodesk Revit Architecture 2015: Autodesk Official Press. Sybex. ISBN: 9781118862858

Lovell, Lucy J.; Davies, Richard J.; Hunt, Dexter V.L. (2023) The Application of Historic Building Information Modelling (HBIM) to Cultural Heritage: A Review. Heritage 2023, 6, 6691-6717. Available at https://doi.org/10.3390/heritage6100350

Lui, Zhen; He, Yunrui; Demian, Peter; Osmani, M. (2024) Immersive Technology and Building Information Modeling (BIM) for Sustainable Smart Cities. Buildings 14(6):1765 DOI: 10.3390/buildings14061765

McGraw-Hill Construction (2012) The Business Value of Building Information Modeling (BIM) in North America: Multi-Year Trend Analysis and User Ratings. Key findings from McGraw-Hill Construction's New BIM SmartMarket Research Study. Available at https://www.slideshare.net/slideshow/the-business-value-of-bim/15387171

Murphy, M.; McGovern, E.; Pavia, S. (2009), "Historic building information modelling (HBIM)," Structural Survey, Vol. 27, No. 4, pp. 311–327. https://doi.org/10.1108/02630800910985108

Offield, Luke (2023) Autodesk Revit: The Best in BIM. Seiler Design Solutions. Available at https://www.seiler-ds.com/autodesk-revit-the-best-in-bim/

Peek, Jeff (2024) Ford Piquette Plant, Birthplace of the Model T, Celebrates 120 Years With $500K Grant. Automotive History, News. Hagerty Media. https://www.hagerty.com/media/news/ford-piquette-plant-birthplace-of-the-model-t-celebrates-120-years-with-500k-grant/

Quirk, V. (2012) A Brief History of BIM. Available at http://www.archdaily.com/302490/a-briefhistory-of-bim

Ubisoft (2025) Assassin's Creed, https://www.ubisoft.com/en-gb/game/assassins-creed/games

UK Parliament (2022) Conservation of Elizabeth Tower and Big Ben. https://www.parliament.uk/about/living-heritage/building/palace/big-ben/elizabeth-tower-and-big-ben-conservation-works-2017-/

UNESCO (2000) Assisi, the Basilica of San Francesco and Other Franciscan Sites. https://whc.unesco.org/en/list/990/

CHAPTER 3

Creating an HBIM 3D Model for a City Across Different Eras

This chapter follows the introductory level of the book by outlining the step-by-step process of creating an HBIM 3D model that spans architectural time periods. It discusses the importance of historical research and context in selecting the eras for reconstruction of a heritage building before being ready to create the building. It has been designed to demonstrate how to reconstruct a building that no longer exists rather than one that still exists or partly exists. The reason for choosing a building that no longer exists is fivefold, especially at introductory level:

1. As an introduction to HBIM and architecturally important CAD software, using Autodesk Revit can be quite encouraging in how quickly a building comes together, at the same time getting used to the quite technical looking interface.

2. Having built in Revit, the reconstructed building already includes BIM data and is easier, subsequently, for inputting researched HBIM data.

3. Creating a building from researched archival material only, such as floor plans and sketches, reinforces the need for thorough research for HBIM 3D modelling.

4. Reduces the need for hiring/purchasing expensive kit for scanning a building, gaining permissions to do so and learning more advanced technical software to create the building from the converted mesh/surface.

CHAPTER 3 CREATING AN HBIM 3D MODEL FOR A CITY ACROSS DIFFERENT ERAS

5. Buildings that no longer exist are prime buildings for people that want to know more about them. The reconstructed building helps visitors/users to understand the size and importance of the building that used to be part of the city/landscape/community. There is more query over a building that no longer exists because it is generally harder to imagine than ruins and, obviously, existing buildings.

The building I will use as the working model for the practical chapters is the family home of Jane Austen, "Steventon Rectory." The building no longer exists, except for a pump marking where the building once stood at Steventon (see Figure 3-1). There is also a debate over how the Rectory looked among the various Jane Austen societies and fans.

Figure 3-1. *Photograph of the site of Steventon Rectory (detail), showing a pump, the only remaining object from Jane Austen's time. Nicolson (22-23), courtesy of Stephen Colover (Walker, 2007)*

Included alongside the Steventon Rectory will be an example by a Digital Media Design – 3D Visualization student from the University of Winchester, who has been working through the process for recreating Winchester Castle for the Virtual Cities – Winchester project, 1400 period. The castle was ordered to be demolished in 1649 by Cromwell except for the Great Hall, which still exists and houses the history of Winchester Museum. The student's work highlights the importance in researching material to be able to model the castle as accurately as possible and demonstrates how he went about gathering as much material and data as possible.

There will be other examples of previous projects that will help to explain the necessity of different areas of research, mapping out how you will collect and record data as well as practical steps to help you consider how you might start your own project.

Overview of the Reconstruction Process

Creating an HBIM 3D model that spans various architectural time periods requires a structured workflow that integrates historical research, data acquisition, and digital modelling techniques. Below is a step-by-step guide detailing the process, emphasizing the importance of historical context in selecting eras for reconstruction.

Defining the Project Scope and Historical Context

- **Establish Objectives:** Determine the purpose of the HBIM model (e.g., academic research, heritage conservation, virtual tourism, or educational use).
    - For the purpose of this book and the Virtual Cities – Winchester project, I will be required to find a building that no longer exists in Winchester. Due to it no longer existing, it would need to be a building that existed in 1400 or 1800, the two selected time periods of the project. A significant building that no longer exists is Winchester Castle; another is Wolvesey Palace, although there are several ruins for the latter where 3D scanning could be used. As we will be working on recreating without using 3D scanning, i.e., purely using HBIM software, Winchester Castle is the most

suitable. The castle will enable story scenes to be created of Royal events that may have happened and then make use of a "portal" to 1800 to view how the site has changed in that period.

- The second building is going to be a building outside of Winchester but connected via a historically significant person that lived in an existing Winchester building in the 1800s. The Winchester building referred to is 8 College Street, where Jane Austen lived before she died. The building outside of Winchester is Steventon Rectory, which no longer exists. By modelling this building, we have the opportunity to "portal" to and from the two buildings across time, seeing Jane Austen with her family at Steventon Rectory and then at Winchester with her sister Cassandra.

- Therefore, my purpose is a combination of historical fact and storytelling, both architectural and cultural, aimed at engaging tourists/visitors/users interested in the history of Winchester and Jane Austen. Furthermore, enabling them to explore buildings that no longer exist and why they were important.

- **Select Time Periods:** Identify key architectural periods based on historical significance, availability of records, and the evolution of the building in question.

  - With regard to selecting time periods for the Virtual Cities project, the two time periods, 1400 and 1800, were chosen primarily to visualize the significant change and growth in the city over the 400 years, and the availability of maps that were detailed sufficiently to use as a layout of the streets and indication of buildings. The maps chosen can be viewed in Chapter 1, Case Study 2 (Figures 16, 17, and 18). Research also provided a good breadth of information for the two time periods, including John Crook's book of the Cathedral Close buildings (Crook, 1984), Atkinson's paper of Winchester Cathedral Close (1941), and Professor Martin Biddle's "Winchester: A City of Two Planned Towns" (2020).

- I had intended the medieval period as the first time period but then needed to work out a particular century, one that would see most of the cathedral close buildings still in place in 1800, such as the Cathedral, Cheyney House, and Kings gate. One of the maps Biddle had included in his work was for 1400, which lined up well with the building requirements; hence, 1400 was chosen. By choosing 1400 instead of 1350, it would be possible to include the cathedral as it stands today as one of the landmark buildings, resulting in slightly less work in remodeling such a large building. The Nave and Choir were remodeled in the 1400s to the perpendicular style, and the West Front remodeled between 1350 and 1410. There was also the additional possibility of significant events, such as the Royal visit of Henry IV in 1403 when he married Joan of Navarre.

- The reason for choosing 1800 was similar regarding the availability of detailed maps. For this period, Biddle's (2016) "An Historical Map of Winchester (Town & City Historical Maps)" map was perfect and an excellent resource for the layout of the city, highlighting buildings that no longer existed and partly existed, the newer buildings, and street changes. The time period also coincided with Jane Austen's time period; she moved to live in 8 College Street, Winchester, in 1817. The idea is to create a pinpoint in time before Jane took lodgings at 8 College Street, i.e., in 1800, and then enable a portal to another pinpoint in time during 1817 when Jane moved in and was there with her sister Cassandra, before she died. Users/visitors would then also be able to portal back in time to when Jane was a child with her family at Steventon Rectory. This would enable visitors to take a virtual peek at aspects of Jane's early life and end of life.

- For your own project, considerations such as those above are important for mapping your starting point, i.e., what building(s) (unless already known) and what material is available to work with in laying out the city/environment chosen for a particular date. Another consideration was what events happened in that time period.

- Stories engage all audiences; they are cross generational, so creating the environment for stories to be told makes sense for engaging all types of visitors and users. Gathering social and cultural material for each of the time periods is therefore a crucial, albeit time-consuming, aspect for ensuring an engaging virtual city. You need to be selective though, find the buildings that people would like to know more about, and search for those stories as well as the historical significance of different buildings.

- **Conduct Preliminary Research:** Gather information about social, cultural, and technological factors that influenced architectural styles in the selected eras.

  - Gathering research material could probably form the most time-consuming part of the project. Although it would be a good idea to ensure you have archivists, historians, and architects helping you, I have found that also doing your own research helps you to understand how you could model the building, i.e., the structure, the materials, known and typical details. This has been the case for students working on the Virtual Cities project. The research they needed to undertake to recreate their chosen building led to a much better understanding about what they were modelling, how it was built, and the materials used. In doing this, they also came across conundrums such as when a tower changed from being D-shaped to circular or square and discrepancy in maps or floor plans, i.e., a tower showing on one illustration, but not another, although of a similar time period (see Figures 3-2 and 3-3).

    Finding further research about other buildings of the same period in the local area helped them to fill in missing detail.

CHAPTER 3   CREATING AN HBIM 3D MODEL FOR A CITY ACROSS DIFFERENT ERAS

Winchester Castle in the 12th and 13th centuries

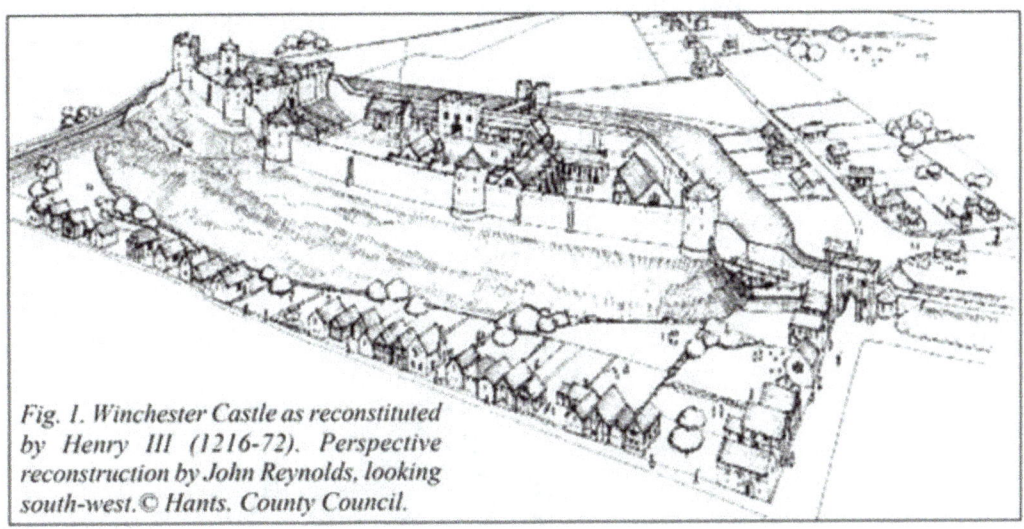

Fig. 1. Winchester Castle as reconstituted by Henry III (1216-72). Perspective reconstruction by John Reynolds, looking south-west.© Hants. County Council.

Figure 3-2. *Winchester castle in the 13th Century – look to the top right bend of the castle wall, there is not a tower situated there highlighted by student Tomas Dulkys in his research for recreating Winchester Castle (Dulkys, 2024)*

Winchester Castle in the 12th and 13th centuries

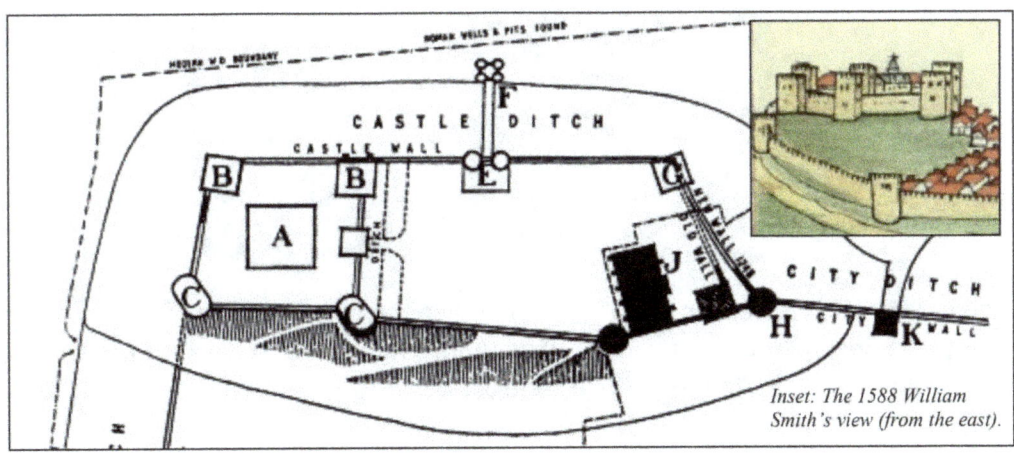

Inset: The 1588 William Smith's view (from the east).

Figure 3-3. *Winchester Castle plan view in the 13th century showing a square tower in the top right bend of the castle wall as "G" (Black Tower). Also highlighted by student Tomas Dulkys in his research (Dulkys, 2024).*

123

- It required further research as to what should be modelled, i.e., with or without the tower. The Black Tower could also be seen in another map (Speed, 1610) and an engraving by J. Milner shown in Figures 3-4 and 3-5, but in the physical scaled model in the Westgate Museum (Figure 3-6), the tower is missing. It was therefore important to discover the time covered by the physical model as to why the tower wasn't part of the model, i.e., when was the tower built into the curtain wall.

Figure 3-4. *John Speed's c 1610 map of Hampshire showing the layout of Winchester, here just the southwest area highlighting the castle and the square tower previously labelled as "G" in Figure 3-3*

CHAPTER 3   CREATING AN HBIM 3D MODEL FOR A CITY ACROSS DIFFERENT ERAS

Figure 3-5. *J. Milner's 1798 engraving of Winchester Castle from the West, highlighted by student Tomas Dulkys in his research (Dulkys, 2024)*

Figure 3-6. *Reconstruction of Winchester Castle as it may have appeared in the mid-13th century by Castellogy (2025) highlighted by student Tomas Dulkys in his Miro research boards for how to rebuild the castle as a digital model (Dulkys, 2024)*

- The tower appears to have been built after mid-13th century, possibly in the reconstruction of the curtain walls when they were badly damaged in the First Barons' War in 1216, remaining damaged until Henry III's reign. During his reign, Henry III ordered considerable restoration to the castle's defenses, and "by 1248, all the eastern defenses had been reconstructed." The additional research to discover what was or wasn't in place for the time period chosen can easily take time away from modelling and progressing the project, as Tomas discovered, but valuable in understanding how important research is in informing practice and being able to substantiate why certain aspects have been included or not.

On an HBIM level, it is particularly important to ensure those details are as correct as possible. Later periods and styles are obviously easier to source detail for, plus buildings may still exist in part and more detailed sketches available.

Historical Research and Data Collection

- **Archival Research**
    - The above example highlights the need to examine **historical maps**, **architectural plans**, **photographs**, and **sketches** to ensure you have the most correct information and compare those items for any discrepancies. A similar discrepancy regarding how a building may have looked is talked about in Walker's article (2007) about Jane Austen's family home, Steventon Rectory, which also led me to create a quick demo in 2009 to work out how the building may have looked. The information regarding this can be found in Chapter 1 (Figures 1-35 and 1-36) and therefore not needed to be repeated here. It does, though, provide another example where research needs to be thorough and similar to puzzle solving.
    - Another example of heritage puzzle solving was also involved when digitally reconstructing Beaulieu Abbey, Beaulieu, in Hampshire in 2009. There are ruins for some of the Cloister facing buildings but not for the main abbey church. Much like Hyde Abbey, it was an important abbey in the UK, not just Hampshire, initially built in King John's reign. According to the Abbey floor plan by Fowler (1911), the night stairs meant that the physical model in the abbey museum could not quite be right with regard to the cloister roof along the south transept. It was only through building the model digitally with architectural software according to the floor plan that this became obvious, but I still needed to

double-check by reading through Fowler's text and other sketches such as Milner's engraving and Hope and Brakspear's (1906) perspective sketch of Beaulieu Abbey (see Figure 3-7).

- Elevations are not often available for older buildings, so working through textbooks for possible heights is necessary. If part of the building remains, then measuring the size of the stonework and counting "bricks" for overall height might be possible. If a full wall is still available, then 3D scanning would be really helpful for determining the height once the scan has been taken into Revit or a 3D modelling program.

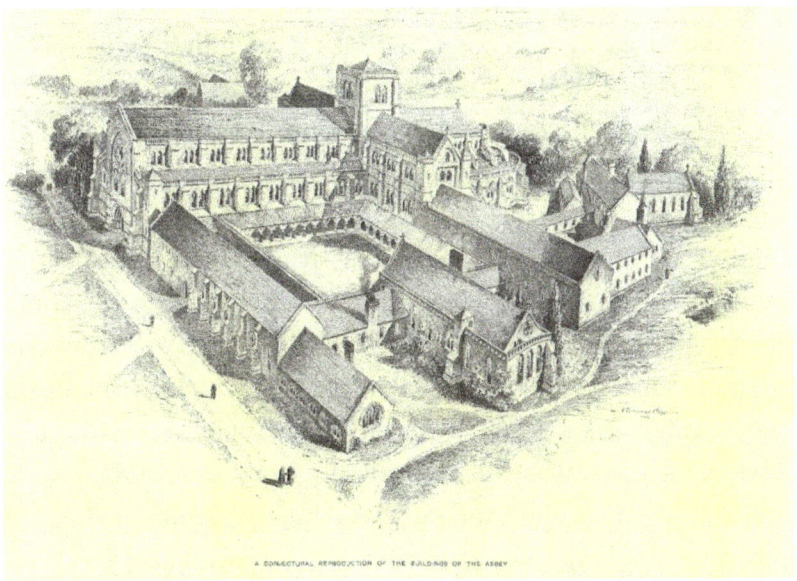

Figure 3-7. *A conjectural reconstruction of the buildings of the abbey (Hope & Brakspear, 1906)*

- Consult primary sources, for example, old tax records, blueprints, archaeological records, local and county records, local historical books, local history groups, local planning departments, and, if relevant, estate documents. Fowler's 1911 book of Beaulieu Abbey provided valuable information regarding the history of the abbey, and this book alongside Hope and Brakspear's 1906 book *The Cistercian Abbey of Beaulieu in the County of Southampton* helped in being able to ensure the 3D model could be as accurate as possible at three different periods. These were determined from archaeological surveys undertaken from 1900 to 1906 when Hope and Brakspear's book was published. Archival documents such as the "Houses of Cistercian monks: Abbey of Beaulieu," in A History of the County of Hampshire: Volume 2 (Doubleday, 1903), which includes the Annals of Waverley, from British History Online, also helped in finding out more about the monks and their activities, which in turn helped to provide stories for visitors to engage with while exploring the history of the abbey.

- Review secondary sources such as written work that provides technical information and principles for building styles and vernacular architecture, academic papers, and restoration case studies. With regard to Virtual Cities and the buildings reconstructed for Winchester, research regarding the local material, a particular style of flint, and stone walling was necessary. The flint walling textures available via texture libraries such as Quixel/Megascan (now Fab in Unreal) were not suitable, nor were the stone, brick, and flint. The pattern of the three types of material is specific to Hampshire. Details such as this can often be found in architectural/restoration documents. Without this detail, the buildings would look wrong, and for HBIM embedded data, it is really important to ensure that the details are correct as well as looking visually correct. More information about materials and textures can be found in Chapter 6's "Incorporating Historically Accurate Vernacular Materials and Textures" section.

- **Site Investigation (If Possible)**
  - Conduct laser scanning (LiDAR) or photogrammetry for existing structures. Unfortunately, most of the buildings I have worked on have not had much or nothing in the way of existing structures to scan, and I have therefore not invested in 3D scanning equipment. It is extremely useful for sites that have ruins; the scans can often help determine materials, height, depth, decay/

repairs, and finer detail. There are companies that will undertake this for you rather than perhaps investing in the equipment required for what could be just one project.

- Take field measurements if parts of the building still exist. When I was reconstructing Beaulieu, I was able to take measurements of the south wall of the nave and the remains of the chapter house arches, frater, and dorter (now the museum) and was surprised to find the measurements coincided with metric units. For example, the arches along the south wall were exactly 10 meters wide. In some ways, I should not have been surprised as the abbey was built by French stonemasons. The onsite measurements at Wolvesey Palace were also useful in conjunction with English Heritage's dimensioned elevations of the ruins. Visiting the site and taking measurements also help in understanding the site and how the stonework looks and feels, valuable for recreating the texture for the digital model, and something not ascertained from reading/viewing texts.

- **Consult Experts**

  - Historians, archaeologists, and architectural conservators can provide critical insights into construction techniques and material use. I was very lucky in being able to work with a geologist when we worked in reconstructing Hyde Abbey (see Chapter 2, Case Study 4). His knowledge on the type of stone that was used to build Hyde Abbey and then where that would have come from was extremely valuable, especially in making sure the material used in the digital reconstruction was of an appropriate color and texture.

  - Being able to talk with Lady Mary Montagu-Scott and Beaulieu's archivist Susan Tomkins about Beaulieu Abbey and having access to information not generally available were inordinately helpful. Their combined knowledge of the abbey was extremely valuable in being able to replicate the abbey, and the stories of the monks with confidence in the information being as accurate as possible considering the age of the abbey.

CHAPTER 3   CREATING AN HBIM 3D MODEL FOR A CITY ACROSS DIFFERENT ERAS

Scoping the Reconstruction Process

The next two sections provide further steps in what should be considered during the planning and reconstruction process. What I would say at this point is to determine whether you are creating this HBIM model on your own, or with a team, or perhaps you have access to experts who will be happy to help you. Your project may be too large/involved for just one person, but if there is no timescale, i.e., more of a personal ongoing project, then maybe it is fine continuing on your own. If a project with a deadline and/or a client project, then it is really important to set out how big a team you will need and the skills required to ensure deadlines are met. This is also necessary if applying for funding. Once you have decided on your HBIM project and the buildings/site involved, you should scope each of the buildings, how you will model them and therefore the skills required. Will you sub-contract to access the skills needed or buy in that expertise, i.e., employ short term or invest long term? From my experience, having a consistent team who you know and can trust with regard to experience and the necessary skillsets to meet goals/deadlines, flexible with those skillsets and have a similar work ethic, cannot be beaten in being able to produce a project on time.

What has helped me considerably with each of the reconstructions is a project spreadsheet that includes all the sources of data, where they were sourced and when, permissions asked, etc. The same spreadsheet (via different tabs) also includes an object record sheet, i.e., the buildings that are needed, their important dates, who has modelled the building, whether the model is finished, and where it is kept. It also records the materials, the styles, and where those library objects are kept. Since starting Virtual Cities as an HBIM model, the spreadsheet now includes HBIM data, with a growing type/category/code data library to help in embedding data to the Revit and Unreal models. I have made this into a template that is included as a resource on the accompanying web portal to this book.

Selecting the Time Periods for Reconstruction
Importance of Historical Research in Era Selection

In the previous section, I provided an overview of different considerations when selecting your time period. In this section, we will explore the time chosen and how to scope out the research required, what you want your building(s) to demonstrate, i.e., what information you would like your users to engage with, the type of data you want to embed in your HBIM model (or need to embed), and how you will find that data. While doing this, you will also need to think about the following aspects, especially in searching out the material to use:

- **Authenticity:** Ensures the reconstructed model accurately represents past architectural states

    Checking the authenticity of documents you might use is crucial for accurate reconstruction and heritage preservation. This will involve verifying the reliability of archival resources, historical maps, architectural drawings, and written records used to inform the model, generally achieved by cross-referencing multiple sources to confirm details (such as in the example provided in the previous section regarding Winchester Castle's Black Tower), assessing provenance and credibility of documents, and distinguishing between original records and later interpretations.

    Metadata should be maintained within the HBIM model to document the source, date, and confidence level of each piece of information. From experience, any information you find, always make a note of as much detail as possible at the time of finding, including the URL if relevant and the date you accessed the information. I also tend to either screengrab or PDF the information and save to a suitably named folder.

    Additionally, digital tools such as photogrammetry and laser scanning can help validate historical accuracy by comparing archival data with physical evidence from existing structures.

- **Cultural Relevance:** Highlights key moments in a city's or building's history

    The cultural relevance of a building or city is essential in HBIM as it provides context beyond architectural features, linking historical structures to their social, cultural, and historical significance. This type of data involves integrating historical narratives, community memories, and symbolic meanings into the model. This can be achieved by embedding archival texts, oral histories, and historical events within the HBIM database, allowing users to access layered information about a building's past functions, inhabitants, and transformations over time, similar to The Talking Walls' Beaulieu Abbey 2010 application (Beaulieu Abbey -3D Views). Additionally, GIS integration can map cultural connections across a city, while digital storytelling elements, such as interactive timelines or VR experiences, can enhance engagement with the heritage value of the built environment.

- **Educational Value:** Provides a teaching resource for historical architecture and urban development

    HBIM models have significant educational value, serving as both a teaching resource for heritage studies and a practical tool for training students in 3D visualization and architectural modelling. As a teaching resource, HBIM provides detailed, data-rich reconstructions of historical buildings, allowing students to explore architectural history, construction techniques, and cultural heritage in an interactive way.

    For students learning 3D and architectural visualization, HBIM offers hands-on experience in modelling complex structures, integrating archival research, and applying advanced digital techniques such as parametric modelling, photogrammetry, and laser scanning. By working with HBIM, students develop critical skills in heritage documentation, accuracy in digital reconstruction, and storytelling and gamification through immersive visualization, bridging the gap between historical analysis and modern design technologies.

- **Comparative Analysis:** Demonstrates changes in materials, techniques, and styles over time

    Will your building be a model that demonstrates different styles over time, or will it focus on a single period? If the former, will you be able to trace all changes, or will you select specific periods based on available data? Demonstrating changes in materials, techniques, and styles over time in an HBIM model requires careful data collection and interpretation. While records for more modern buildings may be relatively straightforward to obtain, older structures often rely on fragmented archival sources and building surveys. Integrating these diverse data sets can be complex, requiring a way of determining the unknown values where gaps exist and different levels of confidence in modelling each phase. Access to experts such as archaeologists and architectural historians can be invaluable in validating findings and saving time. HBIM phasing tools and timeline-based visualizations can effectively illustrate these transformations, allowing users to explore the evolution of a structure dynamically. However, a balance must be struck between historical accuracy and interpretative reconstruction, particularly when dealing with uncertain or missing data.

- **Preservation Planning:** Assists conservationists in restoration projects

It may be that you are reading this book from a heritage conservation role or similar and need to model a building for preservation and restoration purposes. The main focus of the book is for non-existent buildings and therefore recreating from primarily archival data. Preservation implies that something exists to preserve, and restore, generally to return a building to what it once was (although at what period of time?); therefore, this consideration would most probably be in the area of photogrammetry and laser scanning to recreate the building. Creating buildings for preservation purposes is a growth area and much more recognized since the fire that destroyed the roof of Notre-Dame in Paris (see Case Study 5 in Chapter 2 for more detail). Andrew Tallon, an art and architectural historian, had already completed a top-to-bottom laser scan of the building in 2010, preserving how the building looked, without knowing that it would be valuable for the reconstruction after the fire. There are many other scanned buildings, several for commercial purpose, such as being able to virtually visit and view shops, hotels, and restaurants online, for example, The Dome, Edinburgh (see Figures 1-2, 1-3, and 1-4), detailing the inside and outside in great depth. Adding HBIM data to these models would then make them valuable assets for future restorative work and preservation.

CHAPTER 3   CREATING AN HBIM 3D MODEL FOR A CITY ACROSS DIFFERENT ERAS

Structuring the HBIM Model by Time Period

- **Develop a Periodization Strategy**
  - Having identified your time period(s), the next thing is to start to develop a record, list, or similar to provide an instant reference of the major architectural changes over time and in sequence (e.g., medieval to Baroque, Georgian to Victorian) that have happened to your building(s)/city. Depending on the type of person you are, or who will be tasked with this, the choice of how will vary. I have used spreadsheets and Pinterest boards; my students have used Trello and Miro boards. The bonus with Pinterest is that it will also save the link to the source automatically rather than having to add, which is therefore time saving for initial research scoping. Furthermore, it is visual, which suits me as a visual learner. The material that you then use can be added as a listed record, perhaps as a spreadsheet. Working as a team, just make sure that any documents created are shared as a single source, i.e., not multiple versions on different team members' drives.

    Finding the information has been covered, but there will be aspects of the building (or city) that may not be recoverable. Therefore, there will be a need to make informed decisions for the missing data based on research of that period for which you may want to confirm with experts. Will the building model require all changes across its lifetime, i.e., for conservation and restoration purposes, or will it be for visualization and storytelling within a visitor application? The latter will mean that periods of change can be selected based on evidence available, but obviously not for the former.

    One such example was in reconstructing Hyde Abbey, Winchester. There is very little evidence of what Hyde Abbey looked like other than archaeological evidence and remains in the form of different stones repurposed elsewhere. A historical and archaeological group, Hyde900, provided much of the research plus the reason for the digital reconstruction of the abbey. A set of visuals created by Nick McPherson in his MA research "Hyde Illustrated – Architectural Aspects through History" helped considerably in creating the initial model. We needed to call upon experts such as Dr. John Crook, Professor Martin Biddle, and the Hyde900 team for confirmation of the reconstructed abbey church. In one of these discussions, it was highlighted that the cloister pillars should be smaller in diameter based on stones discovered. There is still, therefore, a certain amount of conjecture in how the abbey and the monastic buildings looked in their day. To resolve some of the queries, I needed to research how other Benedictine abbeys of a similar age were laid out, i.e., where the infirmary and other monastical buildings would be positioned within the curtilage walls. There is a difference in the positioning of these buildings between Benedictine and Cistercian monasteries, plus also the layout of the land, i.e., rivers/streams, that would affect those positions. Information I would not have known without the research but has since helped form a recorded knowledge database about Benedictine and Cistercian monasteries. Not just in the architecture and placement, but also the cultural aspects and stories of the monks' daily lives in the 1100–1500 period. The reason for reconstructing Hyde Abbey and Beaulieu Abbey (Cistercian) was purely visual as 3D digital models for exploring in VR, on screen, and for backdrops to storytelling. BIM and HBIM were not required as visualization projects, but in using Revit initially, the provision of dimensioned plans and elevations has been possible.

- Decide whether to create a single model with changeable phases or **separate models** for different periods. This is important especially in being able to use the building in subsequent applications such as Unreal Game Engine.

CHAPTER 3   CREATING AN HBIM 3D MODEL FOR A CITY ACROSS DIFFERENT ERAS

- As a Revit model, creating the different time point changes as Phases would make perfect sense, i.e., all the changes to the building in one model, which, through Revit, you would be able to access and view, and export those views and data for use in visuals and reports.

- For taking that model into Unreal, there could be an issue in the many additional "hidden" objects that those phased changes represent when taking that model into Unreal Engine.

- Key considerations for using Revit phases in Unreal Engine are shown in Tables 3-1 and 3-2.

Table 3-1. *Phased Revit model (single model with phases)*

Positive	Negative
Efficient for documentation in Revit: Phasing allows you to manage changes over time within one model, making it easier to produce clear visual timelines, reports, and drawings	**Potential Unreal Engine issue:** When exporting the Revit model to Unreal Engine (via Datasmith), all phase data may come through as geometry. Elements marked as "hidden" in Revit's phase views may still be exported, adding unnecessary complexity and clutter in Unreal Engine
Streamlined data management in Revit: Phases are integrated into Revit's view filters, schedules, and materials, making it easier to track historical changes	
Best practice recommendation: If your focus is primarily Revit driven, i.e., documentation and reports, then create a phased model in Revit for efficient management. When preparing for Unreal Engine, filter and export only the visible elements for each phase using view template or custom 3D views	

Table 3-2. *Separate models for different time periods (multiple models)*

Positive	Negative
Cleaner geometry in Unreal Engine: By separating models into distinct time periods before export, you avoid the risk of redundant "hidden" elements	**Increased workload in Revit:** Managing separate models means duplication of shared elements and potential version control challenges
Better performance in Unreal Engine: Since Unreal Engine excels with optimized geometry and minimal overlapping data, separating models may result in improved performance	
Best practice recommendation: If your focus is primarily Unreal Engine driven, i.e., interactive experiences/storytelling/gameplay, consider creating separate models for each phase in Revit. This simplifies the Unreal Engine import process and avoids excess geometry	

Having worked with Revit's Phases, i.e., Demolished, Existing, and Proposed within an architectural practice, I know how valuable the Phasing function is; it is particularly important for construction purposes for builders and architects to understand the current building and what to demolish. Therefore, for heritage conservation use, I know that they can also be useful especially as you can add your own phases such as 1800, 1400, etc., so that effectively in the one model you have only to select the phase you want to view and the model updates to show what the building was like in that time. Taking such a model into Unreal Engine would, as mentioned in the table above, create a problem with meshes sitting inside meshes, creating an overly complex and complicated model.

This is why you need to consider what the building is ultimately going to be used for, i.e., taking into Unreal or staying as a Revit model. Personally, as stated, for heritage purposes in Unreal and storytelling, I would make a copy of the model for the time period I need in my Unreal project and ensure that model contains only that one period of time as a phase before taking it into Unreal. In Unreal, I can create a new level of that period and import the Revit model via Datasmith to that level, i.e., 8 College Street in 1800.

CHAPTER 3 CREATING AN HBIM 3D MODEL FOR A CITY ACROSS DIFFERENT ERAS

I can then go back to another phase in the Revit model, make a copy of that, and also take into Unreal, ensuring that just that one phase is available. I would then create a new level in Unreal and import the latter period model into that new level, i.e., 8 College Street in 1817.

And so on. You still then have your complete all-inclusive model over different times (phases) in Revit intact for conservation/preservation purposes and separate period models in Unreal on different levels for storytelling and visualizing different periods of time. This also then allows you to time travel between the levels, stepping to and fro using the Unreal portal's function as part of your storytelling.

As a practical workflow for exporting a phased model to Unreal Engine, in Revit, create dedicated 3D views for each phase with only the visible geometry shown. Then use the Datasmith Exporter and export each phase 3D view separately, ensuring only the relevant geometry is exported.

Once in the Unreal Engine, import each model as a unique layer or sequence to manage visibility changes interactively. Below is a step-by-step guide for efficiently exporting a phased Revit model into Unreal Engine using Datasmith, ensuring clean geometry, optimal performance, and smooth phase management.

Step 1: Prepare Your Phased Model in Revit

1. Organize your phases in Revit.

    - Ensure your project's phases are correctly defined in Revit's Phases dialogue.

    - Assign the appropriate phase to each building element (e.g., walls, doors etc.).

    - Use Phase Filters to manage visibility across different time periods.

2. Create dedicated 3D views for each phase to control what is exported:

    - Go to View ➤ 3D View and create separate views for each phase.

    - In each 3D View's Properties panel:

- Set Phase Filter to display only the elements relevant to that phase (e.g., *Show Complete, Show New Only*).

- Use Visibility/Graphics (VG) overrides to hide non-essential categories or annotations.

Tip Name each view clearly (e.g., "Phase 1 – Foundation," "Phase 2 – Extension").

---

3. Check model cleanliness.

   - Purge unused elements (via Manage ➤ Purge Unused) to reduce unnecessary data.

   - Run a geometry check for stray elements or objects that may export unintentionally.

Step 2: Export to Datasmith Using Revit 2024

1. Revit 2024 has Datasmith Exporter included in the Revit software; there is not a Plugin to download as in previous versions of Revit. Please visit this page on Unreal if you have an earlier version of Revit: https://www.unrealengine.com/en-US/datasmith/plugins.

   In Unreal Engine 5.5.4, go to the Edit menu and select Plugins.

   In Plugins search for Datasmith. Make sure they are active by clicking on them (blue tick). If they were not active and you have ticked them on, you may be prompted to restart Unreal.

2. In Revit 2024, export a Phase View.

   - In Revit, switch to your prepared 3D View for the desired phase.

   - Go to the View menu, then Twinmotion.

   - Under Twinmotion, make sure that Autosync is on by clicking on it (it needs to be in color, not gray). Check the Export settings, i.e., the Data groups you want to see in Unreal. Click Synchronise.

CHAPTER 3   CREATING AN HBIM 3D MODEL FOR A CITY ACROSS DIFFERENT ERAS

- Click Export Datasmith.
- Save your Datasmith file in an appropriate location, i.e., Datasmith Folder in your project folder
- Repeat for each phase, ensuring each export has a clear file name (e.g., Phase_1_Foundation.udatasmith).

Step 3: Import into Unreal Engine

1. Create a new project in Unreal Engine.
   - Start a new Blank or Architecture template project.
   - Enable the Datasmith Plugin if not already active (via Edit ➤ Plugins).

Figure 3-8. Unreal Engine Datasmith Plugins

CHAPTER 3   CREATING AN HBIM 3D MODEL FOR A CITY ACROSS DIFFERENT ERAS

2. Import your Datasmith files.

- In Unreal Engine, create a new Level, double-click, and wait for it to open.

- Go to File ➤ Import Datasmith.

- Select the .udatasmith file for Phase 1 and configure:

    - ✓ Import Geometry

    - ✓ Import Materials (if desired)

    - ✓ Import Lights (if applicable)

- While the objects are still highlighted in the Outliner, click on the new folder icon, top right of the Unreal window.

- All your objects will then be contained in that folder.

- Provide a suitable name for the folder – right-click Edit/Rename.

- Repeat for each subsequent phase, i.e., new level for each phase, new folder for all the Phase objects per level

Tip If you intend to use Unreal's materials, i.e., you have created a library of accurate local materials in Unreal Engine, then leave the Import Materials box unticked.

Step 4: Optimize the Unreal Scene, Level by Level

1. Clean up geometry.

    - Unreal Engine may import extra geometry (especially from hidden objects). Manually inspect and delete redundant meshes.

2. Refine materials.

    - Unreal Engine may assign default materials. Use Materials from the drop-down menu (see Figure 3-9), just to add different materials now. We will cover creating Unreal materials in detail in Chapter 6.

CHAPTER 3   CREATING AN HBIM 3D MODEL FOR A CITY ACROSS DIFFERENT ERAS

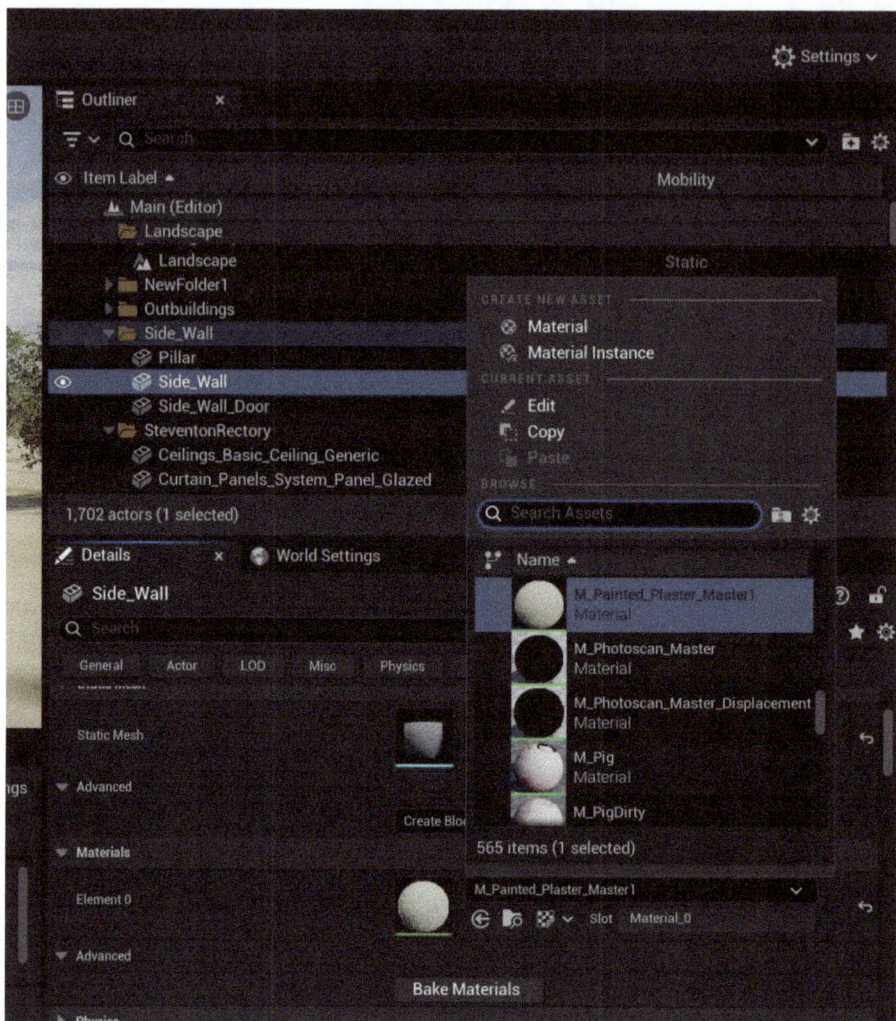

Figure 3-9. *Changing materials in the Details side menu from the available materials in Unreal Engine*

From this last step, you will have created perhaps two to three new levels in Unreal, each containing a Revit phase model. In Chapter 7, we will revisit and start to create steps to portal from one level to another, Using either the Unreal levels you have created here – or the Steventon Rectory and 8 College Street levels you will create in Chapter 6.

CHAPTER 3   CREATING AN HBIM 3D MODEL FOR A CITY ACROSS DIFFERENT ERAS

Create a Phased Rebuilding Plan/Model

Having defined the chronological sequence of additions, demolitions, and modifications of your building/city over time, this segment is aimed at helping you to achieve this effectively in Revit.

Step 1: Understand the Project Timeline

1. Identify the key stages of your project:
   - **Existing Conditions** (Pre-construction)
   - **Demolition Phase**
   - **New Construction Phase(s)**
2. Break down the sequence further if needed (e.g., multiple construction phases).

Step 2: Set up Phases in Revit

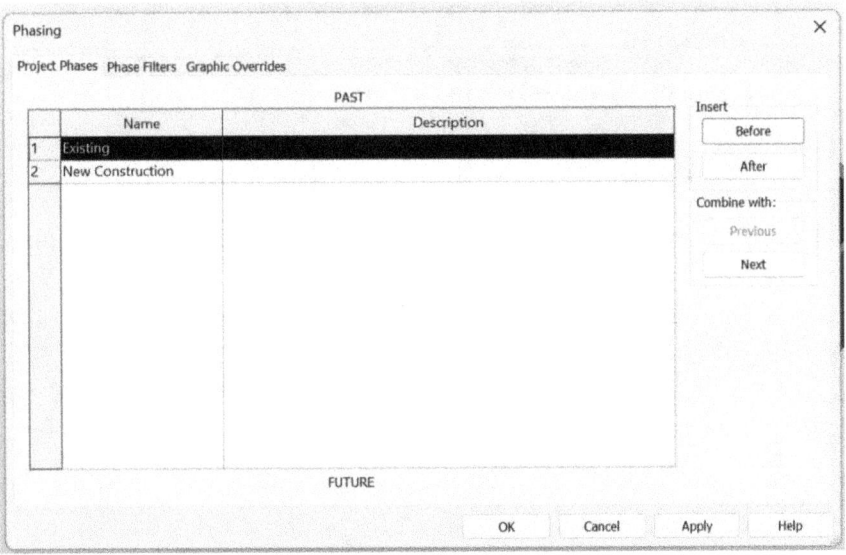

Figure 3-10. Phasing dialogue box for creating new phases

CHAPTER 3   CREATING AN HBIM 3D MODEL FOR A CITY ACROSS DIFFERENT ERAS

1. Open the Phasing dialogue:
   - Go to Manage ➤ Phases.
   - In the Phases dialogue, create each stage as a separate phase. Example:
     - **Existing**
     - **Demolition**
     - **Phase 1 – Foundations**
     - **Phase 2 – Structural Framing**
     - **Phase 3 – Interior Fit-out**
2. Phase filters
   - Set up Phase filters in the same dialogue to control visibility for each stage. Typical settings include
     - **Show All**
     - **Show Complete**
     - **Show New**
     - **Show Previous + Demo**

CHAPTER 3   CREATING AN HBIM 3D MODEL FOR A CITY ACROSS DIFFERENT ERAS

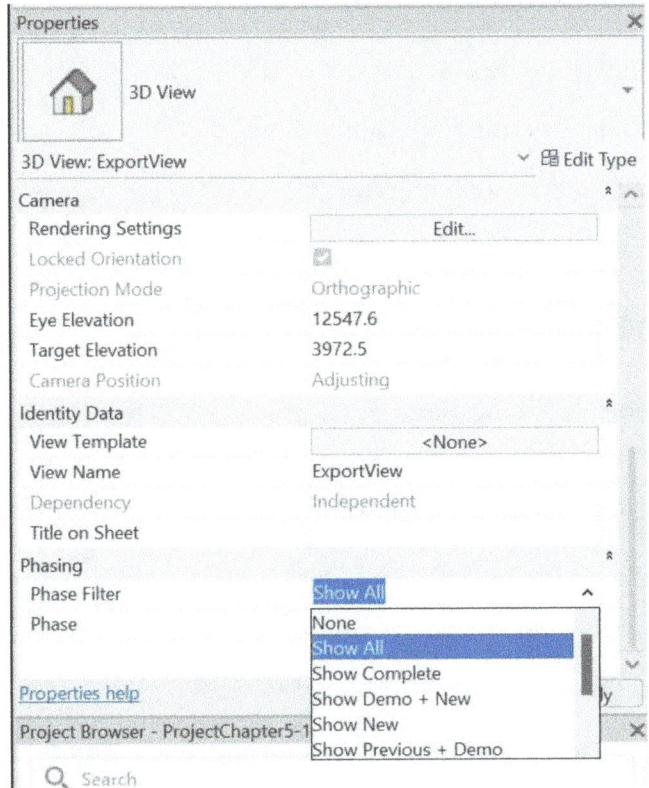

Figure 3-11. *Phase filters available*

Step 3: Assign Phases in Elements

1. Select elements in your model and assign them to the correct phase using the Properties Palette under the Phasing section:

   - **Phase Created:** Assign the phase when the element is built.

   - **Phase Demolished:** Assign the phase when the element is demolished.

   Example Workflow

   - A wall that exists in the current building:
     - **Phase Created:** Existing

- A wall to be demolished during phase 1:
  - **Phase Created:** Existing
  - **Phase Demolished:** Demolition
- A new structure built in phase 2:
  - **Phase Created:** Phase 2

Step 4: Manage View Settings for Clarity

1. Create dedicated **floor plans**, **sections**, and **3D views** for each phase.
2. In each view's **Properties**, adjust
   - **Phase Filter** (to control visibility)
   - **Phase** (to define the active phase)

Recommended Filters for Key Views

- **Existing Conditions Plan:** Use "Show Previous + Demo".
- **Demolition Plan:** Use "Show Demo Only".
- **New Construction Plan:** Use "Show New Only".
- **Final Phase or Completed Model:** Use "Show Complete".

Step 5: Use Phase Graphics for Visual Clarity

1. Adjust **Graphic Overrides** for demolished and new elements to distinguish them.
2. Go to **Manage ➤ Phases ➤ Graphic Overrides** to customize color schemes:
   - **Existing:** Gray
   - **Demolished:** Red (or dashed lines)
   - **New Construction:** Solid black or blue

CHAPTER 3   CREATING AN HBIM 3D MODEL FOR A CITY ACROSS DIFFERENT ERAS

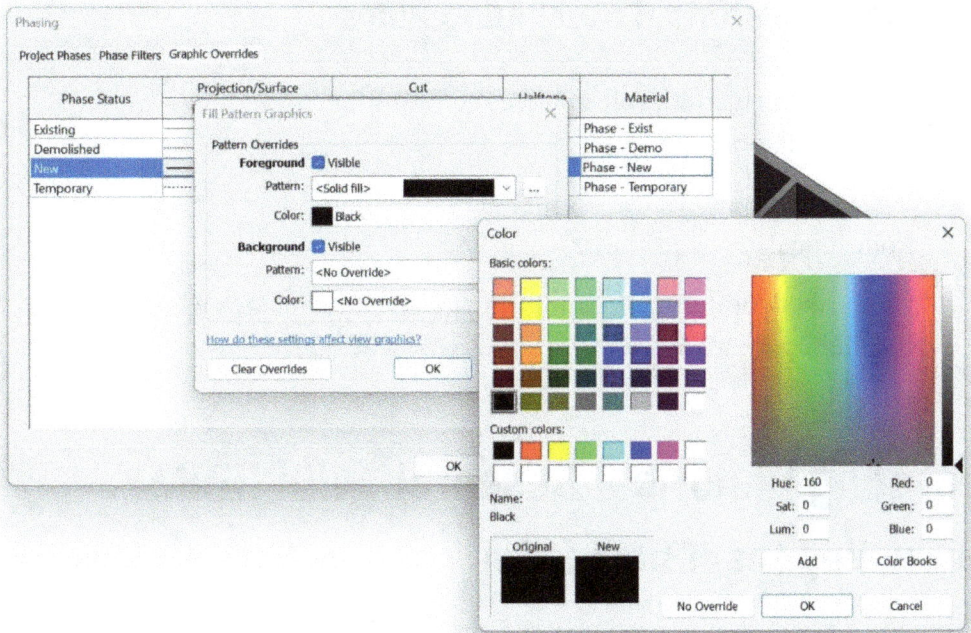

Figure 3-12. *Graphic Overrides for phasing*

Step 6: Annotate the Timeline

1. Use **Keynotes**, **Text Notes**, or **Tags** to label key milestones, especially in construction drawings.

2. **Callouts** can highlight critical changes, like structural upgrades or heritage features being reinstated.

Step 7: Export for Unreal Engine (Datasmith Workflow)

1. Before export:
   - Ensure phases are clearly defined.
   - Consider separating phases into linked models for improved control in Unreal Engine.

More details can be seen in the previous section regarding exporting to Unreal Engine using a Datasmith workflow.

Quick Tips for Historical Rebuilding Plans

- Use **Phasing** to model alternative scenarios for speculative reconstructions.

- For heritage models, use **View Filters** to distinguish original elements from speculative additions.

- Use **Linked Models** to maintain clear phase distinctions when combining multiple datasets (e.g., archival evidence + new data).

Integrating Historical Research with HBIM
Constructing the HBIM Model

In this section, we will start to prepare your Revit HBIM project for construction. You will now have the majority of data you will need to confidently start creating your building, but the Revit environment will probably require changes before you start to build. The following are areas that I recommend checking/adapting to suit your project. Revit is actually quite good at adapting input of imperial measurements to metric and vice versa, but it is infinitely better to ensure you have the settings set to the correct version.

- **Setting up the model environment**
    - Define project base settings (units, coordinate system, levels). Depending on the age of your building, you might need to change project units to Imperial. For some buildings though, this might not be the case, as in the case of Beaulieu Abbey, which was initially constructed with metric units after discovering the dimensions taken from the remaining south wall of the nave tied quite clearly with metric measurements. This was a surprise until I discovered that a French Master Mason was employed for the start of the abbey, with French workers also coming over to Beaulieu to help in the build. The layout, especially the semi-circular apse, is in the French style.

Changing the coordinate system would be valuable if the building is going to be used for conservation/restoration purposes, but if you are going to take the building into Unreal, generally it would be placed according to the map layout. For Winchester City, for example, it was more important to place the buildings according to the map overlaying the landscape, which wasn't set at real-world coordinates. It was set at True North though, which is important for daylight/sun settings, mostly because the Unreal system uses real-time daylight and location settings, and therefore could have an impact on whether it is night or day, sun setting, etc., for your scene, all of which we cover in detail in Chapters 6 and 7.

Hopefully you will have elevational heights for your building, so you would therefore be able to set up initial levels (more can be added or changed as you work through the project, but it is good to make a few levels that you can work with initially).

- **Building the model for each period**

  - **Structure:** Model walls, roofs, columns, and load-bearing elements based on historical construction techniques

    Depending on the time period, the majority of the standard BIM wall types will not be suitable for your building; therefore, it is a good time to create the different wall types you will require in the project. You can do this by duplicating and renaming (with a relevant new name) a wall type and editing its structure and width of each structural element. Then duplicate this (and rename accordingly) for each of the different widths and wall structure types. For the medieval buildings, and knowing I was taking the model into Unreal, I used a wall type without additional faces such as a plaster depth facing a brick wall. This was because it would create overlapping/coplanar faces that can create problems in other programs as well as Unreal. The walls I created in this way still had the structural information available via the standard data fields (with the ability to add more data fields as required), adding BIM/HBIM data to the model. The model could then still be interrogated for data/information once it is in Unreal (via Datasmith) but not with all the additional faces of a full structural wall type included.

For a restoration project, it would perhaps be sensible to create fully as a Revit model as mentioned earlier, but then for the model going into Unreal, it might be worth duplicating and simplifying structures to reduce the adverse effects of overlapping faces. This sounds quite a lot of work, but it would be worth having a full Revit model that provides visual and structural data as a BIM and HBIM model, and a simplified copy that can be used more easily for the interactive experience and storytelling model in Unreal.

- **Materials:** Apply historically accurate textures (stone, timber, plaster, brick). Similarly here, you may have a need for two models depending on what your project requirements.

  - For a full Revit model that can be used for restoration and conservation purposes, building into the BIM objects, for example, walls and historically accurate textures, would be a necessity both visually and for data purposes.

  - For taking into Unreal, in my experience working with students, it would be beneficial for the model to not have materials and to use Unreal's materials and textures, or derivatives of, to create a library of historically accurate materials and textures that can then be applied. More detail about materials can be found in Chapters 6 and 7.

  - Importing different buildings created by different people having used their own version of realistic materials created a bloated material library within Unreal with many duplicates of typical materials such as glass, white paint, brickwork, brass, and similar. I have found that remedying this problem is quite time-consuming, so for our future Unreal projects, the models imported will need to be material-free as much as possible to avoid an excessive amount of unused materials.

- **Architectural elements**
  - Doors, windows, and decorative moldings should match their period-specific styles.

    Even with a growing amount of period style libraries developing from manufacturers with regard to restoration purpose/use in Revit, there will inevitably be windows, doors, moldings, and similar detail that will require modelling. Not all the Revit models available are fully parametric, so there will be a need to adapt or model from scratch. There are some excellent library resources that have been listed in Chapter 6, and by looking through these, you may be able to find a similar style that you can adapt, which may be quicker than starting from scratch. One thing to consider again with regard to structure of the objects is coplanar faces if taking the model into Unreal.

  - Use parametric families in Revit to enable variations across different eras. In creating your objects and knowing that older properties do not always have identical sizing, i.e., windows that have need to be shortened in length or height due to internal changes to partitioning, parametric modelling will make this much more straightforward with just the one object (family file). In Chapters 6 and 7, we go through this in detail for some of the interior and exterior additions to the Steventon Rectory and 8 College Street scenes.

- **Interior elements** (if needed)
  - Ceilings, fireplaces, staircases, and joinery elements.

    As above with regard to available libraries and considerations regarding parametric modelling where possible.

  - Period-specific furniture and fixtures.

    There are even more period style furniture objects and fixtures, but perhaps you may still need to add your own furniture items. There were not as many libraries available when I modelled Dunster Castle, or even Beaulieu, and therefore decided to recreate specific pieces that were of historical interest for each property only. The early concept was to use generic period style pieces for furnishing the rooms, other than those specific historical interest pieces. In this way, I managed to build a personal library of different period objects, some of which have come in handy as reference for remodeling in Revit. Today, there are many more period objects available in Revit, which makes that initial concept much easier to achieve, i.e., modelling historically significant items, but the remaining to be generic. The reason being the time it would take to model every item of furniture would be too costly – perhaps a project worth thinking about for retirement, i.e., creating period style furniture and architectural elements in Revit!

The majority of the furniture objects I have collated over different projects were purchased from libraries such as TurboSquid but were not parametric or Revit based (Dunster was prior to Revit), therefore 3DS Max objects.

- **Integrating HBIM metadata**
  - Attach historical data (e.g., construction dates, restoration records) to elements.

    To attach historical data such as construction dates and restoration records to elements in Revit, the best method depends on how you want to access and manage the information. Here are the most effective methods:

    1. **Custom parameters (best for structured data)**

        Use **Project Parameters** or **Shared Parameters** to create structured fields that store historical metadata.

        - **Project Parameters:** Good for information that stays within the project file

- **Shared Parameters:** Ideal if you need consistency across multiple projects or want to schedule/export the data

How to add custom parameters:

1. Go to **Manage ➤ Project Parameters** (for project specific) or **Manage ➤ Shared Parameters** (for cross-project use).

2. Click **Add**, and choose the **Category** (e.g., Walls, Floors, Windows).

3. Set **Parameter Type** to **Text, Date, or Number** depending on the information.

4. Apply the parameter to elements that need historical data.

Example Parameters: "Original Construction Year", "Restoration Date", "Architect/Builder", "Historical Significance Level"

2. **Key Schedule (for tabular organization)**

If you need a more structured approach for categorizing historical data, a Key Schedule can be useful

- Create a **Schedule** that includes the custom parameters.

- Use a **Key Schedule** to link common attributes to multiple elements (e.g., "Victorian Era" linked to a set of buildings).

Example:

- A "Historical Phases" key schedule could list
    - **Key Name:** "Georgian Restoration"
    - **Construction Year:** "1750"
    - **Last Restoration:** "1995"
    - **Architect:** "John Smith"

3. **Revit families with embedded metadata**

   For custom elements (e.g., historical windows, doors, columns), embed metadata inside **Family Parameters**. We cover Family Parameters in much more depth and practical detail in later chapters; here it is worth knowing that it is possible to create your own for adding embedded metadata to your Revit model.

   - Families can include parameters such as "Year of Origin" and "Renovation Date".
   - You can also add **Instance Parameters** for unique historical notes.

4. **Revit tags and notes (for visual annotations)**

   - Use **Custom Tags** with labels that pull from historical parameters.
   - Add **Text Annotations** in views to highlight specific restoration details.

Validating the Model Against Historical Data

At different points through this chapter, I have mentioned about the importance of checking/confirming accuracy of data you have found and want to use for building your HBIM project. I have found that this becomes more critical once you have visuals of your 3D model, details that on paper make sense but somehow in the making/3D modelling throw up conundrums or just do not look how they should when compared with artistic sketches or similar. It could simply be a single dimension not quite right – or too true an angle. Therefore, once modelled, you may want to put those digital plans, elevations, and 3D details/3D views in front of an expert that can review with more objective and professionally informed eyes (not to say you are not one of these experts, but fresh eyes always help). At the very least, cross-check your model's dimensions with historical records. You also need to check the accuracy of materials, not just dimensions.

I would recommend that there are probably three occasions when you should cross-check the model's accuracy, once the building shell has been created, i.e., before you start adding detail and then when you have added all the detail such as columns/pillars/vaulting/panelling or similar (this was certainly an important stage with regard to Hyde Abbey and the cloister pillars and took additional time and cross-checking to confirm accuracy). The third time would be the "sign off" of the building, i.e., confirmed and ready to use in your scene or publish to Sketchfab, which is a shared repository for models either for use commercially or for heritage collections. In summary, to ensure you have covered all bases regarding the accuracy of your model, please remember to

1. **Cross-check accuracy**
   - Compare model dimensions and styles with historical records.
   - Ensure materials and techniques align with the construction knowledge of the period.
2. **Peer review and expert input**
   - Involve historians and conservation architects for validation.
   - Adjust inaccuracies based on new findings.

Visualization and Interactive Presentation

All your research, data gathering, puzzle solving, and accuracy checking/confirmation lead to creating visuals for others to understand the changes to the building (or city) over time, possibly also of the people that lived in those buildings and aspects of their lives. By now, you/your team will know so much about the building and similar buildings of either a specific moment in time or a series of moments in time, but others will not; they will rely on your visuals. It is only by creating visual scenes – still, animated, interactive, or virtual – that others will get to also have an insight to the life of that building. As the saying goes, "a picture is worth a 1000 words"; in this case, with all the research, your scenes are worth so many more.

I am not too sure that if I had not spent a couple of days research and then a day creating a basic Revit model of Beaulieu Abbey, and a simple Revit-based walkthrough (in places way too fast!), that I would have been able to 'impress' the Beaulieu team sufficiently enough to allow me to work with them to reconstruct the abbey as it was in its heyday, in its construction phase and how it looked as it was demolished. The short video walkthrough provided an animated visual of how the abbey church and its monastic buildings looked, externally and internally. It provoked ideas in how visitors could engage with not just the abbey but the lives of the monks that lived and worked there. I can still remember the look on the archivist's face when she saw the project nearly completed and could see monks sitting in the Nave pews, highlighting the sheer size of the building. It was one of the largest Cistercian abbey churches in the UK, an amazing building.

CHAPTER 3   CREATING AN HBIM 3D MODEL FOR A CITY ACROSS DIFFERENT ERAS

So visualization is incredibly important, and with today's technology developments, it is now very possible for fully interacting with the digital models, exploring the interior, and being able to pick up objects and interrogate those objects or the building for additional information, in a variety of ways. For Virtual Cities – Winchester, visitors/users will be able to portal between different time periods, engage with objects, and engage with avatars and their stories. For this to be successful, the visuals need to be as realistic and accurate as possible. Lighting, textures/materials need to be convincing. Thankfully, Unreal Engine and real-time rendering make this so much easier today than in September 2008 when we were working with Revit and 3DS Max only on the Beaulieu Abbey project when Unreal Engine was not available, nor real-time rendering. All rendering had to be in 3DS Max (or similar such as Maya and Softimage), on a frame by frame basis, each frame possibly taking anything from 30 minutes to 2 hours plus depending on the complexity of lighting and materials.

The following aims to help you with these different aspects:

- **Rendering and animation**
  - Generate realistic visualizations to depict how the building evolved by layering different construction phases in Revit or HBIM. Use phasing tools to segment the different time periods (see the previous section) and apply appropriate materials to show weathering, renovations, or structural changes. Once modelled, export to Unreal Engine or Twinmotion via Datasmith for high-fidelity rendering, adjusting lighting, textures, and environmental effects to enhance realism. Further information can be found under "Digital storytelling."
  - Use Unreal Engine or Twinmotion for immersive experiences by optimizing assets for real-time rendering. In Unreal, leverage Lumen for dynamic lighting and Nanite for detailed geometry without performance loss.

- **VR/AR integration**
  - Develop an interactive timeline-based navigation system using Unreal's Blueprint scripting system. Implement triggers or UI overlays to allow users to select a time period and update the scene dynamically, swapping assets, materials, or entire sections of the model.

CHAPTER 3   CREATING AN HBIM 3D MODEL FOR A CITY ACROSS DIFFERENT ERAS

- Allow users to toggle between different time periods by utilizing visibility layers or morphing animations. In Unreal, this can be achieved using level streaming or Blueprint-based visibility controls, while in Revit, you can predefine view states that show different construction phases for AR integration. You can also use Unreal's 3D portal configuration, which enables you to teleport seamlessly from one level to another: those levels being the different eras/points in time. This is how we are stepping into different scenes within Virtual Cities and is quite effective.

- **Digital storytelling**

  - For visual storytelling in phased heritage reconstructions, blending accurate data with engaging narratives is key. With Unreal or Twinmotion, you can incorporate historical narratives and/or guided tours. The framework below focuses on how to guide the user through the timeline of changes while emphasizing historical narratives.

    1. **Establish a Clear Narrative Structure**

       A compelling reconstruction should combine both historical accuracy and emotional engagement, which can be achieved by defining the following elements:

       Key Milestones: Ensure you have identified pivotal changes in the building's timeline (e.g., original, construction, significant additions, damage, restorations).

       Historical Figures or Events: Tie phases to personal stories (e.g., *"Our lovely kitchen became a billiard room when George Luttrell, my great, great, great, great grandson and namesake, employed Anthony Salvin, a well-known architect of his time to modernise Dunster Castle in the mid-18th Century. The overall modernisation of Dunster apparently cost in the region of £25,350, equivalent to £3.8 million in your time, an amount I cannot comprehend in my time"* (edited from National Trust Dunster Castle Guidebook, 1995).

Cultural Context: Highlight social, political, or artistic shifts reflected in the building's evolution.

Example Structure for a Historical Timeline Narrative

- **Scene 1 (Introduction):** Present original structure as it first appeared.

- **Scene 2 (Conflict/Change):** Showcase key demolitions, additions, or damages over time.

- **Scene 3 (Resolution):** Conclude with the present state or a speculative "ideal" restoration.

2. **Visual Techniques for Phased Storytelling in Unreal Engine**

To emphasize different phases of construction, consider the following possible techniques:

a) **Phased Transparency and Highlighting**

- **In Unreal Engine:**
    - Use **Datasmith Tags** or **Material Instancing** to apply unique materials to phased elements.
    - Employ **Opacity Fades** to gradually reveal demolished or new elements.
    - Use **Outline Materials** (glowing edges) to highlight elements as they appear or disappear.

    Example: As you transition from 18th century architecture to Victorian modifications, it is possible to use a warm color fade to distinguish each phase.

b) **Interactive Elements for Deeper Engagement**

- Introduce clickable hotspots that reveal archival documents, sketches, or voiceovers when a phase is highlighted.

- Use **interactive portals** to transition between phases directly in VR experiences.

  Example: A visitor could "step back" into an earlier phase of the building using an interactive portal, seeing the original layout before additions.

3. **Audio and Environmental Cues**

   Sound design can elevate the storytelling:

   - Introduce **ambient soundscapes** to differentiate time periods (e.g., 18th-century street noise, WW2 air raid sirens).

4. **Curating the Visitor's Journey**

   - Define the intended path your audience should follow.
   - Use **Lighting Cues** or **Pathway Markers** to guide viewers intuitively.
   - Introduce **Points of Interest (POIs)** that reveal historical insights without overwhelming the user.

   Example: A guided VR tour could feature a glowing marker over an 18th-century fireplace prompting the story of its original stone carving.

5. **Testing and Refinement**

   - Regularly test your visual sequences with potential users to ensure clarity.
   - Balance **Educational Content** with immersive engagement to maintain user interest.

Tip Use audience feedback to refine pacing, visual clarity, and narrative balance.

CHAPTER 3   CREATING AN HBIM 3D MODEL FOR A CITY ACROSS DIFFERENT ERAS

Summary

This chapter has provided a combination of guidance and step-by-step processes to help you in scoping out your project. In addition, it helps to understand what needs to be achieved depending on whether you are intending to build a single HBIM model to provide restoration and conservation data, or a simpler constructed model, i.e., less "faces" but still embedded with BIM/HBIM data that will be imported to Unreal Engine.

It will be important to consider whether you have one model that makes full use of Phases providing the life of the building from when it was first constructed to when it no longer exists or lasting to present day. This may be decided for you if working for a company that has provided a project brief, but it might also need you to say what is possible and what isn't, hence this chapter.

To see the different phases, elements of the building will be hidden according to the phase it belongs to, so you would not be able to see more than one time period at a time, other than view captures on Sheets, or exported as visuals. The way this building can be taken into Unreal is by creating 3D views of each of the phases and working through different processes to ensure each 3D view has the other phases turned off completely.

The other option could be several separate models of the building, each of a specific period of time, i.e., stand-alone models that are embedded with data for that period alone. These would be much more straightforward to export to Unreal, i.e., no processes involved in hiding different phases.

It will really depend on the type of project you are involved with or working on and therefore the requirements, your own or your client's, and the skillsets and expertise of your team. It will also depend on the material you are able to use to inform those changes over time, particularly with the periods/pinpoints of time you choose to use.

As well as these considerations, you will need to think about how you are going to share this knowledge with others and how you are going to store the HBIM model, i.e., accessible repositories, and ensure the model's longevity, which would still allow future additions as either new research emerges or restorative changes are made.

Then, of course, how will you visualize the building, will it be stand-alone, or will it be in a typical environment, with the environment also needing to be updated/changed? What stories would you include for visitors to engage with, or do you intend the model to be purely a record for preservation and conservation purposes? Will you be required to share your process/knowledge with different communities via presentations or scholarly articles, or will the output be purely for an interactive application/website?

I hope this chapter has helped you to clarify what you need to consider in scoping out your project and what is possible via different routes.

The next chapter will take you through a step-by step process of data collection required for the Virtual Cities project using the two examples of Winchester Castle and Steventon Rectory mentioned at the beginning of this chapter.

References

Atkinson, Thamas Dinham (1941) Winchester Cathedral Close. Papers and Proceedings. Vol.15 (1), pp. 9–26. Hampshire Field Club & Archaeological Society. https://www.hantsfieldclub.org.uk/publications/hampshirestudies/digital/1940s/vol15/Atkinson.pdf

Biddle, Martin (2020) Winchester: A City of Two Planned Towns. In book: The Land of the English Kin. DOI: 10.1163/9789004421899_004

Biddle, Martin (2016) An Historical Map of Winchester (Town & City Historical Maps), Publisher: The Historic Towns Trust. https://www.historictownstrust.uk/maps/an-historical-map-of-winchester

Castellogy (2025) Image: Reconstruction of the castle as it may have appeared in the mid-13th century, seen from the east. Castles and town walls in England and Wales - Winchester Castle. www.castellogy.com [Accessed Feb. 15, 2025]

Crook, Dr John (1984) The Wainscot Book: The Houses of Winchester Cathedral Close and their Interior Decoration A.D. 1660–1800. Hampshire Records Office for Hampshire County Council, Southampton. ISBN-13: 978-0906680032

Doubleday, Arthur (1903) Houses of Cistercian monks: Abbey of Beaulieu', in A History of the County of Hampshire: Volume 2, William Page, London, British History Online. https://www.british-history.ac.uk/vch/hants/vol2 [Accessed March 5, 2025]

Fowler, Sir James Kingston (1911) A History of Beaulieu Abbey, AD 1204–1539. The Car Illustrated. London

Hope, W.H. St John and Brakspear, Harold (1906) The Cistercian Abbey of Beaulieu in the County of Southampton. An original article from the Archaeological Journal. Volume 63, pp. 129–186. Royal Archaeological Institute, London

McPherson, Nicholas (2015) Hyde Illustrated – Architectural Aspects through History MA thesis. Personal copy provided in person.

Milner, J. (1798) Winchester Castle from the West Engraving, History and Survey of the Antiquities of Winchester Vol. II, p. 473 image published in The Castle Studies Group (CSG) Journal No 33, p. 228, 2019-2020

National Trust (1995) Dunster Castle, Somerset Guidebook (Purchased by the author in 1995)

Speed, John (1610) Map of Hampshire published in Theatre of the Empire of Great Britain, 1611. Hampshire Cultural Trust. https://collections.hampshireculture.org.uk/object/john-speeds-map-hampshire-1611

Walker, Linda Robson (2007) Why Was Jane Austen Sent away to School at Seven? An Empirical Look at a Vexing Question. Persuasions On-Line, JASNA. http://www.jasna.org/persuasions/on-line/vol26no1/walker.htm

CHAPTER 4

Step One: Data Collection

This chapter explores the crucial phase of data collection for historical building reconstruction. It covers various data sources, such as historical documents, archives, photogrammetry, and LiDAR technology, emphasizing the importance of accurate and comprehensive data collection in the HBIM process. The purpose of this chapter is to equip readers with the necessary knowledge and tools to gather historical data effectively, as accurate data is the foundation for successful HBIM reconstruction.

We will do this by working through two quite different examples of buildings that no longer exist, which also belong to two different time periods, each spanning approximately five to ten years across the stated year, allowing for a little flexibility in the data available.

The first building is Steventon Rectory, Steventon, in Hampshire, the home of Jane Austen's family. The building no longer exists, no evidence at the site other than a pump in the field. Therefore, we will need to discover when it existed, i.e., when it was constructed, when the Austin family lived there, and when it was demolished. This building will be linked to Virtual Cities – Winchester via a story related by Jane Austen while she is staying at 8 College Street in 1817, the place she is known to have stayed in before she died.

The second building is Winchester Castle, Hampshire. A historically significant building that also no longer exists except for the Great Hall and the base of the North Tower. This building was chosen by one of the students, Tomas Dulkys, as his client project, the client being Virtual Cities. Tomas is a mature student, studying Digital Media Design – 3D Visualization. His research needed to discover how the castle looked in approximately 1400 (across five to ten years of 1400) to tie in with the two stated time periods of the Virtual Cities – Winchester 1400 and 1800 project.

CHAPTER 4 STEP ONE: DATA COLLECTION

Gathering Historical Documents, Architectural Plans, and Visuals

We have covered quite a bit of detail about data required, the type of data, and how important it is to ensure the accuracy of information you use to reconstruct your building/city, so now we will put this in action. This section will provide the methods used to determine the most accurate data to work with and how that data is recorded ready to access when we want to embed that information within the model. We will also need to ensure we retain the source of the data for future reference and for requesting permissions to use if being published with the model.

Steventon Rectory

Although I have already completed a satisfactory level of research to enable the earlier Jane Austen Demo, there is a need to clarify information. I know Jane Austen lived there with her family, when that was, when her father retired, and when they left the Rectory to move to Bath. There is quite a breadth of information available on these aspects of Jane's life and family. But there is much more information required to be able to model the interior of the Rectory and ensure the earlier assumed information from the external sketched views available is correct, or at least sufficiently correct. There are a significant number of Jane Austen Societies and organizations that have already completed thorough research into the life of Jane Austen and her writing. Researching their sites and publications and going to talk with them would probably provide a wealth of information, which would help in this regard.

I also need to find more details with regard to the style of the period in which the Rectory was built, i.e., which period does it belong to? Information regarding the period in which it was built will help with detailing windows, doors, roof, chimneys, etc. In doing so, I can perhaps also discover the materials used. If I cannot find when the Rectory was built, how else would I find out what period style to use? I could do this by researching other buildings in the area that still exist from before the Rectory was demolished and searching for planning permission documents, conservation reports, listed building status, and historical vernacular.

Why does the original Rectory no longer exist? A new one was built across from the original Rectory and higher up. Why? For the purpose of modelling the building, you might think this may not matter, but perhaps it was falling into disrepair? If this was the case, then the interior would need to be presented as such, i.e., this information would have an impact on how we presented the interior details.

So what do I need to find out? Table 4-1 shows a list of the information (in no particular order) I need to be able to confidently model the Rectory, externally and internally.

Table 4-1. Steventon Rectory research list for modelling data

Externally	**Internally**
Building shape	Internal layout
Building construction details	How many bedrooms
Window construction details inc. positions	How many other rooms/what were they and how were they positioned
Door construction details inc. positions	Does it have a kitchen/where
Roof construction detail inc. positions	Does it have a bathroom/where
Chimney construction details inc. positions	If not a bathroom, where were the toilets and how did they wash or take a bath
Porch construction details	Was there electricity
Wall construction details	How did they heat their water
Where were their electricity lines attached if they had electricity	Where was water drawn from, i.e., a pump, did they have a water butt/well?
If they had a well and or pump, where were they situated	What material lined the walls, if any
If they had a water butt, did the house have guttering that fed into it	What were the partitions constructed of
Are there external buildings, what was their purpose	What were the internal doors construction – were they painted, or wood preserved
What were the external buildings' construction material	How many staircases

(*continued*)

CHAPTER 4   STEP ONE: DATA COLLECTION

Table 4-1. (*continued*)

Externally	Internally
What would the state of repair be like in Jane's time	What was the construction of the staircases, sizes, materials
Were there plants climbing the walls	What was the ceiling height of the rooms? Was this different for upper floors to the ground floor
Were there trees/shrubs against the house	Was there an attic
What was the layout of the grounds immediately around the house, drive, fencing etc	Were there bedrooms/rooms in the attic
What was the drive material	How many fireplaces
Fencing, wood or metal, what did it look like	Were there fireplaces in the bedrooms/which bedrooms
Which way did the building face with regards to sunlight	What did the fireplaces look like – were they different for each of the rooms,
Was the Rectory built on flat ground or sloped, i.e. would there be a difference in levels internally	How were the rooms furnished – were there curtains, how were they fixed, did the rooms have skirting boards etc
What were the external heights, i.e. wall, doors, windows of all the buildings	Which family members had which bedroom – may determine the way in which it is presented
Would there have been a damp proof course	Were any rooms used for purposes not related to a typical home i.e. prayer room/classrooms (based on being a rectory and possibly a school)

For the internal layout, it would be sensible to create a typical BIM room schedule including known furniture items and accessories. For the rooms where this information cannot be found or confirmed, I would look to homes of a similar nature and period and furnish with generic period items. For an activity in VR or on screen, I could leave a couple of room types empty with a library of assets for users to furnish the room as they wish.

CHAPTER 4   STEP ONE: DATA COLLECTION

Winchester Castle

The research for Winchester Castle was undertaken by Tomas Dulkys, which he has compiled using a Miro Board, which has been valuable for not just compiling his information but also using for presenting to his client and the necessary progress presentations to his tutors and peers. From this, I am able to share with you how Tomas planned his research and where he went to find the data he required to model the castle. Tomas has chosen to continue the project across the two semesters; the final deadline for the project is May 2025; therefore, he will have completed the project by the time the book has been written.

The project overview entailed:

1. Objective

    a. **Goal:** To create an accurate 3D model of Winchester Castle as it would have appeared in the 1400s

    b. **Purpose:** To showcase the architectural and historical significance of Winchester Castle during the medieval period

2. Scope

    a. **Focus:** The project will focus solely on the 3D modelling aspect, using 3DS Max to recreate the castle's structure and details.

3. Key features

    a. **Historical Accuracy:** Emphasis on using historical references and accurate architectural details.

    b. **Detailed Modelling:** High level of detail in the 3D model, including textures and materials that reflect the period.

    c. **Research Based:** The model will be based on thorough research including historical maps, images, and architectural studies.

4. Tools and software

    a. **3DS Max:** Primary software for creating the 3D model

    b. **Additional Tools:** Any other software or tools that might be used for texturing or rendering

CHAPTER 4　STEP ONE: DATA COLLECTION

5. Expected outcomes

    a. **3D Model:** A detailed and historically accurate 3D model of Winchester Castle

    b. **Documentation:** A report or presentation detailing the research process, modelling techniques, and historical references used

Tomas is a Digital Media Design – 3D Visualization student and wanted to enhance his 3DS Max skills over the course of this project instead of using Revit. This is absolutely fine, especially as the model will be taken into Unreal Engine as a significant asset for the Virtual Cities – Winchester 1400 level. BIM/HBIM data can be added in Unreal, and I know that this model, by not being a Revit model, will not include hidden objects; it will be just the one model, i.e., not a phased model.

The areas that Tomas set out to research were mostly external, sourcing information for how the castle elements would have looked. I have translated a few of the information boards on his Miro Project to the list shown in Table 4-2.

Table 4-2. *Winchester Castle research list for modelling data*

Externally	External Measurements
Overall Building shape	Westgate Dimensions
Curtain Wall construction/details	Curtain Wall dimensions
Windows/arrow slits construction/details inc. positions	Upper Bailey Donjon (Walled complex)
Door construction/details inc. positions	Overall Castle Measurements
Roof construction/detail inc. positions	The Great Hall measurements
Towers – how many and shape	Tower measurements
Gatehouses/keeps construction/details	Arrow slit measurements
Wall construction/details	Door sizes
The Great Hall construction/details	Merlon measurements
Great Chapel construction/details	Crenel measurements
The King's Chambers construction/details	
The Queen's Chambers construction/details	

(continued)

Table 4-2. (*continued*)

Externally	External Measurements
The Great Bridge construction/details	
The Buttery construction/details	
The Pantry construction/details	
The Almonry construction/details	
The Salsary construction/details	
The Great Kitchen construction/details	
The Chapel of St. Judoc construction/details	
The Chapel of St Thomas construction/details	
Buttress construction/details	
Corbels construction/details	
Crenellation/Battlement construction/details	
Staircase construction/details	

For being able to detail the interior, Tomas will need to research further information which may be more difficult to discover and possibly require researching typical details of castles built in the same style and period. The majority of the information covered up to the 13th century (1200s), and we really need the reconstructed 3D castle model to refer to the 1400s. There is information relating to the South East and North East towers dated 1370 and a basic map outline of the city in 1400. There is also documentation relating to dilapidation due to lack of funds for the upkeep of the castle in the late 1300s. The combination of this data may mean we can present the castle how it looked in the mid-1300s but with signs of disrepair, for the 1400 period.

Aspects that Tomas would need to review and add to his research for the 2nd part of the project are therefore listed in Table 4-3.

Table 4-3. *Winchester Castle additional research list for modelling and visualization*

External	Internal
What was the state of repair like in 1350–1400	How many rooms were there
Were there plants climbing the walls	What did the royal chambers look like
Were there trees/shrubs against the curtain walls	What material lined the walls, if any
What was the layout of the grounds immediately around the main entrance/Westgate	How many fireplaces
Which way did the building face with regard to sunlight	Were there fireplaces in the bedrooms/which bedrooms
	What did the fireplaces look like – were they different for each of the rooms
	How were the rooms furnished – were there curtains, how were they fixed
	What was the ceiling height of the rooms, was this different for upper floors to the ground floor
	How many staircases
	What was the construction of the staircases, sizes, materials
	How were the service buildings furnished
	What furniture would there have been through the living quarters?

Recording the Data for Embedding into the Unreal Scenes

For both buildings, the resulting information for the different elements listed will need to be recorded alongside the values discovered. For Virtual Cities, I created a spreadsheet that has/will help us to record all the data collated, the sources, permissions requested, the categories involved, and similar for each of the buildings modelled. In addition to the HBIM data, tabs are provided for the different elements of the project. There is a project object library tab, buildings tab, Unreal scenes tab, website creation tab and then data type and codes, and BIM/HBIM Object categories. The last two tabs provide information for inputting abbreviated data. Having worked with BIM for a number of years and HBIM for the heritage reconstructions, the spreadsheet has evolved over the years to include more and more data, more latterly the permissions' columns. Previously this used to be just references, ensuring that all work was referenced to its source; for academic purpose, this was generally fine, but now we have set up Virtual Cities Ltd and another Ltd company, "Time Tourist" (and writing this book); it is much more important to gain permissions for work that might be used commercially/published commercially. The working spreadsheet for Virtual Cities has been adapted for this book to show just the two buildings involved rather than all of them and can be sourced from the accompanying website.

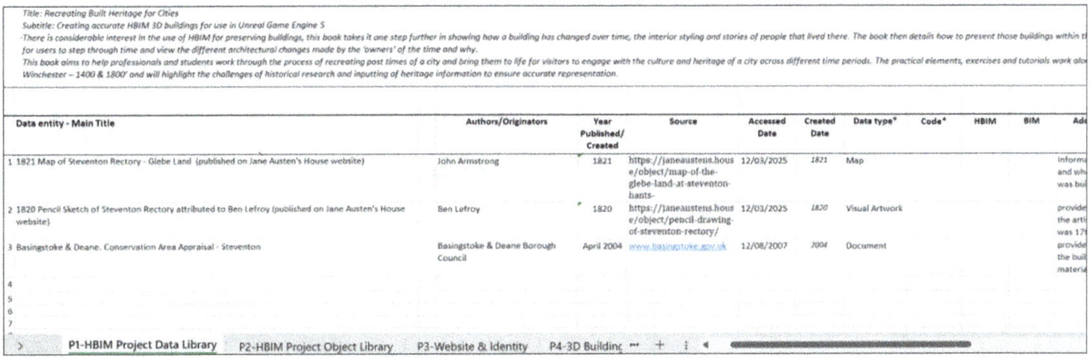

Figure 4-1. Virtual Cities' HBIM Project Data Library (by the author, 2024)

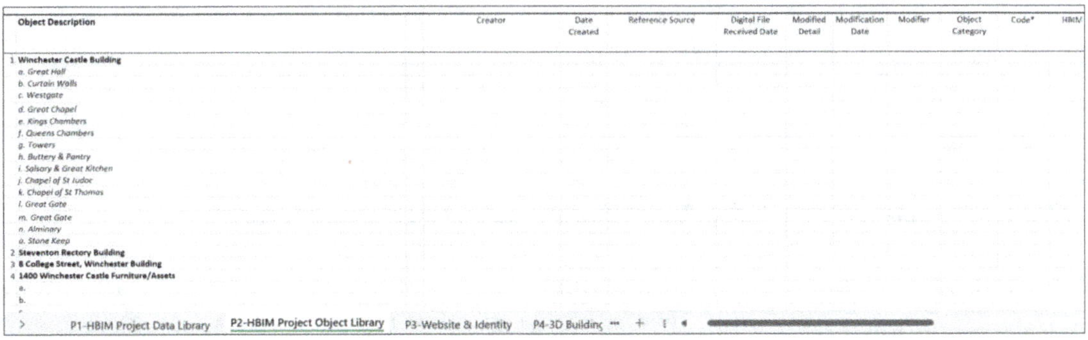

Figure 4-2. Virtual Cities' HBIM Object Data Library (by the author, 2024)

CHAPTER 4   STEP ONE: DATA COLLECTION

This is the way I generally work; it is not a common standard for HBIM data; this is still being discussed nationally and internationally, i.e., what data should be recorded and how. The debate is on how the multiple variants of objects on historical buildings can be standardized. I am not sure they can be other than via subcategories of subcategories, as many as needed, and flexibility to include data discovered at a later date. In the meantime, the spreadsheet included may help for your project in keeping everything recorded in one file.

VIRTUAL CITIES - HBIM DATA LIBRARY - TYPE, CATEGORY & CODE		
DATA TYPE	CATEGORY	CODE
Archaeological Surveys (Architectural Plans)	Architectural Drawings	AD-A
Architectural Blueprints	Architectural Drawings	AD-B
Architectural Details	Architectural Drawings	AD-D
Architectural Elevations	Architectural Drawings	AD-E
Architectural Floor Plans	Architectural Drawings	AD-F
Planning Permission drawings	Architectural Drawings	AD-P
Energy Analysis	Analysis Records	AR-E
Light Analysis	Analysis Records	AR-L
Bill of Materials	Construction Detail	CD-B
List of Materials	Construction Detail	CD-L
Existing Digitisation Assets	Digital Asset	DA-E
Historical Films	Moving Image	MI-H
Video Footage	Moving Image	MI-V
Cadastral Maps	Maps	MP-C
Historical maps	Maps	MP-H
Historical Urban Plans	Maps	MP-U
Early Photogrammetry	Photogrammetry	PG-E
Aerial Imagery	Photographic Image	PI-A
Colour Photographs	Photographic Image	PI-C
Drone Imagery	Photographic Image	PI-D
··· P4-3D Buildings P5-Unreal Scenes & PM	**Data Type & Code**	BIM-HBIM Object C

Figure 4-3. *Virtual Cities' HBIM Data Library – Type, Category & Code (by the author, 2024)*

Finding the Answers and Substantiating Data

We now have a more defined list of data queries we need to answer to help us accurately model the interior and exterior.

One aspect that was easy to answer was for modelling the interior of Steventon Rectory, and that was about washing, water, and toilets. This was partly based on knowledge built from personal experience. My parents moved into a tied house, an old Cornish rectory, when I was in my early teens. This house was very similar in many ways to the Rectory the Austen family lived in, although it was considerably smaller, i.e., just two main reception rooms and what could have been a back scullery and two large bedrooms and a small box room between. There was an impressive central entrance hall and staircase. The reason for mentioning is that in my research regarding how to model the interior of Steventon Rectory, thinking specifically about whether there were bathrooms, running water, and toilets, I remembered my time at Lamorran Rectory and the lack of any form of sanitation. The water was mainly from the nearby pump (approx. five minutes walk away) and the very large water butt against the front side of the house. The only toilet was a tiny garden hut that had a wooden bench with a bucket-sized hole, under which was a bucket (I won't go into how or where this was emptied!).

Figure 4-4. Lamorran Rectory, Cornwall, showing the garden "hut" that used to serve as our only toilet

Lamorran was a micro hamlet, two semi-detached cottages right on the creek edge, going up the hill from the creek was the church and small cemetery with a bell tower, and immediately behind was the rectory, with a courtyard of barn-type buildings between the road and the rectory.

Figure 4-5. *The parish of Lamorran. The rectory is circled in red. The buildings to the east are farm buildings. To the south west of the church is the old bell tower. Below this a pair of semi-detached houses. There used to be a Manor, but it was just a ruin in the woods along the road to the west when we lived at Lamorran.*

There was not any form of mains supply except for electricity, which was supplemented by a standby generator. One of the reception rooms had a multifuel range and cooker socket and became the room we cooked, ate, and washed in. The other large room became a storage room of unpacked boxes and an old organ that my father was learning to play. A far cry from the convenience of bathrooms and living/private spaces families have today. Washing was a case of a strip wash in front of the range, with the door locked to keep other family members from just walking in. Going to the toilet at night, my sister and I had a bucket in the room to save traipsing across the lawn with a torch to the dark, cobweb-infested hut, which in the dark felt far too close to the cemetry wall and bell tower.

Figure 4-6. *The church of St Moran right next to the garden "hut"*

This was in the 1970s, so I can only imagine the Austens had similar experiences with Steventon Rectory, but instead of being an exception, it was how people lived, albeit with metal bathtubs and china chamber pots, and no electricity.

Supporting this, I also thought of my grandparents' house in London and their experience of having to go outside to the shed in the courtyard, again in the dark. Furthermore, the house my mother lives in now, a Victorian semi-detached "villa," when it was built, there was a scullery/back kitchen with taps and a ceramic sink with a wooden draining board but no evidence of a bathroom; the toilet was the shed at the side of the house. One of the four bedrooms was converted to a bathroom in the late 1970s; the outside toilet is still used, but at least there is an inside one now.

Figure 4-7. *The toilet on the right is almost identical to our old toilet at Lamorran except made of brick instead of stone. The toilet on the left is identical to the one at my mother's house.*

The outside toilet and lack of a bathroom are well documented in historic house layout books, although a detail easily overlooked when creating historic interiors, i.e., not really thought about, nor do we as adults generally want to involve this aspect of life in our cultural stories. Children, though, are intrigued by the history of toilets. Horrible histories and medieval stories about how people went to the toilet are generally guaranteed to get them giggling and exclaiming.

Therefore, in answer to my research query on bathrooms and toilets for Steventon Rectory, personal experience and historical records prove that they did not exist, and therefore, the interior modelling will not need to include room space for sanitary appliances.

It would be good if most of the queries were as simple. Another query re Steventon Rectory was finding out the period of the building, i.e., when it was constructed. This would help in understanding the materials used, the style of the house, and internal layout. This was not as straightforward, and after considerable research, I found three mentions of the 16th-century rectory from different Jane Austen Societies/Blogs (Jane Austen Society, 1997; Book Lady Deb, 2010; Walker, 2007). I also discovered the reason Jane's brother Edward demolished the family home was mostly due to dilapidation and possibility of being flooded from the same sources. Therefore, building a new rectory on the other side of the road higher up made sense. The original rectory being at the bottom of a slope was quite likely to flood with extremely heavy rainfalls. The building was 200–250 years old, being built in the 16th century, and therefore, quite possible that it was suffering dilapidation.

CHAPTER 4　STEP ONE: DATA COLLECTION

For Winchester Castle, Tomas had a list of measurements he needed to find and details of the different buildings, how they were constructed, and the materials used. Table 4-4 shows the measurements he has managed to find so far; the sources of measurements can be seen in Dulkys' notes in Figure 4-7.

Table 4-4. *Winchester Castle measurements*

Externally	External Measurements
Westgate dimensions	60 feet (18 m) length; 20 feet (6 m) width; 60 feet (12 m) height
Curtain wall dimensions	9 feet (2.7 m)
Upper Bailey Donjon (Walled complex)	100 feet (30 m) x 100 feet (30 m) square
Overall castle measurements	850 feet (259 m) length; 250 feet (76 m) width; 55 feet (16.8 m) height. Approx. 4 acres (1.6 hectares) overall
The Great Hall measurements	110 feet (33.5 m) length; 55 feet (16.8 m) width; 55 feet (16.8 m) height
Tower measurements	North Apex Tower (Lower Ward) outer dia. 43 feet (13 m); inner dia. 30 feet (9 m); wall thickness 6.6 feet (2 m) Round Apex Tower (known as the Round Tower) approx. 40-60 feet (12-18m) Tall
Arrow slit measurements	4 inches (10 cm) wide; 6 feet (1.8 m) high
Door sizes	
Merlon measurements	4–5 feet (1.22–1.52 m) wide; 3–7 feet (0.9–2.13 m) high
Crenel (Castellation) measurements	2–3 feet (0.61–0.91 m) wide

Tomas also needed to research the materials which for the Great Hall, and therefore possibly other buildings of the castle, consisted of flint with stone dressing; see Figures 4-8 and 4-9.

CHAPTER 4   STEP ONE: DATA COLLECTION

Figure 4-8. *The Great Hall, Winchester (courtesy of Dulkys, 2024)*

CHAPTER 4 STEP ONE: DATA COLLECTION

Figure 4-9. Remains of the Henry III Round Apex Tower and Curtain Walling, Winchester (courtesy of Dulkys, 2024)

The information for the above was resourced across approximately 17 resources according to Tomas' Research board, ranging from local history documents to British History Online, plus a visit to The Great Hall and to the Hampshire Records Office. Academically, Wikipedia is generally not allowed as a reference, although we know students may well use this as a starting point for further research (see Figure 4-10 for Tomas' Reference Miro Board). As the client and his previous lecturer, I was impressed to see the effort he had gone to with recording the sources and his visit to The Great Hall and Records Office. It shows a proficient level of proactivity, research, and a logical yet creative method of recording the data. It also highlights individuals will use methods that make sense to them if not provided with a system to use.

Across the many heritage organizations, historical architectural practices, and academia organizations working on HBIM, there will be many systems, either developed or in development, to record similar researched sources of HBIM data. Trying to

179

standardize the various systems is an ongoing task, again by different organizations, national and international. Until such a system is standardized, I am certain, with the growth of reconstructing digital twins, lost heritage reconstructions, and similar, there will be further individual/organizational data records developed. Feel free, therefore, to either use the spreadsheet resource on the accompanying website or follow Tomas' more visually aesthetic system or develop your own. As long as the data is recorded, it can always be amended to a standardized system at a later date.

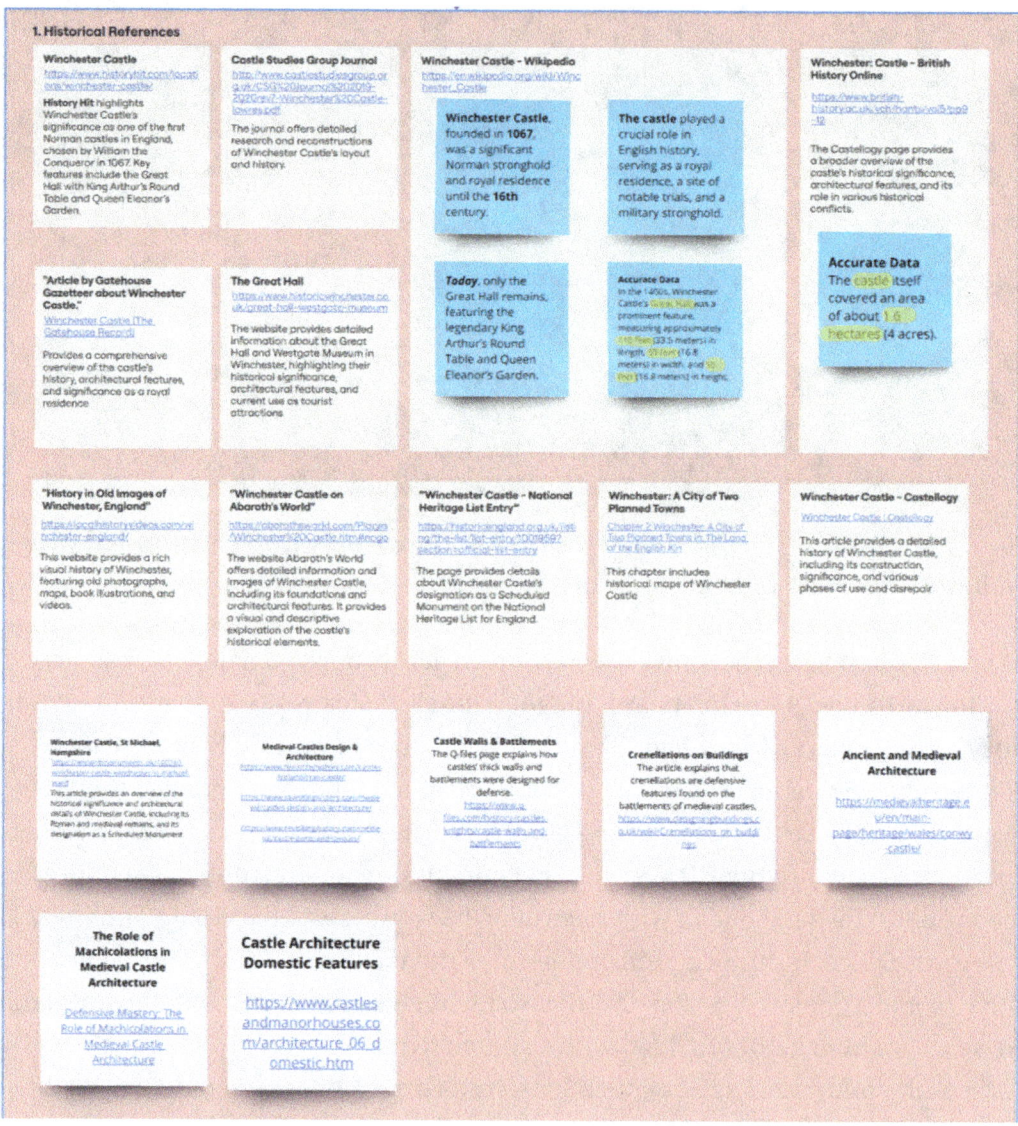

Figure 4-10. *Virtual City CP Research Reference Miro Board (courtesy of Dulkys, 2024)*

The data we use will still require substantiation, and as previously mentioned, in my experience, building the basics with some detail and presenting/showing local historians, archaeologists, conservationists, and heritage architects your progress and why, i.e., the derivation of your data resources, produces more impactful, valuable results.

Further results of research answering the query lists above can be found on the accompanying website under "Research Informing the Project."

Section Summary

The examples of Steventon Rectory and Virtual Cities – Winchester illustrate the depth of research required, from architectural details to historical context, and the importance of addressing data gaps through various research methods. This section also highlights the complexities of data standardization in HBIM and advocates for meticulous data recording, irrespective of the system used, to ensure adaptability for future standardized systems. Ultimately, it underscores that thorough research and well-substantiated data are foundational to impactful and valuable historical reconstructions including the necessity of source retention for future reference and usage permissions.

The following section provides information about using photogrammetry and LiDAR. Although as yet unused in Virtual Cities – Winchester, we are planning to make use of these technologies for helping to map the textures of the ruins of the castle, castle wall, Wolvesey, St Mary's College, and similar. It would also be valuable in scanning the structure of the remaining tower and cellar if we are able to gain the permissions required. Therefore, step-by-step how-to's have been included and recommendations regarding equipment.

Utilizing Photogrammetry and LiDAR Technology

For Steventon Rectory, other than interior artifacts that may still exist from Jane's family life at Steventon, which she may have taken to Bath and subsequent homes, there is no need for the use of photogrammetry or LiDAR/3D scanning. According to a record of the Steventon Rectory auction sale of family items on May 5, 1801, most of the home assets were sold with a later auction for the animals and farm equipment held in September (Jane Austen Society, 1997). This is a useful record for recreating the assets for the family home, but most likely modelled from scratch rather than through scanning.

CHAPTER 4   STEP ONE: DATA COLLECTION

It may be possible to scan aspects of The Great Hall, or perhaps the complete building as it currently stands. The 1400 model would have been different; there were multiple dormer windows that were later removed when the hall was adapted in the mid-1300s, the previously lowered walls being built up between the dormers and a plain parapet added. Therefore, as a simple box-shaped structure, it was straightforward to model. Scanning, though, would pick up the roof structure which may not have changed too much since the mid-1300s amendments, although the building has been re-roofed several times. It would also pick up on the material which we could then re-use for texturing other buildings. A scan may already exist from dating the timbers/structure, so we will need to research this further.

Another element that could be scanned is the remains of the Round Tower, which would also pick up on the cellar below and attached curtain walling. To do this, we will need permission and bring in a company to do this for us, not having the equipment to use. From memory, I believe the University may have LiDAR, so it could be a project for the archaeology students, unless, of course, this has already been done, possibly by the University, Hampshire County Council, or a local history/archaeology organization.

We could definitely use photogrammetry for artifacts within the Great Hall and will look to do this for Tomas' 2nd phase of his client project.

Personally, I am in awe of the technology now available for scanning buildings, the use of drones, and similar, which then creates excellent results as 3D models of the interior and exterior of buildings. I have watched the development of scanning and LiDAR (and similar) since first starting The Talking Walls in 2004. LiDAR was first used for imaging buildings in the 1960s, long before The Talking Walls and my interest in heritage architecture. It was initially designed for topographic mapping and military applications. However, its use for detailed building imaging and architectural documentation became more prominent in the 1990s, when advancements in laser scanning technology made it feasible for high-resolution 3D mapping.

One of the earliest notable applications in built heritage documentation was in the late 1990s and early 2000s, when projects began using terrestrial laser scanning (TLS) to capture precise 3D data of historical structures. This was further enhanced in the 2010s with the integration of LiDAR into drones and mobile mapping systems, significantly improving efficiency and accessibility. In the 1990s and early 2000s, LiDAR equipment was prohibitively expensive for most SMEs. Terrestrial laser scanners (TLS) cost anywhere from £100,000 to £300,000, which would make them more feasible/accessible for large institutions, government agencies, and well-funded research projects.

Other factors that made LiDAR challenging for SMEs at the time included

- **Computational Requirements:** Processing large point clouds required high-end workstations, which added to costs.
- **Specialist Training:** LiDAR data required expertise in point cloud processing, which was a niche skill.
- **Limited Software Options:** Early software was not as user-friendly or widely available, making workflows complex.

By the 2010s, costs started to decrease significantly with the rise of cheaper, portable scanners and drone-mounted LiDAR, making it more feasible for SMEs and independent practitioners. Today, LiDAR solutions range from high-end systems to more affordable options like mobile-based LiDAR (e.g., iPhone Pro models with built-in scanners).

The following have been recommended as SME-friendly LiDAR solutions covering different price ranges and applications:

1. **Handheld and Mobile LiDAR Scanners** (affordable and versatile)

    - **Leica BLK2GO** (£50,000): High-end but portable, great for real-time indoor and outdoor scanning
    - **GeoSLAM ZEB Horizon** (£35,000–£45,000): Good for rapid mapping and heritage sites
    - **Apple iPhone/iPad Pro** (built-in LiDAR) (~£1,000+): Limited range but useful for small-scale scans and quick site capture with apps like Polycam or SiteScape

2. **Drone-Mounted LiDAR** (mid-range for surveying and mapping)

    - **DJI Zenmuse L1** (£10,000–£15,000, plus drone): Good entry-level option for aerial scans with RGB camera integration
    - **YellowScan Mapper** (£30,000+): Compact and accurate for larger site scans, commonly used for archaeological and heritage work

3. **Terrestrial Laser Scanners** (best for accuracy and built heritage)

    - **Leica BLK360** (£20,000): Lightweight, easy to use, and great for historic buildings

    - **Faro Focus S350** (£30,000+): High-precision long-range scanner, often used in HBIM projects

    - **Trimble X7** (~£25,000): Automated registration, making it user-friendly for SMEs

4. **Open Source and Budget LiDAR Sensors** (for R&D and prototyping)

    - **Livox MID-40** (£1,500): Affordable for custom-built applications but requires software development

    - **Intel RealSense L515** (£400, now discontinued but available secondhand): Good for close-range scans, but not high accuracy

For SMEs, a good balance of affordability and usability would be Leica BLK360 for terrestrial scanning, DJI Zenmuse L1 for drone-based mapping, and GeoSLAM ZEB for mobile scanning. Scanning can be costly, especially with permissions involved. Therefore, if you already have the measurements, modelling from scratch might be the more practical and controlled option. You could always incorporate photogrammetry for textures if you want to bring in real-world surface detail without the expense of a full LiDAR scan. Below are considerations for knowing when to use LiDAR/photogrammetry and when to model from scratch.

When to Model from Scratch

1. Model in Revit/3D software if

    - The building is simple or modular (e.g., modern structures)

    - You have incomplete scan data, making manual reconstruction easier

    - The final asset needs precise parametric control for HBIM or analysis

- The building is fictional or heavily reconstructed (e.g., missing historical structures)

Best Hybrid Workflow

- Use scan data as a reference for scale and proportions.
- Model clean geometry in Revit or Blender for easier editing.
- Import into Unreal Engine for visualization.

When to Use LiDAR or Photogrammetry

1. Use LiDAR if
   - You need precise structural geometry (e.g., walls, columns, facades)
   - The building has clear, solid surfaces (good reflectivity)
   - You need data for BIM workflows (Revit-friendly)
   - The site is complex or inaccessible, making manual measurement difficult
2. Use photogrammetry if
   - You need high-detail textures and organic shapes.
   - The object/building has a lot of surface detail (e.g., statues, ornate facades).
   - You are working in a real-time visualization environment (Unreal Engine).
   - Budget constraints make LiDAR too expensive.

Best Hybrid Workflow

- Use LiDAR for structural accuracy (walls, floors, roofs).
- Use photogrammetry for fine details (decorations, materials).
- Merge datasets in RealityCapture, Agisoft Metashape, or CloudCompare before cleaning in Blender/Revit.

Should you decide to use LiDAR and photogrammetry and want to take the scans into Unreal, not having done this before, then the following step-by-step workflow should help you, ensuring efficiency and high-quality results.

Step 1: Preparing LiDAR Data for Unreal Engine

LiDAR data is typically in point cloud format (LAS, E57, PLY) and needs to be processed before Unreal can use it.

1.1 Convert LiDAR Point Cloud to Mesh

Software: Autodesk Recap Pro, CloudCompare, or Blender

- Import your .LAS or .E57 file into Autodesk Recap Pro (or CloudCompare for open source).
- Clean and filter the data (remove noise, unnecessary points).
- Export as a .FBX or .OBJ mesh (Unreal cannot handle point clouds directly).
- If needed, use Blender or MeshLab to simplify the mesh (i.e., reduce the poly count).

1.2 Optimize Mesh for Unreal

- Use Blender's Decimate Modifier or MeshLab to reduce polygon count.
- Keep important structural features but remove excess data.
- Export as FBX (best for Unreal Engine).

Step 2: Preparing Photogrammetry Data for Unreal Engine

Photogrammetry scans tend to have high poly counts and need optimization.

2.1 Process the Photogrammetry Scan

Software: RealityCapture, Agisoft Metashape, Meshroom

- Import photos and generate a 3D model with textures.
- Export as high-poly OBJ or FBX.

2.2 Clean and Optimize the Mesh

Software: Blender, ZBrush

- Retopologize the mesh (reduce polygons while keeping details).
- Bake high-poly details into normal maps for performance.
- Create LODs (Levels of Detail) for better real-time rendering.

Step 3: Importing into Unreal Engine

3.1 Import Mesh into Unreal Engine

- Open Unreal Engine (UE5 recommended).
- Use Datasmith (for Revit models) or import as FBX (for processed scans).
- Enable Nanite for high-poly scans (UE5 only).
- Adjust scaling and positioning in the viewport.

3.2 Apply Materials and Textures

- If using photogrammetry, ensure textures are applied correctly.
- Convert high-res textures into PBR materials using Substance Painter or UE's material editor.
- Use Normal Maps and AO Maps to enhance surface details.

Step 4: Enhancing and Optimizing in Unreal Engine

4.1 Use Nanite for Large Models

- If your model is very detailed, enable Nanite for real-time optimization.
- Nanite handles massive polygon counts efficiently, improving performance.

4.2 Improve Performance

- Add level of detail (LOD) models for distant viewing.
- Use HLOD (Hierarchical LODs) for large environments.
- Optimize lighting with Lumen (UE5) or baked lightmaps (UE4/UE5).

4.3 Add Interactivity and Storytelling

- Use Blueprints for interactive exploration.
- Add VR compatibility if required.
- Implement Unreal's Sequencer for cinematic storytelling transitions.

Summary: Best Workflow

1. LiDAR → Autodesk Recap/CloudCompare → Blender for cleanup → Unreal Engine (Nanite if UE5).
2. Photogrammetry → RealityCapture/Metashape → Blender (retopo and texture baking) → Unreal Engine.
3. Revit Models (if applicable) → Export via Datasmith → Unreal Engine.
4. Optimize with Nanite, LODs, and Blueprints for best performance.

Example Workflow for Integrating a Scanned Historical Building into Unreal Engine

Here you will find an example workflow for integrating a scanned historical building such as one of the houses for the Virtual Cities – Winchester project into Unreal Engine. This process focuses on using LiDAR for structure and photogrammetry for details, optimizing the model for real-time rendering.

Case Study Project: A historical townhouse with intricate facades and interior details
Goal: To create an optimized, interactive Unreal Engine scene

Step 1: Capturing the Historical Building

1.1 LiDAR Scan for Structural Accuracy

Equipment: Terrestrial LiDAR scanner (e.g., Leica BLK360, Faro Focus)

- Scan the exterior and interior of the building to capture walls, columns, and rooms.

- Export as .E57 or .LAS (point cloud format).

1.2 Photogrammetry for Surface Details

Equipment: DSLR camera or drone

- Take overlapping high-resolution photos (80% overlap).

- Capture ornate facades, textures, and decorations separately.

- Import into RealityCapture or Agisoft Metashape to create a high-resolution 3D model.

Step 2: Processing the Scan Data

2.1 Convert LiDAR to Usable Mesh

Software: Autodesk Recap Pro/CloudCompare

- Import the LiDAR point cloud.

- Clean the data (remove noise, misaligned scans).

- Export as .FBX or .OBJ mesh.

2.2 Optimize the Photogrammetry Model

Software: Blender/ZBrush

- Retopologize the photogrammetry mesh (reduce polygon count).
- Bake high-res details (normal maps, ambient occlusion).
- Export as optimized FBX with textures.

Step 3: Importing into Unreal Engine

3.1 Setting Up the Project

Software: Unreal Engine (UE5 recommended)

- Create a new Unreal project (use Nanite enabled for high-res models).
- Import LiDAR structure as an FBX.
- Import photogrammetry details separately for better material control.

3.2 Optimizing the Building Model

- Enable Nanite for high-poly assets (e.g., facades).
- Apply LOD (level of detail) settings for performance.
- Use Datasmith if working with a Revit model.

3.3 Applying Materials and Lighting

- Convert photogrammetry textures into PBR materials using Unreal's Material Editor.
- Use Substance Painter for texture refinement.
- Set up Lumen (UE5) or baked lighting for realistic shadows.

Step 4: Enhancing the Experience in Unreal

4.1 Adding Interactivity with Blueprints

- Create interactive buttons to display historical information.
- Set up VR compatibility for immersive exploration.
- Implement Sequencer for historical reconstructions (e.g., time-lapse of building changes).

4.2 Optimizing Performance

- Use HLOD (Hierarchical Level of Detail) to reduce draw calls.
- Implement Occlusion Culling to load assets only when visible.
- Optimize collision meshes for smoother navigation.

Step 5: Final Export and Deployment

- Package the project for PC, VR, or WebGL.
- Export cinematic sequences using Unreal's Movie Render Queue.

Summary Workflow

1. LiDAR Scan → Clean in Recap Pro/CloudCompare → Export as FBX
2. Photogrammetry → Process in RealityCapture → Retopologize in Blender
3. Unreal Import → Enable Nanite, LODs, and Materials
4. Interactivity → Add Blueprints for storytelling, VR compatibility
5. Optimize and Deploy → Package for PC, VR, or Web

CHAPTER 4   STEP ONE: DATA COLLECTION

Common Issues When Importing LiDAR Data into Unreal Engine

When importing LiDAR data into Unreal Engine, common problems include crashes with large files, color issues, flickering, and performance issues, especially in VR, requiring careful file format selection and plug-in configuration to ensure smooth integration.

Below is a more detailed breakdown of potential problems and solutions.

File Size and Engine Crashes Problem: Large LiDAR point cloud files (e.g., over 90GB) can cause Unreal Engine to crash, particularly during import or when running in VR.

Solution

- **Further Reduce File Size:** Edit the point cloud files to result in even smaller point cloud files or try decimating the data before import.

- **Optimize LOD:** Experiment further with the level of detail (LOD) settings in the LiDAR plug-in to reduce the number of points rendered at a distance.

- **Use a Stable Engine Version:** There are reported issues with specific Unreal Engine versions, so try using a version known to be stable with LiDAR point clouds, such as 5.0.3.

Color Issues Problem: Colors in LiDAR point clouds might not render correctly, appear as incorrect colors, or disappear altogether.

Solution

- **Verify Color Data:** Ensure the LiDAR file contains color data and that the import settings in Unreal Engine are configured to read and display the colors correctly.

- **Use Supported File Formats:** Experiment with different file formats such as .LAS, .LAZ, and .E57 to see which one renders colors best.

- **Check for Missing Data:** If colors are missing, it might be because the point cloud file itself does not contain color information.

Performance Issues Problem: Rendering large point clouds can lead to performance drops and stuttering, especially in VR.

Solution

- **Optimize Point Cloud:** Try reducing the number of points in the scene by using LODs, or by removing unnecessary points.

- **Disable Motion Blur:** Motion blur can cause flickering or performance issues with point clouds, so try disabling it.

- **Adjust Rendering Settings:** Experiment with different rendering settings in Unreal Engine, such as the point cloud budget and frustum culling, to optimize performance.

- **Use a Lower-Overhead Environment:** Consider using a programming environment with lower overhead, like OpenGL using LWJGL or similar gaming library, if performance is critical.

VR Issues Problem: Crashes or other issues may occur when running LiDAR point clouds in VR, especially with certain versions of Unreal Engine.

Solution

- **Use a Stable Engine Version:** As mentioned above, try using a version of Unreal Engine known to be stable with VR and LiDAR point clouds.

- **Optimize for VR:** Ensure that the point cloud is optimized for VR by reducing the number of points and using appropriate LOD settings.

- **Check for Plug-in Compatibility:** Make sure that the LiDAR point cloud plug-in is compatible with the version of Unreal Engine and the VR platform you are using.

Alignment Issues Problem: LiDAR point clouds might not align correctly with other assets or terrain in Unreal Engine.

Solution

- **Use a Consistent Coordinate System:** Ensure that all assets and point clouds are using the same coordinate system.

- **Reproject Data:** If necessary, use tools like GDAL to reproject the LiDAR data to a coordinate system that is compatible with Unreal Engine.

- **Fine-Tune Transformations:** Experiment with transformations in Unreal Engine to align the point cloud with other assets.

Collision Issues Problem: Collision with the point cloud might not work as expected or might cause performance issues.
Solution

- **Build and Enable Collision:** Make sure to build and enable collision for the point cloud asset.

- **Adjust Collision Complexity:** Experiment with different collision complexity settings in Unreal Engine to optimize performance.

- **Use a Collision Mesh:** Consider creating a separate collision mesh for the point cloud to improve performance.

In my experience with a handheld 3D scanner, albeit with a full-size clay horse and not a building, parts of the surface where the sun was coming through and lighting sections of the model had an impact on the resulting point cloud. It showed gaps and would not form a mesh for that area (see Figure 4-11). It was quite frustrating working out why, but once I did, I was able to revisit and re-scan, making sure the model was completely in the shade. Nonetheless, there were still a few gaps which I needed to manually "knit" to form a full model and prepare it for 3D printing. Admittedly, this was in 2014, the handheld scanner was a reasonably new Artec Scanner. A later experience with a tomb in Malmesbury Abbey was with my Samsung mobile, which resulted in a really good, almost instant, clean 3D model, although my colleague's iPhone scan was much better. I have yet to use LiDAR for a building, colleagues have though, and it is impressive what can now be achieved.

CHAPTER 4   STEP ONE: DATA COLLECTION

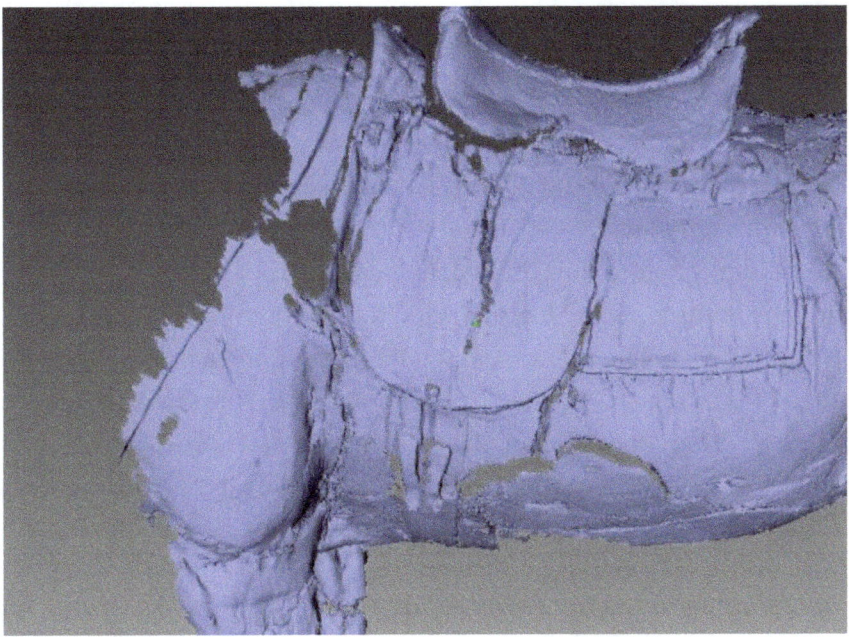

Figure 4-11. *3D scan of clay horse showing gaps where sunlight had caught the model (Wilson, 2015)*

Section Summary

In Chapter 2, there are several case studies demonstrating the use of LiDAR (or similar) and photogrammetry, which may also be used in deciding how this can add to your project. The case studies may also help to understand the workflows used, what, if any problems occurred, and how they may have resolved them. There are several issues that can occur as highlighted above, but there is also a growing resource of people's experiences with LiDAR, photogrammetry, and 3D scanning that should help you take this further.

The next section is about collecting geographic and spatial data, which for Virtual Cities was so important to be correct. Winchester is mostly hilly, 200 feet above sea level, with various waterways in the valley. Modelling by hand in Unreal Engine, i.e., using landscape sculpting, would not have been sufficiently accurate for the precise placing of buildings. We will cover how we created the landscape as well as where and how to collect the data required.

CHAPTER 4   STEP ONE: DATA COLLECTION

Collecting Geographic and Spatial Data

It doesn't really matter whether you start recreating the building first or creating the topography/landmass for your city or creating the immediate context for your individual buildings, i.e., you do not have to wait for the building to be completed before collecting the geographic and spatial data. For Virtual Cities – Winchester, students had already created a few buildings before the Unreal Landscape was in place.

In creating the landscape for Unreal, I tried many options and plug-ins, one or two much easier to work with than others, but what I might find easy to understand and work with might not be a good method for someone else. Therefore, in this section, I will include a couple of different methods; you may already know one or two yourself; they are just a guide, and more options are becoming available all the time. One such option is an Unreal open source plug-in called Cesium. Cesium originated in aerospace to track moving objects in space; it was spun out as an independent company in 2019. When I first saw what it could do, I thought, yay, all the hard work of collecting maps, making sure they were the right scale, negated. It was all there, a topographical surface (Google Maps), 3D geospatial map complete with trees and buildings (the buildings can be hidden), why use anything else?

Figure 4-12. *Cesium 3D Geospatial plug-in for Unreal, a quick test for suitability for Virtual Cities – Winchester (Wilson, 2025)*

CHAPTER 4   STEP ONE: DATA COLLECTION

After an evening of downloading and going through the simple steps of activating it within Unreal Engine, grabbing the coordinates of College Street, Winchester, and inputting to the Cesium dialogue box latitude and longitude fields, and hey presto, a 3D version of Winchester is visible. After exploring various queries such as "are you able to hide the buildings," I realized that however impressive and perfect for modern-day quick visualizations and backdrops (see quick result for Winchester in Figure 4-12), it was not going to be of help to me for the Virtual Cities project. Why? It is of modern day, and although you can hide the buildings, you cannot edit the topography; you cannot paint, push, and pull in Unreal; it is not (yet!) possible. Nothing is ever that easy in 3D unfortunately. If you would like to try/use for your own projects, I have added a step-by-step guide at the end of this section.

Therefore, back to the more involved methods of collecting geospatial data, maps, and visuals of how the city looked in 1400 and 1800. There are many options with regard to data sites to collect your height and map data; it is literally a minefield of knowing which is the best for detail, low or no cost and then the methods used to choose and export that data, the data type, what grayscale depth it needs to be, and so much more.

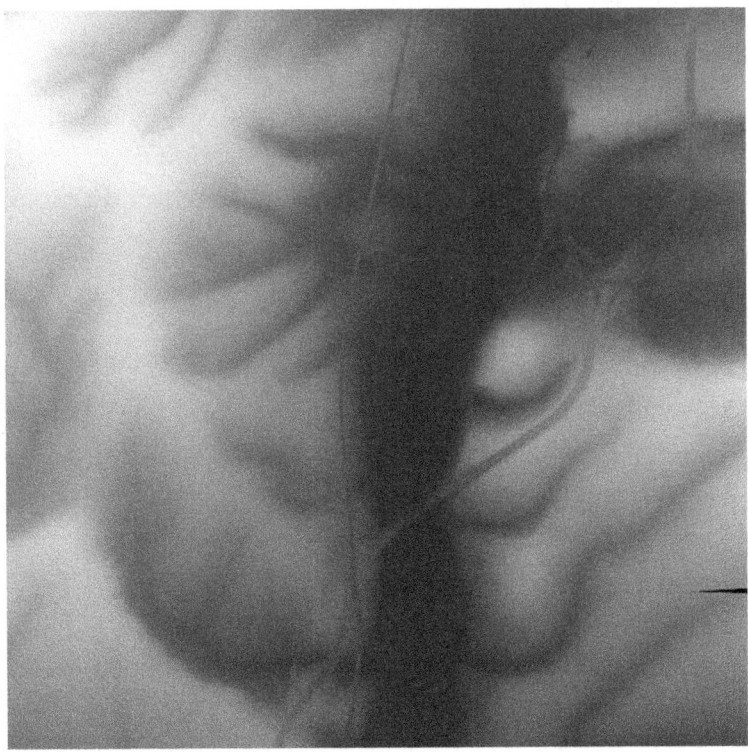

Figure 4-13. *Grayscale heightmap for current-day Winchester (Wilson, 2021)*

197

CHAPTER 4   STEP ONE: DATA COLLECTION

To obtain accurate Digital Elevation Model (DEM) data for a specific location, such as Winchester, for use in Unreal Engine, the following provides a list of key sources and considerations:

Key Data Sources

- **Data.gov.uk**
    - This UK government website is a valuable resource for open data, including environmental data. You can find DEM datasets provided by agencies like the Environment Agency.
    - Specifically, the "SurfZone Digital Elevation Model (DEM) - 2m" dataset is mentioned. While it is focused on coastal areas, it is provided by the environment agency, and they are a good source of data.
    - It is crucial to check the dataset's metadata for coverage, resolution, and licensing information to ensure it meets your Unreal Engine project's requirements.

- **Environment Agency**
    - The Environment Agency is a primary source for environmental data in England, including LiDAR and elevation data. Their datasets are often high quality and suitable for terrain generation.

- **Ordnance Survey (OS)**
    - The Ordnance Survey is the national mapping agency for Great Britain. They offer various digital terrain data products, though some may require licensing.
    - OS data is known for its accuracy and detail, making it ideal for precise terrain modelling.

- **LiDAR data**
    - Light Detection and Ranging (LiDAR) data provides highly accurate elevation measurements. Search for LiDAR data repositories or providers that cover the area you are working with.

- **Commercial providers**
    - Several commercial providers specialize in supplying DEM and terrain data. These providers may offer higher-resolution or customized datasets.
- **Local surveys**
    - For very high detail, localized surveys can be commissioned. There are companies that specialize in this.

Considerations for Unreal Engine

- **Resolution**
    - Determine the required resolution for your terrain. Higher-resolution data results in more detailed terrain but also larger file sizes.
- **File format**
    - Unreal Engine supports various terrain data formats. Ensure the DEM data is available in a compatible format or can be converted. Common formats include GeoTIFF.
- **Coordinate system**
    - Pay close attention to the coordinate system of the DEM data. Unreal Engine requires consistent coordinate systems for accurate terrain rendering.
- **Data processing**
    - DEM data may require processing before it can be used in Unreal Engine. This may involve clipping, resampling, or converting the data.

CHAPTER 4 STEP ONE: DATA COLLECTION

Recommendations

- Start by exploring the data available on Data.gov.uk and the Environment Agency's website.

- If you require high-resolution data or specific coverage, consider contacting the Ordnance Survey or a commercial provider.

- When working with DEM data in Unreal Engine, utilize the Engine's terrain tools to refine and customize the terrain to your project's needs.

I had already collected the maps we would use for 1400 and 1800 Winchester that showed the layout of the city. I also needed to find the topography data to go with the city maps, for both periods of time. For this, I researched and tried several sites and methods. The Winchester terrain was modelled in 2022, using Google Maps. In revisiting the Beaulieu Abbey/Beaulieu Village reconstruction, I tried which created a map with height data in Adobe Photoshop, which could then be exported. For Hyde Abbey, it was another system again. Each year seems to bring new terrain/height map generators, free and paid for applications. There are several now within Unreal Engine, such as SynTerra by SynPlanet launched in March 2025, a free plug-in with Unreal Engine 5.5.

The map created for Virtual Cities – Winchester was for a section of Winchester as an initial prototype. The section covered a quadrant that included Winchester College/College Street, between Kingsgate Street and Wolvesey Castle and the Cathedral Grounds (see Figure 4-14). We now need to expand the mapping to fully cover the city and therefore can use a more up-to-date system for creating a more detailed terrain.

CHAPTER 4   STEP ONE: DATA COLLECTION

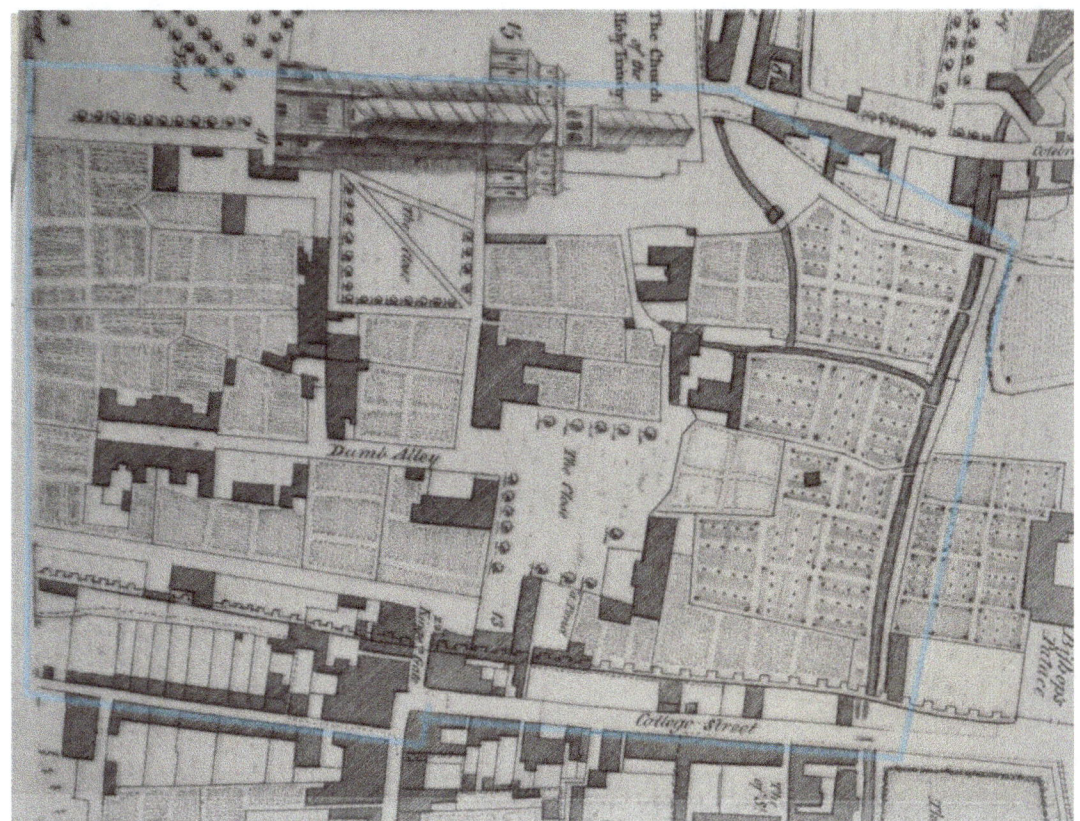

Figure 4-14. *Prototype section of Winchester 1750–1800 using a combination of overlaid maps*

In the various tutorials you can find on YouTube, Unreal, Udemy, and elsewhere, the process is generally for modern-day real locations or for game environments, not how the environment was in past eras. Much like BIM and HBIM, the difference in what is needed to create a digital twin of the city in approx. 1400 and again in 1800 is quite significant. Below you can see the GIS map of Winchester, followed by the 1800 map, which was overlaid in Unreal Engine. This is followed by a perspective view of the 1800 prototype and then the 1400.

CHAPTER 4 STEP ONE: DATA COLLECTION

Figure 4-15. *Winchester City GIS Export Map – 3DS Max perspective view tying in with the overlaid 1800 map in Figure 4-16*

Figure 4-16. *Winchester City 1800 Map – 3DS Max perspective view with the map sized to fit with the GIS modern-day map in Figure 4-15*

CHAPTER 4   STEP ONE: DATA COLLECTION

Figure 4-17. *Virtual Cities – Winchester prototype view – looking across Winchester Cathedral Close 1800s*

Figure 4-18. *Virtual Cities – Winchester prototype view – looking along Canon Street to College Street with the Castle wall 1400s*

Creating past landscapes in Unreal Engine introduced interesting challenges compared to replicating a modern terrain. While the fundamental process of importing and manipulating heightmaps remains the same, the focus shifts toward historical accuracy and artistic interpretation. The process below covers the additional considerations required, and the work involved.

CHAPTER 4   STEP ONE: DATA COLLECTION

Heightmap Data Limitations

- **Historical accuracy**
    - Direct Digital Elevation Models (DEMs) from the 15th century do not exist. Therefore, you will primarily rely on modern DEM data as a base.
    - However, you will need to account for significant landscape changes over time due to
        - Erosion and sedimentation
        - Deforestation and agricultural practices
        - Urban development and infrastructure
    - This means that the heightmap data you get from modern sources will need to be heavily edited.
- **Artistic interpretation**
    - Historical maps and illustrations can provide valuable insights into the general topography of the area during the 15th century.
    - You will likely need to use Unreal Engine's sculpting tools to reshape the terrain based on historical references and artistic vision.

Terrain Modification and Detailing

- **Emphasis on natural features**
    - 15th-century landscapes were predominantly natural, with fewer human-made structures.
    - There will be more of a focus on creating realistic woods, forests, rivers, hills, and other natural features.

- **Historical vegetation**
  - Research the types of trees and vegetation that were prevalent in the region during the 15th century.
  - Use Unreal Engine's foliage tools to populate the landscape with historically accurate vegetation.
- **Limited human settlement**
  - Human settlements were smaller and less dense than modern towns.
  - There would have been pigs, chickens, and similar often kept in what would be gardens in the outlying city areas, also small hamlets which later were enveloped by the city.
  - Use historical references to accurately depict the architecture and layout of these settlements.
- **Material creation**
  - Creating materials that reflect the time period is very important. There was not tarmac then, but earth, stone, and other natural materials.

Key Considerations

- **Historical research**
  - Thorough research is crucial for creating an accurate 15th-century landscape.
  - Consult historical maps, illustrations, and texts to understand the topography, vegetation, and settlements of the region.
- **Artistic license**
  - While historical accuracy is important, artistic license may be necessary to fill in gaps in information and create a visually compelling scene.

- **Unreal Engine tools**
  - Unreal Engine's landscape sculpting tools, foliage tools, and material editor are essential for creating a realistic and immersive 15th-century landscape.

- **Procedural generation**
  - Using procedural generation tools within Unreal Engine can greatly help in the creation of large areas of forest and other natural features.

In Summary

- The process starts with obtaining a base heightmap but then diverges significantly into historical research and artistic interpretation.

- You will spend much more time sculpting, texturing, and populating the landscape with historically accurate details than a modern scene. With Game scenes, it can almost be anything you want, but to create a historically accurate scene, you will need to do significant research for each time period portrayed.

Having completed as much research as possible for your HBIM project, considered your workflow and how much work may be needed re sculpting and painting, and finished collating the data and maps, Depending on the data collected, you may now need to combine them, especially if you are creating two different time periods. I used a combination of different methods and multiple tools. These included Autodesk Revit and Adobe Photoshop to scale and align the 1400 map with the 1800 map. I tried this in Photoshop first, which is how I did this for Hyde Abbey maps, but I then used Autodesk Revit to align them in more detail, using Revit's dimensioning tools and scale referencing. There are other ways of doing this, which I have listed below, but sometimes using tools you know and use regularly does make sense even if they may take a little longer; the learning curve is not as steep.

GIS-Based Georeferencing (Most Accurate and Scalable)

If the historical maps have identifiable landmarks that still exist today, you can georeference them in QGIS or ArcGIS:

- **Step 1:** Import the modern city map with known geospatial coordinates (e.g., OpenStreetMap or satellite imagery).
- **Step 2:** Load the historical maps as separate raster layers.
- **Step 3:** Use the Georeferencer Tool to align key landmarks (churches, roads, rivers, etc.) with their modern counterparts.
- **Step 4:** Export the georeferenced images at the same resolution for direct use in Unreal Engine.

Best for: Accuracy, alignment at different scales, and future expansion (GIS can handle many historical layers)
Downside: Requires familiarity with GIS software

Using Revit or AutoCAD for Alignment (CAD Workflow)

If your project is Revit based, you can align maps more precisely in AutoCAD or Revit before importing into Unreal:

- **Step 1:** Import all maps as raster images into AutoCAD or Revit.
- **Step 2:** Scale each map using known reference distances (e.g., a road width that exists in all maps).
- **Step 3:** Align maps using a common base point (e.g., a central square or riverbank).
- **Step 4:** Export them as aligned images (or as geometry layers if needed).

Best for: Architectural workflows, ensuring maps stay to scale with accurate distances
Downside: Requires CAD knowledge

Image Processing Automation with OpenCV (Fastest for Large Projects)

If you have multiple maps and want to automate alignment, you can use Python with OpenCV for feature-based matching:

- **Step 1:** Convert all maps to grayscale.
- **Step 2:** Use SIFT (Scale-Invariant Feature Transform) or ORB (Oriented FAST and Rotated BRIEF) to detect common landmarks across maps.
- **Step 3:** Use Homography Transformation to warp each historical map onto the modern city layout.
- **Step 4:** Save and import the aligned maps into Unreal.

Best for: Automating map alignment across multiple time periods
Downside: Requires coding skills

Blender Projection Mapping (For 3D Surface Alignment)

If you want to maintain topographic accuracy while aligning maps:

- **Step 1:** Import a 3D terrain model of the modern city (from LiDAR or elevation data).
- **Step 2:** Import the historical maps as texture layers.
- **Step 3:** Use Blender's UV Project Modifier to project each map onto the terrain.
- **Step 4:** Export the textured planes for Unreal Engine.

Best for: Ensuring historical terrain shifts are preserved
Downside: Requires Blender knowledge

Which One to Choose?

- If you want accuracy and scalability, use GIS (QGIS or ArcGIS).
- If you work in Revit/AutoCAD, align maps there for precision.

- If you have many maps and need automation, use OpenCV.
- If you're dealing with topography, use Blender projection mapping.

Creating the Landscape

To create a realistic UK landscape in Unreal Engine 5, you will need to use heightmaps and satellite imagery to create a 3D terrain and then add textures and assets to represent the specific location. The following takes you through step by step to build your landscape in Unreal Engine.

Creating Your Landscape in Unreal Engine

- **Create a New Landscape**

    In the Unreal Editor, select "Modes" ➤ "Landscape" to open the Landscape tab and create a new landscape object.

- **Import Heightmap**

    In the Landscape tab, select the "Import" button in the "Heightmap" section and import your DEM.

- **Adjust Landscape Settings**
    - **Size and Resolution:** Set the size and resolution of your landscape based on your DEM data and desired level of detail.
    - **Material:** Choose a base material for your landscape.

- **Texture Painting**
    - **Landscape Painting Mode:** Enter Landscape Painting Mode to paint textures onto your landscape.
    - **Target Layers:** Select the textures you want to paint with.
    - **Use Satellite Imagery:** Use your satellite imagery as a reference to paint textures and details.

- **Add Assets**
  - **Place Static Meshes:** Add static meshes to represent buildings, trees, and other objects in your landscape.
  - **Use Landscape Layers:** Use Landscape Layers to add more detail and variation to your landscape.
  - **Consider Procedural Generation:** Explore using procedural generation techniques to create more complex terrain features.
- **Refine and Optimize**
  - **Adjust Lighting and Shadows:** Set up realistic lighting and shadows to enhance the visual fidelity of your landscape.
  - **Optimize Performance:** Optimize your landscape for performance to ensure smooth gameplay.

Tips for Realism

- **Use High-Quality Assets:** Use high-quality assets to create a more realistic environment.
- **Pay Attention to Detail:** Pay attention to the details of your landscape, such as the texture of the ground, the shape of the trees, and the placement of buildings.
- **Experiment with Different Techniques:** Experiment with different techniques to create a unique and realistic landscape.

Example

If you wanted to recreate your local small village or market town, you could

1. Obtain a DEM and satellite imagery of the village
2. Create a landscape in Unreal Engine and import the DEM
3. Paint textures based on the satellite imagery, using materials that represent grass, fields, and roads
4. Place static meshes of buildings, trees, and other objects

5. Add details such as fences, walls, and other small objects

6. Adjust lighting and shadows to create a realistic atmosphere

Cesium Step-by-Step Guide

I promised to provide a quick how-to for Cesium for Unreal Engine 5, allowing you to bring real-world geospatial data into your projects. Here is a step-by-step guide:

1. Prerequisites

- **Unreal Engine 5:** Ensure you have Unreal Engine 5 installed.
- **Cesium ion Account:** You will need a Cesium ion account to access and stream geospatial data. You can create a free account at Cesium ion.
- **Internet Connection:** Cesium relies on streaming data from the internet.

2. Installing the Cesium for Unreal Plug-in

- **Unreal Engine Marketplace**
    - Open the Epic Games Launcher.
    - Navigate to the "Marketplace" tab.
    - Search for "Cesium for Unreal".
    - Click "Install to Engine".
    - Select the Unreal Engine 5 version you are using.
    - Click "Install".
- **Enable the Plug-in**
    - Open your Unreal Engine 5 project.
    - Go to "Edit" ➤ "Plugins".
    - In the "Plugins" window, search for "Cesium for Unreal".

CHAPTER 4   STEP ONE: DATA COLLECTION

- Enable the plug-in.
- Restart Unreal Engine when prompted.

3. Connecting to Cesium ion

- **Cesium ion Token**
    - Log in to your Cesium ion account.
    - Go to your user settings (usually in the top-right corner).
    - Select "Access Tokens".
    - Create a new access token. Give it a descriptive name (e.g., "Unreal Engine").
    - Copy the generated access token.
- **Unreal Engine Connection**
    - In Unreal Engine, go to "Window" ➤ "Cesium" ➤ "Cesium Quick Add."
    - Alternatively, within the content browser, right-click, and under the Cesium tab, select "Cesium 3D Tileset".
    - In the "Cesium Quick Add" or "Cesium 3D Tileset" panel, you will see a field for your Cesium ion access token.
    - Paste your access token into the field.
    - If you are creating a 3D Tileset, you will then need to paste the asset ID of the Tileset you wish to import from your Cesium ion account.

4. Adding Geospatial Data

- **Cesium ion Assets**
    - In Cesium ion, browse the available assets (e.g., 3D Tilesets, terrain, imagery).
    - Find the data you want to use in your Unreal Engine project.

CHAPTER 4   STEP ONE: DATA COLLECTION

- If you are using the quick add panel, you can select from some of the most popular assets directly within unreal.
- **Adding to Unreal Engine**
  - In Unreal Engine, use the "Cesium Quick Add" panel or the "Cesium 3D Tileset" actor to add the desired assets to your scene.
  - If you have copied the asset ID, you can paste that into the 3D Tileset actor.
  - The data will be streamed into your scene.

5. Adjusting Settings

- **Georeferencing**
  - Cesium for Unreal automatically georeferences the data.
  - You can adjust the georeference settings in the "Cesium Georeference" actor to fine-tune the placement and orientation of the data.
- **Appearance**
  - Adjust the appearance of the terrain and imagery using Unreal Engine's material editor and other tools.
- **Performance**
  - Cesium streams data in real time, so performance can be affected by internet speed and the complexity of the data.
  - Optimize your scene by adjusting LOD settings and other performance-related parameters.

Key Considerations

- **Internet Connectivity:** Cesium relies on a stable internet connection for streaming data.
- **Cesium ion Data Limits:** Be aware of any data usage limits associated with your Cesium ion account.

CHAPTER 4   STEP ONE: DATA COLLECTION

- **Coordinate Systems:** Cesium handles coordinate system transformations automatically, but it is essential to understand the coordinate systems used by your data.

- **Performance Optimization:** Large geospatial datasets can impact performance. Optimize your scene for smooth rendering.

By following these steps, you can successfully set up Cesium for Unreal Engine 5. You can find more information on the Cesium website Quick Start guide: `https://cesium.com/learn/unreal/unreal-quickstart/`.

If you want to hide the buildings and add your own buildings, then the following will be helpful.

Cesium: How to Hide Buildings by Disabling the Cesium OSM Buildings Layer

With thanks to the Cesium Community, the following steps will help you to hide the buildings that come with the Cesium Map data (Cesium Community, 2025):

- **Disabling Cesium OSM Buildings**

    - In CesiumJS, you can disable the Cesium OSM Buildings layer by setting viewer.scene.globe.imageryLayers.get(0).show = false;.

    - In Cesium for Unreal, you can disable the Cesium OSM Buildings layer by unchecking the "Show Buildings" check box in the Cesium for Unreal plug-in settings.

- **Using Cesium ion**

    - Cesium ion includes access to curated global 3D content including Cesium World Terrain, Bing Maps imagery, and Cesium OSM Buildings.

    - You can combine these assets with your own data to see it in a geospatial context and share the results securely with your colleagues or make them available through your apps.

- **Custom Terrain**
    - If you need to create a custom terrain with buildings, you can upload your desired building models to your Cesium ion account and place them in your terrain at specified coordinates.
    - You can also add the Cesium Terrain option and ensure that the terrain you generated is being added to the Cesium viewer correctly.

Section Summary

In this last section, we have explored the collection of geographic and spatial data for historical reconstructions, detailing methods to create accurate digital landscapes. It discusses various tools and data sources, from the open source Cesium plug-in for Unreal Engine to government resources like Data.gov.uk and the Ordnance Survey for DEM data. Emphasizing the challenges of recreating historical landscapes compared to modern ones, it outlines the importance of artistic interpretation, historical accuracy, and the use of Unreal Engine's terrain modification tools. The text also provides a step-by-step guide to creating landscapes in Unreal Engine and using the Cesium plug-in, concluding with key considerations for optimizing performance and ensuring historical fidelity in virtual world-building.

References

3D Map Generator (2021) Create Your Own 3d Map in Photoshop 3D-Mapper. https://www.3d-map-generator.com/

Book Lady Deb (2010) Jane Austen Steventon Parsonage redux. Jane Austen in Vermont Blog https://janeausteninvermont.blog/tag/steventon-rectory/

Cesium (2023) Bring the real world to Unreal Engine. https://cesium.com/platform/cesium-for-unreal/

Cesium (2023) Cesium for Unreal Quickstart. https://cesium.com/learn/unreal/unreal-quickstart/

CHAPTER 4   STEP ONE: DATA COLLECTION

Jane Austen Society (1997) Sale of items at Steventon rectory (image taken) Jane Austen Collected Reports 1986-1995 https://archive.org/details/austencollreport_1986_1995_202004/page/n5/mode/2up

Walker, Linda Robson (2007) Why Was Jane Austen Sent away to School at Seven? An Empirical Look at a Vexing Question. Persuasions On-Line, JASNA http://www.jasna.org/persuasions/on-line/vol26no1/walker.htm

CHAPTER 5

Step Two: Pre-processing

This chapter discusses the pre-processing stage, where data is cleaned, aligned, and prepared for integration into the HBIM model. The chapter takes a technical angle, addressing data management and preparation for use in the subsequent stages of reconstruction. The purpose of this chapter is to ensure that readers understand the critical role of pre-processing in creating an accurate and cohesive HBIM model, thus avoiding potential issues in the later stages.

In the first section, "Data Preparation," we will work through putting a template together in Revit, one for the 1800s Steventon Rectory model and another for the 1400s Winchester Castle model.

The "How to Manage Incomplete or Missing Data" section will provide practical strategies that will help in being able to mitigate these gaps and ensure the model remains as accurate, credible, and useful as possible. The approaches are not about "filling in the blanks" arbitrarily, but more about using informed methods to create plausible and justifiable representations when certain aspects are not known.

The last section "Georeferencing and Aligning Datasets" will include different processes for creating the topography for the immediate area of each building and other methods to achieve the same result. I need to create the map, the 3D topography data, and the visual landscape plus in the case of Winchester, the layout of the streets, and then how this is taken into Unreal Engine, ensuring that the embedded data is also taken through. This will mean that the Unreal project will also need to be set up, materials and data fields ready for using as a template for the following chapter where we start to construct the 3D building models.

CHAPTER 5   STEP TWO: PRE-PROCESSING

Data Preparation

The initial phases of an HBIM project, particularly data acquisition and pre-processing, can be considerably time-consuming due to the unique and often intricate nature of historic buildings and the potential scarcity of reliable documentation. By establishing a solid foundation of clean, aligned, and georeferenced data, the pre-processing stage directly enhances the overall reliability and adaptability of the resulting HBIM model. Furthermore, a streamlined pre-processing workflow significantly improves the efficiency of HBIM management by simplifying subsequent tasks and reducing the reliance on overly precise measurements and complex geometric modelling in later stages. Therefore, even though we have reviewed and worked through collecting/collating data, we now need to make sure it is completely ready to use. In this, I mean prepare the software to make it easier to record the data we have collated, such as creating the wall types, window styles, finishes, and similar in Autodesk Revit (or whichever program you are using).

I was always taught in early days of CAD to create templates of the items you will need to use, the fonts, line types, drawing sheets, etc., to ensure consistency across all drawings/projects, thereby not having to recreate each time. BIM has taken care of a significant amount of this within programs such as Autodesk Revit and Graphisoft ArchiCAD, as standard and using standards, for example, Industry Foundation Classes (IFC), ensuring semantic interoperability, enabling the HBIM model to be effectively exchanged and utilized across different platforms and by different stakeholders. As we saw in the previous chapter, choosing appropriate file formats for different data types is a key aspect of data storage best practice.

Implementing a robust version control system such as Git, (which stands for Global information tracker, commonly used by Unreal Engine) is also essential for tracking changes and maintaining data integrity through the model's life cycle. This includes regularly backing up all project data to prevent data loss due to hardware failure or other unforeseen events. Furthermore, it will be crucial to consider the long-term archival requirements of the heritage data, ensuring that the information can be preserved and accessed by future generations for research and conservation purposes. We have used CD-ROMs, then DVDs, Zip drives, and large storage external hard drives over the years, each promising long-term storage/archival use. Unfortunately, it turns out (for me anyway) that many of these storage solutions are not as long term as hoped for, with data no longer accessible, files not reading, drives not seeing the files, and similar. Cloud storage is now the preferred route, although it is worth remembering that cloud storage is ultimately a computer-based system relying on a network of servers somewhere, which could also break or be broken into. Personally I still save to a dedicated external drive as well as cloud storage – just in case in the hope that at least one will still be safe and accessible.

In this section, therefore, we will work through putting a template together in Revit, one for the 1800s Steventon Rectory model and another for the 1400s Winchester Castle model.

The first step in your template is to ensure units and data attribute fields have been created so that it is all ready to use and not delay progress in drawing the model(s). With this, I mean attributes such as material composition, historical alterations, and structural conditions, where possible. Creating data object parameters for HBIM (Historic Building Information Modelling) information, especially for nonstandard materials like those found in historic structures, requires a thoughtful and structured approach. Here is a detailed step-by-step guide.

Phase 1: Understanding the Requirements and Defining the Data

Step 1: Identify the Specific Nonstandard Material(s)

- Clearly define the nonstandard wall material(s) you need to document. Examples include
  - Wattle and daub
  - Cob
  - Rubble stone with lime mortar
  - Timber framing with infill (specify infill type)
  - Specific types of historic brick or plaster with unique compositions, for example, Hampshire Flint and Stone Walling

Step 2: Determine the Relevant Properties and Characteristics

- For each nonstandard material, brainstorm the properties and characteristics that are important to capture for your HBIM project. Consider the following categories:

CHAPTER 5   STEP TWO: PRE-PROCESSING

- **Physical Properties** (several of these may apply for conservation purposes only, but if you have the information, then it would be good practice to include, time allowing):
  - Composition (e.g., percentages of clay, straw, lime, aggregate types and sizes)
  - Dimensions (e.g., thickness, layer structure)
  - Weight/density
  - Texture (e.g., rough, smooth, porous)
  - Color (potentially with links to color palettes or spectral data)
  - Moisture content (if relevant and measurable)
  - Thermal properties (conductivity, resistance, specific heat capacity – if data is available or needs to be estimated)
  - Acoustic properties (absorption, transmission – if relevant)
  - Fire resistance (if documented or estimated)
- **Material State and Condition**
  - Current condition (e.g., good, fair, poor, deteriorated)
  - Type of deterioration (e.g., cracking, erosion, biological growth)
  - Extent of deterioration (e.g., percentage of affected area)
  - Previous interventions/repairs (type, date if known)
- **Historical Information**
  - Construction date/period (if known or estimated)
  - Original construction techniques
  - Source of materials (if documented)
  - Cultural significance related to the material
- **Analysis and Assessment Data**
  - Results of material analysis (e.g., XRF, microscopy)
  - Structural performance data (if available or assessed)
  - Hygrothermal performance data (if modelled or measured)

- **Visual Documentation Links**
  - Links to photographs
  - Links to drawings or sketches detailing the material

Step 3: Prioritize Data Requirements

- Not all identified properties will be crucial for every HBIM project. Prioritize the data based on your project goals, such as
  - Conservation planning
  - Structural analysis
  - Energy performance modelling
  - Historical interpretation
  - Cost estimation

Step 4: Define Data Types and Units

- For each property, determine the appropriate data type (e.g., text, number, integer, boolean, date, URL, selection from a list).
- Specify the units of measurement (e.g., mm, kg/m^3, °C, W/mK). Consistency in units is crucial for data accuracy and interoperability.

Phase 2: Creating the Data Object Parameters in Your BIM Software

The specific steps will vary depending on the BIM software you are using (e.g., Revit, ArchiCAD, Vectorworks). However, the general principles remain the same. The initial steps for then accessing Parameters assumes you have some knowledge of Revit; if not, then once you open Revit, choose the Architectural Template from the drop-down menu.

CHAPTER 5   STEP TWO: PRE-PROCESSING

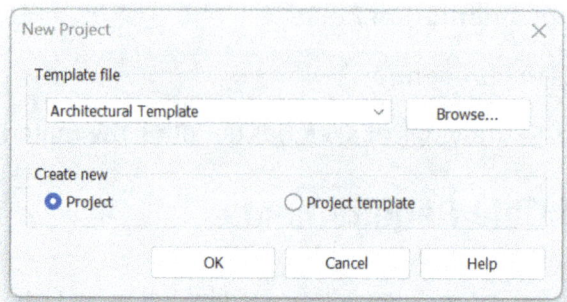

Figure 5-1. *Creating a new architectural project in Autodesk Revit*

Revit will open with the standard architectural elements and tools. The first thing I do is to make sure the Units are the Units I want to work with for the project, so go to Manage and Project Units, and change to suit your preferred system.

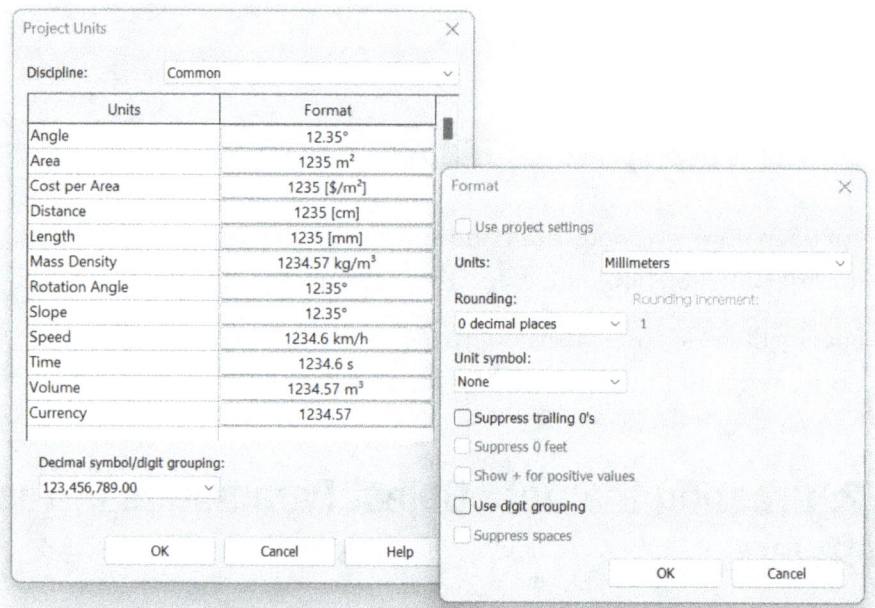

Figure 5-2. *If you need to change/check the project units, go to Manage/Project Units; the standard setting for a Metric project is millimeters*

There are a range of Revit tutorials for new users and advanced users from the Autodesk site and various Revit experts online, but not many specifically in the use of HBIM data; therefore, I will focus on HBIM data only for the step-by-step guides such as the following for HBIM Data objects/parameters guide.

Step 5: Accessing Parameter Management

- In Revit, you will primarily work with two types of parameters; you will find them under the Manage tab:

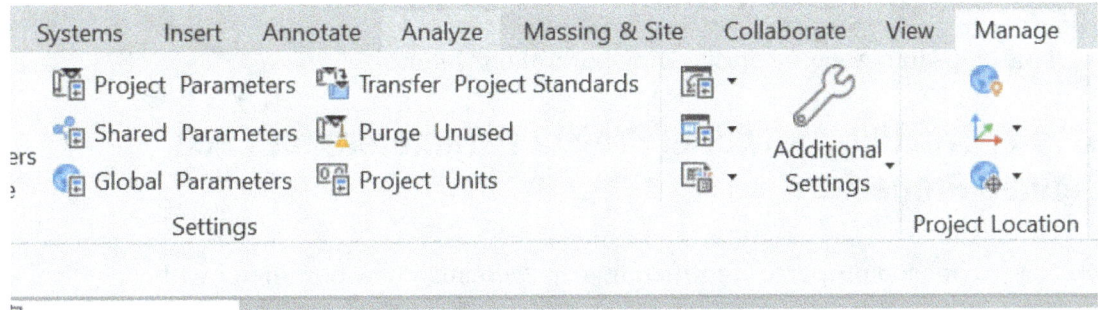

Figure 5-3. Part of the Manage tab showing where Project and Shared Parameters can be found

- **Project Parameters:** These are specific to the current Revit project file (.rvt). You can access them via the Manage tab on the Revit ribbon; then click on Project Parameters. Use them if the nonstandard materials are unique to this project.

- **Shared Parameters:** These are defined in an external text file (.txt) and can be used across multiple Revit projects and families. This is the recommended approach for HBIM to ensure consistency and interoperability if you anticipate working with similar historic materials in other projects. You can access the Shared Parameters file via the Manage tab; then click on Shared Parameters.

Step 6: Creating New Parameter Groups (Optional but Recommended)

- In both Project and Shared Parameters dialog boxes, you can create Parameter Groups to organize your custom parameters logically. When creating a new parameter, you will assign it to a specific group.

Examples

- "Historic Wall Material Properties"
- "Wattle and Daub Specific Data"
- "Cob Material Analysis"

This helps in managing and finding parameters later.

Step 7: Creating Individual Project Parameters for Each Defined Property

- For each property identified in step 2, create a new parameter with the following considerations:
    - **Name:** Use a clear and descriptive name (e.g., "Wall Material Composition - Clay Percentage", "Cob Density", "Rubble Stone Mortar Type"). Avoid abbreviations unless they are universally understood within your team.
    - **Discipline:** Choose the appropriate discipline (e.g., Common, Structural, MEP). This often influences the available parameter types and units.
    - **Data Type:** Select the appropriate data type as defined in step 4 (e.g., "Text" for composition details, "Number" for density, "Integer" for year).
    - **Group Parameter Under:** Use the drop-down to select which section of the Edit Type properties box you would like to see this data. Identity Data is often used for additional information and makes sense for the HBIM information.
    - **Category Association:** Link the new parameters to the relevant BIM categories (e.g., "Walls"). This ensures that these parameters are available when you select or work with wall elements in your model.

CHAPTER 5   STEP TWO: PRE-PROCESSING

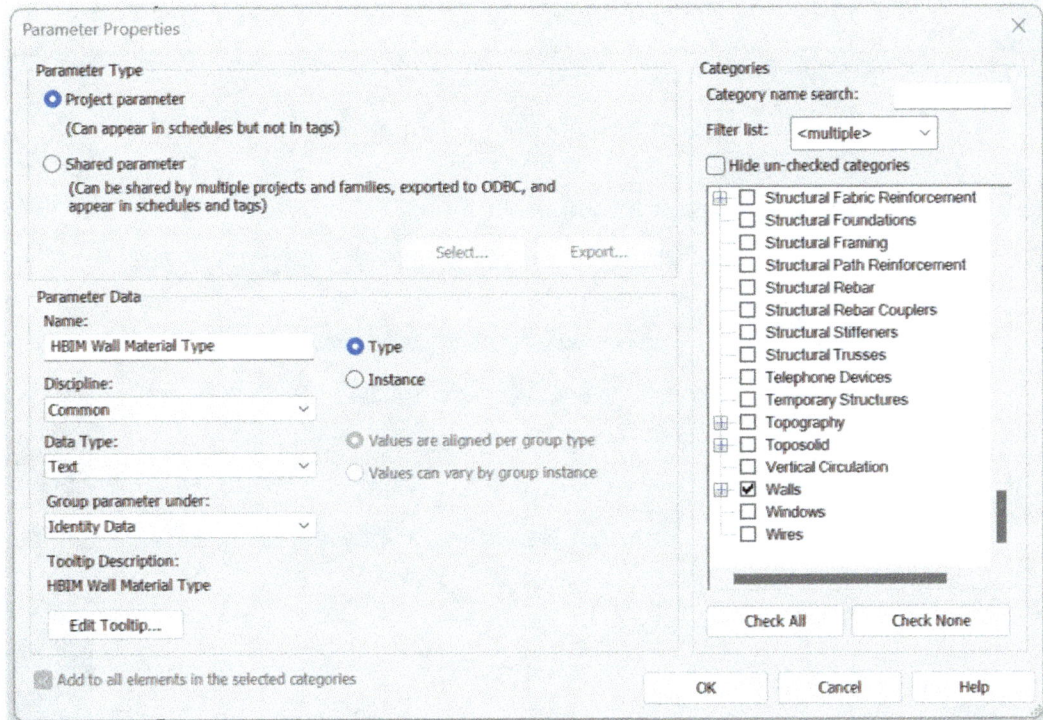

Figure 5-4. *Project Parameters dialogue box using Type so that it is common across the Project, but this Project only*

You will see this Project Parameter "HBIM Wall Material Type" now listed in each of the Wall Types such as the Basic Wall "Wall-Ext-215Bwk", ready for adding your information in Figure 5-5.

225

CHAPTER 5   STEP TWO: PRE-PROCESSING

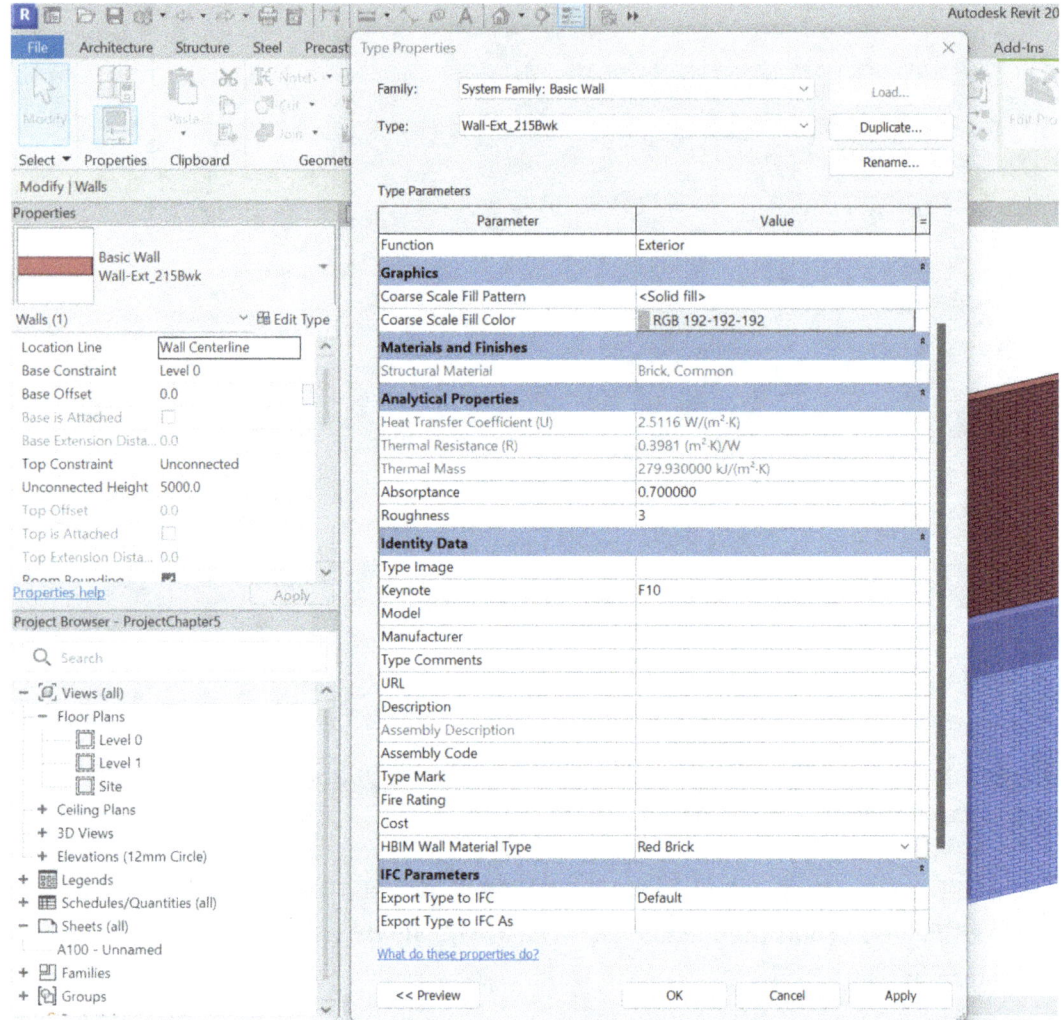

Figure 5-5. *The new Project Parameter "Type" added in the Edit Type dialogue box*

You can create a Project Parameter using Instance, which will add the Parameter to the Properties box, not the Edit Type dialogue box, as shown in Figure 5-6, again for all wall types you create.

Project Parameters, Type and Instance, will be found only within the current project, i.e., they cannot be used in a different project.

If you had different objects that shared a common data such as a particular wood, you can choose the different categories, i.e., doors, windows, stairs, etc., under the Categories in the Project Parameter box, and then each category object would list the data field for adding your HBIM information, as shown in Figure 5-7.

CHAPTER 5 STEP TWO: PRE-PROCESSING

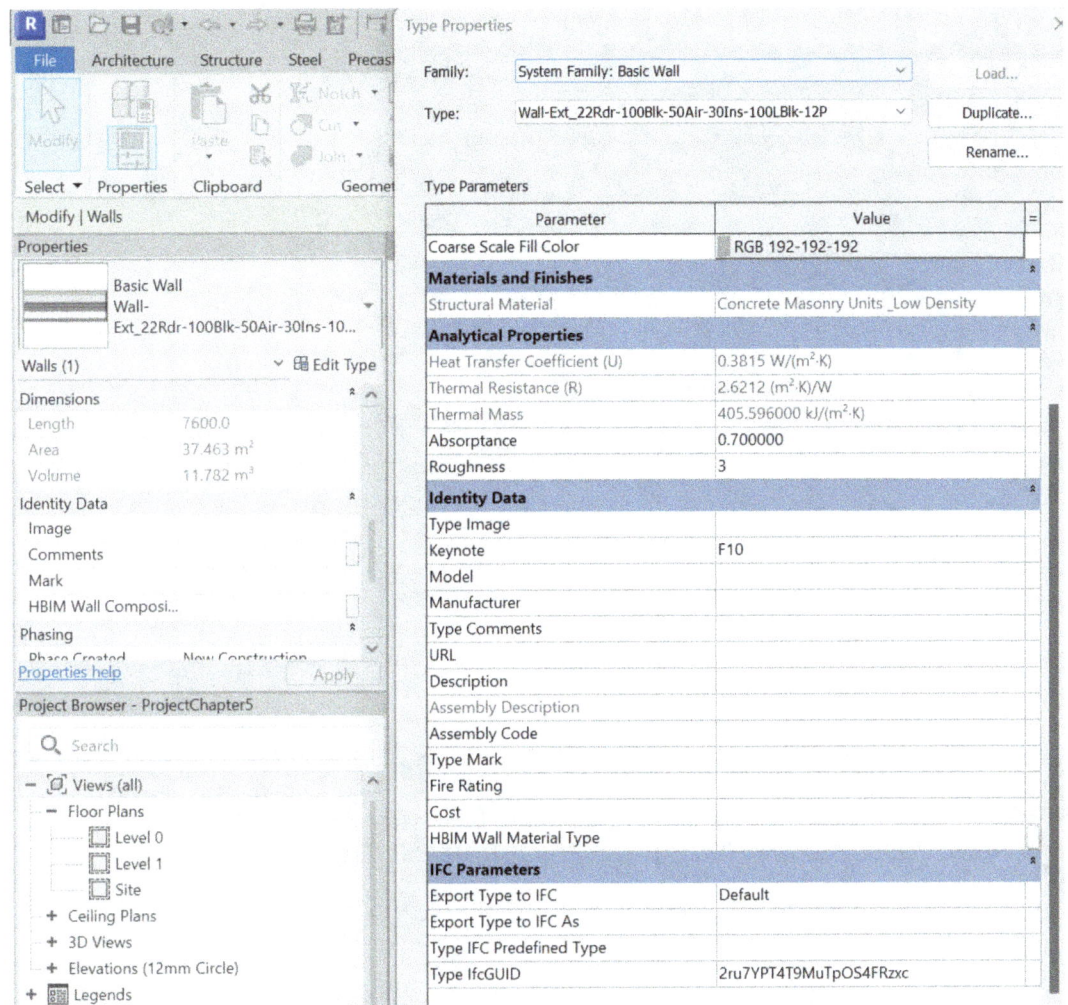

Figure 5-6. *The Project Parameter "Instance" showing in the Properties box and the "Project Parameter Type" showing in the Edit Type dialogue box*

CHAPTER 5   STEP TWO: PRE-PROCESSING

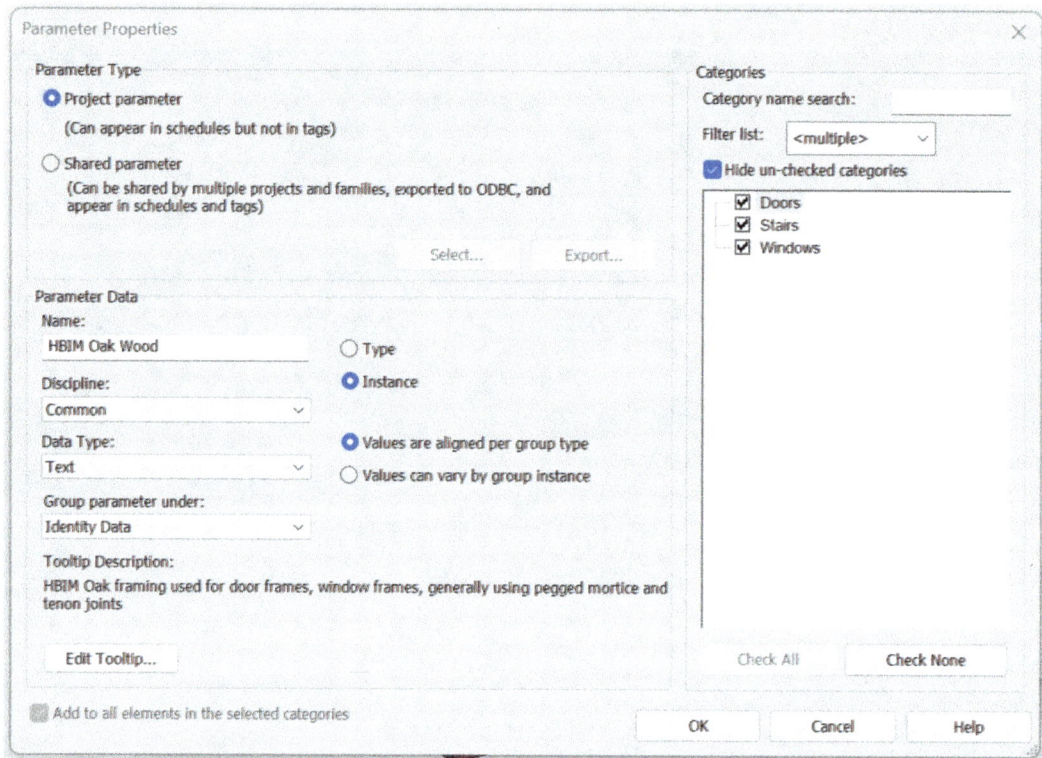

Figure 5-7. *Creating a Project Parameter Instance to show in the Properties box for Windows, Doors, and Stairs, i.e., using multiple categories*

1. **Using Shared Parameters**

    1. In the Shared Parameters dialog box, if you haven't already, create a new Shared Parameter file by clicking Create… and saving it to a location accessible to your team.

    2. Create a New "Group" by clicking New under Groups; name appropriately. It will then appear as the "Parameter Group".

    3. Under the desired Group (created in step 6), click New… to create a new parameter.

    4. **Name:** Enter a clear and descriptive name (as discussed in the general guide).

CHAPTER 5   STEP TWO: PRE-PROCESSING

5. **Discipline:** Choose the appropriate discipline (e.g., Common, Structural, MEP). This often influences the available parameter types and units.

6. **Data Type:** Select the appropriate data type (e.g., Text, Number, Integer, Yes/No, Length, Area, Volume, Material, URL).

7. **Group Parameter Under:** Use the drop-down to select which section of the Edit Type properties box you would like to see this data. Identity Data is often used for additional information and makes sense for the HBIM information.

8. Click OK to create the shared parameter. Create as many as needed.

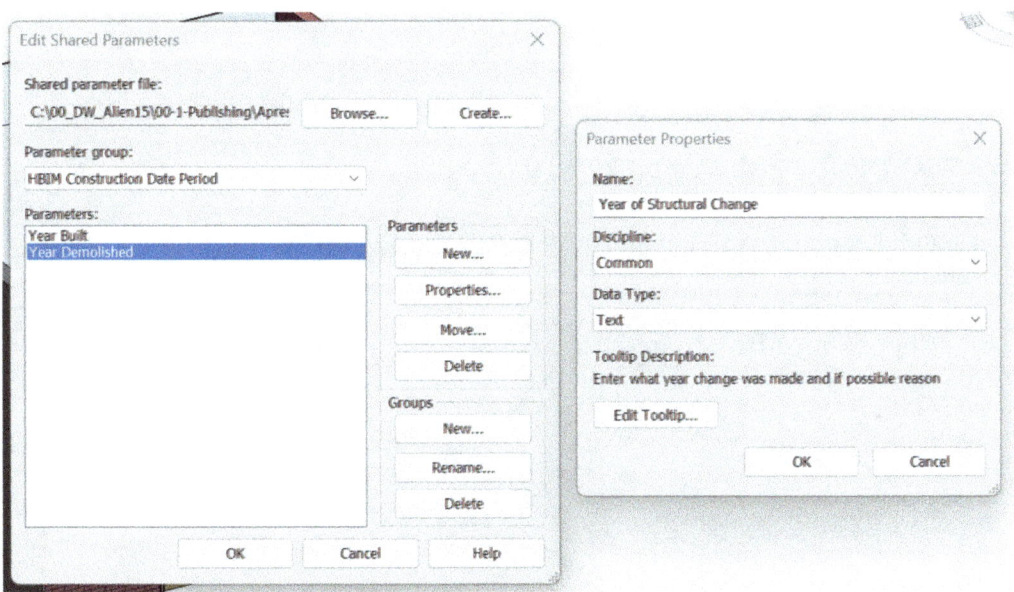

Figure 5-8. *Creating Shared Parameters to add to your project*

229

CHAPTER 5   STEP TWO: PRE-PROCESSING

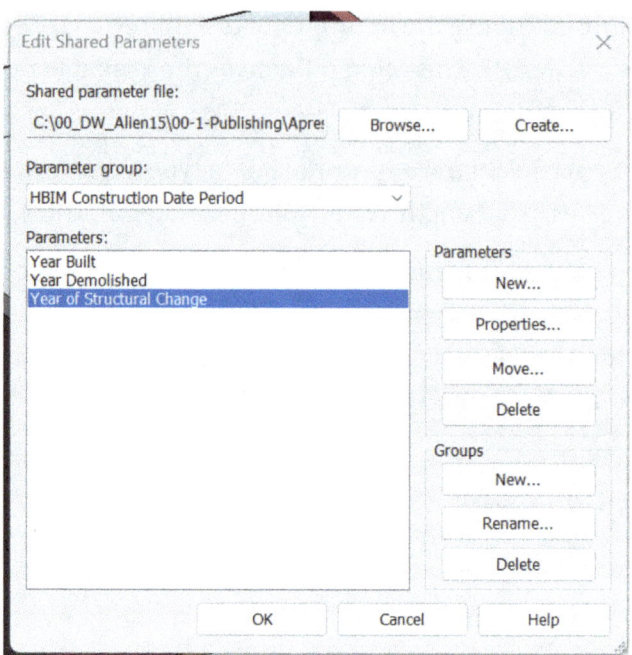

Figure 5-9. *The list of shared parameters created*

9. Once ready, go to Manage/Project Parameters, create new Shared Parameter, and click Select.

10. Choose one of the Shared Parameters created above (1–8).

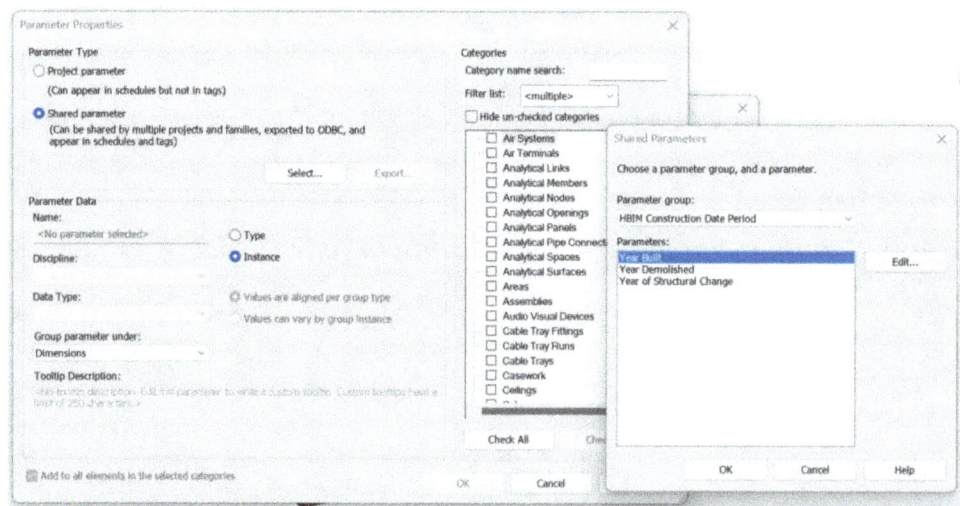

Figure 5-10. *How you connect the shared parameters to Project Parameters using the Shared Parameter type*

CHAPTER 5   STEP TWO: PRE-PROCESSING

11. Select "Identity Data" under "Group parameter under" and then choose the categories you want to see this applied to – see Figure 5-11.

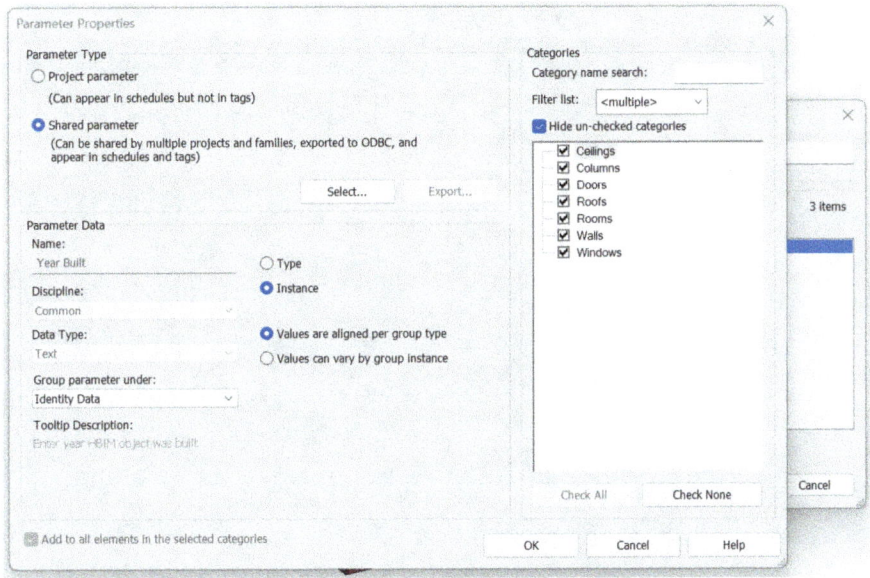

Figure 5-11. *The settings required before clicking OK*

12. Click OK and then select one of the walls drawn and check the Properties. You will see the Shared Data parameters under Identity Data ready for you to add your information.

CHAPTER 5   STEP TWO: PRE-PROCESSING

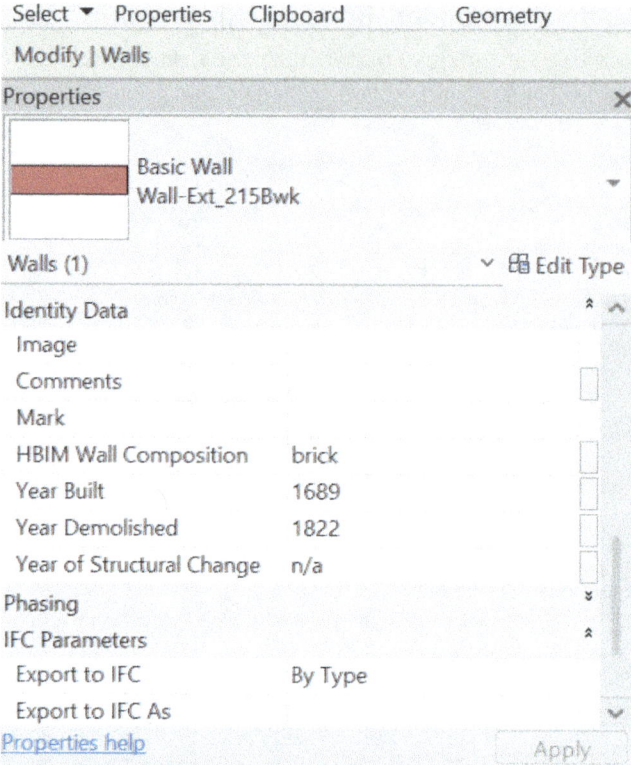

Figure 5-12. Shared Parameter data fields in the Object Properties box

This method allows you to see the list of shared parameters (Year Built, Year Demolished, and Year of Structural Change) in other projects, whereas the first method (step 6) only provides those parameters in the project in which they were created.

13. To see the shared parameters in another project, simply go to Manage/Project Parameters and create a new parameter.

14. In the Project Parameter settings box, choose Shared Parameters; click the select button and you will see the three shared parameters from your other project.

15. Make sure to select Instance, and then under Group parameter under, choose Identity Data.

16. Do not forget to select the categories it will apply to.

17. Repeat for each of the shared parameters.

Step 8: Implementing Value Lists or Look-up Tables (Where Applicable)

- For properties with a predefined set of possible values (e.g., "Condition" – Good, Fair, Poor; "Mortar Type" – Lime, Cement, Mixed), consider using

- **Value Lists (Drop-down Menus)**
    - When creating a Text type Shared or Project Parameter, you can define a list of allowed values. After creating the parameter and associating it with the "Walls" category, select a wall element. In the Properties palette, for your newly created parameter, you can click "Edit..." next to the parameter value. This will sometimes (depending on the exact Revit version and parameter type) allow you to define a list of predefined values that users can choose from.
    - Alternatively, for more controlled value lists, you might consider using Revit Key Schedules. You can create a schedule for a specific category (like Walls) and define key parameters with predefined values. Then, you can link these key schedule values to your wall instances.

- **Look-up Tables (CSV Files)**
    - Revit allows you to import data from CSV (Comma-Separated Values) files to drive parameter values within families. This is particularly useful for complex relationships between material properties (e.g., thermal conductivity based on composition).
    - You would typically create a family parameter (often within a material asset or a specific wall family type) and then link it to a look-up table. While primarily used within families, this concept can sometimes be extended to project parameters with more advanced workflows or add-ins.

Step 9: Adding Constraints and Validation Rules (If Necessary)

- Revit has limited built-in capabilities for direct data validation rules on project or shared parameters in the way a database might. However, you can
  - **Use Formulas:** Within Family Editor (less directly applicable to project-wide material parameters but relevant if you are creating specific wall families for historic materials), you can use formulas to control parameter values based on other parameters.
  - **Utilize Revit Schedules:** You can create schedules that flag inconsistencies or out-of-range values using conditional formatting. For example, you could highlight "Condition" parameters with "Poor" values in red.
  - **Leverage Revit Add-ins:** Several third-party Revit add-ins offer more advanced data management and validation features.

Step 10: Applying the Parameters to Wall Objects in Your Model

- Select one or more wall elements in your Revit model.
- In the Properties palette (usually on the left side of the Revit interface), you will find the parameter groups you defined (e.g., "Historic Wall Material Properties").
- Expand these groups to see the custom parameters you created.
- Enter the specific data for the selected wall element(s) into the corresponding parameter fields.

Phase 3: Data Management and Utilization
Step 11: Establish Data Entry Protocols

- Develop clear guidelines for how and when to enter data into the custom parameters. This ensures consistency among team members.
- Consider using data entry forms or templates if your BIM software allows for it.

Step 12: Quality Control and Data Validation

- Regularly review the entered data for accuracy and completeness. Implement quality checks to identify and correct errors.

Step 13: Utilize the Data for Analysis and Reporting

- Leverage the custom parameters for various HBIM workflows:
  - **Filtering and Selection:** Revit filters allow you to select elements based on the values of their parameters. This can be useful for visually highlighting walls made of specific materials or with particular conditions in your model views.
  - **Schedules:** Revit schedules are a powerful tool for managing and reporting on parameter data. You can create wall schedules that include your custom material parameters. You can then filter, sort, and format this information as needed.
  - **Tags:** You can create custom tags that display the values of your custom material parameters directly on your drawings.
  - **Material Assets:** While your nonstandard materials might not have direct equivalents in the standard Revit material library, you can still create Revit materials that visually represent them. You can then use your custom parameters to store the detailed, nonvisual information about their composition, condition, etc., which goes beyond the standard material properties. You might link these custom parameters to the "Comments" or "Description" fields of the Revit material for easy access.
  - **Visualization:** Use parameter-driven graphics or color-coding to represent material properties or conditions visually in the model.
  - **Analysis Tools:** When exporting data from Revit (e.g., to IFC), ensure that your custom Shared Parameters are properly mapped to IFC properties to maintain data richness in other BIM platforms.
  - **Documentation:** Include the material data in drawings, specifications, and reports.

CHAPTER 5   STEP TWO: PRE-PROCESSING

Step 14: Iterate and Refine

1. As your HBIM project progresses and your understanding of the historic building evolves, you may need to add, modify, or refine your custom parameters. Be prepared to iterate on your data structure.

Example Scenario: Documenting a Wattle and Daub Wall

1. **Identify Material:** Wattle and Daub
2. **Relevant Properties**
   - Core Material (e.g., Hazel, Willow) - Text (Value List: Hazel, Willow, Other)
   - Daub Composition - Text (e.g., Clay: 60%, Straw: 30%, Sand: 10%)
   - Daub Thickness (mm) - Number (Unit: Length)
   - Condition - Text (Value List: Good, Minor Cracking, Significant Damage, Missing)
   - Evidence of Repair - Boolean (Yes/No)
   - Repair Type (if Yes) - Text
   - Photographic Link - URL
3. **BIM Software Implementation (General Steps)**
   - Open Parameter Manager.
   - Create a Group: "Historic Wall Material - Wattle and Daub".
   - Create individual Shared Parameters with appropriate names, data types, and units, linking them to the "Walls" category.
   - For "Core Material" and "Condition", define value lists.
   - Apply these parameters to the wattle and daub walls in your model and fill in the data.
4. **Utilization:** Generate a schedule of wall conditions, filter walls needing repair, and link to condition assessment reports.

Key Considerations for HBIM and Nonstandard Materials

- **Data Standards:** Be aware of any relevant national or international HBIM data standards or guidelines that might influence your parameter creation.

- **Interoperability:** Consider how your data might be exchanged with other software or stakeholders. Using shared parameters enhances interoperability.

- **Flexibility:** Design your parameters to be flexible enough to accommodate variations within nonstandard materials.

- **Documentation:** Thoroughly document your custom parameters, their definitions, data types, and units for future reference and team collaboration.

- **Collaboration:** Engage with conservation specialists, material scientists, and other experts to ensure you are capturing the most relevant and accurate data.

By following these steps, you can create a robust and informative set of data object parameters to effectively document the unique characteristics of nonstandard materials within your HBIM projects. Remember that the specific implementation will depend on your chosen BIM software, so consult its documentation for detailed instructions.

Using Revit, by focusing on Shared Parameters, it will ensure a more consistent and manageable approach to documenting your historic building information. Remember to share established and clear protocols for your team on how to use these parameters if you are not working on this project alone.

Walls

Walls are another category that you can pre-edit as part of your project preparation. By now you should have a clear idea of the buildings you will be creating and the different wall structures, i.e., thickness, whether there are air gaps, insulation, or similar. In very old buildings such as castles, abbeys, and old stone houses, the walls are not always as complex as modern wall structures, but often they are much deeper. The French Farmer's cot we go to in France has 500 thick stone walls, the middle of which is much smaller stone, but solid, i.e., no air gap. The beams are mostly tree trunks/massive limbs (and curved), not the straight rough sawn thick beams that have been used to add a second story. Therefore, to build in Revit, we would have to appropriate modern wall styles and edit them to suit, as much as possible, i.e., the curved beams would be a little more difficult to accurately recreate unless using LiDAR or photogrammetry.

If you have not been able to find out the depth/structure of some of the walls, you can research typical depths reasonably easily online and work with the expert opinions found. For example, Steventon Rectory was built in the late 17th century, and according to research, the typical size of a brick at that time was 2.5 inches. The wall thickness tended to be either a single brick (9 inches [228.6mm]) or 1.5 bricks (13.5 inches [343 mm]) for domestic buildings (English Heritage, 2012; FRAG, 2021; Maybank, 2019; Yorke, 2017). Therefore, not knowing the wall thickness of Steventon Rectory, but knowing that it was brick, I can use either of those thicknesses.

If you have access to a floor plan, the thickness of the wall layouts can also guide you. This has been particularly useful when rebuilding abbeys that have floor plans created from archaeological surveys, and remaining walls such as at Beaulieu Abbey. For Winchester Castle, there is still part of one tower and part of the curtain wall still existing. We also know that a tower built in the 12th century had 14-feet-thick [4267 mm] walls; it is likely therefore that the other towers were of a similar thickness. The east wall of the Great Hall is 9 feet 2 inches thick [2804 mm], which is shown on a floor plan of the "County Hall" (the Great Hall) (British History Online, 1912) that also has a scale included; therefore, we can deduct what the sizes are and apply them to other castle buildings.

In Revit, we therefore need to create walls ranging in thickness from 228 mm to 4267 mm and materials such as red brick, flint, and ashlar mentioned in the HBIM information data fields. I say mentioned because I will add the material in Unreal; adapting and using Unreal materials will work much more effectively with its lighting and other systems. In Revit, I generally use just a color and not an image. By using the same-colored material, once all the buildings have been imported to Unreal, the plan is not to have hundreds of different materials taken through. This has happened with the Virtual Cities – Winchester prototype where students have created their own materials either in Revit or Blender, and now the material library is absolutely huge.

Another aspect is the structure of the wall. Although Unreal can handle a large number of polygons, it is still worth considering whether the additional polygons created by an internal structure to a wall type are going to be relevant within your Unreal scene.

CHAPTER 5   STEP TWO: PRE-PROCESSING

For example, are you going to show cut throughs of the wall(s)? If not, as in the case of Virtual Cities – Winchester, I can specify in the data fields which the makeup of the wall comprises. I could even supply a detail image of the structure, perhaps with annotation tags to the different construction materials which users can access through the Edit Type/Properties data fields. This method would then keep just the outside polygons, making it a simpler model for Unreal.

The following is a step-by-step guide for duplicating and editing wall types to represent different wall thicknesses and keeping the structures as single structures, which can be used for Steventon Rectory and Winchester Castle.

Wall Duplicating and Editing Step-by-Step Guide

1. Choose a single structure wall type such as "Basic Wall, Wall-Ext_215Bwk" from the drop-down of different wall types.

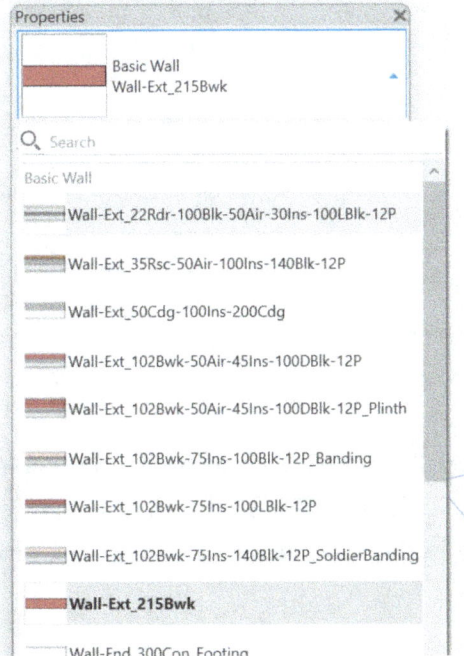

Figure 5-13. *Properties drop-down list of wall style*

2. First thing you need to do before you do anything else is to click "Duplicate" so that you do not overwrite the templated wall type.

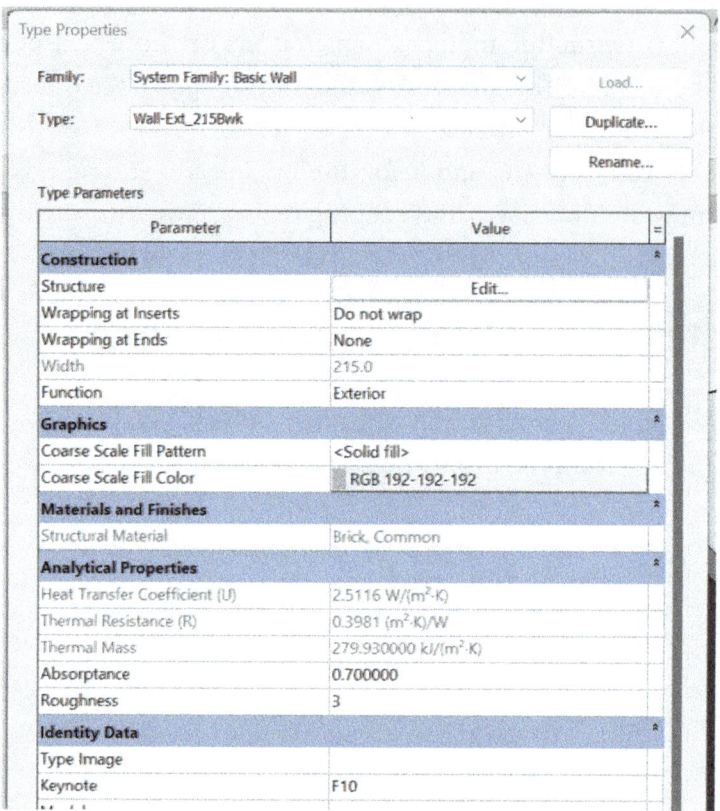

Figure 5-14. Make sure to use the Duplicate button to save overwriting the existing file

3. Name your new wall type with a name you will recognize as being relevant to a particular building perhaps, or city, village, etc., and make sure you add the wall thickness so you know which wall size it is.

CHAPTER 5   STEP TWO: PRE-PROCESSING

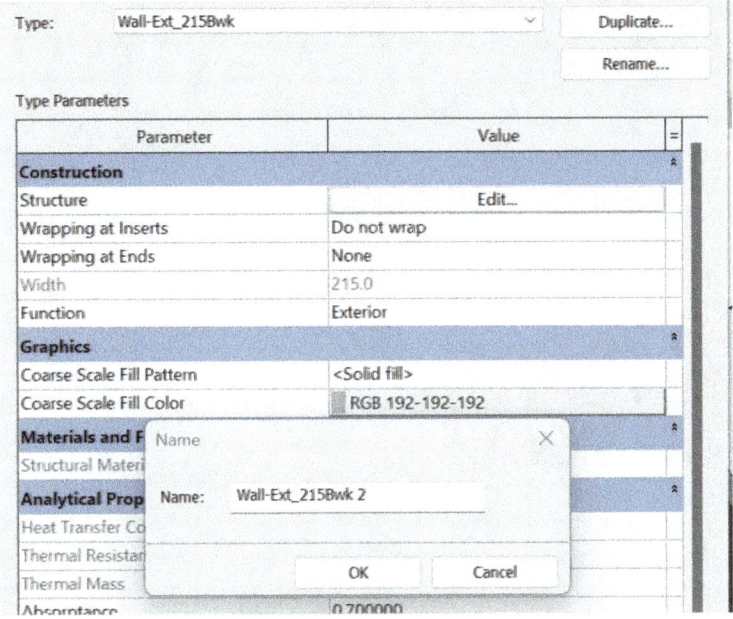

Figure 5-15. *Name your new Wall Type appropriately with the thickness included*

4. Only then should you click "Edit Type"; then click the "Edit…" field next to Structure.

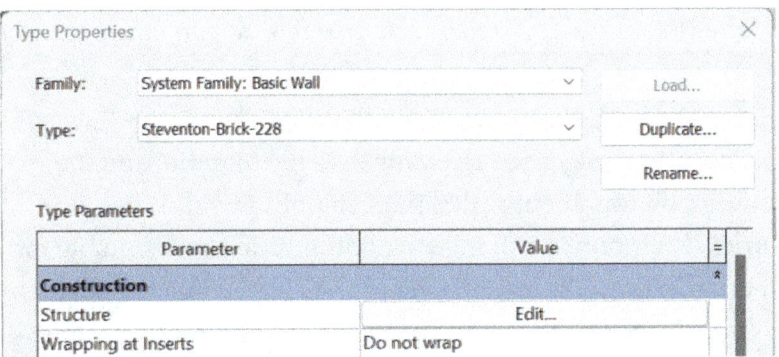

Figure 5-16. *The "Edit" field for updating the wall thickness*

5. This will open the "Edit Assembly" dialogue box; if you click the "Preview" bottom left, an image of the wall structure will appear; as a single structured wall, it will show as a solid shape, which is what will be best for Unreal Engine but not necessarily your Revit model if you are using your model in Revit only.

241

CHAPTER 5   STEP TWO: PRE-PROCESSING

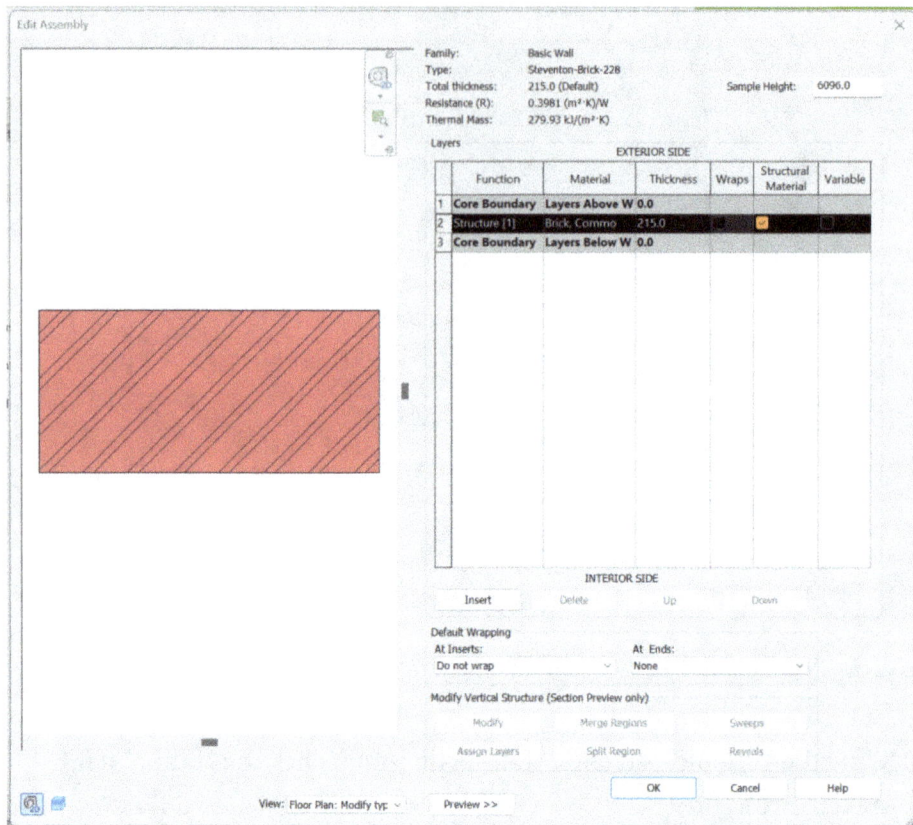

Figure 5-17. *The Preview pane on the left and where you edit the thickness of the wall*

6. The aspects you may need to change are the Material and the Thickness. If I was keeping this in Revit only, I would keep this as "Brick, Common" or change to another Brick type suitable for the period of the Rectory at Steventon. As I am going to take this into Unreal, I will change the material to a common color-only material. This is where, if you haven't already decided to have a model in Revit and a model you will use for Unreal, then perhaps it is a good idea to consider this now before you start changing all your materials to a common color for Unreal. What you could do is build initially for Revit, and then have a full Revit model for Sketchfab or similar and then make a copy and convert your materials for Unreal. I will show here how to change for Unreal, as you will also need to create the common material.

242

CHAPTER 5 STEP TWO: PRE-PROCESSING

- Click the "215.0" under Thickness and then change to the size you need, as stated in the new name, i.e., 228.

	Function	Material	Thickness	Wraps	Structural Material	Variable
		EXTERIOR SIDE				
1	Core Boundary	Layers Above W	0.0			
2	Structure [1]	Brick, Commo	228.0		✓	
3	Core Boundary	Layers Below W	0.0			

Figure 5-18. *The Wall thickness is now changed from 215 mm to 228 mm*

- Then to change the material, click "Common, Brick"; three little dots appear, and it opens to the Material dialogue box.
- The first thing, again before anything else, is to Duplicate the material, which will keep the brick metadata but allow you to change the material. I have called mine "Common Colour".

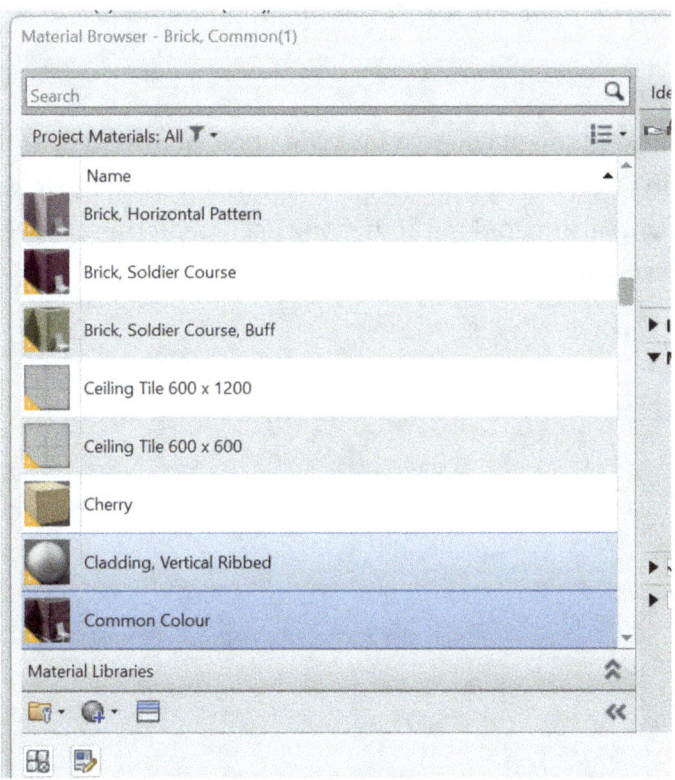

Figure 5-19. *Access the Revit Material by clicking on the Sphere with the +sign*

243

CHAPTER 5   STEP TWO: PRE-PROCESSING

- Now I can change the Appearance by removing the image by choosing color using the side down arrow next to the image name. I have chosen the darker gray under Basic colors.

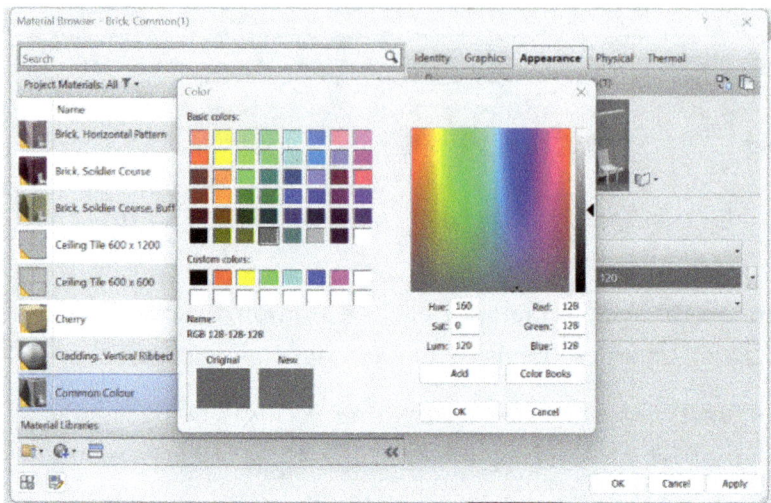

Figure 5-20. *Material Browser for changing the Appearance to a single color material*

- I have also changed where it says what type of brick it is to "Revit Common Colour Grey" so that I will know it is from Revit when it is in Unreal and looking at the long list of materials. I have also unchecked the tick box for "Relief Pattern".

CHAPTER 5   STEP TWO: PRE-PROCESSING

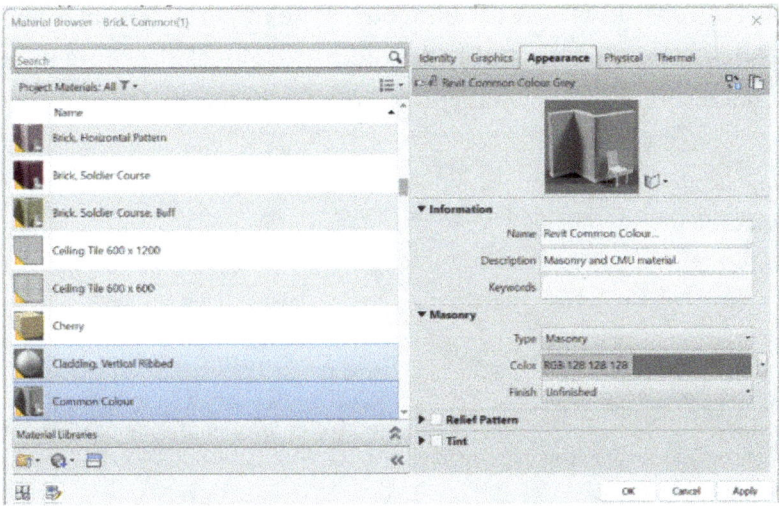

Figure 5-21. *The Appearance tab for adapting the color*

- I can still use the graphical appearance settings as these do not appear to translate through to Unreal as a separate asset like the material image/texture does. You can do this by simply clicking "Use Render Appearance" under the Graphics tab and the color will change to the same gray chosen in the Appearance tab.

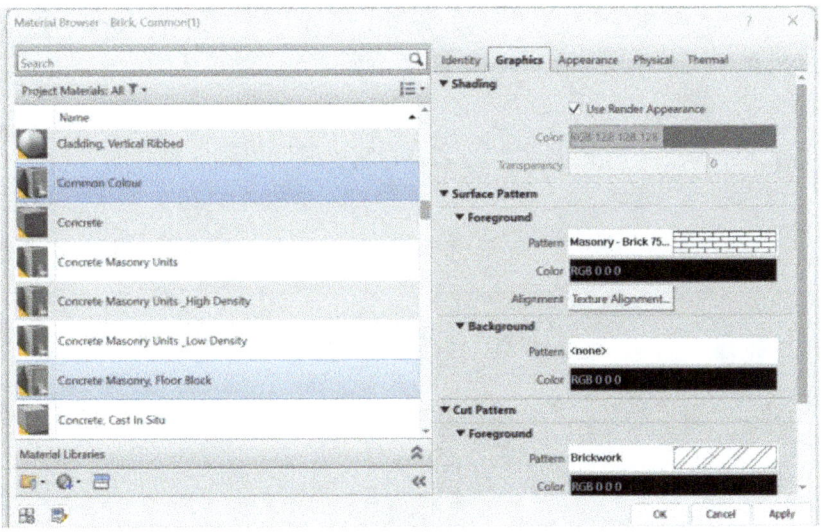

Figure 5-22. *The Graphics tab and ticking the "Use Render Appearance"*

245

CHAPTER 5   STEP TWO: PRE-PROCESSING

- Click "Apply" and "OK" to come out of the material box and you will go back to the Edit Assembly dialogue box. Check the other settings to make sure they are what you want, and then click OK.

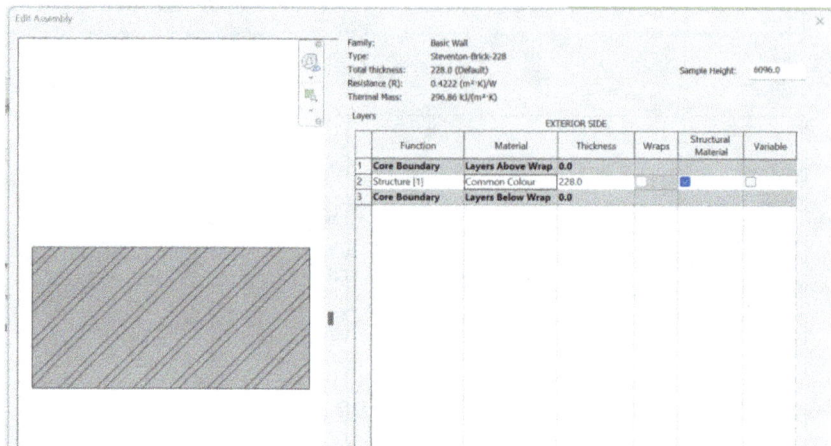

Figure 5-23. *Having applied your material changes, click OK to go back to the Edit Materials box*

- The box closes to your Type Properties box where you can also add or change the data if necessary to the various data fields.

246

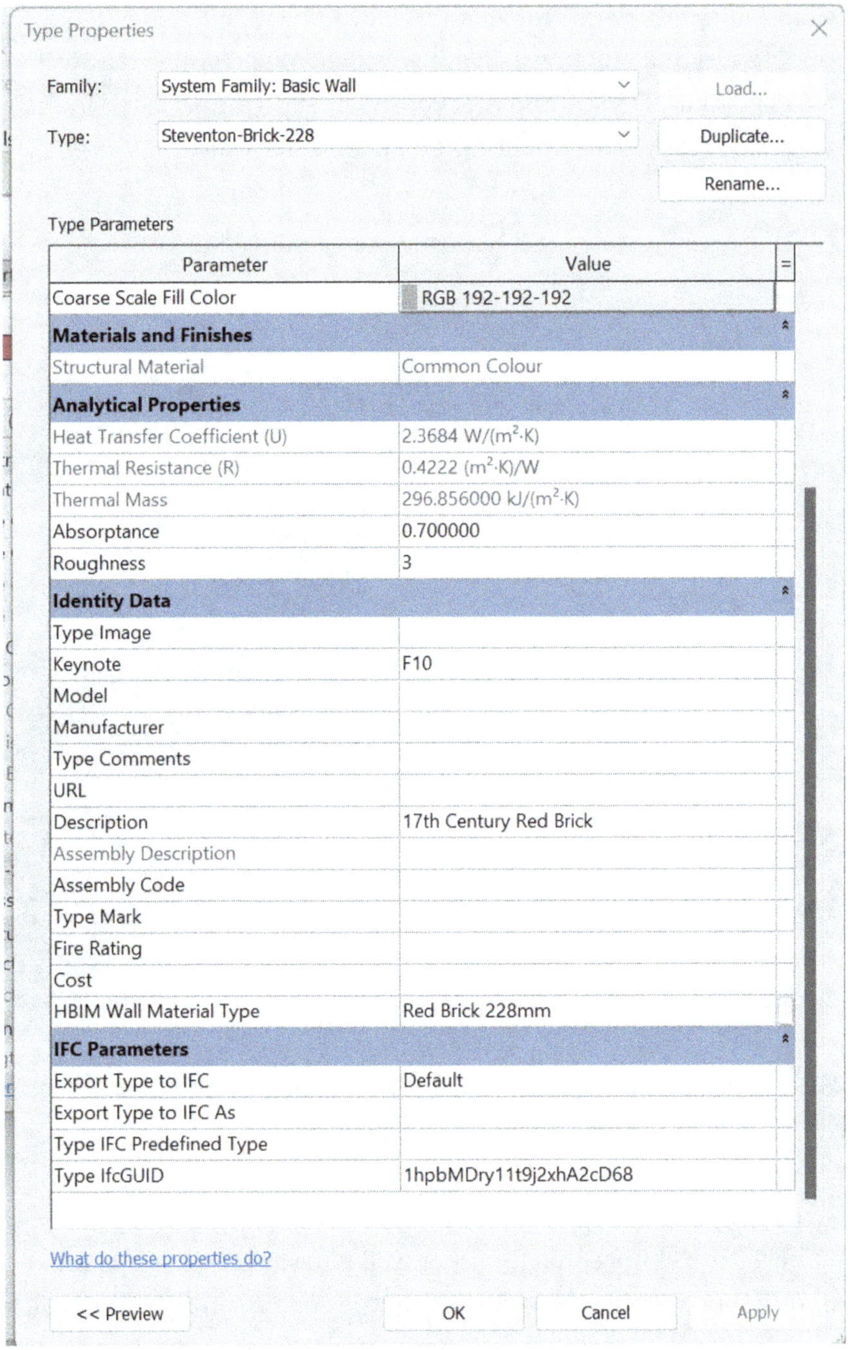

CHAPTER 5   STEP TWO: PRE-PROCESSING

Parameter	Value
Coarse Scale Fill Color	RGB 192-192-192
Materials and Finishes	
Structural Material	Common Colour
Analytical Properties	
Heat Transfer Coefficient (U)	2.3684 W/(m²·K)
Thermal Resistance (R)	0.4222 (m²·K)/W
Thermal Mass	296.856000 kJ/(m²·K)
Absorptance	0.700000
Roughness	3
Identity Data	
Type Image	
Keynote	F10
Model	
Manufacturer	
Type Comments	
URL	
Description	17th Century Red Brick
Assembly Description	
Assembly Code	
Type Mark	
Fire Rating	
Cost	
HBIM Wall Material Type	Red Brick 228mm
IFC Parameters	
Export Type to IFC	Default
Export Type to IFC As	
Type IFC Predefined Type	
Type IfcGUID	1hpbMDry11t9j2xhA2cD68

Type Properties — Family: System Family: Basic Wall — Type: Steventon-Brick-228

Figure 5-24. *The revised Type Properties box for adding further data*

CHAPTER 5   STEP TWO: PRE-PROCESSING

- Click OK and in your Project, the wall you have selected will have updated so that you now can see your new Wall Type and how it looks in your 3D View and that your Wall Type is also listed in the drop-down ready for updating/using for other wall.

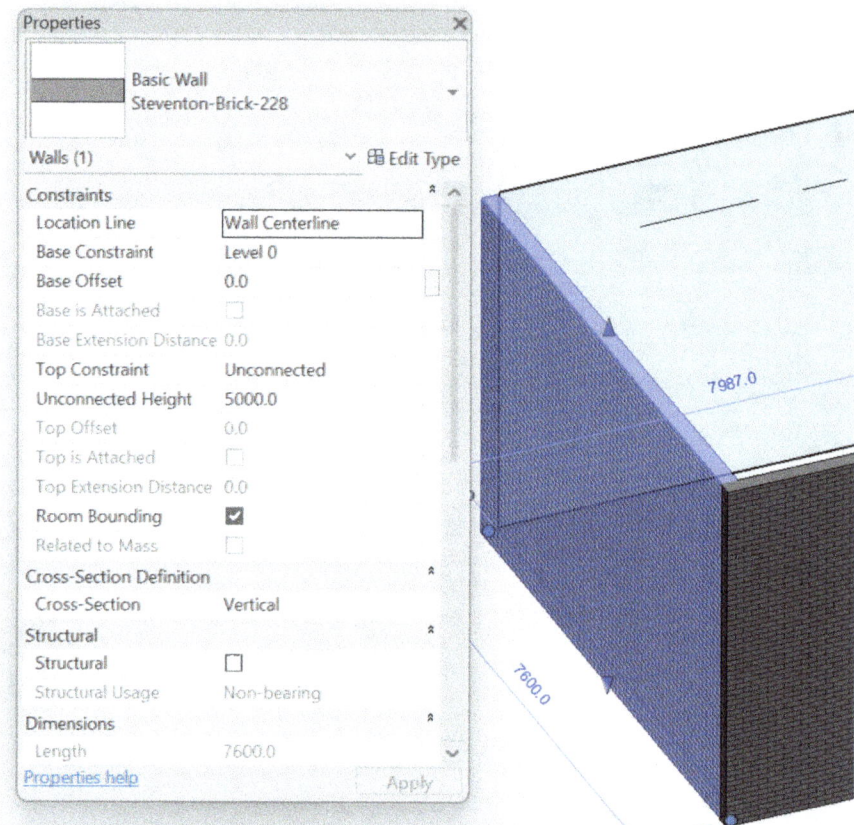

Figure 5-25. *The material change in the 3D view and the Properties box for the Wall Type*

- Having created the Common Colour Grey material, you will now be able to choose that for other wall types you create that are different in structure/thickness to the current one, i.e., you will not have to go through that part of the process for each wall type. You can also duplicate your current wall type and rename to reflect a different thickness as shown in Figures 5-26 and 5-27.

CHAPTER 5   STEP TWO: PRE-PROCESSING

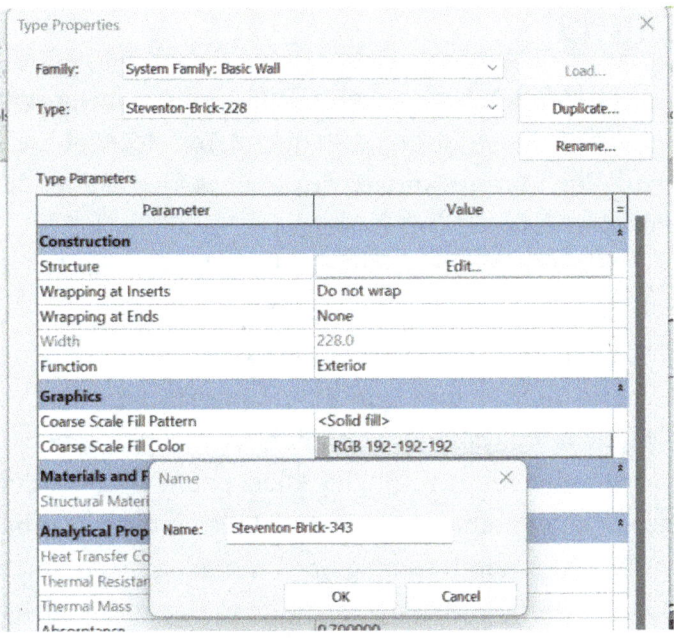

Figure 5-26. *Making further versions of the changed Wall Type using Duplicate and naming appropriately with the Thickness*

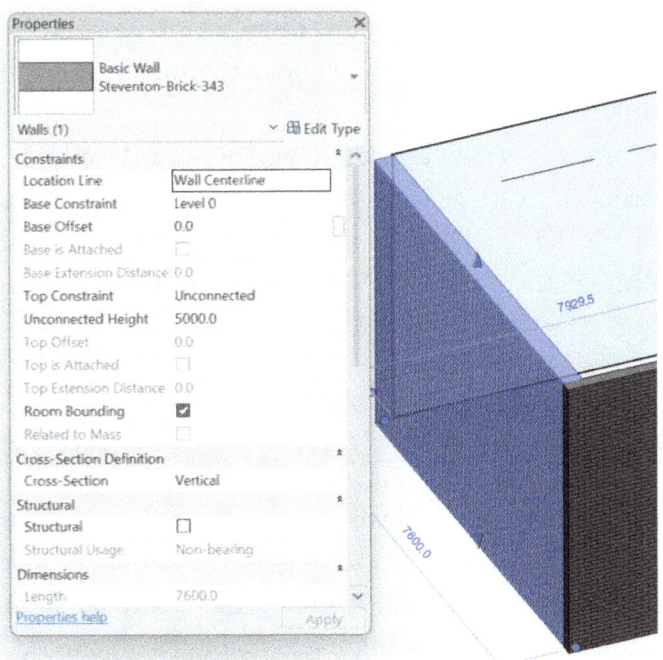

Figure 5-27. *The new Wall Type in place*

CHAPTER 5   STEP TWO: PRE-PROCESSING

Section Summary

Data preparation is a foundational step in any HBIM project, ensuring accuracy, efficiency, and long-term value. It begins with organizing clean, georeferenced data and establishing clear workflows for software environments such as Autodesk Revit. Creating templates for elements such as wall types, windows, and materials ensures consistency, drawing from early CAD practices now enhanced by BIM standards, i.e., IFC.

A critical focus is on preparing custom data object parameters, especially for nonstandard historic materials. This involves identifying relevant material properties (e.g., composition, moisture, structural condition), prioritizing data based on project goals (e.g., conservation or analysis), and defining appropriate data types and units. These parameters are implemented through Project or Shared Parameters in Revit – Shared Parameters being preferable for interoperability and multi-project use.

The document outlines a step-by-step guide for managing parameters, including naming conventions, grouping, and assigning them to categories such as walls. It explains how to use value lists, lookup tables, and scheduling tools to facilitate data entry and validation. Further, it advises on visualization and exporting practices, ensuring HBIM data remains accessible and meaningful throughout the project life cycle.

Examples such as documenting a Wattle and Daub wall illustrate the process of defining detailed metadata fields and linking them within Revit. Key considerations include interoperability, flexibility, thorough documentation, and collaboration with conservation experts.

Finally, the section covers the duplication and editing of wall types in Revit to match historical structures such as Steventon Rectory or Winchester Castle. It explains how to modify wall thickness, replace material images with solid color representations for Unreal Engine, and manage material libraries efficiently for performance in game engines.

How to Manage Incomplete or Missing Data

In historical reconstruction projects, dealing with incomplete or missing data is inevitable. By applying the following key strategies, you should be able to manage uncertainty responsibly, encourage critical engagement with the model, and lay the groundwork for future information as and if it becomes available:

- **Triangulation of Sources:** Drawing on multiple types of evidence (e.g., photographs, written records, maps, oral histories, architectural patterns) to infer likely features or dimensions. When one source is incomplete, another may provide a clue that helps piece together the missing information.

- **Typological Comparison/Historical Precedent:** You can choose to infer missing information based on documentation of similar historic buildings from the same period, region, architect, and construction type. This method relies on architectural typologies and historical norms to make educated assumptions about style, materials, or spatial arrangements. I would still gain expert opinion before committing.

  - Appropriate use would be when detailed historical research provides strong evidence for typical materials, dimensions, or construction techniques. It does, though, require careful comparison and justification.

- **Documenting Assumptions and Certainty Levels:** Clearly noting areas where assumptions are made, perhaps through metadata tags or visual markers in the model and grading the confidence level of each element. Transparency is crucial for conservational record rigor and future changes.

- **Expert Judgment**: As mentioned earlier, consulting with historians, archaeologists, architects, or local heritage groups may provide insights not found in formal archives. They can provide support or verification by using their expertise to estimate missing values based on visual inspection, historical context, and understanding of building behavior. This interdisciplinary collaboration can also help to bring to mind overlooked data or validate speculative elements, for example, the pillars expert discussion at Hyde Abbey mentioned in the "Overview of the Reconstruction Process" section in Chapter 3.

  - Appropriate use would be when other methods are not feasible. It is important, much like referencing, that the advice is clearly documented as expert opinion.

CHAPTER 5   STEP TWO: PRE-PROCESSING

- **Using Parametric or Modular Design**: When details are missing, parametric modelling techniques or modular components can be used to suggest likely configurations without locking the model into a single interpretation. These can be swapped or updated as new evidence emerges.

- **Versioning and Iterative Modelling**: Maintaining versions of the model that reflect different levels of data completeness or different thoughts/options for the missing aspect(s), allowing users to explore multiple scenarios. This could then also help users understand how interpretations evolve over time.

- **Leaving Space for the Unknown**: Occasionally it might be appropriate to leave parts of the model blank, ghosted, or abstracted to visually indicate uncertainty and therefore avoid misleading the viewer. You can visually represent the missing data by using transparent or dashed elements or specific color codes. This would also help to reinforce the idea that historical reconstruction is a process rather than a finished product. By omitting the missing data, though, be aware it can limit the functionality of analysis and simulation tools that require complete datasets.

  - Appropriate use would be when the impact of the missing data is significant and any addition highly speculative, or when the focus is on highlighting areas needing further investigation.

Ultimately, transparency is paramount. Clearly communicating the presence of missing data enables users to understand the limitations and interpret the results accordingly. The temptation to make assumptions on how to fill in those gaps, for an HBIM model in particular, could result in the model being viewed as invalid, not trustworthy and therefore negated. For purely visualization purposes, in past projects, incomplete information may have been "passed over" by ensuring the camera views are focused only on the areas that are known, hiding the incomplete areas. With the ability to roam, either on desktop, walkthroughs, or in VR/XR, the complete model would normally be accessible; therefore, "hiding" would not be possible without questions being asked, i.e., why can that area not be accessed?

A Step-by-Step Guide – Student Based

Our students have been taught 3D modelling for primarily visualization purposes. We explained that missing information should prioritize visual plausibility and historical accuracy within the constraints of their project time and available resources. The following step-by-step guide is what we encourage students to work through, which may be helpful here:

Step-by-Step Guide (For Students to Consider Regarding Missing Data)

1. **Thorough Initial Investigation** (within the time frame and resources of the student client project module):

    - **Maximize Existing Documentation** – start by reviewing/revisiting all available resources:

        - **Measured Drawings**: Search for any existing plans, elevations, or sections, even if incomplete.

        - **Photographs**: Analyze historical and contemporary photographs for clues about missing elements, materials, and finishes. Make sure to pay attention to details such as window patterns, roof lines, and decorative features.

        - **Historical Maps**: These provide context about the building's layout and surrounding environment.

        - **Written Records**: Look for any historical descriptions, inventories, or local history accounts that might mention the missing features.

        - **Online Archives**: Explore digital archives of historical societies, libraries, and museums.

CHAPTER 5   STEP TWO: PRE-PROCESSING

- **Site Visit** (if feasible): If access to the building is possible, conduct a careful visual survey. Note existing materials, construction techniques, and any remaining fragments that could suggest the form of missing elements. Take detailed photographs of surviving details.

- **Sketching and Note-Taking**: Document all findings with sketches and detailed notes.

2. **Prioritization Based on Visual Impact**: Since the primary goal set is visualization, focus on filling in the information that would have the most significant impact on the visual representation of the building. This could include

   - **Major Geometric Elements:** Missing walls, roof sections, significant openings (doors and windows)

   - **Key Architectural Features:** Columns, arches, cornices, decorative moldings

   - **Dominant Materials and Finishes:** Wall materials (brick, stone, plaster), roofing materials, windows and door materials

3. **Employing Visual Inference and Historical Precedents**

   - **Visual Continuation:** If a feature is partially visible, extrapolate its likely form based on the existing parts. For example, if a section of a cornice is intact, assume the missing parts follow a similar pattern.

   - **Symmetry and Repetition:** Historic buildings often exhibit symmetry and repeating elements (e.g., window types, spacing of columns). Use these patterns to infer missing components.

   - **Analogies with Similar Buildings:** Research well-documented historic buildings of the same period, style, and location. Look for comparable architectural features, materials, and construction techniques that could reasonably be applied to the building you are modelling. Cite the precedents you are using in your documentation.

- **Common Building Practices:** Understand typical construction methods and materials used during the building's era. This can help in making educated guesses about concealed elements or missing details.

4. **Simple and Justifiable Imputation Techniques:** For visualization, prioritize methods that are visually plausible and can be justified based on the available evidence:

    - **Direct Modelling Based on Inference:** If you can confidently infer the geometry of a missing element based on visual continuation or symmetry, model it directly. Clearly document your reasoning.

    - **Applying Standard Materials and Finishes:** If the material of a surviving element is known, and there is no evidence to suggest otherwise, assume the same material for missing but similar elements. For example, if a section of brick wall exists, assume missing wall sections are also brick.

    - **Using Generic but Period-Appropriate Details:** If specific details are missing (e.g., window tracery patterns), research typical window designs of the period and use a representative, albeit generic, pattern. Acknowledge that this is an approximation.

    - **"Placeholder" Elements:** If the form of an element is entirely unknown, consider using a simplified "placeholder" element to indicate its presence without making a definitive statement about its appearance. For example, a simple rectangular block to represent a missing outbuilding if its exact dimensions are unknown.

5. **Documentation Is Key for a Student:** Crucially, as a student, you must meticulously document all instances of missing information and the rationale behind your decisions for filling those gaps. This demonstrates your understanding of the limitations and the assumptions you have made. Your documentation should include

- Clear identification regarding which parts of the model are based on incomplete or missing data.

- Explain the sources of information (drawings, photos, precedents) used to inform your assumptions.

- Describe the techniques you have used to replace missing data values with estimated values, allowing for analysis using complete datasets you employed (visual continuation, analogy, etc.).

- Acknowledge the level of uncertainty associated with the information used in place of the missing data.

6. **Seek Feedback:** Share your model and documentation with instructors or peers. Their feedback can help identify areas where your assumptions might be questionable or where further investigation is needed.

Example Scenario

Imagine you are modelling a historic house and a section of the roof is missing in all available drawings and photos. For visualization purposes, you might

- **Examine Surviving Roof Sections:** Note the roof pitch, material (e.g., slate tiles), and any visible details like eaves or dormers.

- **Research Similar Houses in the Area from the Same Period:** Look for common roof shapes and materials.

- Based on this research, infer a plausible roof shape and material for the missing section.

- Document that the roof form in this area is an informed assumption based on surviving evidence and regional architectural precedents.

Adding Data As It Becomes Available

Once you have exported your model to Revit, and then a few months or more later, missing data has been sourced and verified, how do you go about updating the amended Revit model to Unreal? The best method is via Datasmith Direct Link from Revit to Unreal Engine.

CHAPTER 5　STEP TWO: PRE-PROCESSING

This is a nondestructive workflow, where updates to your Revit model can be pushed to Unreal without starting from scratch each time. Additional HBIM data enrichment such as the shared parameters discussed in the previous section can be changed or updated in Revit and re-exported and reimported via Datasmith and the parameter values will be refreshed with the new or amended data. Your materials in Unreal that you have used on the previous import can be preserved, i.e., the re-import does not override existing ones. The "Preserve Data" option in Datasmith enables your materials to be retained via a material substitution table to pick which materials you want to replace with Unreal's materials.

The following is a breakdown of the workflow to maintain that dynamic link between Revit and Unreal.

Step-by-Step Workflow for a Revit–Unreal Link (Update-Friendly)

1. **Install Datasmith Exporter for Revit**
    - Go to Unreal Datasmith Exporters and download the Datasmith Exporter for Revit plug-in that matches your version of Revit. You can only use for Revit versions up to 2024, which can then only be used for Unreal Engine versions up to 5.2.

Figure 5-28. *Unreal Engine's Autodesk Revit Exporter window*

CHAPTER 5   STEP TWO: PRE-PROCESSING

- **For 2024+ versions of Revit, please see Step 2, 3, and 5.**
- Install it and make sure it appears in Revit as a new ribbon tab.

2. **Export from Revit As a Datasmith File (.udatasmith)**

   - In Revit, go to the Datasmith tab. Click Export 3D View.
   - Choose a 3D view that is clean and ready for export (no working views).
   - Save the .udatasmith and accompanying folder somewhere accessible.

Note   For 2024+ versions of Revit, you will need to lock your 3D view.

- Set up your 3D view and hide annotation categories such as text, levels, and similar.
- Click the Lock 3D View icon on the bottom view options bar – house symbol next to the glasses – and choose the "Save orientation and lock view" option.

Figure 5-29.   The bottom view options bar with the Lock 3D View icon

- Under the top Ribbon Bar, choose the View Tab and go the Twinmotion drop-down menu and ensure Auto Sync is active; if not, then click to make active.
- Go back to the Twinmotion drop-down menu and then select Export to Datasmith File.

CHAPTER 5   STEP TWO: PRE-PROCESSING

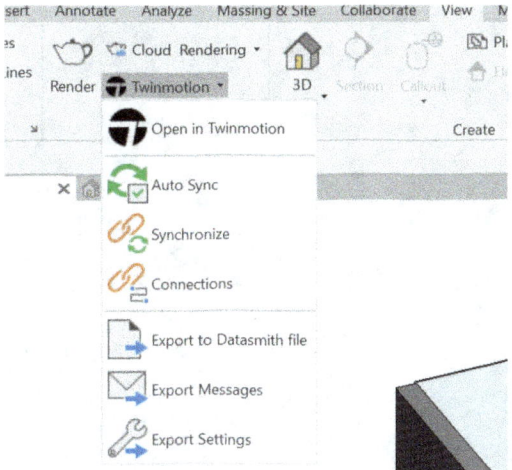

Figure 5-30. *Twinmotion drop-down window*

Tip   Make sure to export from the same 3D view every time to maintain consistency.

---

3. **Import Datasmith File into Unreal Engine**

   - In Unreal, make sure Datasmith plug-in is enabled (it is by default in Architectural templates).

CHAPTER 5   STEP TWO: PRE-PROCESSING

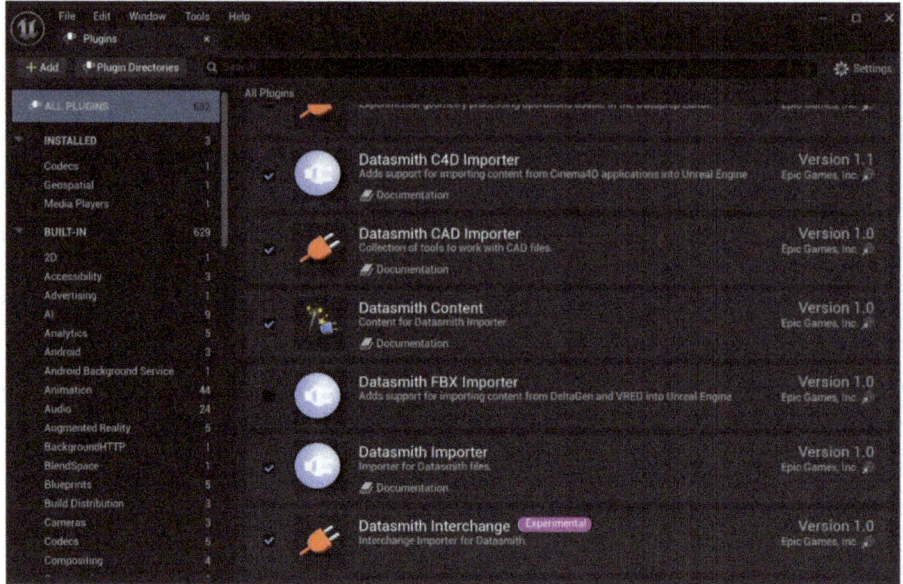

Figure 5-31. *Unreal Plugin window under the Edit tab*

- Go to File ➤ Import Datasmith and select your .udatasmith file.
- Choose to import into a new or existing level. Unreal will create a folder structure with all the geometry, materials, and hierarchy intact.

Figure 5-32. *The imported Revit model using the Datasmith plug-in*

Note For using Revit versions up to Revit 2024 and Unreal Engine 5.2, there is a different process.

- Please follow the instructions on the link provided below for Revit 2023 as I do not have Revit 2023 on my machine. The Unreal Engine "Exporting Datasmith Content from Revit" (`https://dev.epicgames.com/documentation/en-us/unreal-engine/exporting-datasmith-content-from-revit-to-unreal-engine`) provides the process via screengrabs so you can see the changes in Revit 2023 and Revit 2024.

4. **Enable Reimport Support**

   When importing the .udatasmith file, Unreal automatically tracks the source path.

   Later, if you update the Revit model and export a new .udatasmith from the same view and overwrite the old file, you can

   - Right-click the Datasmith scene in Unreal's Content Browser.
   - Choose Reimport to bring in the updates.

CHAPTER 5   STEP TWO: PRE-PROCESSING

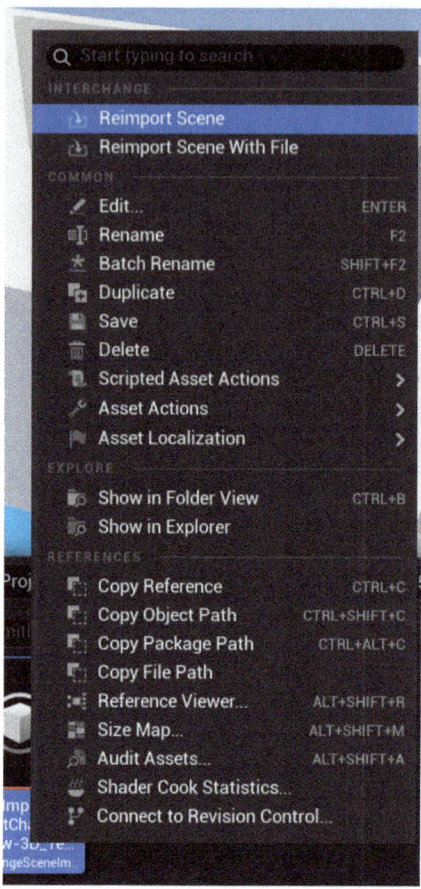

Figure 5-33. *The Reimport window shows after right-clicking on the scene in the Content Browser folder*

This keeps materials, lightmaps, and custom changes (where possible) intact.

5. **Using the Datasmith Direct Link (Optional for Twinmotion or Bridge Workflows)**

If you are using Twinmotion or Unreal Engine with Twinmotion Bridge, you can try Live Link, which enables real-time syncing:

- **In Revit:** Use the Twinmotion plug-in (Direct Link).

- **In Unreal:** Use Twinmotion for Unreal Engine (TM4UE) to sync.

However, Direct Link does not support full UE scene control – it is more limited than the manual Datasmith workflow for complex UE projects.

CHAPTER 5   STEP TWO: PRE-PROCESSING

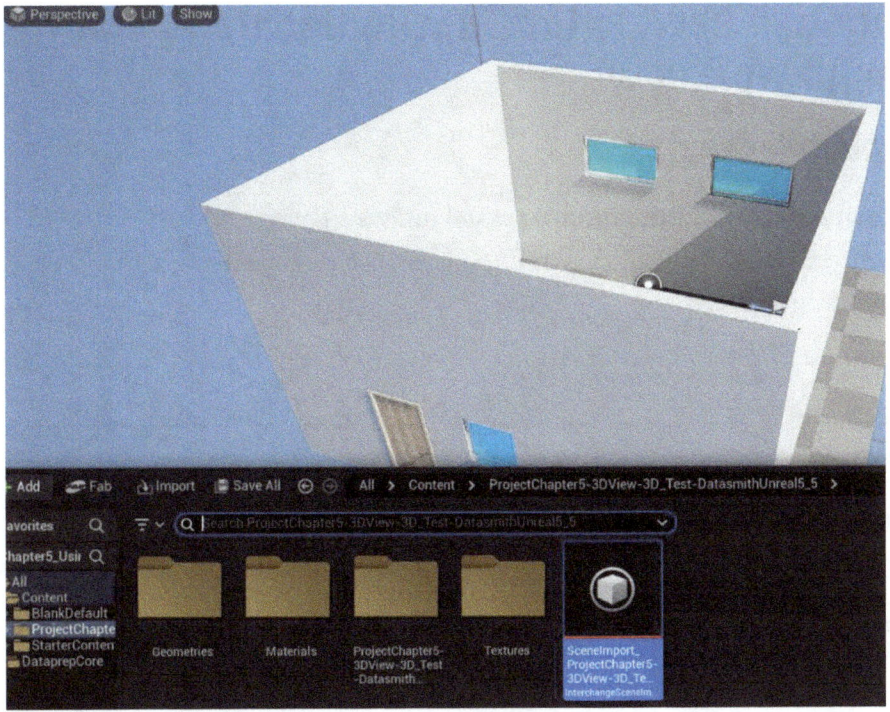

Figure 5-34. *The reimported file and the changes made coming through from Revit*

Note   I have found that this is not yet consistent with the versions I have used (Revit 2024 and Unreal Engine V5.5.4). You can instead use the export file again with any changes and then reimport file by right-clicking on the scene file in the Content Browser as outlined above. Unfortunately Version 5.3.1, my other version, and presumably Version 5.2 being an older version again, does not see the Datasmith file ".udatasmith" exported from Revit in Windows Explorer; therefore, I was not able to import to Unreal. I have tried with the Beta Interchange Format ticked and unticked in the Plugin window and restarted as prompted, but still no luck. You might have better luck, but for me, it did not work.

263

CHAPTER 5   STEP TWO: PRE-PROCESSING

Mini Tutorial: Revit to Unreal with Update-Friendly Datasmith Workflow

What You Will Create

A small Revit model (a simple room or small building) exported and imported into Unreal Engine 5 using Datasmith, with updates from Revit reflecting in Unreal without reimporting from scratch.

Prerequisites

Tool	Version
Autodesk Revit	2024
Unreal Engine	5.5 or later
Datasmith plug-in in Unreal	Enabled (Architectural template includes it)

Step-by-Step Tutorial

Step 1: Create a Simple Revit Model Using Revit 2024

1. Open Revit.
2. Create a new project using the Architectural Template.
3. Model a basic room:
    - Walls and floor.
    - Add a door and a window.
    - Place a few furniture items if you would like (e.g., table, chairs).
4. Name your 3D view clearly, e.g., "Export_View".

CHAPTER 5   STEP TWO: PRE-PROCESSING

Figure 5-35. *Locked 3D View ready for exporting*

Tip   Hide categories you do not want (like 2D annotations) from this 3D view.

Step 2: Export to Datasmith

1. Go to the View Tab ➤ Click Twinmotion to access the drop-down menu.

2. Select your "Export_View".

3. Save the .udatasmith file and accompanying folder to a clear location (e.g., Documents/DatasmithTest/).

Step 3: Import into Unreal Engine

1. Open Unreal Engine.

2. Start a new project using the Architectural Visualisation Template.

3. In Content Browser, go to File ➤ Import into Level.

4. Select the .udatasmith file you exported.

5. Choose a folder name and level to import into.

6. You should see your Revit model appear in the viewport.

265

CHAPTER 5   STEP TWO: PRE-PROCESSING

Figure 5-36. *Your Revit model live in Unreal*

At this point, everything from Revit should be live in Unreal.

Step 4: Customize in Unreal (Optional)

1. Add lighting (sunlight, spotlights, etc.).

2. Apply custom Unreal materials to a few surfaces.

3. Add a camera or a player start point.

CHAPTER 5   STEP TWO: PRE-PROCESSING

Figure 5-37. *Unreal Material added to the imported Revit floor*

Try not to move the actual geometry from Revit yet; this keeps reimport clean.

Step 5: Make a Change in Revit

1. Go back to Revit.

2. You will notice that the Unreal floor material does not show in Revit.

3. Modify the model, e.g., move a wall or change a window type.

4. Save and re-export the same 3D view to the same .udatasmith file, overwriting it.

267

CHAPTER 5   STEP TWO: PRE-PROCESSING

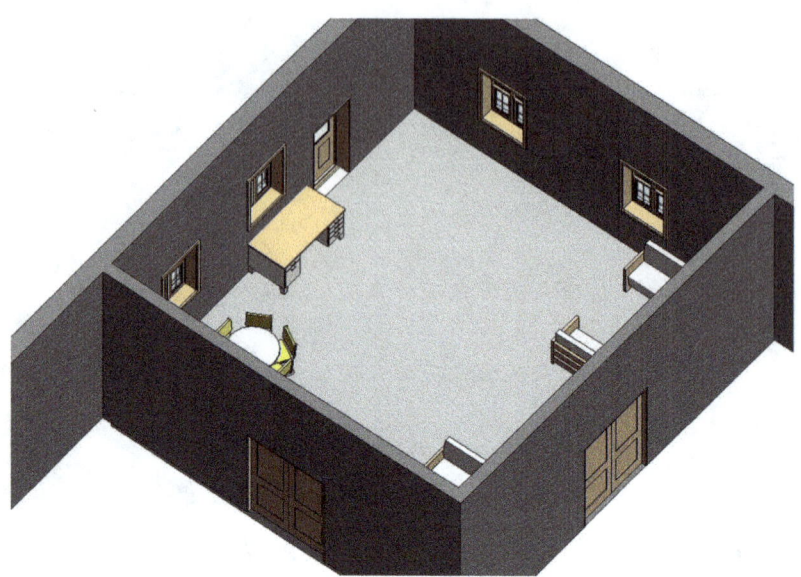

Figure 5-38. *In Revit, make a change, save then using the Twinmotion drop-down, and export the Datasmith file*

Step 6: Reimport in Unreal

1. In Unreal, go to the Content Browser.

2. Locate the imported Datasmith Scene file (YourSceneName.uasset).

3. Right-click it ➤ Reimport.

4. Watch as your model updates in place, without needing to redo materials or settings!

Figure 5-39. *The reimported Revit file updating the change made in Revit, now visible in your Unreal Engine scene*

Bonus Test: Custom Elements

Try placing a plant, light, or particle effect in Unreal outside the Revit model folder. Then reimport the Datasmith scene and verify that your Unreal-specific assets stay intact.

Section Summary

In historical reconstruction projects, managing incomplete or missing data is both inevitable and critical. A responsible approach involves drawing on multiple sources such as photographs, written records, maps, oral histories, and architectural patterns to piece together gaps in documentation. This triangulation helps ensure that when one source is incomplete, others may provide the clues needed for informed reconstruction. A complementary strategy involves comparing the building in question with typologically similar structures from the same period, region, or architectural tradition. This allows educated assumptions about features such as materials, dimensions, and layout, though such assumptions should always be backed by expert consultation where possible.

CHAPTER 5   STEP TWO: PRE-PROCESSING

Transparency is essential in this process. Any assumptions made during modelling should be carefully documented, whether through metadata, color coding, or confidence grading within the HBIM model. When expert judgment is used such as advice from historians or archaeologists, it must be recorded clearly as opinion to preserve the scholarly integrity of the model. Where uncertainty is high, parametric or modular modelling techniques are useful, as they allow the representation of possible configurations without committing to a single version. Maintaining multiple versions of the model that reflect varying degrees of certainty is also helpful, both for future revisions and for educating users about how historical interpretation evolves over time.

In some cases, it may be better to leave certain areas of a model visually abstracted or ghosted to signify missing data. While this may limit certain simulation tools, it helps avoid the risk of misrepresenting speculative elements as factual. This is particularly important in immersive environments such as VR, where users can explore the full model and would likely notice, and question, any inconsistencies or inaccessible areas.

For students working primarily on visualization projects, a guided process is recommended. This begins with thorough research into available documentation, including drawings, photos, historical maps, and site visits if feasible. Visual impact should guide the prioritization of which missing data to address, focusing on major structural and stylistic elements. Students are encouraged to use visual cues, symmetry, and repetition to infer missing parts, while drawing analogies with well-documented buildings of the same style and period. Where needed, simplified placeholders can be used, as long as they are clearly identified as nondefinitive. Importantly, students must document all assumptions, sources, and techniques used to address missing data and seek feedback to strengthen their approach.

Once additional data becomes available, integration into an existing Unreal Engine model can be managed efficiently using the Datasmith workflow from Revit. By exporting from a locked 3D view in Revit to a .udatasmith file and reimporting into Unreal, changes to geometry or HBIM data can be updated nondestructively. Materials and scene structure remain intact, ensuring the continuity of visual and technical fidelity. This approach supports iterative modelling while maintaining a dynamic link between design tools and visualization platforms.

A quick reference for best practice for an Update-Resistant workflow can be found in Table 5-1.

Table 5-1. *Best practice reference for linking Revit to Unreal to ensure an Update-Resistant workflow*

Tip	Why It Matters
Use consistent naming in Revit	Prevents object duplication or mismatches during reimport
Do not move actors around in Unreal if you plan to reimport	It will reset positions based on Revit origin
Add lighting, materials, foliage, etc., outside the Datasmith hierarchy	Keeps them unaffected by reimport
Lock down the Revit 3D view used for export	Changing it will affect export consistency

Georeferencing and Aligning Datasets

GIS (Geographic Information Systems) plays a crucial role in HBIM by georeferencing historical data, integrating spatial datasets, and aligning reconstructed models within real-world coordinates.

GIS integration in HBIM is used to

- Georeference historical maps and plans
- Align point clouds, CAD, and photogrammetry with real-world coordinates
- Manage spatial metadata (e.g., material decay, urban context)
- Facilitate analysis and visualization of historical building locations

For 2D data pre-processing, you will need to convert rasterized historical maps or scanned drawings into vector-based CAD files. You can achieve this by possibly using AutoCAD Raster Design or QGIS. You will also need to ensure the 2D content is at the correct scale and coordinates are correctly referenced. You can align historical maps and floor plans to real-world coordinates using QGIS (GDAL georeferencing) or ArcGIS Pro if you have access to the latter. You can also use Autodesk Revit's "Specify Coordinates" if you have the real-world coordinates to hand. Cross-referencing the modern survey data with historical maps will also need to be worked on, correcting any changes to the landscape, i.e., removing/editing roads for the 1400s in my case.

CHAPTER 5   STEP TWO: PRE-PROCESSING

Below is a step-by-step guide for georeferencing historical maps and drawings, covering key tools and methods:

Step 1: Import Historical Map into GIS
Software: QGIS (Free) | ArcGIS Pro (Paid)

- Load historical raster images (TIFF, JPEG, PNG) into QGIS/ArcGIS.
- Ensure the image covers the correct geographic area.

Step 2: Assign Control Points (Ground Control Points – GCPs)

- Identify known reference points (churches, roads, riverbanks) in both the historical map and a modern map (OpenStreetMap, satellite imagery).
- Use the Georeferencer Tool (QGIS) or Georeferencing Toolbar (ArcGIS).
- Select at least four to six control points for accurate transformation.

Step 3: Apply Transformation and Save Georeferenced Image

- Choose a transformation method:
  - Affine (for simple distortions)
  - Polynomial (1st or 2nd order) (for moderate distortions)
  - Thin Plate Spline (TPS) (for highly distorted images)
- Save as GeoTIFF (georeferenced raster file).

Output: Georeferenced map that aligns with real-world coordinates

If you are not sure how to convert your 2D CAD drawings (your historical floor plans or site maps) ready for GIS integrations by assigning them spatial coordinates, the following steps provide a method to follow.

Converting 2D CAD Drawings for GIS Integration

Step 1: Import CAD File into GIS

- In QGIS: Use "Add Vector Layer" → Import .dwg/.dxf.
- In ArcGIS: Use "CAD to Geodatabase" tool.

Step 2: Assign CRS (Coordinate Reference System)

- If no coordinate system exists, manually assign one matching the real-world location (e.g., OSGB36 (EPSG:27700) for UK projects).

Step 3: Align CAD Drawing to GIS Map

- Use the Georeferencer Plugin (QGIS) or Spatial Adjustment Tool (ArcGIS).
- Match known reference points (building corners, road intersections).
- Apply transformation and export as Shapefile (.shp) or GeoJSON (.geojson) for GIS compatibility.

Output: CAD drawings correctly positioned within the GIS environment

If you are using point cloud data, the following steps will help you to align for spatial analysis in GIS.

Integrating Point Clouds with GIS

Step 1: Prepare Point Cloud for GIS

- Convert LiDAR scan (.LAS, .LAZ, .E57) into GIS-compatible format.
- Tools
    - CloudCompare: Export as LAZ (compressed LiDAR format).
    - LAStools: Convert to GeoTIFF DEM (Digital Elevation Model) if needed.

Step 2: Import Point Cloud into QGIS

- Use "LAStools Plugin" → Import .las/.laz files.
- Generate elevation maps or classify data (ground vs. non-ground).

Output: LiDAR scans aligned in GIS for spatial analysis

For HBIM models, the following should help:

Export HBIM Model for GIS

- Convert Revit/Rhino model to GeoJSON or CityGML format.
- Use FME Workbench or BlenderBIM for conversion.

Output: HBIM models aligned in GIS for spatial analysis

CHAPTER 5   STEP TWO: PRE-PROCESSING

The above guides should be helpful in knowing how to use GIS to enhance HBIM by managing historical metadata, particularly regarding the possible uses such as mapping historical material decay data (brick erosion, timber damage), overlaying building evolution timelines in different eras, or creating interactive 3D city models integrating HBIM and GIS layers, as in the Virtual Cities – Winchester project.

The following step-by-step tutorial takes a more detailed approach in case you are not familiar with QGIS.

Step-by-Step Guide: Georeferencing Historical Maps in QGIS

This tutorial will guide you through georeferencing a historical map in QGIS and align it with real-world coordinates.

Required Tools

- QGIS (Free, download from qgis.org)
- A historical map (JPEG, PNG, TIFF)
- A modern reference map (OpenStreetMap, satellite imagery, or shapefiles)

Step 1: Load QGIS and Open a Basemap

1. Open QGIS and create a new project.
2. Add a reference layer (e.g., OpenStreetMap) to help align your historical map:
    - Click "XYZ Tiles" in the Browser panel.
    - Right-click "OpenStreetMap" → Select "Add Layer to Project".
    - This will serve as the reference to align your historical image.

CHAPTER 5   STEP TWO: PRE-PROCESSING

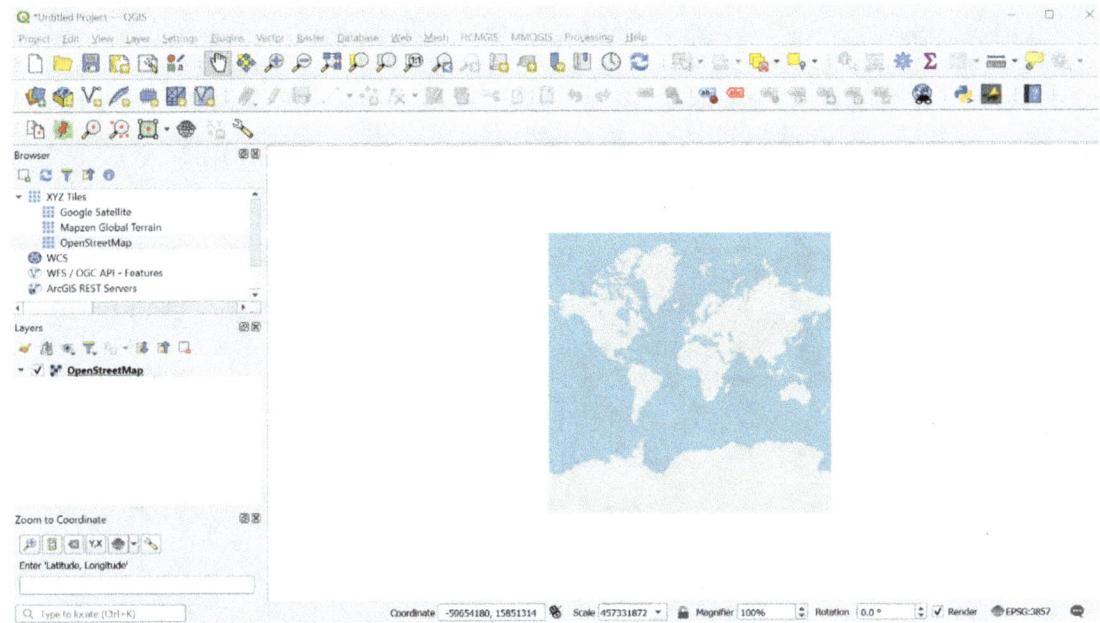

Figure 5-40. Step 1: OpenStreetMap Screen in QGIS

Step 2: Load the Georeferencer Tool

1. In the QGIS Menu, go to "Layer" ➤ "Georeferencer" ➤ "Georeferencer…".

2. In the Georeferencer window, click "Open Raster" and select your historical map (JPEG, PNG, or TIFF).

3. The image will appear in the Georeferencer window, ready for control point selection.

CHAPTER 5   STEP TWO: PRE-PROCESSING

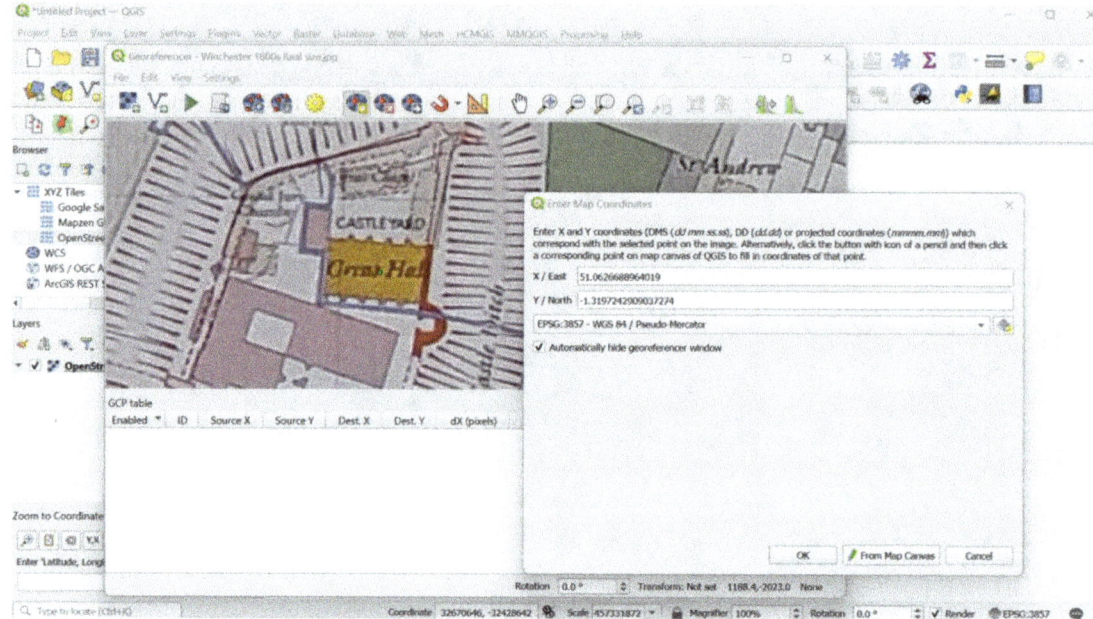

Figure 5-41. *Step 2: The Georeferencer dialogue box with the historical map showing*

Step 3: Assign Control Points (Ground Control Points – GCPs)

1. Click "Add Point" (📍 icon) in the toolbar.

2. Identify a known location (e.g., a church, road intersection, or landmark) in your historical map.

3. Click on that point and enter the real-world coordinates OR select it manually from the reference basemap:

    • Click "From Map Canvas" and find the same location in OpenStreetMap or another reference layer.

    • Click on the correct point in the modern map to get the real coordinates.

4. Repeat this for at least four to six well-distributed points across the image.

5. Once done, click "OK" to save each control point.

CHAPTER 5   STEP TWO: PRE-PROCESSING

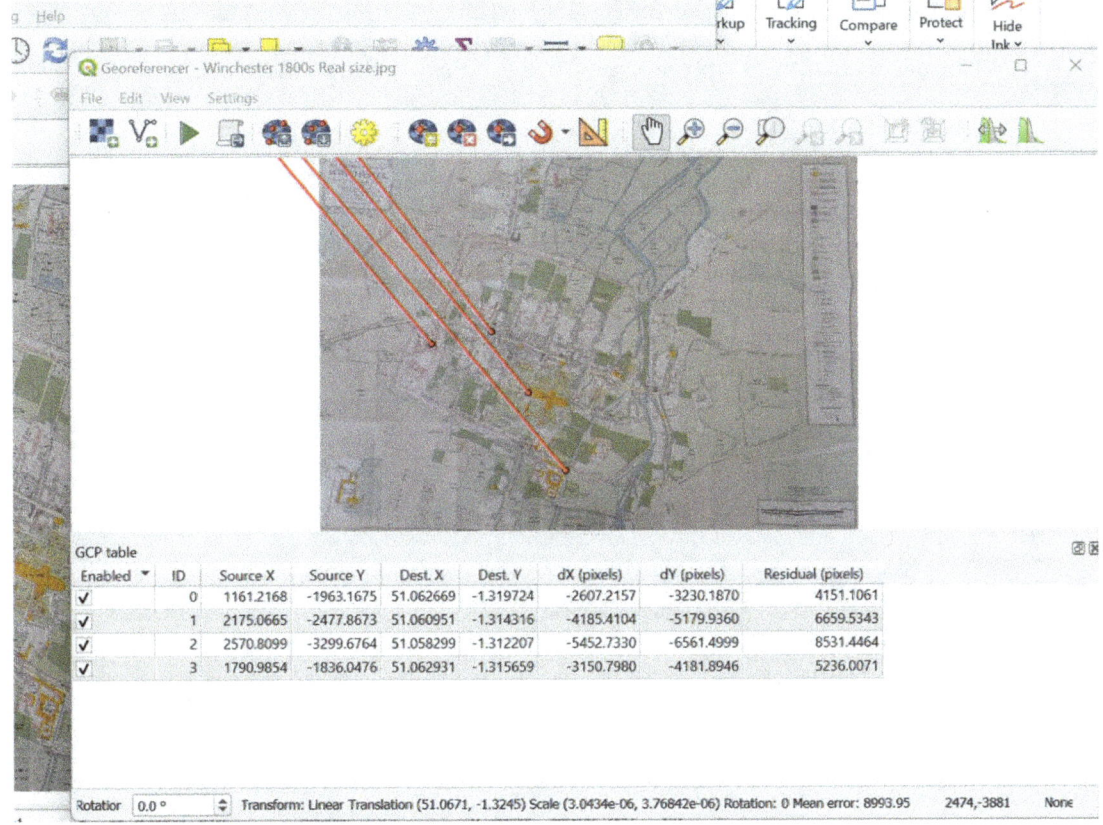

Figure 5-42. *Step 3: Adding real-world coordinates in Georeferencer*

Step 4: Apply Transformation and Georeference

1. Go to Settings in the Georeferencer and click "Transformation Settings" (⚙ icon).

2. Choose a transformation method (based on image distortion):

    • Affine (for minimal distortion)

    • Polynomial 1st Order (for slight warping)

    • Thin Plate Spline (TPS) (for highly distorted historical maps)

3. Set the output coordinate system (CRS):

    • Click "Select CRS" ➤ Choose an appropriate system (e.g., EPSG:4326 (WGS84) or EPSG:27700 (OSGB36 for the UK)).

CHAPTER 5   STEP TWO: PRE-PROCESSING

4. Set the output file format to GeoTIFF (.tif).

5. Choose a compression package from the Profile drop-down.

6. Click "Validate".

7. If you want to generate a PDF Map as well, choose a file path for it.

8. It is also a good idea to tick "Save GCP points" and "Load in Project when done".

9. Close the Transformation Settings dialogue box.

10. Click "Start Georeferencing" (green right-facing triangle in the menu bar) to process the transformation.

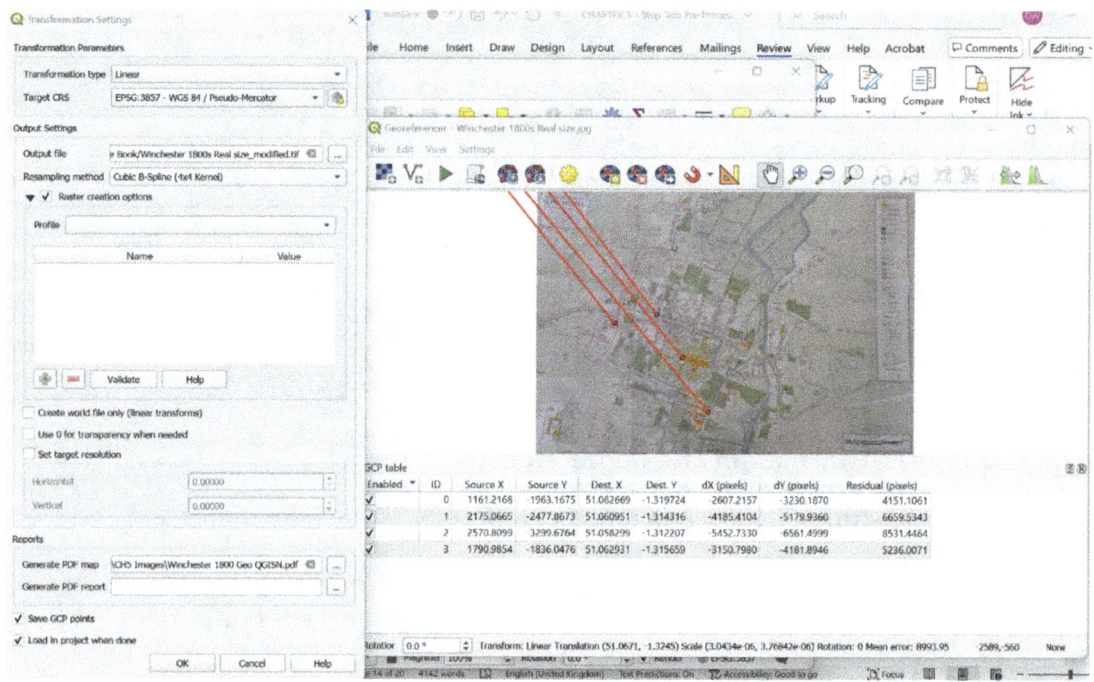

Figure 5-43. *Step 4 showing the Transformation Settings dialogue box*

Step 5: Verify the Georeferenced Map

1. Close the Georeferencer window.

2. In QGIS, if you did not tick Load in Project when done, click "Add Raster Layer" and load the new GeoTIFF file.

3. The historical map should now align correctly with the reference layers.

4. If adjustments are needed, reopen the Georeferencer, refine control points, and reapply the transformation.

Next Steps

- **Vectorize Historical Maps:** Convert features like old roads/buildings into vector layers.

- **Overlay GIS Data:** Add archaeological records, building footprints, or land-use layers.

- **Export for HBIM:** Save georeferenced maps as GeoTIFF or vector layers for integration into CAD/Revit.

After exploring various methodologies, including those above, for generating 3D terrain models of real-world locations and subsequently mapping urban layouts, including road networks and infrastructure, I have found Autodesk Revit to be my preferred software solution. This preference stems primarily from its seamless integration with my existing BIM workflow for building design. Utilizing Revit for terrain modelling significantly streamlines the project by ensuring accurate alignment and contextualization of building models within their site.

Specifically, Revit's Toposurface tool (evolving into the more robust Toposolid feature in Revit 2024) offers versatile methods for terrain creation. It readily accommodates point cloud data from surveying or photogrammetry, allows for the import of existing digital terrain models (DTMs) from various sources, and, crucially, provides the flexibility to define terrain through user-defined elevation points. This latter capability is particularly valuable when adapting contemporary terrain to historical map information, enabling the accurate reconstruction of past landscapes. The ability to directly manipulate elevation points offers a granular level of control, facilitating the incorporation of subtle topographical nuances and the integration of historical features that may no longer be present in the modern landscape.

Furthermore, leveraging Revit for both buildings and terrain fosters a cohesive project environment, simplifying collaboration and ensuring data consistency across all aspects of the design.

CHAPTER 5   STEP TWO: PRE-PROCESSING

There are several methods using GIS (QGIS and ArcGIS as examples) and which can be easily found online with YouTube videos demonstrating how to use the software to create modern-day landscapes using high-resolution raster elevation models (DEM/DTM/DSM), satellite data, LiDAR, and full geospatial metadata. For historical landscapes though, the resulting terrain from these methods would require considerable unpicking, i.e., removal of roads, changes in courses of rivers, lack of buildings, and similar. Therefore, finding a process that provides a good result with a less convoluted process and minimal, if any, cost (if Revit is already part of your toolkit) could be really valuable and time-saving. The method for creating the terrain data that I use is through the use of CADmapper, free to use/download and really quite simple to use, especially compared to other systems. The data can be exported via a DWG to open in AutoCAD for cleaning layer information, and then taking to Revit, or as a DXF, which can be taken straight into Revit.

CADmapper simplifies terrain extraction by pulling OpenStreetMap and SRTM/NASA elevation data and wrapping it in a CAD-friendly format (DWG/DXF), with ready-made contours and optional buildings/roads. Autodesk Revit also expects CAD input, i.e., Revit's Toposolid tools are designed to work easily with 2D contour lines with Z values, which DWG/DXF provide, meaning that translation is not required. CADmapper also abstracts away a lot of geographic data processing, i.e., you do not need to work with projections, coordinate systems, and raster formats.

QGIS and ArcGIS are more involved in how they work and what they produce. These types of programs offer greater precision and flexibility, working directly with high-resolution raster elevation models. You are working closer to the raw data, which can mean more control, and therefore more steps. You often start with a GeoTIFF, .asc, or .las file (raster or point cloud) that must be

- Georeferenced
- Cropped/clipped to your area
- Converted to a mesh, contour lines, or 3D surface
- Aligned to a suitable coordinate reference system (CRS)

These platforms do not natively talk to Revit, so you have to convert terrain to DXF/SHP/OBJ or other readable formats, possibly remap the coordinates to align with Revit's origin and clean geometry to make it Revit-ready. The output is richer. QGIS/ArcGIS allows resolution down to 1 m or sub-meter precision with LiDAR. Plus you can combine terrain with land-use, geology, flood risk, and building footprints. You would need to use these methods for environmental analysis, planning infrastructure modelling, and large-scale civil projects. In Table 5-2, you can see the points made above highlighting the tradeoff in using one or the other.

Table 5-2. *Comparison table in using CADmapper versus QGIS/ArcGIS for Revit use*

Feature	CADmapper + Revit	QGIS/ArcGIS + Revit
Setup complexity	Very low	Moderate to high
Geographic accuracy	Medium (~30 m SRTM data)	High (1 m+ with DEM/LiDAR)
Terrain detail	Basic contours	Detailed surfaces or full 3D mesh
Workflow integration	Direct to Revit	Needs format conversion
Best for	Conceptual site modelling	Precision GIS + infrastructure work

If you need a quick site model for design concepts or visualization, or a simple terrain without the geographic coordinate fuss and high resolution is not critical, then it would be good to use CADmapper and Revit.

If you need accuracy and modern-day realism, have access to LiDAR or custom elevation datasets, and need to do a terrain analysis, then you would be better to use QGIS/ArcGIS workflows. In addition, if you will be working with civil engineers, urban planners, or surveyors, then again, QGIS/ArcGIS (or similar) would be the better option.

For the work I do and the Virtual Cities project, my goals are generally to use the terrain as a base for visualizing and modifying historic environments (different roads, settlements, etc.) and export to Unreal Engine where I can visually enhance, sculpt, and re-contextualize. The terrain needs, therefore, to be a framework, not a precise modern survey. My focus in using CADmapper is based on accessibility, time-efficiency, and reproducibility, for educational, creative, or heritage environments where budgets are tight, time is limited, and where users are not always technical specialists.

To sum up why CADmapper to Revit is my working option, the following points may help you to also decide which route is best for you:

CHAPTER 5   STEP TWO: PRE-PROCESSING

1. **Fast and clean base terrain**
   - CADmapper provides basic but consistent elevation contours (30 m SRTM or better in some areas).
   - That is sufficient for terrain shape, especially when you will edit/augment it for different centuries.
   - Revit Toposolid gives you a clean, mappable surface to anchor buildings, landmarks, and assets.

2. **You do not want modern detail**
   - QGIS/ArcGIS often starts with high-res contemporary data – useful, but full of modern noise:
     - Contemporary roads, land use
     - Buildings that did not exist
     - Trees, hydro features, etc., that are hard to untangle

   You would have to spend extra time cleaning or reinterpreting those – which may not add value when you are *remaking history* anyway.

3. **Easy path to Unreal**
   - Revit to Unreal Engine (via Datasmith) is solid and familiar.
   - The result is a nice, parametric surface that Unreal can render and enhance.
   - You can overlay period-specific features on top (roads, buildings, rivers).

4. **Low friction entry point**
   - CADmapper is free and easy to use.
   - Revit is often already available in academic/architecture contexts.
   - Datasmith plug-in for Revit to Unreal is free and powerful.

CHAPTER 5 STEP TWO: PRE-PROCESSING

5. **Cross-skill compatibility**

    - Works for architects, historians, designers, and visualizers
    - Does not need heavy GIS knowledge
    - Leaves room for creative workflows (sculpting, narrative overlays, etc.)

6. **Modular and scalable**

    - You can always add GIS later.
    - You can upgrade terrain detail if needed.
    - It suits both solo and collaborative projects.

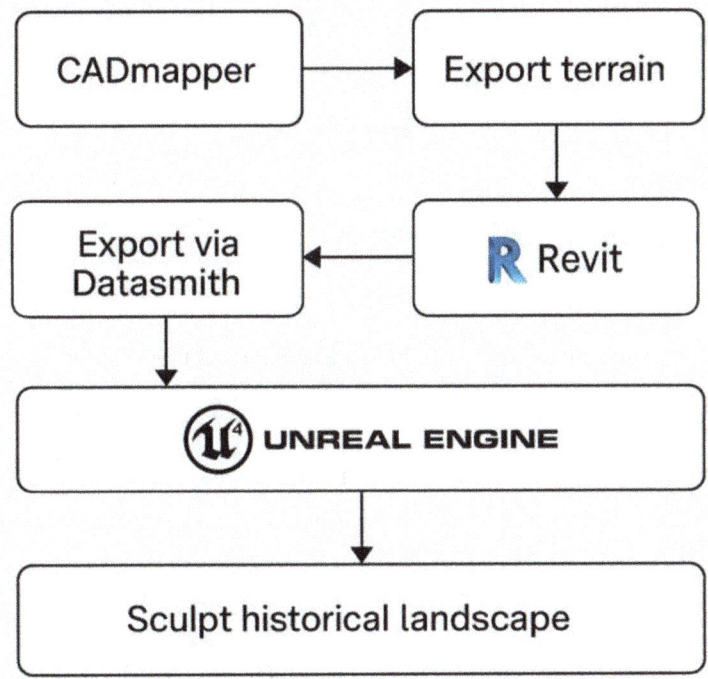

Figure 5-44. *My workflow for Virtual Cities – Winchester and other projects*

The following is a step-by-step guide to using CADmapper to create a Toposolid in Revit (2024 or newer). This method is perfect for getting accurate topography data from real-world locations into your Revit project.

283

CHAPTER 5 STEP TWO: PRE-PROCESSING

Step-by-Step Guide: Using CADmapper to Create a Toposolid

Tools you will need:

- **CADmapper** (https://cadmapper.com)
- **Autodesk Revit** (2024+ for Toposolid support)
- **Optional: AutoCAD** (for file prep/cleaning)

Step 1: Download Terrain Data from CADmapper

1. Go to https://cadmapper.com.
2. Search for your location, type in a city, address, or drag the map.
3. Resize and place the selection box over the area you want to import.
4. Under "What would you like to include?", select
    - Terrain
    - Buildings (optional)
    - Roads (optional)
5. Under "Model export for:", choose "AutoCAD (.DWG)".
6. Click Download; after a few seconds, it will give you a .zip file.
7. Extract the .zip; it contains a DWG file with terrain contours and other data.

CHAPTER 5   STEP TWO: PRE-PROCESSING

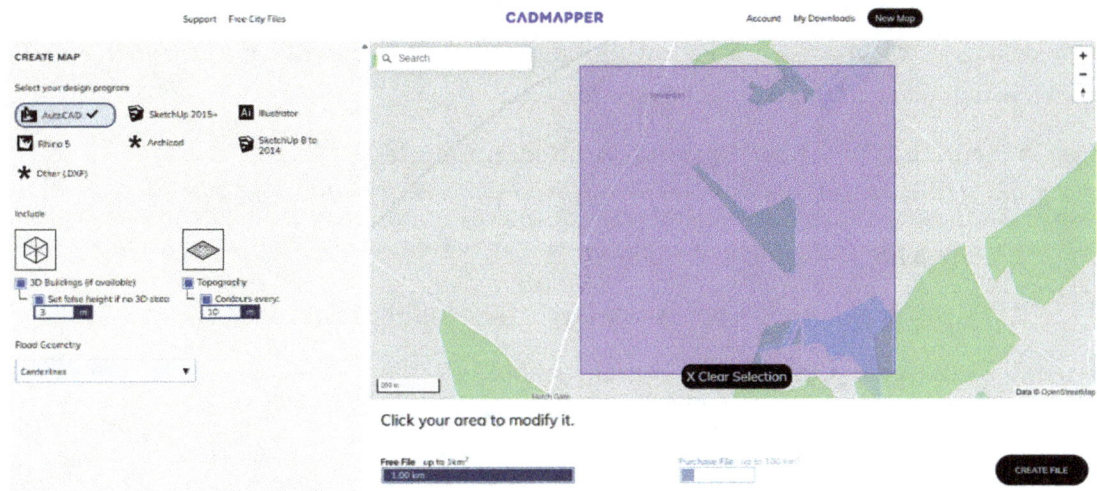

Figure 5-45. CADmapper screen showing a map of Steventon, near Overton, Basingstoke, and a 1 km² drawn to cover the area where Jane Austen lived with her family. The settings are as stated above

This is an online program, and therefore not an additional program to download to your machine unlike QGIS. You would choose the "Other (.DXF)" if you did not have AutoCAD and only a Revit license; the process follows the same steps for this first step.

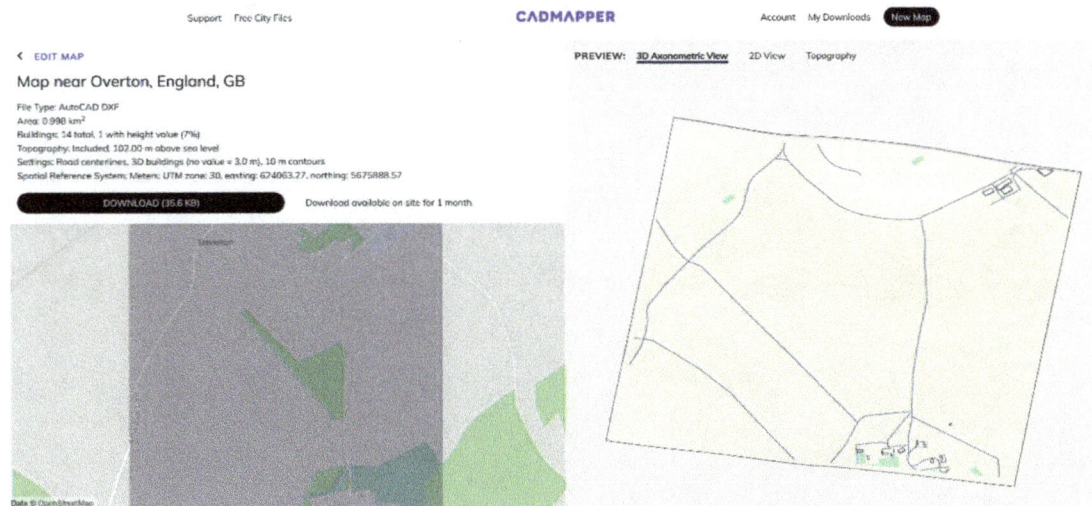

Figure 5-46. This image shows the next screen once you have clicked "Create File"; it will take a few seconds to process the map and then you will be presented with the map on the right shown as a 3D Axonometric view

285

CHAPTER 5   STEP TWO: PRE-PROCESSING

You can click on the 2D View to explore the image and the Topography tab will provide a view of the contours. Follow the steps in step 1 to download a zip file to your folder, which you can then extract to see the data.

Step 2: Clean the DWG File (Optional but Recommended)
Use AutoCAD if available for easier cleanup, but you can skip this if the file is simple.

1. Open the DWG file in AutoCAD.
2. Turn off or freeze unnecessary layers (like buildings or roads).
3. Make sure only contours remain visible.
4. Use OVERKILL to clean duplicates (optional).
5. Save the cleaned DWG.

Note   In CADmapper, even if you choose AutoCAD, the file still exports as .DXF. This may be because I do not have AutoCAD on my machine, as I use Revit for all 2D as well as 3D work. I can use Autodesk's DWG TrueView to open a DWG or a DXF for viewing but viewing only; it will not save any changes made. I have taken a screengrab to show you the Layer changes you can make in AutoCAD. The changes can be made and saved using Revit as also shown in Figure 5-47.

CHAPTER 5   STEP TWO: PRE-PROCESSING

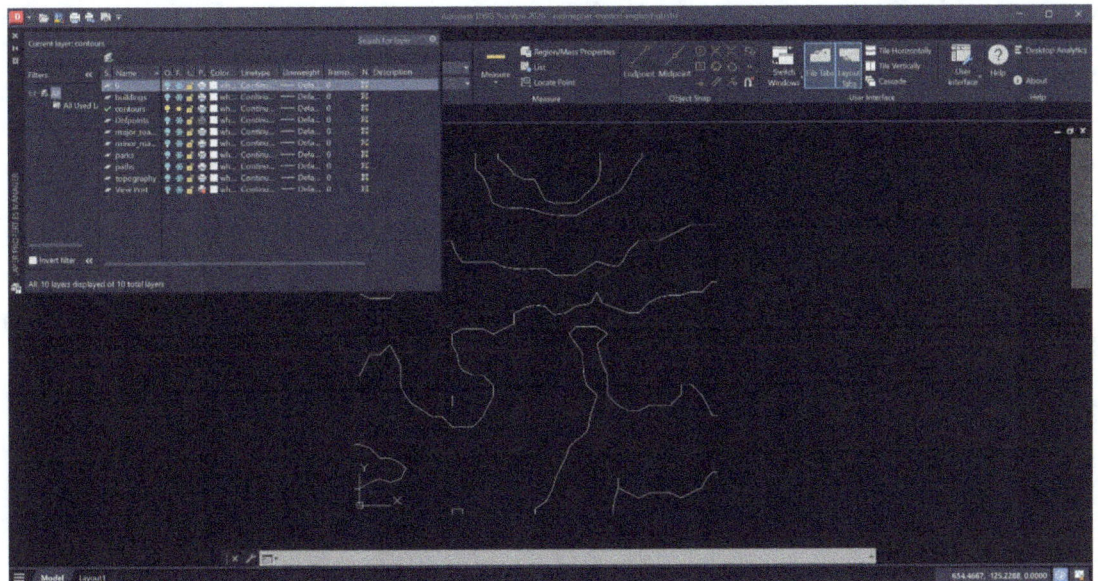

Figure 5-47. *Autodesk's free software for viewing DWG and DXF files, "DWG TrueView". The image shows the layers that you can freeze/turn off before taking into Revit*

Choose either step 3A or step 3B depending on whether you have used AutoCAD to turn off Layers to show only the Contours Layer as above, or you have taken the DXF direct to Revit.

Step 3A: Import into Revit (Cleaned in AutoCAD)

1. Open Revit (2024+ project).
2. Go to a 3D View or Site Plan.
3. Insert ➤ Import CAD
   - Select your cleaned DWG file.
   - Import it using
     - Auto – Origin to Origin
     - Preserve colors (or not, up to you)
     - Current View Only: OFF
4. The contour lines should now appear in your Revit model.

287

CHAPTER 5   STEP TWO: PRE-PROCESSING

Step 3B: Import into Revit (Not Cleaned in AutoCAD)

1. Open Revit (2024+ project).

2. Go to a 3D View or Site Plan.

3. Insert ➤ Import CAD

    - Select your DXF file.

    - Import it using

        - "Specify" Layers to import (drop-down to choose, see Figure 5-48)

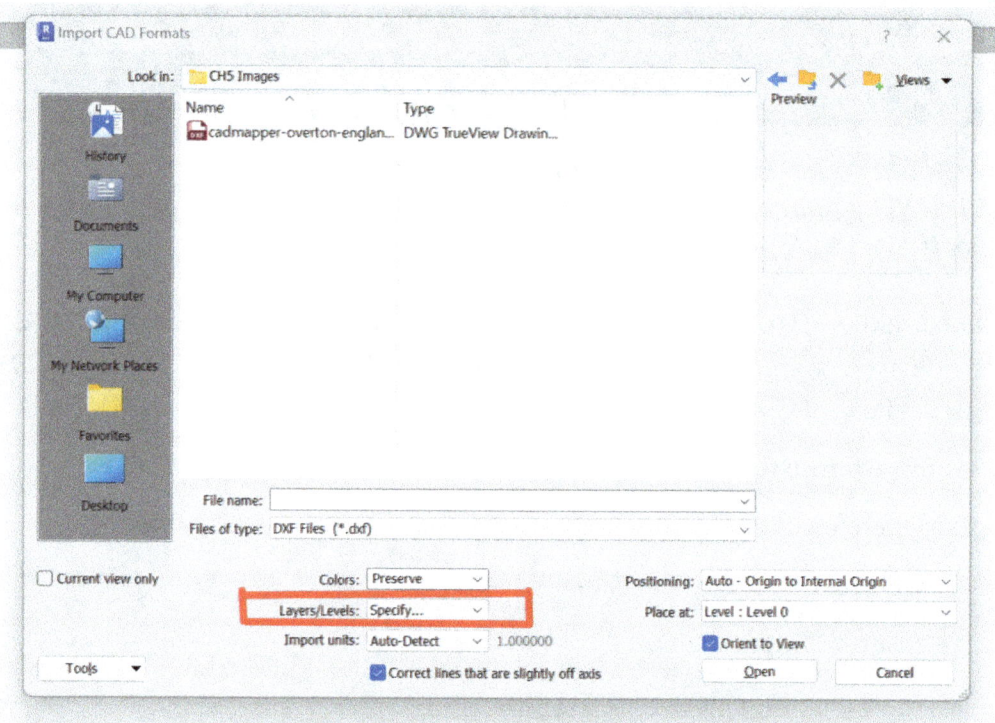

Figure 5-48. *Importing DXF file direct to Revit, choosing the "Specify" Layers option*

- Auto – Origin to Origin

- Import units – Meters (not Auto-Detect)

CHAPTER 5 STEP TWO: PRE-PROCESSING

- Preserve colors (or not, up to you)

- Current View Only: OFF

• Click to import and a dialogue box will appear with the layers where you can then tick off the layers not required, either by choosing None and then ticking on Contours or by manually deselecting. The two images below show what the dialogue box looks like when first appearing and then once you have selected just the Contours Layer.

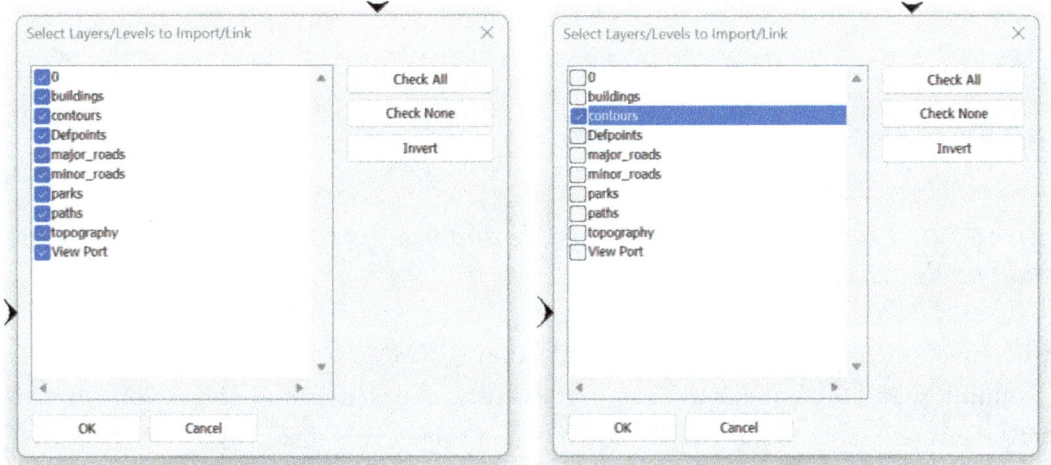

Figure 5-49. *Deselecting all layers except for the Contours Layer, which is needed for creating the Toposolid*

4. The contour lines should now appear in your Revit model.

CHAPTER 5   STEP TWO: PRE-PROCESSING

Figure 5-50. *Contour lines are now visible and having used Meters as the Units, should be the correct size*

If you are unsure, use the measure tool in Google Maps for the distance between contour lines, and then check in Revit that the distance is the same. If not, you can use Revit's reference scale to scale up or down to suit the correct distance.

Step 4: Create the Toposolid

1. Go to Massing & Site ➤ Toposolid.

2. Choose Create from Import ➤ select Import Instance

3. Click on the imported CAD (DWG) contours.

CHAPTER 5   STEP TWO: PRE-PROCESSING

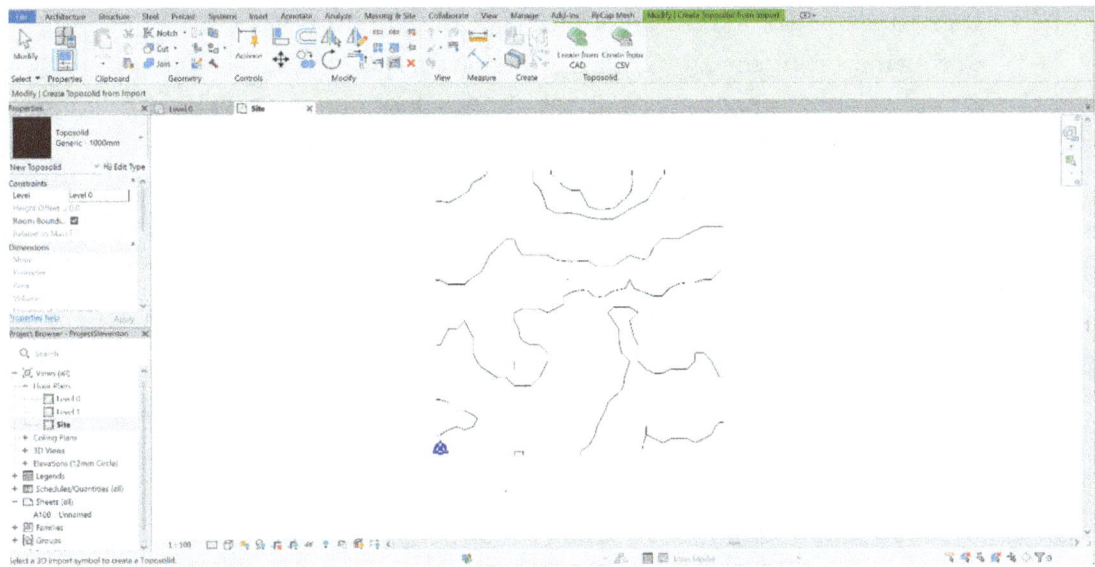

Figure 5-51. Create a Toposolid by selecting the "Create from CAD" option in the top menu bar and then selecting the contour DWG or DXF import

4. Revit will ask which layers to use – select the layer(s) that contains the contour lines (usually named like Contours, Topo, etc.).

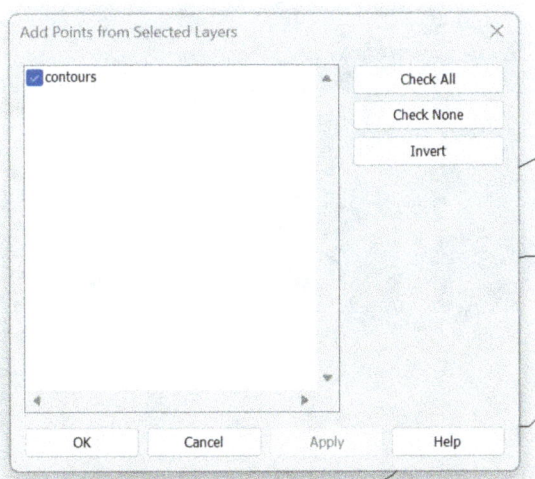

Figure 5-52. Select the Contours Layer for creating the Toposolid

291

If you had not deleted the other Layers prior to importing, or during importing the DWG or DXF, then at this point, you can still choose to ignore the Layers and just choose the Contours Layer. This can be useful should you wish to include roads and paths to trace over to create those entities within Revit.

5. Click Finish.

Revit will generate a Toposolid using those contour lines!

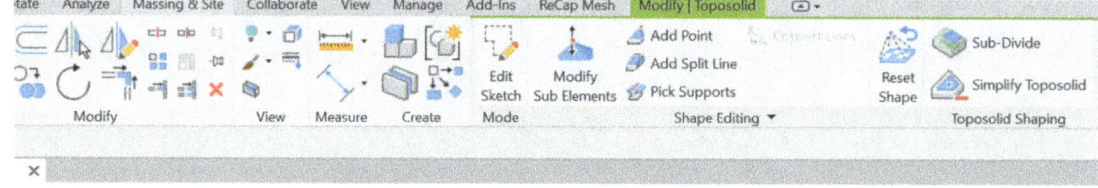

Figure 5-53. *The selected Toposolid shows as blue, while it is selected, you can then modify the material as in step 5 below*

Step 5: Final Touches

- **Adjust Materials:** You can modify the Toposolid material from the Properties panel.

- To change to Grassland, go to Edit Type in the Properties panel and choose Grassland from the drop-down menu.

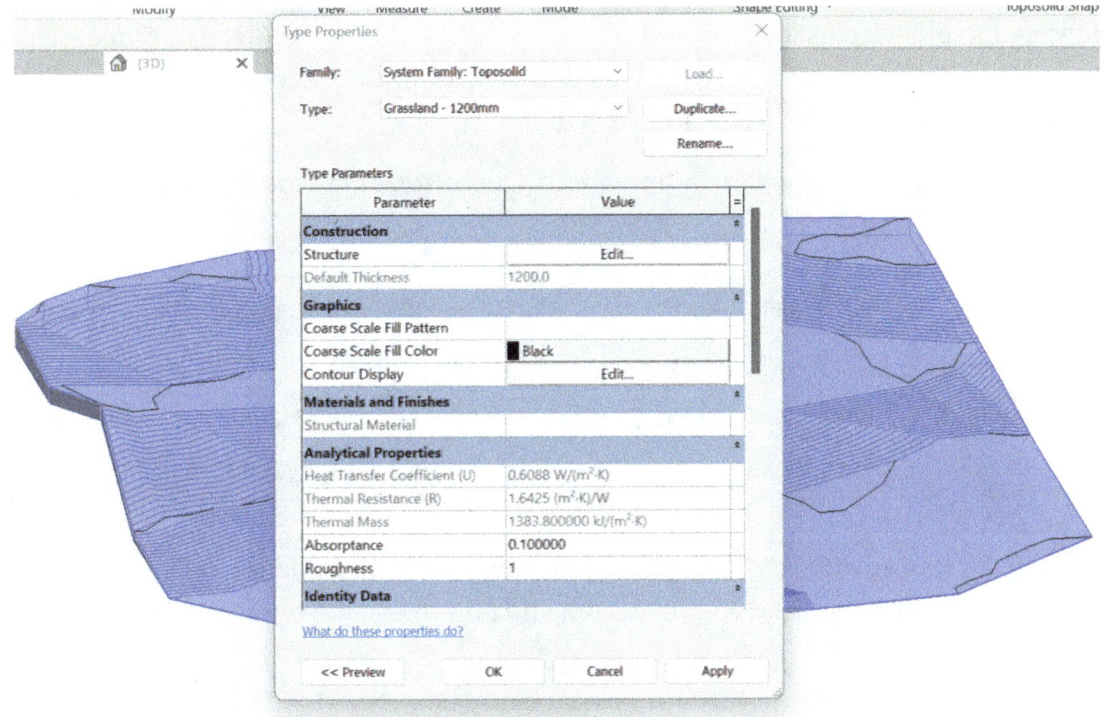

Figure 5-54. Selecting Grassland to change the properties of the Toposolid

- **Add Site Components:** Trees, roads, pads, etc.
- Cut sections to inspect the terrain.

Optional Bonus: Link Instead of Import

If you plan to update the DWG in AutoCAD and reflect changes in Revit, use Link CAD instead of Import CAD. It is a smarter workflow for large projects.

CHAPTER 5   STEP TWO: PRE-PROCESSING

My next step is generally to import the Revit file to Unreal Engine using Datasmith so that I can use Unreal's sculpting tools to reshape features that changed historically, i.e., carve medieval or Regency/Georgian roads, regrade areas before industrial earthworks, and alter waterways and rivers. I would not add trees in Revit, or roads/paving unless they are depth based. It would be better to sculpt, and texture painted in Unreal. The depth-based objects such as pavements can be created in Revit using the Toposolid Subdivide feature. In Unreal, I would have a historic map overlay and work with the information provided by the map and artistic views/sketches to mold the terrain to suit the period. Table 5-3 is my suggested workflow for creating a historical city or village terrain as created for Winchester and Steventon.

Table 5-3. *Suggested workflow for recreating a historic city/town/village*

Stage	Tool	Purpose
Terrain base	CADmapper + Revit	Get elevation and clean geometry
Overlay analysis	QGIS/Blender/Photoshop	Georeference old maps to guide changes
Sculpt and modify	Unreal Engine Landscape Editor	Rebuild rivers, roads, and fields as they were
Place assets	Unreal Engine	Historic buildings, trees, street furniture

For progressing with your terrain, the following steps will guide you in how to export from Revit to Unreal using Datasmith and how to edit the terrain as a Landscape in Unreal.

Sculpting Imported Revit Terrain in Unreal and Using Historic Maps As Overlays

1. **Export Revit Toposolid to Unreal (via Datasmith)**

   Setup

   - Use Datasmith Export Plugin for Revit.

   - Export as .udatasmith.

   - In Unreal, install the Datasmith plug-in, then import the file into your scene.

Result

- You get your Toposolid as a static mesh.
- BUT – Unreal's Landscape Sculpt Tool only works on Landscape assets, *not* static meshes.

2. **Convert Static Mesh to Landscape**

You have two good options:

Option A: Use Unreal Plug-in "Mesh to Terrain" (Recommended)

1. Enable the "Editor Mesh Utilities" plug-in (it comes with UE).
2. In the Landscape Tool, choose
    - New Landscape ➤ Import from Mesh
    - Select your Revit terrain mesh
3. It will bake the mesh into a heightmap and generate a real Landscape Asset you can sculpt.

Now you can use

- Sculpt, Smooth, Flatten, Erosion
- Landscape Layers for historic overlays

Option B: Export Heightmap from Revit via Intermediate Software

1. Export terrain as OBJ or FBX from Revit.
2. Bring into Blender, Rhino, or 3DS Max.
3. Use tools to bake the mesh into a grayscale heightmap image (16-bit PNG).
4. Import into Unreal Landscape using
    - Landscape ➤ Import from file ➤ Heightmap

This works if you want more control over resolution or shaping before Unreal.

3. **Bring in Historic Maps As Overlays**

   This is brilliant for sculpting terrain based on historic features like old roads, rivers, canals, walls, etc.

   In Unreal

   1. Add a Plane or Decal over the terrain.
   2. Apply your historic map as a material/texture (JPEG, PNG).
   3. Align and scale it using transform tools.
   4. Or import the map as a Texture Layer in the Landscape tool (for painting/splat mapping guidance).

   Use it as a visual sculpting guide or even bake it into the material later.

4. **Sculpt the Landscape**

   Now you are in Unreal's Landscape Mode:

   - Use "Sculpt" to raise earth where hills or embankments once were.
   - "Flatten" for cut roads or riverbanks.
   - "Erosion" for more naturalistic forms.
   - Add new features like trench lines, medieval roads, and old building plots.

5. **Add Period-Specific Assets**

   You can now add

   - Historic buildings (hand-modelled or asset packs)
   - Period-appropriate vegetation
   - Roads from old layouts
   - Water features (Unreal Water System)

   You are reconstructing the lived space, not just terrain.

CHAPTER 5   STEP TWO: PRE-PROCESSING

Final Tips

- If using old maps, georeference them in QGIS or Blender with projection mapping, then export for alignment in Unreal.

- Keep Z scaling realistic; Unreal sometimes exaggerates verticals.

- Consider Landscape Material blending for painting different historic ground types (mud, cobble, pasture, etc.).

Section Summary

This section has explored the role of georeferencing and terrain generation as a foundational element of HBIM projects focused on real-world sites, particularly those set in historical contexts. Rather than relying on imagined landscapes typical of game design, the aim here is to create plausible, research-informed environments grounded in actual geography and historical reference. This process allows historical buildings and streets to be anchored meaningfully within the landscape, enabling richer interpretive reconstructions and more immersive visual storytelling.

Various methods were discussed for bringing terrain into modelling workflows, including detailed GIS-based techniques (using QGIS or ArcGIS) and more accessible alternatives like CADmapper. While QGIS and ArcGIS offer high-resolution data and powerful analytical capabilities – essential for applications like environmental or flood risk analysis – they also require greater technical skill, additional processing time, and conversion steps to integrate with software like Revit.

For heritage and educational projects where time, budget, and expertise may be limited, the CADmapper-to-Revit workflow offers a lightweight, scalable alternative. It provides fast access to terrain data, including elevation contours, which can be easily imported into Revit's Toposolid tool (especially from version 2024 onward). This terrain can then serve as a base to situate historical buildings and evolve the scene over time. Because the workflow integrates smoothly with Unreal Engine via Datasmith, it also supports dynamic terrain sculpting and texture painting for more accurate historical representations.

While precision is always a consideration, particularly for archaeological or infrastructural modelling, historical urban scenes often prioritize interpretive accuracy – such as showing the evolution of roads, rivers, or urban layouts – over precise contemporary survey data. This means that plausibility, consistency, and narrative purpose can be weighted more heavily than exact measurements. In these cases, sculpting tools in Unreal can be used to reshape terrain, allowing features like medieval roads or lost waterways to be reintroduced visually.

Ultimately, the goal is to create a landscape that serves as a coherent stage for historical buildings and the stories they embody. The terrain does not need to be flawless in technical terms, but it must feel authentic and believable. Streamlining the terrain preparation stage gives more time and creative energy to the interpretive elements – the stories, people, and architecture that audiences care about most. In my experience, the people engaging with your scenes are more interested in the buildings, the people, and the stories; they will not necessarily be inspecting the terrain. For those working in heritage, education, or visualization, this method offers an efficient, flexible, and accessible entry point into integrating terrain and geospatial data into HBIM and immersive environments.

References

British History Online (1912) Winchester: in *A History of the County of Hampshire: Volume 5*, ed. William Page (London, 1912), *British History Online*. https://www.british-history.ac.uk/vch/hants/vol5/pp9-12 [accessed April 2025]

English Heritage (2012) Practical Building Conservation Mortars, Renders & Plasters. Editors: Henry, Alison and Stewart, John. English Heritage, Ashgate/Routledge. ISBN: 978-0-7546-4559-7

FRAG (2021) Dating Houses. Peterborough Archaeology, Fane Road Archaeology Group. https://peterborougharchaeology.org/dating-houses [Accessed April 2025]

Maybank, Geoff (2019) Traditional Brickwork. Building Conservation Articles, Cathedral Communications Limited. https://www.buildingconservation.com/articles/traditional-brickwork/traditional-brickwork.htm [Accessed April 2025]

QGIS (2025) Spatial without Compromise – QGIS download. https://qgis.org/ [Accessed April 2025]

Unreal Engine (2025) Datasmith Export Plugins. Epic Games. https://www.unrealengine.com/en-US/datasmith/plugins [Accessed April 2025]

Yorke, Trevor (2017) How to Date Buildings: An Easy Reference Guide. Publisher: Countryside Books. ISBN: 9781846743436

CHAPTER 6

Step Three: Building the 3D Model

This chapter focuses on the actual construction of the HBIM 3D model. It covers the selection of appropriate HBIM software, creation of building geometry, and incorporation of textures and materials. The chapter combines technical details with a creative angle, as building the 3D model requires both technical skills and an artistic understanding of architecture. The purpose is to guide readers through the process of building the HBIM model and developing a visually appealing representation of historical architecture.

Starting to Build with Your HBIM Software

In the following practical exercise, you will be creating an HBIM building from scratch i.e. it is a building that no longer exists, with very little pictorial evidence, and the images available have question marks over them as they differ in how the building is portrayed. This building is Steventon Rectory, in Hampshire, UK, where Jane Austen lived for her formative years. The information to reconstruct Steventon Rectory is collated from written resources such as memoirs and letters about and from Jane Austen and her family life at Steventon Rectory. As previously mentioned, Steventon Rectory is linked to Virtual Cities – Winchester through the narrative of Jane Austen's life before she came to Winchester and stayed in 8 College Street before she died and was then buried in Winchester Cathedral. It also makes a very good use case regarding the lack of evidence and therefore the interest and expert opinion that may result once an initial building has been produced.

CHAPTER 6   STEP THREE: BUILDING THE 3D MODEL

Data entity - Main Title	Authors/Originators	Year Published/ Created	Source	Accessed Date	Created Date	Data type
JA-1 1821-Map-Steventon-Rectory-Glebe-Land (published on Jane Austen's House website)	John Armstrong	1821	https://janeaustens.house/object/map-of-the-glebe-land-at-steventon-hants-1821/#&gid=1&pid=1	12/03/2025	1821	Map
JA-2 1820-Sketch-Steventon-Rectory-Front-attributed-to-Ben-Lefroy (published on Jane Austen's House website)	Ben Lefroy (Anne Lefroy's Sketch?)	1820	https://janeaustens.house/object/pencil-drawing-of-steventon-rectory/	12/03/2025	1820	Visual Artwork
JA-3 1820-Sketch-Steventon-Rectory-Rear-attributed-to-Ben-Lefroy (published on Jane Austen's House website)	Ben Lefroy (Anne Lefroy's Sketch?)	1820	https://janeausteninvermont.blog/tag/steventon-rectory/	12/03/2025	1820	Visual Artwork
JA-4 1741-Map-Estate-Steventon	?					
JA-5 1840 Tithe Map - Steventon	?					
JA-6 Unlocking secrets from Jane Austens Steventon home - BBC News	BBC News	2012	https://www.bbc.co.uk/news/uk-england-hampshire-20678244	12/03/2025	2012	News Report
JA-7 1902-Sketch-B-College-Street	Jane Austen: her home & her friends' written by Constance Hill and Illustrated by Ellen Hill, which was published by The Bodley Head in 1902	1902	https://janeaustens.house/object/original-pen-and-ink-drawings-by-miss-ellen-g-hill/			Visual Artwork
JA-8 Steventon Rectory – Jane Austen in Vermont	Janeite Deb jasnavermont@gmail.com	2010	https://janeausteninvermont.blog/tag/steventon-rectory/		2010	Blog
JA-9 Archaeology Greets Jane Austen. By unearthing her birthplace and first home.	Deborah Charlton	2017	https://www.janeaustenbooks.net/products/17409		2017	Book
JA-10 Jane Austen's China and the Steventon Archaeological Dig	Jane Odiwe, Jane Austen Centre	2015	https://janeausten.co.uk/blogs/jane-austen-life/jane-austens-china-and-the-steventon-archaeological-dig		2015	Blog
JA-11 Map Steventon Late 19th Century	Basingstoke & Deane Borough Council	April 2004	www.basingstoke.gov.uk	12/08/2007	2004	Map
JA-12 Basingstoke & Deane. Conservation Area Appraisal - Steventon	Basingstoke & Deane Borough Council	April 2004	www.basingstoke.gov.uk	12/08/2007	2004	Document
JA-13 The Village of Steventon. Journal of the Jane Austen Society of North America - Persuasions #19.	Joyce Bown	1997	www.jasna.org		1997	Article
JA-15 Parishes: Steventon', in A History of the County of Hampshire: Volume 4, ed. William Page	British History Online	1911	www.british-history.ac.uk/vch/hants/vol4/p p171-174	19/04/2025	1911	Online Archive
JA-16 Parson Austen's Daughter.	Helen Ashton	1967			1967	
JA-17 Voices from the World of Jane Austen Publishers David & Charles CPI Bath Press, Newton Abbot, Devon. ISBN-13: 978-0-7153-2379-3	Malcom Day	2006				Book
JA-18 Archaeology in Hampshire Annual Report 2012,	Hampshire Field Club and Archaeological Society	2012				
JA-19 Historic England 2020 Farmstead and Landscape Statement: Hampshire Downs. Hampshire Downs Chalk and Limestone Mixed	Historic England, Jeremy Lake, Bob Edwards	2020	https://historicengland.org.uk/research/results/reports/8153/HampshireDownsChalkandLimestoneMixed	19/04/2025	2020	Statement Document
JA-20 Why Was Jane Austen Sent away to School at Seven? An Empirical Look at a Vexing Question. Persuasions On-line V.26 No.1 A publication of the Jane Austen Society of North America,	Linda Robinson Walker	2005	http://www.jasna.org/persuasions/on-	2006	2005	Article

Figure 6-1. *The author's project spreadsheet showing the list of resources that will be used in reconstructing Jane Austen's family home, Steventon Rectory. (The project spreadsheet is included in the lesson files on the accompanying website.)*

Due to the lack of building and building remains, I obviously cannot use 3D scanning, LiDAR or similar; therefore, I am building it in Autodesk Revit and will then take it into Unreal, without textures, ready to use Unreal Engine's textures, which will be adapted to provide a used/more dilapidated finish that Revit materials generally produce. I have added the resources I am going to use to my spreadsheet, although as I work through the building, I may need to add to this list, for example, 16th/17th-century typical styles and sizes (see Figure 6-1).

The version of Revit I will be using is 2024, and the Unreal Engine version will be 5.5.4 (April 2024). The combination of the two programs will ensure that Datasmith works seamlessly between the two, with Datasmith/Twinmotion settings built into Revit 2024, and in Unreal Engine, the plug-in is readily available when using the Architecture template. The following step-by-step exercise will be from an Introductory level in both programs, suitable for beginners and therefore also students.

CHAPTER 6   STEP THREE: BUILDING THE 3D MODEL

Building Steventon Rectory – Step-by-Step Exercise
Step 1. Starting Your Project in Autodesk Revit 2024

1. Choose the Architectural template.

2. Under Manage and Project Units, I have changed the units to feet and fractional inches due to the age of the building and therefore the available measurements.

Note To convert to Imperial, there is a simple calculator online, but if you type in the Metric measurement, Revit will convert it for you to feet and inches if you have selected this as your Project Unit.

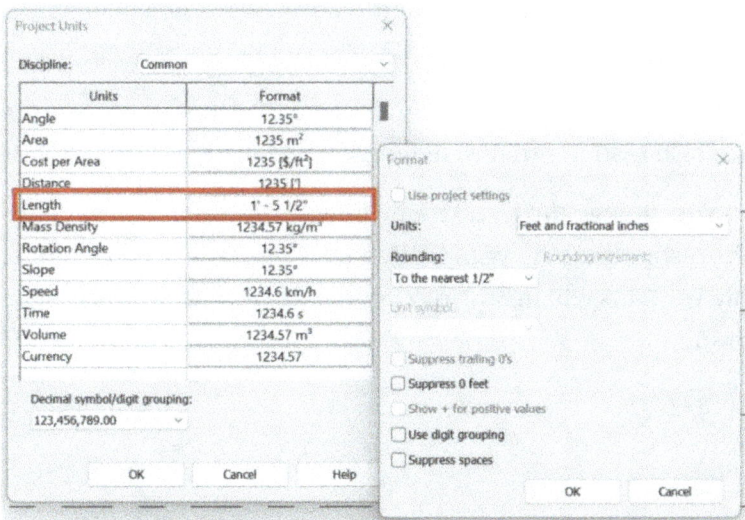

Figure 6-2. *Changing units to feet and fractional inches*

3. I have also added Levels for the different floor levels of the building.

CHAPTER 6   STEP THREE: BUILDING THE 3D MODEL

Note   For these heights, I have researched typical floor levels/ceiling heights for buildings of this period. While I am building, these will be fine and can always be adjusted should future research provide different sizes, or when shown to architectural experts and historians, they may provide changes to those sizes which can be implemented without too much trouble. This is one of the nicest aspects of Revit; elements such as walls are set to go from one level to another, i.e., from ground to top floor/roof, and therefore, if a level changes height, everything attached to that level will adjust to the new information, walls, floors, ceilings, beams, and so on.

4. When you create your levels, try to make sure they link with each other so that you can move them as one out to the side. To do this:

    - Check each elevation so that the Level heads will be outside of the building.

    - Also make a point of naming them so that they will make sense but also read in order of height.

    - As you change the Level name, it will ask you if you want all Corresponding Views to be Renamed, generally you should say Yes. This will mean your ceiling views will also be renamed to suit.

Figure 6-3. Elevational view showing the Levels and changed level names

302

CHAPTER 6   STEP THREE: BUILDING THE 3D MODEL

Figure 6-4. *Project Browser showing the Floor Plans and the Ceiling Plan names updated to suit*

Step 2. Start Building the Rectory

I do not have a floor plan available, only a map showing the outline shape of the building, albeit very tiny. The map does have a scale that will be valuable in working out the footprint of the Rectory and outlying buildings; see below. I also have notes from the Archaeology in Hampshire Annual Report 2012, which states:

"The first known historical record regarding Steventon 'Rectory' building dates to January 1696 and tells how the house stood within Glebe Land. It consisted of two bays of building and was extended at the west end and part of the south side over a cellar. From the Austen family letters we know that refurbishment of the building was completed in the second half of 1768. The building was demolished probably in the second half of 1822 and/or early 1823 leaving no trace in the Glebe Land landscape, excepting some surface rubble."

The outline in the Glebe map reflects the statement, so again, a good map to use for creating the footplate. I also now know that part of the south side was built over a cellar.

303

CHAPTER 6   STEP THREE: BUILDING THE 3D MODEL

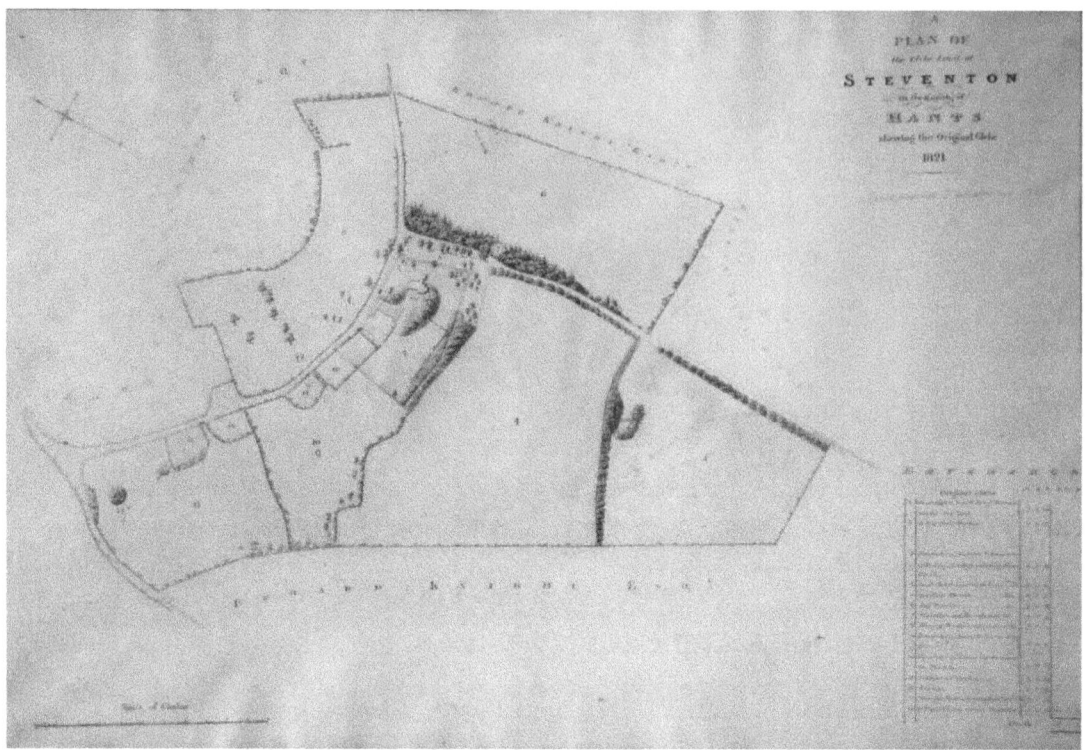

Figure 6-5. *Plan of Steventon, Hampshire, 1821 (Jane Austen's House, 2025)*

1. In Revit, use Insert/Import Image and select the center of the Site plan by clicking on the project space.

Note As mentioned above, the map of Steventon Rectory Glebe has a scale, which, although difficult to read, is a "Scale of Chains." A "chain" equates to 66 feet, and the scale goes up to 10 chains from 0, so we need to scale the map up from its initial import size of 36 feet 10", as shown below, to 660 feet.

2. Use the Model Line command on the Architecture tab and draw a line from the "0" mark on the left-hand side of the scale across to the end of the scale on the right as shown in Figure 6-6.

3. Draw another line from the end point of the 36'10" model line just drawn and type in 660 for the end point and press return, i.e., do not click to place.

CHAPTER 6　STEP THREE: BUILDING THE 3D MODEL

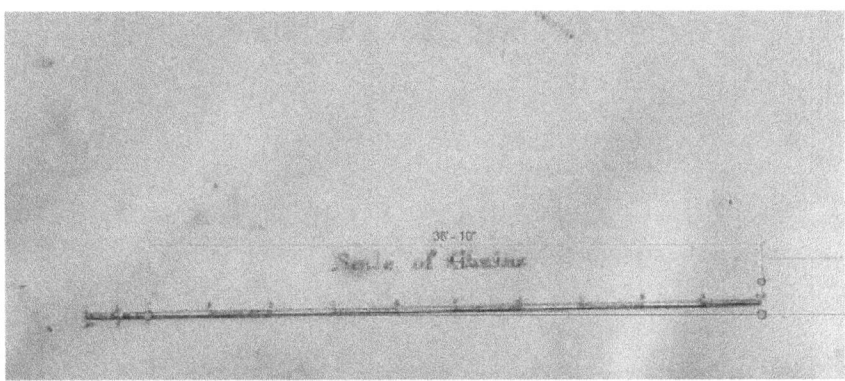

Figure 6-6. *Scale of Chains legend showing the image has imported at a much smaller scale*

4. Zoom out to see the full line.

5. Select the map and use CTRL to add to your selection and select the shorter 36'10" line. You do not need to select the 660' line.

6. With those items selected, go to Scale/Reference and choose Graphical on the options bar.

7. Select the End Point of the short line, then the other end of the short line for the next point of reference, then the end of the 660' line for the final reference point.

8. The map's scale legend will now be at the 660' scale, and therefore a more correct scale for starting to model the buildings.

Note　The map image has most likely been scanned and/or photocopied and therefore is likely to be distorted from its true scale, for example, as you can see, the line is slightly angled. You may need to adjust sizing should evidence come to light about the true size, for instance, later archaeological evidence.

CHAPTER 6   STEP THREE: BUILDING THE 3D MODEL

Figure 6-7. *The result of scaling up the map using the scale provided and Scale Reference command*

9. Select the map and using the Move command, move the building area to the center of the elevation marks, or as close as possible.

Figure 6-8. *Moving the map to center the building outline within the elevation marks*

10. The model lines can be deleted.

    The map shows North off to the top left; you therefore might want to rotate the map so that the North arrow faces North. To do this:

11. Draw two model lines as shown below: one along the north arrow line and another straight North from the end point of the first line.

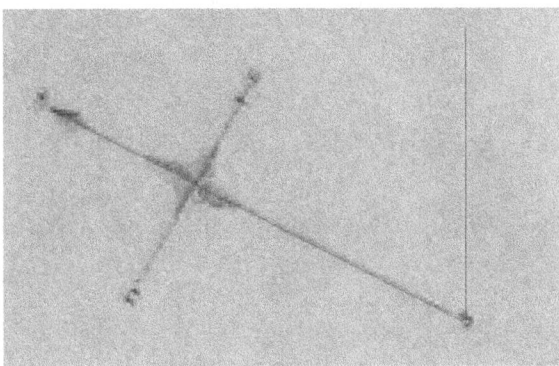

Figure 6-9. The two model lines drawn to use for rotating the map to actual North

12. Select the angle North Line and using CTRL, click on the map.

13. Using the Rotate command, select Centre of Rotation 'Place' on the green Options bar.

14. Select your first point of Rotation as the joint end point of the two lines, the second point as the arrow line end point, and the final point, choose the end point of the true North line.

15. The map and angled line will rotate to line up to the Project North line as shown in Figure 6-10.

CHAPTER 6 STEP THREE: BUILDING THE 3D MODEL

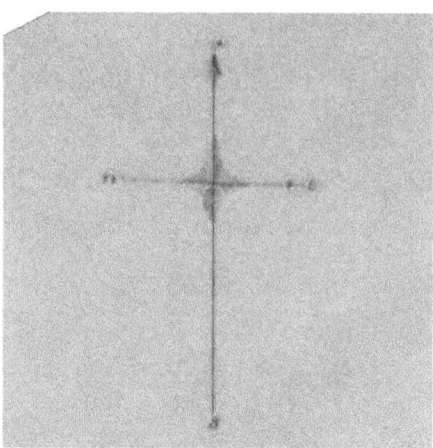

Figure 6-10. *The map is now aligned to actual North*

16. You can then move the map again so that the building is centered within the elevation marks as shown in Figure 6-11.

Note If the map had shown the building footprint to be straight lines at the original angle, I may have decided to draw the outline walls and then rotated the walls and map as above. As the footprint was already at a slight angle, then it did not matter as much. The problem with an image rather than a vector .dwg or similar is that it becomes pixelated when zoomed in, so defining the true outline becomes more difficult. For a visualization project, an inch or two out of place is not a problem. For a conservation/restoration project, having the more precise measurement would be ideal; therefore, research for sizes, lengths, area, or similar would be good to do. I have read many books, articles, and blogs regarding measurements for Steventon Rectory and have not found any unfortunately. This map and its scale are (to date) the only resources. Should further evidence be found, then it would not be a problem to update the Revit model, and via Datasmith, update the Unreal model with the latest information.

CHAPTER 6　STEP THREE: BUILDING THE 3D MODEL

Figure 6-11. *The map has been moved to be near/within the elevation marks*

17. Once you have the map in the right position, you can choose the "Pin" command to lock the image into position and prevent it from being selected going forward.

Figure 6-12. *(a) The Pin command highlighted, (b) the result once applied to the map*

CHAPTER 6   STEP THREE: BUILDING THE 3D MODEL

Step 3. Rectory Walls

1. For the Rectory walls, the next step is to choose your premade External Wall and draw a rectangle that is straight and roughly the right size to cover the main part of the building; see Figure 6-13.

2. Use Rotate/Place reference to rotate the rectangle to the shape of the pixels and then adjust each wall to make sure it fits the outline as much as possible and looks true to the lines of the pixels; see Figure 6-14.

3. To do this, make sure you move the center of rotation to the end of one of the walls and then use the other end to rotate to align with the pixels, similar to how you rotated the map.

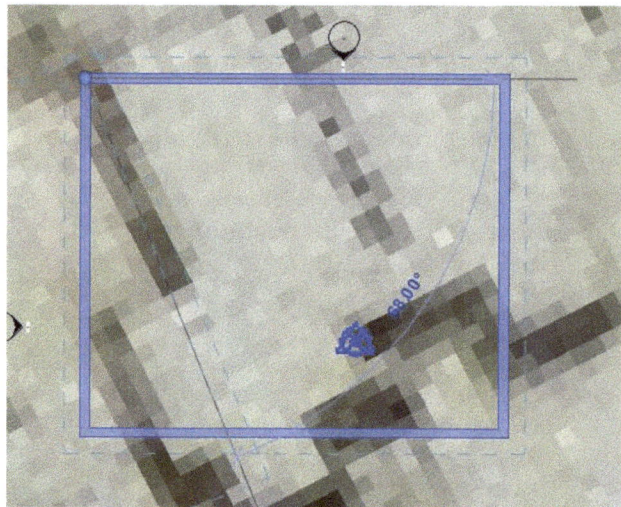

Figure 6-13. *Create a rectangle with your wall command, ensuring the building has "true" corners*

CHAPTER 6   STEP THREE: BUILDING THE 3D MODEL

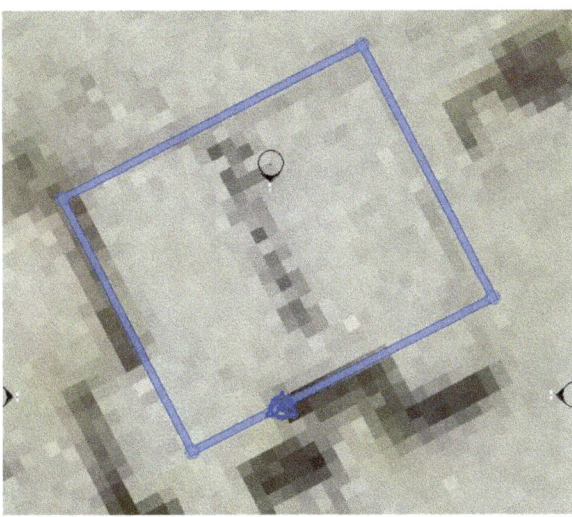

Figure 6-14. *Rotating the rectangle to align with the image pixel outline of the building*

4. You can repeat the same rectangle commands above to add the extensions to the main building outline or draw individual lines. The latter might now be quicker because you have the rectangle already drawn. This is because Revit recognizes perpendicular while you are drawing lines.

5. Roughly draw the shape using the perpendicular snap option; you can always nudge using the arrow keys to move individual walls to tie in with the pixelated outline; see Figure 6-15.

CHAPTER 6   STEP THREE: BUILDING THE 3D MODEL

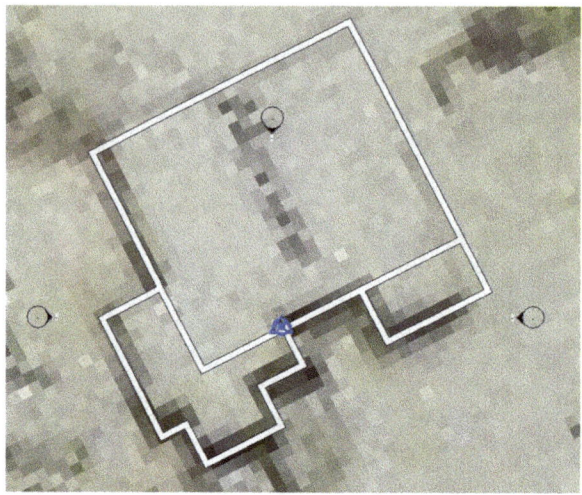

Figure 6-15.   *The initial walls following the image's pixel outline of the building*

Having drawn your external walls, you will now see in one of your elevation views that, unless you chose the walls to go to a Level before drawing them, they will probably be on an "Unconnected" height as in Figure 6-16.

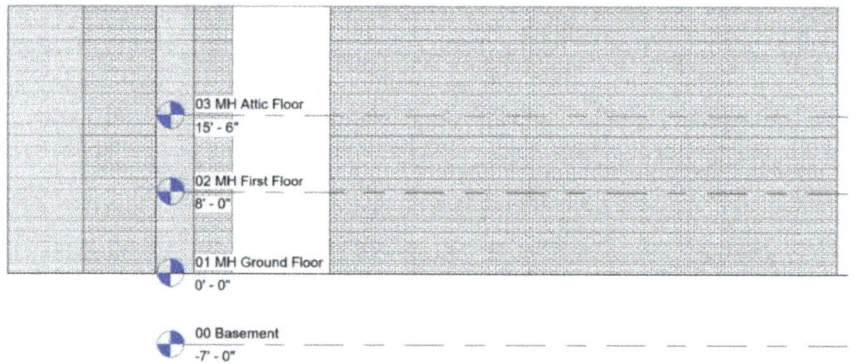

Figure 6-16.   *Elevational view with walls at an Unconnected height*

CHAPTER 6   STEP THREE: BUILDING THE 3D MODEL

6. To quickly change them to the upper level, do a crossing selection, right to left, to select the tops of the walls

7. Go to the Properties box and change to the Attic Floor level by clicking on Unconnected and choosing the correct level.

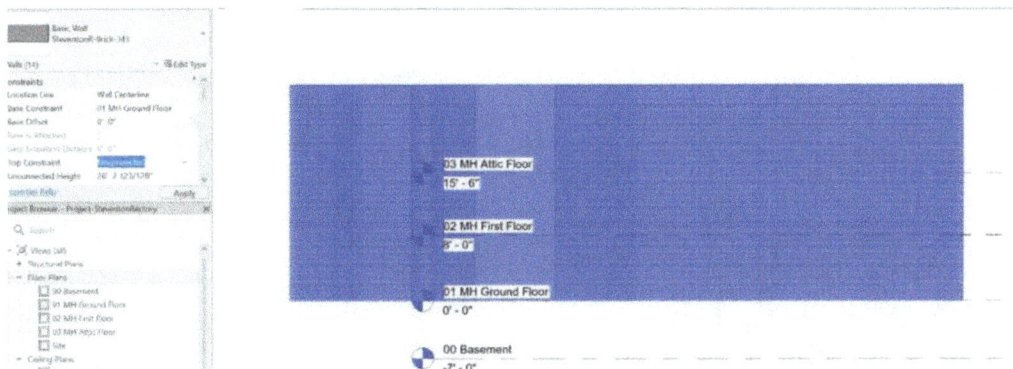

Figure 6-17. *Changing the height of the walls in the Properties box*

8. The walls will automatically change in height to that of the level chosen.

9. You can also move the level heads out further to the left so they are not embedded in the walls as in Figure 6-18.

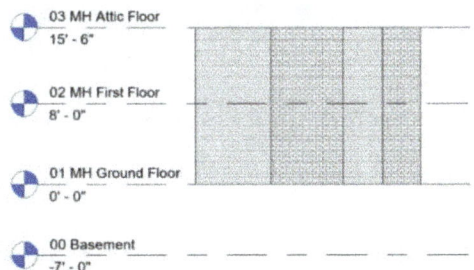

Figure 6-18. *Elevation view showing the walls at the top-level height and the level heads moved out to the left*

If you cannot see all your walls, it will mean that the Elevation view has been clipped, which is easy to change to be able to see all the walls:

CHAPTER 6   STEP THREE: BUILDING THE 3D MODEL

10. Go to a Plan view, i.e., ground floor, and click on the nose of the elevation mark/circle and go to the Properties box.

11. A line will appear. Scroll down and look for the Extents section.

12. Now look for Far Clipping and click "Clip with Line" and in the drop-down, choose "No Clip".

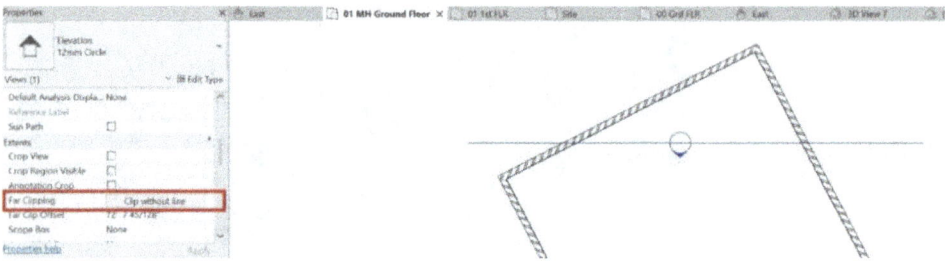

Figure 6-19. *Changing your Far Clipping elevation view*

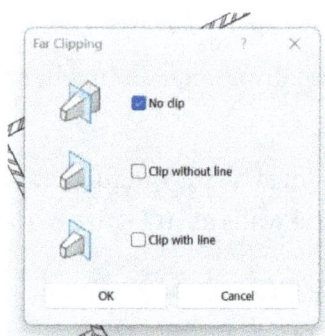

Figure 6-20. *The "No Clip" option, which will enable depth of view of all your objects*

13. You should now be able to see all the walls on that elevational view. Do this with each elevation mark to ensure you can see all of your building in each Elevation.

CHAPTER 6 STEP THREE: BUILDING THE 3D MODEL

Note You could always move the elevation marks out further, but the above method is easier and will ensure that regardless of any further building or site work, you will always see your drawn objects. If an elevation mark is in the way on a Plan view, obviously you can move it away. **Please do not delete, as your view of that elevation will also be deleted.**

14. Open a default 3D view and look at your model. You will see that the map does not show in this view; it has only come into the Site view where you inserted it as an image earlier.

15. You may notice that not all walls show brick on the outside. This will be because the wall needs reversing, having been drawn left to right/anticlockwise.

Figure 6-21. *The wall showing as the inside rather than the outside (no pattern visible like the side wall)*

16. Go to your floor plan and click on the wall and you will see a symbol of two opposing arrows.

17. Click on this and the wall will flip to show the Plaster on the inside and Brick pattern on the outside; see Figure 6-22.

CHAPTER 6   STEP THREE: BUILDING THE 3D MODEL

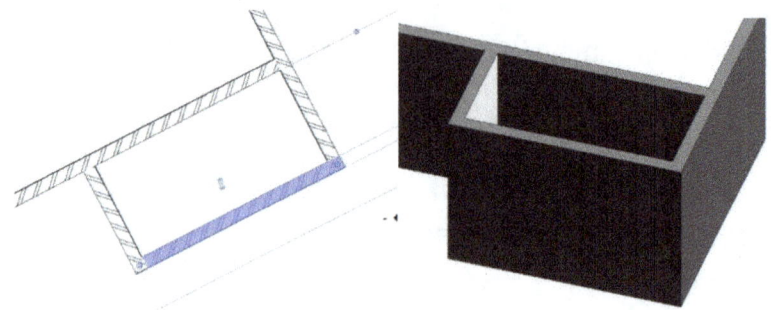

Figure 6-22. *(a) The wall has now been flipped using the arrows visible in floor plan view and (b) the wall now showing the external pattern in the 3D view*

Before we go any further, I thought I would mention the possibility of either building the walls from ground to top as single height walls and applying a texture in Unreal that depicts rows of brick and rows of flint, or building the walls as separate rows, i.e., layers of walls that can then be individually applied as either a brick or a flint texture. It is not clear whether Steventon Rectory was built with brick quoins, base and top, a framework of brick in that sense, with the interior of the framework all flint as in the first and the second image below, or built with rows of both with the brick quoins, base and top, as in the third image below.

Figure 6-23. *Images a, b, and c highlighting the different methods used for brick and flint walling*

Should you wish to build a layered wall, rather than use a texture, then please follow the instructions below.

CHAPTER 6   STEP THREE: BUILDING THE 3D MODEL

A Layered Wall of Brick and Flint

First of all, you will need to know the height of the brick used in the era involved. According to Maybank (2019), the late 16th-century bricks were between 1.25" and 2.25" in height. Not knowing without a sample being available, perhaps from an archaeological dig, then for this purpose (which can be changed should information be found at a later date), I am going to use a mid-range height of 2" (50.8 mm), making a 3-course row a height of 6" (152.4 mm), although also with grout at approximately 3/8ths of an inch (9.5 mm). Therefore, the 3-course row overall height will be approximately 7.1" (180.9 mm).

Now that this height is known, you will need to create Reference Levels for the different wall types to attach to.

1. Go to an Elevation view and select Level at the far end of the Architecture tab.

2. Once selected, you have the option (Options bar) to create a Plan view or not.

Note   Plan views will appear in your Project Browser, whereas a Reference Level (a non-Plan view) will not, but they will be visible in your elevations. The Level circle heads will also be black, not blue once deselected.

---

3. You can change the side of the Level Head by ticking on the little square just off to the side of the Level Head so that the symbol is on the other side to the Floor Levels for ease of viewing as shown below.

4. You can also adjust the height if not correct, simply by selecting the line and changing the dimension to suit, or the dimension text under the name of the Level.

CHAPTER 6   STEP THREE: BUILDING THE 3D MODEL

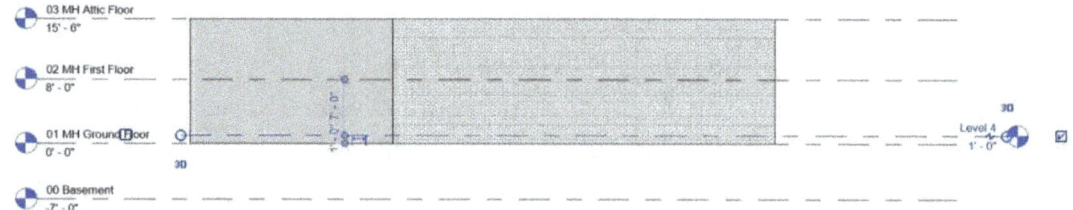

Figure 6-24. *Adding a Reference Level for your brick or flint wall to attach to*

In the third image (Figure 6-23c), the flint appears to be twice the height of the brick; therefore, use your judgment to decide on the right measurement. I have used 2' 1" for Flint Height and 7" for Brick Height.

5. On this basis, you will need to create a reference level for each row of brick and flint and a corresponding wall that starts from the top of, say, brick and is attached to the top of flint for a flint row, then a row of brick from the top of the flint attached to the top of brick – as in Figure 6-25.

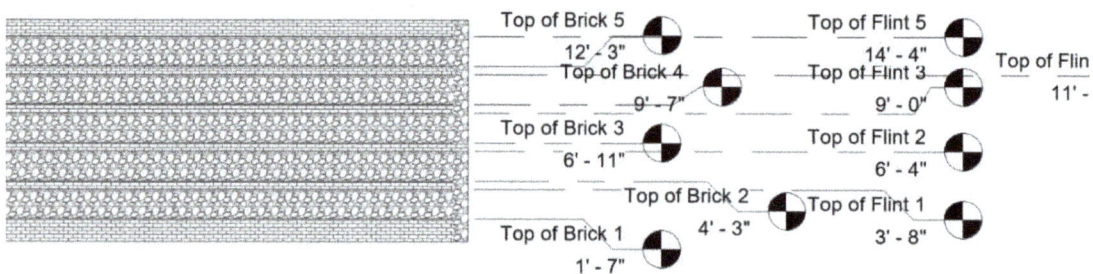

Figure 6-25. *Rows of brick and flint as individual elements with the associated reference levels*

6. You will need to use an elevation for adding the reference levels at the right heights and then use the Ground Floor plan to create the walls.

CHAPTER 6 STEP THREE: BUILDING THE 3D MODEL

7. When you draw a wall over the top of the other, once drawn, make sure you have it selected (an error message will appear to say the wall is in the same place of another).

8. To change this and make sure it is correct, while selected, go to Properties and choose the base level, i.e., Top of Brick 1, from the drop-down menu.

9. Then for the attached to, instead of Unconnected, choose Top of Flint1.

10. The error message will disappear, and your new wall will be on top of the initial wall.

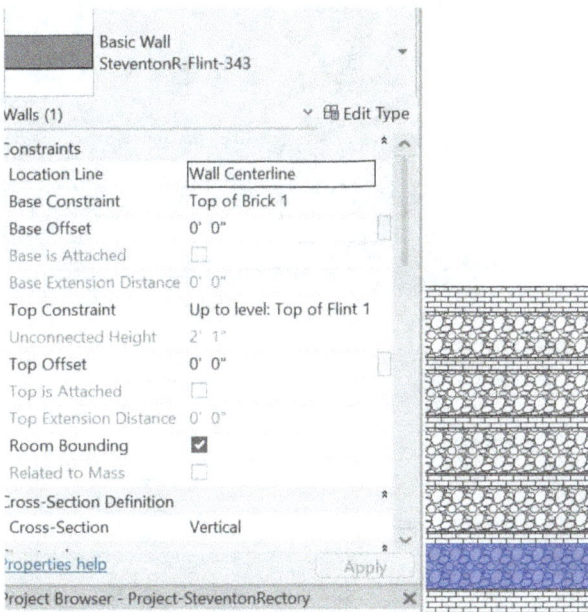

Figure 6-26. *Properties box showing the Base Constraint and Top Constraint*

This is going to take time, as you will then need to repeat for all the external walls. One good aspect for doing it this way is that you are able to schedule the types of walls and therefore how much flint and brick has been used in the construction.

Another way would be to make a new wall type called a stacked wall.

319

CHAPTER 6   STEP THREE: BUILDING THE 3D MODEL

11. There are two by default in Revit 2024, so you can choose one, duplicate, and choose Edit Structure.

12. There will be different wall types shown which you can change to layer the flint and brick wall types you have already created.

13. This will become a Wall Type which you can choose to replace the walls already drawn, therefore quicker overall.

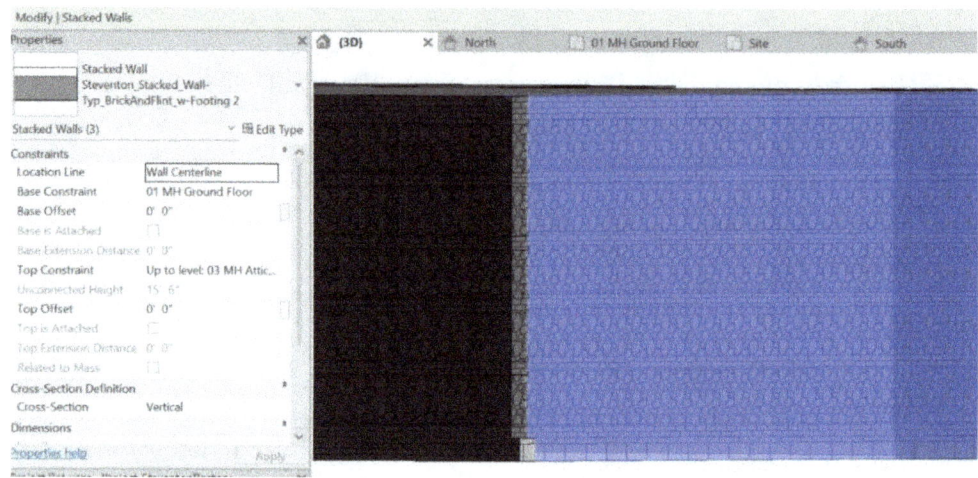

Figure 6-27. *Stacked Wall Type applied to the walls*

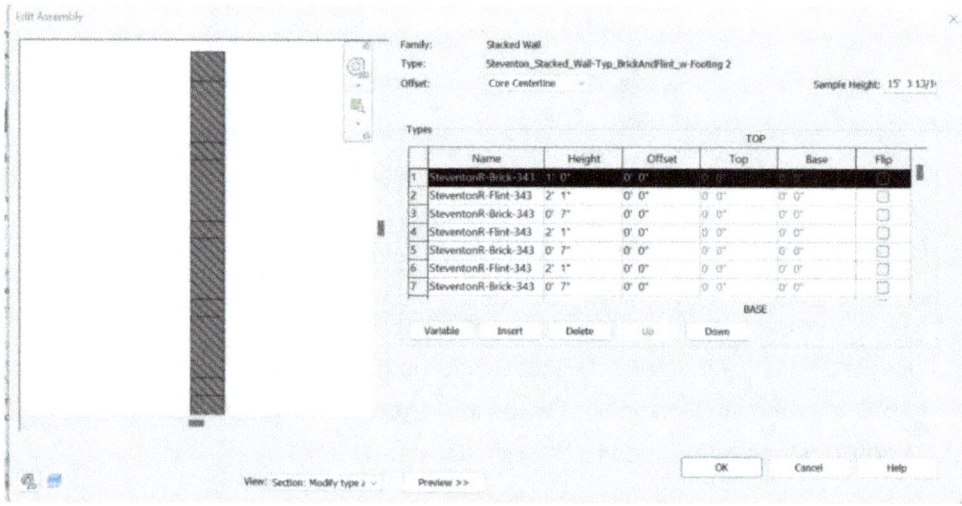

Figure 6-28. *The stacked wall structure with the different walls and their heights*

CHAPTER 6   STEP THREE: BUILDING THE 3D MODEL

I have exported both types to Unreal Engine using Datasmith, and each wall structure enables you to apply separate materials to the different layers/rows. Figure 6-29 shows the Stacked Wall type in Unreal, albeit only as a test at this point and therefore not the correct materials.

Figure 6-29. *Image showing the Stacked Wall type in Unreal Engine with each layer accessible as a separate object for applying individual materials*

Both methods will also list each wall type separately in a Wall Schedule (see Figure 6-30). For a Revit model, the Stacked Wall type would be the easier and quicker method.

\<Wall Schedule\>					
A	B	C	D	E	F
Type	Width	Length	Volume	Area	HBIM Information
SteventonR-Brick-343	1' - 2"	52' - 3"	2.76 m³	8 m²	
SteventonR-Brick-343	1' - 2"	52' - 3"	26.68 m³	75 m²	
SteventonR-Brick-343	1' - 2"	5' - 2"	3.10 m³	9 m²	
SteventonR-Brick-343	1' - 2"	8' - 3"	4.09 m³	12 m²	
SteventonR-Brick-343	1' - 2"	8' - 3"	4.69 m³	13 m²	
SteventonR-Brick-343	1' - 2"	8' - 4 1/2"	4.29 m³	12 m²	
SteventonR-Brick-343	1' - 2"	7' - 5"	3.20 m³	9 m²	
SteventonR-Brick-343	1' - 2"	20' - 2 1/2"	10.32 m³	29 m²	
SteventonR-Brick-343	1' - 2"	52' - 0"	1.00 m³	3 m²	
SteventonR-Brick-343	1' - 2"	52' - 0"	1.00 m³	3 m²	
SteventonR-Brick-343	1' - 2"	52' - 0"	1.00 m³	3 m²	
SteventonR-Brick-343	1' - 2"	52' - 0"	1.00 m³	3 m²	
SteventonR-Brick-343	1' - 2"	52' - 0"	2.03 m³	6 m²	
SteventonR-Brick-343	1' - 2"	15' - 1 1/2"	0.27 m³	1 m²	
SteventonR-Brick-343	1' - 2"	15' - 1 1/2"	0.27 m³	1 m²	
SteventonR-Brick-343	1' - 2"	15' - 1 1/2"	0.27 m³	1 m²	
SteventonR-Brick-343	1' - 2"	15' - 1 1/2"	0.27 m³	1 m²	
SteventonR-Brick-343	1' - 2"	15' - 1 1/2"	0.27 m³	1 m²	
SteventonR-Brick-343	1' - 2"	15' - 1 1/2"	0.46 m³	1 m²	
SteventonR-Brick-343	1' - 2"	24' - 0"	0.46 m³	1 m²	
SteventonR-Brick-343	1' - 2"	24' - 0"	0.46 m³	1 m²	
SteventonR-Brick-343	1' - 2"	24' - 0"	0.46 m³	1 m²	
SteventonR-Brick-343	1' - 2"	24' - 0"	0.46 m³	1 m²	
SteventonR-Brick-343	1' - 2"	24' - 0"	0.46 m³	1 m²	

Figure 6-30. *Wall Schedule example*

CHAPTER 6   STEP THREE: BUILDING THE 3D MODEL

Now that we have the external wall types created, we can add the floors, doors, and windows. We can also work on adding the cellar to the south wing and other structural elements. The floor would most likely have been flagstones laid on compacted earth, flint, or chalk and the upper floors made from timber joists covered with oak planks. The windows may have been sash or casement windows, and the doors oak, possibly painted.

Step 4. Floors

1. To create the ground floor, choose the Ground Floor Plan and go to Architectural tab and Floor command.

Note   If you have not used Revit before, Revit comes with a set of commands termed Sketch mode, which allows you to create a sketch or outline of what you want to create and set the properties of it, and then in order for it to be created, you need to make sure to click on the green tick shown below.

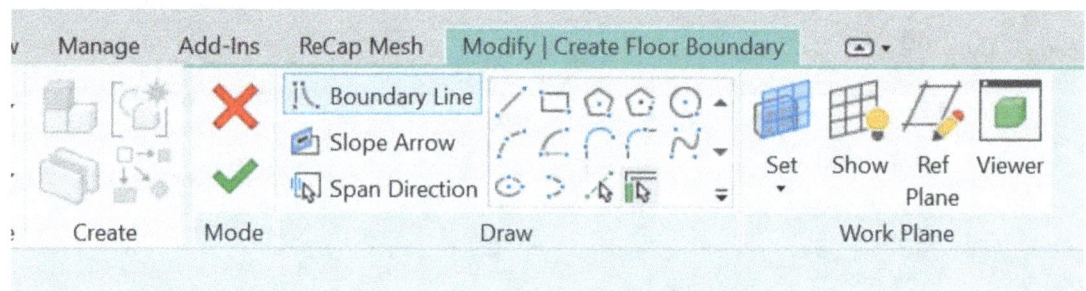

Figure 6-31. Sketch mode's Modify commands showing the green tick to complete or red cross to cancel

2. Using the "Pick Walls" drawing tool, select the external walls of the building if you want the complete footprint to be flagstones. (You can always edit the floor outline later if you discover that some areas are a different floor type.)

CHAPTER 6   STEP THREE: BUILDING THE 3D MODEL

Note   If you click the Tab keyboard button just once (i.e., do not keep depressed), you can select a chain of walls – walls that are connected to save you picking each wall individually. For this shape, not all of the walls are selected, so you can then pick the others individually using the CTRL key (add to selection).

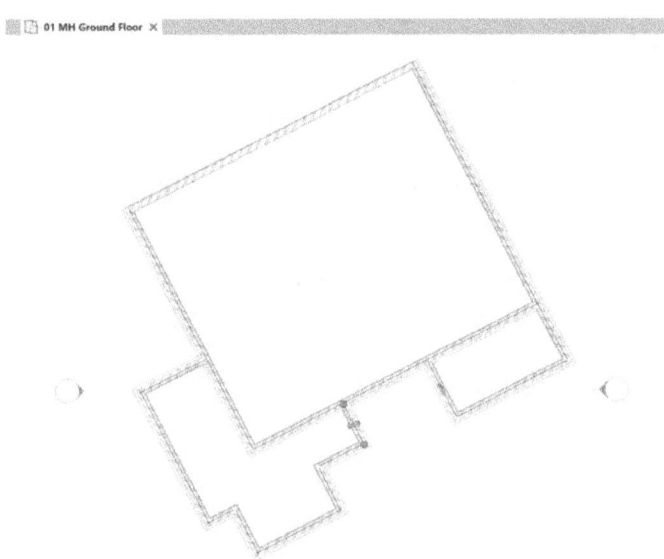

Figure 6-32. Floor command with all walls selected – showing as red

The current selection would not make the floor, i.e., if you were to select the green tick to finish, you would see that an error message appears bottom right of your screen.

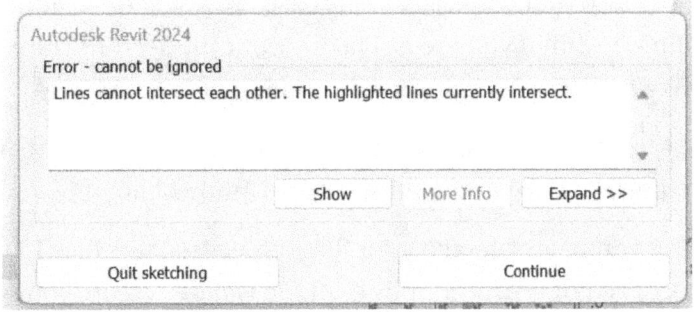

Figure 6-33. Error message appears because the lines intersect in places

As you are going to create a floor to the external walls, and to the inside face of the walls not to the centerline of the walls, you have a couple of things to do, so click Quit Sketching on the error message to start the command again.

3. This time, once you have chosen Pick Walls, look at the Options bar and tick off "Extend into wall (to core)".

4. Then also look at the type of floor in the Properties box and choose your floor type if you have already created your Flagstone Floor Type.

5. If you have not yet created your floor, choose one of the Floor Types, and edit the structure to suit what the floor would be, i.e., compacted earth/sand and flagstone finish.

6. Remember to always duplicate a core material before editing the properties. My floor looks like Figure 6-34.

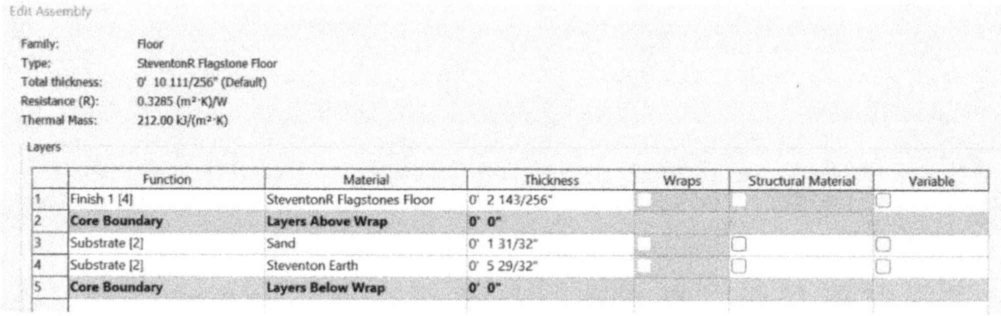

	Function	Material	Thickness	Wraps	Structural Material	Variable
1	Finish 1 [4]	SteventonR Flagstones Floor	0' 2 143/256"			
2	Core Boundary	Layers Above Wrap	0' 0"			
3	Substrate [2]	Sand	0' 1 31/32"			
4	Substrate [2]	Steventon Earth	0' 5 29/32"			
5	Core Boundary	Layers Below Wrap	0' 0"			

Family: Floor
Type: SteventonR Flagstone Floor
Total thickness: 0' 10 111/256" (Default)
Resistance (R): 0.3285 (m²·K)/W
Thermal Mass: 212.00 kJ/(m²·K)

Figure 6-34. Steventon Rectory Flagstone Floor structure

7. Remember also that materials in my case are going to be added in Unreal Engine, but if you are not taking your model into Unreal, then make sure you use appropriate materials in Revit.

8. Change the option that takes your floor into the center of the wall by selecting the Wall Faces option in the Options bar.

9. Make sure you have selected your floor type, then use Pick Lines and select each of the interior lines of the walls to create your outline again.

10. It should now look like Figure 6-35.

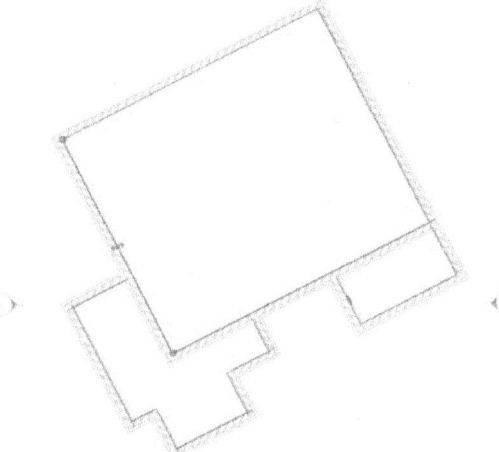

Figure 6-35. *The inner line of the walls selected to create your floor*

You will notice that not all lines meet and some intersect, so your floor will still not create.

11. Use the "Split with Gap" and "Trim/Extend" modify commands to create a continuous external outline.

12. Split the long line that forms the bottom of the main house square.

13. Then use Trim/Extend to Corner to fillet the lines together to make the image shown in Figure 6-36.

CHAPTER 6   STEP THREE: BUILDING THE 3D MODEL

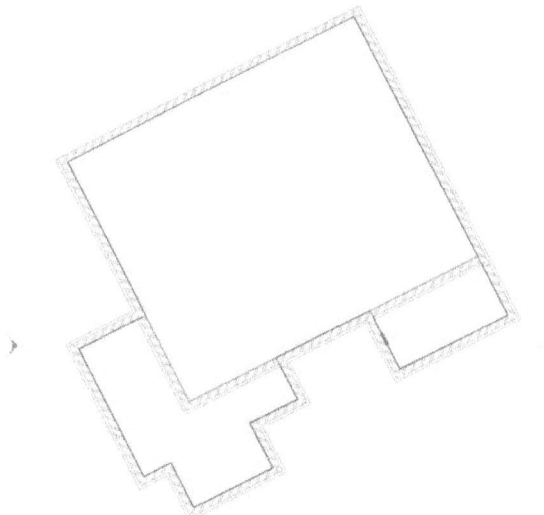

Figure 6-36. *One complete, outline without intersections or gaps is needed to create the floor*

14. You can now select the green tick to complete the creation of the floor.

15. If you go to your 3D view, you will see the floor at the base of the walls, but only internal to the wall outlines.

Note   It is sometimes difficult to select the floor in a Plan view, so going to a 3D view or Elevation view makes it easier to select if you need to edit the outline.

16. In a Plan view, put your mouse arrow on the inside edge of the wall and cycle through the selection of what is sitting under your mouse by using the Tab key, tapping on the Tab key rather than keeping it depressed.

17. Eventually your floor will show up in the bottom left corner of your screen, and once it does, click to select.

18. To save repeating the process for the First Floor, you can copy the ground floor up to the first floor and then change its properties by choosing your Timber Floor type.

19. The way to copy the floor up is by using an elevation view.

20. Select the floor.

21. Use the Copy command in the Modify area and copy from the endpoint of the Ground Floor Level up to the endpoint of the First Floor Level.

22. You can also copy up to the Attic Floor Level.

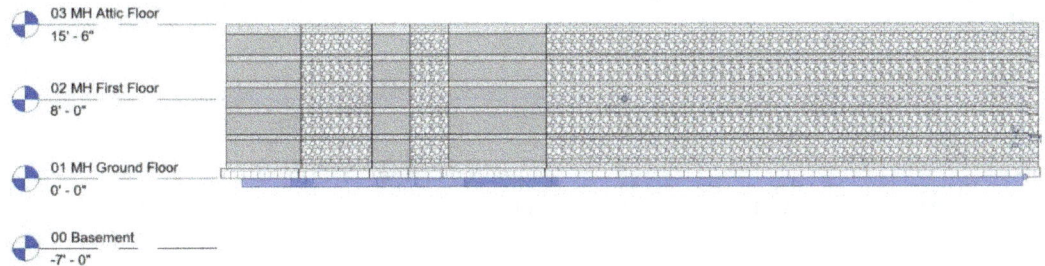

Figure 6-37. Selecting the Ground Floor and copying up to the other floors using the endpoint of the Level lines as reference

23. In a 3D view, you can pick the floor by going to the edge of the floor, not the center, and then choose your timber floor.

24. To see the first floor, you may need to hide the Attic Floor, so while you have the Attic Floor selected, right-click and choose Hide in View/Element.

CHAPTER 6   STEP THREE: BUILDING THE 3D MODEL

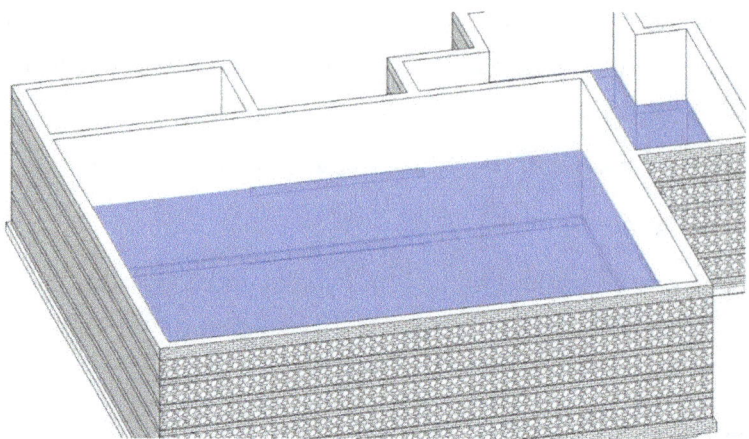

Figure 6-38. *Hide the Attic Floor to see the First Floor; select by going to the edge of the floor*

25. You can also hide the first floor as you will need to work on the ground floor soon, and in a 3D view, you will not be able to see the ground floor while the first floor is visible.

Step 5. Windows and Doors

For the windows, the front sketch of the Rectory (see Figure 6-39) shows a slight curve caused by the bricks at the top of the window, and therefore, we do not need to find a curved pre-made sash window but a straightforward rectangular window that would be appropriate and match the style drawn. There is an excellent site "NBS Source" for traditional sash windows, and it provides the Revit family for each window style. The window style I have chosen is NBS Mumford Wood Ltd. Wood Window Units, Conservation Spring Sash Window.

1. Extract the zip file once downloaded; you will see the family file.

2. Go to Revit and open the family file. You will see it is a Revit 2015 file so Revit will upgrade, and you will then be able to see the family file in Revit.

CHAPTER 6   STEP THREE: BUILDING THE 3D MODEL

***Figure* 6-39.** *The sketch of Steventon Rectory that we are using to reconstruct the building (image courtesy of Jane Austen's House, 2025)*

I do not have the actual size of the windows, so we need to approximate the size in relation to the size of the building, the spacing shown in the sketch, and guidance regarding typical sizes of windows of the period. The ground floor windows are slightly larger than the first-floor windows, and the tops of the windows will be slightly higher than the door/porch. The door I have used is also from the NBS site, the only traditional door available; it will do for now; I can always adjust/change later if it is found that it is the wrong type of door for the Rectory.

CHAPTER 6   STEP THREE: BUILDING THE 3D MODEL

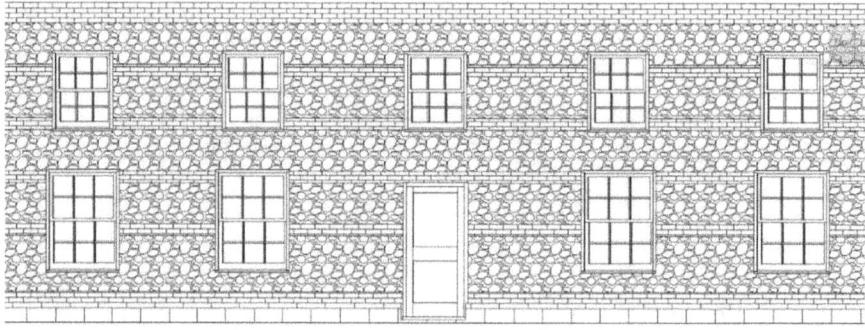

Figure 6-40. *Sash windows and front door added to the front of the house (the front faces North)*

To be able to add windows to the rest of the building, I really need to lay out the internal walls to form the rooms as described in the letters and memoirs of Jane, her sister Cassandra, and her niece Anna Lefroy, so that I do not place windows that might be in the way of a partition: "The dining parlour was on the right-hand side as you went in and my father's study was on the left, with a window looking down the strawberry walk. The parlour was a real parsonage room, with a worn carpet and old furniture, not very choice; there were family pictures on the walls; we kept the best tea-service in a cupboard in the corner. My mother liked to sit in the parlour of a morning, with the door open so she could see and hear whoever came and went, and she would keep the younger children with her while she did her darning and mending" (Ashton, 1967).

"She [Jane's mother] had her dairy and her poultry yard behind the house and always kept Alderney cows. She would go into the kitchen and train young maids in the ways of a gentleman's house. We baked our own bread and brewed our own beer" (Ashton, 1967).

From the last part of the memory, I would make a guess that the kitchen was at the back of the house, near to the dairy. I have also researched the interior layouts of buildings and parsonages of the period. This visual research supported the guess regarding the kitchen at the rear of the property. You might want to sketch out the interior plan based on your own research of your building or go straight to creating the interior walls. Should you need to adjust, it is quite straightforward at any time through the project to edit/amend; therefore, making a start straightaway is not a problem.

Figure 6-41. *Ground Floor Layout based on memoirs and typical layouts for houses of the period showing the addition of windows, doors, and chimneys*

As you may be able to see from the Ground Floor Plan (Figure 6-41), I have amended the South extension on the left to tie in more faithfully to the rear sketch view showing the two extensions in Figure 6-42. I am not sure if this will be correct with

CHAPTER 6   STEP THREE: BUILDING THE 3D MODEL

regard to the two outlying buildings, but I was not too sure how the sketch could show a two-story extension that connects to the roof of the main house as shown, without making the other two shapes single story, and aligning the main extension shape to just within the main building's left length of wall. This is where the discrepancy in sketches doesn't help, but I will run with it for now, seek expert opinion once the initial building model is complete while also checking for later evidence, and then adapt if needed.

Figure 6-42. *Rear view sketch of Steventon Rectory (image courtesy of BookLady Deb, 2010)*

I have also placed doors, an interior door option from the NBS file. The placement is mostly from my previous experience as an architectural spatial planner/designer, thinking about flow and normal use of the room. These also may need to be adjusted, but it is a start and will provide visuals for discussion once completed.

3. Doors and windows are easy to add.

4. Click on the Architecture tab; choose Door or Window.

5. Select the type you are going to use in the Properties tab.

6. Then hover over the wall where you want to insert the door or window; click to place.

Note If you select the external edge of the wall, the window should be placed facing the right way. In Plan view, once inserted, and selected, you will see the double flip arrows. If they are on the outside of the wall, they are facing the right way. The doors have additional flip arrows; one set flips direction, i.e., into the room or out of the room, and the other set flips the way the door swings open, i.e., left to right. You can also use dimensions under the Annotation tab to measure exactly how they are placed, or you can use the keyboard's arrow keys to nudge along the wall. Doors and windows are "wall hosted"; therefore, they will only fit into a wall – slightly obvious – but I have seen people trying to place the same way as furniture objects to then move to a wall, which, of course, will not work.

Step 6. Chimneys

Chimneys also needed to be added (they are freely moving objects, not wall hosted – although there are some models available that are wall hosted). The only reference for the chimney placements was the two sketches: the front sketch (Figure 6-39) and the rear sketch (Figure 6-42), which shows a reasonably central chimney, two chimneys on the far side, and one on the gable end of the larger extension.

I have placed those chimneys roughly as shown with Revit's basic chimney model.

1. Go to the Architecture tab and Component and choose Place a component.

2. The chimneys are not yet in the template, so you will need to use the Load Family command, which you can see on the Modify bar on the right-hand side.

3. Click Load Family, and it should take you out to the Revit Family Library, a set of folders that has various typical family models of objects, such as Doors, Windows, Beams, Casework, and similar.

4. Look for the Speciality Equipment folder; it used to be there, but if you cannot find it, I have included several different types of chimney in the lesson files for Steventon Rectory on the accompanying website for this book. Go to the lesson files and choose the "Fireplace_and_Chimney_8618" file (which has been used in this exercise).

CHAPTER 6   STEP THREE: BUILDING THE 3D MODEL

> **Note**   If you do not have any Library folders, you can go to www.autodesk.com/revitcontent to download the content for your Revit version, by following their instructions. You can also access Revit families from other sites such as RevitCity.

5. Once the chimney has loaded, you can place in position, making sure the fireplace is facing the right way.

6. You can adapt the height, width, and depth using the Properties box.

Step 7. Staircases

In Figure 6-41, you can see I have already added a central staircase to the first floor and another staircase to the cellar accessed via a door to the under-stair space. The ground floor therefore could have looked something very similar to the layout in Figure 6-43.

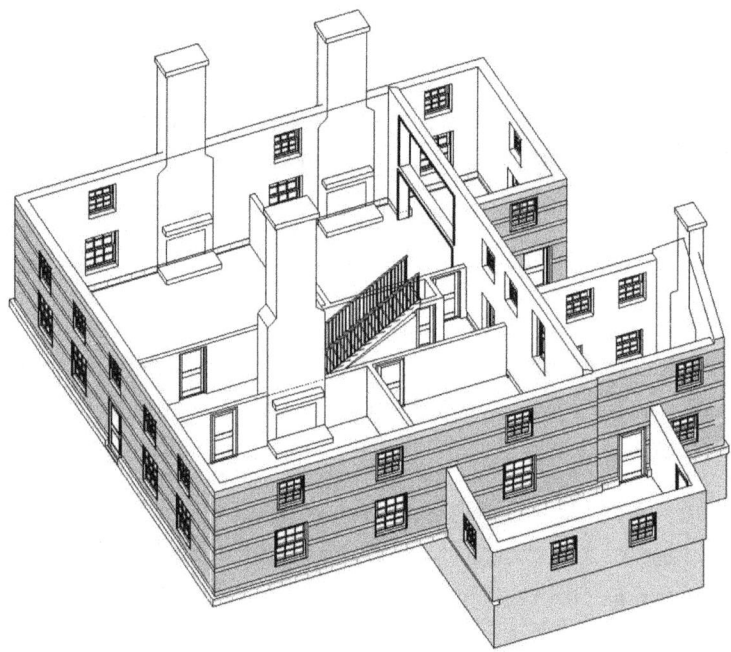

Figure 6-43. *3D view of the ground floor (first floor and attic floor (timber) hidden to see the layout)*

CHAPTER 6   STEP THREE: BUILDING THE 3D MODEL

This can be viewed by hiding in view the first floor and attic floor if they were copied up from the ground floor earlier.

1. To Hide in View, select the floor by selecting the edge, not the middle of the floor, and then right-click and choose "Hide in View"/Element.

2. To create your first staircase, from the ground floor to the first floor, go to the Ground Floor plan.

3. In the Architecture tab, choose the Stair command.

4. The Modify tab will appear and show a range of options for the stair shape – the straight run type should already show as highlighted; therefore, you can click "Run".

5. Check in the Properties box for the Stair Properties Type. The one used in this model is Assembled Stair Residential-Left-Saddled.

6. Make sure the Base Level is Ground Floor, and the Top Level is First Floor as shown in Figure 6-44.

Figure 6-44. *Stair Properties*

CHAPTER 6   STEP THREE: BUILDING THE 3D MODEL

7. Click to place the first point of your staircase (the bottom step) and draw along the full length of the line until the complete set of 15 risers is shown. (It should state 15 Risers Created/None Remaining in gray by the staircase). Click to place the full staircase.

8. While still in Sketch mode (you will see the green tick and red cross at the top of the screen), align/move the staircase to its correct location, aligning with the right-hand wall as shown in Figure 6-45.

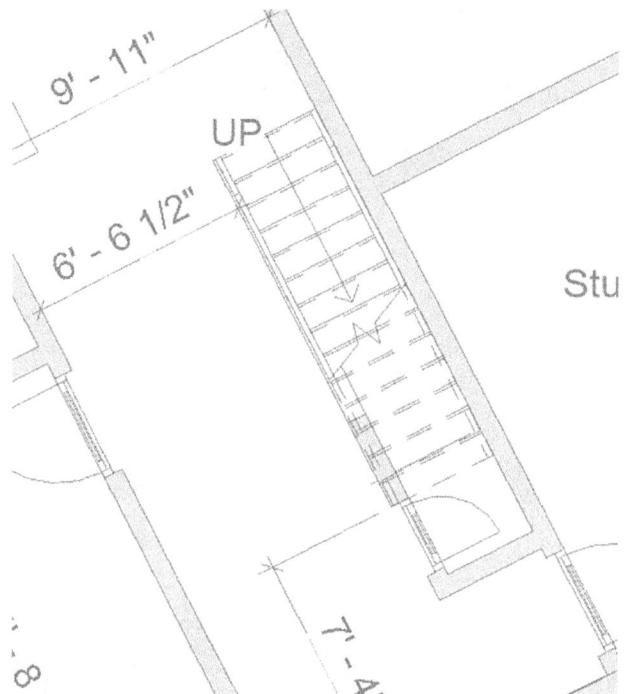

Figure 6-45. *Aligning your stair run to the right hand wall and suggested measurements*

9. Once happy with its location, click on the green tick to complete your staircase.

Note If you want to adjust the width of your staircase, select the completed staircase and choose Edit Staircase in the Modify bar. Select the staircase again and you will see an arrow appear on each side of the staircase (Plan view), and in the Properties box, you can see that you are now able to edit the width either with a measurement or adjust by moving the arrows.

We should now adapt the stair wall on the left to fit with the slope of the staircase, although we could leave it as a solid wall to the top. This is a good opportunity to know how to edit the shape of a wall though. To do this:

10. You will first need to create a section view to see the wall and staircase.

11. Go to the View tab and select the Section command.

12. On the Ground Floor plan, draw a line with the Section tool from alongside the wall and the bottom of the staircase toward the end of the corridor.

13. You should see the section line showing on the floor plan (Figure 6-46).

CHAPTER 6   STEP THREE: BUILDING THE 3D MODEL

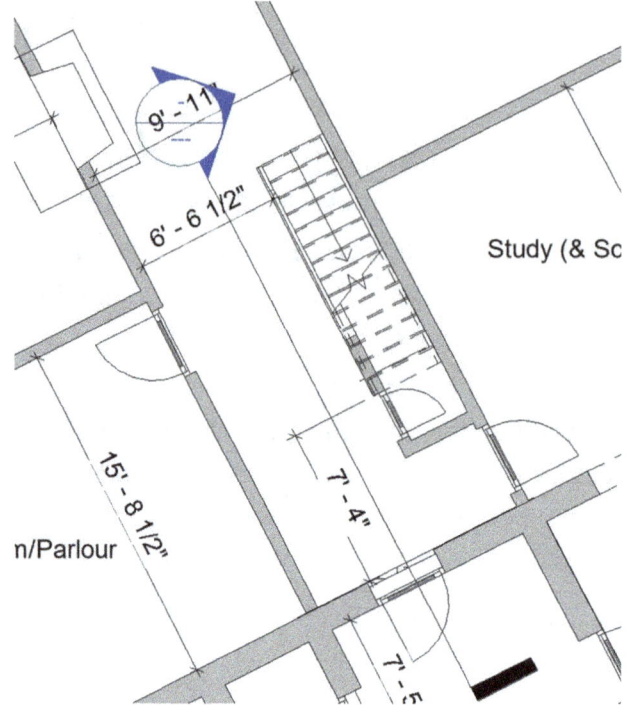

Figure 6-46. *Your newly created section line, looking at the wall and staircase*

14. In the Project Browser, you will now see a Section View (just after the Elevations).

15. Double-click on "Section 1" and it will open to show the wall in front of the staircase.

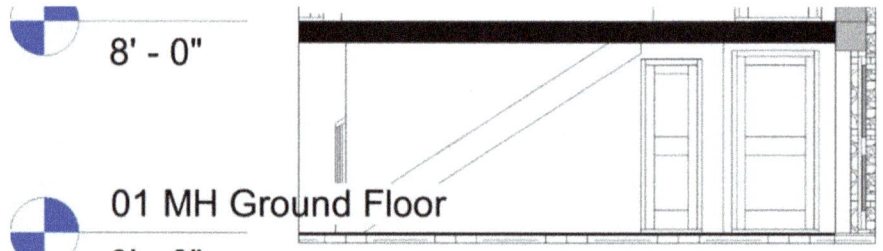

Figure 6-47. *Your Section 1 view of the staircase and wall*

16. Select the wall in front of the staircase; it will turn blue.

17. On the Modify bar, you will see the Edit Profile command.

CHAPTER 6   STEP THREE: BUILDING THE 3D MODEL

18. Select this command and your blue wall will go into sketch mode where you can edit the profile to fit the slope of the staircase.

19. Use Pick Lines to choose the sloped staircase edge and the upright line at the top edge of the stairs as in Figure 6-48.

20. Use the Trim/Extend command to fillet as shown in Figure 6-48 – remember to choose the lines parts you want to keep.

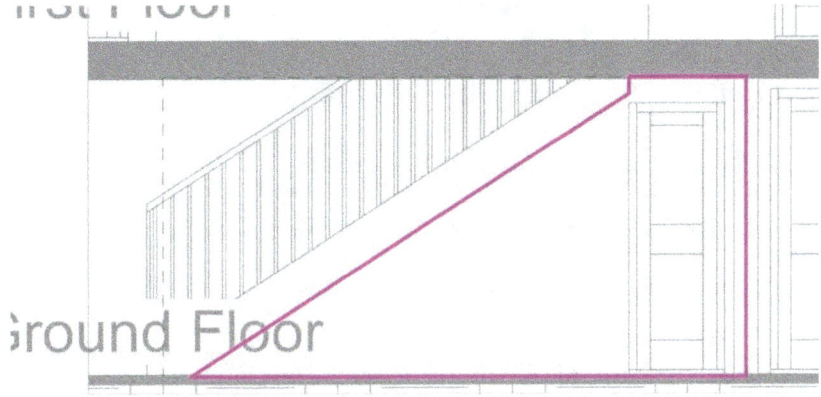

Figure 6-48. *New profile of the stair wall*

21. Delete the remaining vertical line of the profile on the far left.

22. Click on the green tick to complete the new profile.

23. To see this in 3D, go to the View tab and choose 3D View/Camera.

24. Click to place your camera view (first click places where you stand; second click places your focus – make sure to place beyond where you want to see so that the view is not clipped).

25. Your camera view will appear, which you can still edit/rotate to ensure you see your staircase and new profiled wall.

In the default 3D view, you can see that I have also created the brick basement walls. I know there was a cellar, and it was under the south side of the Rectory, but not how large. I have made it across the whole of the south, rather than a small section. There are comments made about storing produce in the cellar, such as vegetables and fruits from the garden and beer that they brewed.

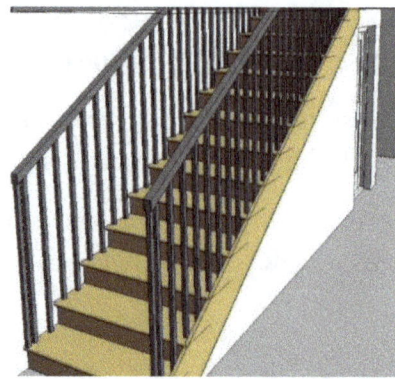

Figure 6-49. *Camera view of your staircase and sloping wall*

26. To create the basement walls, go to the Ground Floor Plan – this will make it easier for you to trace the ground floor outline.

27. I have used brick walls only to create the basement walls; choose which wall type you want to use and create your first wall by drawing over the top of one of the ground floor walls at the south of the main building.

28. While the wall is highlighted, go to the Properties box and choose the Basement Level for Base Level and Ground Floor for Top Level.

29. Then use the "Create Similar" command on the Modify bar for the remaining walls and you will see that the new walls are created using the Basement Level as the Base Level.

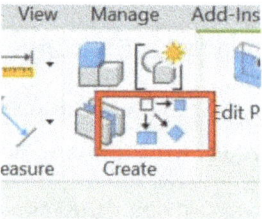

Figure 6-50. *The Create Similar command*

30. The Basement Level outline that I have created is shown in Figure 6-51, following the outline of the extensions and going across the main building in a straight line from the northern edge of the side single story extension to the East wall of the main building.

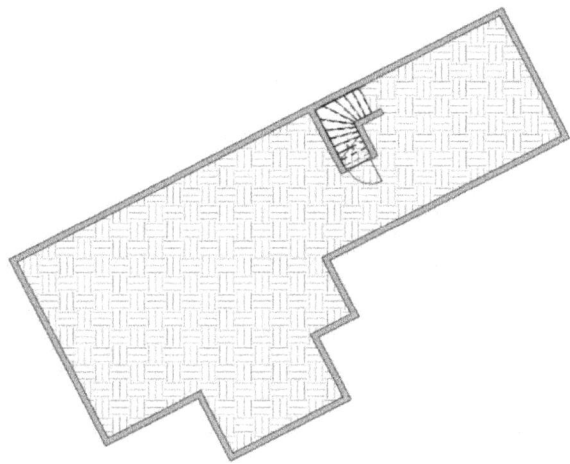

Figure 6-51. *Outline of the Basement Level with the stairs included, using a Left Hand Winder stair shape*

Step 8. Second Floor Layout

Once reasonably happy with the structure and layout of the ground and basement floor, the next is to work out the layout for the next floor. The family had domestic help in the form of a "manservant, (who doubled as a gardener) and two maids, as well as a washerwoman and a daily help" (Day, 2006). It was highly probable that the manservant and the two maids stayed at the house. In most historic references, books and films, for example, household staff were usually housed in the attic or basement, but I cannot find a definite mention that this was the case for Steventon Rectory. Nonetheless I expect this could be the most plausible spaces to consider for the staff. It is known that the Rectory was at the bottom of a slope with comment about damp and the lane occasionally flooding; therefore, logical thinking would assume that the basement would be too damp to be a suitable living space, so the attic would be the better option for the staff. This also then keeps the bedrooms on the first floor for the family.

CHAPTER 6   STEP THREE: BUILDING THE 3D MODEL

To start, the first floor needs to be unhidden and then edited to create a "hole" for the stairwell.

1. Once the floor is selected, click on Edit Boundary and you will see the red sketch lines.

2. Create a rectangle using Pick Lines choosing the edges of the staircase.

3. Click on the green tick to see your new stairwell hole.

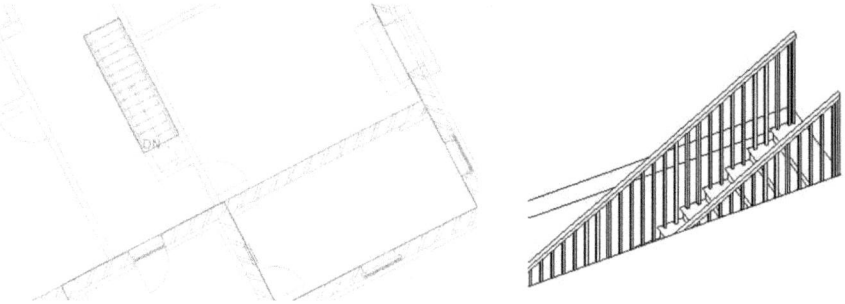

Figure 6-52. *Creating the stairwell "hole" in the first floor by editing the Floor sketch*

Now, using your best judgment, create bedrooms for the parents and the seven children living at the house, using your partition wall type. We know that Cassandra and Jane shared a bedroom and as they grew up, they changed their dressing room to a private drawing room. It is quite possible that some of the brothers also shared bedrooms. George lived elsewhere, so it was just the seven children. I would also expect Mrs. Austen to have a dressing room. Figure 6-53 shows my thinking about the layout of the rooms.

CHAPTER 6   STEP THREE: BUILDING THE 3D MODEL

Figure 6-53. *Assumed layout of Steventon Rectory first floor*

Figure 6-54. *3D view of the first floor showing the spaces for each room*

CHAPTER 6   STEP THREE: BUILDING THE 3D MODEL

Now that the first-floor layout is completed, we can create the 2nd storey stairs, roof, and the attic space.

The first step is to create the second storey staircase, i.e., from first floor to attic floor.

4. Create another staircase following the same direction as the previous staircase with the Stair command.

5. I also created a door on the first floor in the end wall as shown below to be able to access the stairs from the hall. The Attic rooms would generally be used by the house staff and would therefore have a door to keep it separate.

6. To be able to see the wall and where the previous stair is situated on the first floor and align the second, you will want to see the floor below.

7. To do this, go to the Attic Floor Plan Properties and then to the Underlay section and change the Range: Base Level option to the First Floor.

8. You should then see a grayed outline of the first floor showing in your Attic Floor Plan.

To be able to see if the walls around the staircase line up, you might want to create a camera view looking toward the base of the new staircase on the first floor. You could also create a sectional view by using the Section command. This is really easy.

CHAPTER 6   STEP THREE: BUILDING THE 3D MODEL

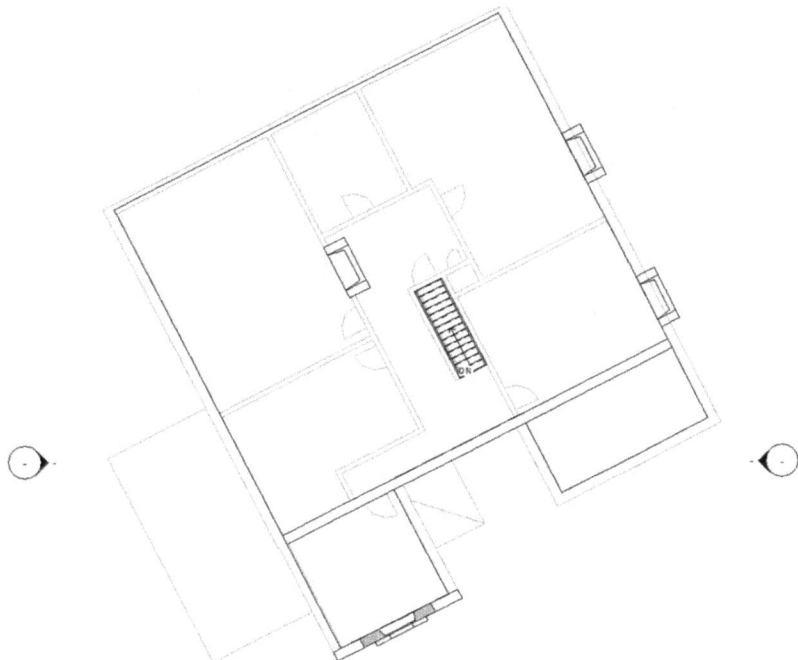

Figure 6-55. *The attic floor showing the grayed outline of the first floor and the second storey staircase*

9. Click on the command which can be found under the View tab.

10. Draw a line where you wish to see a sectional view.

Note   It will depend on which way you draw the line as to which direction the view faces; if facing the wrong way, just use the flip arrows to make it face the other direction.

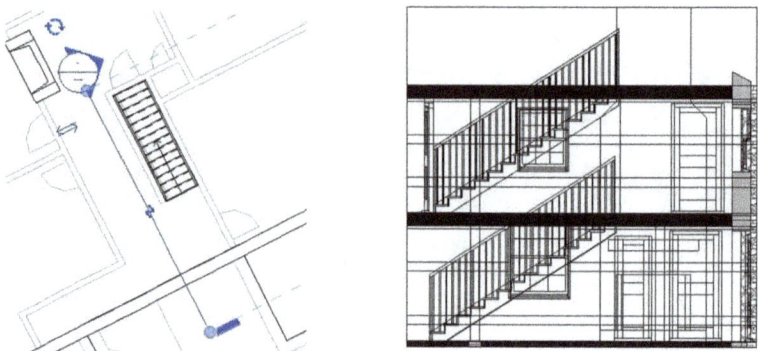

Figure 6-56. *(a) Creating a section and (b) the resulting section displayed as a wireframe*

You can use the Wireframe option in the bottom of the screen display options to be able to see the staircases and how they align to the floors.

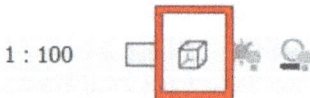

Figure 6-57. *View options can be found at the bottom of the screen.*

Step 9. Creating the Roof

Before we create the layout of the attic, we should create the roofing so that we know what head height we may have into the eaves. For now, we will not create the beams, just the roof. We can add further detail to the model once we have the basics in place.

We will create the main roof first and then the two extension roofs, which we will then tie into the main roof.

1. Go to the Roof command and once again we go into Sketch mode.

2. On the Options bar, you can create an overhang for the roof; you can also choose your roof type.

3. Using the Pick Walls command and pressing once on the Tab button, you can select all of the outside walls of the main house; click to select. You will see a pink line slightly offset externally to the walls.

CHAPTER 6   STEP THREE: BUILDING THE 3D MODEL

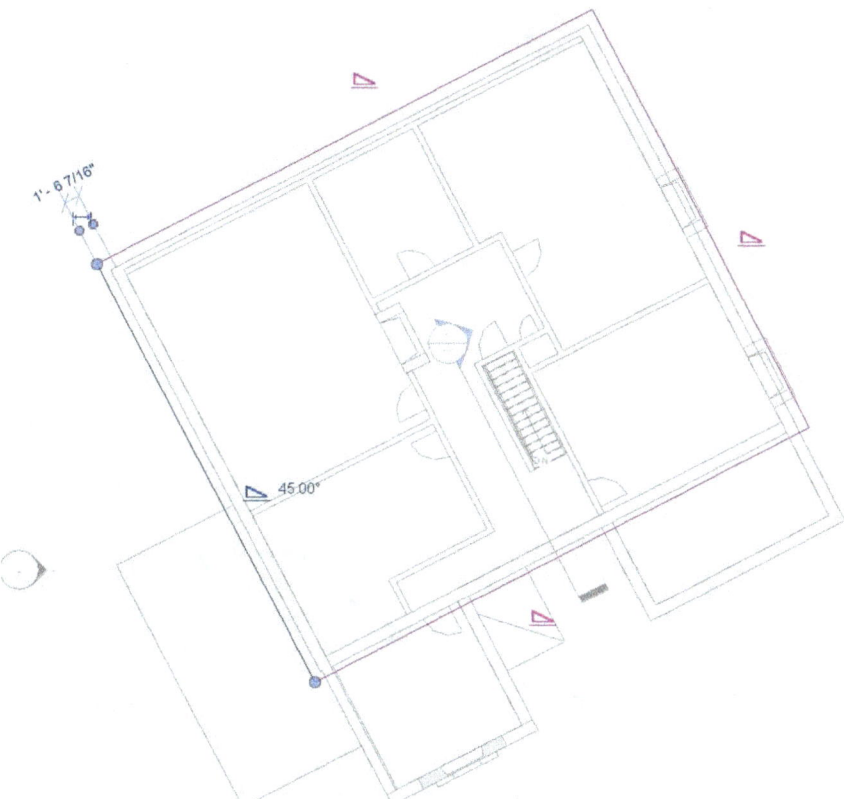

Figure 6-58. *Creating the outline of the main roof*

4. To make this roof work and look similar to the sketches, I found that the sides of the roof should have an angle of 45 degrees, and the front and back should have an angle of 27.5–30 degrees. The combination of these angles provided the longer ridge which tied in with the sketches.

5. To change the angles, select the pink line and go to Properties and type in the new angle; the default is usually 30 degrees.

6. Do this for each line and then click on the green arrow to complete the roof.

7. The roof will show as partly drawn due to the clip height view setting; it is perfectly okay, i.e., complete, not with a hole, as you will see if you go to the 3D view, which does not have a clip height setting.

CHAPTER 6   STEP THREE: BUILDING THE 3D MODEL

8. For the extension roof on the right (from south view), repeat the process in selecting the walls.

9. This time, the line that will meet the main roof should not have an angle symbol, so click on that line and on the Options bar, and deselect Defines Slope.

10. You should just have three lines with the angle. I have each of these lines set at 40 degrees.

11. Click the green tick and complete your extension roof.

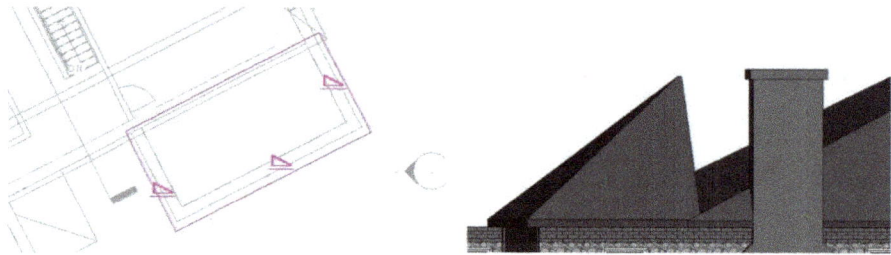

Figure 6-59. *Creating the shorter extension roof (right from rear view)*

12. You will see that in the 3D view, the roof does not join the main roof; instead, it stands up right on the side that should reach the main roof.

13. To make this work, you need to use the Join Roof command, which is part of the geometry section of the Modify ribbon.

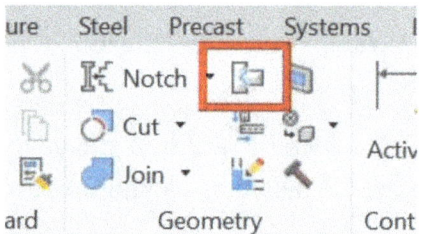

Figure 6-60. *Join Roof command*

14. In the 3D view, rotate the view so you can clearly see the edge of the unfinished roof and the face it will join of the main roof.

CHAPTER 6   STEP THREE: BUILDING THE 3D MODEL

15. Select the Join Roof command and select an edge of the unfinished roof.

16. Then select the face of the main roof.

17. You will see that the extension roof will extend to the main roof cleanly as shown in Figure 6-61.

Figure 6-61. *The completed extension roof*

18. The process now needs to be repeated for the second larger extension.

19. This is a gable ended roof so there will be two lines that you will need to deselect in the Defines Slope option in the Options bar. They are the same line that will touch the main roof and then the opposite line.

20. The sides are set at 45 degrees.

21. Your roof should look like this once you have clicked the green tick.

CHAPTER 6   STEP THREE: BUILDING THE 3D MODEL

Figure 6-62. *The second extension roof before joining to the main roof*

22. Repeat the Join Roof command and the roof will extend as before and tie into the main roof cleanly.

Note   What you will need to do now that is different to the previous extension is to get the wall to reach the gabled roof. There is another command for this, and it does not involve stretching the roof up, or telling the roof to go to the Ridge level (should you have created one); it is much simpler.

---

23. With the wall selected, you will see in the Modify ribbon at the end, there is an option to Attach to Top/Base.
24. Select the command and then select the Gable roof and the wall will immediately extend and fit to the gable roof.

CHAPTER 6   STEP THREE: BUILDING THE 3D MODEL

Figure 6-63. *Attaching the wall to the Gable roof using the Attach to Top/Base command*

25. Using the Roof command, go to the Ground Floor plan and create a single sloped roof for the single story side extension and then a two-sided sloped roof for the kitchen porch entrance as highlighted in Figure 6-64.

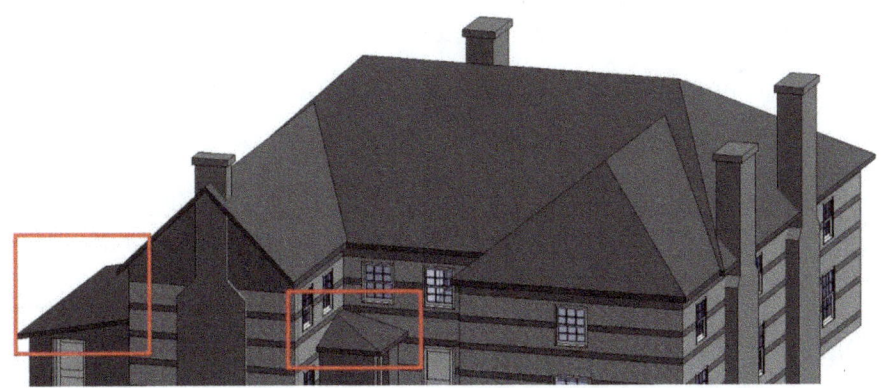

Figure 6-64. *The side single story roof and the kitchen porch roof*

You might need to adapt the height of the outside wall of the single story extension and the angle of the sloped roof to ensure the roof does not finish on a window.

351

CHAPTER 6   STEP THREE: BUILDING THE 3D MODEL

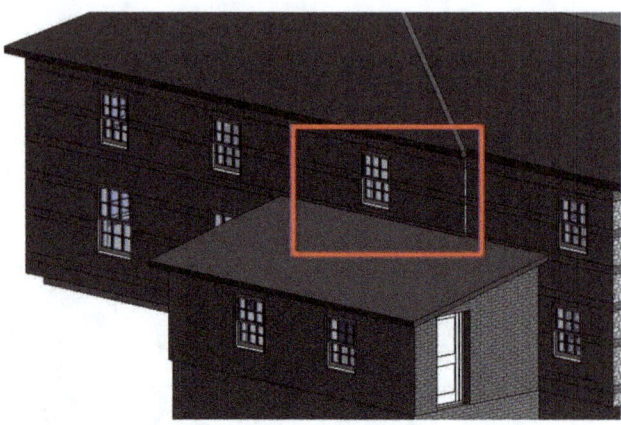

Figure 6-65. *Ensuring the single story roof fits below the window by changing the angle of the roof and possibly the height of the outside wall*

To know how much headroom you have on this floor, you can add a figure to check the height.

26. Go to the Architecture tab while in the Attic Floor Plan and Load Family.

27. Navigate to the Entourage folder where there is a choice of a male or female.

28. Select one and place near the stairs in the attic.

29. Then go to a 3D view and select the roof.

30. It will show as blue semi-transparent, which will mean you can very quickly see whether the figure's head is hitting the roof or not.

Note   Remember there will be beams as well to consider with regard to headroom.

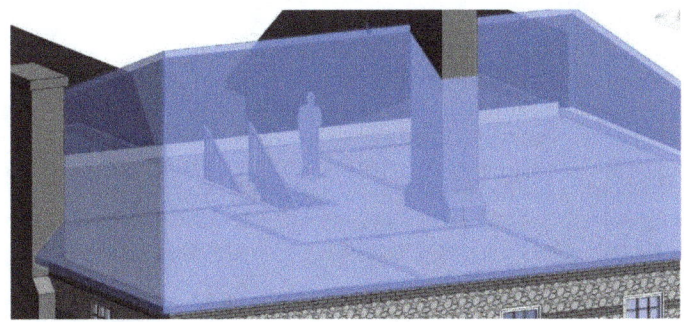

Figure 6-66. *Checking standing height in the eaves*

Step 10. Attic Layout

We may need to do a turn on the stairs similar to my model; otherwise, the figures would have to bend as they come up the last step or two. The Austens had a manservant and two maids that probably lived in, so we need to design a layout that would accommodate at least three rooms, possibly more for anyone else that may stay, such as the boys that came to be taught by Jane's father.

Figure 6-67 shows the new staircase as a right turn and how it has been positioned so that there is headroom at the top of the stairs.

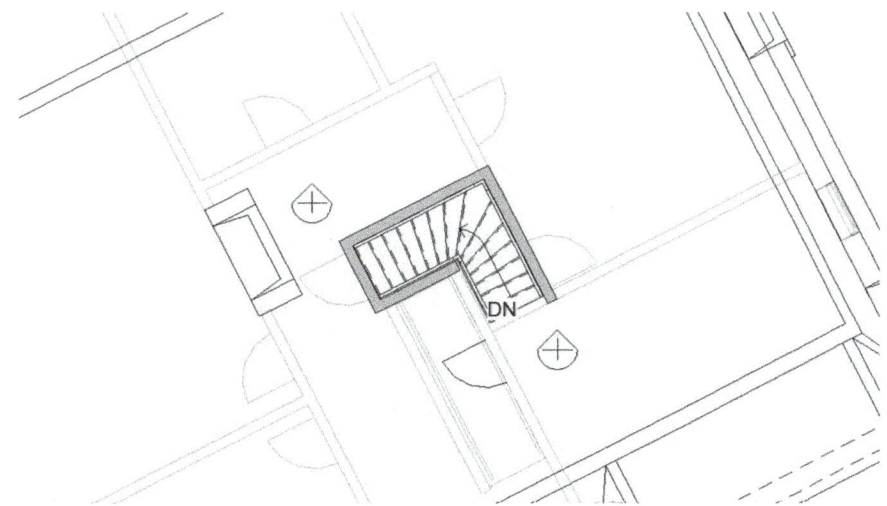

Figure 6-67. *The new staircase configuration to the attic space*

CHAPTER 6   STEP THREE: BUILDING THE 3D MODEL

To do this, you will need to

1. Select the attic staircase and delete.

2. Then use the "L-Shaped Winder" stair.

3. Place in a similar position to the one shown. You may need to rotate to fit the right direction.

4. Once in place, you can create partition walls around the stairwell as shown.

5. Then select those walls and attach them to the roof using the "Attach to Top/Base" command on the Modify Wall tab.

6. The walls will then shape to the slope of the roof.

I have designed the layout of the attic so that there is a corridor around the central part of the attic with the doors as close as possible to the slope but still within headroom height. The rooms look quite large, but there will be a wall against the eaves which will reduce the sizes. Plus there will also be a ceiling in each room, most of which will be sloped. The areas where head height is too low may well provide storage/cupboard space.

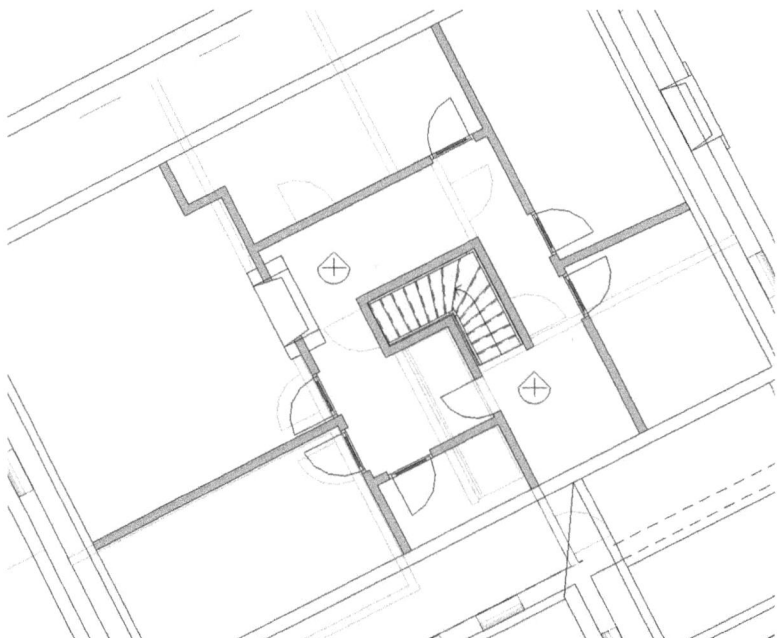

Figure 6-68. *The layout of the room spaces in the attic*

CHAPTER 6   STEP THREE: BUILDING THE 3D MODEL

7. Each wall will need to be attached to the roof as with the staircase walls.

8. When you look at the 3D view, check to see if any doors are peeping through the roof. If they are, move them closer into the center.

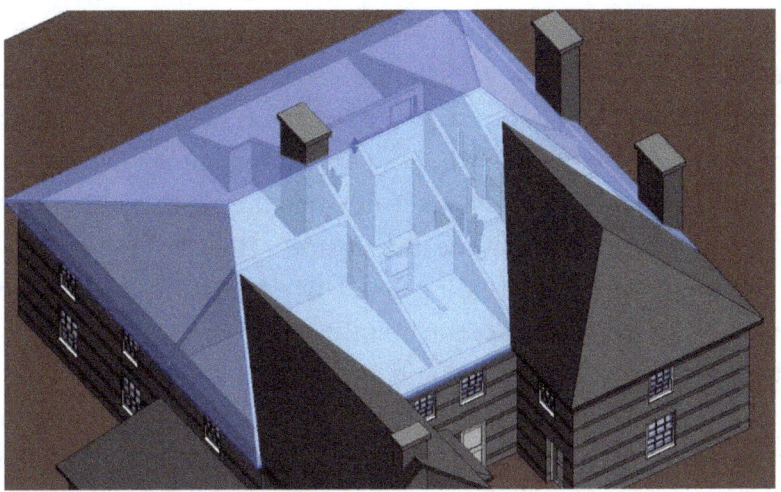

Figure 6-69. *The Attic Layout fitting to the slope of the main roof*

You now have the main structure of the building, i.e., floors, external and internal walls, chimneys, windows, doors, and stairs. There are still structures to add, such as the walls for the eaves to enclose the attic rooms, as well as the roof joists and ceilings which we will cover later. Ceilings in each of the rooms, any panelling, built-in storage, fireplaces, and other similar detail we can add in the next section. Furthermore, in the following section, we will be adding the HBIM data for the structures created in this section and the next, which should be straightforward, having collated the information prior to starting the 3D building of the Rectory.

Section Summary

In this section, "Starting to Build with Your HBIM Software," you have laid the groundwork for reconstructing Jane Austen's Steventon Rectory inside *Autodesk Revit 2024*, with a live Datasmith link to *Unreal Engine 5.5.4*. Because no physical remains

CHAPTER 6   STEP THREE: BUILDING THE 3D MODEL

exist, you collected indirect evidence – memoirs, letters, archaeological notes, and an 1821 Glebe map. You then used that map's scale to position, scale, and rotate an image correctly in Revit, giving the project a historically defensible footprint.

You then set up the modelling environment: switching project units to feet and inches, adding floor levels, and drawing an outline of exterior walls before fine-tuning each segment to the faint pixel outline. A key decision point was whether to represent the period's flint-and-brick fabric with a single textured wall or with true layered/stacked wall types; the tutorial showed both methods so you can choose speed or material quantification later.

With the shell in place, you established the structure: flagstone and timber ground floors, timber upper floors, with sash windows and doors from the NBS library, basic fireplaces, and two stair runs plus a staircase down to the noted south-wing cellar. Throughout, you used Revit's sketch-and-modify tools (Pick Walls, Trim/Extend, Attach to Top/Base) and quick view tricks (hiding floors, wireframe sections, camera views) to be able to view and edit the interior of the building.

Interior room layouts on the ground and first floors were inferred from period parsonage/rectory plans and family descriptions, reserving front parlor, study, and dining parlor downstairs and allocating seven children's and parents' chambers above. Attic accommodation was planned for the manservant and two maids. The upper floor staircase was remodeled as an L-shaped winder to preserve headroom, partitions were attached to the roof slopes, and a quick entourage figure confirmed usable eaves height.

Finally, you created three pitched roofs – with different slopes to match sketch proportions – and joined them seamlessly, then attached gable walls and added smaller porch and lean-to roofs. Every choice was made with future revision in mind, i.e., if later archaeological data is discovered and alters sizes or materials, Revit's level-based walls and the Datasmith AutoSync will propagate those edits to Unreal without breaking custom materials or metadata.

What you now have is a fully parametric HBIM core: foundations, walls, floors, stairs, openings, chimneys, cellar, and roof, ready for the HBIM metadata you will add in the next section, and for the vernacular materials and textures, you will explore in the 'Incorporating Historically Accurate Vernacular Materials and Textures'. Equipped with these methods, you can repeat the workflow for other lost buildings.

In summary, you have taken a site that no longer exists and laid down the digital structural bones for it in a way that is flexible, accurate, and respectful of its sources.

CHAPTER 6   STEP THREE: BUILDING THE 3D MODEL

Creating a Detailed Building Geometry

In the previous section, we covered the basics of creating Steventon Rectory using the Glebe map and two historical sketches as the points of reference for size and external look. In order for this building to "feel real" and representative of the era in which Jane and her family lived at the Rectory, there is much more to add. Most of this can be added in Revit, such as interior structural elements and external details. For example, we know that the building had dormer windows, which we have not yet added. There would also have been either brick or stone quoins, door furniture, fascias/soffits/bargeboards, guttering, and similar. Internally, there could have been exposed beams in places, panelling, architraves, shutters, skirting, built-in shelving, wall niches, window sills, and similar.

To add such detailing, we will need to source images and information regarding the style/type of detailing relevant to the period. We know that there is not much evidence about this type of information for Steventon Rectory, but as in the walls, we can resource from similar buildings of the time that have been written about. We could also resource from film footage of Jane Austen's books such as *Pride and Prejudice*, which was written while Jane lived at Steventon Rectory. Although we need to be careful which film footage due to the interpretation of the style of the film, we need to select authentic "real" styled environments, rather than more glossy or modern versions.

We will also need to be careful about how we construct the details, ensuring a clean geometry for taking through to Unreal Engine via Datasmith.

Therefore, in this section, we will cover the following.

Setting the Stage: The Essence of 16th/17th-Century Building for Storytelling and Recording for Future Information

- **Establishing the Level of Detail (LOD):** Clarifying the architectural detailing discussing the process of refining the wall construction, i.e., how much detail is required for the level of storytelling intended in Unreal Engine.

- **Door and Window Detailing:** This is a key area for visual richness in the storytelling and for HBIM recording.

CHAPTER 6   STEP THREE: BUILDING THE 3D MODEL

- **Shaping the Living Spaces:** Making these look more real and lived in than blank walls. For example, wall panelling, the structural finish between walls and floor, walls and ceiling, what would this have been? Were there Dado and Chair rails, built-in shelving, inglenooks, style of fireplaces, etc.?

- **Defining the Facade:** Ensuring the roof elements are visually correct for the period and locality will be important in conveying an image similar to the sketches already known by Jane Austen fans and experts. The roof geometry, dormers, and quoins through to the door furniture and porch framework may provoke comment and lack of trust in the authenticity of the research and resulting building if not visually correct and in the style of the property and period.

To be able to do the above, the following aspects are where I still need to research to ensure historical accuracy, as much as possible due to the Rectory no longer existing.

Considerations for Further Research: Detailed Architectural Elements

a. **Structural Detailing**

- Exposed beams or ceiling structures (vaults, joists)

b. **Doors and Windows**

- Period-appropriate frame profiles, mullions, and casements
- Consideration of glazing, shutters, and ironmongery

c. **Interior Panelling and Trim**

- Wainscoting, plaster detailing, cornices
- Period-authentic joinery (stairs, skirting, architraves)

d. **Fitted Elements**

- Fitted kitchen furniture (e.g., fixed cupboards or scullery features)
- Built-in shelving, wall niches
- Library shelving: built-in versus stand-alone

e. **Exterior Architectural Detailing**

- Dormer windows
- Roofing details, i.e., soffits, fascias, and guttering
- Window surrounds, sills, lintels, and quoins
- Doors and porch detailing
- Chimney stacks, decorative gables or eaves

In recreating the building, I also need to be conscious of how much detail. For example, the more detail may result in requiring making assumptions that may, when presented to experts, cause them to discuss/debate whether the detail is correct for the time, period, and state of the building. Furthermore, I need to think about how to portray aspects that perhaps will not be needed in the storytelling and visualization aspect but may be a firm requirement for being able to use the model for conservation/archival information. For example, the makeup of the partition walls. Do we model the walls as timber framed with wattle and daub, although not seen as they are covered by plaster, wallpaper, or panelling, or do we simply state this in the HBIM data fields and include cut-through illustrations? My leaning is toward the latter, i.e., state as HBIM data and include illustrations of the internal makeup. The reason for this choice is because of the complexity of the model that this would result in, possibly making it unwieldy for exploring seamlessly, i.e., no lag in recreating real-time scenes. If you can imagine perhaps 75 buildings with this level of detail, each trying to update as you explore and move through the scenes, then you might appreciate why this choice. It is back to the consideration of detail versus the storytelling; the majority of "explorers" will be focused on the story rather than the physical internal structure of walls. The textual information and an illustration pop-up window may be sufficient in this regard.

Interior Visual Reference

Before I start adding the internal detail, I will source images to provide period style and guidance. From quick research, it would appear that the 1995 series of Pride and Prejudice was the most historically correct with regard to the period, in costume and interiors (Marino and DeMeo, 2021). For the moment, I am not interested in costume; that will come later once the model is in Unreal. Unfortunately, it does seem that costume is the focus of much of the research regarding the period, with interiors shown much more about the larger country houses such as Pemberley and the Bennet's family home at Longbourn. The portrayal of Longbourn (in reality Luckington Court, near

CHAPTER 6   STEP THREE: BUILDING THE 3D MODEL

Chippenham, Wiltshire) (Movie World Map, 2025) seems to be a little grander than the Austen's family home, which has been recorded as "a little dilapidated." The Bennet's family home in the 2005 Pride and Prejudice film presents the Bennet's home as more of a rural country family home, almost farm holding, much like I imagine, based on the comments regarding the state of Steventon Rectory, the dairy, and other external buildings that kept animals and farm equipment. Mrs. Cassandra Austen, Jane's mother, also sounds as though she is very practical, doesn't sit still for long as she is constantly working on keeping the house and dairy running smoothly.

Therefore, the images I feel I should work with are not as grand as those portrayed for the 1995 Bennet's family home (see Figure 6-71), but perhaps also not as rural, i.e., pigs in the house, as the 2005 film version (Marino and DeMeo, 2021) (see Figure 6-70).

Figure 6-70. *The scene showing a pig walking through the house in the 2005 Pride and Prejudice version (Marino and DeMeo, 2021)*

The above image also shows a flagstone floor and shabby finish to the paintwork on the walls, and a planked wooden door. There is considerable discussion about the differences between the above version and the 1995 version, although personally I think the view in Figure 6-70 is of the scullery/dairy rather than the house. Therefore, it would be good to find different scenes that may show the style of decor of maybe the Drawing Room and or the Dining Room. Below is a scene of both versions concerning the Drawing Room and then the Dining Room with comparisons of the two.

Figure 6-71. *Still from the 1995 Pride and Prejudice Mini Series showing the Drawing Room with Miss Bennet and Mr. Darcy (Mistress of Pemberley, 2023)*

CHAPTER 6   STEP THREE: BUILDING THE 3D MODEL

Figure 6-72. *Still from the 2005 Pride & Prejudice film showing Mrs. Bennet and her daughters in the Drawing Room (Mistress of Pemberley, 2023)*

Comparing the Drawing Rooms, it is easy to spot the sofa cover in a state of disrepair in the lower image, the carpet is slightly wrinkled, the walls are completely panelled, and there is a wood floor in the 2005 screenshot. In the 1995 version, the panelling only goes one-third up the wall with wallpaper covering the remainder. I cannot see the floor to know if it is carpeted, but I know from another clip that there are no curtains at the window.

CHAPTER 6   STEP THREE: BUILDING THE 3D MODEL

Figure 6-73. *Still from the 1995 Mini Series with Miss Bennet and her father in the Dining Room (Sanborn, 2008)*

Figure 6-74. *Still from the 2005 film showing the Bennet family in the Dining Room (Mistress of Pemberley, 2023)*

363

CHAPTER 6   STEP THREE: BUILDING THE 3D MODEL

The second pair of images highlights the less formal dining room in the 2005 version; the walls are fully panelled, wood floor shabby paintwork in the room through the doorway. Again I cannot see the windows with regard to curtains; the table is bare wood and informally laid. The 1995 version shows wallpaper and lower panelling, curtains, and a tablecloth with a much more formal table setting.

Now I know that these are representing a fictional place and family, but there is a possibility that Jane Austen called upon her own family life and surroundings in the portrayal of the Bennet family and family home. In doing so, she is likely to have fabricated not just the story of the Bennet family and their comings and goings but also lifted the level of her own surroundings. Her books are stories of her time, therefore plausible to use to gauge how her own home may have looked; there just needs to be some rationality between the two visually different interpretations of Pride and Prejudice. The 2005 film location house for Longbourn, the Bennet family home (Groombridge Place, Kent), is more in line structurally with Steventon Rectory unlike Luckington Court (Wiltshire) (Movie World Map, 2025), which bears no similarity structurally. Again, it is worth remembering that once modelled, we can present to the experts and gain their opinion with regard to the decor and other visual aspects of the model.

My decisions for each room with regard to detail can be seen in Table 6-1. I have also added the detail for the exterior that we will work through in this section along with one room example, which can be repeated to complete each of the rooms.

Table 6-1. *Structural detail to add room by room*

Room Name	Walls	Floors	Ceilings	Windows	Doors
Ground Floor					
Dining parlor	Panelled and fireplace with mantle Skirting Candle sconces	Polished timber with carpet	Plaster and cornicing/moldings	Painted sash with internal folding shutters and ironmongery Curtains and drapes	Panelled with ironmongery
"Best" parlor room	Part panelling painted and wallpaper and fireplace with mantle Painted skirting Candle sconces Picture/Dado rail	Polished timber with carpet	Plaster and cornicing/moldings	Painted sash with internal folding shutters and ironmongery Curtains and drapes	Panelled with ironmongery
Drawing room	Part panelling painted and wallpaper and fireplace with mantle Painted skirting Candle sconces Picture/Dado rail	Polished timber with carpet	Plaster and cornicing / moldings	Painted sash with internal folding shutters and ironmongery Curtains and drapes	Panelled with ironmongery

(*continued*)

Table 6-1. (*continued*)

Room Name	Walls	Floors	Ceilings	Windows	Doors
Study	Panelled and fireplace with mantle Skirting Candle sconces Shelving	Polished timber with carpet	Plaster and cornicing/moldings	Painted sash with internal folding shutters and ironmongery	Panelled with ironmongery
Hall	Part panelled with wallpaper Skirting Candle sconces Picture/Dado rail	Flagstones	Plaster and cornicing/moldings	n/a	Panelled with ironmongery
Kitchen	Painted and fireplace/cooking range Candle sconces Shelving Pantry cupboard Copper apron sink	Flagstones	Beams and plaster	Side opening casement and ironmongery	Panelled with ironmongery
Buttery/dairy	Painted Candle sconces Shelving Storage cupboard Copper apron sink	Flagstones	Beams and plaster	Side opening casement and ironmongery	Panelled with ironmongery

(*continued*)

Table 6-1. (*continued*)

Room Name	Walls	Floors	Ceilings	Windows	Doors
First Floor					
Bedroom 1	Painted panelling	Polished timber and carpet	Plaster and cornicing/ moldings	Painted sash and ironmongery Curtains	Panelled with ironmongery
Dressing Rm 1	Part panelling and wallpaper	Polished timber and carpet	Plaster and cornicing/ moldings	Painted sash and ironmongery Curtains	Panelled with ironmongery
Bedroom 2	Panelling	Polished timber and carpet	Plaster and cornicing/ moldings	Painted sash and ironmongery Curtains	Panelled with ironmongery
Bedroom 3	Painted panelling	Polished timber and carpet	Plaster and cornicing/ moldings	Painted sash and ironmongery Curtains	Panelled with ironmongery
Dressing Rm 2	Part panelling and wallpaper	Polished timber and carpet	Plaster and cornicing/ moldings	Painted sash and ironmongery Curtains	Panelled with ironmongery
Bedroom 4	Panelling	Polished timber and carpet	Plaster and cornicing/ moldings	Painted sash and ironmongery Curtains	Panelled with ironmongery
Bedroom 5	Panelling	Polished timber and carpet	Plaster and cornicing/ moldings	Painted sash and ironmongery Curtains	Panelled with ironmongery
Hall/landing	Part panelling and wallpaper	Polished timber	Plaster and cornicing/ moldings	N/A	Panelled with ironmongery

(*continued*)

Table 6-1. (*continued*)

Room Name	Walls	Floors	Ceilings	Windows	Doors
Attic Floor					
Room 1	Painted Candle sconces Shelving Storage cupboard	Polished timber	Plaster and cornicing	Painted casement and ironmongery Curtains	Panelled with ironmongery
Room 2	Painted Candle sconces Shelving Storage cupboard	Polished timber	Plaster and cornicing	Painted casement and ironmongery Curtains	Panelled with ironmongery
Room 3	Painted Candle sconces Shelving Storage cupboard	Polished timber	Plaster and cornicing	Painted sash and ironmongery Curtains	Panelled with ironmongery
Room 4	Painted Candle sconces Shelving Storage cupboard	Polished timber	Plaster and cornicing	Painted sash and ironmongery Curtains	Panelled with ironmongery
Cupboard	Painted and shelving	Polished timber	Plaster	N/A	Panelled with ironmongery
Basement					
Overall space	Brick painted, shelving and candle sconces	Compacted earth	Beams	N/A	Panelled with ironmongery

(*continued*)

Table 6-1. (*continued*)

Room Name	Walls	Floors	Ceilings	Windows	Doors
Exterior					
Front (north)	Brick and flint, stone quoins	N/A	N/A	N/A	Panelled with ironmongery
Rear (south)	Brick and flint, stone quoins	N/A	N/A	N/A	Panelled with ironmongery
Side (east)	Brick and flint, stone quoins	N/A	N/A	N/A	N/A
Side (west)	Brick and flint, stone quoins	N/A	N/A	N/A	N/A
Single storey	Brick	N/A	N/A	N/A	Panelled with ironmongery
Rear porch	Brick	N/A	N/A	N/A	Panelled with ironmongery

Adding Detail to Steventon Rectory – Step-by-Step Exercise

Step 1. Exterior Detail – Dormers

1. Double-click in the project browser to open the Attic Floor Plan.

2. If you have not already done so, create partition walling to close off the eaves for each room.

3. In doing so, you may need to adjust some of the room names, for example, I now have four rooms and a cupboard. This was done by making the previous Room 2 and Room 3 one room (now Room 2) and changing Room 5 to a cupboard (it was too small for a room).

CHAPTER 6 STEP THREE: BUILDING THE 3D MODEL

4. Once you have these walls in place, you can create new short walls, as shown in Figure 6-75, which will create the dormer framework.

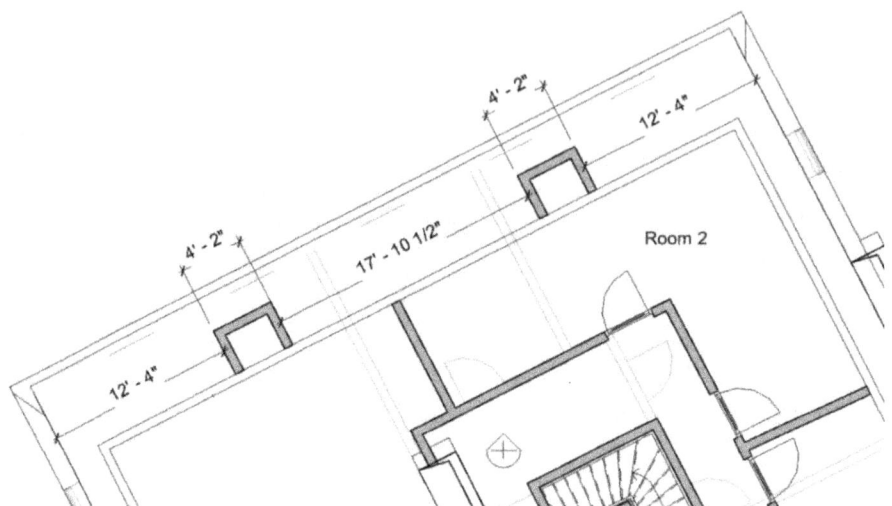

Figure 6-75. *The dormer walls at the front (North) view of the house*

5. When you look in the default 3D view, you will see the walls poke through the roof. This is as it should be.

6. Now create a roof for the first dormer. Go to the Roof command, and in the options bar, create an overhang (I have used 12").

7. Use Pick Walls and select the three walls.

8. Then use Pick Lines and select the inner cut roof line.

9. For the front of the dormer and rear, deselect "Defines Slope" as shown in Figure 6-76.

CHAPTER 6   STEP THREE: BUILDING THE 3D MODEL

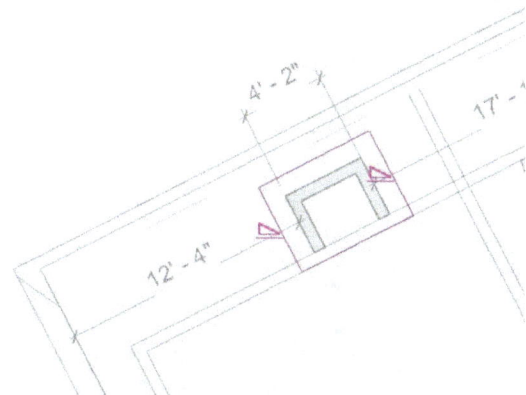

Figure 6-76. *Selecting the outline for the Dormer roof and deselecting the "Defines Slope"*

10. Select the green tick to complete your first Dormer roof.

11. While the roof is still selected (blue), go to Properties and change the level from 03 MH Attic Level to your 05 MH Head Height level.

12. Go to your 3D view and you will see the roof now sitting above your walls, although there might be a gap as in the view in Figure 6-77.

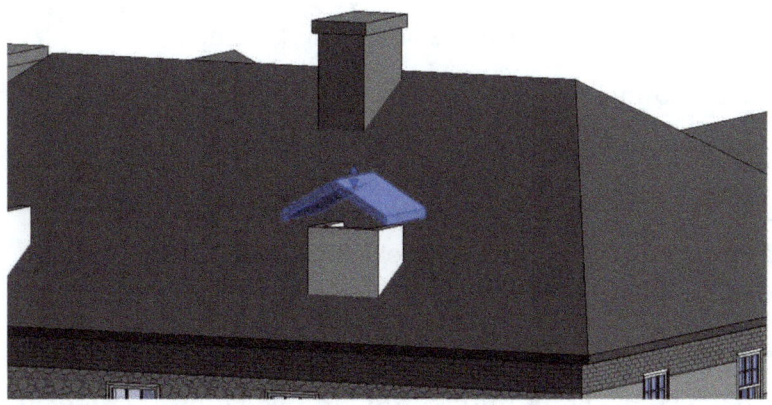

Figure 6-77. *The Dormer roof sitting above the dormer walls*

CHAPTER 6   STEP THREE: BUILDING THE 3D MODEL

13. Select the three walls for the dormer.

14. While selected, go to the Attach to Top/Base command and then select the new dormer roof. The walls should reach the roof and close the gap.

Figure 6-78. *The dormer window attached to the roof*

15. There are a couple of things to change now that we can see what the overall size is:

    - The pitch of the dormer compared to the sketch.
    - The height of the dormer is possibly too high.

16. Select the dormer roof and go to the Properties box.

17. Change the slope/angle of the roof to 40 degrees.

18. Change the height of the dormer roof so that it is a little lower. To do this, with the dormer roof selected, change the 0'0" "Base Offset from Level" to -1'6".

19. Check your dormer in the 3D view again to see if the proportions look right. I thought the dormer window was a little too wide, so I have changed the width dimensions as in Figure 6-79.

CHAPTER 6   STEP THREE: BUILDING THE 3D MODEL

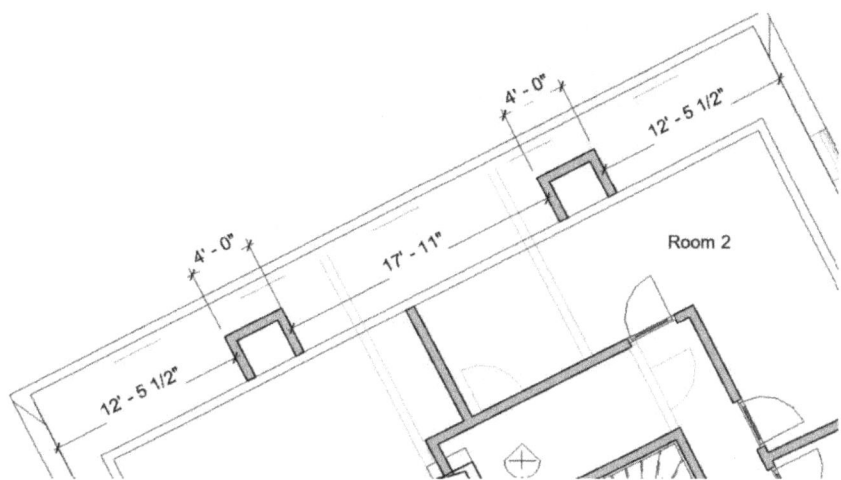

Figure 6-79. *Update dimensions for the dormers.*

20. We will now join the dormer roof to the main roof using the "Join Roof" command. Select the dormer roof and then select the Join Roof command under the Modify Geometry tool section.

21. As the roof is selected, select a rear edge of the dormer, and then select the face of the main roof.

22. Your dormer roof will stretch to the main roof and will look similar to Figure 6-80.

Figure 6-80. *The dormer roof is now attached to the main roof*

CHAPTER 6   STEP THREE: BUILDING THE 3D MODEL

23. You will notice the walls will also need to reach the main roof. To do this, go to your 04 MH Eaves Height Floor Plan to see the walls and select a side dormer wall and stretch (ensuring it stays perpendicular) toward the inside of the main roof as in Figure 6-81.

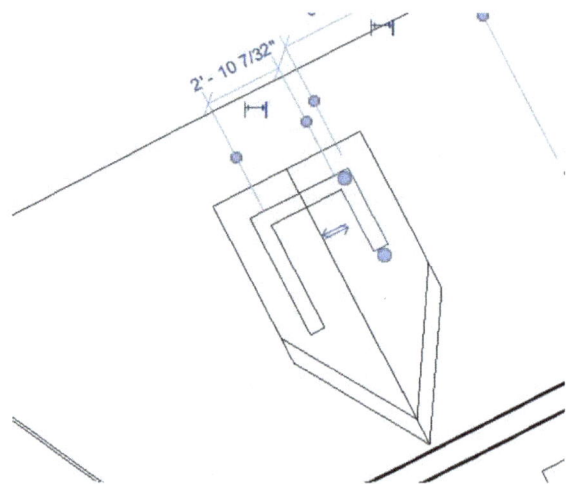

Figure 6-81. *Adapting the dormer walls to reach the main roof*

24. You can repeat the above commands to create the dormer roof for the 2nd dormer.

25. Once you have done this, you will need to add your casement window. I have used the NBS resource again and chosen the following casement window: Heritage Casement Windows - Timber Casement Window (https://source.thenbs.com/product/heritage-casement-windows/7BN43wj4aVZGtSgcWBnWwn/qhd6Eaz41QugmsMXKbxyPZ). I have included this file with the exercise files on the website.

26. Load the Casement window family file to the project – you can do this by opening the extracted RFA file (double-click). Revit will say it needs to upgrade the file; select okay. Once open in Revit, click the "Load into Project" command on the far right of the menu bar.

CHAPTER 6   STEP THREE: BUILDING THE 3D MODEL

27. The window will now be available in your project, although you will need to adjust the size. You can insert the window using the Attic Floor Plan.

28. Once placed, go to the Properties box and choose "Duplicate" to make a copy of the window type. I named it 630x800mm as this will be the size for the dormer window.

29. Once named, click Edit Type and scroll down to find "Operation", under IFC Parameters. Change the option to SinglePanel.

30. Remembering that Revit will adapt your metric measurements to the correct feet and inches, change the Rough Width to 630 mm and Rough Height to 800 mm.

31. Change the FirstMullionOffset to half the width of the window, i.e., 315 mm.

32. Change the TransomOffset to the height of the window, i.e., 800 mm (see Figure 6-82).

CHAPTER 6   STEP THREE: BUILDING THE 3D MODEL

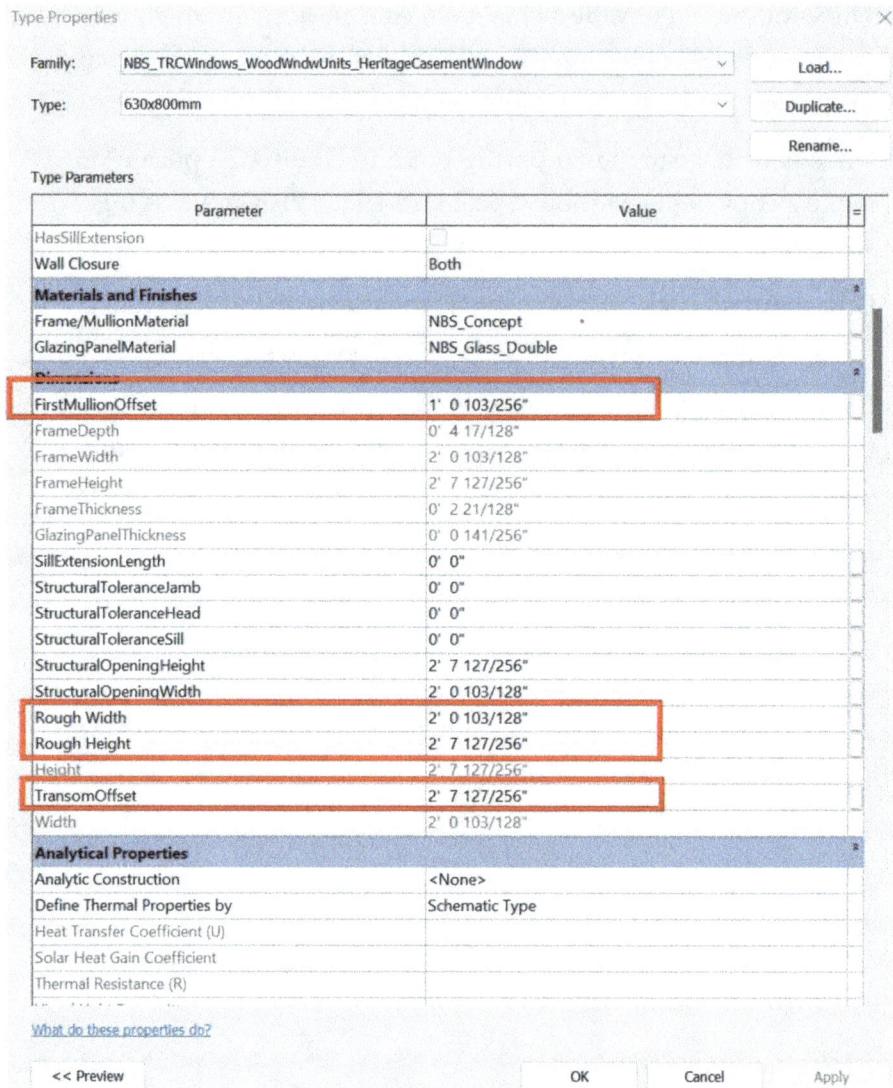

Figure 6-82. *Editing the measurements of your Dormer casement window, sourced from the NBS Heritage Windows website*

33. Now click Apply and OK to come back to the main Properties box.

34. In the Properties box, check that the window is on your Attic Floor level and the Sill Height is at 3 feet.

35. Go to your default 3D view and you should now see your new casement window sitting appropriately within the dormer frame.

CHAPTER 6 STEP THREE: BUILDING THE 3D MODEL

36. You can now add the same window to the 2nd dormer either by selecting the type again or by using the "Create Similar" command.

37. Remember to change the Sill Height for the 2nd dormer window.

Figure 6-83. *The two dormers completed*

Step 2. Exterior Detail – Fascias, Bargeboards, Guttering, and Soffits

In Revit, the sequence for adding soffits, fascias, and guttering is important; it is also important to make sure the lines meet so that they automatically join as corners. Therefore, we will start with the soffits to the main and extension roofs.

Soffits

1. Go to your Attic Floor Plan.

2. Go to the Roof command on the Architecture tab, and using the down arrow, select Soffit.

3. Using Pick Lines, select the outer edge of the main roof and the extension roofs as in Figure 6-84.

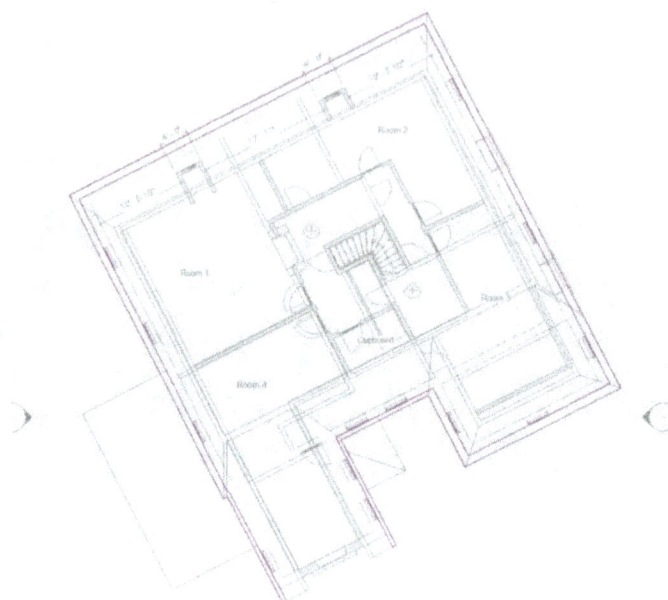

Figure 6-84. *The outline for the Soffit using Pick Lines*

4. Click the green tick to complete the soffit.

5. Go to the Properties box and change "Height Offset From Level" to -0' 3 ½" so that it sits just below the roof edge.

6. Check in the 3D view that this is the case; if not, adapt and edit to fit.

Figure 6-85. *The soffit in place, rear view*

Fascias

1. Open your 3D view; we will use this view to create the fascias.

2. Go to the Architecture tab and then the Roof command and drop-down to Fascias.

3. Select the top edge of the soffit and continue to select until you have the complete top lines showing as fascias.

Figure 6-86. *The fascias in place, the bottom edge of the gable shows this clearly*

Guttering

1. With your 3D view still open, go to the Roof command again and select Guttering from the drop-down.

2. Now select the top line of the fascia to place your guttering.

Note You can use the "Add/Remove Segments" option on the Modifier bar if you miss a segment or add too many. Picking the lines might also be easier if the roofs are hidden from view. If you leave the command and then go back to it to add more, make sure you choose Add/Remove Segment, and then select the new missing top line to add.

We still need to add the downpipes for the guttering. To do this, we first need to load into the project a Pipe elbow.

Figure 6-87. *The roof now has soffits, fascias, and guttering*

3. Go to the Architecture tab, and then click on Component.

4. Go to the Load Family option and navigate to the Pipe folder.

5. There are three folders within the Pipe folder; choose "Fittings" and then "Generic".

6. In Generic, you will find "M_Elbow-Generic"; select and it will load into the Project.

7. Now go to the Systems tab and select the Pipe command.

8. Go to the Properties box and click Edit Type.

9. In the Edit Type, click the "Edit" button for "Routing Preferences".

10. Under "Elbow" where it says None, click to access the drop-down menu and select the M_Elbow-Generic type.

11. Under Size, instead of None, select from the drop-down options 32 mm.

12. Click OK, and again Okay to come out of the Edit Type box.

To be able to draw your guttering, you will need to create a view in which you can draw your downpipe against the house. As the building is at an angle, the quickest way to do this is to create a new elevation mark and therefore View.

13. Go to the View tab and halfway along the Menu bar you will see the Elevation command. Click to select.

14. In your Ground Floor plan, place the new elevation mark facing the rear gable end of the building.

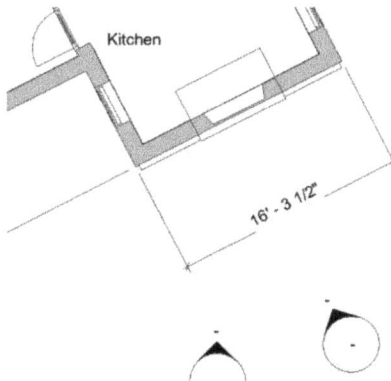

Figure 6-88. *The new elevation mark pointing to the gable end wall of the extension*

15. You will see the new Elevation View 1-a under your Project Browser's Elevation category; double-click to select.

16. The view is now a straight on view ready for you to draw your downpipe. Go to the Systems tab and choose the Pipe command.

17. Go to the left side of the extension and start to draw your pipe from the center at the end of the gutter tray, down the slope toward the wall a little way and then draw straight down to the base of the wall.

18. Your view may show this as a series of lines rather than a pipe. If that is the case, choose the "Fine" view option at the base of the screen and it will show as pipe.

19. If the pipe looks to be very big, check your Options bar once you have selected all of the downpipe – the diameter should be 32 mm.

CHAPTER 6   STEP THREE: BUILDING THE 3D MODEL

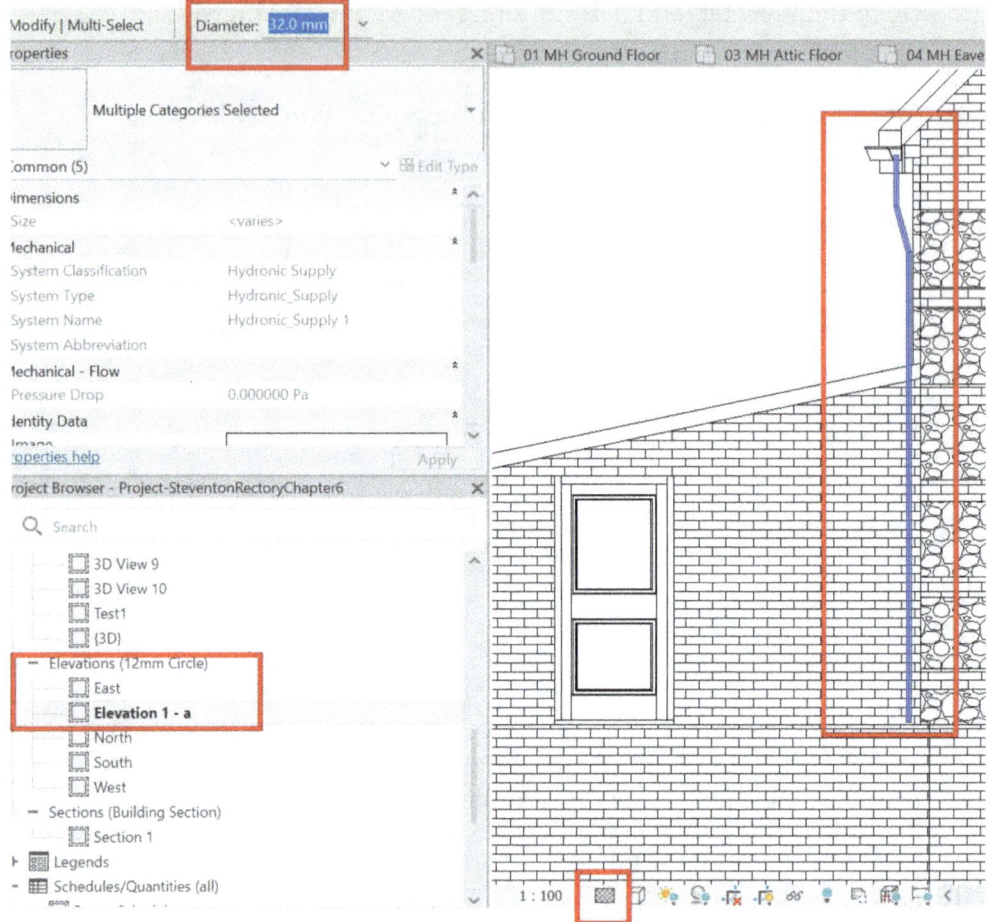

Figure 6-89. *New Elevation View enabling you to draw the downpipe against the building and highlight areas you need to check regarding size and viewing the pipe*

Once you are happy with your downpipe, you can then copy and mirror to other corners of the building.

Step 3. Exterior Detail: Windows, Sills, Lintels, and Quoins

For these details, I plan to use library families where possible to speed up the process. There are many online tutorials that cover the creation of the different family files you may use in your model, allowing you to tweak to match the detail you are replicating. For the introductory level of this book and knowing I may still need to adapt as a result of expert reviews, the use of pre-made families seems sensible.

Therefore, for the quoins, I am using an Exterior Quoin family from RevitCity. There used to be one included with Revit many versions ago, but this and other library family files appear to have disappeared. RevitCity does seem to have included some of the library files, but it does take a little bit of searching to discover them.

For the Curved Brick Headers, I am using another family "Curved Brick Lintel" from RevitCity. The family allows you to change the curve, width, and brick size, which is really helpful. Both this and the Exterior Quoin family file have been included with the exercise files on the website accompanying the book.

Lintels

1. To add the Window Lintels to your windows, you need to open the Curved Brick Header.rfa file in Revit.

2. Once opened, immediately go to "Load Family to Project".

3. In your project file, click on the Modify arrow to stop from placing the lintel immediately.

4. Go to one of your additional Elevation views that looks squarely onto the North front of the building. Remember to double-click to open the view.

5. Zoom into one of the top windows.

6. Select Component on the Architecture tab, and the Lintel, as the last component loaded, should be there to select.

7. You may be asked to select a "Work Plane" to place your lintel above the window. If so, you can pick the wall as the work plane. Once the work plane is selected, you can then place the lintel in the middle top of the window as in Figure 6-90.

CHAPTER 6   STEP THREE: BUILDING THE 3D MODEL

Figure 6-90. *Curved Brick Lintel in place on a first-floor window*

8. You may need to adjust both the width and the curve to fit the size of the window. For the window shown, go to Properties and then Edit Type to change the sizes. The Properties/Edit Type settings are shown in Figure 6-91.

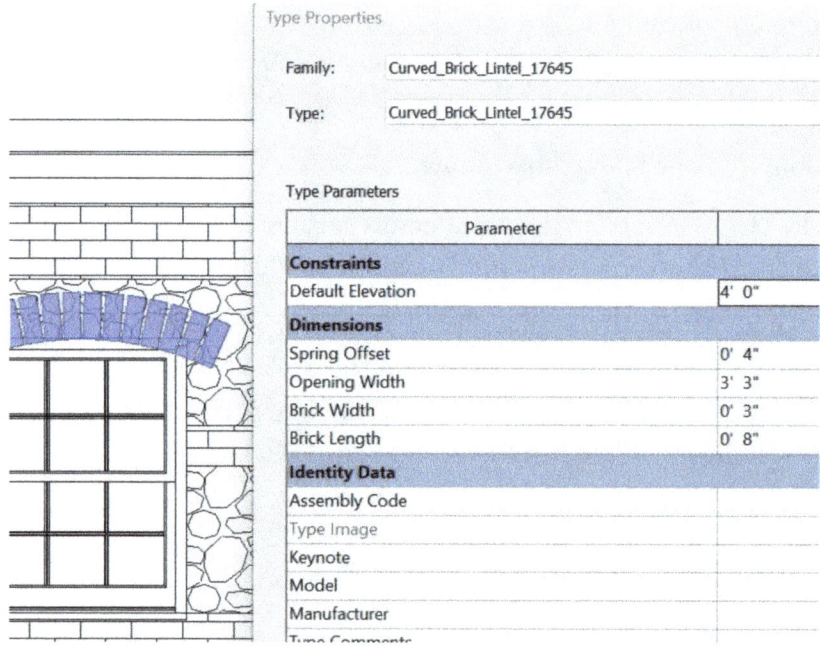

Figure 6-91. *The Property settings for the first-floor curved lintel*

384

9. For the Ground Floor Windows, repeat, but before changing the sizes, duplicate the family type and name appropriately to save overwriting the first-floor lintels.

10. The settings I used for the Ground Floor windows are shown in Figure 6-92.

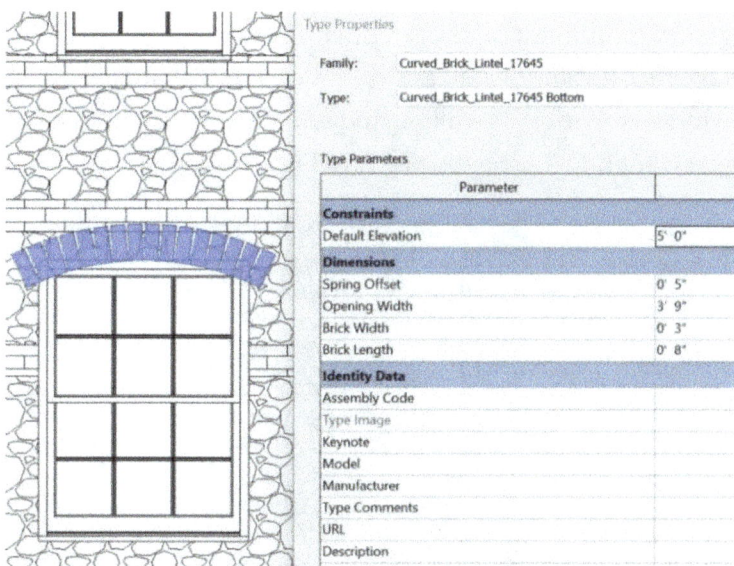

Figure 6-92. *The settings for the Ground Floor curved lintel*

Sills

It is not particularly easy to see if there are sills in the sketch, but it might be good to place external sills, which we can always amend later if needed. Research on 17th-century windows shows that the sill extended to the sides of the window; therefore, for the window type we have used, we will need to add a separate sill. It is possible to extend the depth of the sill of this window type, but not the width without widening the whole window.

I have found a separate sill on Library Revit (`https://libraryrevit.com/rvt/exterior-precast-window-sill/`) which works well with the window type once some sizes have been changed.

CHAPTER 6   STEP THREE: BUILDING THE 3D MODEL

1. Open the downloaded Exterior Precast Window Sill family file in Revit.

2. Select "Load into Project" straightaway.

3. In your project file, click on the Modify arrow so that you do not place the lintel.

4. Now go to Component on the Architecture tab and select the Exterior Precast Window Sill and go toward one of the ground floor windows. The sill is wall hosted and may want to place lower than you want it to. Place anyway (see Figure 6-93).

Figure 6-93. *Sill before height change*

5. Once placed, you can now edit the measurements including "Elevation from Level". My measurement for this is 2' 2".

6. Also change the Length to 4' 4" so that it extends either side of the window.

7. Go into the Edit Type settings and make sure the Top Edge Height is set at 0' 0". My other measurements can be seen in Figure 6-94.

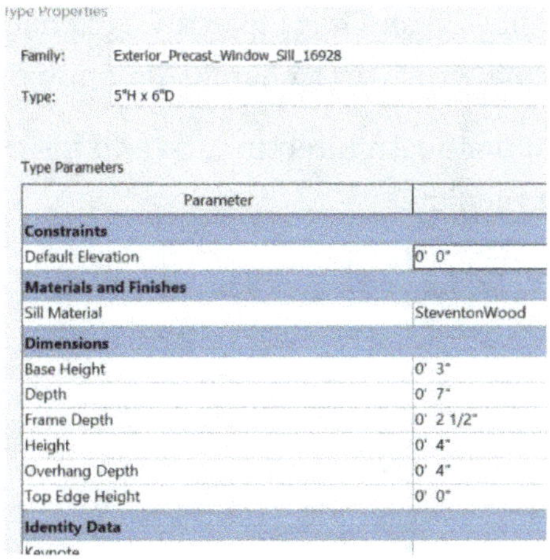

CHAPTER 6   STEP THREE: BUILDING THE 3D MODEL

Type Properties	
Family:	Exterior_Precast_Window_Sill_16928
Type:	5"H x 6"D

Type Parameters	
Parameter	
Constraints	
Default Elevation	0' 0"
Materials and Finishes	
Sill Material	SteventonWood
Dimensions	
Base Height	0' 3"
Depth	0' 7"
Frame Depth	0' 2 1/2"
Height	0' 4"
Overhang Depth	0' 4"
Top Edge Height	0' 0"
Identity Data	
Keynote	

Figure 6-94. *The Edit Type settings*

8. Once the first is done, you can copy this to each of the ground floor windows that are the same size.

9. You will need to duplicate the type for the first-floor windows and name appropriately. The width will change if your first-floor windows are narrower like mine. My setting for Width is 3' 8"; all other settings except Elevation from Level are the same. Elevation from Level for my project is 1' 2 57/64".

10. There are many windows but only two types which will make it quicker to copy/repeat the above to fit all the windows.

Quoins

1. Similar to the lintel, open the downloaded family file "Exterior Quoin.rfa" in Revit.

2. Select "Load into Project" straightaway.

3. In your project file, again click on the Modify arrow so that you do not place the quoin, unless you have already opened your Ground Floor plan ready to place the quoin on a corner of the building. If you haven't done this, then do so now.

CHAPTER 6   STEP THREE: BUILDING THE 3D MODEL

4. The quoin is wall hosted and has flip arrows to change faces, making it easy to place and then change direction once placed.

5. Go to Component on the Architecture tab and the quoin should be there to use immediately.

6. Place the quoin on one of the corners of the main building.

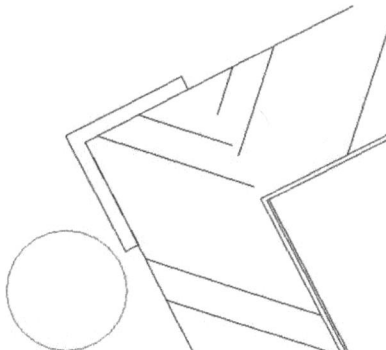

Figure 6-95. *The quoin placed on the front west corner of the building*

7. Go to an elevation or 3D view and you can see the quoin array does not meet the roof so you will need to adjust the sizes to suit. The following sizes are good for my building, although I have adjusted the height of the levels due to the ground floor rooms needing to be higher in height. My Floor Levels are now as shown in Figure 6-96.

CHAPTER 6   STEP THREE: BUILDING THE 3D MODEL

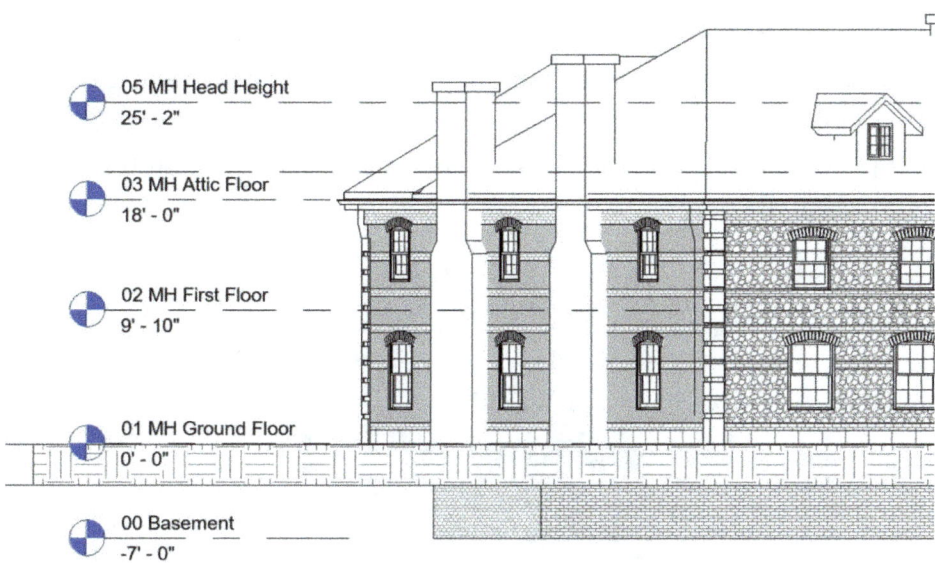

Figure 6-96. *Revised Level Heights due to internal ceiling heights*

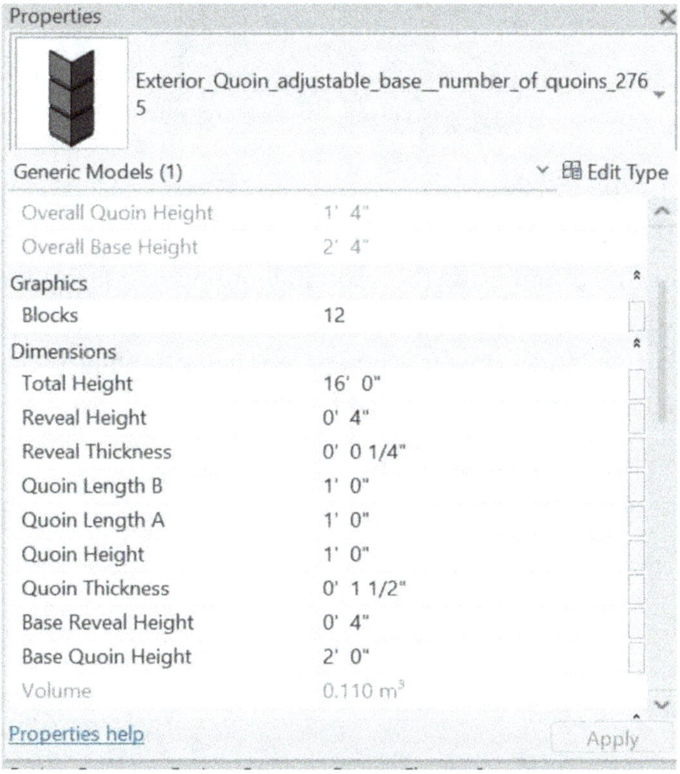

Figure 6-97. *Sizes for the quoin in the Properties box*

8. The most important to change is the number of blocks once you have the right size of block. For the moment, I am assuming the size of the stone quoins. I am hoping to find evidence of what the sizes were so that I can adjust before sending the model for expert opinion. The resulting quoin, therefore, should look something like Figure 6-98.

Figure 6-98. *The finished quoin*

9. Now copy the quoin using the Ground Floor plan to the other corners of the main building and extensions. You will need to use the flip arrows and adjust placement to make sure they are facing the right way and are aligned to the wall.

10. You shouldn't need to add them to the rear kitchen porch or the single story side building.

11. The Rectory is beginning to look very smart – but this is Revit; we can make it look more dilapidated once we are in Unreal.

CHAPTER 6   STEP THREE: BUILDING THE 3D MODEL

Figure 6-99. *The Rectory's progress so far*

What is missing from this front view is the porch, which is created from latticed wood, typical of the period. I could not find one that would be good to use, so we will create our own using a Mass shape.

Front Porch

1. Go to your Ground Floor plan and focus on the front face of the building.

2. Go to the Massing & Site tab and choose the "Place Mass" command.

3. A message will appear to say about showing the mass form; just click on close; it may then say there are no mass forms loaded, do you want to load one. You do; it should then provide you with a choice of shapes. Select the one that looks like London's Marble Arch.

4. Place it at the front of the house in your Ground Floor Plan. It should look like Figure 6-100 and is very large, so we will need to align it to the front wall and resize it.

391

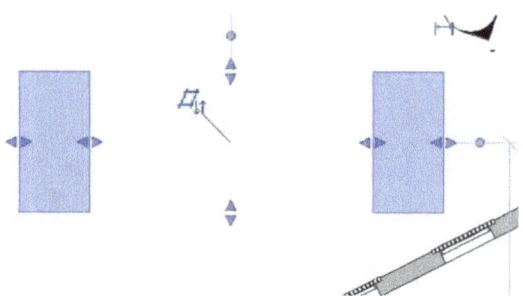

Figure 6-100. *The M_Arch Mass placed in the Ground Floor Plan*

5. Align to the front wall by using Rotate/Reference.

6. Go into the additional elevation view that looks square on to the front wall and you will notice the Mass Form is very high as well as wide. Using the different arrow heads, resize to one that covers the front door with a little space either side and above. The one below has the following settings in the Properties box.
We are going to transform the two sides and front faces of the mass to Walls. The wall type we will choose is Curtain Wall Exterior Glazing, which will enable us to create a diamond trellis pattern for the grids. We will then transform the top face of the mass to a roof.

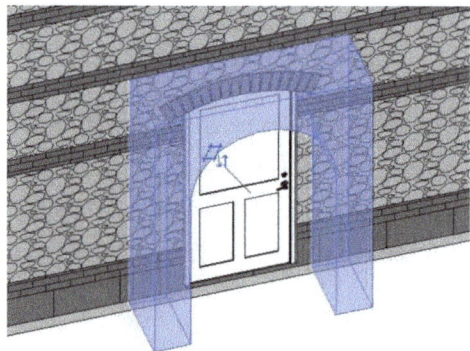

Figure 6-101. *The resized M_Arch Mass*

CHAPTER 6   STEP THREE: BUILDING THE 3D MODEL

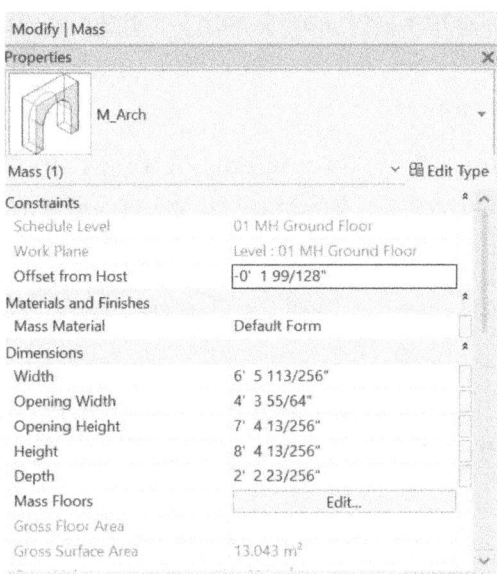

Figure 6-102. *Settings for the resized mass*

7. Select your mass and then go to Massing & Site.

8. Select the Wall option and then select the front face and two sides. You should see a few grid lines but not many.

9. To change the grid pattern, go to Edit Type and duplicate the Curtain Wall and add a relevant name.

10. In the Edit Type box, you now need to alter the Vertical and Horizontal Grids Spacing to 0' 6" and tick Adjust for Mullion Size. Leave Layout as Fixed Distance.

11. Click OK.

12. In the Properties box, scroll down to Vertical Grid and Horizontal Grid. You will see the number of grids has now changed and is grayed out. What you need to change is the angle for Vertical and Horizontal to 45 degrees.

13. Now when you look at your mass, you will see there are more grids and they are angled correctly forming a diamond pattern.

393

CHAPTER 6   STEP THREE: BUILDING THE 3D MODEL

14. To make the grids have substance, you will need to add Mullions to each of the grid lines. Go to the Architecture tab and click on the Mullion command.

15. A choice of Mullion Type is required, but we will duplicate one to make a smaller version. Choose the 30 m square mullion and duplicate; name it 20mm.

16. Where it says Thickness in the Edit Type box, type in 20mm. Then click OK.

17. Now select each grid line; you can use Select All, but as there are a few very small grid lines, it will come up with messages to say that they need to be deleted, and the Select All does not seem to cope with that as much as selecting the individual grid lines. Remember to add the uprights, top and bottom grid lines, as well as the angled grids. The result should look similar to Figure 6-103.

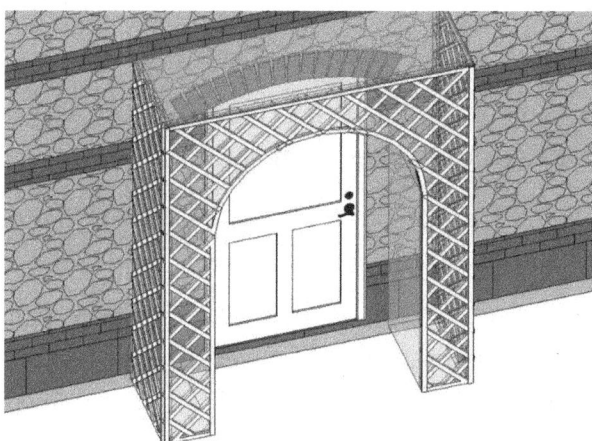

Figure 6-103. *The diamond trellis Front Porch after selecting the curtain walling grid lines*

18. If you see a mesh of grid lines in front of the mullions, look at your Ground Floor Plan and flip the arrows so that the mesh sits on the inside.

CHAPTER 6   STEP THREE: BUILDING THE 3D MODEL

19. Now you can select the mass again and go to Massing & Site.

20. Pick the Roof option and select the top face of the mass – it will convert to a solid roof.

21. You can also add a fascia to the Roof edge as you did with the main roof of the house.

22. Now go to Massing & Site tab and click on the Show Mass Form and Floor command, and by doing so, it should turn off visibility of the mass, leaving just the Porch elements.

Your Front Porch should look fairly complete now. Using the Massing and Curtain Walling tools has made it much simpler to create the porch pattern than modelling as a family file.

Figure 6-104. The finished porch

Chimney Stacks

We are now going to add detail to our chimneys' stacks. In the sketch, it shows an outline of what appears to be round chimney pots that stand on a base that is slightly smaller than the top lip of the stack. We have the top lip, and we could find or create a chimney stack that includes the two pots and base. Instead, I have used RevitCity again and have downloaded a family file of a base with the option for two or one pot (Chimney Cap with Pots 14425.rfa) which we can place on top of the current chimney stack. This file is included in the online exercise files for the book. The pots are roundish; they are faceted brick as opposed to clay pots, but we may be able to change this, although Hampshire is well-known for its decorative brick chimney pots/stacks, so for now, we can leave as brick and check with the experts later and adapt if necessary.

Internally, do make sure your chimney stack's fireplaces are far enough into the room to show the fireplace void.

Figure 6-105. *Chimney stack position in the wall to ensure visibility of the fireplace void*

1. Download and open up the Chimney Cap with Pots 14425 family file.

2. Load into your project.

3. Immediately click on the Modify arrow before accidentally placing in your walls.

4. Go to a Plan view so that you can see the chimney stacks.

5. Now go to Component on the Architecture tab and select the Chimney Cap. It will offer one or two pots, choose the two pots and place on one of your chimney stacks.

6. If like my project the building is at an angle, you will now need to rotate the Chimney Cap to fit the stack.

CHAPTER 6   STEP THREE: BUILDING THE 3D MODEL

7. Looking at a 3D view, you may find that the Chimney Cap needs to be moved up in height. The best way to do this is by using your Elevation views. The height for my Chimney Cap on the stack to the north-east side of the building (they are all different heights) is 3' 6" from the 05 MH Head Height level. It is also 28' 8" Offset from Host.

8. You may also find that the base is too large for the Stack top. You can use the arrows to resize. My settings are 3' width and 5' length.

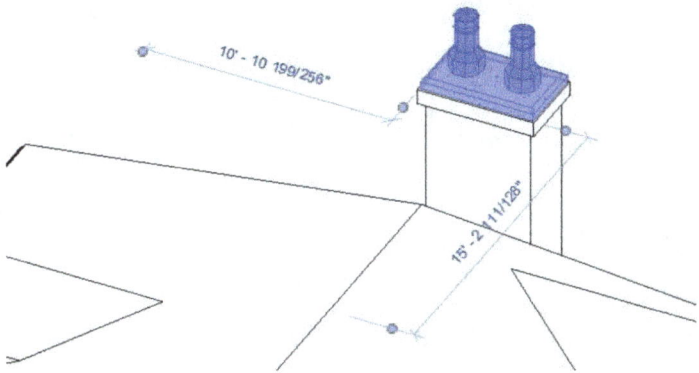

Figure 6-106. *The new Chimney Cap with Pots in place on top of the chimney stack*

9. If you click on Edit Type for the Chimney Cap, you can change the materials for the Chimney Pots and the Cap. Remember to always duplicate materials rather than overwrite.

CHAPTER 6   STEP THREE: BUILDING THE 3D MODEL

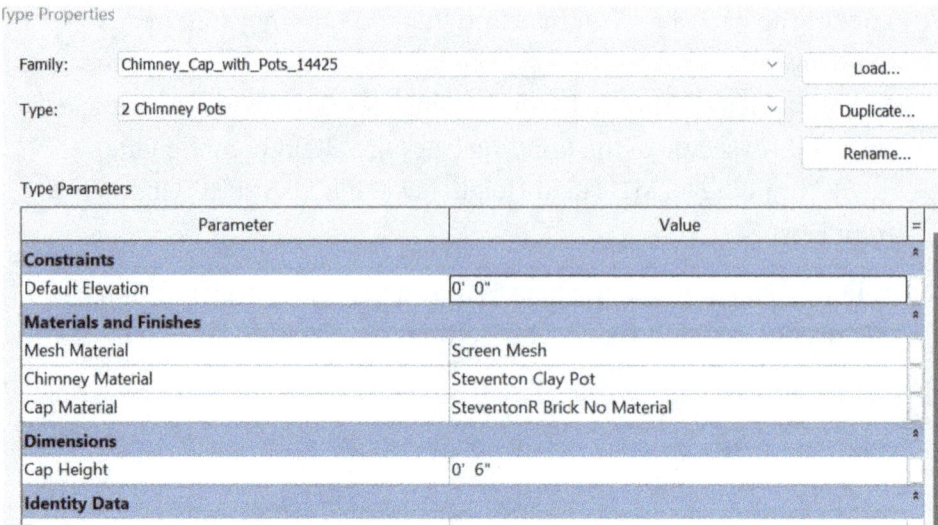

Figure 6-107. *Changing the material for the Chimney Cap and Pots*

10. You can also click on the Chimney Stacks and change the materials for the Stack and Cap to your brick material.

11. Either place or copy using reference points to add the Chimney Cap and Pots to the other chimneys. Remember to use your Elevation Views to make sure each one is sitting flush with the top of the stack.

Figure 6-108. *Checking the heights are flush with the stacks in an Elevation View*

12. Once you have placed all your Chimney Caps and updated the materials for your Chimney Stacks, your roof should now look similar to Figure 6-109.

CHAPTER 6   STEP THREE: BUILDING THE 3D MODEL

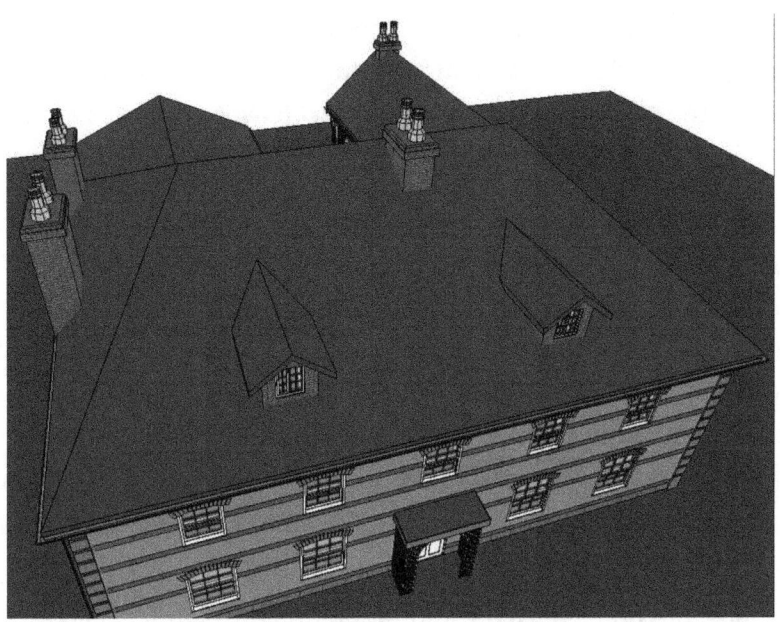

Figure 6-109. *The completed roof with chimney caps, pots, and stacks*

Interior Details

For this introductory exercise, we will now move on to the Interior. The example we will create for the interior detail is just one room, covering the following which should then provide sufficient information for working on the other rooms according to Table 6-1. The room which we have more available visual resource from film clips and sketches is the Drawing Room. This is the room that was used for going to after dinner and for receiving visitors. For the Virtual Cities – Winchester project, the storytelling aspect for Jane Austen is to visit 8 College Street to see Jane and her sister, and as Jane or Cassandra talks about family life at Steventon, possibly the time that she wrote Pride and Prejudice, the user/virtual visitor can be "portalled" back in time to Steventon Rectory to see a family scene in the Drawing Room according to the memory being recounted. In addition, as a "visitor," albeit virtual, it would tie in well with the use of the room. Therefore, recreating the interior for this room will allow testing this scene once in Unreal.

CHAPTER 6   STEP THREE: BUILDING THE 3D MODEL

According to the memoirs and letters previously mentioned, the Dining Parlor was on the right as you entered the house, and the Study on the left, which would place the Drawing Room on the left at the rear, and the "best" parlor opposite leading into the Kitchen and Dairy. Therefore, we will be focusing on the room at the left rear of the property.

Step 4. Interior Details: Ceilings and Floor Finish

Before we can add panelling to the room, we will need to add a ceiling and any possible coving the room may have had, although this can be added afterward. You will have noticed that the Project Browser has a category for Ceiling Plans similar to Floor Plans. It is often easy to select a ceiling plan instead of a floor plan and vice versa and wonder why you cannot see things you expected. A little note to make sure you know which one you are in at all times.

1. To check the room space prior to modelling the ceiling, in your Ground Floor Plan, create a Camera View (under 3D View).

   - Click to place where you would stand with a camera as your first point.
   - The second point needs to be beyond the walls so that you do not clip your view and therefore not see the walls.

2. The camera view will open, and if not showing enough of the room, select the rectangle sides and stretch out – do not stretch too far as the view will become distorted; you can always take another view.

3. Check on the height of the casement opening which opens into the extension. If you think it should be higher or lower, or wider/narrower, change the height or width setting in the Edit Type box. Remember that the other openings would also change, so you may wish to duplicate the type and create a new name so that the other openings do not change.

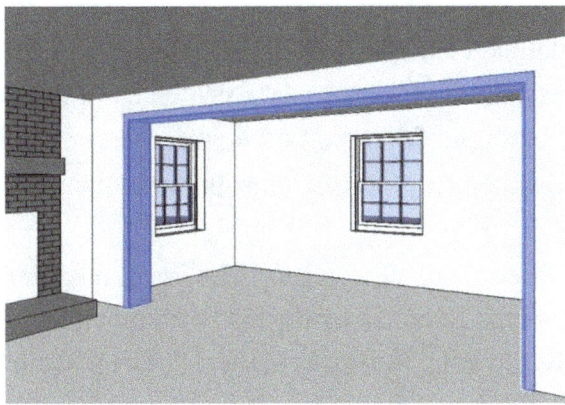

Figure 6-110. *Checking on the casement opening in the drawing room space.*

4. Now go to the Project Browser and expand the Ceiling Plans category and double-click your Ground Floor ceiling plan.

5. You will notice that it looks different to your Ground Floor plan, i.e., lack of door opening swings and similar detail. This should help to remind you which plan you are in.

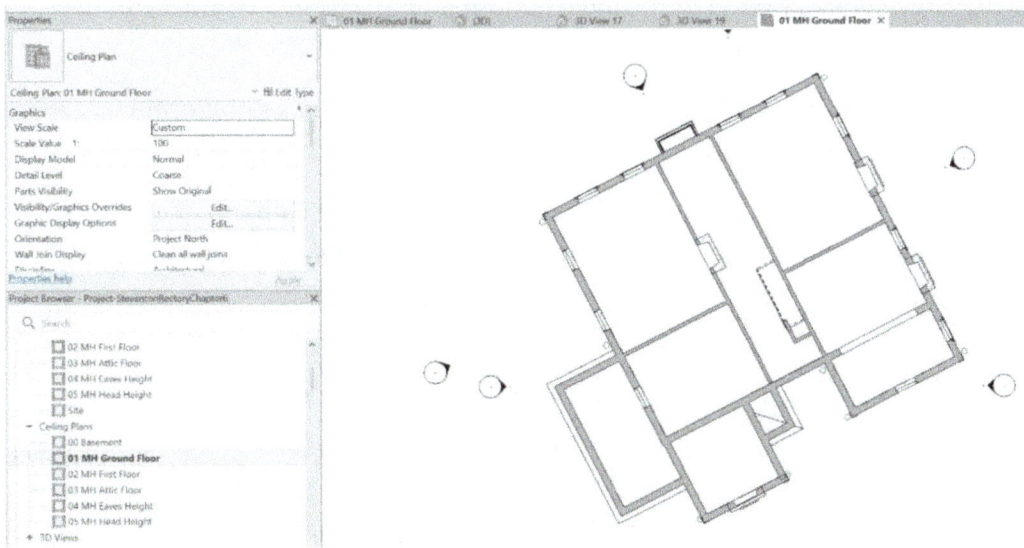

Figure 6-111. *The ceiling ground floor plan showing the lack of detail generally found on the Ground Floor plan*

> **Note** There are a couple of ways to create the ceiling and ceiling types. You can create a ceiling either using the "Automatic Ceiling" command or the "Sketch Ceiling" command. Automatic Ceiling offers quick placement within enclosed spaces, but Sketch Ceiling provides more flexibility for complex or irregular shapes.

You also have two types of ceiling category. The first is a basic type which is a simple planar ceiling that allows you to add a texture to it without worrying about additional depth – excellent for visualization purposes in Unreal. The second type is a compound ceiling that offers three different ceiling types, each having a depth and structure, similar to walls in that sense. The latter category can be useful for providing more structural detail and visual information via sectional details of the ceiling. Being mindful of additional faces within Unreal, for this exercise, I am going to use the first category "Basic Ceiling Generic."

Ceilings

1. Each room may be different (treatment or height), so we need to create a separate ceiling for each room. For this room, we are also going to use Sketch mode.

2. Select the Sketch Ceiling command and then the Pick Lines option to draw the sketch.

3. On the Options bar, there is an Offset option, but we do not need this, nor do we need to lock the ceiling. Make sure you have chosen the Basic Ceiling Generic type and then start to select the inside edge of the walls.

4. You will notice that there are longer lines than you need as the pink line of the sketch line runs the length of the wall selected. Before you click the green tick to finish, you will need to fillet all the lines that overlap and make a single break in the outside wall line to fillet the middle linework to the outer. You will also find that in effect you are creating two ceilings, one either side of the extension wall with the cased opening (see Figure 6-112).

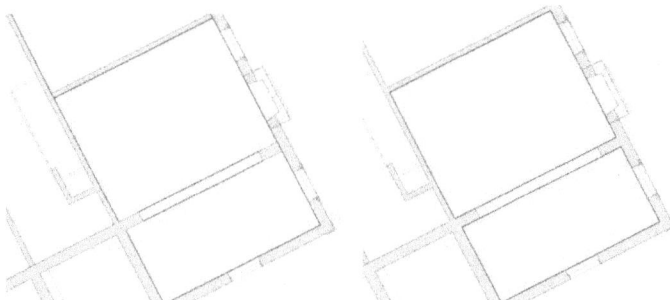

Figure 6-112. *Before and after making a break in the external pink line and then filleting to create two enclosed spaces*

5. Once you click the green tick to complete your ceiling, the ceiling will show as blue where it is still selected.

6. While it is still selected, go to your Camera View and check on its height. You may want to change the height if you know what the ceiling height should be for your building.

7. I have changed my height to 8' 9", which is approx. 2438 mm, a reasonable height for the Drawing Room.

Note Research provides a generic 8' for ceiling heights in the 17th century for similar rooms, rising to 9' plus after 1994 (Borson, 2010). There is no need to add a central lighting rose, as the houses did not have electricity at this time. We will add wall sconces to the panelling instead.

Floor Finish

The flooring was timber, possibly worn with a polished patina of wear, my assumption working with the "dilapidated" condition mentioned by Edward Knight. It most likely would have been covered by a large carpet, although not completely covered, most likely a central carpet with the polished timber showing around the edges. The texture for the timber floor we can create in Unreal, so what we could do with adding here is the central large carpet.

CHAPTER 6   STEP THREE: BUILDING THE 3D MODEL

1. To create the carpet, we will use the Floor command and create a new Floor Type.

2. Select the Floor command, and using Pick Lines, pick the four main walls of the room.

3. Fillet them so that it is a complete rectangle.

4. Using the arrow keys, nudge the side in so that the carpet is central with a border around the carpet.

5. Before you click complete, i.e., the green tick, go to the Floor Types and choose a simple structured floor and duplicate, and name accordingly, i.e., Steventon DrawingRm Carpet.

6. Click on Structure 'Edit'.

7. Change the Substructure to Finish 1 [4].

8. Change the Material. I chose Default Floor Area Face; it seemed appropriate, and duplicate, naming it to Carpet or Steventon Drawing Rm Carpet.

9. Change the height to 2 mm (it will change to 0' 0 5/64").

10. Click OK.

11. This should now be selected for your carpet so now you can click the green tick to complete the sketch.

12. In the Properties box, change the Height Offset from Level to 1 mm (0' 0 5/128").

CHAPTER 6　STEP THREE: BUILDING THE 3D MODEL

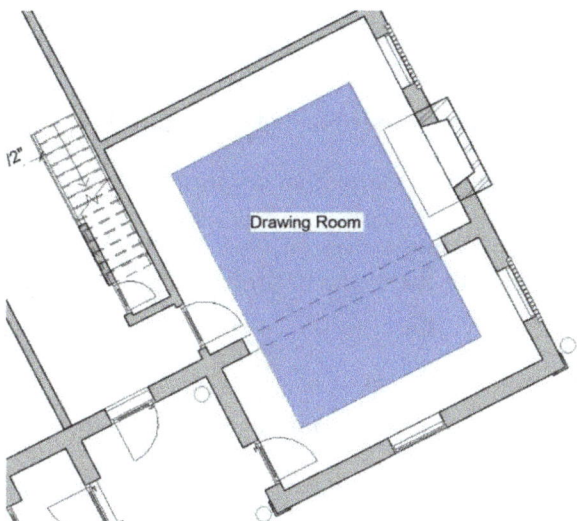

Figure 6-113. *The completed carpet in the drawing room*

Note When this is taken into Unreal, you should be able to place a suitable patterned texture to fit this separate floor object, leaving the timber floor as timber floor. By having the 1 mm offset, there will not be coplanar interference in the textures once in Unreal.

Step 5. Interior Details: Panelling and Trim

Panelling was most likely in each of the rooms, especially knowing that the Rectory suffered with damp; therefore, we can either create full height panelling as in the film clip from the film or half height panelling as in the mini series. I think for practicality's sake, there was a mix on ground and first floor. In Table 6-1, I have put the Drawing Room as part panelling and wallpaper.

Panelling

In order to see the interior of your Drawing Room, you have the camera views, but another way of viewing the interior is by using the Section Box. This is available in 3D views by going to the Properties box and scrolling down to Section Box.

405

CHAPTER 6   STEP THREE: BUILDING THE 3D MODEL

1. Click on the Section Box and double arrows will appear on each edge.

2. Use these to reveal the different levels of the building.

3. You can also pull them in to create a cut through.

4. Using a Top View, you can select the Section Box and Rotate Reference to align with the angle of the building. A really useful feature and saves creating multiple camera views.

5. To retain the sectioned 3D view, simply rename the 3D view appropriately and create a new Default 3D View.

6. For adding to a presentation board, you can also hide the Section Box. See Figures 6-114 and 6-115 for the different view settings for the Section Boxes.

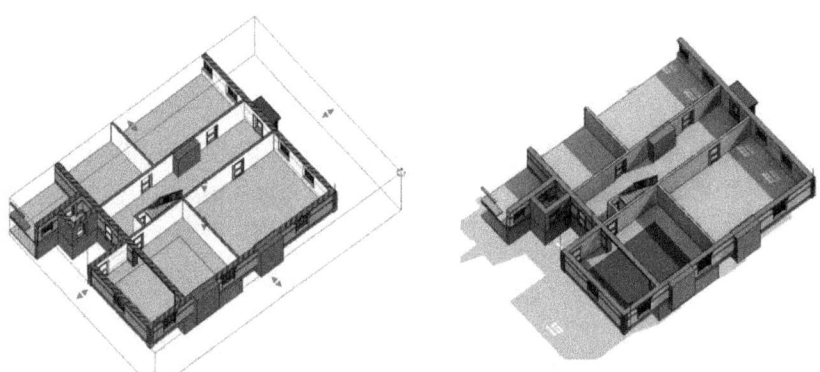

Figure 6-114 and Figure 6-115. *The Section Box with the arrows for resizing the section and the difference in View settings for presenting cut throughs of the building*

7. This function will be very useful for adding the panelling. Therefore, use the section box to "trim" the building to just the Drawing Room.

CHAPTER 6　STEP THREE: BUILDING THE 3D MODEL

8. I am using pre-made panelling sourced from Blackbee 3D (https://blackbee3d.com/product/wall-trim-6/), which saves me time even though it costs $4.99. The file is height adjustable and therefore could be used for full panelling as well as part panelling. The file has been included in the exercise files on the website accompanying this book.

9. Download the file "WallTrim6.rfa" and open in Revit.

10. Load into your project.

11. The panelling works by going from corner to corner of each wall, the same as if you were drawing a line. Remember to draw the lines in a clockwise direction or the external face will be facing the wall.

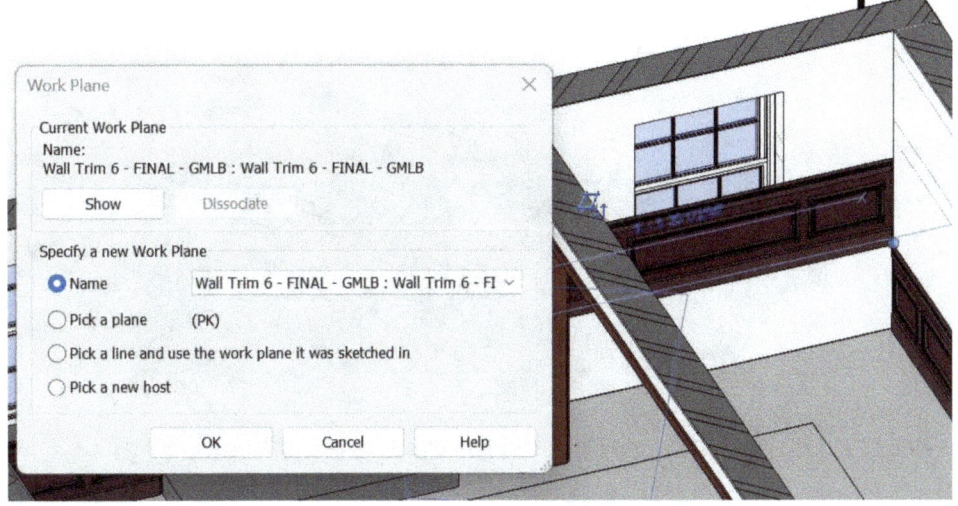

Figure 6-116. *Changing the work plane for the panelling*

12. Check your Section 3D view to see how the panelling looks. There are two things that you might need to correct:

    a. The height of placement, i.e., too high by not being hosted on the right Work Plane

    b. The top of the panelling covers part of the windows.

407

CHAPTER 6   STEP THREE: BUILDING THE 3D MODEL

13. Changing the work plane of the panelling: Select the panelling, and on the Modify panel, far right, you will see Edit Workplane. Select.

14. A dialogue box appears with options to "Specify a New Work Plane"; click on the drop-down field next to "Name" and choose your Ground Floor plan.

15. Changing the height of the panelling: Select the panelling and go to the Properties box.

16. Select Edit Type and change the Height under the Dimensions category. My setting is 2' 6".

Note   Your panelling should now look correct and tie in with the window sills.

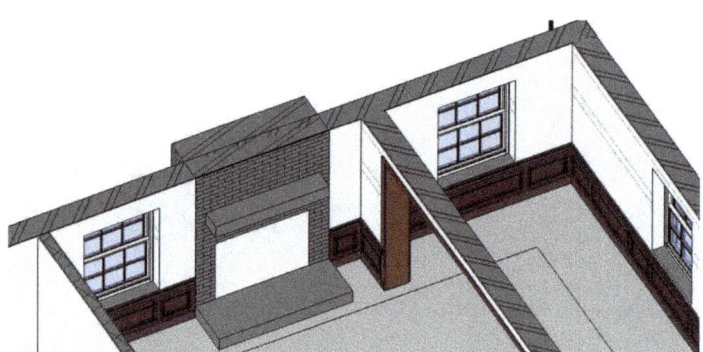

Figure 6-117. The panelling completed for the Drawing Room

Wall Finishes

The external face of the wall (with the casement opening) in the extension part of the room shows as flint and brick, but it will need to be plaster. There is a command that enables you to "Split the Face" of the chimney which you can then apply a different finish. Unfortunately, the chimney will not work with this command to change the brick due to the way the chimney has been created as an extrusion. We can change it in Unreal Engine, so not a problem to leave as brick for now.

CHAPTER 6   STEP THREE: BUILDING THE 3D MODEL

1. Select the External Wall that has the casement opening.

2. Go to the "Split Face" command in the Geometry section.

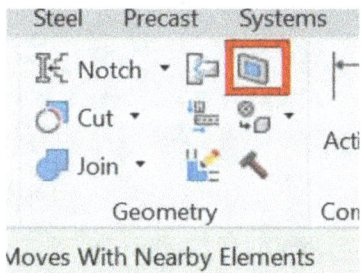

Figure 6-118. The "Split Face" command

3. Click on one of the faces of the stacked wall.

4. It will change to what looks like sketch mode, but the lines are orange, not pink.

5. Draw a line along the corner edge from the top of the rectangle shown in orange to the bottom of the orange rectangle.

6. Click on the green arrow to complete. You will think nothing has changed, but you need to now "Paint" the split face.

7. Select the "Paint" command (underneath the Split Face command) and then select a plaster or white render material from the box that appears.

8. Now click on the Split Face; it will change to that material, but the rest of the external wall outside of the room remains the same.

9. You now need to do that for each of the stacked wall sections, on both sides of the casement opening.

CHAPTER 6   STEP THREE: BUILDING THE 3D MODEL

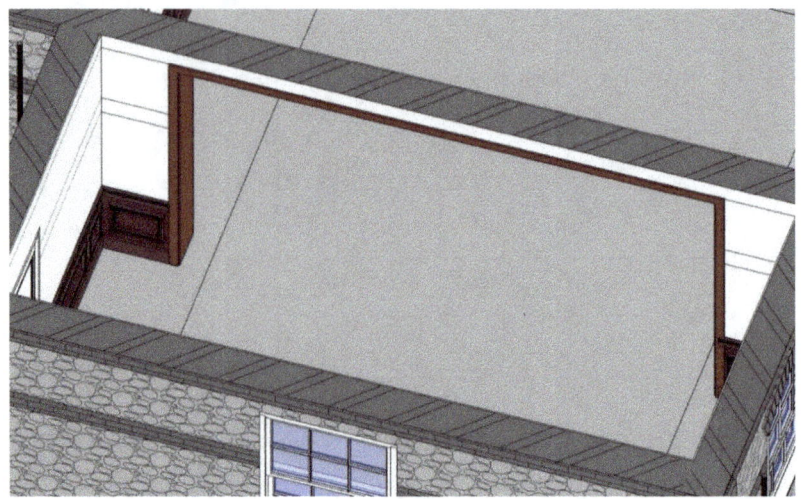

Figure 6-119. *The external wall interior faces now changed to match the rest of the room using Split Face and Paint*

Note We will add the correct textures such as wallpaper once we are in Unreal Engine. If you are not taking the model into Unreal, you can use the Split Face and Paint commands to create insets of different textures.

Coving

We can use the Sweep command with a profile to create the coving. There are many profiles included with Revit, and several more detailed profiles online, or you can create your own. For this, you will need to pick a path (the walls) and then choose/draw a profile that will flow along the path, creating your coving. I have used one of a set of ten profiles, each with different heights.

1. To do this, open a Profile family, and then load into the project.

2. Once in the project, the profile(s) will sit there waiting to be used.

3. To create the Coving Sweep, go to Component on the Architectural tab, and click to select "Model in Place".

4. A dialogue box appears for you to select an appropriate category; for the coving sweep, select Walls, and click Okay.

CHAPTER 6 STEP THREE: BUILDING THE 3D MODEL

5. You will be prompted for a name – I named mine Coving DrawingRm1.

6. You will then be in an extended sketch mode – extended because you first have to create a path and then either choose a profile or create your own.

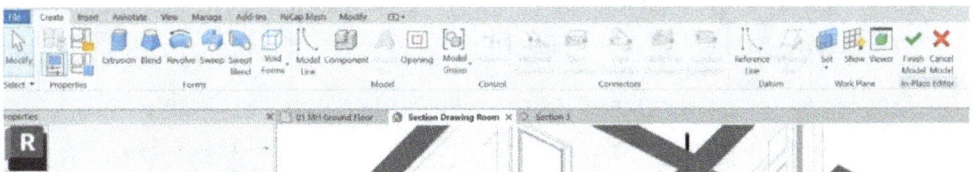

Figure 6-120. *The extended Sketch mode for the "Modelling in Place" command*

7. Choose the Sweep option on the left of the toolbar.

8. This will take you further into Sketch mode to create the sweep path. Use the Pick Path on the right of the toolbar command and select the lines making up the walls of the extension similar to Figure 6-121. You only need to select one edge per side and then fillet them together to create a closed loop.

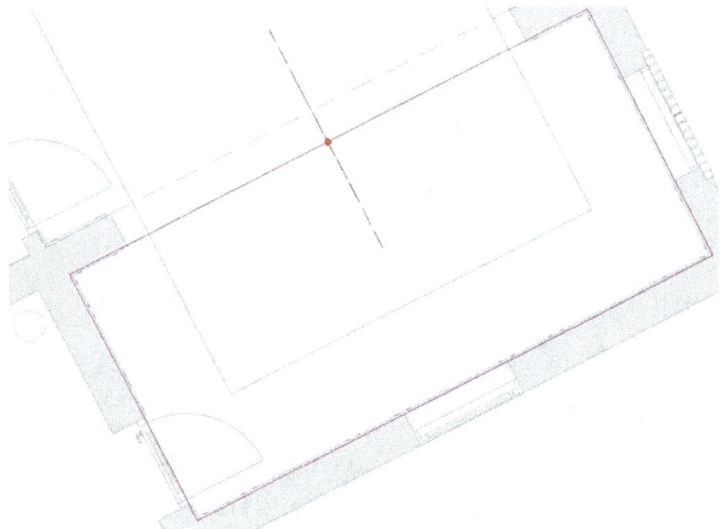

Figure 6-121. *The Pick Path used on the Ground Floor, forming a closed loop/path*

411

9. Click on the green tick to go back to the overall Sketch mode at the same time completing the Sweep Path sketch.

10. On the right of the toolbar, you will see "Profile" with different options. You can Select Profile, Load Profile, and Edit Profile. As we have a Profile loaded, you can click on the drop-down <By Sketch> and choose the Profile you have loaded. I am using "PackTen – Moulding 3:08" Height".

11. Once selected, you can see there are options regarding Offsets and Angle, but these are fine as they are for this Profile. You can also change the Profile should you wish to.

12. If you are happy with your settings, you can click on the green tick to complete the Profile sketch.

13. Now click the green tick to "Finish Sketch".

14. Go now to your 3D Section view and you may see that your Coving Sweep is not the right height; we also do not know the material.

15. To change the height, select the Coving Sweep.

16. In the Modify bar, you will see "Edit In-Place"; select to enter Edit mode.

17. In the Properties box, change the Vertical Height to suit – mine is 6'3" to face onto the ceiling.

18. You will be able to see this more clearly in a Section View:

    - Open the Ground Floor plan.
    - Go to the View tab and select the Section command.
    - Draw a line that will provide a sectional view of the Drawing Room.
    - Go to the new Section View and change the View settings at the bottom of the screen to Fine Detail and Hidden Line. You may need to switch between Hidden Line and Wireframe to select your Coving Sweep.

CHAPTER 6   STEP THREE: BUILDING THE 3D MODEL

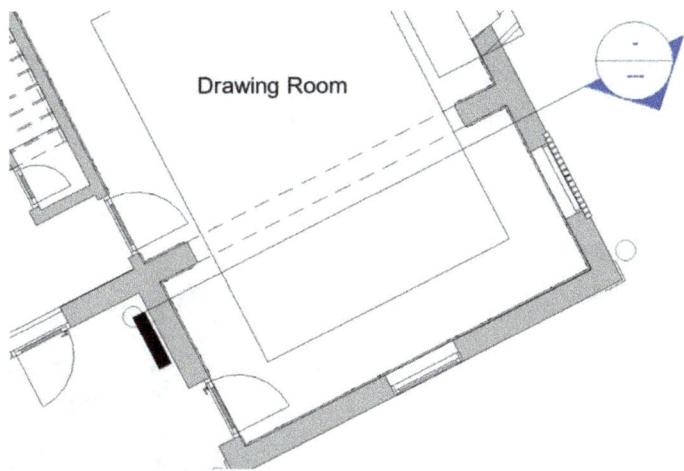

Figure 6-122. *The Section View line for seeing how your Coving Sweep is fitting with regard to height*

19. You may also notice that the Coving Sweep is not showing the curves of the profile. This is most likely because the Profile is facing into the wall.

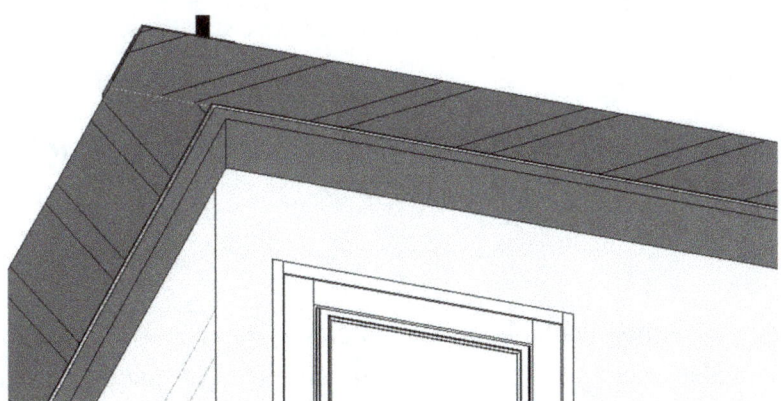

Figure 6-123. *The Coving Profile is facing into the walls and needs to be "flipped"*

20. To flip the Profile, go to Edit in-Place again and re-select the Profile to see its settings in the Properties box.

21. Scroll down a little and you will see under the "Profile" section "Profile Is Flipped".

CHAPTER 6   STEP THREE: BUILDING THE 3D MODEL

22. Tick the check box and immediately in your 3D Section View you will see the Profile detail facing the room interior.

23. Click on the green tick for "Finish Model" to come out of Edit In-Place.

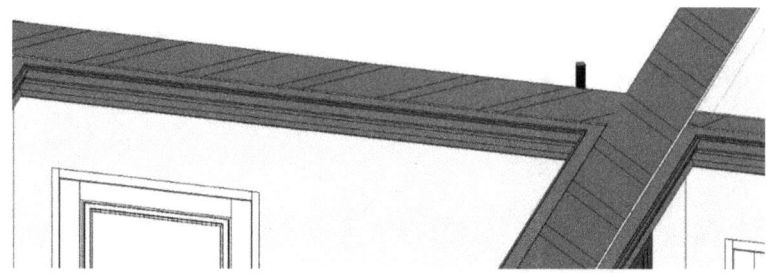

Figure 6-124. *The Coving Profile now faces the correct way.*

24. You can use the same command to complete the larger end of the Drawing Room, and the other rooms, perhaps using different Profiles.

25. The Sweep command can also be used for creating Picture Rails and Moldings to door panels and door frames, skirtings, and similar.

Step 6. Interior Details: Fitted Elements – Built-In Shelving, Wall Niches

Wall Niches

There are a few wall niches available online which you can use, as in the case for this exercise. You can also create your own using the Model in Place command again, but this time using the Extrusion options. By creating as a family file, you can ensure that it is parametric, and wall hosted, and able to be used in other projects.

The wall niche I have used is a parametric model from RevitCity and is included in the exercise files on the website accompanying this book. I have added simple extrusions as additional shelving within the wall niche.

1. Download and open the family file "Arched Wall Niche 11234".

2. Load into your project.

3. In the Ground Floor Plan, place your wall niche. I have placed it to the left of the door in the Drawing Room.

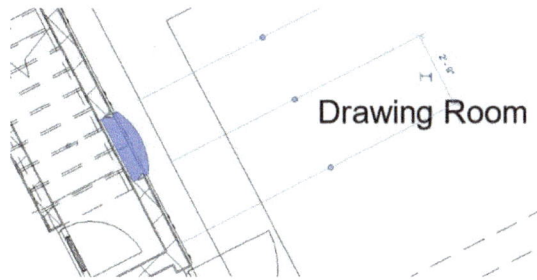

Figure 6-125. *The Arched Wall Niche placed left of the door into the Drawing Room*

4. To work with the niche further, create a Section View of this wall, making sure the section line is drawn from bottom upward for the section to face the wall.

5. Open your Section View and resize the cropping so that you are only seeing the Ground Floor, the Niche, and the Door.

6. You can resize the Niche using the Edit Type settings. My measurements have changed to 2'6" wide, 3' 6" high, and 5 ½" for the Niche Depth.

Figure 6-126. *The wall niche placed and resized*

Wall Framing for the Niche (Also Useful for Door Frames)

We are now going to create a sweep to provide framing around the wall niche.

1. In your Section View (as above image), go to Component (Architecture tab) and choose Model in Place.
2. Choose "Walls" as the Family Category and create a unique name for the Framing Sweep. I named mine "ArchedNicheFraming" and click OK.
3. You will be in the first part of Sketch mode. Before you select the Sweep command, click on "Set" work plane to get the drop-down options and choose "Pick a Plane".
4. Hover over the Drawing Room wall in your Section View until the door and the arch are outlined in blue and the tool tip says that it is the partition wall that is being selected and click to accept. This is so that the sweep and profile know how the path should flow and not twist.
5. Now you can go to Sweep and Pick Path. Select the uprights and the two arched segments only, i.e., it is not a closed loop and does not need to go around the sill.
6. Select the green tick to return to the overall Sweep sketch mode.
7. Now pick a Profile by clicking on the drop-down <By Sketch>.
8. Click on the green tick to go back to the overall Sketch mode.
9. Click Finish Sketch to complete the Niche Framing sweep.

Built-In Shelving

Now we will create the shelving within the niche:

1. Go to your Section View so that the Niche is face on to you.
2. Go to Component and select Model in Place.
3. Choose Generic for the Family Category and provide a name, i.e., Niche Shelving.

CHAPTER 6   STEP THREE: BUILDING THE 3D MODEL

4. In the overall Sketch mode, go to the right and select "Set" and choose Pick Work Plane as before, making sure you hover and then select the partition wall as your work plane.

5. Now go to Extrusion. Select Rectangle to draw a slim rectangle from one side of the niche side to the other.

Figure 6-127. *The Extrusion rectangle from one side to the other*

6. In the Properties box, change the Extrusion End to -0' 5" so that it extrudes into the niche from the front.

7. We are going to make copies of this extrusion. Use the modify arrow to drag a selection window over the rectangle.

8. Use the Copy command under Modify, to copy this rectangle up a couple of times to make three shelves.

9. Click the green tick and then again to Finish Model.

10. You can use your Ground Floor Plan and Section View to adjust the sizes and how the shelves fit in the niche by using the arrows.

CHAPTER 6   STEP THREE: BUILDING THE 3D MODEL

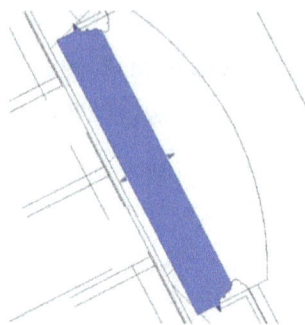

Figure 6-128. *Ground floor plan and shelving*

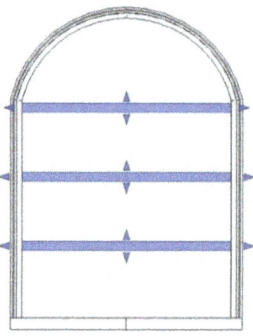

Figure 6-129. *Section View of shelving*

Picture Frames

We are now going to add a couple of picture frames which will make it easier to add images once in Unreal Engine. You can create the picture frames in Unreal if you prefer, but I think it would be a good idea to show how to do this in Revit as well. The frame only needs to be quite simple in shape, as the image that will be applied can also include the frame decoration rather than modelling it and creating many more polygons. I am going to add two picture frames to the end wall, either side of the window.

1. Navigate to Section View of the end wall.

2. Go to Component and Model in Place (unless you have picture frames as models already, in which case simply place them).

3. Choose Generic again and provide a suitable name, i.e., Picture Frame.

4. Set your work plane to be the end external wall. If you are not sure, hover near the corner of the window and then press tab singly until wall and the type are mentioned in the bottom left corner of the Revit scene; then select.

5. Go to Extrusion and create a large rectangle on the wall to the side of the window.

6. Go to Properties and change the remembered negative amount to a positive amount, i.e., 0' 1". While you are there, you can see the work plane grayed out so you can check that you are on the right work plane.

7. Now create another rectangle inside the first, which will extrude negatively to create the frame border.

8. Go to the Properties and change the extrusion to -0' ½" and then click Finish Model.

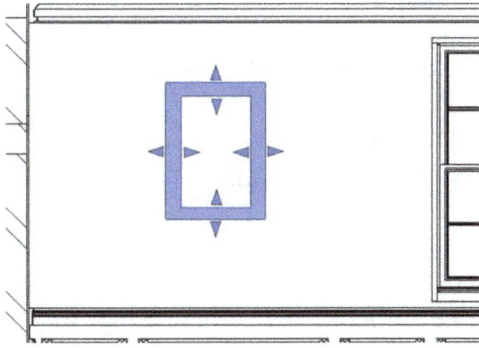

Figure 6-130. The completed Extrusion for the picture frame

9. You will probably need to go to the Ground Floor plan to check if the frame is slightly embedded in the wall. If so, it will be because the work plane has picked up the centerline of the wall rather than the outside face.

10. To adapt if this is the case, use the arrows to reposition the front face and then adjust the back face of the picture frame to meet the front of the wall face.

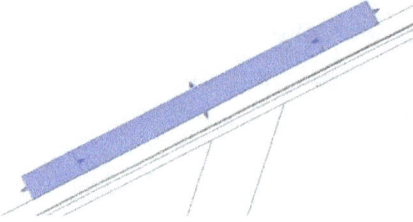

Figure 6-131. *Plan view of the frame*

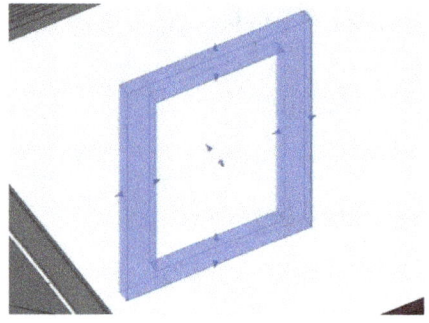

Figure 6-132. *3D view of the picture frame*

11. Once you are happy with its placement and the size, you can copy across to the other side of the window. The material can be added in Unreal Engine.

12. You can use this model across the building for further pictures and change the sizes by adjusting the arrows rather than re-making.

Figure 6-133. *The finished picture frames, coving, and panelling on the end wall*

Wall Candle Sconces

Lighting was by candlelight or paraffin lighting; therefore, there would have been wall sconces as well as table lamps and candlesticks.

For this room, we will add a couple of candle-based sconces to each of the walls. I have used "Classical Candle Wall Sconce RA 2010 10306" downloaded from RevitCity. There is a slight oddity with this file in that you cannot see it placed until you view the Site plan, and then also using Wireframe view setting. Once you know this, it is quite simple to add and copy around the Drawing Room, rotating to align to each wall. I have placed several knowing that if there are too many, I can simply delete the extras once in Unreal Engine. The family file has a light source, so they should provide the type of lighting a candle would supply.

This file has been included for the exercise on the accompanying website. In addition, another candle sconce is included should you wish to have options for different rooms. The second sconce is "wall Sconce Candle 17079", also from RevitCity.

Figure 6-134. Wall sconces added, shadows and Consistent Shading view settings applied

The commands worked through in this introductory exercise for the Drawing Room at Steventon Rectory should be sufficient for adding interior elements and details to the other rooms, and exterior details. It is time-consuming, more so when you start to add furniture, but very much worthwhile for seeing the end result and have various rooms completed in which to provide stories of the people that lived here.

Congratulations if you have managed to create Steventon Rectory to this stage; other than myself, no one else has done this to date. Reconstructing a building that has nothing left to refer to other than a few sketches, written memoirs, letters, and stories is not easy and takes considerable research. Well done!

CHAPTER 6   STEP THREE: BUILDING THE 3D MODEL

In the next section, we will add the HBIM data for this room and then take this model into Unreal Engine. There we will add historically accurate materials and textures and demonstrate how to create these materials. We may also add a few items of furniture, but mostly we will focus on also working out how to view the HBIM data we have inputted for the built objects and materials.

Section Summary

In this section, "Creating a Detailed Building Geometry," you have begun the process of adding historically informed architectural detail to your Steventon Rectory model in Revit, moving from core structural geometry toward a richer and more authentic visualization.

Working from both historical inference and comparative research, you have now established a rationale for including features like quoins, dormers, lintels, and chimneys, as well as internal elements such as panelling, coving, fireplaces, and shelving, focusing particularly on one key interior: the Drawing Room. This was selected because of its storytelling potential and the amount of visual reference available, especially from film interpretations of *Pride and Prejudice*.

We have been careful throughout to balance historical accuracy with practical constraints. Where definitive evidence was lacking, we made cautious inferences based on similar buildings, film sets, and 17th-century architectural norms, while acknowledging the need to adapt based on expert review. This included being selective about period dramas (e.g., preferring the 1995 *Pride and Prejudice* for its relative historical fidelity) and being mindful of assumptions that might later be questioned.

A key consideration was level of detail (LOD): how much to model versus how much to communicate through metadata or illustrative pop-ups in Unreal. This was especially important when dealing with unseen structural makeup like wattle-and-daub partition walls, where performance and storytelling needs outweighed the benefit of geometric complexity.

Practically, you made strong use of Revit tools such as component families, sweeps, profiles, and wall-hosted elements to add detail cleanly. You imported external assets (e.g., NBS casement windows, custom quoins, and chimney caps from RevitCity) and modified them thoughtfully for size, placement, and materiality. Features such as dormer roofs, decorative fascias, and guttering were built systematically and then joined or trimmed using Revit's parametric controls.

Internally, you experimented with camera views and section boxes to place and verify panelling, flooring, and cornices. You also modelled items like picture frames, wall niches, and candle sconces to enhance the lived-in appearance of the Drawing Room, laying the groundwork for later storytelling scenes in Unreal Engine.

By the end of this section, your Rectory model has evolved from a foundational shell into a richly detailed, historically plausible environment. You now have a well-organized workflow for continuing the interior detailing across other rooms. In the next section, you will embed HBIM metadata, take your model into Unreal, and begin experimenting with materials, textures, and interactive storytelling elements.

Incorporating Historically Accurate Vernacular Materials and Textures

This section covers how to incorporate HBIM data and historically accurate materials in both the Revit-only model and the model that will be imported to Unreal Engine via Datasmith. Through the previous sections' exercise in recreating Steventon Rectory, I have mentioned about creating a duplicate model. When exporting models from Revit to Unreal Engine, it is tempting to retain every material from the original project. However, as previously stated, this often results in a bloated Unreal project filled with redundant or poorly optimized materials. To avoid this, through building in Revit, we have applied a simple gray override to the entire Steventon Rectory model in Revit. This keeps the import clean and allows us to assign high-quality, reactive materials directly in Unreal Engine, where they are designed to interact seamlessly with real-time lighting, reflections, and environment settings.

CHAPTER 6   STEP THREE: BUILDING THE 3D MODEL

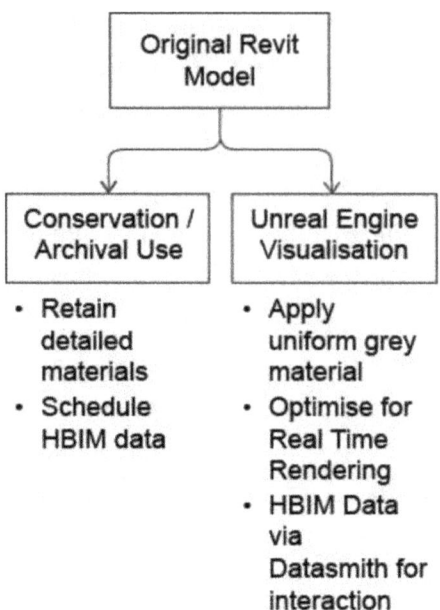

Figure 6-135. *Revit model and purpose considerations*

This workflow not only improves performance but also gives you full creative control inside Unreal, where material behavior is far more flexible and powerful than in BIM tools.

Should you be someone who is keen to retain the model for conservation and preservation purposes only, you might still want to take it into Unreal and set among a realistic environment. This model would still need to have a minimal number of materials.

If you have no requirement for importing into Unreal, then you can duplicate the model and change the default gray to the Revit materials, unless you have already made that decision before starting to model.

Either way, creating historically accurate textures and materials for a 16th to 17th century Hampshire village parsonage in Unreal Engine involves several stages: historical research, reference gathering, material creation, and implementation in Unreal Engine. In previous sections, we have worked through how to collate this material and categorize the data sourced, so we should be able to use this information to find or create the textures and apply to the model and the HBIM data fields. In this section, we will work through a detailed breakdown of how to approach both interior and exterior textures to add to the Revit model in Unreal and as HBIM data in both Revit and Unreal. We will also work through how to interact with the HBIM data in Unreal.

CHAPTER 6   STEP THREE: BUILDING THE 3D MODEL

First of all, we need to add the HBIM data to the Revit family objects in the model of Steventon Rectory. For the exercise, I am going to focus on just one room, the Drawing Room, which is where the family will be to receive visitors. You may have been adding this data as you went along, but in case not, the objects to which I have added HBIM data are listed in Table 6-2 followed by an image of the Drawing Room structural details completed.

Table 6-2. Drawing Room components list

	Drawing Room	**Total**
1	Casement windows	3
2	Internal doors	1
3	External doors	1
4	Door handles	4
5	External walls	4
6	Internal walls	2
7	Floor	1
8	Ceiling	1
9	Coving	8
10	Fireplace	1
11	Mantle	1
12	Corbels	2
13	Wall panelling	11
14	Cased opening	1
15	Wall candle sconces	18
16	Picture frames	2
17	Wall niche	1
18	Wall niche shelves	3
19	Carpet	1

CHAPTER 6   STEP THREE: BUILDING THE 3D MODEL

Figure 6-136. *The completed details added to the Steventon Rectory Drawing Room*

Your HBIM data shared parameters may be titled differently to mine, but as a guide for the exercise, the ones I added are as follows using two object examples showing the information that generally remains the same with the information fields that might change.

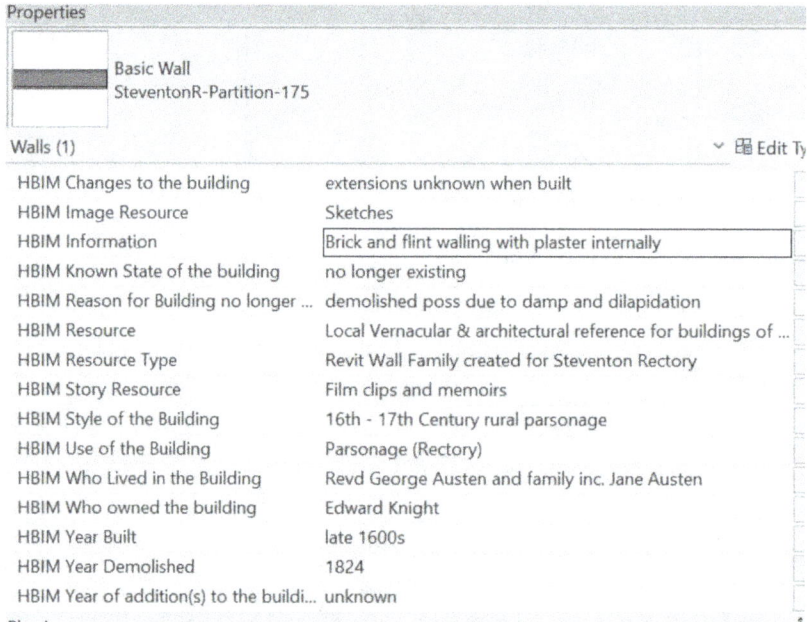

Figure 6-137. *The Basic Wall Properties box showing the HBIM data fields with the relevant data*

CHAPTER 6   STEP THREE: BUILDING THE 3D MODEL

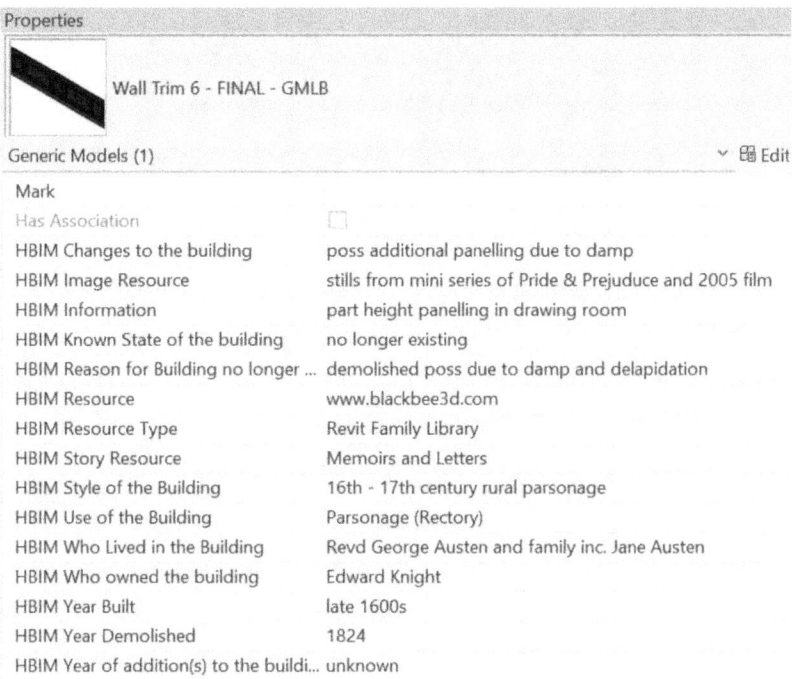

Figure 6-138. *The Wall Panelling Properties box showing the difference in data for the HBIM data fields*

What you will find is that the Stacked Walls Properties box does not include the HBIM data fields to add relevant information. The Stacked Walls category does not show up in the listing for applying the shared parameters. This is because the individual walls that make up the stacked wall will contain the data and will schedule accordingly.

CHAPTER 6   STEP THREE: BUILDING THE 3D MODEL

Figure 6-139. *Properties box of one of the Stacked Walls highlighting lack of HBIM data fields*

SteventonR-Partition-175	0' - 7"	29' - 10 1/2"	2.77 m³	16 m²	
SteventonR-Partition-175	0' - 7"	20' - 7 1/2"	2.90 m³	17 m²	Brick and flint walling with plaster internally
SteventonR-Partition-175	0' - 7"	20' - 10 1/2"	2.94 m³	17 m²	
SteventonR-Partition-175	0' - 7"	44' - 0"	5.45 m³	32 m²	Brick and flint walling with plaster internally
SteventonR-Partition-175	0' - 7"	43' - 4 1/2"	5.55 m³	32 m²	
SteventonR-Stone-343	1' - 2"	15' - 1 1/2"	0.53 m³	1 m²	
SteventonR-Stone-343	1' - 2"	10' - 6"	0.23 m³	1 m²	
SteventonR-Stone-343	1' - 2"	15' - 0 1/2"	0.34 m³	1 m²	
SteventonR-Stone-343	1' - 2"	15' - 0 1/2"	0.34 m³	1 m²	
SteventonR-Stone-343	1' - 2"	20' - 7 1/2"	0.63 m³	2 m²	
SteventonR-Stone-343	1' - 2"	52' - 0"	0.95 m³	3 m²	
SteventonR-Stone-343	1' - 2"	44' - 0"	1.47 m³	4 m²	
SteventonR-Stone-343	1' - 2"	52' - 0"	1.57 m³	4 m²	
SteventonR-Stone-343	1' - 2"	54' - 6"	1.81 m³	5 m²	
Wall-Ext_215Bwk	0' - 8 1/2"	8' - 1 1/2"	1.00 m³	5 m²	
Wall-Ext_215Bwk Steventon	0' - 8 1/2"	4' - 1"	0.01 m³	0 m²	

Figure 6-140. *Part of the Wall Schedule highlighting the different wall types but not the "Stacked Wall", only the components of the Stacked Wall*

Once you have the HBIM data fields completed, you can then make sure all the materials show as a standard gray color ready for exporting to Unreal via Datasmith. When the model is in Unreal, you can apply materials, replacing the gray color. Before you do this, it is important to make sure you have those materials ready to apply; therefore, you need to make a record of what materials are needed and where you will apply them. The following Interior and Exterior common material types will help you focus on finding the right images, or as close as possible.

Common Exterior Materials (16th- to 17th-century Hampshire)

- **Timber-Framing:** Oak was dominant. Wattle and daub infill.
- **Thatched Roofs:** Local straw or reed
- **Clay-Based Tiles:** Clay tiles were common in the southeast of England.
- **Flint and Brick:** Flint was often used with brick cornering or quoining.
- **Limewash:** Exterior walls were often whitewashed with lime.
- **Lead or Wooden Gutters, Wooden Window Frames with Leaded Glass.**

Common Interior Materials

- **Plastered Walls** (lime plaster, sometimes painted with earth pigments)
- **Wooden Floors:** Elm, oak boards
- **Stone Flagging:** In kitchens or service areas
- **Fireplaces:** Large stone or brick fireplaces with iron fixtures
- **Beams and Ceilings:** Exposed oak beams, sometimes chamfered. Occasionally plaster ceilings with coving

CHAPTER 6   STEP THREE: BUILDING THE 3D MODEL

Further research at places such as the Weald and Downland Living Museum, Hampshire Archives, and Historic England's vernacular building reports (mentioned in the previous chapter) would be useful for authentic visual and documentary references.

You therefore need to gather texture references for

- Oak timber (weathered and fresh)
- Lime plaster and limewash
- Wattle and daub variations
- Thatch and handmade tiles (possibly)
- Clay and slate tiles
- Flint stone with mortar
- Flint and brick walling
- Iron
- Marble (possibly)

Creating Materials and Textures

You can either source textures from Unreal's Fab marketplace (recently created combining Unreal's marketplace, Sketchfab, and Quixel Megascans), photograph and process your own, or create them from scratch. You can do this by any of the following:

Using Photogrammetry (Optional but Accurate)

- Photograph real 16th to 17th century structures with even lighting.
- Use RealityCapture, Meshroom, or Agisoft Metashape to generate textured meshes or texture maps.
- Extract albedo, normal, roughness, ambient occlusion (AO), and height maps.
- Clean them up in Photoshop or Substance Designer.

Procedural Texture Creation (Substance Designer or Painter)

- Create tile-able materials such as
  - Timber beams (with sapwood edge and weathering)
  - Wattle and daub (with surface cracks and straw bits)
  - Flint with lime mortar patterns
- Use Substance Designer to simulate age effects:
  - Moss accumulation
  - Water staining
  - Pigment fading
  - Smoke staining near fireplaces

The following provides a good list of sources for Pre-made Base Textures:

- Fab
- Textures.com
- AmbientCG
- CGAxis
- 3DTextures.me
- Poliigon
- ShareTextures
- TextureCan

Note You can modify these to add historical context, for example, you can tone down the glossiness, layer hand-applied textures, or adjust scale and roughness.

CHAPTER 6   STEP THREE: BUILDING THE 3D MODEL

Implementation in Unreal Engine

The following provides tips for creating your materials in Unreal Engine. Its master materials are designed to work seamlessly with the lighting system, enabling quick interaction with the environment and essential for real-time rendering.

When you import the textures to Unreal, ensure that you

- Import albedo, normal, roughness, height, and AO maps.
- Set correct texture compression for each (normal map compression for normals, for instance).

Creating Material Instances

- Use the Material Editor to create
  - Master materials with parameters for weathering, dirt, and moss
  - Material functions for tiled normal details or blend layers (e.g., moss over wood)

Vertex Painting (Optional for Detail)

- Use Runtime Virtual Textures or Vertex Paint to manually apply
  - Dirt, moisture near ground
  - Smoke near chimneys
  - Wear in footpaths or thresholds

Adjust Physical Properties

- Set realistic roughness and specular values:
  - **Limewash:** High roughness, very low metallic
  - **Timber:** Slightly reflective but varied
  - **Thatched roof:** Diffuse, porous
  - **Clay Tiled Roof:** Slightly reflective but varied with a mid-level of roughness

CHAPTER 6   STEP THREE: BUILDING THE 3D MODEL

Interior Details in Unreal

- **Wood Panelling and Flooring:** Use tiling wood grain with displacement if needed.

- **Plaster Walls:** Add subtle cracking, soot stains, and discoloration or use textures that already include this, i.e., flaking paint.

- **Stone or Brick Fireplaces:** Use detailed normal and AO maps; maybe add emissive fake glow for firelight.

- **Leaded, Sash, or Casement Glass Windows**
    - Use a translucent material.
    - Add subtle bumpiness/warping via a normal map.
    - Simulate internal reflection from hand-blown imperfections.

Optional Advanced Tips

Light and Color Accuracy

- Use Lumen or Ray Tracing with natural daylight profiles to match the historic interior lighting feel (mostly daylight with warm hearth/fire and candle light).

- Use desaturated or earth-toned color palettes, for example, bright; synthetic colors are anachronistic.

The following takes you through step by step to create a realistic master material in Unreal. You can apply the materials to basic shapes modelled in Unreal, rather than to Steventon Rectory, initially. It would also be good practice to make a library of the materials you will use and name logically so you know exactly which ones you are looking for to apply to specific objects. Once you have perfected your materials and created your material library, you can import Steventon Rectory and simply apply your newly made materials.

CHAPTER 6   STEP THREE: BUILDING THE 3D MODEL

Step-by-Step Guide to Creating Master Materials in Unreal

The following is a step-by-step guide to creating historically accurate materials in Unreal Engine 5, featuring red brick and flint walling, plaster, panelling, and other internal features, remembering the age of the building, therefore including weathering and damage.

Step 1: Prepare Your Texture Maps

You will need texture sets for

- Plaster walling, most probably limewashed
- Timber oak floors, panelling, doors, and window frames
- Flint and brick walling
- Roof slates

Where to source:

- Fab
- AmbientCG
- Texture Hub
- Or create in Substance Designer

Step 2: Create a Master Material

1. Open Unreal Engine.
2. Click the +Add command in the Content Browser and choose *Material*.
3. Name it: M_SR_InteriorFlooring_Master.
4. Double-click the named material to open it in the Material Editor.

CHAPTER 6　STEP THREE: BUILDING THE 3D MODEL

Step 3: Set Up Base Material Nodes

1. Texture Samples: Add the six texture sets (BaseColour, Normal, Roughness, AO, Specular, Gloss) by dragging each one in from the Content Browser material folder.

2. Once the texture is dragged in, connect it to the relevant node in the main panel.

3. Do this one by one so you know which one is which to be able to connect to the right node input.

4. Once all six are in the Material Editor Graph and connected to the main panel, it should look like Figure 6-141.

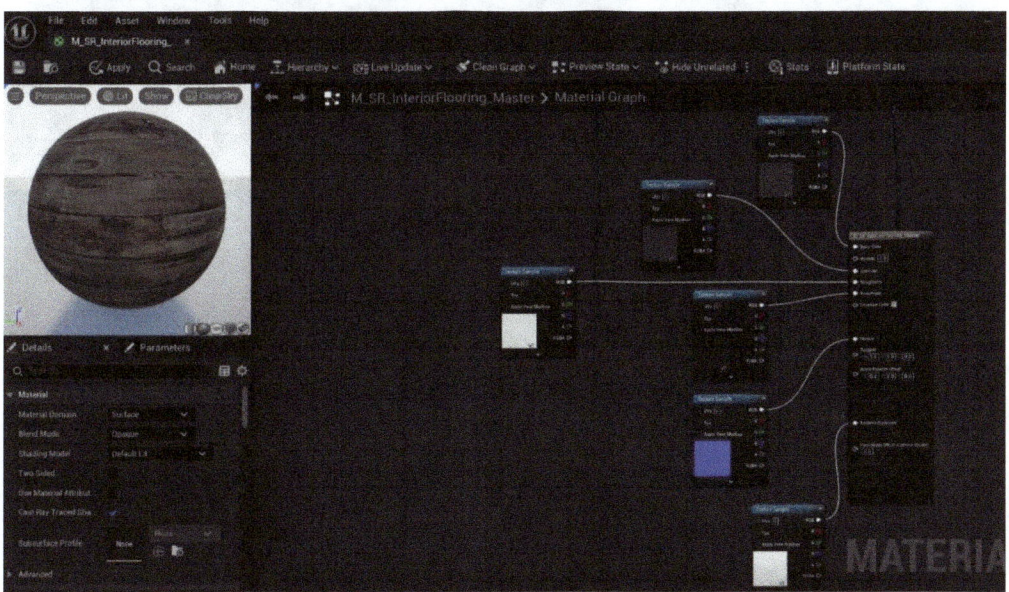

Figure 6-141. Connecting the textures to the main panel to create you Master Material

5. UV Tiling: Add Texture Coordinate node → Multiply by using the U Tiling and V Tiling arrows to control scale.

6. Connect to UV input of each texture sample.

435

CHAPTER 6   STEP THREE: BUILDING THE 3D MODEL

7. You can do this by right-clicking and choosing Duplicate, placing each Duplicate to a TextureSample and connecting the input and output nodes to "UV" on the TextureSample.

8. You will need to do each one so that all the TextureSamples are the same.

9. Your Material Editor Graph should now look like Figure 6-142.

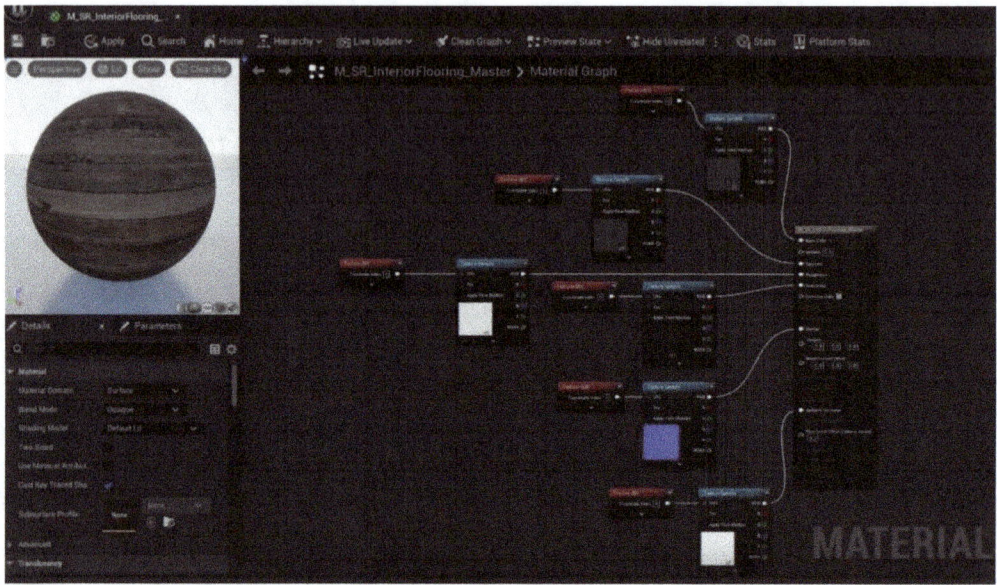

Figure 6-142. *Texture Coordinates added to each TextureSample*

10. Create a simple box and apply the newly made material to the Box's Material slot.

11. Check to see if it looks at the right scale for the box; if not, adjust the UV Tiling until it does.

Now that you have one material, you can import your model of Steventon Rectory using the Datasmith export option in Revit.

Step 4: Importing via Datasmith

1. Open the default 3D view; you need to be in a non-cropped default 3D view to export to Datasmith.

2. Go to the View menu and you will see the Twinmotion option in the Presentation panel.

3. Click the down arrow and click Autosync.

4. Go back to the list on the drop-down and this time, click the Export to Datasmith file.

5. Save to your folder ready for importing to Unreal.

6. Open Epic Games Launcher and choose a new Architecture project.

7. You can choose the Archviz template if you do not want to immediately start with creating your own lighting. (If you choose the Archviz template, you will need to hide the geometry and notes that it comes with).

8. Make sure you check or change the path where the project will be saved and name your project before clicking Create.

9. Go to Edit Menu and then Plugins to check that Datasmith is enabled.

CHAPTER 6   STEP THREE: BUILDING THE 3D MODEL

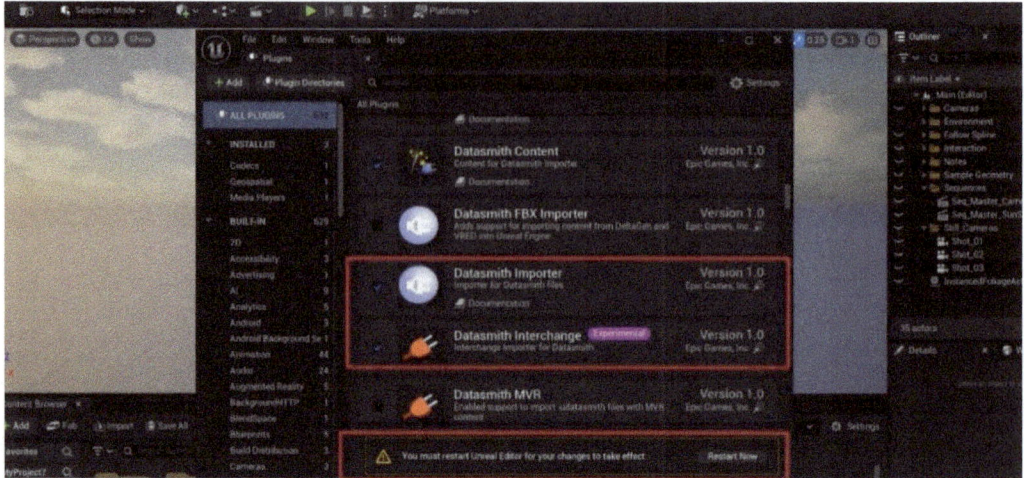

Figure 6-143. *Activating the Datasmith Importer plug-in and the new Datasmith Interchange plug-in*

10. If you select the Datasmith Interchange plug-in, you will need to restart Unreal.

11. Once back in Unreal, go to File, Import to Level, and navigate to where you saved your Revit Datasmith file – the file extension is .udatasmith.

Figure 6-144. *The Revit Datasmith exported file*

12. Choose "Content" as the base directory, and click OK.

13. The Import Scene dialogue box appears; check the information and then click Import.

CHAPTER 6 STEP THREE: BUILDING THE 3D MODEL

14. There may be some error messages, but these will mostly be about renaming duplicate materials.

15. You should see your model in the project window.

Figure 6-145. *The imported complete Datasmith model in the project window*

16. Zoom into the house and the Drawing Room; you will see it gradually lights up and the candle sconces emit light. Explore the building and you will notice that rooms will gradually lighten with the daylight seeping in.

17. If you do not want to see the light icons and other helpers, you can click on the menu bars in the window (top left) and choose Game View.

Figure 6-146. *Inside the Drawing Room, ready for adding materials*

439

CHAPTER 6   STEP THREE: BUILDING THE 3D MODEL

Step 5: Adding Your Material and Creating Additional Materials

1. Navigate to see inside the Drawing Room and focus on the floor.

2. Apply your Master Material to the floor of your model: Select the Floor object in the Outliner, or by clicking on the object in the Unreal workspace.

3. Go to the Details section below the Outliner and scroll down to Materials. My floor has two material slots, one for top face and for the bottom face.

4. Click on the first slot with the down arrow and search for your new Material. Once found, select and the material will show applied to the floor. Repeat for the second slot.

5. Your material can be seen, and it may look the wrong size (see Figure 6-147). If this is the case, go back to the Material Editor Graph and change the Texture Coordinates, click Apply, and adapt until the flooring looks more realistic.

Figure 6-147. *The new material on the floor, but it does not look realistic*

6. You will find that having to change each of the six Texture Coordinates is time-consuming and would be much easier to just have one to change. Choose one and move out to the left and then delete the others.

CHAPTER 6   STEP THREE: BUILDING THE 3D MODEL

7. Connect the one on the left to each of the TextureSamples instead and try to ensure there are not too many lines crossing over (see Figure 6-148).

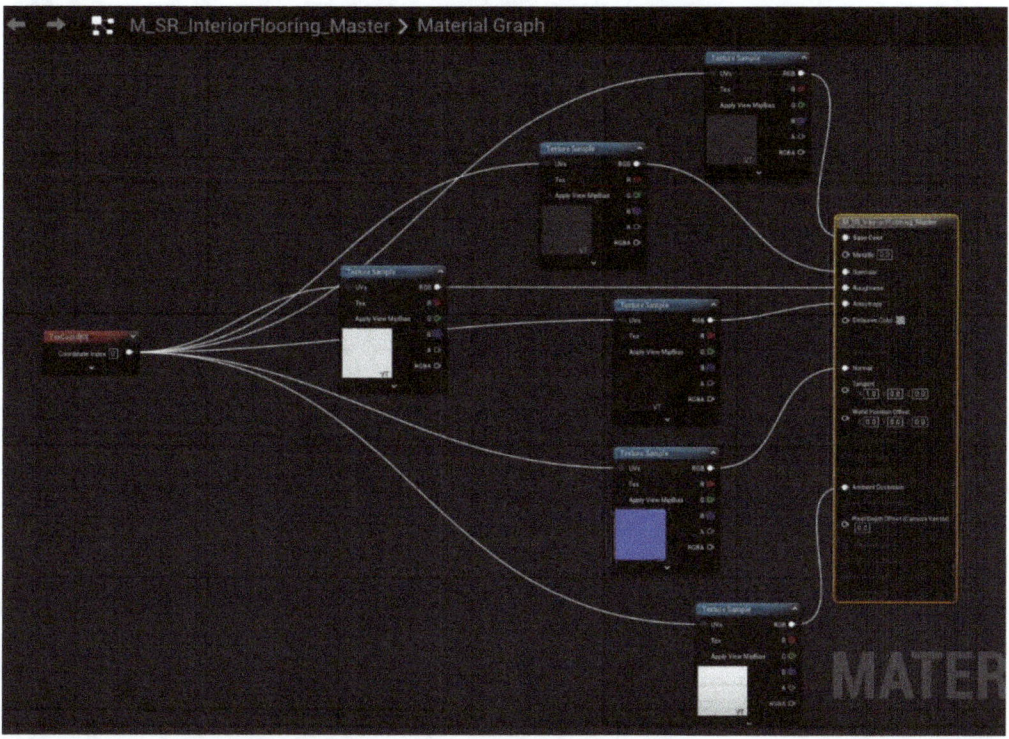

Figure 6-148. *Using just one Texture Coordinate panel for all the TextureSamples, making it easier to adjust all*

8. Now it is much simpler to adjust the coordinates until the tiling appears more realistic for your floor as in Figure 6-149. The setting I chose was 0.2 for the U and V Tiling.

441

CHAPTER 6   STEP THREE: BUILDING THE 3D MODEL

Figure 6-149. *A more realistic sizing of the planking for the floor*

9. The floor looks okay but probably looks too worn for the Drawing Room, so you can duplicate your material and rename so that it doesn't overwrite your original material as you may want to use this material elsewhere. With the duplicated material, you can now change the Texture Samples.

10. Open up the new material and click the BaseColour Texture Sample.

11. On the left panel, you will see the details of the TextureSample, which is where you can change the texture.

CHAPTER 6   STEP THREE: BUILDING THE 3D MODEL

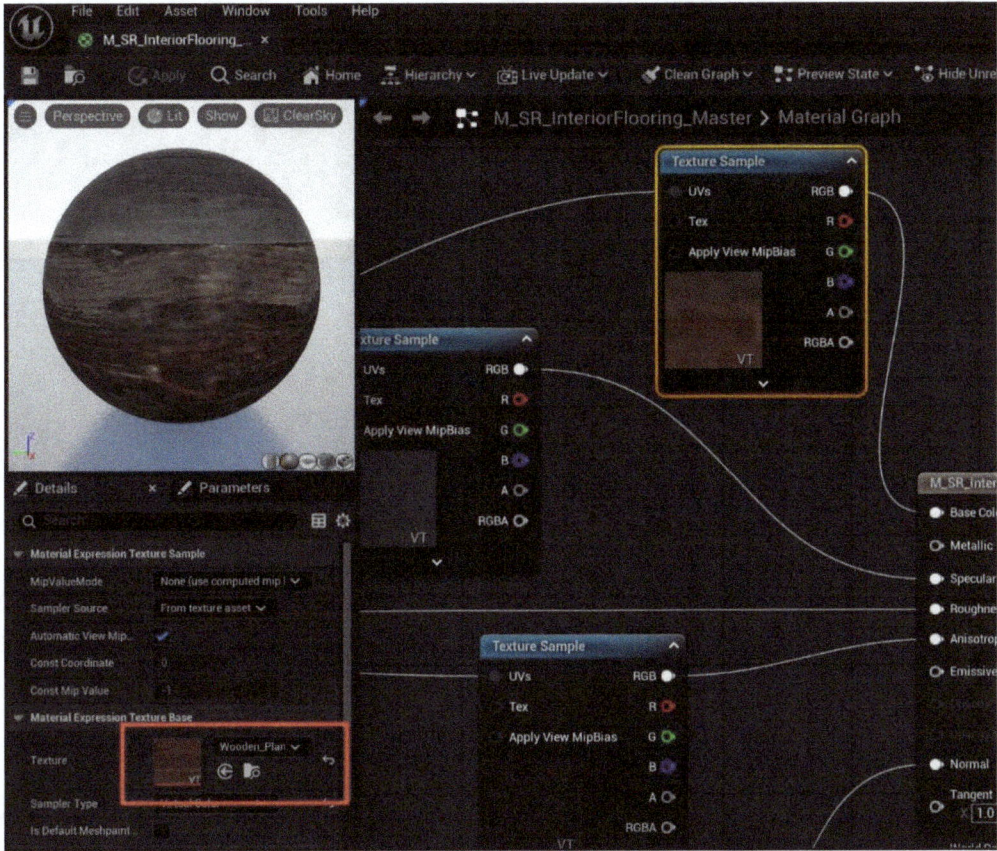

Figure 6-150. *Highlighting where to change the texture sample*

12. Click on the arrow next to the texture file to then navigate to the texture you want to use – here I have used "Worn_Wooden_Planks".

13. Do this for each of the Texture Samples ensuring you use the correct texture type for each one. Then click Apply, Save All, and check your floor.

443

CHAPTER 6   STEP THREE: BUILDING THE 3D MODEL

Figure 6-151. *The updated floor finish (Worn_Wooden_Planks)*

You can repeat the Master Material process above for creating the remaining materials to complete the Drawing Room and external walls/roof. The materials I have used are shown in Table 6-3 and are included in the lesson files folder on the website.

Table 6-3. *Materials created and where they are used*

Object	Nodes Used	Textures Used
Floor	New Master Material: BaseColour, Specular, Roughness, Anisotropy Normal, Ambient Occlusion	Worn Wooden Planks: BaseColour, Specular, Roughness, Gloss, Normal, AO
Panelling	Unreal Engine Material: BaseColour, Roughness, Normal	Unreal Engine Material: M_Wood_Walnut using T_Wood_Walnut_D (BaseColour & Roughness), T_Wood_Walnut_N
Interior Walls	New Master Material: BaseColour, Specular, Roughness, Anisotropy Normal, Ambient Occlusion	Flaked Paint Wall: BaseColour, Specular, Roughness, Gloss, Normal, AO

(continued)

Table 6-3. (*continued*)

Object	Nodes Used	Textures Used
Exterior Walls Flint sections of Stacked Wall	New Master Material: BaseColour, Specular, Roughness, Normal, Ambient Occlusion	Flint Wall: Adobe Stock 26718723 BaseColour, Adobe Stock 26718723 Bump, Adobe Stock 26718723 Normal
Exterior Walls Red Brick sections of Stacked Wall	New Master Material: BaseColour, Specular, Roughness, Normal, Ambient Occlusion	Brick Wall Worn: RedBrick BaseColour, Gloss, Normal, Roughness, Specular
Brick Window Headers	New Master Material: BaseColour, Specular, Roughness, Anisotropy Normal, Ambient Occlusion	Single Red Brick: Adobe Stock 363626587 BaseColour, Adobe Stock 363626587 Normal, Adobe Stock 363626587 Roughness, Specular, Gloss
Quoins	New Master Material: BaseColour, Specular, Roughness, Normal, Ambient Occlusion	Brick Wall Worn: RedBrick BaseColour, Gloss, Normal, Roughness, Specular
Roofing	New Master Material: BaseColour, Specular, Roughness, Normal, Ambient Occlusion	Roof Slates: BaseColour, Specular, Roughness, Normal, Ambient Occlusion
Guttering	New Master Material: BaseColour, Specular, Roughness, Anisotropy, Normal, Ambient Occlusion	Scratched Painted Metal: 4K Gloss, 4K Normal, 4K Mask
Fascias	New Master Material: BaseColour, Specular, Roughness, Anisotropy Normal, Ambient Occlusion	Fine Grained Wood: BaseColour, Rough, Normal, AO

(*continued*)

CHAPTER 6 STEP THREE: BUILDING THE 3D MODEL

Table 6-3. (*continued*)

Object	Nodes Used	Textures Used
Niche	Unreal Engine Material: BaseColour, Metallic, Roughness	Unreal Engine Material: Ml_White using M_Simple_Opaque: using Colour
Niche Shelving	Unreal Engine Material: BaseColour, Metallic, Roughness	Unreal Engine Material: Ml_White using M_Simple_Opaque: using Colour
Coving	Unreal Engine Material: BaseColour, Metallic, Roughness	Unreal Engine Material: Ml_White using M_Simple_Opaque: using Colour
Doors	Unreal Engine Material: BaseColour, Roughness, Normal	Unreal Engine Material: M_Wood_WalnutVert using T_Wood_Walnut_D1R (BaseColour & Roughness), T_Wood_Walnut_DXVert
Door Handles	New Master Material: BaseColour, Specular, Roughness, Anisotropy, Normal, Ambient Occlusion	Scratched Painted Metal: 4K Gloss, 4K Normal, 4K Mask
Window Frames	New Master Material: BaseColour, Specular, Roughness, Anisotropy Normal, Ambient Occlusion	Fine Grained Wood: BaseColour, Rough, Normal, AO
Window Glass	Unreal Engine Material: BaseColour, Specular, Roughness, Opacity, Refraction	Unreal Engine Material: M_Glass using ColourGlass
Picture Frames	New Master Material: BaseColour, Specular, Roughness, Anisotropy Normal, Ambient Occlusion	Fine Grained Wood: BaseColour, Rough, Normal, AO
Cased Opening	Unreal Engine Material: BaseColour, Roughness, Normal	Unreal Engine Material: M_Wood_Walnut using T_Wood_Walnut_D (BaseColour & Roughness), T_Wood_Walnut_N

(*continued*)

CHAPTER 6 STEP THREE: BUILDING THE 3D MODEL

Table 6-3. (*continued*)

Object	Nodes Used	Textures Used
Mantle	New Master Material: BaseColour, Specular, Roughness	White Marble: Ziarat White Marble 4K BaseColour, 4K Normal, 4K Roughness, 4K Specular, 4K Gloss
Corbels	New Master Material: BaseColour, Specular, Roughness	White Marble: Ziarat White Marble 4K BaseColour, 4K Normal, 4K Roughness, 4K Specular, 4K Gloss
Candle Sconces	Unreal Engine Material: BaseColour, Roughness, Normal	Unreal Engine Material: M_Metal_Gold using T_Metal_Gold_D (BaseColour & Roughness), T_Metal_Gold_N
Carpet	New Master Material: BaseColour, Specular, Roughness, Anisotropy Normal, Ambient Occlusion	Dusty Carpet Material: BaseColour, Specular, Roughness, Gloss, Normal, AO

Figure 6-152. *The materials to create in Unreal Content Browser*

With these materials applied, you should be able to achieve a similar set of images to the following:

CHAPTER 6   STEP THREE: BUILDING THE 3D MODEL

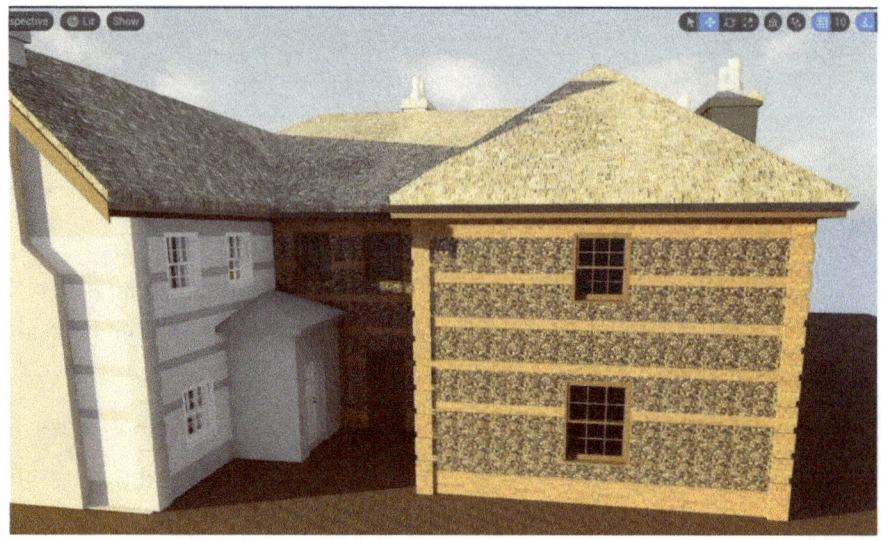

Figure 6-153. *External view of Steventon Rectory's Drawing Room*

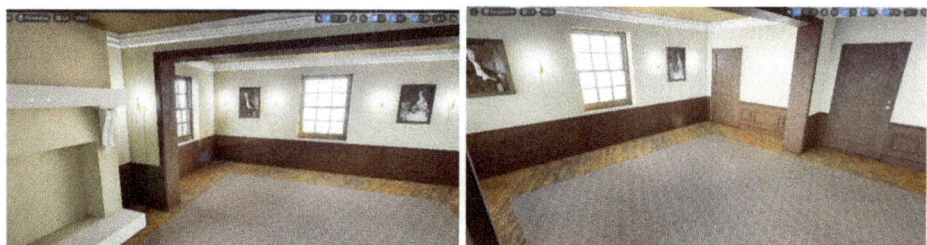

Figure 6-154. *Internal views of the Drawing Room*

If you need to make a copy of a material so that the UV Tiling can change for example, you can either do this by opening up the original version and Save As with appropriate name, or create a material instance.

Step 6: Create Material Instance

1. Right-click M_SR_RedBrick_Master → *Create Material Instance.*

2. Call it M_SR_RedBrick_Test.

3. Apply to a test wall mesh.

4. Adjust parameters:
   - Tiling
   - Blend intensity
   - Dirt

5. You should then be able to see the changes, but you will not have changed the original.

Note The benefit of Material Instances is that they reduce the number of materials that need to be stored in memory.

Section Summary

In this section, "Incorporating Historically Accurate Vernacular Materials and Textures," you have worked through the process of considering what you will need for adding materials to your Steventon Rectory model, researching and collating the textures and images you need, and then using those to create Master Materials in Unreal and apply them to the model.

The focus has been on just one room as discussed in the previous section, the Drawing Room. The materials were focused on structural items and a couple of wall items. Adding furniture will come later once the model has been verified by experts. It will also keep the model easier to manipulate while adding/adapting other structural elements.

There is very little known of Steventon Rectory, particularly visually, so there is much reliance on memoirs, letters, and film clips, which takes time sifting through, but very much worthwhile in order to achieve as realistic a model as possible. In the last week, among this research, I now have a new book based on an archaeological dig by Deborah Charlton, which provides a few critical measurements and further structural information. In Chapter 8's section "Refining the HBIM Model," we will revisit the size of the model and make any adjustments necessary.

The HBIM data we have added may also need to change, and further shared parameters might be required. By using the Export to Datasmith option in Revit (with AutoSync enabled), we can maintain a live connection between the Revit model and the Unreal Engine project. This means that when changes are made in Revit – such as geometry updates or the addition of shared parameters – they can be reflected in Unreal without having to reimport the entire model or reassign materials manually. As long as the materials and metadata assignments are handled correctly using Unreal's Datasmith Reimport and Material Override system, these updates will not overwrite custom work done inside Unreal. HBIM elements that rely on shared parameters will be preserved as long as they are consistently defined in Revit and mapped correctly through Datasmith metadata settings.

Based on what you have learned so far will enable you to build further structurally realistic models using Revit, and take them into Unreal Engine for enhancing visually internally and externally. In the next chapter, we will work through the process in adding external surroundings to place the building in context. In addition, we will work through the methods for accessing the HBIM data and add a story to link Steventon Rectory to 8 College Street, creating a portal to jump to the different places and time periods.

References

Ashton, Helen (1967) Parson Austen's Daughter. Collins, London

Borson, Bob (2010) Ceiling Heights and "Scoreboard", Life of an Architect. `https://www.lifeofanarchitect.com/ceiling-heights-and-scoreboard/` [Accessed May 2025]

Day, Malcolm (2006) Voices from the World of Jane Austen. David & Charles Ltd., Devon. ISBN-13: 978-0-7153-2379-3, ISBN-10: 0-7153-2379-2

Jane Austen's House (2025) Map of the glebe land at Steventon Hants 1821. Map originated by John Armstrong. `https://janeaustens.house/object/map-of-the-glebe-land-at-steventon-hants-1821/` [Accessed March 2025]

Jane Austen's House (2025) Pencil Drawing of Steventon Rectory (image:1820-Sketch-Steventon-Rectory-Front-attributed-to-Ben-Lefroy). `https://janeaustens.house/object/pencil-drawing-of-steventon-rectory/` [Accessed March 2025]

BookLady Deb (2010) Jane Austen - Steventon Parsonage redux. (image: Steventon Parsonage - LeFroy sketch rear view) Jane Austen in Vermont, Random Musings of a Janeite. `https://janeausteninvermont.blog/tag/steventon-rectory/` [Accessed March 2025]

Marino, Anya; DeMeo, Lucy (2021) Pride & Prejudice: 1995 or 2005? The Looking Glass, Montrose Student Newspaper. `https://lookingglass.montroseschool.org/arts-entertainment/2021/12/05/pride-prejudice-1995-or-2005/` [Accessed April 2025]

Maybank, Geoff (2019) Traditional Brickwork. Building Conservation Articles, Cathedral Communications Limited. https://www.buildingconservation.com/articles/traditional-brickwork/traditional-brickwork.htm [Accessed April 2025]

Mistress of Pemberley (2023) YouTube's Mistress of Pemberley. Video clips of Jane Austen's book adaptations as films and series. https://www.youtube.com/@Mistress.of.Pemberley [Accessed April 2025]

Movie World Map (2025) Movie Locations – Where was Pride and Prejudice Filmed? Movie World Map. https://www.movieworldmap.com/movies/pride-and-prejudice/ [Accessed April 2025]

Sanborn, Vic (2008) Pride and Prejudice 1995, China Pattern at Longbourn (image: The Bennets dining at Longborn). Jane Austen's World Blog. https://janeaustensworld.com/2008/08/26/pride-and-prejudice-1995-china-pattern-at-longbourn/ [Accessed May 2025]

Links to Revit Family Objects

RevitCity – https://www.revitcity.com/index.php
Library Revit – https://libraryrevit.com/
Blackbee 3D – https://blackbee3d.com/product/
NBS Source UK – https://source.thenbs.com/product/

Links to Materials and Textures Assets

https://texturehub.co.uk
https://www.fab.com
https://textures.com
https://ambientcg.com/
https://cgaxis.com/
https://3dtextures.me
https://www.poliigon.com/textures/
https://sharetextures.com/textures
https://texturecan.com

CHAPTER 7

Step Four: Adding Context

This Chapter explores the crucial role that urban and landscape context plays in the reconstruction of historical buildings using HBIM. While much attention is often placed on the architectural detail and structural accuracy of individual buildings, it is equally important to recognize that these buildings did not exist in isolation. They were embedded within dynamic and evolving urban environments, shaped by natural landscapes, social infrastructure, and cultural practices. To achieve meaningful and immersive reconstructions, HBIM must therefore extend beyond the building envelope to incorporate the broader spatial and societal frameworks in which these structures once operated.

By examining the integration of surrounding topographies, adjacent built forms, transportation, and historical patterns of land use, this chapter demonstrates how HBIM can provide a more nuanced and contextually rich understanding of the past. It considers how environmental features and city planning conventions influenced architectural decisions, how socio-political conditions shaped spatial arrangements, and how buildings interacted with the rhythms of daily life. For example, in medieval towns, you would typically find the church and lord's castle at the center or highest point, showing their social importance, while craftspeople and merchants lived in specific quarters based on their trade. In modern cities, political decisions determine where you can build homes versus businesses versus factories, which shapes how people move through and experience the city. Imagine you are looking at a city from above. The way buildings, neighborhoods, roads, and public spaces are arranged isn't random, it reflects the values, laws, and power dynamics of the people who built it. Spaces are not neutral. They are physical expressions of who has power, what a society values, and how people are expected to interact with each other. Understanding this helps us see how buildings and city layouts can either reinforce existing social patterns or potentially challenge them. This holistic approach allows for reconstructions that not only visualize heritage buildings with technical precision but also communicate their function, significance, and meaning within a larger urban and cultural system. Ultimately, the purpose of this Chapter is to emphasize the value of contextual awareness in HBIM practice. By foregrounding the relationship between buildings and their historical settings, readers are encouraged to move beyond object-focused modelling and toward historically grounded digital environments that foster deeper engagement, interpretation, and storytelling.

Integrating Surrounding Landscapes and Urban Features

This section provides the process of creating the Steventon Rectory environment in Unreal for enabling the storytelling of a memory being discussed by Jane and Cassandra at 8 College Street in Regency Winchester. Jane spent her last months before she died from her illness in lodgings at 8 College Street. The memory will be based on an event that took place at their family home Steventon Rectory. We will use an event recorded in the memoirs and letters from different members of the family that has a good level of detail to be able to expand the story and recreate a suitable virtual reconstruction. The book is focused on HBIM data and reconstructing buildings that no longer exist using Revit and Unreal, but for people to engage with the data, the best way is to build stories that bring that data alive. Therefore, we are building the immediate environment of Steventon Rectory and 8 College Street, for a more engaging way for "visitors" to explore buildings, the occupants, and surroundings. By doing so, visitors/users may learn more of past cultures.

Having built the "bones" of Steventon Rectory, you are able to continue to add details to each room according to use. For this exercise, we will take the building as it stands, i.e., with just the drawing room detail added, and start to place the environment. We will capture the immediate area of the Rectory from the Glebe map of 1821 and, using research from the memoirs and letters, reconstruct the area so that the "visitor" can walk up to and around the house, see the outbuildings, the elm trees Jane talks about, the strawberry walk that Reverend Austen can look out on from his study, and the start of the path up to the church and the part of Steventon Lane seen from the front of the house.

You already have Steventon Rectory in Unreal, so you could start with this file, but it might be more prudent to save a copy of the Unreal project so that you can always go back to just the Rectory model.

CHAPTER 7   STEP FOUR: ADDING CONTEXT

Copying Your Project

1. In your Unreal Project (UnrealProject_Chapter6), go to the Content Browser. Right-click on "Content".

2. Select "Show in Explorer". It will take you to File Explorer and the exact location of the Content folder.

3. Select the root folder "Unreal Projects"; see Figure 7-1.

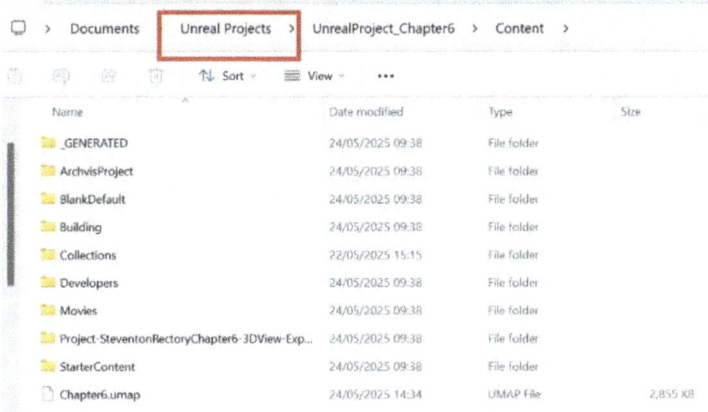

Figure 7-1. *Where to find your project for copying/backing up in File Explorer*

4. Right-click on your Project folder and copy then paste. You will see a copy of the folder created.

Figure 7-2. *The new copy created*

5. Rename the project folder appropriately. I am simply changing the chapter number to 7 and deleting the word copy for this exercise (a copy can be found in the lesson files online).

6. Double-click to open the folder. You will see that the Unreal file is still called Chapter 6; rename this to your new project name and then the png file.

7. Close your current Chapter 6 project and open the new project (Chapter 7) which you will see listed in Epic Games Launcher.

8. Your new project is completely the same, and therefore, you can add the landscape to this project and know that you still have the original project as a backup if required.

Initiating the Landscape for Steventon Rectory

Your next step is to create the landscape for the Rectory. We covered how to create landscapes in Chapter 4, in the "Collecting Geographic and Spatial Data" section, and following the exercise under "Creating the Landscape," create your landscape for Steventon Rectory. To create the Landscape, it would be a good idea to hide the rectory model so that you can see what you are doing more easily. To do this, just click on the eye next to the top hierarchy for the Rectory.

It would also be good to crop the Glebe map to remove the writing on the right side, but do not worry if you use the whole map; it will only be used as a guide for adding the rectory model, landscape objects, and texture painting.

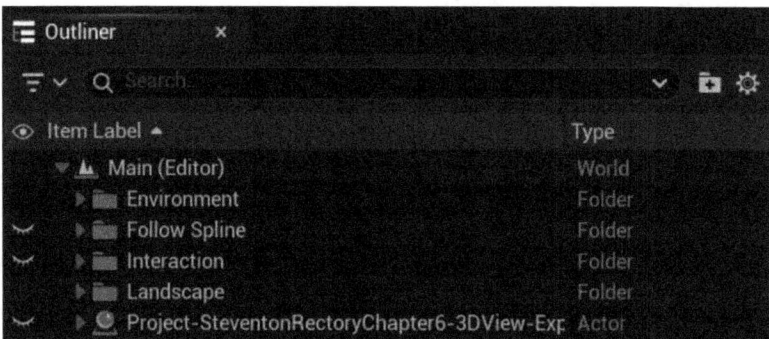

Figure 7-3. Hiding the Steventon Rectory model to work on the Landscape

Once you have done this, you will need to create a new Landscape object in your Unreal Project, and then import your Height data map, and adjust if required. If your map looks very mountainous, do not worry, you will be able to scale the height down once it is a Landscape object.

CHAPTER 7   STEP FOUR: ADDING CONTEXT

Layering Images to Guide Placement of the Rectory

1. To work with adding map layers, it would be best in a Top view.

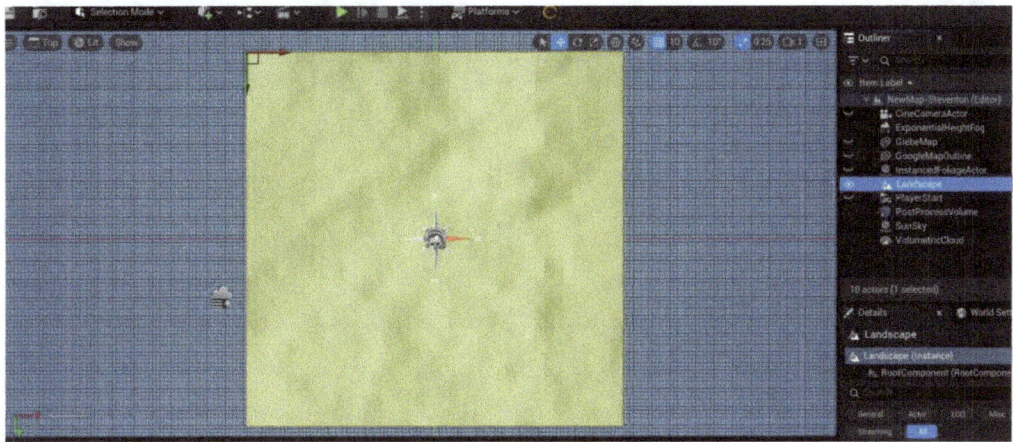

Figure 7-4. Top view of the Landscape object

2. Once in a Top view, create a rectangle by going to Modelling Mode.

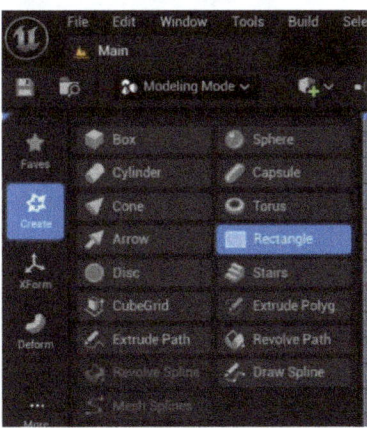

Figure 7-5. Modelling Mode to create a rectangle

3. Click Create and accept the basic shape. Once the rectangle is place, you will need to scale it to match the size of your Landscape object.

457

CHAPTER 7   STEP FOUR: ADDING CONTEXT

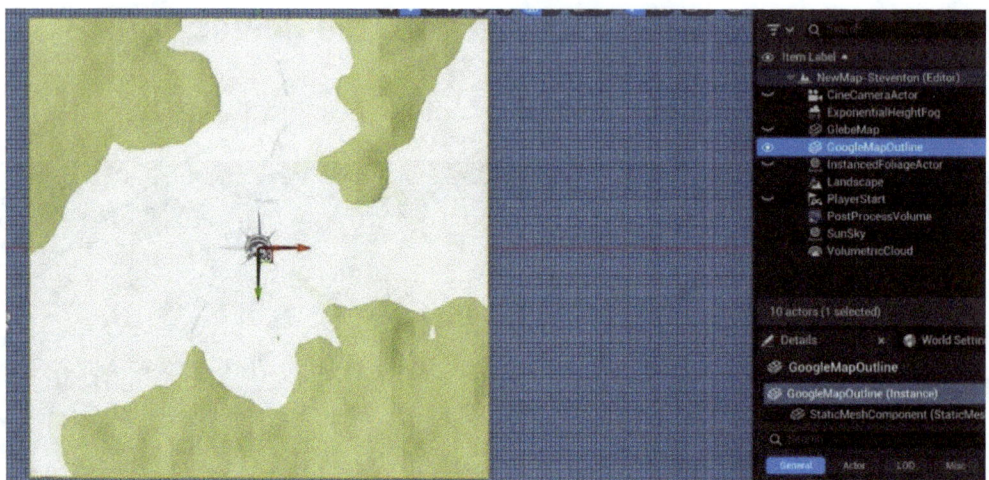

Figure 7-6. *The Google Map rectangle in place*

4. Name the rectangle appropriately. This will be for adding the Google Map image.

5. You will need to create another rectangle for the Glebe map. This time change the size/scale of the rectangle to suit the proportions of the Glebe map, i.e., it is not square.

6. You also need to change the Blue field for Location to be 10 so that you can see the new rectangle (it will be on the same plane as the previous rectangle otherwise).

7. Next, you need to import to the Content Browser the Google Map tile and the Glebe map image.

8. Once imported, create each one as a basic image Material (the same as the Picture Materials in the last chapter).

9. Click on the first rectangle and add the Google Map Material to the Material slot.

10. Repeat with the second rectangle and use the Glebe Map Material.

You will notice that the Glebe map is not at the right angle, i.e., it is not facing true north as in the Google map and the Landscape therefore. The Glebe map needs to be scaled and rotated so that it matches the Google image below. To check progress in aligning the Glebe map with the map below, you can hide and unhide until happy with the positioning.

458

CHAPTER 7   STEP FOUR: ADDING CONTEXT

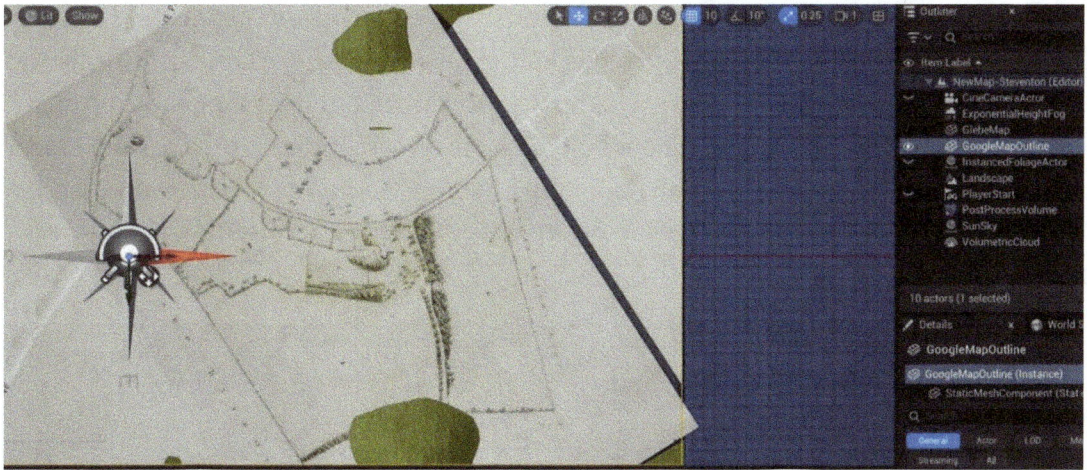

Figure 7-7. *Positioning, scaling, and moving the Glebe map to match the Google map below*

Be careful with skewing the Glebe map when you are scaling/resizing the rectangle. It can skew out of shape if the proportion is not retained. The settings I used for the above image are in Figure 7-8.

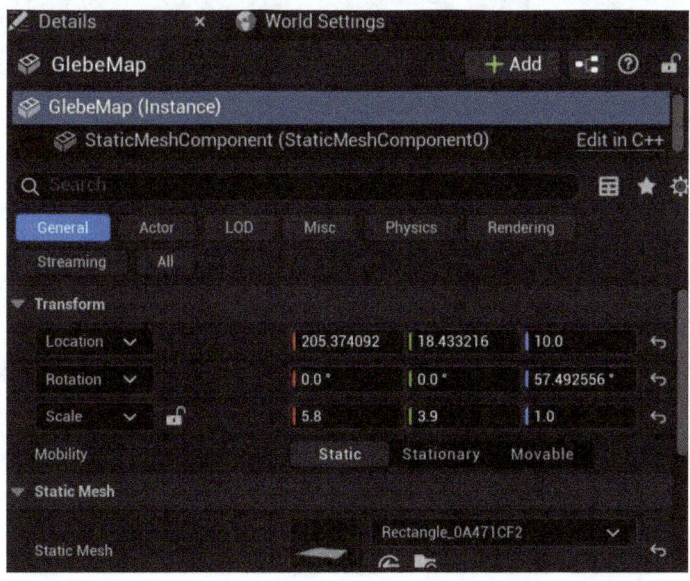

Figure 7-8. *Settings for the Glebe Map after it has been positioned to match the Google map*

459

CHAPTER 7   STEP FOUR: ADDING CONTEXT

You can now return to Perspective view and unhide the Steventon Rectory model. You will probably notice that the Rectory is far too big, or rather the Landscape is far too small. You might think it is okay to scale the Rectory down, but then the real scale for adding furniture, people, and similar would be incorrect. To make sure this is the case, I have added a silhouette of a woman (from the Building/Geometry folder if you used the Archviz template). If the house was too big, then she would be miniscule, as it is, she is the right size.

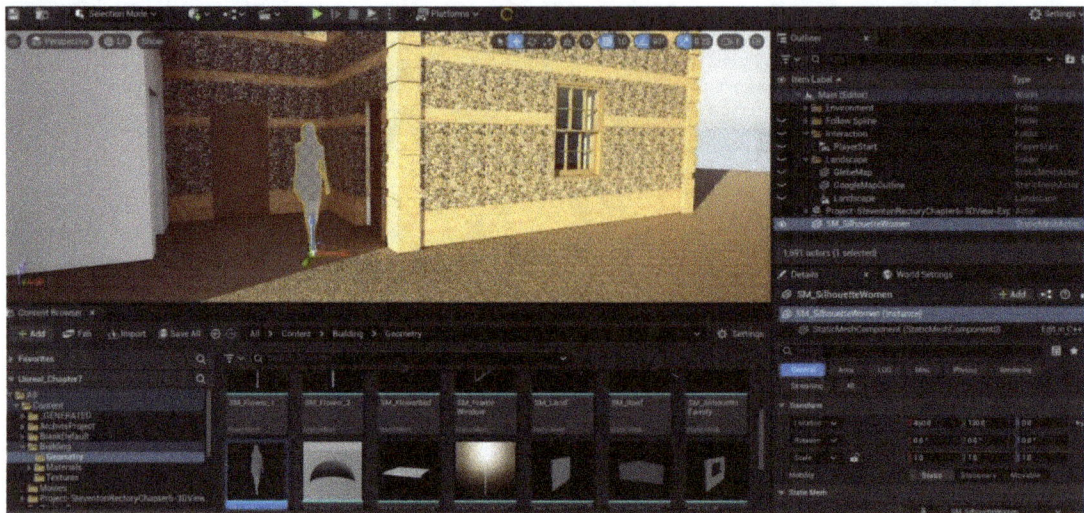

Figure 7-9. *Checking the size of the Rectory with reference to the size of the Landscape and map objects*

You will therefore need to resize the Landscape objects so that the Rectory fits on the Glebe map's outline of the building. It may take a few tries, but it will be worth it to see the building sitting where it should be. The settings that work for my Exercise file can be seen in the following images for Landscape, Google map, and Glebe map.

CHAPTER 7   STEP FOUR: ADDING CONTEXT

Figure 7-10. *Landscape updated settings from being scaled to fit the Rectory size*

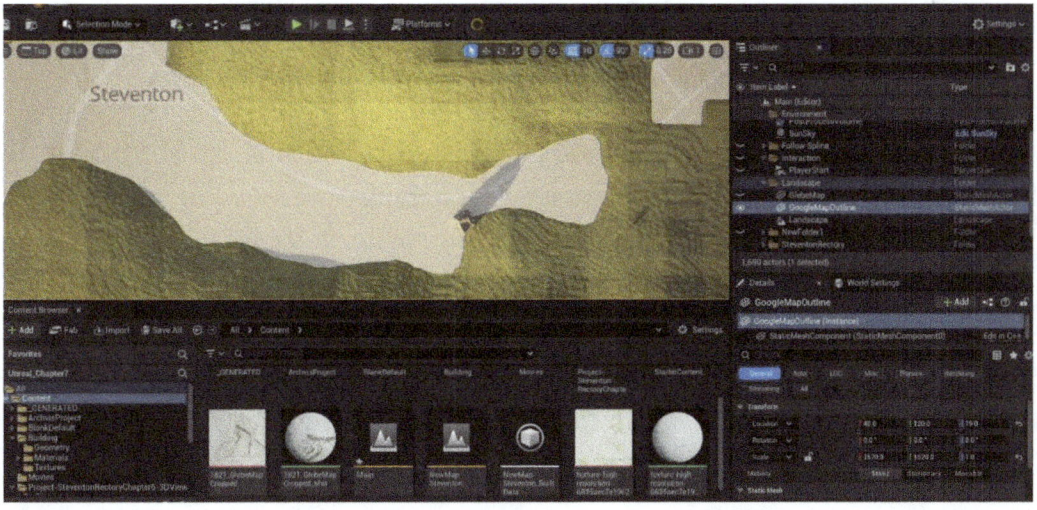

Figure 7-11. *Google map with updated settings after being scaled to fit the Rectory*

CHAPTER 7   STEP FOUR: ADDING CONTEXT

Figure 7-12. *Glebe map with updated settings after being scaled to fit the Rectory*

As you may be able to see in your own file and the images from mine, there will need to be some adjustments of the landscape surface to ensure the landscape is not going through the walls. In reality, a level foundational pad would be built and the ground landscaped away from the building to ensure good drainage of surface water. The Landscape Sculpting tools are therefore necessary before adding further detail. We will work through these as well as painting the landscape surface to add the road past the house, the track up to the church, and the sweep of the drive. We will also add a few trees, shrubs, and plants as part of the Landscape tool process. Using Unreal Engine's modelling tools, we can also add garden walls and possibly the outbuildings, although these might be quicker in Revit.

CHAPTER 7   STEP FOUR: ADDING CONTEXT

Figure 7-13. *Steventon Rectory in position but the landscape needs modifying for the model to sit on the land all-round the building*

In the image above, you can see that I have not added all the external materials yet; you may have already done so and therefore have a more complete front aspect. We still need to ask for verification; therefore, adding the materials and the landscape objects will help to provide a richer visualization for engaging with and exploring externally and internally.

Developing Your Steventon Rectory Rural Landscape

Before you start using the Landscape tools, it would be a wise decision to make a copy of the Project, which will not only create a backup of where you have got to so far but also allow tracking back should the file crash or make a mistake that cannot be undone. We covered this previously, but to add quickly here, go to File Explorer and navigate to where you are saving your projects. Copy the folder of your Project, then paste and rename the folder and then the Unreal Engine Project file icon and .png in the folder root. Then open up your new project file or download my version from the lesson files on the website.

Epic Games provides a wealth of information for working with Unreal Engine, so I will focus on the tools you will need just to build aspects for starting to "bed" your building into the landscape and sufficient detail to be able to continue to add elements to complete your Steventon Rectory scene. Remember that we are building a scene for a

463

visitor to have context when they portal in from 8 College Street, so it does not need to be the complete area brought in as a landscape object, simply the immediate area around the Rectory. You will start with the ground the Rectory is sitting on.

Step by Step Modifying and Adding to Your Rural Rectory Landscape

In this exercise, you will create the landscape to tie in with the Glebe map detail; you will need to have the following images open to guide you: Front and Rear Sketches by Anna Lefroy and the 1821 Glebe map (in Chapter 7 Lesson files).

Step 1: Sculpting your immediate surroundings

1. Select Landscape Mode from the drop-down menu, top left of your window.

2. You have three options for Landscape Mode: Manage, Sculpt, and Paint. You will need Sculpt.

3. You will be presented with a range of tools under Sculpt; each has a set of options, i.e., Brush Type and Falloff, Size and Strength.

4. Your brush size is important; you may have a largish brush size set by default; this is good for large landscaping projects, but you will need to decrease this size considerably for working around the Rectory.

5. The Brush Type is also important; the default and first tool is Sculpt; this may be okay, but it might be better to use Smooth or Flatten for creating the base the Rectory sits on. If you want to create a sharp edge, the second Falloff option would be the one to use, or a smooth edge, obviously use the first option. It is good to experiment first if you haven't used these tools before. You can undo each brush stroke, so it is always good to test, undo, test, undo etc., before going too far and then not able to undo completely.

CHAPTER 7 STEP FOUR: ADDING CONTEXT

6. Select the Flatten tool. You will be presented with a different option set, including "Flatten Mode". As you want to raise the landscape in the far right of the front of the Rectory, choose Raise, and then for the rear, you will need to use Lower. If you want to be cautious, then use a 100 (approx.) Brush Size. To ensure you do not create a mountain (Raise) or a deep hole (Lower), you can set the Flatten Target to 0.0, which should be ground floor level of the Rectory.

7. You will need to hide the Google Map Outline object, which can stay hidden.

8. You will need to hide/unhide the Glebe map object and hide/unhide the Rectory to view progress.

9. When you have done a few strokes with the Raise tool, hide the Rectory and you may see the surface has become uneven, little furrows possibly. To change this, you can switch to the Smooth tool and increase the brush size to 200 to smooth the "rivulets."

10. Using a combination of these two tools and hiding/unhiding, continue to sculpt the land under the building so that it is flat and not intruding into the Rectory.

Note Remember that the front of the Rectory had a sweeping drive, yet looking at the landscape, the land falls down to the road from the house, so there will need to be a gentle slope at the front of the house before then levelling out for the sweeping drive. The roadside of the drive may also have a further gentle slope before the fencing to the road.

The following two images show the Rectory and landscape meeting all around the building base and the same level across the base of the house. At some point, you will need to create a cellar and therefore use Sculpt or Flatten with sharp falloff to create the depth of cavity required for the height of the cellar.

Figure 7-14. *The ground now meets the Rectory around the base*

Figure 7-15. *The same view with the Rectory hidden to see the flatten base*

The next step is to paint the surface with suitable materials. For example, the base will need to be flattened earth; the sweeping drive will also be earth but with small stones, possibly slightly muddy. At the back of the house, there would probably also be a similar surface for walking to the outbuildings, possibly with a little grass mixed in.

CHAPTER 7   STEP FOUR: ADDING CONTEXT

In the Chapter7-Unreal project (in the lesson files), you will find a Master Material "M_Grass_Landscape_New" created for the Landscape. The Master Material has a different Material Graph to other materials, which enables it to paint the surface of the landscape with those other materials. If you open that project file and find the Master Material, when you double-click on it to open the material graph, you will see how different it looks. There are four textures and their associated normals that are linked with a Landscape Layer Blend node (one for the textures, one for the normal). The Landscape Layer Blend is then linked to the relevant nodes in the Material Result main panel. The textures and normal are also linked on the left to a Landscape Coordinate node.

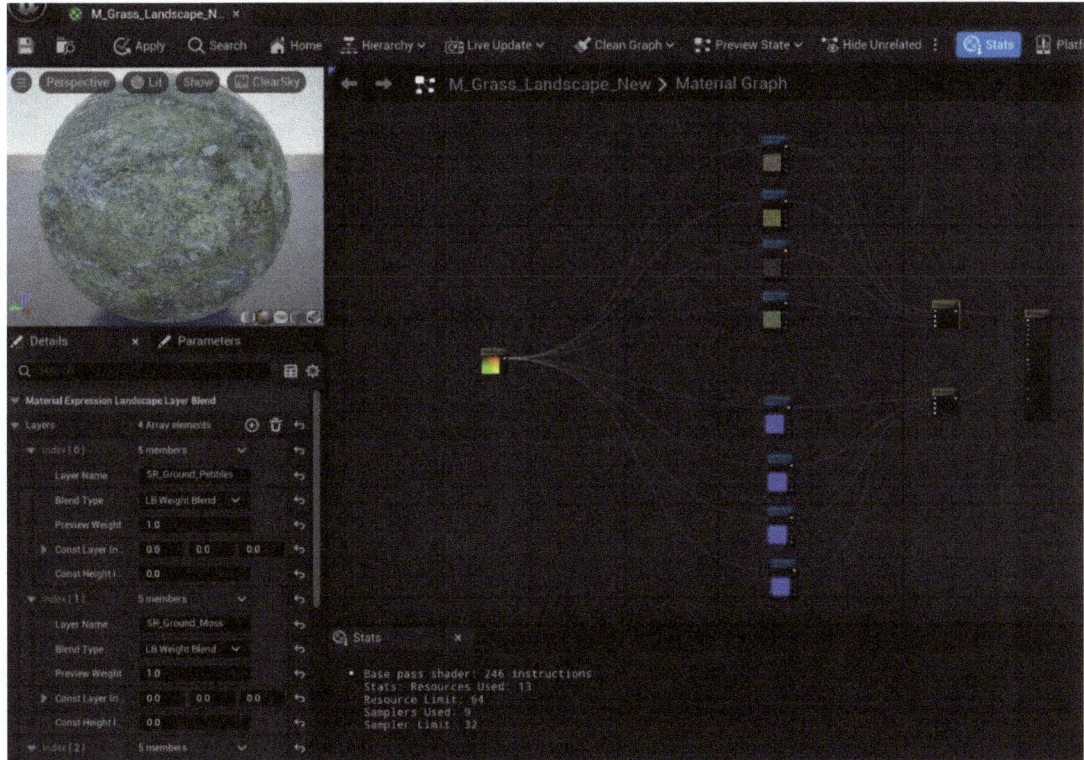

Figure 7-16. *Landscape Master Material*

The textures and normals used are shown in Table 7-1, sourced from the Environment_Set which I have had as part of all my projects for a number of years (also included in the Project file).

Table 7-1. "M_Grass_Landscape_New" components

Material	Texture	Normal
SR_Forest_Grass	T_ground_forest_grass_06_BC_H	T_ground_forest_grass_06_N
SR_Ground_Dirt	T_ground_dirt_02_BC_H	T_ground_dirt_02_N
SR_Ground_Moss	T_ground_moss_03_BC_H	T_ground_moss_03_N
SR_Ground_Pebbles	T_ground_big_pebbles_01_BC_H	T_ground_big_pebbles_01_N

There are many other textures available within the Environment_Set folder in the Content Browser which you may want to use for Foliage, Rocks, and Landscape. I have chosen these, but you can duplicate this material and then change the textures and normal to ones you want to use or build your own Master Landscape material. There is an excellent tutorial with Epic Games for creating your own. The link for this tutorial can be found in the Documentation Glossary at the end of the chapter; see Link 1.

You now need to make your Master Landscape material work in Landscape Painting mode:

1. The first step is to apply the material to the Landscape object.

2. Then select Landscape Mode (top left) and Paint. You will see the options panel for Paint.

CHAPTER 7   STEP FOUR: ADDING CONTEXT

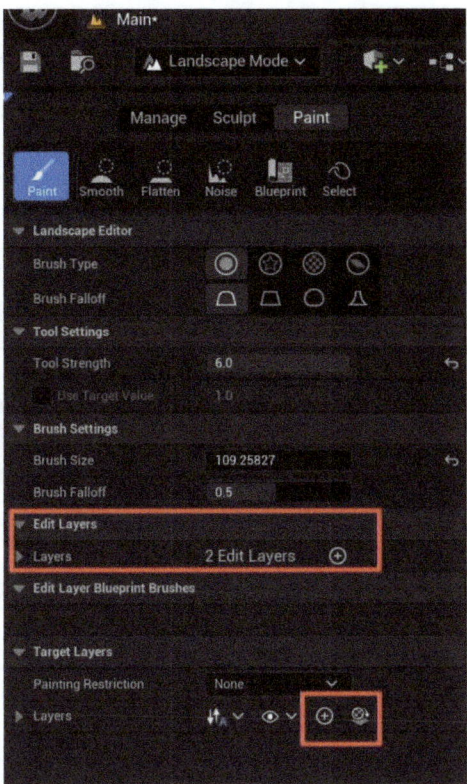

Figure 7-17. *Landscape Mode Paint options*

3. There are new features in this panel for Version 5.5; the one to note is the addition of Edit Layers, which are useful for adding Layers to your Landscape, enabling you to layer paint effects. More about this feature within Epic Games can be found in the Documentation Glossary Link 2.

4. Leave this for the moment; instead go to the last icon in the bottom highlighted area which is the "Create Layers from Assigned Materials" tool. Click on this icon and it will import the textures and normal used in your Master Landscape material. You only need the textures to be listed here, so you can click on the normal layers and select the delete button, leaving just the textures as layers in this area.

469

CHAPTER 7   STEP FOUR: ADDING CONTEXT

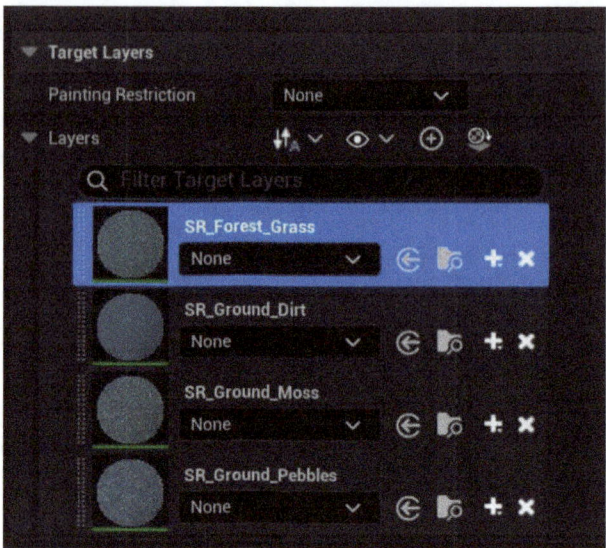

Figure 7-18. *The imported Layers*

5. The next step is to create Layer Info for each of the materials. Click on the Plus sign "Create Layer Info" icon, and a dialogue box appears to choose either Weight-Blended Layer (Normal) or Non-Weighted Blended Layer; choose Weight-Blended.

6. You will be prompted to save the Layer Information in a folder of your choice – I chose the Environment_Set/Environment/Landscape/Materials folder to keep all the information in the same place.

7. Repeat for each Layer – Painting the Landscape will not work until you have done this. You should now see the following showing the new layer information in the Materials folder and the name of the Layer Info in the previous field where it said "None".

CHAPTER 7   STEP FOUR: ADDING CONTEXT

Figure 7-19. *The new Layer Information objects in the Materials folder*

8. Move up to the Edit Layers/Layers section and rename Layer 1 Ground as shown below (if there is not a Layer listed, then click the circled plus icon to create a new layer).

9. Add another layer and name it Paint. You will then have two layers to work with for adding materials to your Landscape surface.

CHAPTER 7   STEP FOUR: ADDING CONTEXT

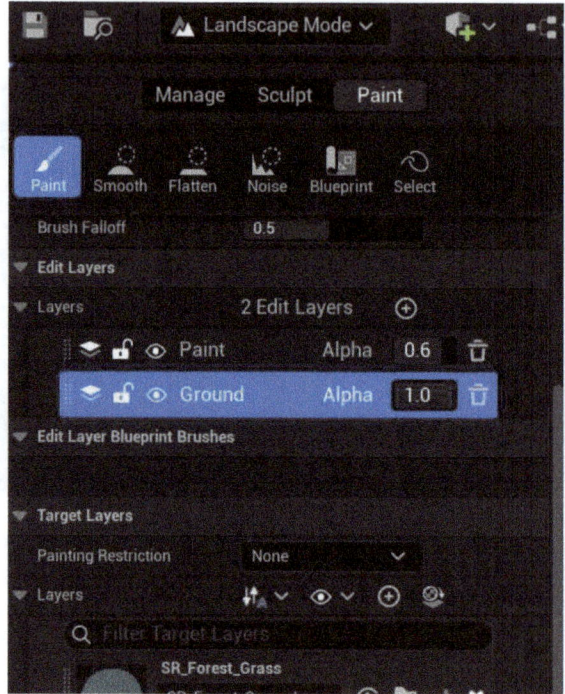

Figure 7-20. *Edit Layers – Adding layers to your Landscape surface*

10. Choose SR_Ground_Dirt Layer and the Ground Layer ready to paint this material onto the surface underneath the Rectory, and for the sweeping drive, backyard area, and lanes – you can add to/change later if you want to, but for this exercise, we will just put the basics in.

11. Check the strength of the tool and the brush size, maybe a smaller brush size to outline the shape of the house and yard and then a larger brush size to "fill" the outline and for the drive and lanes.

12. You also really should generally work in the Top view; make sure you choose "Lit" instead of "Wireframe".

13. You can paint the surface with the Rectory showing and with the Glebe map showing, hiding and unhiding as necessary.

CHAPTER 7   STEP FOUR: ADDING CONTEXT

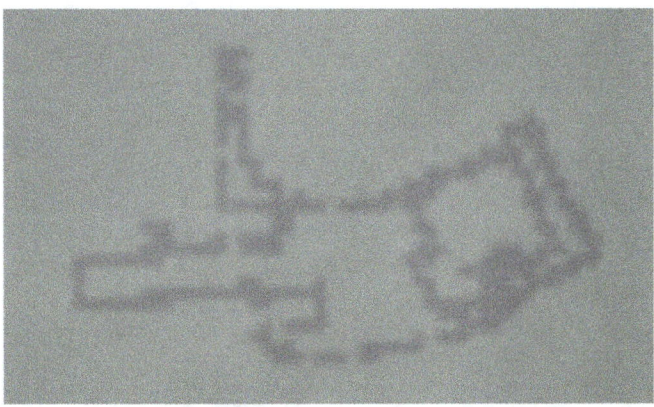

Figure 7-21. *Outline of areas using the Glebe map and the Rectory building*

Figure 7-22. *Top view showing the Glebe map for being able to paint the lanes, yards, and drive*

14. You will notice in Figure 7-23 that the painting looks pixelated which is fine and can be tidied as you start to plant shrubs and trees.

CHAPTER 7   STEP FOUR: ADDING CONTEXT

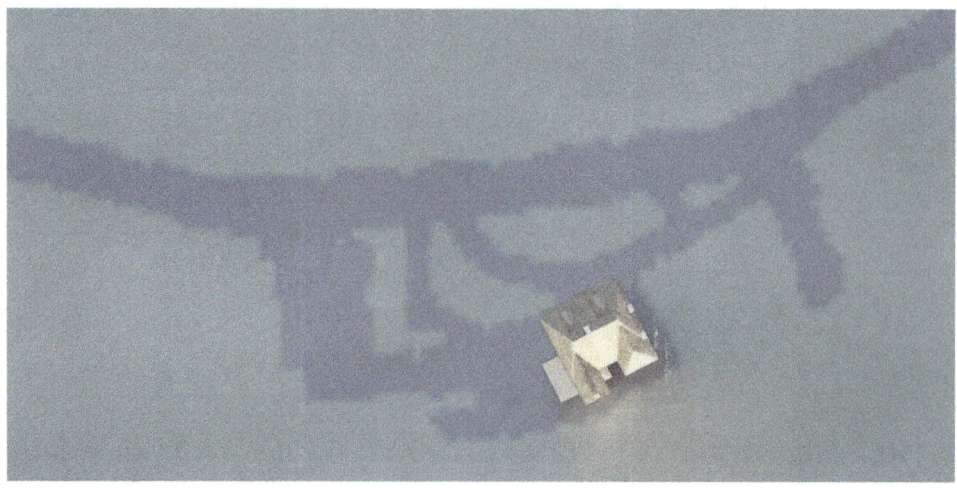

Figure 7-23. *Initial painting areas having used the Glebe map*

15. You can also experiment with Subtractive Blend Mode, which basically subtracts color information of one texture from another. This can result in a darker or desaturated color. The Subtractive Blend can be found as a tick box with each of the Material layers.

16. You can also try the Alpha mode found with the new Edit Layers command. The Alpha mode controls the intensity or blending of a layer, allowing you to influence how much of a layer's effects are applied. It is a value between 0 and 1 (or 100% and 0%), where 1 (or 100%) represents full intensity and 0 (or 0%) represents no effect.

Now to Add Landscape Objects Using Foliage Mode

1. Change Landscape Mode to Foliage Mode. You will see another set of tools (see Figure 7-24). Before you can use this Mode, you will need to create your foliage resource in the area where it says "Drop Foliage Here".

CHAPTER 7   STEP FOUR: ADDING CONTEXT

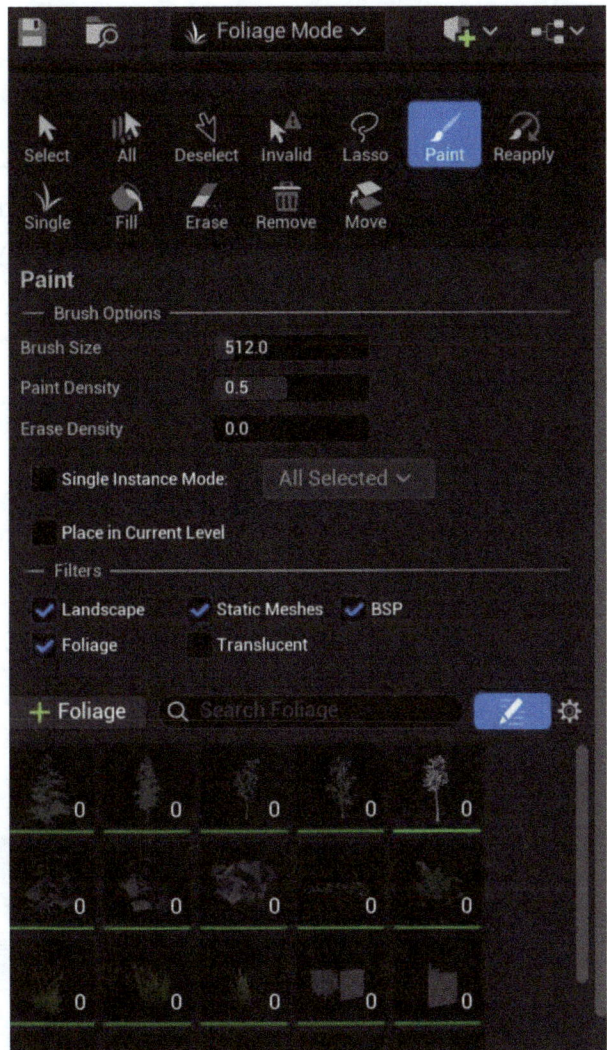

Figure 7-24. *Foliage Paint Options with foliage added*

2. In the Environment_Set folder used for the Landscape materials, there is also a folder for Foliage. For this exercise, you can use the models in this folder.

3. To add them to where it says Drop your Foliage here, choose the plants/trees you want to use and "drag and drop" each one to the space, as shown in Figure 7-24.

4. When the models are dropped in, you will see a thumbnail of each one and a zero in the bottom right corner. The zero will change to be the amount you have added to the scene.

5. In this view, you might not always know how many are selected for adding to your landscape. At the top right you will see a settings icon; click on this to change the thumbnails to a list where you will see a tick box, which may be easier for you to select and know how many types are selected.

6. To begin with, just add one tree. Click on the "Single" tool at the top of the panel, and that only one type is selected.

7. In your project window, make sure the Glebe and Google map outlines are hidden and choose where to place your tree. They can always be moved.

8. If you think it is too tall and would like to change its height, change to Selection Mode, and go to the Details panel on the right of your screen and scale the tree down on the Z scale.

Figure 7-25. *A tall Scots Pine added to your scene*

CHAPTER 7   STEP FOUR: ADDING CONTEXT

9. You can add several types at once, or more than one of the same type, which is great for creating wooded/forest areas, or even just to place and then space out to suit. You need to use the foliage Paint tool for this, adjusting the brush size and density to suit. Then paint an area and the trees will be added. Each one can be resized by using the scale function.

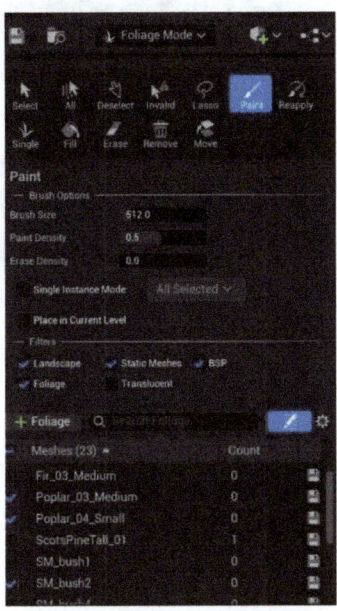

Figure 7-26. *Foliage Paint tool with several types of tree/bush selected*

10. As you can see in Figure 7-27, the trees and shrubs are clumped together wherever you click or paint. To space them out, use the foliage Select tool and then move each to a new space.

477

Figure 7-27. *The result of painting several types and selecting individual trees to space if required*

11. There may be some of the trees that do not render properly; the ones here are from another folder and have perhaps lost their material asset. You can simply delete them in the scene if they are not rendering. If you select the trees while not in foliage Select mode, all the trees will be selected, so be careful to remember to select in foliage Select mode.

CHAPTER 7   STEP FOUR: ADDING CONTEXT

Figure 7-28. *Separating the clump of trees and noticing those that are not rendering properly*

12. You can add grass and flowers in the same way. This is one of the aspects of creating in Unreal that is really enjoyable but very time-consuming, depending on the type of person you are; as a perfectionist, it is possible to spend hours planting your scene, much like planning your garden but on a much larger scale.

13. To paint grass, it is much better to choose several types but not too dense. You can then add individual wildflower plants among the grass.

Figure 7-29. *Painting grass and wild flowers*

CHAPTER 7   STEP FOUR: ADDING CONTEXT

The next objects to add are the outbuildings and side wall

1. Create a new folder in the Content folder for your outbuildings.

2. Select the Modelling Mode to access the basic geometry tools. You are going to use a few of these to create a wall to the left side of the front of the house which will have a door to the path that goes around the side of the house, and a simple outbuilding.

3. To create the wall, go to a top view and turn on the Glebe map.

4. Select the Box tool and click to place in your scene and accept.

5. Navigate to the Outliner where you will find your Box object.

6. Rename it Side_Wall, and using the scaling tool, create a wall to the side of the Rectory.

7. Rotate to be in line with the front of the Rectory.

Figure 7-30. *Creating a side garden wall to the Rectory*

8. For a door, it would be a quick solution to duplicate the front door and move the duplicate (renamed Side_Wall_Door) to the garden wall beside the Rectory. You can change the material and ironmongery to make it look more like a garden door later.

CHAPTER 7   STEP FOUR: ADDING CONTEXT

Figure 7-31. *The duplicated front door in place in the side wall*

9. Check the width of the wall and make sure it matches the width of the door. The Top view is the best view for doing this, and the Wireframe view setting.

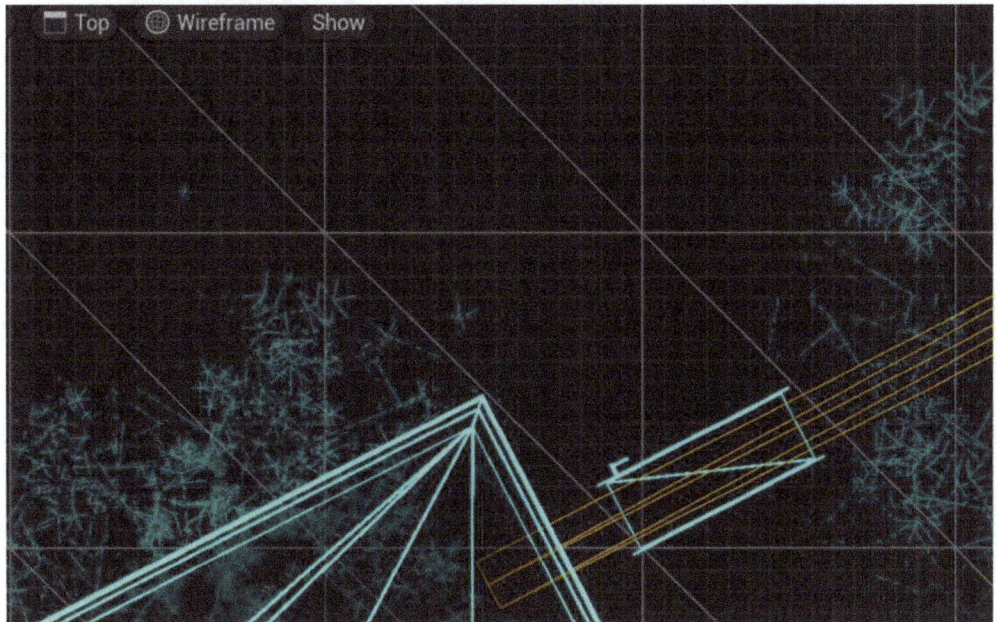

Figure 7-32. *Top view, Wireframe setting to match the wall to the width of the door*

481

CHAPTER 7   STEP FOUR: ADDING CONTEXT

10. This wall may have been tiled at the top, rounded clay or thatched; the sketch we have been using does not show this clearly. One of the sketches of the front does not show a wall, so there is an assumption here that needs clarifying. In the meantime, you need to provide it with a material. For this exercise, perhaps use a rendered brick material, or simply brick. I have used a rendered material. I have also added a Box at the end of the wall as a Pillar, using the same material.

Figure 7-33. The side wall and pillar added with a rendered material

11. To create one of the outbuildings, for this exercise, you will use the Box modelling tool again. Go to Modelling Mode, and then select the Box tool.

12. Place a box and scale to create the outbuilding long rear wall.

13. Use the Copy/Paste Here (right-click commands) and move to the front of the outbuilding. Now scale it back to be a short nib and place to the left, ready to create an opening to this side.

14. Copy/Paste Here this nib and move to the other front side.

15. Copy/Paste Here and place the third nib in the middle of the front face.

16. Copy/Paste Here the rear box and rotate 90 degrees and move to the short right side of the outbuilding. Scale to fit the length of the side shown on the Glebe map.

17. Copy/Paste Here this box and place to the left side of the outbuilding.

Figure 7-34. *The boxes forming the shape of the outbuilding closest to the Rectory*

18. For the material, duplicate the M_SR_InteriorFlooring_Master material and name it M_SR_Outbuilding1_Master.

19. Open up the new material and change the Texture coordinates to 2.0 for U and V Tiling. Save.

20. Apply this material to the Rear and Sides of the outbuilding. The tiling should look okay as vertical planks of wood.

21. Duplicate this new material and keep the same name but add a 1 to the end, i.e., M_SR_Outbuilding1_Master1.

22. Change the Texture coordinates of this second material to be 1.0 for the U and V Tiling. Save.

23. Apply this material to the Front nibs of the building. It is the same texture but a narrower tiling for the narrower nibs.

24. Now create another Box, name it Roof and scale it larger than the shape of the outbuilding. Rotate in Top view to change the angle to match the wooden walls.

25. Go to Perspective view and move the roof box to become the roof. This is going to be a pent roof, a single slope, with the slope to the rear.

CHAPTER 7   STEP FOUR: ADDING CONTEXT

26. Rotate in a side view with the lower edge to the rear of the outbuilding, intersecting with your wooden walls, and slightly higher than the wooden walls at the front.

27. In Figure 7-35, I have already adjusted the rear to fit the lower slope of the roof. For the sides, we need to shape them to the slope of the roof.

Figure 7-35. *Side profile of the outbuilding and the sloped roof*

28. To do this, go to Modelling Mode if you are not still there, and instead of the Create category, select the Deform category.

29. Under Deform, select the Lattice command.

30. Cross a window selection over the front set of vertices.

CHAPTER 7   STEP FOUR: ADDING CONTEXT

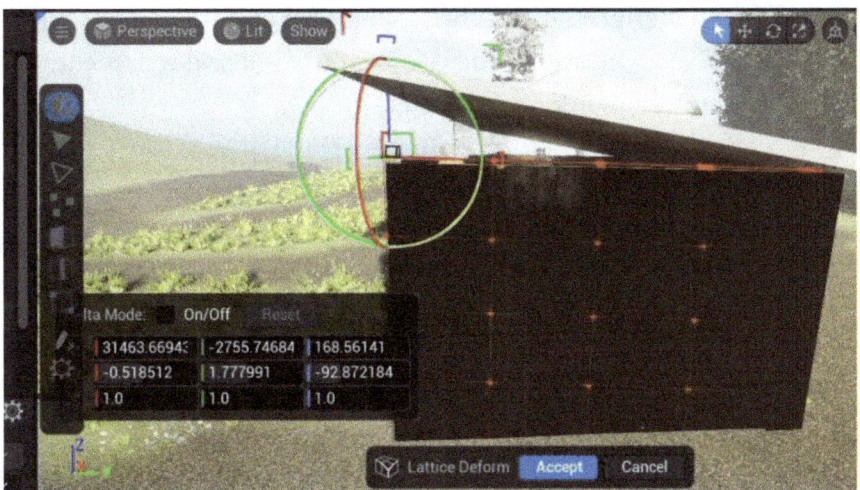

Figure 7-36. *How to select the front set of vertices*

31. Using the blue line with the orb, move the vertices up to meet the underside of the roof.

Figure 7-37. *The vertices moved to fit the slope of the roof*

32. Once you have moved each set of vertices up to meet the roof, click Accept.

33. Repeat for the other side of the outbuilding.

CHAPTER 7   STEP FOUR: ADDING CONTEXT

34. For the roof material, you can create your own or duplicate M_SR_RoofSlates_Master as you did for the wood and rename it M_SR_OutbuildingRoofSlates_Master.

35. Change the Texture Coordinates for the new material to 2.0 for U and V Tiling.

36. Apply to the roof. You will see that it maps the underneath of the roof as tiles too, when it would be better as wood. To change this, copy your roof, and Paste Here so that you can see it in the same space.

37. You might want to resize the depth of each roof object. I changed the depth to 0.1 by changing the Z (blue) Scale field.

38. Move the second roof slightly lower so that two roofs sit together but with a tiny gap between the two to stop any coplanar issues. For the second roof, I have applied the same material as the rear wall.

Figure 7-38. *The completed outbuilding*

39. The outbuilding has plants inside and in front which should not be there. I was over-zealous in my painting of grasses and wildflowers. Another outbuilding attaches to the right-side front of this building that goes down toward the lane. Therefore, the grasses and flowers on the right need to be removed.

40. To do this, go back into Foliage Mode, and using the Select tool, delete the plants in this area before building the next outbuilding. You will find this selects individual plants, but if you use the Lasso tool and a reasonable brush size in the Perspective View, you can delete many plants by sweeping over them with the tool. This tool does not seem to work in the Top View.

41. You can then use the Landscaping painting tool to paint over the grass with a Dirt material before creating further outbuildings.

   The final Landscape object to add that uses a different process to the others shown and which you will find useful for this project and others, involves Landscape Splines. These can be used for adding fencing, railings, and walling. We are going to add wooden post fencing along the Rectory side of the lane. Epic Games has an excellent explanation and how to work with Landscape Splines; a link to the documentation can be found in the Documentation Glossary at the end of the chapter on Link 3.

Figure 7-39. *The scene, far from finished, but looking more bedded into the landscape*

42. Go to Landscape Mode; select Manage; here you will find Splines.

43. To start your spline, you need to click on CTRL and click to place a Control Point.

44. Before you place another Control Point, go to Details on the right. I normally reduce the Half Width to 100 and the Side Falloff to 100. This narrows the width either side, which is perfect for a fence. For a road, it would obviously need to be wider.

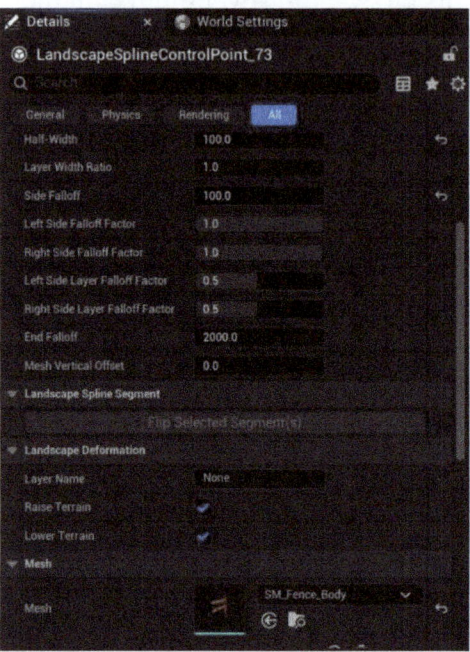

Figure 7-40. *Landscape Spline Details showing the Half Width, Side Falloff, and Mesh input*

45. While in details you can also drag into the Mesh what you want to use to represent your fence. I have used the rail fence available online (A Via Studio/Epic Games, n.d.) This comes with many options, with the mesh and the materials also available.

46. Once the Mesh is loaded, you can then continue to create your control points along your required route, such as along the lane edging fronting the Rectory.

47. As you create the Control Points (CTRL, click), you will see the railing mesh appear; the mesh may not be facing the right direction, but once rotated, they will be fine.

CHAPTER 7 STEP FOUR: ADDING CONTEXT

48. The Control Points may not be vertical, but you can always use the rotate tool to rotate the points correctly.

49. The Top view is useful for keeping the points aligned and checking the line of the Glebe map.

50. You can swap out the mesh object for the Spine Control Nodes, either while experimenting now or later if information is found about the type of front face fencing.

51. To create the following image, I created three separate sets of Splines and went through and checked each fence panel to make sure it was aligned with the following fence panel post. My mesh came in at right angles and therefore had to be rotated, so be aware of this if you use the same mesh (included in the lesson files).

52. Once you have created your spline fencing, you can come out of Landscape Mode to Selection Mode. You can also turn off all the green lines for the spline work by clicking Game View under the Menu Stack, top left of your Project window.

53. You can also take a High-Resolution screenshot which you can access via your Unreal Project folder in Explorer, under Saved.

Figure 7-41. *The railings in place similar to the sketch we have been using as reference*

489

CHAPTER 7   STEP FOUR: ADDING CONTEXT

Section Summary

The work completed in this section has really helped to shape the look and feel of Steventon Rectory within its wider setting, even if we have only begun to scratch the surface of what is possible with landscaping. You have successfully imported historical maps at matching size and scale, using them to accurately position the Rectory and check proportions, which is an essential step that brings a sense of authenticity to the reconstruction.

You have also started to bring the landscape to life by creating and applying landscape materials, painting areas to represent gardens, fields, and old tracks or lanes. By importing objects like trees, grasses, and flowers, you have added depth and atmosphere. This is particularly satisfying when you see the foliage respond to movement in the scene. I still find it rewarding to watch the grass sway and tree leaves rustle; it gives a sense of immersion that is hard to achieve otherwise. You have also started to handle small technical adjustments like nudging trees into place to hide roots. These are exactly the kinds of practical details that add polish and realism.

Of course, there is still more to learn, especially around texture map sizes, lighting, fog volumes, and the sun and sky elements. But now that you have established the foundations, I hope you are beginning to gain an understanding for how these various components work together. Unreal Engine's documentation is an excellent next step for digging into any of these features more deeply.

When I first began working with landscape elements, I made my fair share of mistakes, mainly from diving straight into the tools without fully understanding what each material or layer was doing. Over time, I have built a small library of landscape materials and meshes that I know work well. It saves a great deal of time and reduces frustration, so I would really recommend starting something similar for your own projects. Just be aware of Unreal Engine's version changes; as you may have noticed, version 5.5 introduced some quirks, and with version 6 now released (which I am keen to use for Metahuman creation), I have been weighing up whether to migrate the *Virtual Cities – Winchester* project and *Steventon Rectory* model. It is tempting, but compatibility issues can cause unexpected setbacks, so it is always worth considering the implications of upgrading before taking the leap.

In the next section, we shift the focus to storytelling. You will begin crafting Jane Austen's memory of Steventon as seen from her lodgings at 8 College Street. We will also begin working on the 8 College Street interior, especially the drawing room, and start to populate the street with era-appropriate objects to make the environment feel more grounded in time and place.

CHAPTER 7   STEP FOUR: ADDING CONTEXT

Integrating Urban Features and Infrastructure

In this section, we are going to use a scene (see Figure 7-42) created a couple of years ago of 8 College Street, the house Jane Austen stayed in for a couple of months with her sister while she was ill. She died in Winchester and is buried in Winchester Cathedral. The scene we will revisit does not have HBIM information. At the time it was constructed as a visualization and storytelling scene working with students; therefore, most of the buildings will need revisiting to add the HBIM data and ensure the exterior and interiors are as complete as possible. Many of the street buildings for which information is unknown have been created in Autodesk Revit as simple building shapes, the outlines of which match the 1800s map we have used for reference. You can see these as gray buildings when viewed from above. Additional buildings beyond the immediate area have been deleted so that the focus is on 8 College Street for this exercise.

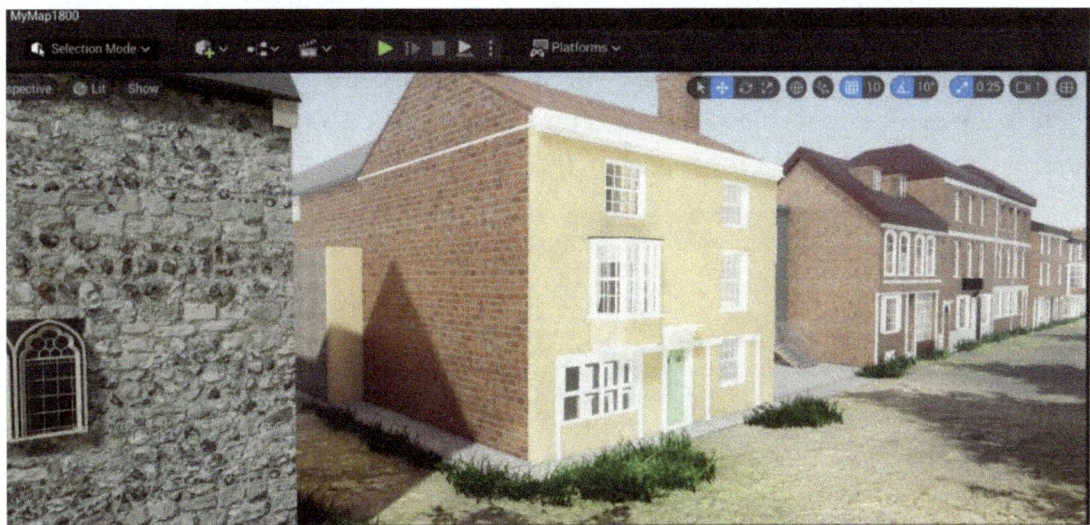

Figure 7-42. *Virtual Cities – Winchester 1800s' 8 College Street with immediate buildings*

The Unreal Project file has been included in your lesson files and contains the 1400 level with the same street available as it was then, plus our newly constructed Steventon Rectory level. The latter was imported to the Virtual Cities – Winchester project using the Migrate command. This process takes the level and all associated assets and copies via pasting the data into the Content folder of the target project – in this case Unreal_Chapter7_Landscape2.

CHAPTER 7   STEP FOUR: ADDING CONTEXT

Note The shortened version of the name "Unreal_Ch7_S2" for the Unreal project icon is mostly due to the restriction of characters for naming. Therefore, when opening via the Epic Games Launcher, if you have downloaded this project file, you will see the shortened file name.

You can access the different Levels in two ways; the first method is by going to File and Recent Levels, where you will see the different Levels listed:

- MyMap1400
- MyMap1800
- Main (the Steventon Level)

The second method is via the Content Browser and finding where the Levels are stored, then double-clicking on the one you want to open. The Levels can be identified with the "mountain" style icon and bottom orange bar. Ensure you save any changes made to the current Level before opening up another Level. You will be able to see which Level you are in by checking the top left of the screen.

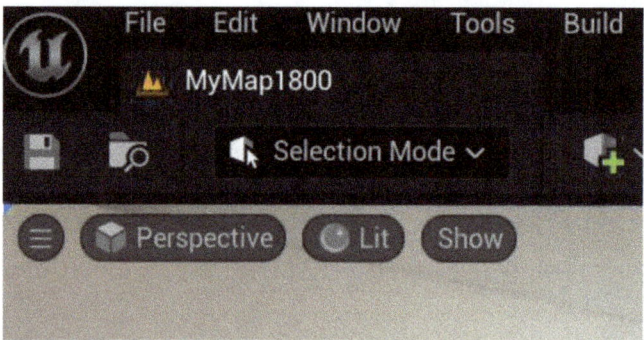

Figure 7-43. *The Level indicator*

Having the different Levels enables you to "portal" between the different levels, and therefore, in a sense, time travel, exploring spaces and how they looked in different times. The Level function also enables the user to portal to different places of the same period, which is what we will create with the Steventon Rectory and Winchester 1800s' 8 College Street. It would not be possible to do this between separate external projects.

- Level "MyMap1800" – Virtual Cities – Winchester 1800

  - What you will notice when you explore this Level are the more urban style features suitable for the Winchester City in the 1800 era, such as the dirt cobbled streets, the remaining city walls, and the additional landscaping assets, some of which we have touched on in the previous section. The streets were cobbled, as were any pavements that might have existed in Winchester in the 1800s. Tar and macadam (tarmac) were not available until the mid-1800s. You will also see the 1800 map we are working with if you hide the Landscape object and the extent of the work required for Virtual Cities – Winchester for the 1800s and 1400s.

- Level "MyMap1400" – Virtual Cities – Winchester 1400

  - You may not need to use this Level for this exercise, but you might want to explore to see the space around College Street before 8 College Street was built. You will be able to see a range of typical medieval houses along Kingsgate Street (right angle to College Street and away from the city) and the castle walls on this side of the city.

- Level "Main" – Steventon Rectory migrated level

  - This is your level that you created as a Project in the previous section.

You can create new blank Levels to try out different lighting, modelling, and maps. I call them practice zones, knowing that you are not damaging aspects of the working Levels. It is good practice to keep them all in the same folder in the Content Browser, i.e., a Levels folder for ensuring they are not accidentally deleted when removing content and saves you from searching through different folders to find the right Level.

For this section's exercise, you will work through creating more detail for 8 College Street and its environment, setting up the Drawing Room in 8 College Street where Jane and Cassandra will eventually be having their conversation, and the portal for going to Steventon Rectory's Drawing Room. You can then also practice creating a portal to see the same space in 1400 Winchester. 8 College Street has a few details already added, i.e., the same as you have done with Steventon Rectory regarding interior structural detail such as panelling.

CHAPTER 7   STEP FOUR: ADDING CONTEXT

We will also add 1800s street furniture and place these in appropriate places to make the streets feel more authentic. During the 1800s, street furniture would probably consist of essential items such as gas lamps, drinking fountains, and possibly milestones. Benches might be common in public squares or parks, while bollards and barriers would be used to manage traffic and pedestrian flow (Artform Urban Furniture, 2022; Historic England, 2022). Personally, I am a great believer in not spending time building items that other people have already created really well. Therefore, as with the windows, candle sconces, and doors, these objects may be able to be sourced on sites such as Fab, Sketchfab, and other 3D Commercial Library sites. Most of the Material and Textures sites also provide models; one of these sites I have used for many years is Turbosquid. You can find the link to Turbosquid as Link 4 in the Documentation Glossary.

We will approach this exercise with as much historical accuracy as possible in mind, using archival references and material cues typical of the Georgian and Regency periods. The aim is to introduce practical workflows for asset creation, texture preparation, and effective placement within the environment.

Table 7-2 is a list of items that should be considered for the Winchester scene; you are welcome to find or create your own examples, or use those included in the lesson files.

Table 7-2. *1800 period essential street items*

1800 Street Item	Description	Source
Street lighting	Gas lamps would be the primary source of illumination, enhancing safety and visibility at night	https://sketchfab.com/3d-models/old-lamppost-gas-lighting-fd8ad3eb4e0a47ab9a7013c4359f2c49
Drinking fountains	Providing access to clean water for residents and visitors, often made from materials such as granite or marble	https://sketchfab.com/3d-models/waterlow-park-drinking-fountain-3eda0d3de352426da6e5eff8af09c7cf
Benches	In public spaces like parks or squares, to provide opportunities for rest and socializing, possibly made from wood or cast iron	https://sketchfab.com/3d-models/bench-a47e206dd6a3406c8faefc6ab3296bb1

(*continued*)

Table 7-2. (*continued*)

1800 Street Item	Description	Source
Bollards and barriers	To help manage traffic, protect pedestrians, and delineate areas within the city	Create from scratch in a 3D program or Unreal – they are simple shapes
Milestones	In smaller cities like Winchester, milestones might be present along main thoroughfares to indicate distances to key locations	Create from scratch in a 3D program or Unreal – they are simple shapes
Horse troughs	Used for watering horses, reflecting on the use of horse-drawn carriages, buses, and cabs	Create from scratch in a 3D program or Unreal – they are simple shapes

8 College Street Drawing Room Interior

We will start with making sure the Drawing Room is completed in a similar vein to Steventon and add a few period items of furniture. Currently the room looks like Figure 7-44.

Figure 7-44. *The Drawing Room at 8 College Street*

CHAPTER 7   STEP FOUR: ADDING CONTEXT

As you can see, the panelling has already been created, a fireplace mantle and wall cupboard; the materials have been added, but you still need to add candle sconces, pictures, and a few items of furniture to make it look like a drawing room that Jane and her sister Cassandra would be in.

Rooms of the period were not overly furnished, so you do not need to add too many items. I suggest the following:

- A sofa/day bed
- A small table with a couple of chairs
- A writing desk for Jane
- A bureau
- A couple of chairs to be beside the fire
- A clock of some description, maybe a small grandfather clock

Similar to the street furniture, the above items of furniture need to be sourced or created. There are a few items of furniture included with the lesson files which may help.

The following images show the room with the above items added with a few extras to make it look more lived in by Jane and her sister.

Figure 7-45. *The Drawing Room with the added furniture items by the window*

CHAPTER 7   STEP FOUR: ADDING CONTEXT

Figure 7-46. *The Drawing Room with the added furniture items by the fireplace*

Figure 7-47. *The Drawing Room with the added furniture items by the door to the hall*

The candle sconces and picture frames can be used from the Steventon model, with the portraits changed and possibly also resized. All the furniture items have been collated in the Outliner under Furniture, with each object stored under its own subfolder. This will make it easier to hide objects as you work around the room if required.

CHAPTER 7   STEP FOUR: ADDING CONTEXT

Copying Content from One Level to Another

1. To copy content from the Steventon Rectory level, go to the Level that has the information you need.

2. Find the content in the Details Panel.

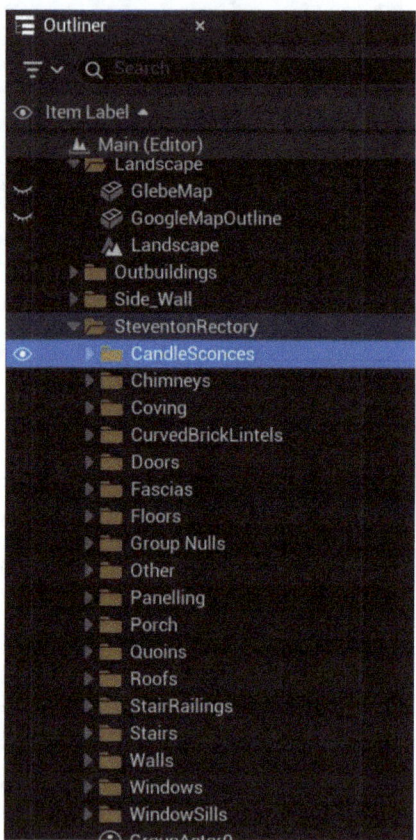

Figure 7-48. *Details Panel – Steventon Rectory and Candle Sconces subfolder*

3. Right-click on the content you want to copy; make sure you have all the information by right-clicking and choosing Select/All Descendants. All the components in the folder will be selected.

4. CTRL-click to add the CandleSconces folder; right-click and choose Edit/Copy.

5. Now go back to the 1800 Level you want the content to be in.

CHAPTER 7   STEP FOUR: ADDING CONTEXT

6. In the Details Panel, choose the folder in which you want to copy the information.

7. Right-click and choose Select/Edit/Paste and you will see the CandleSconces folder now in the 1800 Level.

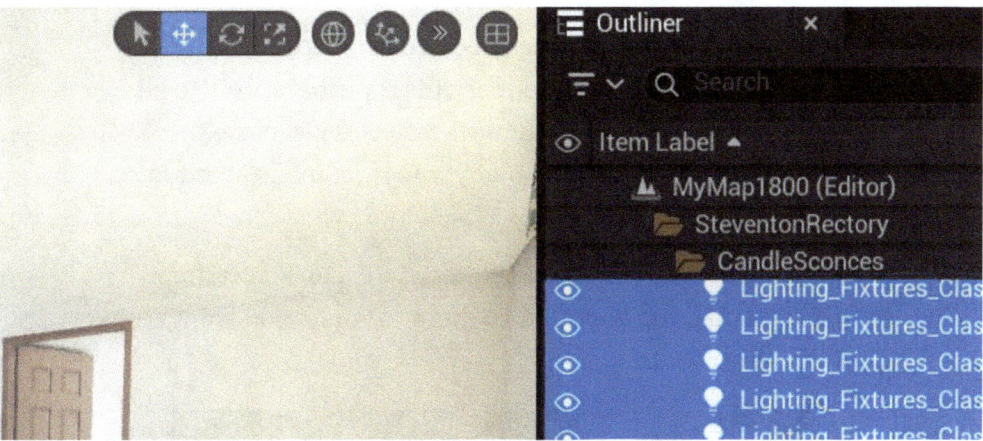

Figure 7-49. *The Copied content now in the 1800 Level*

8. You will now need to position the candle sconces in the Drawing Room; their imported content will obviously be in a different place. Therefore, while all selected, look in the Top view to see where they are located and move them closer to 8 College Street. In a Front or Side view, you can then make sure they are at the right height and right angle to the room.

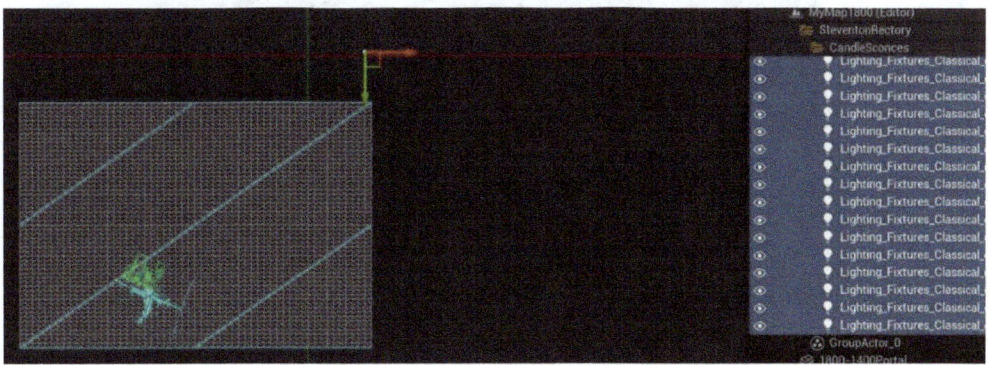

Figure 7-50. *Finding where the imported candles are placed*

9. You will also notice that the scene needs its lighting to be rebuilt (a red message on the screen). To do this, simply go to the "Build" command (top bar menu) and choose to "Build Lighting Only". Time for a coffee break while Unreal rebuilds the lighting. You will see its progress in the bottom right of your screen.

10. Once the Build of the lighting has been completed, you may have a message dialogue box appear; this is probably due to all the planting further away, but for now, you can just close the dialogue box. You can return to it anytime by going to Window/Message Log.

11. Now that the candle sconces can be seen, you can select them individually or in groups and move them to where you want them to be within the room.

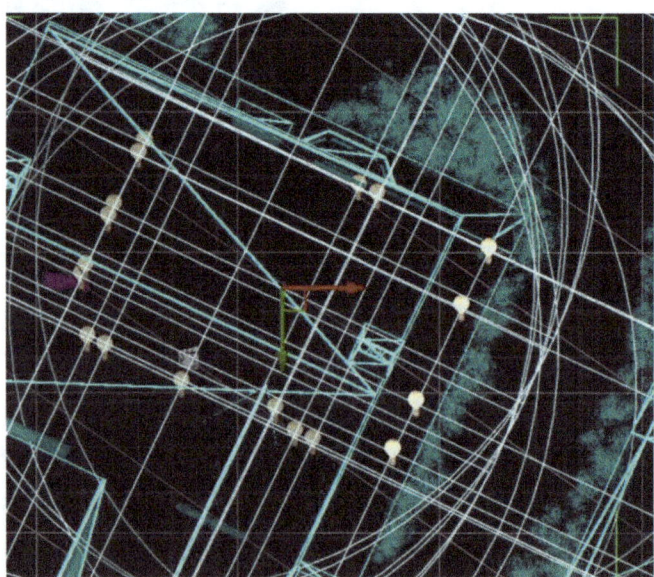

Figure 7-51. *Positioning the imported candles*

CHAPTER 7 STEP FOUR: ADDING CONTEXT

Note The candle lights have been attached to the individual sconces in the project file already, but if you want to attach other instances in the same way, do not use Group; instead use Attach To available on the right-click command. Choose the object that needs to be the child first and then right-click, choose Attach To, and then Attach Actor as Child.

You might find that trying to position each candle and light point is quite time-consuming. Therefore, it might be easier and quicker to put one into position and delete the others.

12. To lower the brightness of the light point, select and in the Details panel, change the Attenuation Radius to 10 and the Intensity Units to Lumens, and then change the Intensity to anywhere between 12 and 15, depending on how bright you want the room to be (Hakimi, 2024; Wuben, 2023).

13. To add the Picture Frame, repeat what you did before, or copy across the content, or create a new Frame and Picture using a different method called Voxel Boolean:

    - Create two Box models, one smaller than the other which you will use to subtract from the larger box.
    - Make sure they are the size you want them to be and can see them in the room for gauging the size.
    - In Modelling Mode still, select the Voxel command.
    - Make sure you have both objects selected; otherwise, Voxel Boolean will be grayed out.
    - Click on Voxel Boolean and you will have your new picture frame.

14. Find a new historical painting/image and import to your Content Browser.

15. Click on the Texture and right-click to "Create Material".

16. Create a rectangle to fit the frame.

17. Apply the new material "HistoricPainting1" to the new rectangle.

18. Once happy with the sizing, make the picture a child of the frame for easy positioning.

Feel free to add other objects if you want to, always making sure they are appropriate for the time period. Your drawing room may look like Figure 7-52 once you have finished.

Figure 7-52. *The completed drawing room scene*

Adding Street Furniture to College Street

To fully immerse the scene's visitors in the historical environment of Winchester, it is essential to go beyond buildings and focus on the everyday details that brought streets to life as previously mentioned. Street furniture such as horse troughs, bollards, lampposts, benches, and signage are crucial visual cues that anchor a scene in its correct time period. The next segment outlines the process of designing and integrating street furniture into your Unreal Engine scene, beginning with a step-by-step guide to creating and placing a horse trough, drinking fountain, and cast-iron bollards.

I usually create 3D models in 3DS Max or Cinema 4D and take them into Unreal Engine as FBX models; therefore, my modelling skills in Unreal Engine have not really been tested that hard – the same may be for you, but it is worth seeing what can be achieved with the toolsets available. If you are not happy with the result, you can either use my models, purchase online, or create in an external program.

Creating a Horse Trough

1. For the Trough, go to Modelling Mode and choose Box and resize to a suitable length and width for a couple of horses to drink from.

2. Do not worry about rotating to suit the street yet; it will make it easier modelling all the components at the angle the shapes come in at.

3. In the Create panel, now choose Capsule and align it with the top of your box so that it runs along the length of the trough. It will be easier to rotate at 90 degrees if you have the Rotation Snap set at 90 degrees (top right of window).

4. The Capsule should be half buried in the Box.

5. Select the Box and then the Capsule.

6. Go to Model set of tools and choose Boolean. The Capsule will have cut the trough to form the basin of the trough.

7. Next, create a Box, or sphere, and create the first "foot" stand of the trough. Once happy with its shape, copy and paste three times (or duplicate – duplicate will mean that if you change the shape of one, the duplicates take on those changes. Copy/paste creates independent shapes).

8. Find or create suitable materials for the trough and feet. I have tried to make my trough look like hewn stone.

Figure 7-53. *The trough so far*

9. Next is the Water Pipe. I have made the water pipe from a series of Torus shapes and Cylinders with a Sphere for the cap.

10. Create a tallish Cylinder (mine is 0.5 height) and place at the end of the trough. Diameter is approximately 0.12 for X and Y.

11. Create a copy of the Cylinder; resize the length (I have X: 1.2, Y & Z: 1.0)

12. Create a copy of the second Cylinder and make it smaller in diameter.

13. Create another copy of this smaller version. These smaller diameter Cylinders will be used as Boolean objects to make the Cylinder a tube. Hide the second copy for now.

14. Create a Torus so that it sits at the base of the tall vertical Cylinder (X & Y: 0.13, Z: 0.2).

15. Create a copy and move it toward the top of the Cylinder.

16. Create a copy and rotate 90 degrees and move to the end of the shorter horizontal Cylinder.

17. Create a sphere and place it at the top of the vertical Cylinder (X, Y & Z: 0.13).

18. For the Pumping Handle, a very basic set of Capsules and Boxes were resized to look like Figure 7-54.

Figure 7-54. *The Basic Water Pump progress*

19. What you need to do now is create the hollowness of the pipe for the water. Select the larger diameter horizontal Cylinder and the smaller Cylinder that is not hidden.

20. Go to Boolean and the larger pipe should now remain as a hollow tube.

21. Unhide the second copy of the smaller Cylinder.

22. Select the end Torus and then the unhidden Cylinder and choose Boolean again.

23. This second Boolean will have created a clean edge to tie in with the hollowed tube.

CHAPTER 7　STEP FOUR: ADDING CONTEXT

Figure 7-55. *The hollowed-out Cylinder and Torus*

24. Apply a material, possibly iron, or painted iron such as the one I have used, which is "rusty_metal".

25. The next step is to put water in the trough: Create a rectangle and place it over the trough and resize so that it covers the basin on each side but does not go through the outside walls of the trough.

26. Move it down so that the water is below the rim of the basin.

27. You will find a Water material in the Content Browser/Starter Content/Materials. I have used the M_Water_Lake option.

CHAPTER 7 STEP FOUR: ADDING CONTEXT

Figure 7-56. *The Water rectangle added to the trough*

28. The Vertical Cylinder and Base Torus could do with a base to sit on, which can be created with another Box and resized to fit. Or you could place grass around the base, hiding its connection to the ground.

29. Finally, making sure all the objects are in a folder (Horse Trough) in the Outliner, select the folder and right-click to choose All Descendants.

30. Once they are all selected, move toward the wall and make sure it is reasonably out of the way but accessible.

31. Having placed your trough, you might want to add two rings to the wall behind to hold the horses' reins while they are having a drink. I have used two Torus rings and two spheres as the connection pin to the wall. The material is m_Metal_Rust.

CHAPTER 7   STEP FOUR: ADDING CONTEXT

Figure 7-57. *The horse trough in place with the two reins rings on the wall*

Adding the Drinking Fountain

1. The model I am importing is free to download on a CC Attribution License. The Drinking Fountain has been created by Artfletch (n.d.) and is a photogrammetry model of Waterlow Park's Drinking Fountain.

2. The model downloaded is a GITF format and therefore can be imported directly into Unreal Engine.

3. This is what I did, and it came in without a problem other than being very large and upside down.

4. First of all, I rotated the Fountain 180 degrees so that it could be seen properly.

5. The fountain then needs to be scaled. On the Scale on each of the axis, change the amount down to 1 and then to 0.1; it should then be the correct size.

6. You can then move it into position. I have moved it to the wall facing 8 College Street.

Figure 7-58. *Repositioning the fountain model*

7. As you can see, some of the grass is growing through it. Go to Foliage Mode and the Select tool and zoom into this area and delete the grasses protruding or simply move the clumps to another area.

8. The Meshes are named Object8 through to Object13. From experience, it might be better to provide unique names that describe the part of the object.

9. The Fountain is exactly what I had in mind and fits well against the opposite wall to 8 College Street.

Creating or Adding the Bollards

In the 1800 Level, the Winchester College model has already been built to include a row of bollards, which you can see in the distance of College Street in Figure 7-59. You could reuse these, although they are one object rather than individual objects. As with the Drinking Fountain, you could import a bollard object, but as it is quite a simple basic shape, the Unreal tools would be good to use to gain more experience with modelling in Unreal and learn to understand their limitations and how they might be useful in adapting or modifying imported models.

CHAPTER 7   STEP FOUR: ADDING CONTEXT

Figure 7-59. *The Drinking Fountain imported in place, scaled and rotated Drinking Fountain*

According to research (Bailey Group, 2022), bollards were originally made of timber. In the late 18th century, old cannons were used on quaysides with the muzzle buried in the ground and the rounded "breech" forming the bollard for rope tying. There were more intricate bollards created late 19th century, mostly made from cast iron (The City Gent, 2023), but for 1800s Winchester, it is best to use the remaining example found at the corner of Winchester Walk and Cathedral Street (Watson, 1998).

Figure 7-60. *Existing 1812 bollard in Winchester, UK (Watson, 1998)*

Ensuring historical accuracy is important for all objects created for embedding realism in your historical visualizations. It might take longer, but without doing the research, I wouldn't have known an 1812 bollard existed in Winchester and therefore have an example to follow. As you can see, it is a simple basic shape, which can be recreated either using a shape profile to revolve or a series of cylinders, torus, and spheres, similar to recreating the water pump for the Horse Trough. Or you could copy the vertical components of the trough pump and adapt to make it look like this bollard. There are often different ways to achieve an end result; there isn't a singular "correct" way, only what you find straightforward in how you want to use your skillset and tools.

Figure 7-61 shows my version which is included in the lesson files.

Figure 7-61. *The bollards situated outside 9 College Street*

Other Entities

In Table 7-2, benches and street lighting are listed; therefore, using either the models provided by the links, your own models, or the models included with the lesson files, place the additional objects to make the streets look more authentic for the time period.

Now that your scene is more or less ready, we can move on to making it possible to portal between the Drawing Room of 8 College Street to the Drawing Room of Steventon Rectory.

CHAPTER 7   STEP FOUR: ADDING CONTEXT

Creating the Portal Between 8 College Street and Steventon Rectory

Creating a portal to transition between levels in Unreal Engine 5.5 involves a few steps. The general idea is to set up a collision volume (your portal), and when the player overlaps it, the engine will load another level completely replacing the current one. Obviously, you will need two levels for this to work, which we have, but do remember this if you are starting a different project.

There are two methods for doing this:

1. **Open Level:** Replaces the current level with a new one
2. **Level Streaming:** Loads/unloads levels while staying in the same persistent world

We will be using the first method as the most appropriate for creating a portal to Steventon. Below is a step-by-step guide to create your portal using this method. After this guide, you will find the method for Level Streaming in case you would like to explore how this method works.

There are many tutorials online that demonstrate how to create special effects for your portal, which can be quite effective if you are creating a game. For this project, the idea is to be the visitor and walk through a door to see a scene, with the door generally open in the scene. You can experiment with an additional effect of the door opening if you wish; there are YouTube videos that explain how to do this. For this project, we will rely on doors already open.

Step-by-Step Guide for Creating an Open Level Portal (Simple Portal System)

1. Open the Level Blueprint.

    (If you do not know how to do this, if you are new to Unreal, it is the icon at the top of your working window in between add to project and cinema icon.)

2. The next step is to add a teleport trigger so that when you trigger, it will teleport you to another location: Create a Trigger Volume and place in your scene, i.e., where you want to enter the room.

CHAPTER 7   STEP FOUR: ADDING CONTEXT

(You will find Trigger Volumes under Add to Project/Volumes. You can also find it under Place Actors in the Place Actors panel if you have this open.)

3. Resize and reposition it to create a portal doorway. For this project, it has been placed in the doorway of the Drawing Room of 8 College Street.

4. Rename your Trigger Volume to "TriggerVolumeToMain" so that you will recognize this from any other TriggerVolume created as being the one to use for this portal.

5. Make sure your Trigger Volume is selected in Outliner.

6. Go to the open Level Blueprint and right-click in the Event Graph area and you will see "Create a Reference to the Trigger Volume". Go to (don't click) the "Add Event for Trigger Volume to Main" and expand the arrow.

7. Expand Collision.

8. Click "Add On Actor Begin Overlap". This node will now appear in your Level Blueprint.

9. Drag a link out of the "On Actor Begin Overlap" right output and type in Teleport.

10. The Teleport node is added to the Blueprint.

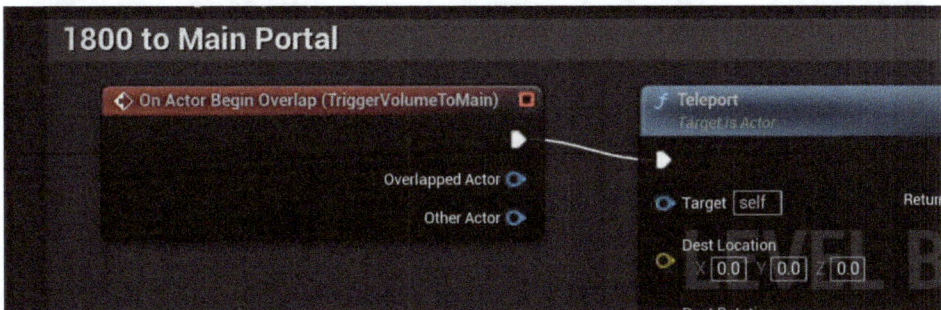

Figure 7-62. *The "On Actor Begin Overlap" node output to Teleport node*

513

CHAPTER 7   STEP FOUR: ADDING CONTEXT

Under the Teleport, you can see it says Target "self". This means that the target is self, not a third-person character. We want to teleport ourselves, not the trigger volume. To do this, we need to create a character actor:

1. Create a basic character actor by going to Add to Project.

2. Expand "Basic" and click Character Actor.

3. Rename Character Actor to "CharacterActorToMain".

4. Place near the Trigger Volume.

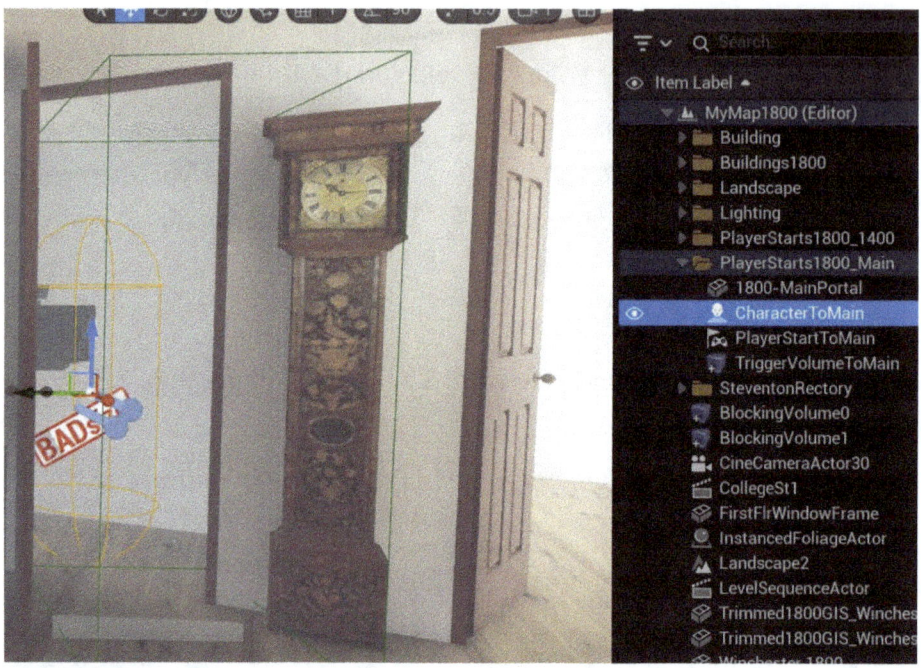

Figure 7-63. *8 College Street Drawing Room doorway with CharacterActorToMain and TriggerVolumeToMain in place*

5. With the CharacterActorToMain selected, go to the open Blueprint and drag a link from the Target in the Teleport panel.

6. Type in Get Player Character.

7. The Get Player Character node will appear already connected to the Target in the Teleport node.

CHAPTER 7   STEP FOUR: ADDING CONTEXT

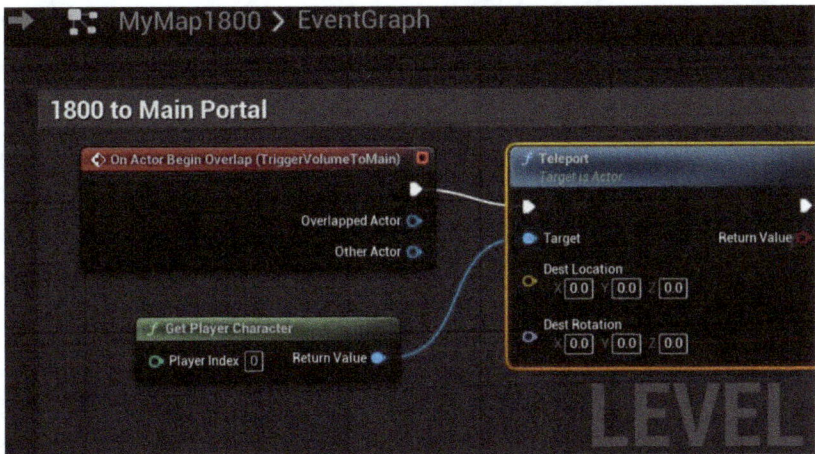

Figure 7-64. *The Get Player Character node added and connected to Target*

8. Now create a Player Start actor: You can find the Player Start Actor in Add to Project.

9. Place and resize to fit around the CharacterToMain actor.

10. Rename to PlayerStartToMain.

11. It is not needed to be selected while working in the Level Blueprint but does need to be in the scene.

12. Next, from the far side of Teleport, drag a link out and type in "Open Level (by name)".

13. The Node will appear. Where it says "Name" in a box field, add the name of the Level you are going to, i.e., Main, which is the Steventon Level.

It is useful and good practice to add a comment box to the set of Nodes, especially here with what is similar/same set of Nodes:

- Select all the Nodes that create the 1800 to Main portal and in the graph.

- Right-click and type in Add Comment.

- A slightly transparent box will appear and prompt you to write the "comment". Here I have used 1800 to Main Portal.

- Click Compile; there should not be any errors if all the Nodes are connected.

515

CHAPTER 7 STEP FOUR: ADDING CONTEXT

Before trying out, go to the Main Level and repeat for its own Level Blueprint and add the Trigger Volume, the Player Start Actor, and the Character Actor, making sure to give them a name that will be different to the 1800 actors. I have used "TriggerVolumeTo1800".

Return to the "MyMap1800" Level. Now you can click the Play button at the top of your screen, and the screen should go through to the Steventon level so that you can explore the scene there. When you click Stop, you should return to your MyMap1800 Level.

Figure 7-65. *The portal view into Steventon Rectory Drawing Room from 8 College Street Drawing Room in Winchester*

Note The Character Actor and Player Actor should not be inside the Trigger Volume, but slightly behind. The Character Actor object (a capsule) sits within the larger Player Start Actor capsule. Both sit in the doorway of each Level's drawing room. As you will be a "virtual visitor," there is no need for a 3D modelled character, i.e., third-person object; "you" will just walk into the room and explore.

For the 1800 Drawing Room to Steventon Drawing Room to work, it has to be the first entry in the Blueprint; even if the links are not attached, the other portal, i.e., 1800 to 1440, would take still take precedence. Hence, you will see in the Level Blueprint that 1800 to Steventon is the first Nodes section. Therefore, make sure that the Steventon Node set is in front of the 1800 to 1400 Node set as in Figure 7-66.

Figure 7-66. *MyMap1800 Level Blueprint showing the 1800 to Main (Steventon) is the first set of Nodes*

You will be working on perfecting how to return to the original level in a future Virtual Cities – Winchester book, but for this exercise, if you right-click on the CharacterActorToMain and choose Snap View To Object, you will see the Drawing Room view again rather than trying to navigate back to this view.

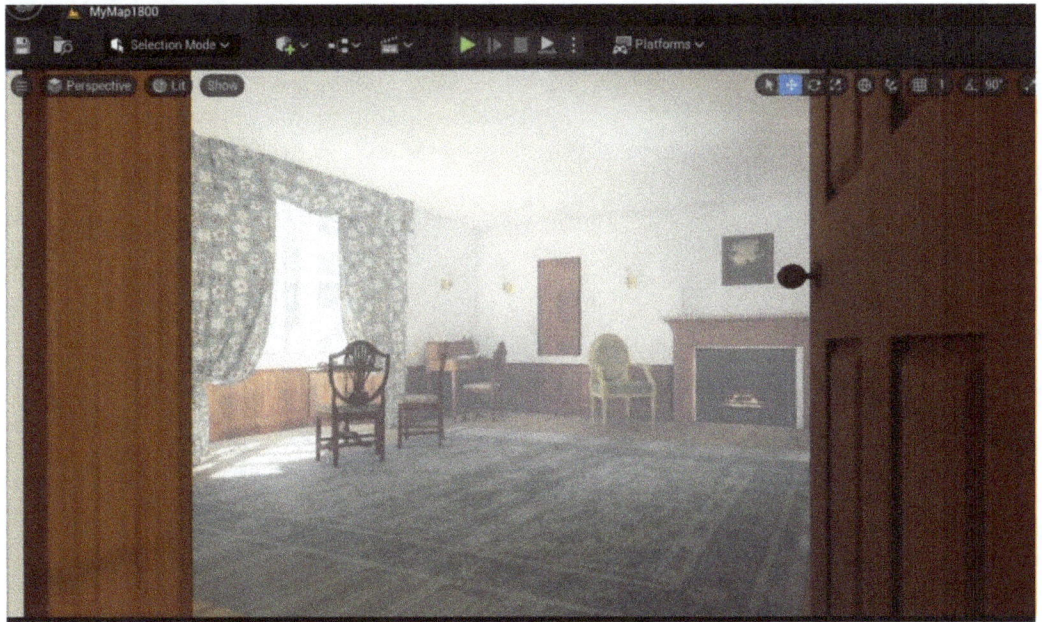

Figure 7-67. *8 College Street Drawing Room view*

The Open Level method works well for scene jumps and historical "leaps" as we are doing in Virtual Cities – Winchester, and for making storytelling engaging. You can also create a reusable blueprint, which is shown below.

Step-by-Step Guide to Create a Reusable BP_Portal

1. **To Create the Blueprint Actor:**
   - Right-click in the Content Browser.
   - Select Blueprint Class ➤ Actor.
   - Name it: BP_Portal.

2. **Add Components**
   - Open the BP_Portal.
   - In the Components panel:
     - Add a Box Collision ➤ name it PortalTrigger
     - Add a Static Mesh (optional, for visual portal)
     - Adjust the shape/size as needed

3. **Expose the Destination Level Name**
   - In the Variables panel:
     - Click + Variable
     - Name: TargetLevelName
     - Type: String
     - Make it Instance Editable and Expose on Spawn (this allows you to change the target level per portal in the Details panel)

4. **Blueprint Logic (Event Graph)**
   - Drag PortalTrigger into the graph.
   - Right-click ➤ Add Event ➤ OnComponentBeginOverlap.
   - Drag off the "Other Actor" pin ➤ Cast To YourCharacter.

CHAPTER 7   STEP FOUR: ADDING CONTEXT

- Then add Open Level (by Name) and connect it.
- Use the TargetLevelName variable as the input.

5. **Place in the Level**

- In either MyMap1800 Level or Main Level, drag in BP_Portal.
- In the Details panel, set TargetLevelName to
  - "Main" (in Winchester)
  - "MyMap1800" (in Steventon)

You now have bidirectional portals using one reusable Blueprint.

There is another method that enables both levels in the same world, for example, walking through a door or elevator and the environment changes without loading screens. It can be useful for a large structure such as a castle tower with floors created as sublevels. This method is provided as a guide below.

Method Overview for Level Streaming (Advanced/ Seamless Transition)

- Create a Persistent Level.
- Add Level1 and Level2 as Streamed Levels in the Levels window.
- Place a trigger box.
- In the Blueprint, use Load Stream Level or Unload Stream Level when overlapping the trigger.

We will cover Level Streaming in more depth in the next book.

Note   Remember that Level and asset/object names are case sensitive; therefore, if your scene is not teleporting, it is worth checking your names.

519

CHAPTER 7   STEP FOUR: ADDING CONTEXT

Section Summary

Congratulations, you have created time travel! No, really. What you have achieved here is something remarkable. You have worked your way from a completely blank Unreal Engine project to building a historically inspired rural environment set in the late 1700s, anchored by a building that no longer exists, and then connected it to a second environment: an urban street in 1817 Winchester. You have now made it possible to move between these two spaces virtually, between times, places, and contexts. That is no small feat.

If you are used to games or game design, the idea of jumping between levels might feel familiar. But what sets your work here apart is that these environments are based on real places and real histories. That brings its own challenges, particularly when it comes to research, accuracy, and making interpretive decisions based on limited historical data. Still, you have navigated this with creativity and care.

Along the way, you have learned how to copy content between levels and use Unreal Engine's built-in modelling tools to create simple shapes. These skills may seem basic, but they are incredibly useful, especially for adding small structural elements or furnishings to your scenes without needing external modelling software. You have also experimented with adding "water" to objects, opening up new possibilities for incorporating rivers, ponds, or streams into future landscapes.

The process of creating portals between levels can feel daunting at first, especially as it involves working with Level Blueprints rather than materials for the first time. But you have now had some experience with key concepts like Trigger Volumes, Character and Player Actors, and aligning those actors correctly across different levels. You have also begun to understand how to manage landscape and building alignment by referencing shared objects and matching their location settings. On top of that, you have encountered two different methods of Level transition: Open Level and Level Streaming, providing you with the flexibility to choose what best suits future projects.

I will be honest: when I first set up portals in the *Virtual Cities – Winchester* project, it took me a few tries to get everything working properly. But the satisfaction of seeing it finally succeed made the effort worthwhile. If your portals did not work perfectly on the first go, don't worry, this is normal. Often it is just a small setting or instruction that has been missed or misunderstood. Take your time, double-check the steps, and trust the process.

In the next section, we will shift gears slightly. You will be working with the HBIM data itself, extracting it using Blueprints and Datasmith nodes and functions, and building a custom User Interface using Widget Blueprints to display this information onscreen. You will also begin crafting the memory-story that allows you to step back in time to Steventon Rectory from Jane Austen's 1817 lodgings in Winchester.

Capturing Historical, Social, and Cultural Context

This last section of Chapter 7 pulls together the last few chapters of learning and creating content. The first part is accessing the HBIM information that was built into the Steventon Rectory model in Chapter 6. We will do this by creating Blueprints, similar to the material Blueprints that you have worked with, but these will be to create a pop-up text box that pulls in the HBIM data we imported via Datasmith from Revit.

There are three elements in extracting and delivering this data to the viewport: a Widget Blueprint, a Heads-Up Display (HUD) Blueprint, and adding further nodes to the Level Blueprint. We will start with the Widget Blueprint, which is then referenced by further Blueprints that you will create.

This will be followed by the reason for engaging with the different buildings and time periods. We will put together a memory of Jane Austen, about her time with the family at Steventon Rectory, using the available information from written memories and letters and put it in a format that can be used as reference for enacting at a later date once Virtual Cities – Winchester has built the family as avatars.

The idea is to cover a memory that will capture the cultural aspects of both periods of time in a way that appeals to most visitors and age groups. The HBIM data will hopefully aid in developing an understanding of the difference in the materials used in building homes to how they are built today. The immediate landscape will also reflect on the differences, not just between city and rural but also in the changes to the landscape over time.

Beginner's Guide: HBIM Data Pop-up Panel in Unreal Engine
Overview

This guide will walk you through creating a pop-up panel that displays HBIM (Historic Building Information Modelling) enhanced data when clicking on objects imported from Revit via Datasmith. You will cover everything from setting up the project to creating the interactive UI.

CHAPTER 7   STEP FOUR: ADDING CONTEXT

Part 1: Project Setup and Preparation

Step 1: Enable Required Plug-ins

1. Open your Unreal Engine project.
2. Go to Edit ➤ Plugins.
3. Ensure these plug-ins are enabled:
   - Datasmith Content (should already be enabled if you imported via Datasmith)
   - UMG (Unreal Motion Graphics UI Designer)
   - Enhanced Input (for modern input handling)
4. Restart the editor if prompted.

Step 2: Verify Datasmith Import

1. In the Content Browser, navigate to your Datasmith import folder.
2. Look for your imported Revit assets.
3. Check that metadata is preserved by
   - Right-clicking on an imported mesh
   - Select Edit or double-click to open the Static Mesh Editor
   - In the Details panel, look for Datasmith User Data section
   - Verify that Revit parameters are listed here

Part 2: Creating the Pop-up Widget

Step 3: Create the UI Widget Blueprint

1. In the Content Browser, right-click in your project folder.
2. Select User Interface ➤ Widget Blueprint.
3. Name it WBP_HBIMPopup (WBP = Widget Blueprint).
4. Double-click to open the Widget Blueprint Editor.

CHAPTER 7   STEP FOUR: ADDING CONTEXT

Step 4: Design the Pop-up Panel

1. In the Widget Blueprint Editor, you'll see the Designer tab.
2. From the Palette panel (left side), drag these elements onto the canvas:

Main Structure

- Drag a Canvas Panel to the root (this should be automatic).
- Drag a Border onto the Canvas Panel.
- Drag a Vertical Box inside the Border.

Content Elements

- Drag a Text widget into the Vertical Box (for the title).
- Drag a Scroll Box into the Vertical Box.
- Drag another Vertical Box inside the Scroll Box (for data entries).

Step 5: Style the Pop-up Panel

1. Select the Border in the hierarchy.
2. In the Details panel, configure
   - Appearance ➤ Background Colour: Set to semi-transparent dark (R:0, G:0, B:0, A:0.8)
   - Appearance ➤ Brush ➤ Draw As: Box
   - Slot ➤ Size: Set to Custom, Size X (Width): 400, Size X (Height): 300
   - Slot ➤ Position: Set to center of screen
3. Select the **Title Text** widget:
   - Content ➤ Text: Set to "Building Information"
   - Appearance ➤ Font ➤ Size: 18
   - Appearance ➤ Colour: White

523

4. Name your widgets for easy reference:
   - **Border:** MainPanel
   - **Title Text:** TitleText
   - **Inner Vertical Box:** DataContainer

Step 6: Create Data Display Function

Creating the Custom Event with Map Input:

1. Switch to the Graph tab in the Widget Blueprint.
2. Create a new Custom Event:
   - Right-click in the Graph.
   - Search for "Custom Event".
   - Name it "PopulateHBIMData".
3. In the Details panel, click the + next to Inputs.
4. Name it "HBIMData".
5. For the Type, you need to
   - Set the type to String initially
   - Click the small arrow next to the Type drop-down to expand it
   - Look for Container Type options
   - Select Map
   - Then set Key and Value types to String
6. Create the data population logic:
   - From the Custom Event, drag out the execution pin (Exec).
   - Search for and add "Clear Children" node.
   - Connect it to the Data Container (you will need to promote this to a variable first).

7. Promote DataContainer to Variable.

    - Go back to the Designer tab.
    - Select the inner Vertical Box (DataContainer).
    - Click "Is Variable" check box in the Details Panel (top bar).
    - This allows you to reference it in the Graph.

Step 7: Creating the HBIMProperties1 Variable in the HBIMDataComponent

1. Create a new variable.
2. Name it "HBIM Properties1".
3. Set type using the same method above in steps 5–6 to create a String-to-String Map.
4. Return to the Graph tab.

Step 8: Getting Map Keys

1. Once you have the Map type set up, you should see

    - Map Keys node (gets all keys from the map)
    - Map Values node (gets all values)
    - Map Find node (finds value by key)

Note If you cannot see these nodes, try the following:

- Right-click in the Blueprint graph.
- Type "Map Keys" in the search.
- Make sure "Context Sensitive" is unchecked in the search box.

Step 9: Complete the Data Population Logic

1. After the Clear Children node, add a For Each Loop node:

    - Right-click and search for "For Each Loop".
    - Connect the Keys map from HBIMData to the Array input.

CHAPTER 7   STEP FOUR: ADDING CONTEXT

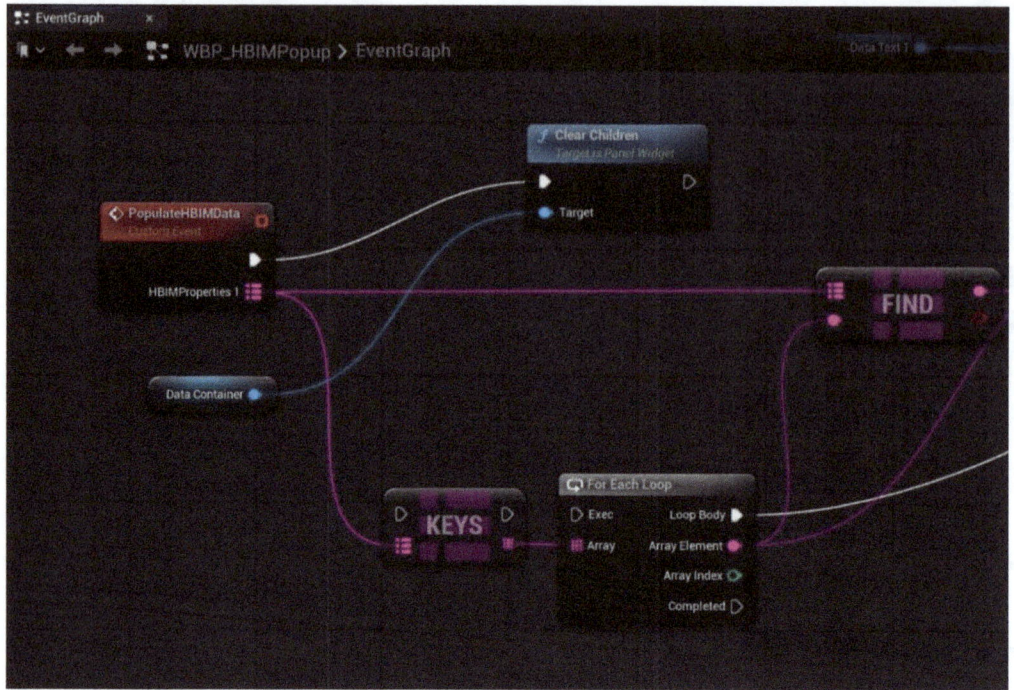

Figure 7-68. *Steps 1–9 configuration in WBPHBIMPopup EventGraph*

2. Inside the loop, create text widgets for each entry:

    - From "For Each Loop" – Loop Body pin, drag and add a Set Text node.

    - There are many Set Texts available; choose the one from the "Text" only category as in Figure 7-69.

CHAPTER 7   STEP FOUR: ADDING CONTEXT

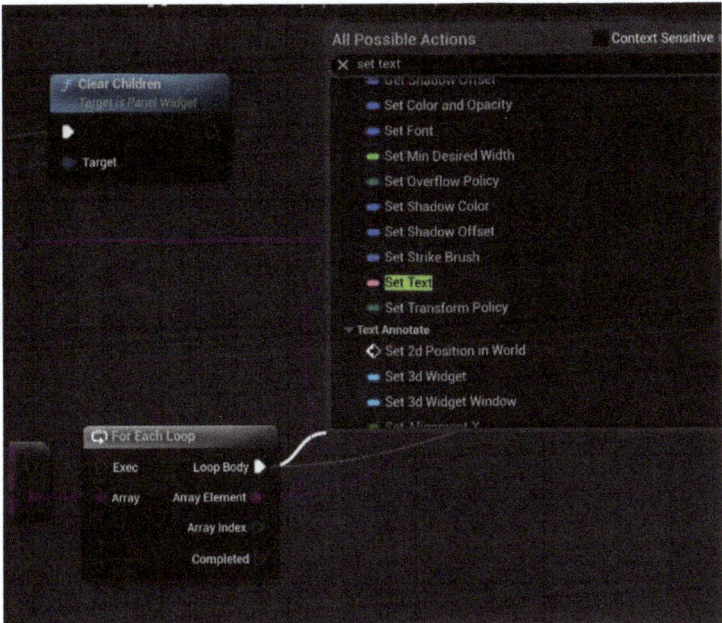

Figure 7-69. *Finding the right Set Text node*

3. Now create a Format Text node:

    • Right-click in the Graph.

    • Type in and add "Format Text".

    • In the Format field box, type in {Key}: {Value}.

    • Two keys will appear: one for "Key" and one for "value".

    • Drag the Key pin out to connect to the "Array Element" output in "For Each Loop" node.

    • Drag the Value pin out to the "Find" map's top output (Value String).

    • Drag the Result output pin from the "Format Text" node to the "Text" input pin in the "Set" node.

4. From the same "Array Element" in "For Each Loop" node, drag a connection to the "Key" input pin in the "Find" map.

CHAPTER 7   STEP FOUR: ADDING CONTEXT

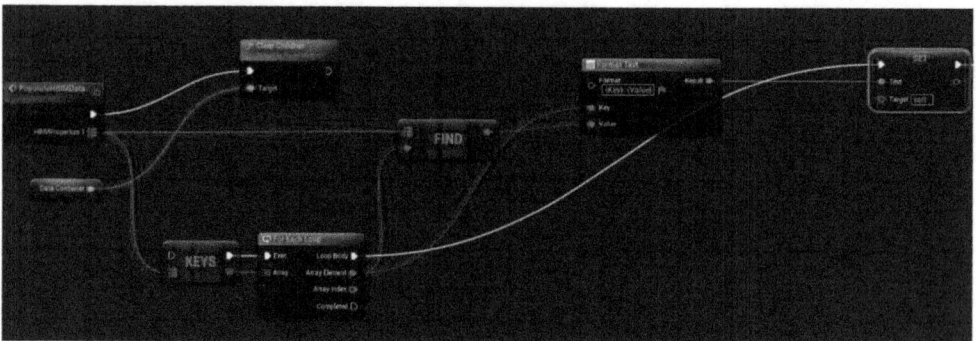

Figure 7-70. *For Each Loop node outputs and inputs*

5. Creating Text Widgets and Visibility:

   In Designer tab:

   - Type in the search "Text".
   - Add a "Text" widget to your "DataContainer" (Vertical Box).
   - Repeat a few times to create several.
   - Name them: DataText1, DataText2, DataText3, etc. Avoid special characters or spaces.
   - Set their "Visibility" to "Hidden" initially.
   - Make them "Is Variable" so you can access them in Graph.

   In Graph tab:

   - Add a "Set Visibility" node to make the Text Widgets visible.
   - Use "Set Text" to update their content.
   - Change "Set Visibility" to Hidden for unused ones.
   - You can create as many Text Widgets as you think you will need for the typical HBIM data display.

6. Connect the Target of Set Text to the now visible Data Text 1 variable.

7. Remember to compile at each stage. Compile and save.

At this stage, the flow should be the following:

- Loop gives you a key.
- Map Find uses that key to get the corresponding value from your map.
- Format Text combines key + value into "Key: Value" format.
- Set Text displays the formatted result.

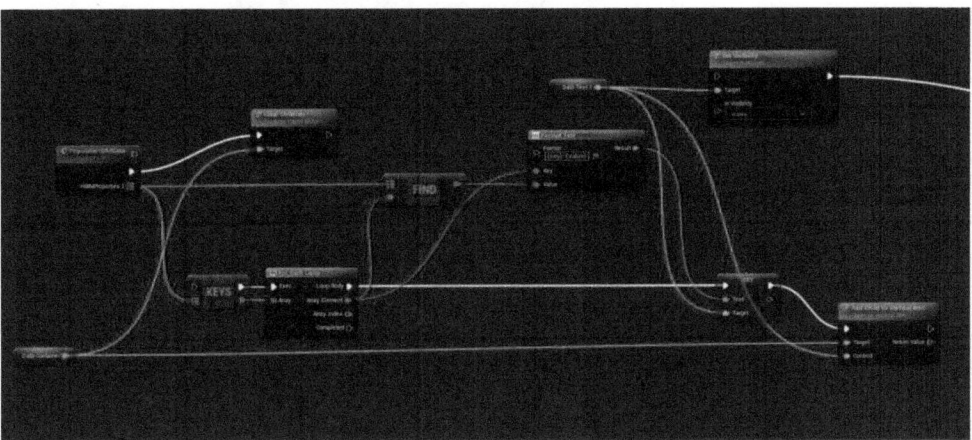

Figure 7-71. Progress stage after adding Text Widgets and setting visibility

To test what happens:

1. **Call the Event:** You need to trigger "PopulateHBIMData" somehow (maybe from BeginPlay, a key press, or another event).

2. **Check the Output:** Look at your "Data Text" widget to see if it displays the formatted key-value pairs.

3. **Verify Visibility:** Confirm the text becomes visible when the process completes.

Potential issues to watch for:

- The For Each Loop will only show the LAST key-value pair since each iteration overwrites the previous text.
- If you want to display ALL properties, you will need to link them instead of replacing.

Part 3: Creating the Interaction System

Step 10: Create Actor Component for HBIM Data

1. In Content Browser, click the Add button and create a Blueprint Class.

2. Choose "Actor Component" as parent class.

3. Name it "HBIMDataComponent".

4. Open the component blueprint.

Step 11: Set Up HBIM Data Storage

1. In the new "HBIMDataComponent" blueprint, switch to the Graph tab.

2. Create a variable in the left panel:

    - **Name:** HBIMProperties

    - **Type:** Map (String, String) the same as you have done previously.

    - Make it "Instance Editable" and "BlueprintReadOnly".

3. Create a function to extract Datasmith metadata:

    - Add a new Function called "ExtractDatasmithMetadata".

    - Add an input parameter: "StaticMeshComponent" (Object Reference).

    - Add an output parameter: call it "MetadataMap".

    - Make sure it is a "Map of String and String" as other examples.

Step 12: Implement Metadata Extraction

1. In the "ExtractDatasmithMetadata" function:

    - From "StaticMeshComponent" pin, drag and get a "Static Mesh" node.

    - From the output of Static Mesh, drag and search for "Get Datasmith User Data" node. This returns an array of user data objects.

The Get Datasmith User Data node returns a Map (dictionary) of user data, where each entry contains

- **Key:** The name/identifier of the user data
- **Value:** The actual user data object

You need to iterate through each of these key-value pairs to extract the metadata from ALL user data objects, not just one.

2. Right-click and find the "Get Datasmith User Data Keys and Values for Value" node.

3. Add this node and connect the Return Value from "Get Datasmith User Data" to the "Object" pin of this new node.

4. From the Return Value output of "Get Datasmith User Data", drag to find "Find Soft References to Object" (tick Context Sensitive to find it easily – the context-sensitive search is really your friend in Unreal; it shows you exactly what nodes are compatible with your current data types).

5. Connect the Exec output of the "Find Soft References to Object" node to the Exec input of "Get Datasmith User Data Keys and Values for Value".

6. From the Out Keys array pin of the "Get Datasmith User Data Keys and Values for Value", drag to type in to select a "For Each Loop" node.

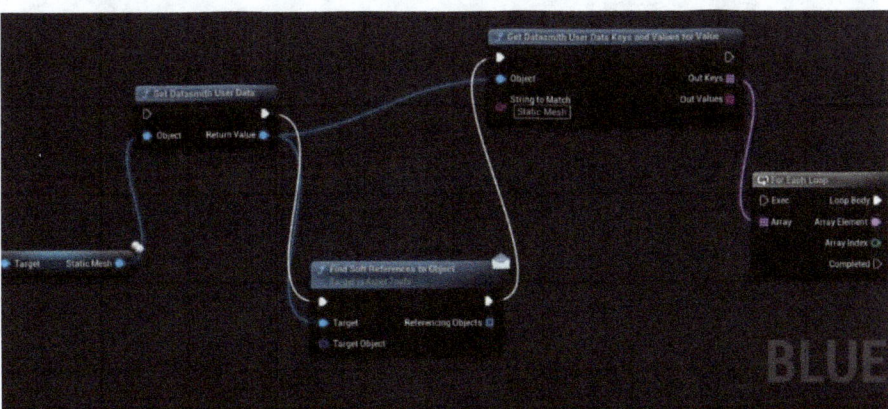

Figure 7-72. *Getting Datasmith data*

CHAPTER 7   STEP FOUR: ADDING CONTEXT

7. From the Array Element of the "For Each Loop" node, add a Map/Find node.

8. From the Loop Body pin, drag to add a Set Text node (use the same one as before, i.e., under the Text category).

9. From the Return Value output of Find, add a Format Text node.

10. In the Format text node, type in {Key}: {Value}.

    - Two keys will appear: one for "Key" and one for "value".

    - Drag the Key pin out to connect to the Return Value output in the "Find" node if it isn't already connected.

    - Drag the Result output pin from the "Format Text" node to the "Text" input pin in the "Set" node.

11. Connect the Text input of the Set Text node to the Result output of the Format Text node.

12. Compile and save.

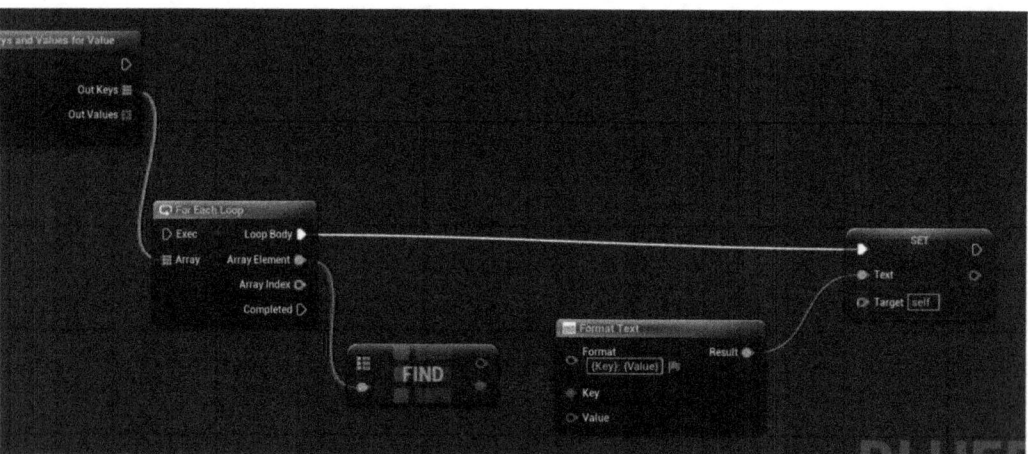

Figure 7-73. For Each Loop, Find, and Format Text nodes

Step 13: Create Click Detection Blueprint

1. Go to the Content Browser and use Add to create a new Blueprint Class based on Pawn or Character (Character has been chosen for this example).

CHAPTER 7 STEP FOUR: ADDING CONTEXT

2. Name it "HBIMViewer".

3. Double-click to open the new Blueprint.

4. Add a "Camera Component" for first-person view.

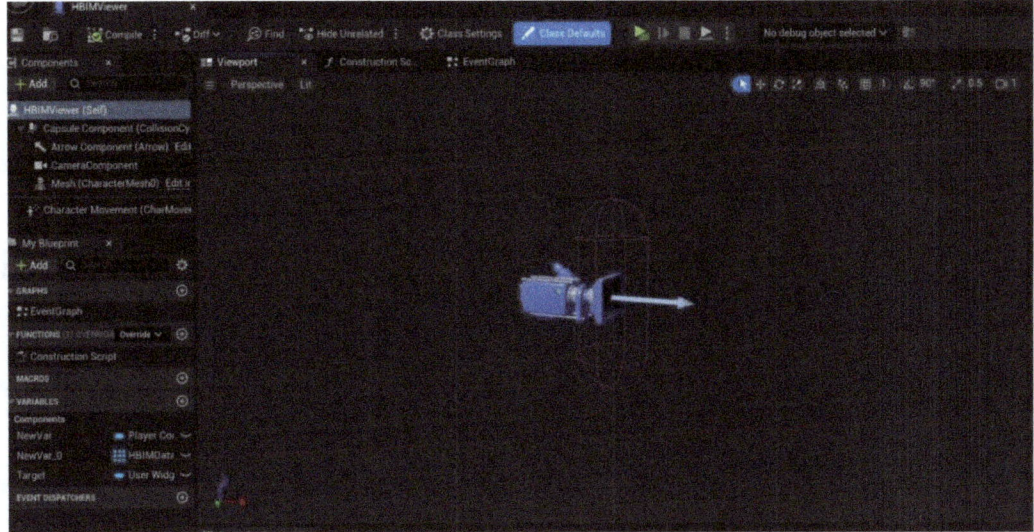

Figure 7-74. *HBIMViewer Camera Component*

Step 14: Implement Click Detection

1. In the "HBIMViewer" blueprint, add click detection:

   • In the Event Graph, add "Event Begin Play".

   • Add a "Show Mouse Cursor" node; connect with the "Event Begin Play node".

   • From the "Show Mouse Cursor" node's Target, drag and add a "Get Player Controller".

   • Connect the Target to Return Value of "Get Player Controller" if not connected.

   • Add an Enable Clicks Event from the Exec output of the "Show Mouse Cursor" node.

   • Connect the Target to Return Value of "Get Player Controller".

   • The Return Value should be connected to both of the new nodes.

CHAPTER 7   STEP FOUR: ADDING CONTEXT

2. Add click handling:

    - Right-click and add an "Event Left Mouse Button" event.
    - From the mouse event, add a "Print String".
    - Right-click and add "Get Hit Result Under Cursor by Channel".
    - Set "Trace Channel" to Visibility.
    - Connect Trace Complex to "Enable Click Events" output pin.

3. Check if clicked object has HBIM data:

    - From "Hit Result" output, get "Break Hit Result".
    - Expand the "Break Hit Result" and find "Hit Actor".
    - Drag from Hit Actor to add "Get Components By Class" node.
    - Use the Component Class drop-down to find "HBIMDataComponent".
    - Drag the Return Value array pin out to add a Set Value node.
    - Compile and save.

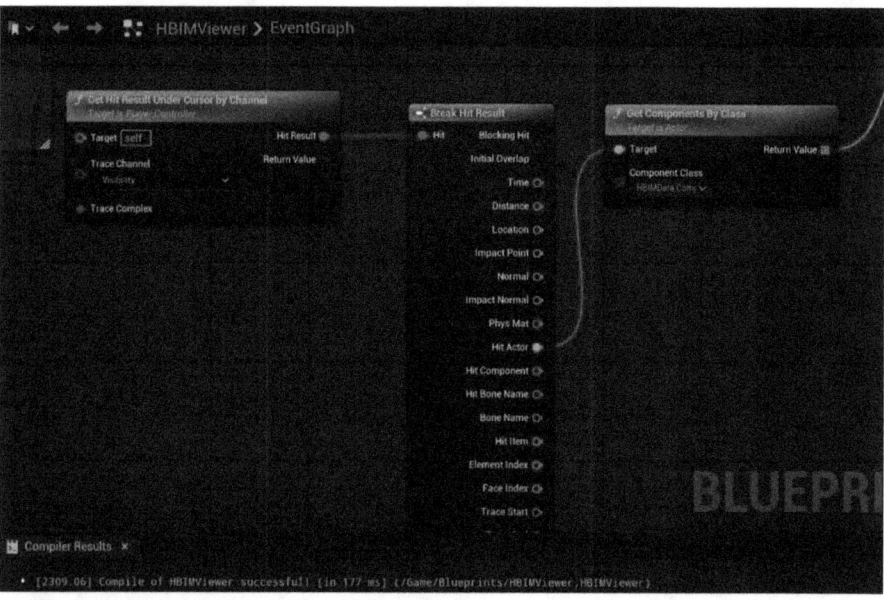

Figure 7-75. *Break Hit Result and Hit Actor to get components*

Step 15: Create Widget Manager

1. Create a new Blueprint Class based on Game Mode Base.
2. Name it "HBIMGameMode".
3. Add a variable for the popup widget:
   - **Name:** CurrentPopup
   - **Type:** "WBP_HBIMPopup" (Object Reference)

Step 16: Implement Pop-up Display Logic

1. In HBIMGameMode, create function "ShowHBIMPopup":
   - Input: HBIMData (Map of String, String)
   - Check if CurrentPopup is valid; if so, remove it from viewport.
2. Create new WBP_HBIMPopup widget:
   - Call PopulateHBIMData on the widget.
   - Add widget to viewport.
   - Store reference in CurrentPopup variable.
3. Create function HideHBIMPopup:
   - Check if CurrentPopup is valid.
   - Remove from viewport.
   - Set CurrentPopup to None.

Part 4: Connecting Everything Together

Step 17: Set Up the Game Mode

1. Go to Edit ➤ Project Settings.
2. Under Game ➤ Default Modes, set Default Game Mode to your HBIMGameMode.
3. Set Default Pawn Class to your HBIMViewer.

CHAPTER 7   STEP FOUR: ADDING CONTEXT

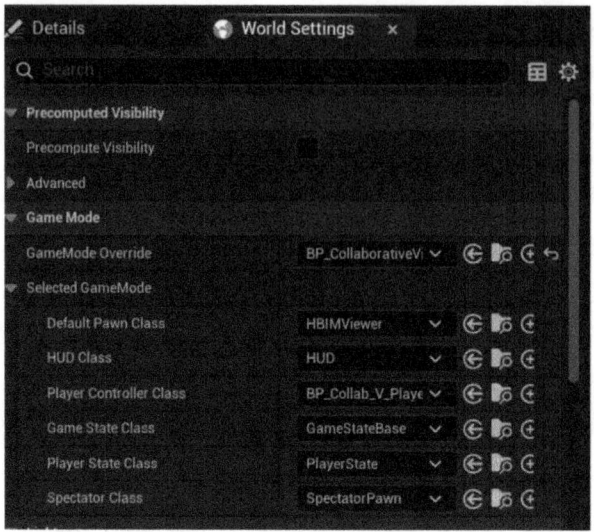

Figure 7-76. *World Settings tab (next to Details, bottom right)*

Step 18: Add HBIM Components to Your Revit Objects

1. For each imported Revit object in your level:

    - Select the actor in the World Outliner.

    - In the Details panel, click Add Component.

    - Add HBIMDataComponent.

    - The component should automatically extract Datasmith metadata.

CHAPTER 7   STEP FOUR: ADDING CONTEXT

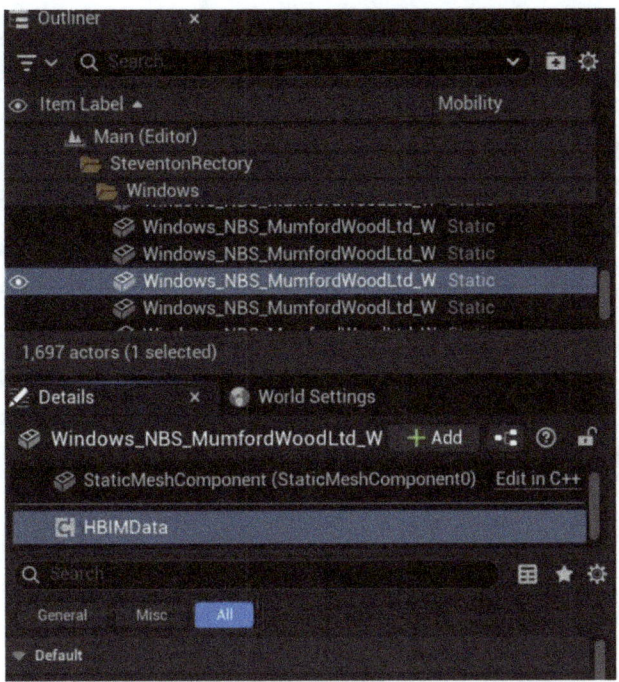

Figure 7-77. *Adding HBIMData Component to the relevant meshes*

Step 19: Complete the Click Handler

1. In your HBIMViewer blueprint, complete the click detection:

    • Add a "Show HBIMPopUp" node by typing this in the search box.

    • From this new node, drag the Target output to add "Cast to HBIMGameMode".

    • The Exec keys should also be connected.

    • From the "Set Value" node, connect the Exec output to the Exec input of "Cast to HBIMGameMode".

    • From the HBIMData array input of "Show HBIMPopUp", drag to get the "HBIMProperties1" variable.

    • From the Show HBIMPopUp Exec output, drag to "Add to Viewport".

    • Drag Target out add a 'Promote to Variable'

537

CHAPTER 7   STEP FOUR: ADDING CONTEXT

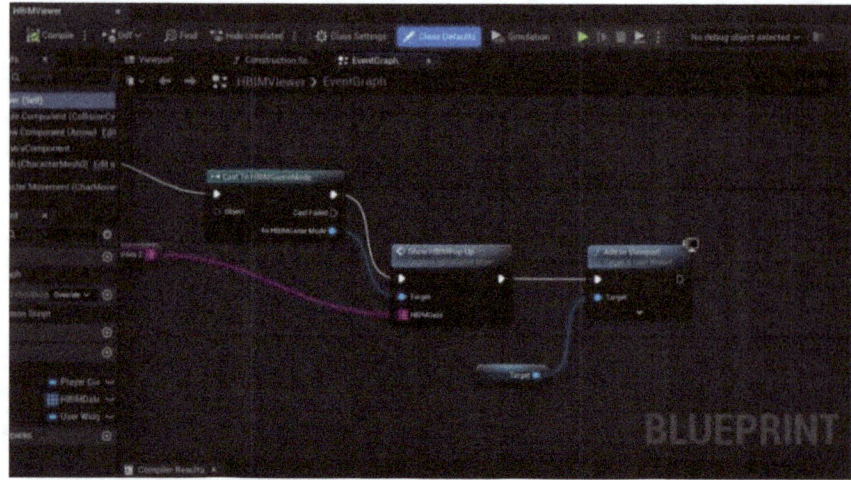

Figure 7-78. *Additional nodes for HBIMViewer*

Step 20: Add Close Button to Popup

1. Return to the WBP_HBIMPopup widget.
2. In the Designer tab, add a button to the top right of the Border.
3. Add Text to the button with "X" or "Close".
4. In the Graph tab, add an "On Clicked" event for the button.
5. Get Game Mode reference and call HideHBIMPopup.

Figure 7-79. *Data Pop-up Window result*

Part 5: Testing and Refinement

Step 21: Test the System

- **Play** your level.
- Click on imported Revit objects.
- Verify that the popup appears with correct HBIM data.
- Test the close functionality.

Step 22: Troubleshooting Common Issues
if Popup Doesn't Appear

- Check that HBIMDataComponent is added to clicked objects.
- Verify click detection is working (add print statements).
- Ensure Widget Blueprint is properly configured.

If no data shows in popup:

- Verify Datasmith metadata was imported correctly.
- Check that ExtractDatasmithMetadata function is working.
- Add debug prints to see what data is being passed.

If styling looks wrong:

- Adjust Border size and positioning.
- Check text formatting and colors.
- Ensure scroll box is properly configured.

Step 23: Advanced Enhancements
Add filtering:

- Create check boxes to show/hide certain property types.
- Filter by Revit categories (walls, doors, windows, etc.).

Improve visual design:

- Add icons for different property types.
- Use different colors for different data categories.
- Add background blur effect.

CHAPTER 7   STEP FOUR: ADDING CONTEXT

Add interaction features:

- Right-click for context menu.
- Highlight selected object.
- Show multiple objects' data simultaneously.

Summary

You have now created a complete system that

1. Detects mouse clicks on imported Revit objects
2. Extracts HBIM metadata from Datasmith imports
3. Displays the data in a professional pop-up panel
4. Provides user-friendly interaction

The key components are

- **WBP_HBIMPopup:** The UI widget that displays data
- **HBIMDataComponent:** Extracts and stores Revit metadata
- **HBIMViewer:** Handles user input and click detection
- **HBIMGameMode:** Manages popup display state

This system is extensible and can be enhanced with additional features like filtering, multiple selection, and advanced styling as your project requirements grow.

Creating the Story for the Time Travel to Steventon Rectory

As mentioned previously, to engage with Virtual Cities – Winchester example content, we are revisiting a scene in Jane Austen's last few months before she died at Winchester, in 8 College Street. The concept is that Jane and her beloved sister Cassandra are reminiscing memories of their time at Steventon Rectory with their parents and brothers. To ensure as much accuracy as possible for the story, the references used are from the memoirs and letters written by Jane and other members of the family.

In future, the intention is to also include realistic avatars of Jane, Cassandra, and other family members, but for now and the example for this book, we will simply write the story and provide a visual outline as reference.

The story needs to be an engaging story in order for "virtual" visitors to want to portal from 8 College Street to Steventon Rectory. Although it may be possible that our virtual visitors may just want to explore Steventon Rectory and walk around a building that unfortunately no longer exists. There are many Jane Austen fans across the world; therefore, being able to "visit" Steventon Rectory from wherever they are, would be a great opportunity for them. The work I have always been interested in and have crafted over the years, is creating buildings, and building story scenes, ambient sounds, and now technology is available to be able to build an avatar Austen family, all of which could result in an exciting and engaging reason for visiting virtually.

The question is – what story will we use that will be achievable? There are a couple of stories that may be possible.

We could talk through a memory of what the house looked like, rooms, etc., so that as visitors virtually visited and explored, they could still hear Jane's voice saying about each of the rooms. This would tie in nicely with the architectural aspects of the content that has been created, but to do this would mean each of the rooms would need to be modelled in detail, which is a little too time-consuming for the book.

We could make more of the card games and charades the family used to play of an evening after supper, which, from the description regarding a candle-lit table, probably means they were in the Dining Parlor.

We have added details to both the drawing rooms, so we need to find a memory that makes use of these rooms.

The following is an abbreviated extract from Ashton's (1967) *Parson Austen's Daughter* (pages 47–51) and would make a good scene as a memory by both Jane and Cassandra about their cousin Jane Cooper's wedding breakfast at Steventon Rectory. There would be many guests filling the rooms including the Drawing Room, therefore a choice of people to discuss among the memory telling by Jane and Cassandra at 8 College Street. Fashion, Christmas preparations, food, weddings, mourning, the cold winter, the naval officers, and the impending war with France all make good topics for cultural context and learning.

The Wedding Breakfast at the Rectory in 1792 for the wedding of Cousin Jane Cooper to a naval captain Thomas Williams. Doctor Cooper, Jane Cooper's father, had died on the day the wedding was initially set, so it was postponed for a few weeks. A

CHAPTER 7 STEP FOUR: ADDING CONTEXT

cold December morning, Revd George Austen, Jane Cooper's Uncle, married them at the church followed by the wedding breakfast at the Rectory. Cassandra was chief bridesmaid. A quiet wedding with very little white satin and very few lace veils because of the bride's recent mourning. Edward was in Kent with his wife and her first baby Fanny; Frank had not yet returned from his first voyage in the China seas. Young Charles had come up from the Naval Academy for his Christmas leave. A baby-faced boy, with a most-engaging grin. He was just in time for the wedding, and with him on the Portsmouth coach arrived a crowd of naval officers in all the glory of blue uniforms, gold epaulettes, laced waistcoats, and velvet socks to support Captain Williams. James had ridden over to help his father perform the service and made one of his long prosy speeches at the breakfast afterward. His wife had stayed at home, from the fact that she didn't want to be seen, may have been because she was heavily pregnant. Twenty-one-year-old Henry was down from Oxford. He sat with Madame la Comtesse de Feuillide (Eliza) laughing and whispering at something that nobody else could hear. Cassandra was 18 and Jane was 16.

This now needs to be written as a scene with Jane's and Cassandra's voice, leading from the drawing room in College Street to the drawing room in Steventon Rectory.

The following is a draft scene script that aims to capture the sisters' voices and create that portal effect from College Street to Steventon Rectory. It also aims at capturing the intimate conversation between Jane and Cassandra while creating a "portal" effect. The script focuses on

1. **Establishing the setting** at 8 College Street with the sisters in their familiar, comfortable dynamic

2. **Creating a natural transition** through memory and storytelling that takes visitors from Winchester to Steventon

3. **Incorporating all the historical details** from our research – the naval officers, family members, the mourning context, and the wedding breakfast atmosphere

4. **Using authentic voices** based on what we know of their personalities – Jane's wit and observation, Cassandra's steadiness and warmth

5. **Providing technical notes** for implementing the virtual experience

The script is structured to allow visitors to experience both the intimate sister relationship and the grand family gathering, while giving them reasons to explore the virtual Rectory rooms created. The dialogue naturally highlights specific details that could be interactive elements in virtual environment.

Jane and Cassandra: A Memory of Cousin Jane's Wedding – A Scene Script for Virtual Steventon Rectory Experience

Setting: The drawing room at 8 College Street, Winchester. Late afternoon light filters through the windows. Jane sits in her chair, looking frail but alert. Cassandra sits nearby with her needlework, though her hands have grown still as they talk.

JANE: *(gazing toward the window, a slight smile playing on her lips)* Cass, do you remember that December morning? When we had such a crowd at the Rectory for Cousin Jane's wedding breakfast?

CASSANDRA: *(setting down her needlework)* How could I forget? The coldest morning imaginable, and yet the house felt so warm with all those people filling every room. You were only 16 then but already observing everyone with those sharp eyes of yours.

JANE: Indeed I was! *(laughs softly)* Though I confess I was rather more interested in watching the naval officers than the bride herself. Such magnificent uniforms – all that blue and gold threading through our humble drawing room like exotic birds that had lost their way.

CASSANDRA: You always did notice the details others missed. I was so concerned with my duties as chief bridesmaid, ensuring poor Jane Cooper looked presentable despite her mourning dress. Very little white satin, as you'll recall.

JANE: *(voice taking on a storytelling quality)* Ah, but the drawing room... Cass, close your eyes and picture it with me. Can you see it?

[TRANSITION: The scene begins to shift, the modest Winchester drawing room fading as the grander Steventon drawing room materializes around them]

CASSANDRA: *(voice softer, more distant)* Yes... I can see it perfectly. The morning light streaming through those tall windows, and Papa moving between the guests with such dignity, ensuring everyone felt welcome despite the circumstances.

JANE: The poor dear bride, trying to appear joyful while still in half-mourning for Uncle Cooper. But Captain Williams – such a gallant figure! Do you remember how he kept glancing at her as if she were the finest prize he'd ever captured at sea?

CASSANDRA: *(chuckling)* And our Charles! Just arrived from the Naval Academy, that baby face of his trying so hard to look grown-up among all those seasoned officers. He was so proud to be included in their number.

JANE: *(with growing animation)* But the best entertainment was watching Henry with Cousin Eliza! Even at 21, he thought himself so sophisticated, whispering and laughing with Madame la Comtesse. The way they carried on, you'd think they were sharing state secrets rather than mere gossip.

CASSANDRA: While James made one of his interminable speeches. *(sighs fondly)* Poor James, always so earnest, so determined to say the right thing that he said far too much of it.

JANE: *(eyes sparkling with mischief)* And do you remember the naval officers' reactions? They stood so straight and polite, but I could see some of them fighting not to fidget. Captain Williams kept shooting glances toward his bride as if to say, "Surely this cannot go on much longer?"

CASSANDRA: The drawing room fairly hummed with conversation once James finished. Ladies comparing their winter preparations, the gentlemen discussing Napoleon's ambitions... and through it all, the servants moving like dancers, ensuring everyone's cup stayed filled despite the crowd.

JANE: *(leaning forward conspiratorially)* I spent half the morning tucked in that corner by the pianoforte, watching everything unfold like a play. The way Mrs. Lefroy kept adjusting her lace cap, how the youngest naval officer kept tugging at his waistcoat, the careful way everyone avoided mentioning Uncle Cooper's death directly...

CASSANDRA: You were already storing it all away, weren't you? Even then, I could see you cataloguing every gesture, every conversation for future use.

JANE: *(with a wistful smile)* Perhaps I was. Though I never imagined then how precious such ordinary moments would become. The simple joy of having our family gathered together, the house full of voices and laughter...

CASSANDRA: *(reaching for Jane's hand)* Edward with his new little Fanny, Frank still at sea but soon to return, Charles so eager to prove himself a man... We were all so young, so certain that such gatherings would happen again and again.

JANE: *(squeezing Cassandra's hand)* But they did happen again, dearest Cass. In a way, they're happening still. Here, in this quiet room, we can walk through every chamber of our dear Rectory whenever we choose. We can hear Papa's voice in the breakfast parlor, Mama's laughter in the kitchen, the boys thundering up and down those narrow stairs...

CASSANDRA: *(softly)* And cousin Jane, radiant despite her mourning dress, finally finding happiness with her Captain Williams.

JANE: Yes. In the end, love conquered mourning, didn't it? As it should.

[The Steventon drawing room slowly fades, returning to the simpler surroundings of 8 College Street, but somehow the space feels larger, filled with the warmth of memory]

CASSANDRA: *(after a peaceful pause)* Shall I ring for tea?

JANE: *(settling back in her chair with a contented sigh)* Yes, please do. And Cass? Thank you for remembering with me. It makes the past feel less past, somehow.

CASSANDRA: *(rising to pull the bell cord)* Always, my dear Jane. Always.

[End Scene]

CHAPTER 7   STEP FOUR: ADDING CONTEXT

Technical Notes for Virtual Experience

Visual Transitions

- Gradual fade from Winchester drawing room to Steventon drawing room as memory deepens.
- Subtle lighting changes to suggest morning light versus afternoon light.
- Crowd of wedding guests can be suggested through shadows and voices rather than full avatars initially.

Audio Elements

- Layered conversations and laughter during the wedding breakfast section
- Period-appropriate background sounds (clock ticking, fire crackling, distant church bells)
- Jane's voice becoming more animated during storytelling, Cassandra's remaining steady and warm

Interactive Opportunities

- Visitors can explore the drawing room while hearing the conversation.
- Details mentioned in dialogue (pianoforte, windows, furniture arrangement) can be highlighted.
- Option to "follow" the memory deeper into other rooms of the Rectory.

It is hoped that the above script will create a virtual experience that allows Jane Austen fans to "visit" Steventon Rectory through an immersive storytelling experience. In addition, allow those interested in the built information of Steventon Rectory access to the historic built elements through the use of the additional widget and blueprints.

Section Summary

This section marks an exciting milestone; it concludes the core modelling work needed to tell the story we want users to experience when they visit *Virtual Cities – Winchester*. The focus here has been on bringing Jane Austen's final months at 8 College Street to life, allowing visitors not just to step into her world in 1817 Winchester but also to access a powerful memory shared with her sister. That memory leads them back to Steventon Rectory and into a recreated scene from her cousin Jane Cooper's Wedding Breakfast, making time travel not just possible, but meaningful.

Alongside the storytelling, users also have the opportunity to access detailed information about the architecture itself: how the buildings were constructed, the materials used, when they were altered or demolished, and other historical building data embedded through HBIM in the original Revit models. This adds an additional layer of depth, giving those with an interest in architecture and heritage a way to explore the technical and historical detail alongside the narrative.

In this section, you have learned a great deal about working with Blueprint Classes, Blueprint and Widget scripting, and how to use nodes, functions, and variables to connect data and interface elements. Some of this has gone beyond the basics, but it has all been essential to successfully extract and display the HBIM data from your Datasmith model.

You have also had to engage in a fair amount of debugging, checking your Blueprints to make sure the flow and outputs are working as intended. In developing this section myself, I tried several methods for extracting Datasmith data and settled on the one that made the most sense for this project's needs. But it is clear that for larger projects, such as the full Winchester application which will eventually include over 75 buildings, we will need to continue researching the most efficient ways to extract and manage HBIM data at scale.

At this stage, you now also have a complete script for the memory scene, including the elements that help bring the storytelling moment to life. This is a great time to reflect on whether there are more details you would like to model or add to the rooms of Steventon Rectory to enhance the immersion.

In the next chapter, we will revisit both properties, particularly Steventon, armed with feedback from experts. I have sent floor plans and screenshots to professionals with expertise in Jane Austen's life and Regency/Georgian-era architecture. Their feedback may lead to rethinking room sizes, functions, window types, structural details, or even construction materials. It is also likely they will identify HBIM data fields that I had not considered, fields that matter more to heritage professionals, architects, or conservationists than to someone coming from a heritage visualization background like mine.

CHAPTER 7   STEP FOUR: ADDING CONTEXT

So the next steps involve listening to that feedback, reviewing the models in Revit, and making changes accordingly. It is all part of an iterative and collaborative process, something that lies at the heart of meaningful heritage interpretation.

Documentation Glossary

1. In creating your own Master Landscape material, there is an excellent tutorial by Epic Games which you can find here: https://dev.epicgames.com/documentation/en-us/unreal-engine/landscape-materials-in-unreal-engine

2. More about Edit Layers new feature adding Layers to your Landscape, enabling you to layer paint effects, can be found on the following Epic Games link: https://dev.epicgames.com/documentation/en-us/unreal-engine/landscape-edit-layers-in-unreal-engine

3. Epic Games has an excellent explanation and how to work with Landscape Splines: https://dev.epicgames.com/documentation/en-us/unreal-engine/landscape-splines-in-unreal-engine

4. Most of the Material and Textures sites also provide models; one of these sites I have used for many years is Turbosquid: https://www.turbosquid.com/Search/3D-Models/free

References

Ashton, Helen (1967) Parson Austen's Daughter. Collins, London
Bailey Group - Artform Urban Furniture (2022) The History of Street Furniture. March 2022. https://www.artformurban.co.uk/news/post/the-history-of-street-furniture.html#:~:text=Historically%20our%20streetscapes%20were%20enriched,firstly%20at%20Pall%20Mall%2C%20London [Accessed June 1, 2025]

Bailey Street Furniture Group (2022) What are the origins of bollards? Posted on March 15, 2022. https://www.bsfg.co.uk/What-are-the-origins-of-bollards [Accessed June 1, 2025]

Hakimi, David (2024) Lumens Calculator: How to Determine Total Required Lumens for Your Space. Insights by Alcon Lighting. https://www.alconlighting.com/blog/residential-led-lighting/how-do-i-determine-how-many-led-lumens-i-need-for-a-space/ [Accessed May 31, 2025]

Historic England (2022) From Lamp Posts to Litter Bins: The Stories Behind England's Street Furniture. Street furniture's deceptively simple, everyday functionality ensures the generally smooth operation of the public realm, as well as often providing subtle local character and style. The Historic England Blog, Historic England. Jan. 21, 2022. https://heritagecalling.com/2022/01/21/from-lamp-posts-to-litter-bins-the-stories-behind-englands-street-furniture/ [Accessed June 1, 2025]

The City Gent Feb (2023) Bollardology! Symbols & Secrets, Walking the City of London. https://symbolsandsecrets.london/2023/02/09/bollardology/ [Accessed June 1, 2025]

Wuben (2023) How Many Lumens is a Candle? Flashlight Knowledge, WubenLight Inc. https://www.wubenlight.com/blogs/flashlight-knowledge/how-many-lumens-is-a-candle [Accessed May 31, 2025]

Images

Prodiger, Michael (2023) Historic Picture in 8 College Street in Constable's Wivenhoe Park, Essex, the house is part of the landscape. *This picture was commissioned by Major General Francis Slater-Rebow, owner of Wivenhoe Park. ©Bridgeman (Image credit: Bridgeman Images).* https://www.countrylife.co.uk/luxury/art-and-antiques/the-english-country-house-as-seen-in-the-art-of-turner-dickinson-and-more-262407 [Accessed May 31, 2025]

Watson, Charles (1998) Historic England: Bollard At The Corner With Winchester Walk. Bollard at the corner with Winchester Walk, Cathedral Street. Image by Charles Watson (1998), published November 24, 2023. https://historicengland.org.uk/listing/the-list/list-entry/1378459 [Accessed June 1, 2025]

CHAPTER 7   STEP FOUR: ADDING CONTEXT

3D Models

"Waterlow Park Drinking Fountain" (https://skfb.ly/owT9Q) by artfletch is licensed under Creative Commons Attribution (http://creativecommons.org/licenses/by/4.0/). https://sketchfab.com/3d-models/waterlow-park-drinking-fountain-3eda0d3de352426da6e5eff8af09c7cf [Accessed June 3, 2025]

A Via Studio (n.d.) A Via Studio's Splined Mesh Tool – Fence Panel. Epic Games. https://www.fab.com/listings/f1a2bd89-f18c-4eee-8e11-a35a314bca65

CHAPTER 8

Step Five: Post-processing and Analysis

This chapter focuses on post-processing and refining the HBIM model, conducting further research via feedback on the Steventon Rectory model created, and assessing the structural integrity and preservation needs. The chapter adopts a problem-solving angle, addressing the challenges and considerations involved in the final stages of the HBIM process. The purpose is to emphasize the importance of quality control, historical accuracy, and research validation in the HBIM model. It prepares readers to critically analyze the outcomes of the reconstruction and ensure it is a model that can be used for conservation and preservation as well as engaging users in storytelling.

The chapter's first section covers how to refine the model created of Steventon Rectory, validating the researched information through the completed initial draft. It is always easier to gain opinion from visuals recreated from textual information, or sketches that present just one view. Being able to see a building in plan, elevation and 3D views allow more thorough validation of known facts. The section also takes you through the reimport process from Revit to Unreal to ensure work created in Unreal is not overwritten.

The second section is more theoretical than practical but equally important in assessing accuracy and preservation requirements for recording HBIM data. In addition, it looks at the available databases and frameworks for knowing what HBIM data to record and the best methods and templates to use initially.

CHAPTER 8   STEP FIVE: POST-PROCESSING AND ANALYSIS

Refining the HBIM Model

When refining a Heritage Building Information Modelling model based on expert feedback, the following points are generic key aspects you should consider checking:

1. **Geometric Accuracy and Detail**

    - Dimensional precision of structural elements, decorative features, and architectural details

    - Level of detail (LOD) appropriate for the project's intended use and documentation standards

    - Accuracy of complex geometries like vaults, arches, irregular masonry patterns, and ornamental elements

    - Proper representation of deformation, damage, or structural irregularities

2. **Historical and Archaeological Fidelity**

    - Chronological accuracy reflecting different construction phases and historical periods

    - Proper attribution of architectural styles, techniques, and materials to their respective eras

    - Integration of archaeological findings and stratigraphic evidence

    - Documentation of alterations, additions, and modifications over time

3. **Material Properties and Characterization**

    - Accurate representation of traditional building materials and their properties

    - Proper modelling of material degradation states and pathologies where possible

    - Consideration of original construction techniques and craftsmanship methods

4. **Semantic Information and Metadata**

    - Enrichment of model elements with historical, cultural, and technical information
    - Proper classification and categorization of building components
    - Integration of archival documents, historical drawings, and photographic evidence
    - Inclusion of conservation history and intervention records

5. **Structural and Conservation Assessment**

    - Incorporation of structural analysis findings and stability assessments
    - Documentation of damage patterns, crack mapping, and deterioration processes
    - Integration of conservation recommendations and intervention priorities
    - Monitoring data integration for ongoing heritage management

6. **Data Quality and Validation**

    - Cross-referencing with multiple data sources for verification
    - Resolution of discrepancies between different survey methods or historical sources
    - Ensuring consistency across different model components and phases
    - Validation against existing documentation and comparative studies

7. **Interoperability and Standards Compliance**

    - Adherence to heritage documentation standards and best practices
    - Compatibility with conservation management systems and databases
    - Proper file organization and naming conventions for long-term preservation
    - Integration capabilities with GIS systems and digital heritage platforms such as QGIS and ArcGIS

CHAPTER 8   STEP FIVE: POST-PROCESSING AND ANALYSIS

Thoroughly checking these aspects ensures the refined HBIM model serves as a comprehensive digital twin that accurately represents both the physical reality and cultural significance of the heritage building. Some of the above are covered in more depth in the next section "Assessing Historical Accuracy and Preservation Needs." Other aspects are more suitable for buildings still in existence where modelling has possibly included photogrammetry or LiDAR.

For this section, we will cover how to validate the model from external feedback and how we progress with the feedback received, i.e., choosing to refine and adapt the model to suit feedback.

Revisiting the model to refine it will depend on the expert feedback received. If you have been diligent in your research and implementation, it may be possible that there is very little that needs to be changed. Nonetheless, it is still a process that every designer or architectural 3D modeller should thoroughly work through. It could also be possible that in the post model checking, new evidence becomes available and changes elements of the model considerably.

The first step for the Steventon Rectory model was to reach out to experts in the different areas where feedback is required, i.e., aspects you are not certain of or where there is a question mark over the authenticity of the resource material. It can be daunting, as a student or novice, approaching experts and asking for their feedback, and then a little dismaying to find that the feedback is going to result in considerable changes to the 3D model that you have already spent hours researching and creating.

The feedback areas that were of concern for the Steventon Rectory model were Jane Austen House

- Confirmation that the building followed the correct archival sketches. There is considerable debate about how the Rectory looked, so before publishing the model, it was important to know if the model was the general consensus in external appearance.

- Confirmation regarding the story script regarding the facts building the story.

- Furniture at 8 College Street; was Jane's writing desk part of the furniture in the portal scene to Steventon Rectory, in which case the model needs to be created?

CHAPTER 8 STEP FIVE: POST-PROCESSING AND ANALYSIS

Archaeo Briton – regarding their 2011 archaeological dig results

- Overall size of the building and outbuildings
- The internal layout of rooms – are they as mentioned in the available archival information?
- Materials for the exterior and interior walls, are they shown as correct – the same materials for all walls?
- Sash or Casement windows?
- Was there a bow window on both floors or just the ground floor of the rear right wing?

HBIM professionals

- HBIM Data fields – what type of information was relevant to include to comply with the London Charter principles

The queries for feedback were sent to the three different groups of experts: Jane Austen House, Archaeo Briton, and HBIM professionals.

Feedback has been received regarding three aspects from Jane Austen House; details of the above aspects requested sent were

- What is the general opinion of the sketches regarding Steventon Rectory as there does seem to be a bit of a debate concerning them, i.e., knowing which one to follow most closely.
- Another aspect is the story constructed from an event "wedding breakfast for Jane Cooper's wedding" at Steventon Rectory in 1792, extracted from Ashton's (1967) *Parson Austen's Daughter* (pages 47–51). This has been posed as a memory being discussed between Jane and Cassandra looking back at time at Steventon Rectory with the family. I attached the scene script for information. It would be helpful if this could be looked at in case I have been too imaginative/assumptive in their discussion, i.e., Jane calling Cassandra "Cass." I know Jane was quite ill in her last few months, therefore also a little concerned that she would even be able to have this kind of chat with Cassandra.

- Last aspect is whether anyone knows whether Jane's writing desk (and other furniture) at Chawton was at 8 College Street, or whether it remained at Chawton while she was in Winchester.

With regard to the story script, the feedback received advised that the wedding breakfast was not such the large affair described by Ashton, according to Le Faye's (1869) book *Jane Austen: A Family Record*. It did occur but was a much quieter, smaller event:

> *Captain Williams arrived at Steventon to claim his bride in December and the marriage took place on the 11th, the service being taken by Mr Austen's old pupil Tom Fowle – now in Holy Orders like his father and alder brother – and with Edward Cooper, Cassandra and Jane as witnesses. The Leighs of Adlestrop gave the bride a cloak worth £5.16s.8d. and the newly-married couple set off for the Isle of Wight, where Captain Williams's mother had a cottage in Ryde.*
>
> —Le Faye, 1869

It was also requested by Jane Austen House that the reminiscing was made apparent in that it is a piece of creative writing rather than fact. The outcome is that I will adjust the script to make more of the wedding gift from the Leighs, i.e., the cost and what such a beautiful cloak it was. There will also be a comment to state that it is creative writing and not factual when the user chooses to observe the reminiscing only or portal to Steventon while listening to the story.

With regard to the writing desk, it was agreed that Jane's writing desk at the Jane Austen House in Chawton would most probably not have made the trip to Winchester, owing primarily to Jane's health and not carrying any furniture with them.

This means that the scene at 8 College Street, Winchester, can remain unchanged.

Opposing views from experts can also be difficult to manage and know which route to follow. For example, the two sketches used to model the external look and shape of Steventon Rectory were confirmed by Charlton (2017) as a result of the archaeological dig undertaken in 2011 by Archaeo Briton, a community dig led by Charlton. The confirmation of the larger looking Rectory (nine front windows) by Julia (Anna Lefroy's daughter) supported my view considering the number of rooms and the two rear wings noted in different archival records. The smaller looking rectory sketches by Revd James Austen's daughter Anna Austen who had lived at Steventon Rectory, and Ben Lefroy (Anna's husband), appeared to be too small to house so many rooms. Maybe it was just the angle of the sketch and the trees hiding more than immediately thought, i.e., there are two further windows for each floor, hidden by the trees.

CHAPTER 8   STEP FIVE: POST-PROCESSING AND ANALYSIS

The feedback from Jane Austen's House experts at Chawton is that the sketches by Anna Lefroy are the most reliable in how the Rectory would have looked. I am told that in *Jane Austen: A Family Record* (Le Faye, 1869), Le Faye writes that the larger house was specifically drawn by Anna's daughter Julia, based on her 76-year-old mother's memory for a book by Edward Austen Leigh, *A Memoir of Jane Austen*. Anna, in sending with a letter to Edward for the book, described the drawing as "more pretty than true."

As previously stated, the intention was to arrange a meeting with Archaeo Briton's leading expert, Debbie Charlton. It was requested and kindly accepted and arranged. During this meeting, discussion regarding several aspects, primarily the overall size, room sizes, room positions, and sketches used, took place. Charlton confirmed the size of the house and which sketches she considered were the most realistic considering her own research and archaeological findings. The outcome of the discussion resulted in revisiting the model for a variety of changes, which can be seen in Table 8-1.

Table 8-1. Revisions to Steventon Rectory – Archaeo Briton feedback

No.	Current Model Space	Changes
1	Sizes of rooms and overall layout	Overall matches the dimensions of the rooms in the book
		Change the rooms to the dimensions in the book
		Change the layout to the book sketch – ground floor only
		No known sizes for the rear of the building and therefore layout
2	Front door	Move the door to one side – right, two windows on the left, as in the book sketch
		Set the front door back
		Remove porch
3	Ground floor drawing room	Move to the front of the house, left as you enter the house
		Door from drawing room to dining room
4	Jane and Cassandra's bedroom/dressing room	Swap the bedroom space with the dressing room/drawing room space
5	Attic	Not for servants but for boarders and storage

(*continued*)

Table 8-1. (*continued*)

No.	Current Model Space	Changes
6	Dormers	Possibly three dormers
7	Main stairs	Move to new corridor running to left toward the rear of the house
		Need to change all staircases to tie into the cellar and attic changes
8	Side building	Agrees regarding single story, also not brick but wooden, substantial with corner beams and structure as the roof was most likely red flat clay tiles
9	Main Rectory roof	Red clay flat tiles fixed with peg holes
10	Cellar	Possibly just under East corner
11	Exterior	Bring the right tree further forward to the side of the house – a horse chestnut
		Fir trees hid the house from the lane
		Wall was most likely a mud wall with a door near the side of the house
		Path at left side of the house was made of bricks
		Definitely brick and flint walls

The general outcome of which sketch to work with was that the larger house was the most probable for two reasons. The first reason was based on the archaeological evidence of the foundations and therefore the size of the Rectory. The second reason was due to the Memoir, the book written by James Edward Austen, in which the author decided to use the larger house sketch, presumably because it was agreed to be the most suitable likeness by at least two of the people that lived in the house, James Edward and Anna Lefroy, for a book that was about Jane Austen (Austen-Leigh, 1870). Why would Jane's nephew choose an image that did not represent the Rectory, to be in such an important book? James is listed as the author, although his sister Caroline, half-sister Anna, and their cousin Cassy Esten Austen were also involved in the writing of the book. Anna knew the Rectory well; she had lived there as previously mentioned; the others would have known Jane most at Chawton House. Steventon Rectory wasn't demolished until seven years after Jane's death, so it was probable that the younger nieces and nephews may still have seen the Rectory before it was demolished.

Therefore, for this exercise and for working with Steventon Rectory for Virtual Cities – Winchester and based on the archaeological findings by Charlton in 2011, we will work with the larger sketch, bearing also in mind that maybe the smaller sketches' trees were hiding a larger part of the Rectory. From the discussion with Charlton, it was decided that there were most likely only six windows at the front, instead of the nine in the larger house sketch. Charlton also confirmed about the porch and having seen the original sketches commented that the porch appeared added rather than part of the original sketch. Anna says in her letter to James with the sketch that her daughter had made it look prettier, but no clear explanation as to what parts this referred to; therefore, this could have been the porch, especially where it is on other sketches of the Rectory.

There is compelling evidence for each view; therefore, it may be in future that changes to the front may be required again, once the consensus is definite in how the front view looked, i.e., six or nine windows, and porch or no porch. It would not take much to change now that we have the rest of the building layout agreed.

The following images show the changes made in Revit before using Datasmith to reimport to Unreal. It took approximately a working day to make the changes in Revit.

CHAPTER 8   STEP FIVE: POST-PROCESSING AND ANALYSIS

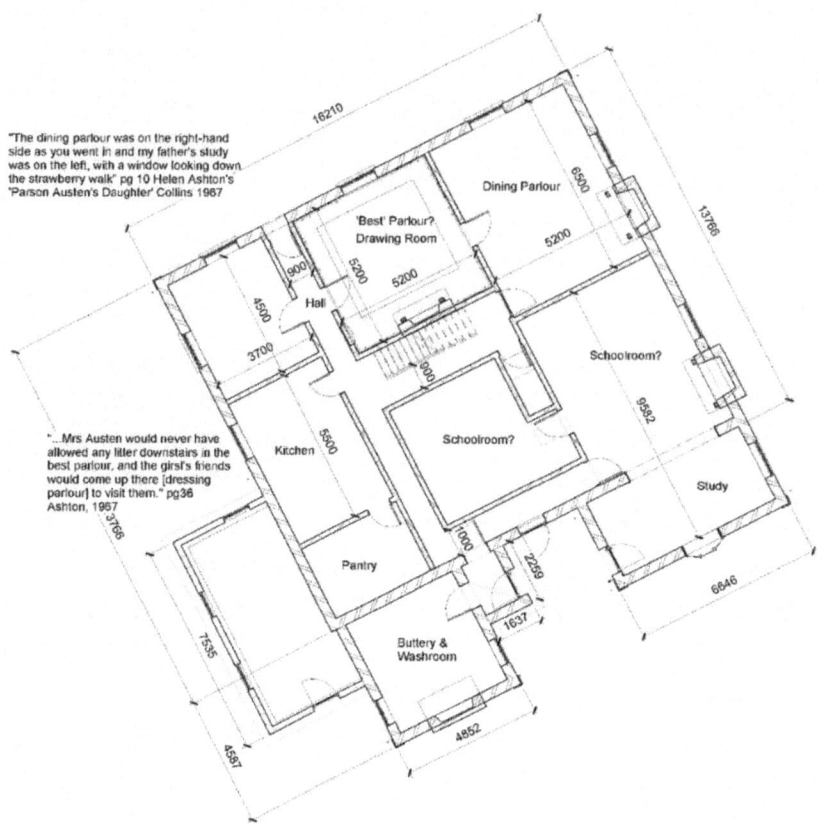

Figure 8-1. *Ground floor*

CHAPTER 8   STEP FIVE: POST-PROCESSING AND ANALYSIS

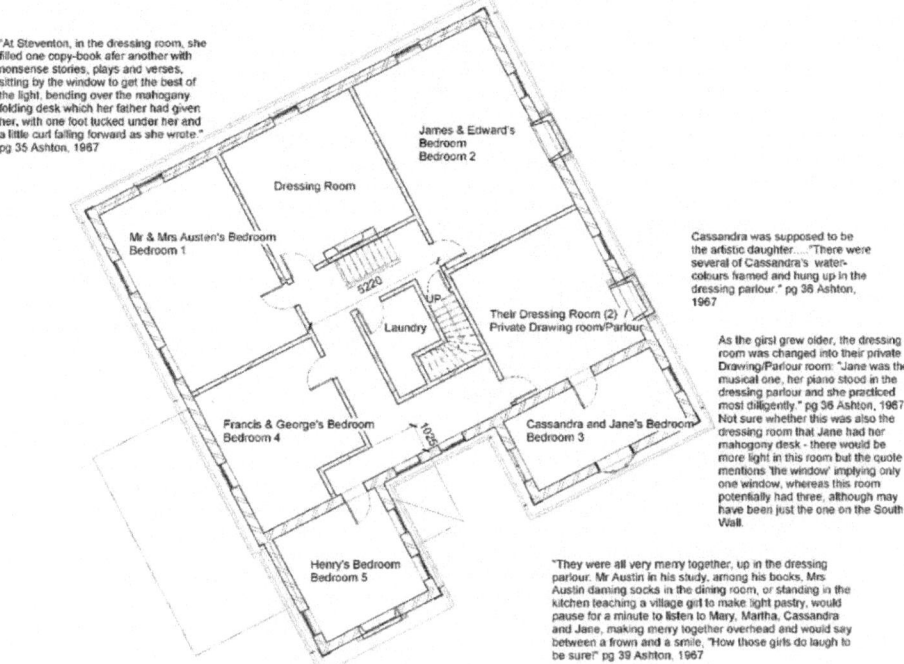

Figure 8-2. First floor

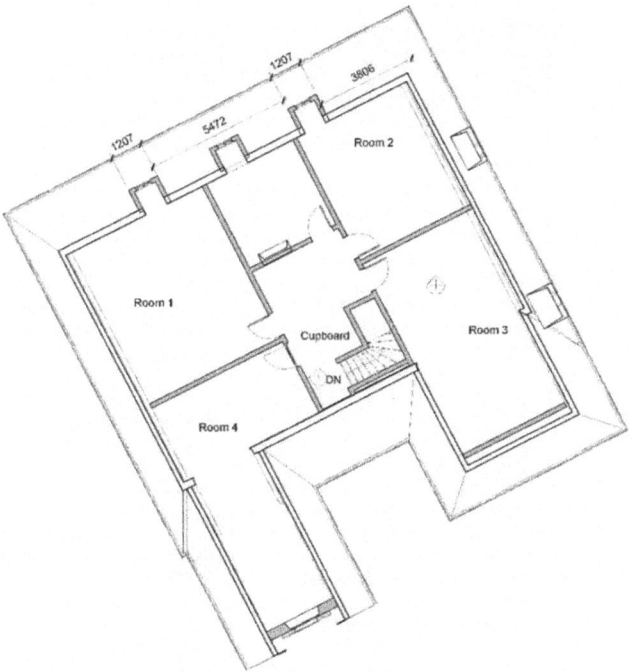

Figure 8-3. Attic floor

561

CHAPTER 8   STEP FIVE: POST-PROCESSING AND ANALYSIS

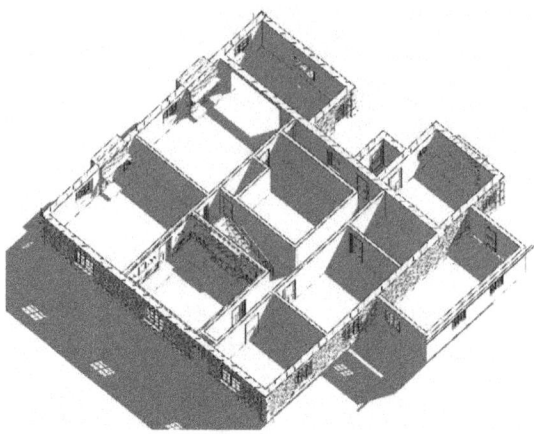

Figure 8-4. Ground floor 3D section

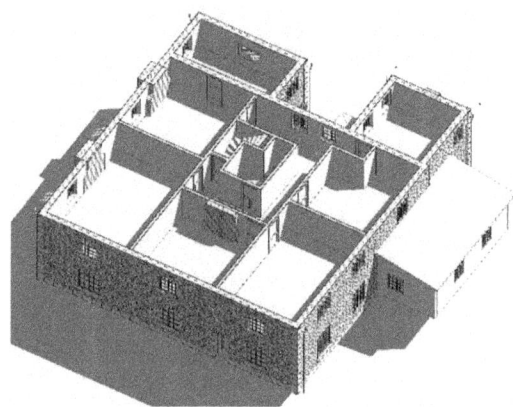

Figure 8-5. First floor 3D section

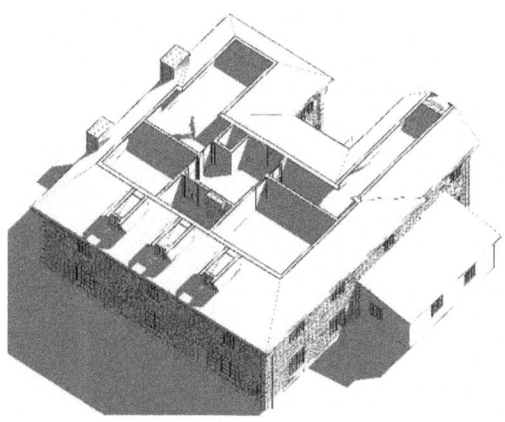

Figure 8-6. Attic floor 3D section

CHAPTER 8   STEP FIVE: POST-PROCESSING AND ANALYSIS

Figure 8-7. *Sketch by Hill (1904)*

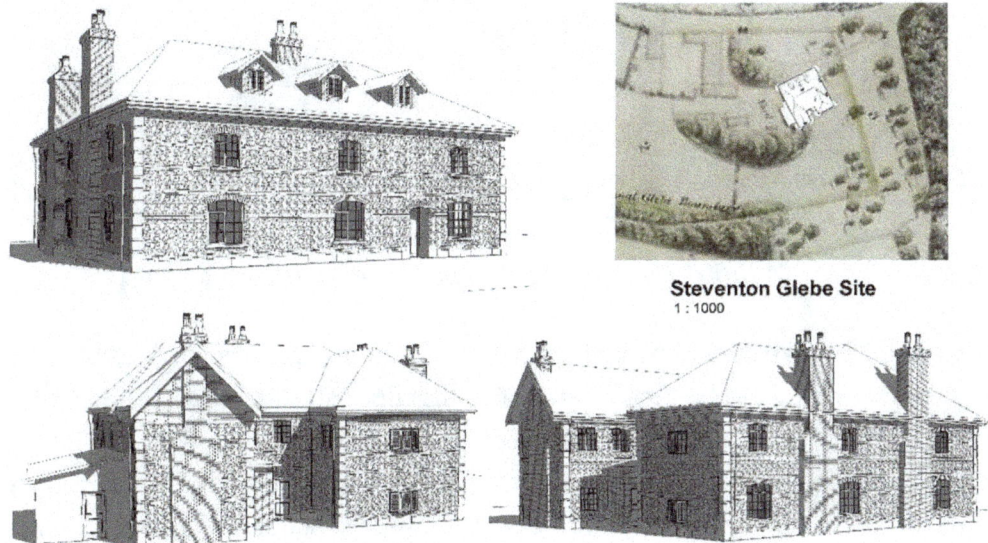

Figure 8-8. *3D views of the front, rear, and east sides of the Rectory with the site map*

CHAPTER 8   STEP FIVE: POST-PROCESSING AND ANALYSIS

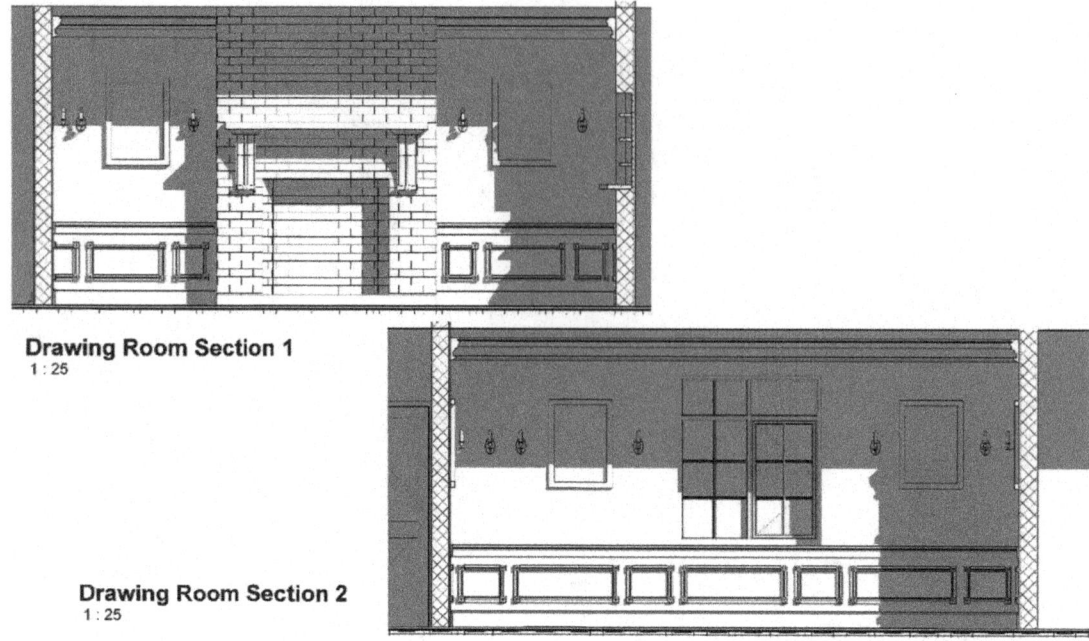

Figure 8-9. *Sectional interior views of the repositioned drawing room*

If you want to make the changes shown above in the images, the dimensions shown on the ground floor should be the first step. The first floor should follow the same ground floor partitioning to a certain degree, but feel free to create your own layout. There are ridge tiles still to add to the different roofs, glass to the upper part of the front door, the additional outbuildings, and more landscape planting/terracing to add to the site. Other than the ground floor, it is mostly conjecture and interpretation from the memoirs and letters written by Jane and her family in later years.

Exporting via Datasmith from Revit to Unreal

1. Once you are happy with the layouts for each floor, then you need to make sure you are in a default 3D view in Revit, i.e., a 3D view that is not cropped. If you have the 3D view saved from the previous export via Datasmith and named and therefore saved as a locked view, you can use this view instead.

2. Make sure it is the only view open, i.e., close all other views.

3. Once done, go to the Twinmotion menu under View.

CHAPTER 8   STEP FIVE: POST-PROCESSING AND ANALYSIS

4. Make sure that Autosync is on by clicking on it (needs to be in color, not gray).
5. Check the Export settings, i.e., the Data groups you want to see in Unreal.
6. Click Synchronise.
7. Click Export Datasmith.
8. Save by overwriting your previous Datasmith file (a good idea to rename the previous Datasmith if you want to check/test first).
9. If you want to make sure you keep a record of the current Unreal project version, go to Explorer and select the folder of your current Unreal Project.
10. Select the complete folder and copy.
11. Paste and rename the copy file to be the archive/old version.
12. Go to Epic Launcher and open your original version (this is to ensure the Datasmith file recognizes the file name of the project.
13. Once open, go to your Steventon Rectory Level.
14. When it has loaded, go to the Quick Add button and drop-down to "Datasmith".
15. Choose "File Import".
16. When prompted, only select the Meshes; deselect materials, lights, cameras, and animations.
17. Choose to save in your Steventon Project folder in the Content Browser.

Note   If like mine, it did not write over the previous Rectory, instead adding the latest version to the scene, then it may be because the link did not synchronize properly. Not a problem though, follow the next steps to make sure the new version is moved to the right space, i.e., on top of the other one – do not delete the other one yet, you might need it for knowing what materials have been used for what objects.

CHAPTER 8   STEP FIVE: POST-PROCESSING AND ANALYSIS

18. Look in the Outliner and you should see the new Rectory items listed. Select all of them and then click on (top right) add New Folder; all the items will now sit in that folder. You can leave it as New Folder for now.

19. Make sure all the items listed in the folder are selected.

20. Go to the 4 viewports option (top right grid of the Viewport).

21. Navigate to where the new rectory has been placed – usually 0,0,0, i.e., the intersection of the main red and green grid lines.

22. Using your four views and the move constraint arrows, move the new rectory to the old one.

23. Zoom in and make sure it is aligned with the sides of the old rectory.

24. In your right or front viewport, make sure it is on the right level, i.e., sitting at the right height.

25. Now that you have it in place, you can go to the folder of the original rectory and turn it off from view.

26. You will now need to add the materials as before, but this time your materials are already made, so it is just a case of reapplying to the new rectory.

27. For the candle lights, I duplicated the ones from the previous rectory and placed the duplicates within the New Folder.

28. You will need to move them from the old drawing room to where it is now positioned.

29. I changed the Roof texture material by "saving as" the current roof material, saving it as M_SR_RedFlatTiles, and then changing the Textures to the Red Flat Tiles textures included in your lesson files.

30. The tiling coordinates will need to change; my settings are U Tiling 0.5, V Tiling 0.2.

CHAPTER 8   STEP FIVE: POST-PROCESSING AND ANALYSIS

31. Once you have finished adding your materials externally and internally, copied your lights over, etc., to the new Drawing Room, you can then choose Edit/Delete for removing the previous Rectory from the Outliner.

32. You might want to experiment with lighting, adding more landscape, adding fir trees to the front, etc.

Congratulations – you have revised the model and brought it into Unreal without overwriting the complete Level, or materials. Your Unreal Project scene may now look like the following images:

Figure 8-10. *West to East sweep of the drive – Steventon Rectory*

Here you can see the porch no longer exists and there are six windows and three dormers. Fir trees have been added to the front, and the tree on the right has been moved closer to the house, creating the shade. You may also be able to just see on the right; the red brick side building is now wood. Unreal basic cubes were added and changed in height to use as corner upright beams, also added along the length of the building for giving structural strength for the clay tiles on its roof. I have moved grass and flowers away from the repositioned door so that there is a clear path up to the door from the sweep. Other than this, no further changes have been made to the landscape. This is something you can continue to work on in your own time, as will I ready for the Virtual Cities – Winchester scene and being able to portal here from Winchester.

CHAPTER 8   STEP FIVE: POST-PROCESSING AND ANALYSIS

Figure 8-11. *East to West sweep of the drive – Steventon Rectory*

Figure 8-12. *Rear view showing the end of side wooden building*

Figure 8-13. *Rear view showing rear entrance and Study Bow Window*

CHAPTER 8 STEP FIVE: POST-PROCESSING AND ANALYSIS

Figure 8-14. *The repositioned Drawing Room now at the front of the Rectory*

Figure 8-15. *The Drawing Room window overlooking the lane*

CHAPTER 8   STEP FIVE: POST-PROCESSING AND ANALYSIS

Figure 8-16. Looking into the Drawing Room window and repositioned front door entrance

HBIM Data Feedback

The final request concerned the type of HBIM data that users/experts would expect or hope to see included. The main information that has come back is to look at the London Charter for the Computer-Based Visualisation of Cultural Heritage information and common metadata standards such as LIDO, EDM/ Europeana, and CARARE for guidance.

- Lightweight Information Describing Objects (LIDO) is an XML harvesting scheme according to their handout; its intention is for delivering metadata for various services. It incorporates standards such as "the CDWA Lite and museumdat schemas and has been aligned with the SPECTRUM collections management standard."

- Europeana Data Model (EDM) is specifically designed to facilitate the uploading of cultural heritage data to the Europeana platform. It ensures that it can be shared and reused across different institutions and platforms within the cultural heritage sector. It also provides a consistent way to represent and manage cultural heritage data, including 3D models for access through Europeana.

- Connecting Archaeology and Architecture in Europe (CARARE) is an accredited aggregator for Europe and advises providers in the areas of metadata standards, schemas, and data quality including data analysis and metadata mapping.

CHAPTER 8   STEP FIVE: POST-PROCESSING AND ANALYSIS

I was also pointed to the Heritalise Project, part of Echoes, a European Union and UK Research and Innovation funded project that started in January 2025, to "revolutionize documentation and understanding of cultural heritage by advancing digitalization and AI-powered tools." This does seem to be more about the tools and development of components than a standard for HBIM.

The two pointers provided have clarified what type of HBIM information is generally required and are based on the London Charter and LIDO. We look into the London Charter principles in the next section, although what would be good here is to see an example of the principles of the London Charter put to use for a heritage object. This would help in ensuring the information included in Virtual Cities – Winchester and Steventon Rectory adhere to those principles. The only example of an HBIM data record other than examples of pipelines, frameworks, or processes used to collate data (Bakken Storeide et al., 2023), is the following "inventory form for ancient city walls" that forms part of an article published in *Heritage Science*. The article is for the city Walls of Pisa, "A HBIM Pipeline for the Conservation of Large-Scale Architectural Heritage: The City Walls of Pisa" (Giuliani et al., 2024). The Inventory Form is comprehensive in the data required and is particularly helpful in understanding what we might need to include for the Castle Walls in the Virtual Cities – Winchester project.

CHAPTER 8   STEP FIVE: POST-PROCESSING AND ANALYSIS

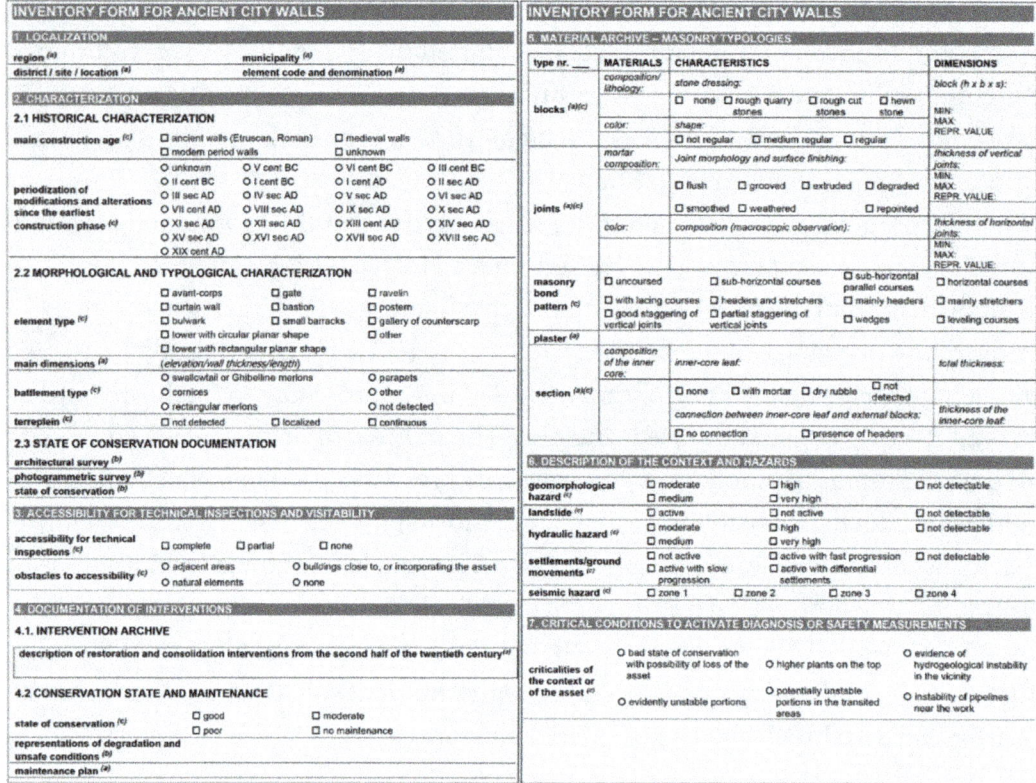

Figure 8-17. *Inventory form for ancient city walls (Giuliani et al., 2024)*

The following LIDO image also helps to understand the type of data normally required/expected for a single LIDO record.

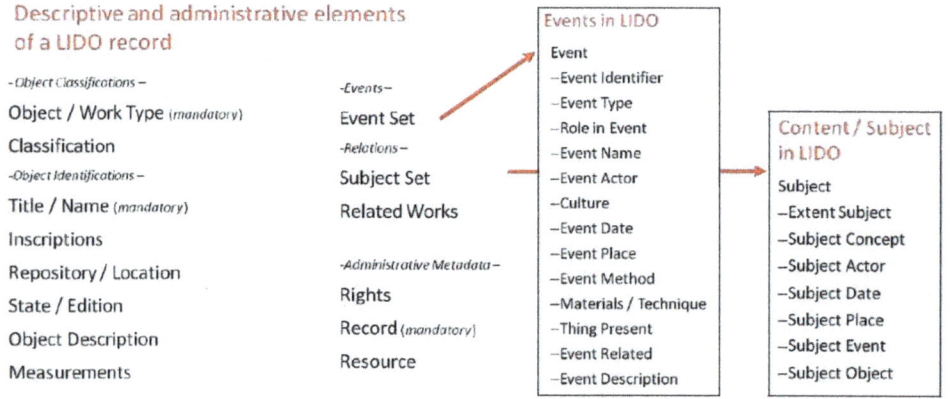

Figure 8-18. *LIDO's breakdown of a single LIDO record (LIDO, 2025)*

This format could certainly help in starting to record HBIM data for a 3D creator who may have no experience of recording HBIM data or have a full understanding of what is entailed/required. I have also found that the recording of photogrammetry, point clouds, LIDAR data, drone footage, and similar, i.e., scans of existing buildings, or ruins, although providing rich data of the objects. For this introduction to building heritage models that no longer exist, it does make the recording more straightforward, although the researched resources might be many more and require more involved clarification and verification.

Section Summary

This section outlines the process of refining an HBIM 3D model using expert feedback, using the Steventon Rectory reconstruction as a case study. It begins by identifying general criteria for HBIM refinement, including geometric accuracy, historical fidelity, material representation, metadata enrichment, structural assessment, and standards compliance.

The feedback process involved consulting three expert groups: Jane Austen House, Archaeo Briton, and HBIM professionals. Feedback prompted several key changes, especially to the Rectory's layout and external features, to align the model with archaeological findings and credible archival sources. A particular challenge was deciding between conflicting sketch interpretations of the building's appearance; ultimately, the version supported by archaeological evidence and literary memoirs was selected, albeit with flexibility for future adjustments.

Practical changes were made in Revit, with revisions exported to Unreal Engine via Datasmith. The section includes step-by-step instructions for managing Datasmith exports and replacing assets in Unreal without overwriting existing environments. It concludes with a discussion on the types of HBIM metadata needed for wider cultural heritage interoperability, referencing standards such as the London Charter and LIDO and suggesting frameworks for effective data documentation.

The next section covers how best to assess historical accuracy and preservation needs. We take a deeper look at the London Charter for the Computer-Based Visualisation of Cultural Heritage, specifically its principles and how its standards may be used to develop a growing need for an HBIM data and model repository by a wide range of creators.

CHAPTER 8   STEP FIVE: POST-PROCESSING AND ANALYSIS

Assessing Historical Accuracy and Preservation Needs

Assessing Historical Accuracy

Digital heritage reconstruction, while offering powerful preservation and accessibility, requires careful attention to historical accuracy and the preservation needs of the original artifact or site. Thorough documentation of your reconstruction process, including the software, methods, and data sources, is vital for ensuring transparency and reproducibility, enabling you to check thoroughly for historical accuracy. By doing this, it would also provide an opportunity to specify what is known recorded fact, what is conjecture, and what may be missing and how it has been resolved.

In the previous section, we covered about gaining expert feedback on your model and how you have interpreted the information found, and the feedback received. In previous projects, I would have considered that the projects were completed at that stage, i.e., receiving and implementing feedback, checking and checking again to make sure the feedback provided has been actioned.

For HBIM projects, thoroughly assessing the historical accuracy of the model, the scene context, the storytelling, and artifacts is an added step that for some may seem too much, especially with regard to time and therefore cost to the project. It is important though for future use, so it is worth making sure additional time is added to the project so that the model is going to be accurate and comply with the London Charter principles.

In your historical accuracy assessment, there are areas to consider such as phasing of the building, i.e., were there structural changes to the building, or perhaps different historical events that involved change of ownership, hand whether these have been recorded. For example, Steventon Rectory is now known to have had three significant refurbishments, and the left side (from the front) was an Elizabethan wing (Charlton, 2017). It is possible, therefore, that the style of the interior would most likely not be the same throughout, perhaps lower ceilings in the Elizabethan wing for example. The construction material of the walls may also not be the same due to the time they may have been built. For example, Charlton (2017) states that from a mention made in the 1768 insurance cover, the south side wall was of plaster.

Assessing historical accuracy in digital heritage projects, therefore, involves going beyond general plausibility or visual coherence. It requires a structured process of validation against historical evidence, expert consensus, and methodological transparency. The following approaches can be used to systematically assess the historical accuracy of HBIM or other reconstructed models:

1. **Source Cross-Referencing and Triangulation**

    Each element of the reconstruction, whether it is material texture, architectural form, or object placement, should be traced back to at least one verifiable source. Where possible, multiple sources should be used to triangulate historical data. This can include

    - Archival documents (e.g., maps, estate records, drawings)
    - Archaeological reports
    - Contemporary written descriptions
    - Iconographic sources (e.g., paintings, engravings)
    - Photographs (where available)

    All assumptions made in the absence of direct evidence should be clearly flagged as conjecture. The process of triangulation helps confirm accuracy and highlights discrepancies or gaps in the historical record.

2. **Accuracy Mapping and Categorization**

    You could introduce an *accuracy key* or visual overlay system within the model or its documentation, indicating the level of certainty for each component. A common categorization includes

    - Known (based on verifiable evidence)
    - Interpreted (based on indirect or partial evidence)
    - Conjectural (no direct evidence, based on stylistic norms or context)

    This kind of mapping is especially useful in HBIM environments, where metadata can be embedded into each model element.

CHAPTER 8   STEP FIVE: POST-PROCESSING AND ANALYSIS

3. **Expert Peer Review**

   Formalizing expert feedback as a peer review process strengthens the assessment. You consider using

   - External audits of selected components by specialists (e.g., conservation architects, historians)
   - Using review checklists that align with known historical facts and conventions
   - Documenting not just the feedback, but your rationale for accepting or rejecting suggestions

   This helps establish scholarly rigor, especially for reconstructions that may be used in education or public engagement. It also provides a trusted and transparent resource for future queries regarding elements of the modelling and research process.

4. **Temporal Consistency and Phasing Validation**

   As noted with Steventon Rectory, changes over time affect historical accuracy. Assessments should therefore also include

   - **Timeline Checks:** Do the modelled features match the era they claim to represent?
   - **Phase Separation:** If multiple time periods are represented, are they clearly delineated?
   - **Material and Construction Logic:** Are materials and techniques consistent with what was available or typical during that phase?

   Phasing sequences in HBIM can support this by letting users toggle between historical states. Here you also have to consider if you are "snap-shotting" a specific time of the building for storytelling purposes or showing the life of the building more relevant for conservation and preservation purposes, an aspect mentioned when at the Revit modelling stage in Chapter 6.

5. **Contextual Plausibility Checks**

   We have covered the importance of this previously; here it needs to be transparent in your record keeping. Therefore, check any interior elements or detail that has not been fully verified and question whether it makes sense contextually.

   - Compare with contemporary buildings of similar status, location, and function.
   - Use period-appropriate architectural handbooks or treatises to support reconstruction decisions.
   - Check against known social or economic constraints of the time (e.g., could the building owner afford ornate plasterwork?).

   This step is especially useful for filling in gaps responsibly.

6. **Documentation and Justification Logs**

   Maintain a living document or an embedded notes log that justifies each significant decision made in the reconstruction. This may include

   - Choice of sources
   - Reasoning for conjectural elements
   - Conflicts in the historical record and how they were resolved

   This documentation not only aids assessment but makes the reconstruction *transparent*, *repeatable*, and open to future revision.

By combining cross-referencing, documentation, expert review, and visual categorization, you can produce reconstructions that are not only visually engaging but also academically robust. For projects where budget or time is constrained, even a partial application of these methods can significantly improve the trustworthiness of the final output.

Table 8-2 is an example table showing how historical accuracy might be assessed for individual elements in a reconstruction project using Steventon Rectory as a hypothetical case. The format combines the source references, accuracy category, expert feedback, and justification log for each key element.

CHAPTER 8   STEP FIVE: POST-PROCESSING AND ANALYSIS

- Under Model Element, add the feature or object being recreated
- Under Evidence Source(s), add citations, images, or documentation used to inform the model.
- Under Accuracy Category, add the classification, i.e., *Known*, *Interpreted*, or *Conjectural*.
- Under Expert Feedback, add what the specialists said, and if they confirmed or questioned the reconstruction.
- Under Justification/Notes, add your rationale for the different modelling decisions, including any caveats.

Table 8-2. Example table: assessing historical accuracy in HBIM reconstruction

| Model Element | Evidence Source(s) | Project: Steventon Rectory | | Justification/Notes |
		Accuracy Category	Expert Feedback	
South Side Wall Finish	Charlton (2017): archival text noting plaster wall	Known	Confirmed by archaeologist	Used plaster material texture. Source is clear, aligns with regional building norms
Left Wing Structure	Charlton (2017); 17th C. estate records	Interpreted	Confirmed by archaeologist	Elizabethan wing likely. Floor heights adjusted; ceiling beam style changed to beams showing
Interior Room Layout	No floor plans found; occasional description in memoirs and letters – general rectory layout inferred	Part Interpreted, part Conjectural	Proposed rechecking against similar rectories, archaeological data, and archival texts	Based layout on descriptions in memoirs and comparable Regency rectories in Hampshire. Marked as "part Interpreted, part Conjectural"

(continued)

Table 8-2. (*continued*)

Model Element	Evidence Source(s)	Project: Steventon Rectory Accuracy Category	Expert Feedback	Justification/Notes
Roof Tile Type	Site photos of remaining tile fragments; regional norms	Interpreted	Feedback: red clay flat tiles with pin hole fixing	Red clay pantiles used; consistent with early 18th C. restorations
Kitchen Chimney Stack	18th C. sketch by Austen descendant (partial)	Interpreted	Historian suggested keeping original placement	Retained chimney location; sketch consistent with written descriptions
Wall Paint Color	No evidence found	Conjectural	Advised use of neutral tones; avoid strong hues	Used muted color palette based on social class and period conventions
Furniture Style	Jane Austen Museum references; archival inventories	Interpreted	Positive feedback, suggestion for refinement	Mixture of plain and elegant Regency and Georgian styles, marked as "Interpreted"

The Pluses and Minuses of Virtual Reconstructed Scenes Relating to Historical Accuracy

When creating camera views, videos, and animated paths, you are able to choose what the viewer sees; therefore, it has been possible to "hide" areas where information could not be found to complete fully. This has been the case for many early projects before it was possible to create scenes in interactive Game Engine environments. It was also possible to "fudge" areas where the construction just wasn't working smoothly, i.e., gaps because walls or roofs wouldn't connect properly.

This is not possible now; your Unreal Engine virtual viewer can explore all aspects of the scene should they wish to, so every part/element of your scene needs to work, be plausible, and as far as possible be contextually correct. An example is our work with Malmesbury medieval town, which was an early project using Unreal Engine. When creating the scenes and adding grass and flowers, I noticed that quite few of buildings had grass growing through the wooden floors or the walls. Additional time working with each building to remove the wayward grass was required for each building that the camera path visited. For the distant buildings and nonvisited buildings, the grass would have been fine to leave as it would not be seen by the camera "tour". Furniture and items to make the place looked lived in were only added to those buildings that you chose as the creator of the "tour". The Unreal Engine Malmesbury scenes were not available to walk through and explore at will, so it was okay to do this.

Virtual Cities – Winchester will be available to explore at will; therefore, there can be no fudging, and the 75 buildings across the two eras that will be "open to the public" need to be accurate in how they look internally and externally. The building and recording for each of the buildings will form a significantly sized project database. By undertaking the historical accuracy checks for each building, each story and site overall will result in a valuable resource for educational, cultural, and preservation purposes, and a large database. Admittedly, it will take a significant amount of time to create this level of detail and ensure validity. Imagine the same project with 75 buildings showing their full lifespan of construction, changes in purpose and therefore the various refurbishments. Currently, I would say this is not feasible and perhaps also too confusing to work through by the user/virtual visitor. Although you could create a Level for each significant change to the building and your viewer could then choose to portal to the different phases of the building. Therefore, again, consider the use of your project; is it going to be as I refer to as a lifespan project, or a single point in time? Are you going to allow your users to wander at will or will they be on prescribed camera paths?

You can also see why the National Trust and other heritage organizations present their properties or rooms in "a moment in time"; it would not be possible to visually present the room across different periods of change or use, easily. This can be done though, via interpretation panels using reconstruction images, old photos, and similar archive material, but not physical changes to the room. Bear this in mind for your Unreal Engine projects. Similar to the Popups for the HBIM data, you can create Popups for images to show how the room/building looked in a previous or future "moment in time" rather than constructing different levels for the same building.

For example, having chosen 1400 and 1800 Winchester, I know that Winchester College, in College Street, has changed significantly since it was first built, sometimes several times within the century, such as the change to the frontage to College Street in the mid-1800s, i.e., the Headmasters' House. I have had to decide on specific moments in time that can be used for each of the eras to ensure the project is feasible, both in time and cost. By choosing 1800, it means that the significant frontage changes to College Street in 1839–1842 would not be seen unless a 1900 Winchester was also created. It can, though, be added in the HBIM data regarding changes to the building and be shown as a pop-up archival image.

What I get excited about with game engines being used for historical recreations is that users can explore and interact with information of their choice. Choice has always been important in my time creating heritage reconstructions. Users can move freely through the environment, exploring areas and objects not dictated by a camera path. What they interact with is entirely up to them. I remember creating three camera paths/tours for Dunster Castle, one by the lord of the Manor providing information about this home, one by the cook who provided information about the costs of things in relation to her role as a cook. The third was a tour done in reverse because of generally seeing things differently when our route is changed. There was considerable self-imposed pressure to ensure they saw the most important aspects of Dunster Castle and learned about aspects that were perhaps not on the interpretation panels. There wasn't access to game engines then (1995–1996). I worked with 3DS Max on an 8-gigabyte desktop, so camera paths it had to be, technology (software and hardware) was not advanced enough to cope with much more than this. The research and fact-checking were as important then as now, as there is always an element of interpretation and conjecture when reconstructing buildings that no longer exist.

Preservation Needs

In 2009, a document entitled "The London Charter for the Computer-Based Visualisation of Cultural Heritage" (2009) was formed in response to concerns regarding a lack of standardized approaches to digital visualization in cultural heritage work. As computer graphics and 3D modelling became increasingly popular tools for archaeologists, historians, and heritage professionals, there was a recognized need for rigor and transparency in how these technologies were used.

The Charter's primary purpose was to establish principles for ensuring that computer-based visualization of cultural heritage is intellectually and technically rigorous. It emphasizes the importance of making the research process transparent, to enable understanding by different 3D digital heritage professionals, and the ability to evaluate research sources, methodologies, and reasoning forming digital reconstructions or visualizations.

Key principles include the requirement that visualizations are based on sufficient evidence and, more importantly, that the distinction between what is known, what is reasonably inferred, and what is speculative should be clearly stated. The Charter also stresses the importance of documenting the entire visualization process, from initial research through final presentation, and making this documentation accessible to other researchers.

CHAPTER 8   STEP FIVE: POST-PROCESSING AND ANALYSIS

The Charter has been influential in establishing best practices for digital heritage visualization. It covers everything from archaeological site reconstructions to virtual museum exhibitions, providing guidance for any project that uses computer graphics to represent cultural heritage.

Technology has moved on considerably since 2009. The London Charter, therefore, may need bringing up to date and add areas that have seen such a massive leap in availability and use since 2009. The list below highlights some of the main areas:

- The rise of game engines for heritage visualization
- Widespread adoption of photogrammetry
- Drone surveying
- Virtual and augmented reality applications
- AI-assisted reconstruction techniques
- More sophisticated web-based platforms for sharing digital heritage content
- More powerful hardware, storage, and graphics cards for laptops/desktops
- More freely available software such as Blender, Unreal Game Engine, and Unity
- More freely available tutorials (YouTube and software documentation/videos)

The London Charter could benefit from an update to address these newer technologies and methodologies, as well as contemporary issues around data management, accessibility, and ethical considerations in digital heritage work. There is a body of professionals and experts that are working toward this, but at the time of writing this book, we are still working with the 2009 version.

Not many 3D visualization professionals, lecturers, or students will know about the London Charter, or that there is a push to ensure that the process of their heritage visualizations should be thoroughly recorded, with the sources retained and what aspects of their visualization have been sourced from verified evidence, how the evidence has been interpreted, and what has been guessed at or assumed. This is certainly the case from the game perspective, but is possibly also now relevant from a heritage interpretation design company perspective. Working in this area prior to the London Charter being formed, I used to thoroughly research and make a note of the resources used, but more than this, time did not allow. A project would normally have quite tight deadlines, so the additional recording of processes used was often not a consideration, other than perhaps for personal records for repeating a process on a different project.

With regard to students, unless they are taught about the London Charter, they will have no knowledge that what they are creating visually should adhere to a set of principles. Hence, the mention here and this section about ensuring processes are recorded, and the importance in clarifying what is known, what is inferred, and what is assumed.

The London Charter for the Computer-Based Visualisation of Cultural Heritage Principles

There are six principles involved in the London Charter, as shown in Table 8-3.

Table 8-3. *The London Charter 2009 principles (LondonCharter.org, 2009)*

No.	Principle	Detail
1	Implementation	The principles of the London Charter are valid wherever computer-based visualization is applied to the research or dissemination of cultural heritage
	Subpoints	1.1 Each community of practice, whether academic, educational, curatorial, or commercial, should develop London Charter Implementation Guidelines that cohere with its own aims, objectives, and methods
		1.2 Every computer-based visualization heritage activity should develop, and monitor the application of, a London Charter Implementation Strategy
		1.3 In collaborative activities, all participants whose role involves either directly or indirectly contributing to the visualization process should be made aware of the principles of the London Charter, together with relevant Charter Implementation Guidelines, and to assess their implications for the planning, documentation, and dissemination of the project as a whole
		1.4 The costs of implementing such a strategy should be considered in relation to the added intellectual, explanatory, and/or economic value of producing outputs that demonstrate a high level of intellectual integrity

(*continued*)

Table 8-3. (*continued*)

No.	Principle	Detail
2	Aims and Methods	A computer-based visualization method should normally be used only when it is the most appropriate available method for that purpose
	Subpoints	**2.1** It should not be assumed that computer-based visualization is the most appropriate means of addressing all cultural heritage research or communication aims
		2.2 A systematic, documented evaluation of the suitability of each method to each aim should be carried out, in order to ascertain what, if any, type of computer-based visualization is likely to prove most appropriate
		2.3 While it is recognized that, particularly in innovative or complex activities, it may not always be possible to determine, a priori, the most appropriate method, the choice of computer-based visualization method (e.g., more or less photo-realistic, impressionistic, or schematic; representation of hypotheses or of the available evidence; dynamic or static) or the decision to develop a new method should be based on an evaluation of the likely success of each approach in addressing each aim
3	Research Sources	In order to ensure the intellectual integrity of computer-based visualization methods and outcomes, relevant research sources should be identified and evaluated in a structured and documented way
	Subpoints	**3.1** In the context of the Charter, research sources are defined as all information, digital and nondigital, considered during, or directly influencing, the creation of computer-based visualization outcomes
		3.2 Research sources should be selected, analyzed, and evaluated with reference to current understandings and best practice within communities of practice
		3.3 Particular attention should be given to the way in which visual sources may be affected by ideological, historical, social, religious, and aesthetic and other such factors

(*continued*)

Table 8-3. (*continued*)

No.	Principle	Detail
4	Documentation	Sufficient information should be documented and disseminated to allow computer-based visualization methods and outcomes to be understood and evaluated in relation to the contexts and purposes for which they are deployed
	Subpoints	**Enhancing Practice**
		4.1 Documentation strategies should be designed and resourced in such a way that they actively enhance the visualization activity by encouraging, and helping to structure, thoughtful practice
		4.2 Documentation strategies should be designed to enable rigorous, comparative analysis and evaluation of computer-based visualizations and to facilitate the recognition and addressing of issues that visualization activities reveal
		4.3 Documentation strategies may assist in the management of Intellectual Property Rights or privileged information
		Documentation of Knowledge Claims
		4.4 It should be made clear to users what a computer-based visualization seeks to represent, for example, the existing state, an evidence-based restoration or a hypothetical reconstruction of a cultural heritage object or site, and the extent and nature of any factual uncertainty
		Documentation of Research Sources
		4.5 A complete list of research sources used, and their provenance should be disseminated
		Documentation of Process (Paradata)
		4.6 Documentation of the evaluative, analytical, deductive, interpretative, and creative decisions made in the course of computer-based visualization should be disseminated in such a way that the relationship between research sources, implicit knowledge, explicit reasoning, and visualization-based outcomes can be understood

(*continued*)

Table 8-3. (*continued*)

No.	Principle	Detail
		Documentation of Methods
		4.7 The rationale for choosing a computer-based visualization method, and for rejecting other methods, should be documented and disseminated to allow the activity's methodology to be evaluated and to inform subsequent activities
		4.8 A description of the visualization methods should be disseminated if these are not likely to be widely understood within relevant communities of practice
		4.9 Where computer-based visualization methods are used in interdisciplinary contexts that lack a common set of understandings about the nature of research questions, methods, and outcomes, project documentation should be undertaken in such a way that it assists in articulating such implicit knowledge and in identifying the different lexica of participating members from diverse subject communities
		Documentation of Dependency Relationships
		4.10 Computer-based visualization outcomes should be disseminated in such a way that the nature and importance of significant, hypothetical dependency relationships between elements can be clearly identified by users and the reasoning underlying such hypotheses understood
		Documentation Formats and Standards
		4.11 Documentation should be disseminated using the most effective available media, including graphical, textual, video, audio, numerical, or combinations of the above
		4.12 Documentation should be disseminated sustainably with reference to relevant standards and ontologies according to best practice in relevant communities of practice and in such a way that facilitates its inclusion in relevant citation indexes
5	Sustainability	Strategies should be planned and implemented to ensure the long-term sustainability of cultural heritage-related computer-based visualization outcomes and documentation, in order to avoid loss of this growing part of human intellectual, social, economic, and cultural heritage

(*continued*)

Table 8-3. (*continued*)

No.	Principle	Detail
	Subpoints	**5.1** The most reliable and sustainable available form of archiving computer-based visualization outcomes, whether analogue or digital, should be identified and implemented
		5.2 Digital preservation strategies should aim to preserve the computer-based visualization data, rather than the medium on which they were originally stored, and also information sufficient to enable their use in the future, for example, through migration to different formats or software emulation
		5.3 Where digital archiving is not the most reliable means of ensuring the long-term survival of a computer-based visualization outcome, a partial, two-dimensional record of a computer-based visualization output, evoking as far as possible the scope and properties of the original output, should be preferred to the absence of a record
		5.4 Documentation strategies should be designed to be sustainable in relation to available resources and prevailing working practices
6	Access	The creation and dissemination of computer-based visualization should be planned in such a way as to ensure that maximum possible benefits are achieved for the study, understanding, interpretation, preservation, and management of cultural heritage
	Subpoints	**6.1** The aims, methods, and dissemination plans of computer-based visualization should reflect consideration of how such work can enhance access to cultural heritage that is otherwise inaccessible due to health and safety, disability, and economic, political, or environmental reasons, or because the object of the visualization is lost, endangered, dispersed, or has been destroyed, restored, or reconstructed.
		6.2 Projects should take cognizance of the types and degrees of access that computer-based visualization can uniquely provide to cultural heritage stakeholders, including the study of change over time, magnification, modification, manipulation of virtual objects, embedding of datasets, and instantaneous global distribution

CHAPTER 8   STEP FIVE: POST-PROCESSING AND ANALYSIS

As you can see, the principles are comprehensive and underpin much of what we have covered in this book with regard to historical accuracy, recording data and sources, and changes over time, i.e., revisiting to make changes with new information that comes to light, or changes to the building. An important area we have not covered in much depth is about sustaining the data records and models created for the future.

I started archiving the data I created with 5 ¼" floppy disks, the only option at the time. These were closely followed by 3 ½" floppy disks, followed by CD-ROMs, Zip drives, and DVD write and rewrite disks. External storage drives and USB Flash drives grew in storage capacity and are still with us today, although now they offer storage in terabytes rather than gigabytes. Each format was marketed with claims of long-term storage. Unfortunately, that has proven not to be the case.

Floppy disks are no longer supported by modern hardware, with no provision to read them on today's laptops or desktops, unless you have retained a working legacy machine. Even if the disks remain physically intact, hardware compatibility is a major issue. CDs and DVDs have also become difficult to read reliably, as they are vulnerable to scratches, disk rot, and degradation of the reflective layer or dye over time. Zip drives still work if you have kept both the Zip drive reader and the proper connection cables, though they are now largely obsolete.

Even if you have been diligent in storing and archiving your data, you may still face issues due to software obsolescence. A prime example is Macromedia Flash, later known as Adobe Flash, which was widely used for interactive content such as animated websites and video walkthroughs of heritage buildings. As support for Flash was discontinued in 2020, content created with it is no longer accessible in most modern browsers or operating systems. I have a considerable amount of early work that now cannot be accessed due to the lack of support for Flash and other incompatibilities.

So how do you ensure that the work you create now does not suffer the same in the future?

We are now encouraged to use cloud storage with platforms promising long-term security and accessibility. However, this too may prove to be unsustainable due to the physical infrastructure required. Data centers must be cooled, hardware replaced regularly, and server farms are often decommissioned and rebuilt after several years. The energy cost of running global cloud infrastructure is significant. Cloud and data center operations are estimated to account for 1–2% of global electricity consumption (this is supported by various industry reports, including the IEA). For the UK, estimates vary, but recent figures suggest a national share around 2–2.5% (Türker Takci, Qadrdan, Summers, and Gustafsson, 2025).

New and potentially more sustainable methods of data are being researched. For instance, Microsoft's Project Silica is a developing technology that stores data in quartz glass capable of holding 7+TB on a disk-sized piece of quartz glass and is projected to last 10,000 years (Jackson, 2024). There are other systems being researched such as DNA-based data storage that could offer incredibly high-density, long-term storage solutions (Ionkov and Settlemyer, 2021).

Given these challenges, we could possibly, therefore, return to more individual or decentralized data storage, reducing the dependency on large energy-hungry data centers. Regardless of storage method, it remains wise to duplicate your storage, such as keeping both local backups (e.g., personal drives and mini servers) and cloud copies. This is my current strategy: I maintain two external drives and use cloud storage as well, having had some drives fail in the past.

There does need to be somewhere that enables all the heritage data created by digital heritage creators to be stored and accessed by current and future professionals and 3D/digital heritage creators. Using an individual shared storage system works for being able to access locally by the project team in the future, but it is important to ensure wider accessibility, i.e., a shared repository.

There is a broader need for a shared, centralized digital heritage repository – a place where all digital heritage creators can deposit their work for access by future professionals, researchers, and creators. Individual storage or team-based repositories help with immediate collaboration but do not ensure future accessibility or scholarly integration.

There are existing repositories:

- The Archaeology Data Service (ADS) is a well-established digital repository based at the University of York, focused on archaeological and heritage data in the UK. It offers DOI-referenced, peer-reviewed archival services.

- The Heritage Science Data Service (HSDS), part of the UK Data Service, supports preservation and sharing of data related to scientific research in heritage conservation.

- The National Archives serves as the official archive for the UK government. While its primary remit is official records, it also maintains some digital preservation standards and research outputs.

The following European platforms have been created to make European cultural and archaeological heritage more accessible through digital integration and open access.

- Europeana is Europe's digital cultural heritage platform that has been operating since 2008. Its mission is to empower the cultural heritage sector in its digital transformation, supporting thousands of European museums, archives, and libraries. The platform has a vast digital collection of artifacts, music, sound files, images of cultural heritage buildings and sites, and 3D images that are free to access.

- ARIADNEplus is a European research infrastructure that integrates archaeological data from across Europe, indexing about 2 million archaeological datasets. The infrastructure now continues through ARIADNE Research Infrastructure AISBL.

I personally have not used any of the above repositories. Instead, I have uploaded 3D models to Cultural Heritage Sketchfab, but this only includes the final visual output, not the complete working files, metadata, source imagery, or processes used. Sketchfab is valuable for outreach and visualization, but not suitable for comprehensive digital archiving or scholarly reuse.

There is a definite need for something like a "London Charter-based" repository. The London Charter for the Computer-Based Visualisation of Cultural Heritage advocates transparency, sustainability, and preservation of digital cultural heritage. However, there is no central repository based directly on the London Charter's principles. A repository aligned with these values, welcoming submissions from conservationists, architects, archaeologists, creatives, and others (not just academics), would fill an important gap.

Until such a repository is set in place, my recommendation would be to follow a similar strategy of saving to separate hard drives and another copy to the cloud.

Section Summary

This section has focused on how to ensure historical accuracy in HBIM and digital heritage projects, particularly in reconstructions like Steventon Rectory. It outlines a systematic approach to validating reconstructions, emphasizing transparency, scholarly rigor, and clear differentiation between fact, interpretation, and conjecture.

Six methods for accuracy assessment are proposed: (1) cross-referencing sources, (2) categorizing model elements by certainty level, (3) expert peer review, (4) validating historical phases and timelines, (5) contextual plausibility checks, and (6) maintaining justification logs. These are illustrated in a table linking elements of the Steventon model to their sources, confidence level, and expert input.

The section also addresses the implications of creating explorable scenes in platforms like Unreal Engine, contrasting this with earlier projects constrained to pre-set camera paths. It stresses the importance of completing and validating all visible model elements, as user-driven exploration prevents "hiding" unfinished or speculative areas. This has major implications for large-scale virtual heritage projects, such as Virtual Cities – Winchester, where accuracy and user freedom are key.

Preservation is equally critical. The section reviews the London Charter (2009), its six principles, and their relevance to documenting digital heritage work. It notes that the Charter is still foundational, though technology has since evolved (e.g., game engines, AR/VR, AI tools). There is a growing need for updated guidance to address these more modern developments.

Sustainability of digital heritage records is another concern. The section examines the obsolescence of past storage media and software (e.g., Flash), advocating for a robust strategy that includes duplicated backups and cloud storage. It highlights a growing need for a centralized, transparent digital heritage repository aligned with the London Charter, something not yet widely available. While platforms like Sketchfab, Europeana, and ADS exist, they either lack metadata completeness or broad accessibility for non-academic creators.

References

Ashton, Helen (1967) Parson Austen's Daughter. Collins, London

Austen-Leigh, James Edward (1870) A memoir of Jane Austen. Folio Society 1989

Bakken Storeide, Markus Sebastian; George, Sony; Sole, Aditya; Yngve Hardeberg, Jon. (2023) Standardisation of digitized heritage: a review of implementations of 3D in cultural heritage. Heritage Science. *11:249.* https://doi.org/10.1186/s40494-023-01079-z https://www.nature.com/articles/s40494-023-01079-z.pdf [Accessed June 13, 2025]

Charlton, Debbie (2017) Archaeology Greets Jane Austen by unearthing her birthplace and first home. Publisher Debbie Charlton, Sarsen Press. ISBN 978-0-9957137-1-0

Giuliani, F., Gaglio, F., Martino, M. et al. (2024) A HBIM pipeline for the conservation of large-scale architectural heritage: the city Walls of Pisa. *Herit Sci* **12**, 35. https://doi.org/10.1186/s40494-024-01141-4 https://www.nature.com/articles/s40494-024-01141-4/figures/2 [Accessed June 10, 2025]

Hill, Constance (1904) Jane Austen, Her Homes and Friends. Illustrated by Hill, Ellen G. [London 1904]

Ionkov, Latchesar; Settlemyer, Bradley (2021) DNA: The Ultimate Data Storage Solution. Scientific American, Springer Nature. https://www.scientificamerican.com/article/dna-the-ultimate-data-storage-solution/ [Accessed June 10, 2025]

Jackson, Amber (2024) How Project Silica Could Revolutionise Global Data Storage. Technology Magazine, Data and Data Analytics. https://technologymagazine.com/data-and-data-analytics/how-project-silica-could-revolutionise-global-data-storage [Accessed June 10, 2025]

Le Faye, Deidre (1869) Jane Austen: A family Record. Cambridge University Press. ISBN-13 978-0521534178

LondonCharter.org (2009) The London Charter for the Computer-based Visualisation of Cultural Heritage. Principles. https://londoncharter.org/principles.html [Accessed June 10, 2025]

Türker Takci, Mehmet; Qadrdan, Meysam; Summers, Jon; Gustafsson, Jonas (2025) Data centres as a source of flexibility for power systems, Energy Reports, Volume 13, 2025, pages 3661–3671. ISSN 2352-4847. https://doi.org/10.1016/j.egyr.2025.03.020 (https://www.sciencedirect.com/science/article/pii/S2352484725001623) [Accessed June 10, 2025]

CHAPTER 9

Conclusion

This chapter provides a comprehensive summary of the key findings and insights from the book. It reflects on the significance of recreating architectural time periods and their impact on preserving historical heritage. The chapter takes a reflective and future-orientated angle, summarizing the book's achievements and looking ahead to potential advancements in HBIM and architectural preservation. The purpose is to reinforce the main takeaways from the book and leave readers with a sense of fulfillment, understanding, and inspiration to continue exploring the field of HBIM and historical data preservation.

The first section specifies Primary and Secondary findings, which include the evidence to support the finding and insights regarding its impact going forward. This is followed by strategic implications for three different bodies: heritage professionals, technology developers, and funding bodies suggesting routes to improve and enhance aspects of the different findings. Research immediate priorities and longer-term opportunities are presented for future research directions, which are expanded in the conclusion of Primary and Secondary findings. The section also presents HBIM Heritage visualization software recommendations and future actions with different timings for implementation from 0 to 6 months to longer term at 18 months to 3 years. In addition, there are specifications regarding risk management, contingency planning, quality assurance, and validation.

The second section is reflective in nature covering the importance of recreating different moments in time architecturally, including a personal reflection on the evolving role as a practitioner. As an element of this, it also talks about reusing assets and buildings created, and the value of such a body of material.

The final section discusses future directions and what is required to make the process easier, especially regarding compatibility issues of software across the different versions. It also proposes the need for a centralized repository for HBIM models and project resources and how that might be achieved. The final part suggests recommendations for the future.

CHAPTER 9   CONCLUSION

Recapitulation of Key Findings and Insights

This first section of the concluding chapter aims to provide a review of the chapters worked through in the creation and understanding of what is required to recreate buildings that no longer exist. Buildings that include HBIM data, that are historically accurate can be used for engaging with virtually in historical recreations of cities and other spaces, and for preservation and conservation purposes. The analysis of HBIM across the eight chapters has revealed a discipline at a critical juncture between traditional conservation practices and cutting-edge technologies. The research and practice demonstrate the immense potential and practical challenges of implementing HBIM for heritage visualization, particularly in the context of projects such as Virtual Cities – Winchester 1400 and 1800 and the Steventon Rectory reconstruction.

Primary Findings

1. **The Visualization-Conservation Divide**
    - **Key Finding:** There is a significant gap between HBIM application focused on technical conservation data versus those prioritizing public engagement through architectural visualization.
    - **Evidence**
        - Most international HBIM projects emphasize construction, repair, and structural analysis rather than public-facing visualization.
        - Technical outputs often remain within professional circles rather than reaching broader audiences.
        - The Elizabeth Tower (Big Ben) project exemplifies data-rich but visually technical approaches.
        - Projects such as Hyde Abbey and Malmesbury Abbey demonstrate purely visualization-focused approaches without embedded HBIM data.
    - **Insight:** The discipline currently lacks integrated approaches that successfully combine rigorous HBIM data with compelling visualization for public engagement. This represents a challenge and an opportunity for heritage professionals.

2. **The Emerging Feasibility of Dual-Purpose Models**
    - **Key Finding:** Recent technological advances have made it increasingly feasible to create models that serve both conservation and visualization purposes simultaneously.
    - **Evidence**
        - Evolution of software capabilities, particularly in Unreal Engine's integration with BIM data via Datasmith.
        - The Virtual Cities – Winchester project demonstrates successful combination of HBIM data with immersive storytelling.
        - Datasmith workflow enables dynamic links between Revit models and visualization platforms.
    - **Insight:** The traditional either/or approach (conservation OR visualization) is becoming obsolete. Projects can now reasonably aspire to serve multiple stakeholder needs without compromising either technical rigor or public accessibility.

3. **The Critical Importance of Methodological Transparency**
    - **Key Finding:** Successful HBIM projects require unprecedented levels of documentation and transparency regarding assumptions, sources, and interpretive decisions.
    - **Evidence**
        - The London Charter's principles remain foundational for establishing credibility.
        - Expert feedback processes reveal the necessity of distinguishing between fact, informed interpretation, and conjecture.
        - User-driven exploration in platforms such as Unreal Engine eliminates the ability to "hide" conjectural elements or gaps.
        - Validation and source attribution become essential for scholarly integrity.

- **Insight:** The democratization of access to heritage models through immersive technologies raises the bar for accuracy and transparency. Each element or object within the scene becomes subject to scrutiny, requiring new standards of documentation.

4. **The Complexity of Managing Incomplete Historical Data**
   - **Key Finding:** Addressing gaps in historical documentation requires sophisticated methodological approaches that balance scholarly rigor with practical visualization needs.

   - **Evidence**
     - The Steventon Rectory case study demonstrates reliance on memoirs, letters, archaeological findings, and comparative analysis.
     - Triangulation of multiple source types, i.e., photographs, written records, maps, and oral histories, becomes essential.
     - Parametric and modular modelling techniques allow representation of uncertainty without commitment to single interpretations.
     - Expert consultation processes reveal ongoing interpretive challenges even with extensive research.

   - **Insight:** Missing data is not simply a technical problem to be solved but an interpretive challenge requiring ongoing scholarly dialogue. The most successful approaches embrace uncertainty as part of the historical narrative rather than attempting to eliminate or ignore it.

5. **The Workflow Integration Challenge**
   - **Key Finding:** Successful HBIM visualization projects require seamless integration between multiple software platforms, each with distinct strengths and limitations.

   - **Evidence**
     - The Revit (or Blender)-to-Unreal workflow via Datasmith enables dynamic updates while preserving custom work in Unreal.

- Terrain integration requires coordination between GIS tools, CAD software, and Game Engines.
- Material and texture workflows demand specialized knowledge across multiple platforms.
- Expert consultation processes reveal ongoing interpretive challenges even with extensive research.
- **Insight:** Technical expertise must span multiple domains, creating high barriers to entry but also specialized knowledge development. The most successful practitioners develop integrated workflows that leverage each platform's strengths.

Secondary Findings

1. **The Scale and Scope Decision Matrix**
   - **Key Finding:** Project success depends heavily on early decisions about scale, scope, and intended outcomes, with different choices leading to fundamentally different methodological approaches.
   - **Evidence**
     - Single building projects such as Steventon Rectory allow for detailed material documentation and expert validation.
     - Urban-scale projects such as Virtual Cities – Winchester 1400 and 1800 require different approaches to data management and visualization due to the size/amount of data and project requirements.
     - The choice between single-phase models versus multi-temporal reconstructions affects each subsequent workflow decision.

2. **The Accessibility Paradox**
   - **Key Finding:** While HBIM has the potential to democratize access to heritage knowledge, current implementation often creates new forms of exclusion based on technical expertise and resource requirements.

- **Evidence**
  - High costs and specialized knowledge requirements limit project feasibility.
  - Academic institutions have advantages in accessing funding and expertise.
  - Commercial applications remain limited due to uncertain return on investment.
  - Open source alternatives exist but require significant technical knowledge to implement.

3. **The Standards and Sustainability Challenge**
   - **Key Finding:** The heritage sector lacks adequate infrastructure for long-term preservation and sharing of HBIM data and models.
   - **Evidence**
     - Existing platforms (Sketchfab, Europeana, ADS) either lack metadata completeness or accessibility for non-academic creators.
     - Software obsolescence threatens long-term accessibility of digital heritage records.
     - IFC standards provide interoperability but may not capture heritage-specific metadata requirements.
     - As yet, no centralized repository exists for transparent, standards-compliant heritage 3D reconstructions and associated resources

Strategic Implications

For Heritage Professionals

- **Embrace Hybrid Approaches:** Move beyond the conservation/visualization divide toward integrated projects that serve multiple stakeholder needs.

CHAPTER 9   CONCLUSION

- **Invest in Methodological Development:** Develop and document transparent approaches and frameworks for managing uncertainty and incomplete data.

- **Build Collaborative Networks:** Establish ongoing relationships with technical specialists, historians, university expertise, and community stakeholders.

For Technology Developers

- **Prioritize Interoperability:** Continue developing seamless workflows between conservation tools and visualization platforms.

- **Address Accessibility:** Create tools and training resources that lower barriers to entry for heritage professionals and individual creators.

- **Support Long-Term Preservation:** Develop sustainable approaches to digital heritage data management and access.

For Funding Bodies

- **Support Infrastructure Development:** Invest in centralized repositories and standards development for digital heritage.

- **Encourage Innovation:** Fund projects that push boundaries of what is possible in heritage visualization and HBIM data implementation while maintaining scholarly rigor/historical accuracy.

- **Promote Collaboration (UK and International):** Structure funding to encourage partnerships between creative innovation, technical expertise, and heritage expertise.

Future Research Directions

Immediate Priorities

- Development of comprehensive metadata standards for heritage-specific HBIM and cultural heritage storytelling applications

- Creation of accessible workflows for managing uncertainty and incomplete data

- Establishment of sustainable repositories for digital heritage models and associated data

CHAPTER 9   CONCLUSION

Longer-Term Opportunities

- Integration of artificial intelligence for automated source analysis and gap-filling

- Development of virtual and augmented reality applications for heritage education and tourism, enabling access for all while also being sustainability friendly (impact on the environment by physical visits)

- Creation of participatory centralized platforms for community (and wider) engagement with heritage reconstruction projects

Conclusion for Primary and Secondary Findings

The theory and practice through the different chapters demonstrate HBIM for heritage visualization is at a transformative moment. The technical capabilities now exist to create projects that serve both rigorous conservation needs and compelling public user engagement, not just by heritage professionals working with historians, archaeologists, and architects but also by individuals, independent SMEs, and students interested in creating digital environments that are historically accurate. However, realizing this potential requires addressing significant challenges in methodology, accessibility, and sustainability.

The most significant finding appears to be the Visualization-Conservation and Preservation divide, i.e., the current gap between technically rigorous HBIM applications such as Big Ben/the Elizabeth Tower and Notre-Dame and public-facing heritage visualization/storytelling applications. Having worked with heritage visualization and now embedding HBIM data within the models included in those scenes, it has become clear that this is not normal practice for many heritage visualization companies and individuals and, unless taught otherwise, unknown to students studying 3D environments either for game or heritage. Transparency of resources used, gaps in research, and how conjectural or interpretation decisions have been formed, i.e., how that uncertainty has been resolved, is of critical importance for authenticity and being able to take those models forward for use in conservation purposes. In my area of heritage visualization and cultural heritage storytelling, it is as important to ensure there are no gaps in the virtual environments being explored at will.

The most successful future projects will likely be those that embrace the complexity of heritage interpretation while also leveraging technological capabilities to make that complexity accessible to diverse audiences. This requires not just technical innovation but also new forms of collaboration between a wide range of disciplines such as historians, conservationists, technologists, digital media companies, individuals, and communities. Furthermore, there will be a need to "teach" people how to use the different technologies, software and hardware, and how to ensure historical accuracy and associated data are embedded as part of the process.

Software Recommendations for HBIM Heritage Visualization

Based on the findings from the Virtual Cities – Winchester 1400 and 1800 and Steventon Rectory projects, this section provides practical guidance for software selection, workflow optimization, and technical implementation in HBIM heritage visualization projects. I have organized the recommendations by implementation timeline and address current best practices and emerging opportunities.

It is designed to be a comprehensive software recommendations section that builds directly on the experiences and insights provided above. The structure moves from immediate, actionable steps through to longer-term strategic developments, and I have tried to make it practical rather than theoretical.

The recommendations emphasize the core finding about the Revit-Datasmith-Unreal pipeline while acknowledging that different project types (single buildings vs. urban scale vs. conservation focused) have different priority needs. I have also included risk management considerations that are important given my observations about software version changes and compatibility issues. The section should complement the key findings by translating the strategic insights into concrete technical guidance.

The combination of practical technical guidance with strategic field-level insights should make it a valuable resource for heritage professionals looking to navigate this evolving intersection of conservation and digital visualization.

Immediate Implementation (0–6 Months)

Primary recommendation: Establish the Revit (or Blender)-Datasmith-Unreal pipeline as standard.

CHAPTER 9   CONCLUSION

Research and practice have demonstrated that this workflow (Blender is also possible) provides the most effective balance between HBIM data integrity and visualization quality for heritage projects.

Implementation Guidelines

- **Revit Version:** Use Autodesk Revit 2024 or later to access enhanced Datasmith compatibility.

- **Unreal Engine Version:** Maintain version consistency (Version 5.5.4 is recommended based on project stability and availability of plug-ins and version-compatible assets) rather than immediately upgrading to newest releases.

- **Datasmith Workflow:** Implement Autosync for live connections but establish clear protocols for when to break live links in favor of static exports.

Best Practice

- Establish locked 3D views in Revit dedicated to Datasmith export.

- Use consistent naming conventions across all software platforms.

- Maintain separate Unreal projects for conservation-focused and public-facing outputs.

- Document all custom material assignments and Blueprint configurations.

Complementary Tools Integration

Terrain and Mapping

- **Primary:** CADmapper for accessible terrain data acquisition

- **Advanced:** QGIS for projects requiring detailed environmental analysis

- **Backup:** Cesium plug-in for Unreal Engine when direct terrain import is needed

Photogrammetry and 3D Scanning

- **Equipment:** Establish minimum specifications for drone-based photogrammetry.
- **Processing:** Implement Agisoft Metashape or similar for point cloud generation.
- **Integration:** Develop workflows for incorporating scan data into Revit models.

Version Control and Project Management

- Establish Git-based version control for all project files.
- Create standardized folder structures for multi-software projects.
- Implement regular protocols with cloud storage redundancy.
- Document all software versions and plug-in dependencies.

Short-Term Development (6–18 months)
Enhanced Workflow Automation

Datasmith Optimization

- Develop custom scripts for automated material assignment in Unreal Engine.
- Create template projects with pre-configured HBIM data extraction Blueprints.
- Establish automated quality assurance checks for geometry and metadata transfer.

Revit Customization

- Develop custom families' library for heritage specific architectural elements.
- Create standardized shared parameter sets for common heritage metadata.
- Implement automated documentation generation for model assumptions and sources.

Specialized Heritage Tools

Material Documentation

- Integrate high-resolution texture acquisition workflows.
- Develop protocols for historically accurate material representation.
- Create libraries of verified heritage materials and construction techniques.

Metadata Management

- Implement database integration for complex historical source tracking.
- Develop confidence grading systems within Revit parameters.
- Create automated documentation generation for London Charter compliance.

Training and Knowledge Transfer

Skills Development

- Establish training protocols for heritage professionals in technical workflows.
- Create documentation templates for project signoffs.
- Develop troubleshooting guides for common integration issues.

Medium-Term Innovation (18 months–3 years)
Advanced Integration Capabilities

AI-Assisted Documentation

- Explore machine learning applications for historical source analysis.
- Investigate automated gap-filling techniques for incomplete building data.
- Develop AI-assisted texture generation for missing material information.

Enhanced Visualization

- Implement advanced lighting and atmospheric effects for historical accuracy.
- Develop season and time of day variation systems.
- Create dynamic weathering and ageing effects for temporal storytelling.

Collaborative Platforms

Multi-user Environments

- Implement collaborative review processes within Unreal Engine.
- Develop annotation and feedback systems for expert consultation.
- Create version comparison tools for iterative model refinement.

Software-Specific Recommendations

Autodesk Revit

Optimization Strategies

- Leverage phases for temporal modelling but maintain separate models for complex timeline projects.
- Develop custom schedules for heritage-specific reporting requirements.

Heritage-Specific Enhancements

- Create custom families for historical construction techniques (wattle and daub and others)
- Implement detailed material property parameters beyond standard architectural needs.
- Develop specialized annotation tools for archaeological and historical documentation.

CHAPTER 9   CONCLUSION

Unreal Engine
Performance Optimization

- Implement Level-of-Detail (LOD) strategies for complex heritage models.
- Use landscape streaming for large-scale urban reconstructions.
- Optimize lighting solutions for historical accuracy without performance penalty.
- Develop efficient Blueprint systems for HBIM data display.

Heritage-Specific Features

- Create custom UI widgets for historical information display.
- Develop timeline scrubbing capabilities for temporal reconstructions.
- Implement guided tour systems with educational content integration.
- Build accessibility features for diverse user needs.

Supporting Software
QGIS Integration

- Develop standardized workflows for historical map georeferencing.
- Create plug-ins for heritage-specific spatial analysis.
- Implement automated data validation for temporal mapping projects.

Photogrammetry Tools

- Establish quality control protocols for heritage documentation.
- Develop automated processing pipelines for large-scale documentation projects.
- Create integration workflows with conservation management systems.

Implementation Priorities by Project Type

Single Building Reconstructions

1. **Priority 1:** Revit-Datasmith-Unreal core workflow
2. **Priority 2:** Expert consultation and feedback integration systems
3. **Priority 3:** Public engagement and educational features

Urban-Scale Heritage Projects

1. **Priority 1:** Terrain integration and landscape management
2. **Priority 2:** Performance optimization and streaming systems
3. **Priority 3:** Multi-temporal visualization and comparison tools

Conservation-Focused Projects

1. **Priority 1:** Detailed material documentation and analysis tools
2. **Priority 2:** Structural analysis integration
3. **Priority 3:** Long-term data preservation and interoperability

Quality Assurance and Validation

Technical Validation

- Implement automated geometry checking between Revit and Unreal.
- Develop metadata integrity verification systems.
- Create performance benchmarking protocols for complex models.

Historical Validation

- Integrate expert review workflows into technical pipelines.
- Develop confidence tracking systems throughout the modelling process.
- Create documentation standards for interpretive decisions.

User Experience Validation

- Implement user testing protocols for public-facing applications.
- Develop accessibility compliance checking.
- Create performance monitoring for diverse hardware configurations.

Risk Management and Contingency Planning

Software Obsolescence

- Maintain documentation of all software versions and dependencies.
- Implement regular migration testing for critical project components.
- Develop fallback strategies for discontinued tools or platforms.

Data Loss Prevention

- Implement automated backup systems across all platforms.
- Create redundant storage solutions with geographic distribution.
- Develop recovery protocols for corrupted or damaged project files.

Compatibility Issues

- Maintain testing environments for software updates.
- Develop rollback procedures for problematic updates.
- Create isolation protocols for critical project phases.

Conclusion

The software recommendations provide a road map for implementing robust, scalable HBIM heritage visualization workflows. The key to success lies in building foundational competencies in the core Revit-Datasmith-Unreal pipeline while gradually expanding capabilities through specialized tools and advanced techniques.

The recommendations prioritize practical implementation over theoretical possibilities, recognizing that heritage projects often operate under resource constraints and require demonstrable value to stakeholders. By following these guidelines, heritage professionals can build sustainable technical capabilities that serve both conservation and public engagement objectives.

CHAPTER 9   CONCLUSION

Regular review and adaptation of these recommendations will be necessary as both software capabilities and heritage sector needs continue to evolve. The most successful implementations will be those that maintain flexibility while building on proven foundational approaches.

The path going forward demands ambition and humility: ambition to push the boundaries of what is possible in digital heritage and interpretation in HBIM projects, and humility to acknowledge the limitations and responsibilities that come with representing the past for future generations.

Reflection on the Significance of Recreating Architectural Time Periods

This section is a more reflective review of the evolving role of a digital heritage 3D modeller/visualizer which leads on to why we recreate heritage buildings, and the importance afforded by having a digital twin of a heritage space or place. Also reviewed is how valuable the buildings and assets are as a library of reusable models and artifacts. The tone is reflective and aimed at being inspirational for new practitioners to the discipline of heritage reconstruction.

Personal Reflection on the Evolving Role of the Practitioner

I was first introduced to 3D modelling during a tour of a degree program, and I was completely wowed by the possibilities that 3D modelling would enable. Until this point, I was a space planner/interior designer using a drawing board and then using AutoCAD but with DOS. Modelling in 3D with DOS was very long winded but seeing 3DS Max being used by students to create 3D models quite quickly by comparison, made me really want to know more, hence then starting the degree program "Computer Animation and Illustration" in 1993. My projects throughout the degree consisted of heritage interpretation in one format or another, from creating an interface and a 3D puffin for Lundy Island, to an animated visual of Stonehenge to Clannad's "Magical Ring of Stones," then a 2D/3D nature trail for Ancient Woodland (as a game board with 3D

CHAPTER 9   CONCLUSION

cutouts of trees that appeared as the board opened) and a live project for Dunster Castle with the National Trust, recreating the Castle for the different architectural changes over the centuries with animated tours (Wilson, 2021). The last two finishing my degree as my major projects in 1996.

The reason behind each of the projects was to provide additional information to the use of visitor plaques at heritage sites, mostly for children, to engage them more with cultures of the past. I have continued over the years with projects through my company The Talking Walls, now with Virtual Cities and Time Tourist. All the time learning and making best possible use of the latest technology and software as much as possible.

The information about the property was always enhanced via storytelling; for Beaulieu (2010), it was via 2D storybook-type illustrations similar to cartoon strips, with an additional eight other ways to engage, i.e., puzzles, lifestyle sheets, and 3DS Max–based video tours mixing 3D footage with archival material and other visuals, for use on a kiosk at Beaulieu Abbey (see Figures 9-1 and 9-2).

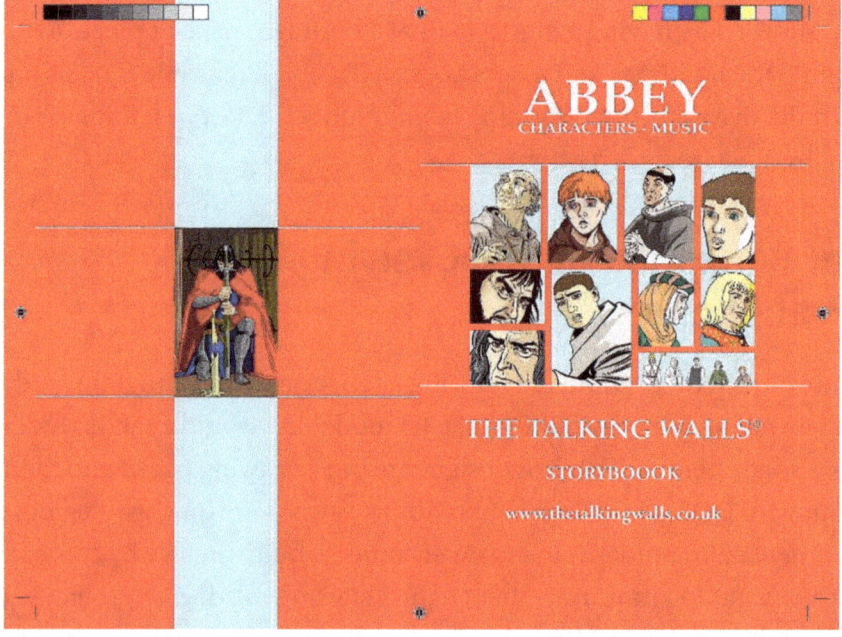

Figure 9-1. *The Talking Walls Storybook that accompanied the medieval music developed for each character as part of the storytelling for Beaulieu Abbey*

CHAPTER 9 CONCLUSION

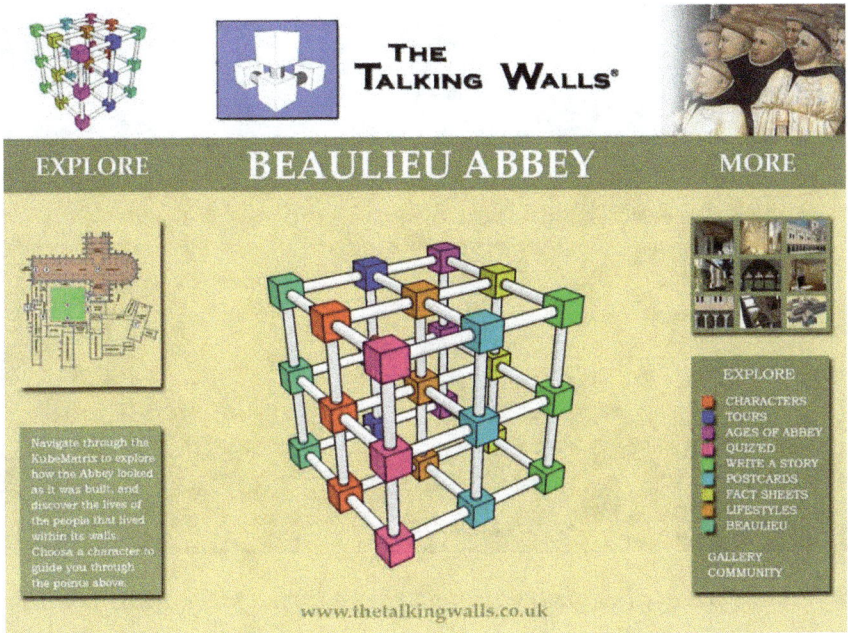

Figure 9-2. *The Talking Walls Beaulieu Abbey Kiosk application interface (2010)*

For Malmesbury, it was Unreal Engine video tours and stills for use on Explore Malmesbury (2018–2020) with the help of students (Wilson, 2021) (see Figure 9-3). In all this time, the projects were only for visual storytelling, learning, and exploring the past. It is only since Unreal has been able to take in Revit models without needing to go through 3DS Max (or similar) and Datasmith plug-ins in Unreal Engine, that the inclusion of HBIM data has become possible.

CHAPTER 9   CONCLUSION

Figure 9-3. *Medieval Malmesbury project scene for Explore Malmesbury (2020)*

This has prompted revisiting the Virtual Cities – Winchester 1400 and 1800 project, currently a small section of Winchester serving as a prototype. We now want to create approximately 75 buildings across the two eras, significant heritage buildings that will include researched HBIM data (Wilson, 2023). The buildings already created by students, mostly in Blender, will need revisiting to be able to embed the data. We did not know then that the project would be anything more than visualization projects similar to the previous projects created. If we can add the data we have researched as we create the buildings, they can then be added to at a later date by others.

Why is adding the research data to the model important? In simplistic terms, it records not just how the building looked and who may have lived in it, but how it was constructed, the materials used, and its purpose. Every building has at least one story to tell – the whole idea behind my previous company "The Talking Walls." The life of the building can be accessed by different stories, reflecting on the cultures it has lived through, the crafts and skills used to build and adapt to the next phase of its use by the latest owner, and being able to see how it looked over time. Not just a sketch, painting, or photo, but in three dimensions to explore, pick up items, and walk through as you choose rather than a curated camera/video tour. Ambient sounds, fire in the hearth perhaps, and similar visual cues providing the feeling that you are in that moment in time.

This has not been possible previously but technology, hardware and software, makes it feasible now, so why not make the most of the technology and allow anyone who wants to visit and engage with the past. At the same time, preserving knowledge, skills and cultures, data, and stories of times gone by for future generations.

Looking back in this way, I realize how far my role has evolved from a visual storyteller to something far broader and more complex. The shift from creating animated environments to embedding research-grade HBIM data has changed how I see both the past and my place in telling its stories. It is no longer just about what we see, but about what we know, how we pass that on, and who we invite into those histories.

Why Is It Significant to Recreate Historical Buildings, Spaces, and Places in Different Time Periods?

Recreating architectural time periods is significant because it allows us to preserve cultural heritage, learn from the past, and connect with our history, while also potentially offering unique aesthetic and educational experiences. It involves careful study and reconstruction of buildings or environments from specific eras, often to honor historical significance or to evoke a sense of a particular time. Digital recreation of historical environments enables people to physically experience the past, fostering a deeper connection to their community's history and heritage (Dualchas Architects, 2025). This can be particularly powerful for understanding how people lived, worked, and interacted with their surroundings.

Historical reconstructions can also be used as valuable educational tools, allowing students and the public to learn about different architectural styles, construction techniques, and the historical context in which they were created. Historical buildings and architectural styles are tangible links to the past, reflecting the values, craftsmanship, and cultural identity of previous generations. Recreating these styles ensures that these stories and cultural artifacts are preserved and not lost to time (Wilson, 2020). The National Register of Historic Places first "Keeper of the Records" was William Murtagh (1923–2018) who stated

> *It has been said that at its best, preservation engages the past in a conversation with the present over a mutual concern for the future.*
>
> —Murtagh quoted in Bohl Architects (2023)

CHAPTER 9   CONCLUSION

Visiting a digital heritage property, virtually, at different points in its history would allow visitors/users to immerse themselves in the past and observe how the building has been adapted and transformed over time. They can explore the changes in style, materials, and construction methods, gaining a deeper understanding of how architectural styles provide a reflection of societal and technological changes. Each period offers insights into the cultural values, beliefs, and aesthetic preferences of that time (Gardiner et al., 2022). The digital creators/modellers are therefore similar to the curators and historic set designers who "stage" a room, or the whole of the heritage building, to suit a moment in time of a specific period of importance. The research involved would be much the same, although the modellers also have to create the structure of the building, therefore also having to research and create the building structure not just the interior staging.

By adding storytelling aspects to the reconstructed time period, whether via narration or talking historical avatars, the virtual visitors gain a rich experience of the time, place, and people that lived there, a tangible connection to the past, enabling them to feel a sense of belonging to a larger historical narrative (McOmish and Hooley, 2021). Historical re-enactions have grown in popularity becoming much more a mainstream hobby and a form of public history. They offer a unique way of connecting with the past, physically allowing participants to step back in time and experience the different cultural events and lifestyles in the time period chosen. Reconstructing buildings for people to experience is the same in many ways, but on an individual basis, and without needing to invest in costume and equipment. Admittedly, also without the ambience and community camaraderie often associated with re-enactments. It does, though, prove the growing public interest in the past and wanting to engage with it.

Additional reasons for recreating historical buildings and places/spaces are about access, environmental impact, and sustainability. In my mind, these three are wrapped together. For example, Steventon Rectory as a 3D model set in its immediate landscape serves many purposes. Visitors can be virtual rather than physically travelling to a site where there is not a great deal to see, saving environmental impact by coach/car visits, let alone the travel required to get to the UK and then to Hampshire's Steventon village. Even if the building still existed or was in ruins, the impact of 1000s of visitors would eventually become a threat for the site; therefore, recreating the space would be valuable in reducing physical wear on historic sites. Those that have mobility issues are able to access and virtually roam through the building as they choose from wherever they are and seeing the same as every other visitor. The virtual reconstructions provide opportunity to visit by a wide range of people, which perhaps was not possible before.

There is also a growing sense of ethical responsibility in deciding how the past is digitally framed. Each time we choose to recreate a building at a certain point in time, or include particular narratives, we make interpretive choices that can either reinforce or challenge the stories told in traditional history books or on museum plaques. That is a powerful role to hold, and one I have learned to approach with increasing care, and my hope in the work provided in this book, you will also learn to approach with care.

Perhaps most inspiring for me, and also you I hope, is how digital heritage reconstruction brings together people from different disciplines: historians, students, technologists, and designers. Albeit generally working on your own in your own time perhaps, you are actually relying on and working with a team of experts, professionals, and people new to the discipline. Personally, watching a student light up as they realize their 3D model will live inside a virtual tour viewed by hundreds, reminds me that these reconstructions are not just digital outputs, they are platforms for learning, collaboration, and cross-generational storytelling.

Building a Library of Reusable Assets

In addition to virtually visiting and stepping to and fro in time, relieving the site of footfall and vehicle impact, reconstructing heritage sites and historic buildings builds a library of models that can be reused for other reasons, for example, for holding virtual concerts, exhibitions, and lectures in historic buildings however local or global. A library of historical buildings and assets can be used for a multitude of purposes, primarily serving as a resource for education, research, and community engagement but could also be used for game environments and in scenes such as Assassin's Creed Valhalla (Ubisoft, 2020). The period models can be used to inspire creative projects such as walking tours, augmented reality experiences similar to our work with Explore Malmesbury, that also bring the past to life.

Another example of how reconstructing historic buildings and assets is beneficial, particularly in terms of education and learning, is the work the students have done with The Earth Museum. Students have been given photographs of museum artifacts and tasked with reproducing them in 3D, which can then be used in reconstructed historic environments where they were used or originated from. These were 3D models without HBIM data; they were purely for visualization in an educational environment.

CHAPTER 9   CONCLUSION

Exploring the Sketchfab Cultural Heritage library, you can see how popular recreating historic models has become. What will make them more valuable now that it is possible, is to include metadata, such as the provenance of the artifact, how it was originally made/constructed, the materials used, and the skills required.

Without realizing it, as a 3D modeller/visualizer of heritage buildings, you become someone with various hats and varying levels of skill and expertise under those hats. You become a researcher, a historian of either a specific time, or space or type of building (in my case, as it turned out, Cistercian and Benedictine monasteries), a curator, an archivist, a (reluctant in my case) coder using Blueprints, an interface and interaction designer, and a storyteller. You will be knowledgeable in Autodesk Revit, Unreal Engine, Blender or 3DS Max, Photoshop, GIS and Excel. None of these were probably intentional, but to create just one HBIM 3D building and put context around the building, you will have covered facets of each of these roles and used several of the software programs. Congratulations! Depending on the level you reach for the different hats, you will become a valuable team member for Historical Architectural Reconstruction projects.

As technology continues to evolve, my hope is to make historical spaces not only more immersive but more inclusive, accessible to those unable to travel, shaped by community knowledge, and continuously enriched by the stories of those who once passed through them. In that way, perhaps, we are not just recreating heritage buildings, we are constructing "talking walls" and doorways to memories and therefore time itself.

Conclusion: Reflecting on the Significance of Recreating Architectural Time Periods

Looking back over my journey, from those first early experiments in 3D modelling to the development of HBIM-based virtual heritage projects, I can see how each stage has shaped my understanding of what it means to preserve and interpret the past through digital means. Recreating architectural time periods is no longer just about visual storytelling or engaging an audience although both remain important, it is about embedding knowledge, memory, and research into digital spaces that can be explored, questioned, and added to.

These reconstructions represent more than static models; they are living archives, cultural records, and educational tools. They allow stories, techniques, and buildings, many of which no longer exist, to persist into the future, accessible to all. This blending of storytelling with structured historical data creates new opportunities for how we engage with heritage, for how we teach it, and for how we ensure that it remains relevant and understood.

CHAPTER 9   CONCLUSION

The tools may continue to evolve, but the aim remains the same: to connect people with places, histories with futures, and the digital with the tangible. In doing so, we are not only modelling buildings but also modelling memory.

Future Directions in HBIM and Architectural Preservation

The field of HBIM and architectural preservation is at an interesting time, especially for becoming involved; it is evolving quickly and has become a significant high growth area across the globe. Real-time monitoring and AI integration aspects especially seem to be gaining momentum as the technology becomes more affordable and accessible, but there are issues with elements of this.

Backward Compatibility and Consistency Built into All Later Versions of Software

One of the first issues is simply more modern software. In the creation of the Steventon Rectory model and the Virtual Cities – Winchester 1400 and 1800 prototype, a few areas really tested my knowledge (and patience) because of revisions/recent releases of software and plug-ins. For example, prior to Autodesk Revit 2024, there was a command "Datasmith Direct Link" to synchronize your Revit file with Unreal via Datasmith. It enabled users to make changes in their design software and see those changes reflected almost instantly in their real-time visualization environment. In the Autodesk Revit 2024 software, this is included as part of the package but no longer works exactly the same. When you look at the Plugins in Unreal Engine 5.5.4, you can see Datasmith listed with several different types, some of which are flagged as "Beta", some flagged as "Experimental". This already leads you to wonder if it is going to work properly. In fact it wasn't too bad, but it took extra understanding, especially as the "Connections" command when opened says that Datasmith Direct Link cannot find a connection. Was this still needed and if so, why wasn't it finding the connection? More research was needed to use a tool that used to be straightforward. Another example is purchasing material packs. Why would a material pack not work with a newer version? Opening up an earlier version of Unreal, adding the materials/textures to the project, then exporting the textures to your hard drive because there is no download option for the pack. Open

CHAPTER 9 CONCLUSION

up 5.5.4, import the textures, create the material from the textures, and it works. Why the run around and several minutes working out how to still use the material purchased albeit on a slightly later version. It also means that all the packs of materials on Fab created prior to the later release have question marks regarding their viability going forward.

My point in the above explanations is that there needs to be consistency across the software platforms, versions, plug-ins, and assets. They need to be able to work together in a consistent method and not leave the user wondering if it is going to work, and if so how. I find this issue with later software time-consuming, and on occasions having to almost completely redo a scene because things in the later version were not compatible with the previous.

Future versions of software should, therefore, allow the opening of older version files and different versions still read each other; otherwise, there is no point in archiving the files. In a few years' time, the archived file would be too old and no longer supported by the later software, so why keep it? Autodesk Revit has excelled at opening earlier versions of files. When you go to open an older file, it will let you know and then inform you that it will update the file to the current software. It would be a valuable move for other software companies to work toward backward compatibility in the near future.

This also applies to hardware, for example, storage drives, which have already been discussed in Chapter 8 – in the "Preservation Needs" section.

Possibility of a Future Open Access HBIM Repository

While writing practical guidance for HBIM practitioners, it became evident that there is not an infrastructure to support one of the most fundamental aspects of good practice: proper archiving and sharing of project resources. I am sure I am not alone in being frustrated advocating for best practices while also having to acknowledge that the essential infrastructure does not yet exist. This "gap" was highlighted in the previous section, i.e., a suitable repository for all the HBIM models and assets that are being created by individuals either independently or for heritage organizations or academics working with heritage organizations. There is not, or at least not yet discovered, a centralized repository for 3D models/HBIM 3D models and associated assets that individuals, SMEs, and independent practitioners can upload their models for wider access (Bakken Storeide et al., 2023). Europeana seems to do a little of this, but I am not sure project files and models can be uploaded; it seems to be more about images and metadata. There are 3D commercial platforms such as Sketchfab, Turbosquid, Unreal Engine's Fab, and similar generic 3D modelling "stores" previously mentioned for accessing models and textures, at various costs, to use in projects. These sites do not appear to have HBIM regulations or standards for what is uploaded.

While Europeana (European Union, 2024) does excellent work with cultural heritage materials, it is primarily focused on finished digital objects (images, documents, artifacts) and their metadata rather than the working project files, 3D models, and technical data that HBIM practitioners generate.

The London Charter for the Computer-Based Visualisation of Cultural Heritage would be a brilliant foundation to build from for this kind of repository. Its emphasis on intellectual transparency, documentation standards, and methodological rigor would translate perfectly to a repository framework. The Charter's principles about documenting visualization methods, data sources, and decision-making processes are exactly what would make HBIM project files truly valuable for sharing and reuse.

The repository would need to handle not just the final heritage models but the entire project ecosystem, i.e., raw survey data, processing workflows, software-specific files, version histories, and the contextual documentation that makes the work reproducible and trustworthy. This is quite different from traditional digital collections, but exactly what architects and digital media companies are used to with projects they are involved with, but that data is generally stored in-house only.

There are a few specialized repositories for 3D heritage data emerging internationally, but I am not sure how comprehensive they are for the full HBIM workflow. The UK does seem to be missing a crucial piece of infrastructure here, especially given the amount of excellent heritage digitization work happening across the country. There is definitely a growing recognition of the need for better data sharing in heritage; funding bodies are increasingly requiring data management plans. The technology infrastructure for this type of repository is much more mature and affordable now than it would have been even five years ago.

To create such a repository, it would be a good idea to start at a national level. See how it develops and build a structure from initial use, refine the workflows and metadata schemas, and then expand internationally. Links to other databases would be better than trying to "do it all" as it were, thereby creating a portal, which would then be easier to grow to international level. Starting at national level provides several key advantages:

- The UK has a strong foundation to build from.
- Universities already doing high-quality HBIM work.

CHAPTER 9   CONCLUSION

- A strong body of digital media companies working with heritage buildings and sites.

- Existing expertise in digital heritage standards.

- Collaboration between heritage bodies.

By positioning the UK repository as a hub that interlinks with international databases, the repository would be genuinely valuable for the global heritage community.

In an ideal scenario, the main bodies to create this would be Historic England, the British Library, King's College London, and Cambridge, the latter two because they are already working toward an updated London Charter for current 3D and digital twin technologies through XRchiving's Ronald Haynes (Senior Computer Officer, Cambridge) and Geoff Browell (Project Lead, Heritage Collections, King's College London). Historic England's policy influence and sector relationships bring institutional authority and national heritage mandate, while the British Library has experience with legal deposit and digital preservation.

The reason for giving this so much thought is because by encouraging students and individuals to learn and create heritage models with HBIM data and understand what data to record and how, I do not have anywhere I can recommend, other than Sketchfab or generic cloud storage to upload their work. The Sketchfab upload would consist of the final model, but this would then lose all the rich data that has been researched to create that model.

From personal experience, students would send me their final model, sometimes forgetting to attach materials, but more importantly none of the references to sources or images/information used would be sent – just the model. Anyone wanting to update that model would effectively be starting from scratch. It is a long enough process as it is, without having to start the "whole," i.e., the research, measurements, etc., all over again. Hence thinking about repositories, researching to find suitable ones and then not finding any that would allow them to upload their material, links to resources as well as the model. Without such a repository, their project files remain on their computer or external hard drive, deleted perhaps as no longer being needed, and then all that work is lost.

Similarly, architectural and engineering companies working with heritage buildings such as the Elizabeth Tower and Notre-Dame, the information and models developed through the course of the project, where is that data now held?

I can imagine one of the first queries would be about copyright and where this would stand in having access to people's models, links to resources, etc. When you consider the information that can already be accessed online, then perhaps this is not going to be such an issue. There are different methods of protection including the various license levels via Creative Commons. Ultimately, other databases already work with copyright, design right, and similar protection for works in the public domain, so the suggested repository should be able to manage the correct rights for the different items.

For someone in the field and producing HBIM heritage buildings, I strongly believe this is an area that requires focus and implementation in the very near future. It is not just what to record but also where to record.

Other Future Areas for Focus and Consideration

There are several interesting directions that look beyond data repositories and software revisions, some of which are

- **AI-Enhanced Documentation and Analysis**

    Machine learning is increasingly being integrated for automated feature recognition, damage assessment, and predictive maintenance modelling. AI can identify structural anomalies, predict deterioration patterns, and suggest intervention priorities based on historical data and environmental factors.

- **Real-Time Monitoring Integration**

    IoT sensors embedded in historic structures are beginning to feed live data directly into HBIM models, creating dynamic digital twins that update continuously. This enables proactive conservation by monitoring structural health, environmental conditions, and visitor impact in real time.

- **Extended Reality (XR) Applications**

    Virtual and augmented reality are expanding beyond visualization to become tools for remote collaboration, training conservators, and enabling public engagement with inaccessible heritage sites. Mixed reality interfaces allow experts to overlay digital information onto physical structures during on-site work.

- **Automated Survey Technologies**

  Advances in photogrammetry, LiDAR drones, and robotic scanning systems are making high-precision documentation faster and more accessible. Autonomous survey systems can now capture data in hazardous or difficult-to-reach areas.

- **Climate Change Adaptation Modelling**

  HBIM models are increasingly incorporating climate projections to simulate long-term environmental impacts and test adaptation strategies for heritage structures facing changing conditions.

- **Blockchain for Provenance and Authenticity**

  Distributed ledger technologies are being explored for maintaining tamper-proof records of conservation interventions, ownership history, and authenticity verification.

These developments suggest HBIM is evolving from static documentation toward dynamic, intelligent systems that actively support decision-making in heritage preservation. The convergence of these technologies opens up possibilities that were not feasible even a few years ago.

Future Recommendations

Digital Twins

- Creating digital twins of heritage buildings that are dynamic representations linked to physical assets to facilitate real-time monitoring and management. Using the digital twin models for creating virtual storytelling, embedding memories and living data (Ioannides et al, 2025).

Publishing and Sharing Findings

- Ensure models are in formats that can be easily shared without disrupting the original model.
- Store the HBIM model in accessible repositories.

- Training material to ensure models are created accurately and include validated metadata.

- Create scholarly articles, presentations, or interactive web applications to share knowledge and experience across disciplines.

Preservation and Future Modifications

- Selecting a FAIR-compliant repository (Findable, Accessible, Interoperable, and Reusable) is a key step in ensuring the long-term preservation of digital assets (Amici and Achille, 2024).

- Long-term storage systems that will not allow the material to decay and remain accessible to be amended and re-archived.

- Ensure model longevity by using open file formats (IFC for interoperability).

Regular Audits

- Ongoing audits and certifications of repositories are necessary to maintain trust and demonstrate ongoing compliance with preservation standards.

Future of Digital Heritage Storytelling – A Personal Aim

As part of future recommendations, there are technologies I look forward to learning, building and making work, i.e., using AI technology and creating avatars for more engaging storytelling scenes. Using Unreal Engine's MetaHumans tool, my next adventure in learning, under my company Time Tourist, is to recreate realistic famous people, such as Jane Austen, and populate them in the buildings they lived in or visited. Virtual visitors can then choose whether to observe the avatars having a conversation such as with Jane Austen with her sister Cassandra or engage with the avatars in conversation, i.e., ask questions. Using AI, the avatars will be able to respond. I have not yet seen an example of this, but I am sure that with the technology we have now, it is possible. We are already creating the HBIM buildings, and in my mind, they need to be "lived-in" rather than empty shells. The people that lived there have stories to tell. For example, my initial company "The Talking Walls" was about exactly this, creating stories of the people that lived in the historic houses, abbeys, and castles. Instead of 2D storybook-style characters, technology now allows 3D versions that can walk, talk, and

CHAPTER 9   CONCLUSION

more importantly respond. I am very much looking forward to the next step and seeing what else the future will make possible in the field of digital heritage, digital twins, HBIM 3D reconstructions and storytelling.

References

Amici, Nicola; Felicetti, Achille (2024) 3D Data Long-Term Preservation in Cultural Heritage. ResearchGate. DOI: 10.48550/arXiv.2409.04507. License: CC BY-NC-ND 4.0. https://www.researchgate.net/publication/383911725_3D_Data_Long-Term_Preservation_in_Cultural_Heritage [Accessed June 16, 2025]

Bakken Storeide, Markus Sebastian; George, Sony; Sole, Aditya; Yngve Hardeberg, Jon (2023) Standardisation of digitized heritage: a review of implementations of 3D in cultural heritage. Heritage Science. *11:249.* https://doi.org/10.1186/s40494-023-01079-z https://www.nature.com/articles/s40494-023-01079-z.pdf [Accessed June 13, 2025]

Bohl Architects (2023) Why Historic Preservation Is Important. Bohl Architects. https://bohlarchitects.com/why-historic-preservation-is-important/ [Accessed June 16, 2025]

Dualchas Architects (2025) Preserving Legacies: The Delicate Balance of Conservation and Historical Architecture - The Importance of Preserving Historical Architecture. https://www.dualchas.com/news/preserving-legacies-the-delicate-balance-of-conservation-and-historical-architecture [Accessed June 13, 2025]

European Union (2024) Shaping the Future of Cultural Heritage. 2024 European Commission. Publications Office of the European Union. ISBN 978-92-68-02517-8, DOI: 10.2777/12321, KI-09-23-174-EN-N. https://www.echoes-eccch.eu/wp-content/uploads/2025/02/shaping-the-future-of-cultural-heritage-KI0923174ENN.pdf [Accessed June 13, 2025]

Gardiner, Sarah; Vada, Sera; Ling Yang, Elaine Chiao; Le Truc, H. (2022) Recreating history: The evolving negotiation of staged authenticity in tourism experiences. Tourism Management, Volume 91, 2022, 104515, ISSN 0261-5177. https://doi.org/10.1016/j.tourman.2022.104515. (https://www.sciencedirect.com/science/article/pii/S0261517722000280) [Accessed June 16, 2025]

Guidi, Gabriele; Frischer, Bernard (2020) 3D Digitization of Cultural Heritage. Chapter in "3D Imaging, Analysis and Applications." September 2020. ResearchGate. DOI: 10.1007/978-3-030-44070-1_13. https://www.researchgate.net/publication/344709655_3D_Digitization_of_Cultural_Heritage [Accessed June 13, 2025]

McOmish, David; Hooley, David (2021) Historic Character and Good Design. Historic England. https://historicengland.org.uk/whats-new/research/back-issues/historic-character-and-good-design/ [Accessed June 13, 2025]

Ioannides, Marionos; Baker, Drew; Agapiou, Athos; Siegkas, Petros (Eds) (2025) 3D Research Challenges in Cultural Heritage V - Paradata, Metadata and Data in Digitisation. Springer. Lecture Notes in Computer Science. ISSN-3349 https://doi.org/10.1007/978-3-031-78590-0. https://link.springer.com/book/10.1007/978-3-031-78590-0 [Accessed June 13, 2025]

Ubisoft (2020) Assassin's Creed Valhalla https://www.ubisoft.com/en-gb/game/assassins-creed/valhalla [Accessed 13-06-2025]

Wilson, Deborah (2020) Curator, Designer and Visitor Interaction in Cultural Heritage Interpretation Design Practice, PhD Design Thesis. Dept. of Digital Technology, University of Winchester. Printed by Sarsen Press

Wilson, Deborah (2021) Digital Heritage Design – Using innovative platforms to recreate heritage environments, Community of Enterprise, Design & Innovation, University of Winchester. https://cedi.uk/digital-heritage-design-unit/ [Accessed June 13, 2025]

Wilson, Deborah (2023) Exploring Digital Possibilities for the Design of Heritage Interpretation & Reconstruction of Times Past, Digital Heritage Interpretation Conference 2023. https://cedi.uk/digital-heritage-interpretation-conference-2023/ [Accessed June 13, 2025]

Index

A

Accessibility paradox, 597
ADS, *see* Archaeology Data Service (ADS)
ADT, *see* AutoCAD Architectural Desktop 1 (ADT)
AI, *see* Artificial intelligence (AI)
AIM, *see* Asset information model (AIM)
Airborne laser scanning, 4
AR, *see* Augmented reality (AR)
Archaeology Data Service (ADS), 589
Architectural preservation
    adaptive reuse, 39
    advantages, 619
    backward compatibility and consistency, 617, 618
    challenges, 38
    collaboration and decision-making, 39
    concept, 38
    considerations, 621, 622
    heritage interpretation and visualization, 39–46
    innovations, 46
    open access HBIM repository, 618–621
    principles, 38
    recommendations, 622, 623
    virtual reconstruction, 38
Architectural time periods
    historical buildings, spaces and places, 613–615
    personal reflection, 609–613
    recreation, 616, 617
    reusable assets, 615, 616

Archival records, 556
ARIADNEplus, 590
Artificial intelligence (AI), 64, 69
Asset information model (AIM), 83
Audio elements, 546
Augmented reality (AR), 39, 50, 64, 68, 156, 157, 621
Authenticity, 131, 554, 600
AutoCAD, 60–62, 207
AutoCAD Architectural Desktop 1 (ADT), 62
Autodesk 3DS Max, 40, 42
Autodesk Revit, 9, 40, 42–44, 62, 67, 206, 218, 280, 605

B

Basilica of Sant'Ambrogio, 13
    BIM elements, 15
    data-driven models, 13
    data sources, 17
    digital data collection, 15, 16
    digital process workflow, 14
    features
        content-rich interaction, 18
        immersive navigation, 17
        multidisciplinary integration, 18
    HBIM models, 16
    impact and insights, 19
    interactive platforms, 16, 17
    methodology, 14
    objectives, 14
    outcomes, 18, 19
    Romanesque architecture, 13

INDEX

Beaulieu Abbey
    Cloister, 41, 42
    East elevation basic model, 43
    kiosk application, 40, 41
    phases, 42
    South elevation basic model, 43
Bentley Microstation, 62
Big Ben
    application, heritage projects, 98, 99
    challenges, 95, 96
    HBIM
        applications, 97
        benefits, 97, 98
        challenges, 96, 97
        YouTube video screenshot, 98
    overview, 95
BIM, *see* Building information modelling (BIM)
Black Tower, 124
BlenderBIM, 9
Blender projection mapping, 208
Budget LiDAR sensors, 184
Building information modelling (BIM), 1
    adaptation, 9, 80
    analysis, 78
    benefits, 82–84
    business Value, 63
    case studies and interviews, 78
    complexities, 76
    cost and resource constraints, 80
    cost management and scaling, 82
    data capture and accuracy, 79
    data integration, 80
    data object parameters, 221–234
    HBIM (*see* Historical building information modelling (HBIM))
    industry architectural software, 5
    leveraging technologies, 81
    literature review, 77
    methodology, 77
    objectives, 77
    parametric modelling, 60
    stakeholder collaboration, 80, 81
    tailored workflows, 81
    3D laser scanning technology, 2

C

CADmapper, 280, 281, 602
    contour lines, 290
    DWG TrueView, 287
    geographic data processing, 280
    vs. QGIS/ArcGIS, 281
    Steventon map, 285
    terrain extraction, 280
    Toposolid, 284–294
    working option, 281–283
CAD software, 61
CARARE, *see* Connecting archaeology and architecture in Europe (CARARE)
Cesium, 196, 197
    adding geospatial data, 212, 213
    adjusting settings, 213
    connecting ion, 212
    considerations, 213
    installing unreal plug-in, 211
    OSM buildings, 214, 215
    prerequisites, 211
    3D Tileset, 213
CharacterActorToMain, 514
Character node, 514, 515
Cheyney House, Winchester, 25
Chimneys, 333, 334
    stacks, 395–399
Church in Iwięcino, Poland

    benefits, 94
    digital deliverables, 91
    digitization process, 91
    historical significance, 90
    horizontal section, object
        projection, 92
    movable object, 93
    overview, 90
    scanned object, 90
    superimposed texture, 92
    vertical section, 93
Church of St Moran, 175
Cloud storage, 218
Compound ceiling, 402
Connecting archaeology and architecture in Europe (CARARE), 570
Content integration, 17
Contingency planning, 608
Coordinate reference system (CRS), 273
CRS, *see* Coordinate reference system (CRS)
Cultural context, 541
Cultural heritage protection, 45

D

Data acquisition, 218
Data collection
    geographic and spatial data
        considerations, 199, 205, 206
        data sources, 198, 199
        grayscale heightmap, 197
        landscape, 196
        limitations, 204
        methods, 197
        recommendations, 200
        terrain modification and detailing, 204, 205
        topographical surface, 196
        tutorials, 201
    recording, unreal scenes, 170–172
    substantiation, 172–181
Data completeness, 252
Data display function, 524
Data preparation
    attributes, 219
    BIM software
        accessing parameter management, 223
        adding constraints and validation rules, 234
        architectural template, 221, 222
        creating parameter groups, 223
        individual project parameters, 224–232
        look-up tables, 233
        project units, 222
        value lists, 233
        wall objects, 234
    considerations, 237
    data types and units, 221
    long-term archival requirements, 218
    management and utilization
        analysis and reporting, 235
        data entry protocols, 234
        iteration, 236
        quality control and data validation, 235
    nonstandard material(s), 219
    properties and characteristics, 219, 221
    reliability and adaptability, 218
    requirements, 221
    standards, 218
    version control system, 218
    walls, 237–248
    Wattle and Daub Wall, 236

INDEX

Decision matrix, 597
DEMs, *see* Digital elevation models (DEMs)
Depth-based objects, 294
Digital elevation models (DEMs), 198, 204
Digital environments, 600
Digital heritage reconstruction, 574
Digital heritage storytelling, 623, 624
Digital heritage visualization, 582
Digital recreation, 613
Digital storytelling, 156–159
Digital terrain models (DTMs), 279
Digital twins, 622
Dilapidation, 176
Disaster recovery, 65
Doll's house model, 5
Dormer framework
    casement window, 374, 376
    deselecting Defines Slope, 370, 371
    metric measurements, 375
    roof, 370, 371, 373
    update dimensions, 373
    walls, 370, 371, 374
    window, 372
Drone-mounted LiDAR, 183
DTMs, *see* Digital terrain models (DTMs)
Dual-purpose models, 595
Dual-time virtual models, Pompeii
    Casa del Centenario, 50, 51
    challenges and limitations, 53, 54
    concept, 47
    data collection and methodologies, 51, 52
    development, 54
    information base and relationships, 53
    northern wall of atrium, 48
    objectives, 47
    technological innovations, 48–50
    visitor experience and impact, 52, 53
    western arm of peristyle, 48
Dunster Castle, 40
Durham Cathedral Plan, 78, 79

E

EDM, *see* Europeana data model (EDM)
Elizabeth Tower, 95, *See also* Big Ben
Environment agency, 198
Environmental degradation, 18
Europeana, 590, 618
Europeana data model (EDM), 570
Extended reality (XR), 621
ExtractDatasmithMetadata, 530

F

Fascias, 379, 380
FEA, *see* Finite element analysis (FEA)
Finite element analysis (FEA), 97
Floors
    command with all walls, 323
    error message, 323
    external walls, 324
    Flagstone, 324
    hide attic floor, 327, 328
    interior lines, 324, 325
    level lines, 327
    materials, 324
    outline without intersections/gaps, 326
    properties, 327
    sketch mode's modify commands, 322

INDEX

G

Game design, 520
Geographic information systems (GIS)
    definition, 271
    integration, 271–274
    methods, 280
    vector-based CAD files, 271
Georeferencing historical maps, 284, *See also* CADmapper
    overlays, Revit Terrain, 294–297
    point cloud, 273, 274
    QGIS, 274–283
        adding real-world coordinates, 277
        dialogue box, 276
        methodologies, 279
        OpenStreetMap screen, 275
        transformation settings, 278
    tools and methods, 272
    2D CAD drawings, 272, 273
GIS, *see* Geographic information systems (GIS)
GIS-based georeferencing, 207
Graphic overrides, 147
Graphisoft ArchiCAD, 61, 62, 218
The Great Hall, Winchester, 177–179, 182
Guttering, 379–382

H

Hampshire Records Office, 179
Handheld and mobile LiDAR scanners, 183
Handheld laser scanners, 4
HBIM, *see* Historical building information modelling (HBIM)
HBIMDataComponent, 525, 530, 540
HBIM 3D model
    architectural elements, 151
    archival research, 126–128
    authenticity, 131
    comparative analysis, 132, 133
    conduct preliminary research, 122, 124, 126
    conjectural reconstruction, abbey, 127
    consult experts, 129
    cultural relevance, 131, 132
    Datasmith Exporter, 139, 140
    educational value, 132
    interior elements, 151, 152
    layout of Winchester, 124
    materials, 150
    metadata, 152–154
    model environment, 148, 149
    objectives, 119, 120
    periodization strategy, 134–138
    phased rebuilding plan/model
        assign elements, 145
        clarity view settings, 146
        export Unreal Engine, 147
        filters, 144, 145
        project timeline, 143
        set up phases, 143, 144
        timeline, 147
        visual clarity, 146
    phased Revit model, 138, 139
    preservation planning, 133
    reasons, 117, 118
    reconstruction process, 130
    site investigation, 128, 129
    structure, 149, 150
    time periods, 120–122, 137
    Unreal Engine, 140, 141
    Unreal Scene, level by level, 141, 142
    validation, 154, 155
    visualization and interactive presentation, 155–159

INDEX

HBIMGameMode, 540
HBIMViewer, 533, 540
Heads-up display (HUD) blueprint, 521
Henry III Round Apex Tower, 179
Heritage BIM, 1
Heritage Science Data Service (HSDS), 589
High-quality assets, 210
Historical accuracy, 551
    advantages and disadvantages, 579–581
    assessment, 574
    construction material, 574
    expert feedback, 574
    reconstructed models, 574–579
Historical building information modelling (HBIM)
    adaptations, 45, 60
    advantages, 73, 74
    analysis, 594
    architectural preservation challenges, 72
    aspects, 552, 553
    audiences, 22
    vs. BIM, 20
    challenges, 70, 71
    characteristics, 22
    collaboration and interdisciplinary applications, 68
    concept, 2, 20
    contextual awareness, 454
    data categories, 65, 66
    data feedback, 570–573
    definition, 1
    early developments, 60–62
    education and training, 75
    evolution, 64
    exporting Datasmith, 564–567
    exterior entrance, 3D scanning, 6
    external feedback, 554
    global developments and applications, 75
    guideline, software and process, 10–12
    holistic approach, 453
    implementation, 65–68
    implications, 598, 599
    information resource, 23, 24
    innovation strategies, 74, 75
    interactive model, 25
    interior space, 3D scanning, 6
    interior space, 360 views, 7
    intrinsic characteristics, 2
    metadata, 16
    milestones, 63–65
    model interaction, 8–10
    nonstandard materials, 237
    open and closed mesh, 8
    origins, 59
    platforms, 4
    point cloud, 7
    pop-up panel, 522–541
    primary findings, 594–597
    professionals, 555
    recommendations
        immediate implementation, 601–603
        project types, 601
    research, 599, 600
    scope, 2
    secondary findings, 597, 598
    simulation, 68, 69
    socio-political conditions, 453
    3D model (*see* HBIM 3D model)
    types, 4
    visualization, 21, 68, 69
    workflow process, 3

Historical recreations, 581
Historical validation, 607
Historic city/town/village, 294
Historic interiors, 176
Hollow mesh, 8
HSDS, *see* Heritage Science Data Service (HSDS)
HUD blueprint, *see* Heads-up display (HUD) blueprint
Hybrid workflow, 185
Hyde Abbey, Winchester, 27, 37
    benefits, 103, 104
    choir space and columns, 103
    cloisters, 102
    and curtilage, 100
    digital deliverables, 101, 103
    digitization process, 100, 101
    historical significance, 100
    King Cnut's Cross image, 104
    Nave, 102
    overview, 99
    site plan, 105

I

IFC, *see* Industry Foundation Classes (IFC)
Incomplete historical data, 596
Incomplete/missing data
    Datasmith workflow, 264–269
    Revit-Unreal link, 257–262
    scenario, 256
    strategies, 250–252
    student based guidelines
        documentation, 255, 256
        feedback, 256
        imputation techniques, 255
        initial investigation, 253, 254

    visual impact, 254
    visual inference and historical precedents, 254, 255
    temptation, 252
Industry Foundation Classes (IFC), 218
Interactive engagement, 21
Interactive opportunities, 546
Interior visual reference, 359–364
Interpretation panels, 581
Inventory form, 571, 572

J, K

Jane Austen House, 554
    aspects, 555, 556
    attic floor, 561, 562
    feedback, 557
    first floor, 561, 562
    ground floor, 560, 562
    reasons, 558
    repositioned drawing room, 564
    sketch, 563
    3D views, 563
    writing desk, 556

L

Lamorran Rectory, 173, 174, 176
Lasso tool, 487
Level blueprint, 521
Level of detail (LOD), 22, 192, 357, 422, 552, 606
Level streaming, 512
Level transition, 520
LiDAR, *see* Light detection and ranging (LiDAR)
LIDO, *see* Lightweight information describing objects (LIDO)

INDEX

Light detection and ranging (LiDAR), 4, 63, 69, 128, 198
    alignment issues problem, 193
    clay horse model, 195
    collision issues problem, 194
    color issues problem, 192
    convert point cloud to mesh, 186
    custom elevation datasets, 281
    factors, 183
    file size and engine crashes problem, 192
    hybrid workflow, 185
    integration, 182
    mesh optimization, 186
    performance issues problem, 192, 193
    price ranges and applications, 183, 184
    Revit/3D software, 184
    scanning buildings, 182
    structural accuracy, 189
    usage, 185
    VR issues problem, 193
Lightweight information describing objects (LIDO), 570–572
Lintels, 383–385
LOD, *see* Level of detail (LOD)
London Charter, 571, 582
    areas, 582
    challenges, 589
    cloud storage, 588
    digital heritage creators, 589
    European platforms, 590
    floppy disks, 588
    principles, 583–587
    repositories, 589, 590
    sustainable methods, 589

M

Machine learning (ML), 64, 69, 621
Malmesbury medieval reconstruction, 27
M_arch mass, 392
Material assets, 235
Medieval Malmesbury project, 612
Medium-term innovation
    collaborative platforms, 605
    integration capabilities, 604, 605
    priorities, project type, 607
    quality assurance and validation, 607, 608
    risk management and contingency planning, 608
    software-specific recommendations, 605, 606
Methodological transparency, 595, 596
Migrate command, 491
ML, *see* Machine learning (ML)
MLS, *see* Mobile laser scanning (MLS)
Mobile and user-centric system for enjoyment (MUSE), 47–49
Mobile laser scanning (MLS), 4
Modelling in place command, 411
Modular design, 252
Multimedia content, 52
MUSE, *see* Mobile and user-centric system for enjoyment (MUSE)
MyMap1400, 493
MyMap1800, 493, 516, 517

N

National Archives, 589
Nondestructive workflow, 257
Notre-Dame Cathedral restoration
    Autodesk Revit exploded view, 112
    benefits, 111

INDEX

collaboration and coordination, 107
collapsed vaults, 108
digital twin model composition, 110
emergency assessment, 106
life cycle, 109
overview, 106
planning, 109
pre-fire model, 107
role of, 106
spatio-temporal tracking, 110

O

Object-based design, 69
OpenCV, 208
Ordnance survey (OS), 198
OS, *see* Ordnance survey (OS)

P

Panelling, 405–408
Parametric modelling, 60, 62, 69, 252
Participatory design, 32
Peer review process, 576
Phased Revit model, 136–139
Phasing validation, 576
Photogrammetry, 7, 15, 55, 63, 69, 128, 131, 430, 508
    clean and optimize mesh, 187
    and 3D scanning, 603
    scan process, 187
    surface details, 189
    and 3D scanning, 603
    tools, 606
    usage, 185
Physical reality, 554
Pilgrim's Hall, Winchester, 21
Planar ceiling, 402
Point clouds, 7, 273, 274

Points of interest (POIs), 104, 159
POIs, *see* Points of interest (POIs)
Polish case studies, 84
Political decisions, 453
Pop-up panel
    creating widget, 522–529
    getting Datasmith data, 531
    HBIMData component, 536, 537
    HBIMViewer nodes, 537, 538
    interaction system, 530–535
    loop node, 528
    project setup and preparation, 522
    result, 538
    testing and refinement, 539, 540
    text node, 527
    world settings tab, 536
Portal effect, 542
Pre-processing
    accurate and cohesive HBIM model, 217
    data preparation, 218–250
    georeferencing and aligning datasets, 271–297
    incomplete/missing data, 250–270
    streamlined workflow, 218
Preservation needs
    contemporary issues, 582
    cultural heritage, 581
    London Charter, 583–590
    principles, 581
Pride and Prejudice film, 360–363
Procedural texture creation, 431
Project management, 603
Project parameters, 223, 225–228

Q

Quality control, 551
Quoins, 387–390

INDEX

R

Realism, 210, 211, 281, 490
RecorDIM, *see* Recording, documentation and information management (RecorDIM)
Recording, documentation and information management (RecorDIM), 1
Remote navigation metaphor, 50
Research validation, 551
Revit–Unreal link
  Datasmith exporters, 257
  Datasmith plug-in, 260
  direct link, 262
  export Datasmith file, 258
  import Datasmith file, 259–261
  lock 3D view icon, 258
  plugin window, 260
  reimport support, 261–263
  twinmotion drop-down window, 259
Risk management, 608
Risk mitigation, 96
Round Tower, 182
Rural rectory landscape
  Alpha mode, 474
  areas outline, 473
  components, 467, 468
  creating side garden wall, 480
  edit layers, 472
  flatten base, 466
  foliage mode, 474–479
  imported layers, 470
  information objects, 471
  lanes, yards and drive, 473
  master material, 467
  outbuilding and sloped roof, 484
  outbuildings and side wall, 480–489
  painting areas, 474
  painting grass and wild flowers, 479
  painting mode, 468, 469
  sculpting immediate surroundings, 464–474
  side wall and pillar, 482
  splines, 487–489
  textures, 468
  wireframe setting, 481

S

Seamless transition, 519
Shared parameters, 223, 228–230, 232, 257, 426
Short-term development
  heritage tools, 604
  training and knowledge transfer, 604
  workflow automation, 603
Sketchfab, 590, 616, 619, 620
Soffits, 377, 378, 380
SolidWorks, 61
Split face command, 409
Stacked wall, 319–321
Staircases
  basement level, 341
  basement walls, 340
  create similar command, 340
  layout, 334
  lines parts, 339
  location, 336
  new profile, 339
  properties, 335
  section line, 337, 338
  sloping wall, 340
  wall, 338
Steventon Rectory, 43, 44, 118, 119, 163–166, 173, 175, 176, 181, 238, 304

INDEX

additional materials, 440–448
aligned map, 308
aspects, 357, 358
attic layout, 353–355
Autodesk Revit 2024, 301, 302
base material nodes, 435, 436
basic wall properties, 426
building, 303–309
chimneys, 333, 334
copying your project, 455, 456
creating master material, 434, 435
creating materials and textures, 430, 431
creating roof
    checking standing height, 353
    completed extension, 349
    extension, 346, 348
    gable, 350, 351
    join command, 348
    outline, 347
    second extension, 350
    shorter extension, 348
    side single story and kitchen porch, 351, 352
drawing room components, 425
elevation marks, 309
evidence, 357
exterior detail
    chimneys' stacks, 395–399
    dormers, 369–377
    fascias, 379
    front porch, 391–395
    guttering, 379–382
    lintels, 383–385
    quoins, 383, 387, 388, 390, 391
    sills, 385–387
    soffits, 377, 378
exterior materials, 429

external view, 448
feedback, 554
feet and fractional inches, 301
first floor layout, 343, 344
floor plans and ceiling plan names, 303
floors, 322–328
implementation, Unreal Engine, 432, 433
importing Datasmith, 437–439
interior detail
    ceilings and floor finish, 400–404
    coving, 410–414
    drawing room space, 401
    external pink line and filleting, 403
    floor finish, 403, 404
    panelling, 405–408
    picture frames, 418–420
    shelving, 416–418
    user/virtual visitor, 399
    wall candle sconces, 421, 422
    wall finishes, 408, 409
    wall framing, 416
    wall niches, 414, 415
interior materials, 429, 430
interior visual reference, 359–364
internal views, 448
landscapes, 456, 457
layering images, 457–463
levels and level names, 302
light and color accuracy, 433
material instance, 448
materials, 444–447
memoirs and layouts, 331
model lines, 307
modelling environment, 356
pin command, 309
repositioned drawing room, 569, 570
research, 358, 359

Steventon Rectory (*cont.*)
   resources, 300
   revisions, 557, 558
   Revit model and purpose considerations, 424
   roofs, 356
   rural landscape, 463–489
   sash windows and front door, 330
   scale of chains, 305
   scale reference command, 306
   second floor layout, 341–346
   sketch, 329, 332
   stacked walls, 427, 428
   stages, 424
   staircases, 334–341
   stairwell hole, 342
   structural detail, 365–369
   sweep of drive, 567, 568
   texture coordinate panel, 441
   texture maps, 434
   time travel, 540–543
   virtual experience, 543–546
   visitor, 454
   wall panelling properties, 427
   walls, 310–322
   windows and doors, 328–332
   wireframe, 346
   wooden building, 568
Structural analysis, 88
Structural integrity, 551
Sustainability, 598, 614

T

The Talking Walls, 26, 43, 44, 182, 612–614, 625
Technical validation, 607
Teleport node, 512, 513
Temporal consistency, 576
Terrain, 602
Terrain modelling, 279
Terrestrial laser scanning (TLS), 4, 182, 184
Textual information, 551
TextureSample, 436
Thin plate spline (TPS), 277
Time-based modelling, 64
TLS, *see* Terrestrial laser scanning (TLS)
Toposolid, 284–293
Toposurface tool, 279
TPS, *see* Thin plate spline (TPS)
Transparency, 251, 252, 270, 600
TriggerVolumeToMain, 513, 514

U

Unreal Engine, 606
   capturing historical building, 189
   changing materials, 142
   data processing, 189
   Datasmith plugins, 140
   default materials, 141
   documentation, 490
   enhancement and optimization, 188
   experience, 191
   exporting, 147
   final export and deployment, 191
   importing, 140, 141, 187, 190
   landscape, 209, 210
   landscape sculpting, 195
   LiDAR, 192–194
   phased model, 138
   real-time rendering, 156
   techniques, 158, 159
   visuals, 67
Update-resistant workflow, 271

Urban environments, 453
Urbanization, 18
User-centered design, 17, 32
User experience validation, 608

V

Vectorworks, 62
Version control, 603
Virtual cities, 8, 9, 119
    architectural time-slices, 25
    background, 26–28
    commercialization, 34, 35
    CP research reference micro board, 180
    design process, 32, 33
    HBIM model, 130
    HBIM project data library, 171, 172
    historical map of Winchester, 31
    iStock purchase, 37
    map creation, 200
    possibility, 33, 34
    prototype, 31
    realistic scenes, 36
    spreadsheet, 170
    time periods, 120
    Winchester 1400, 29, 493
    Winchester 1800, 30, 491, 493
    Winchester prototype view, 203
    workflow, 283
Virtual reality (VR), 16, 39, 64, 68, 97, 156, 157, 270, 621
Virtual reconstruction, 454
Virtual steering by waving, 49
Visual continuation, 254
Visualization
    architectural modelling, 132
    digital media design, 119
    interactive presentation, 155–159
    interiors, 21
    and simulation, 68, 69
    site model, 281
    storytelling, 134, 138
    technology developments, 156
    3D building models, 21
    timeline-based, 133
Visualization-conservation divide, 594
Visual overlay system, 575
Visual transitions, 546
Voxel Boolean method, 501
VR, *see* Virtual reality (VR)

W

Walls
    adapting color, 245
    base and top constraint, 319
    brick and flint, 316–322
    changing height, 313
    drop-down list, 239
    duplicating and editing, 239–248
    elevational view, 312
    external pattern, 316
    far clipping, 314
    image pixel outline, 311, 312
    inside and outside, 315
    material browser, 244
    material changes, 246
    materials, 238
    no clip option, 314
    overwriting, 240
    preview pane, 242
    project preparation, 237
    render appearance, 245
    revised type properties box, 247
    Revit material, 243

INDEX

Walls (*cont.*)
   schedule, 321
   structure, 237, 238
   thickness, 238, 241, 243
   3D view, 248
   top-level height and level heads, 313
   true corners, 310
   type, 249
   versions, 249
Wall Sconce Candle 17079, 421
Wang Temple, Karpacz, 87, 88
   documentation, 89
   HBIM
      implementation, 87
      model benefits, 87, 88
   historical significance and challenges, 86
   innovation, 88
   overview, 86
   3D model, 86
WBP_HBIMPopup, 540
WBPHBIMPopup eventGraph, 526
Widget blueprint, 521
Winchester 1750–1800, 201
Winchester Castle, 119, 123, 125, 163, 167–170, 177
Winchester Cathedral, 21, 491
   drawing room at 8 College Street, 495, 517
      adding bollards, 509–511
      adding drinking fountain, 508–510
      copy content, 498–502
      details panel, 498
      entities, 511
      furniture, 496, 497
      hollowed-out cylinder and torus, 506
      horse trough, 503–508
      imported candles, 499, 500
      items, 496
      level streaming, 519
      methods, 512
      open level portal system, 512–518
      reusable BP_Portal, 518, 519
      street furniture, 502
      water pump, 505
   essential street items, 494, 495
   external projects, 492
   historical accuracy, 494
   levels, 492
   practice zones, 493
   street furniture, 494
Winchester City 1800 map, 202
Winchester terrain, 200
Wireless local area network (WLAN), 50
WLAN, *see* Wireless local area network (WLAN)
Workflow integration challenge, 596, 597

X, Y, Z

XR, *see* Extended reality (XR)

GPSR Compliance
The European Union's (EU) General Product Safety Regulation (GPSR) is a set of rules that requires consumer products to be safe and our obligations to ensure this.

If you have any concerns about our products, you can contact us on

ProductSafety@springernature.com

In case Publisher is established outside the EU, the EU authorized representative is:

Springer Nature Customer Service Center GmbH
Europaplatz 3
69115 Heidelberg, Germany